W9-BAR-340

Special Edition Using XML

Bestseller Edition

Lee Anne Phillips

A Division of Macmillan USA
201 W. 103rd Street
Indianapolis, Indiana 46290

CONTENTS AT A GLANCE

Special Edition Using XML

Copyright© August 2000 by Que

All rights reserved. No part of this book shall be reproduced, stored in a retrieval system, or transmitted by any means, electronic, mechanical, photocopying, recording, or otherwise, without written permission from the publisher. No patent liability is assumed with respect to the use of the information contained herein. Although every precaution has been taken in the preparation of this book, the publisher and author assume no responsibility for errors or omissions. Nor is any liability assumed for damages resulting from the use of the information contained herein.

International Standard Book Number: 0-7897-1996-7

Library of Congress Catalog Card Number: 99-60197

Printed in the United States of America

First Printing: August, 2000

02 01 00   4 3 2 1

Trademarks

All terms mentioned in this book that are known to be trademarks or service marks have been appropriately capitalized. Que cannot attest to the accuracy of this information. Use of a term in this book should not be regarded as affecting the validity of any trademark or service mark.

Warning and Disclaimer

Every effort has been made to make this book as complete and as accurate as possible, but no warranty or fitness is implied. The information provided is on an "as is" basis. The author(s) and the publisher shall have neither liability nor responsibility to any person or entity with respect to any loss or damages arising from the information contained in this book or from the use of the CD or programs accompanying it.

Associate Publisher
Tracy Dunkelberger

Acquisitions Editor
Todd Green

Development Editors
Sean Dixon
Jeff Durham

Managing Editor
Thomas F. Hayes

Project Editor
Leah Kirkpatrick

Copy Editor
Julie McNamee

Indexer
Kelly Castell

Proofreader
Harvey Stanbrough

Technical Editors
Marshall Jansen
Jay Aguilar
Karl Fast
Benoit Marchel
Dallas Releford

Team Coordinator
Cindy Teeters

Media Developer
Craig Atkins

Interior Designer
Ruth Harvey

Cover Designers
Dan Armstrong
Ruth Harvey

Production
Darin Crone
Steve Geiselman

CONTENTS

ABOUT THE AUTHOR

Lee Anne Phillips has been involved in data processing and networking since that happy day the professor of her first programming class at UC Berkeley persuaded her that she had a talent for this stuff and should rethink her planned career in linguistic psychology and tweak bits instead. From UCB she traveled through various incarnations as a mainframe systems programmer, firmware designer, network engineer, software architect, programming and project manager, and finally consultant until she just had to tell somebody about it. She resides in the San Francisco Bay Area—her place of birth—has a bachelor's degree in computer science, and has a great sense of humor. Visit her Web page at `http://www.leeanne.com/`.

DEDICATION

To Alison Eve Ulman, dearest rose among the thorns. Your desperate and transgressive art has inspired my own with clearer vision and profoundest passion.

And to Dangerous Downtown Dave, sweet companion of many years, whose adventurous life took him from the bitter snows of Salt Lake City, Utah, through the empty sunshine of Southern California and into the welcoming fog and rain of the San Francisco Bay Area. He was a rowdy brawler to the end but a gentle and loving friend to his surrogate Mom.

ACKNOWLEDGMENTS

My grateful appreciation to my initial editor at Que, Todd Green, for many patient hours of effort persuading me to rough out the evolving outline and then refine it into a plan. This, in spite of my perfectly natural inclination to revise and extend as I go along, causing stalwart editors to tear out their hair and the noble production crew to weep with frustration.

My thanks especially to Jeff Durham, my development editor, for his helpful feedback and advice; to Jeremy H. Griffith, my technical editor, for catching many fuzzy lapses from clarity and a few outright mistakes; to the countless editors and staff at Que whose many hands and minds have helped turn my words into printable form. If you'll glance at the back of the title page, you'll see a list of some few of their names, and each of them has my undying gratitude.

My gratitude also to the typographers, graphic artists, printers, bookbinders, and all the rest who actually produced the physical book you hold in your hands. And to the delivery people and booksellers of every description whose faith in it has led it to the rack or Web page you found it on.

And of course you, Dear Reader, who might be thinking of buying this book right this minute, I hope! So thank you all, readers, editors, bookstores, printers and everyone. This is the work of many hands and is now in yours.

TELL US WHAT YOU THINK!

As the reader of this book, *you* are our most important critic and commentator. We value your opinion and want to know what we're doing right, what we could do better, what areas you'd like to see us publish in, and any other words of wisdom you're willing to pass our way.

As an Associate Publisher for Que, I welcome your comments. You can fax, email, or write me directly to let me know what you did or didn't like about this book—as well as what we can do to make our books stronger.

Please note that I cannot help you with technical problems related to the topic of this book, and that due to the high volume of mail I receive, I might not be able to reply to every message.

When you write, please be sure to include this book's title and author as well as your name and phone or fax number. I will carefully review your comments and share them with the author and editors who worked on the book.

Fax: 317-581-4666

Email: que.programming@macmillanusa.com

Mail: Tracy Dunkelberger
         Que
         201 West 103rd Street
         Indianapolis, IN 46290 USA

INTRODUCTION

In this Introduction

This book is dedicated to making sense out of the raft of competing (and sometimes conflicting) XML-related standards and proposals afloat on the great sea of XML possibilities. Many of the facilities most needed by users (that's you, Dear Reader) are supplied by means of a half dozen or more differing "standards" with varying degrees of support from only a handful of vendors. It's enough to make you tear out your hair.

But the concepts of XML are about as simple as taking up a red pen and making notes on a text as you read. Unlike HTML, which has a very limited vocabulary, XML gives you almost unlimited freedom to describe your documents in any way you choose.

XML is fast becoming the *lingua franca* of the Web, with new vendors climbing onboard the XML bandwagon every day. This book is designed to help you catch a ride with everyone else.

Many major corporations with significant resources have already invested in XML, among which are some of the heavy hitters in the industry. Microsoft, IBM, SAP, Netscape, Oracle, Sun Microsystems, the US government, the US military—the list reads like a roll call of the top Fortune 5000 companies and major governmental agencies few of us can afford to ignore, even if we don't deal with them directly.

This is a critical time in the development of XML; standards are being proposed and promulgated faster than any one person can keep track of. There are sometimes proposals from World Wide Web Consortium (W3C) members, alternatives from people with no affiliation at all, user group initiatives, and attempts to reconcile them all. This book will help you sort them all out, tell you where to look for more information to help you keep up with new developments as they occur, and help build a conceptual framework to let you fit new bits of information into an existing structure as you go along. Have fun.

Yet everyone online depends on the W3C. Making Web applications that work is hard enough without dealing with a hundred custom systems from different individual manufacturers. Two main approaches are one too many. Like metric and SAE tools, our workbenches are cluttered enough with necessary components without having to worry about whether this particular bolt requires a 19mm or a 3/4 inch wrench.

By promulgating standards, W3C ensures that some basic level of interoperability exists among Web applications. Manufacturers who deviate from the standards risk looking foolish in the long run, however they might try to "spin" their decisions or attempts to impose standards of their own on the rest of the industry.

So XML and its related standards are all compromises between some Platonic ideal methodology and the gritty business of trying to get on with life on the Web. The various working groups within W3C have taken different tacks in some cases, introducing incompatibilities or inconsistencies into the standards themselves, which might or might not be ironed out in the final analysis. In the meantime, we have to get on with our jobs and make Web applications work. And work they will and do. So let's get on with it. After we're up to speed, we're in for a thrilling ride.

Who Should Use This Book

This book is designed for professional Web designers, programmers, database and content specialists, and almost anyone involved in publishing or sharing information over any sort of network. XML and its related standards offer the Web community a valuable and flexible way to organize and share data. Potential user communities include

- Content providers and authors
- Database users
- Programmers
- Web designers
- Scientists and scholars
- Researchers and analysts
- Indexing and search engine providers
- Anyone who wants to learn more about XML and the future of the Web

How This Book Is Organized

There are six major sections to the book:

- Part I, "XML Fundamentals," introduces you to the concepts and facilities needed to use XML and its related standards effectively.
- Part II, "Manipulating XML," examines the tools used to control the structure and presentation of the XML document itself, the Document Object Model, Style Sheets, and SAX, the Simple API for XML.
- Part III, "Integrating XML with Other Technologies," delves into the database and server-side applications XML is particularly suited for. Real-world examples illustrate the nuts and bolts of applications working in the business environment today. In addition, the important issues of online privacy and security are discussed in the context of current industry practices and problems.
- Part IV, "Other Applications of XML," fills in the gaps with discussions of how to integrate existing Web documents with XML using XHTML, ways to create standard descriptive vocabularies using the Resource Description Framework, and multimedia and scientific languages that show how XML or XML-related standards might simplify existing tasks or make possible new interactions as yet undreamed of. Finally, you'll explore how XML can make the Web more accessible for everyone and look at where we might be heading with Web development in the near future.
- Appendices and the special reference pages on the inside front and back covers offer a handy quick-reference to the basics, stripped down to their most essential parts for a quick reminder of how to do a given task or what this or that feature looks like.
- And finally, the bound-in CD-ROM has a selection of the most valuable references and tools for XML production either as freeware, shareware, or demoware together with all

the code from the book and valuable reference documents, such as a Web color chart, the XHTML named entities, and more.

CONVENTIONS USED IN THIS BOOK

This book uses special conventions to help you get the most from this book and from XML.

TEXT CONVENTIONS

Various typefaces in this book identify terms and other special objects. These special type-faces include the following:

Type	Meaning
Italic	New terms or phrases when initially defined. An italic term followed by a page number indicates the page where that term is first defined.
`Monospace`	Code, output, and Web addresses appear in a computer type font indicating these are all things that will either be typed into or appear on the computer screen.
`Bold Monospace`	Specific input the user is supposed to type is in a bold computer type font.

SPECIAL ELEMENTS

Tip from

LeeAnne.com
Words to weave by

Tips are designed to point out features, annoyances, and tricks of the trade that you might otherwise miss. These will help you write XML quickly and effectively.

Note

Notes point out items that you should be aware of, although you can skip these if you're in a hurry. Generally, notes are a way for you to gain some extra information on a topic without weighing yourself down.

Caution

Pay attention to Cautions! These could save you precious hours in lost work. Don't say we didn't warn you.

Each chapter also ends with a "Troubleshooting" or "Getting Down to Cases" element. A "Troubleshooting" section helps you overcome common problem with using XML. A "Getting Down to Cases" section shows you how the subject of the chapter applies to everyday XML development or provides extra information that is interesting or useful.

PART I

XML FUNDAMENTALS

CHAPTER 1

INTRODUCTION TO XML

In this chapter

MAKING ALL THINGS POSSIBLE WITH XML

The Internet community is pouring an enormous amount of energy, money, and effort into developing an extensive suite of related standards centered around XML, Extensible Markup Language, the next generation of document delivery methods on the Web. In 1999 alone, more standards and drafts, almost all XML-related, have been delivered or proposed than in the history of the World Wide Web Consortium (W3C), the body responsible for Web standards. In 2000, several dozen more XML-related standards will be delivered, doubling the number of W3C standards and extending the cohesive power of XML into all corners of the Worldwide Web.

XML and its related standards allow you to replace or extend proprietary tagging systems, such as Allaire's Cold Fusion and Microsoft's Active Server Pages (ASP), with platform-independent languages that fit the problem space of your page precisely. Instead of (or in addition to) inserting special tags or comments explaining what a particular field means, the field itself can be made meaningful to both applications and human readers. So an annotated price list in HTML which might look like this

```
<!--Price list for individual fruits -->
<dl>
  <!-- Fruit -->
  <dt>Apples</dt>
    <!-- Price -->
    <dd>$1</dd>
  <!-- Fruit -->
  <dt>Oranges</dt>
    <!-- Price -->
    <dd>$2</dd>
</dl>
```

can be made to look like this:

```
<FruitPriceList>
  <Fruit>Apples</Fruit>
    <Price>$1</Price>
  <Fruit>Oranges</Fruit>
    <Price>$2</Price>
</FruitPriceList>
```

The above shows a tiny example of what can be accomplished in making data easier to access using XML. Not only is the information less cluttered and more clearly presented, but also the fields are identifiable by a search engine. So, apples to eat can be readily distinguished from the Big Apple (New York City) and the apple of one's eye (a person or thing one is fond of). Whereas we had to fit our HTML data into the Procrustean bed of an HTML definition list to lay out the list in the manner we wanted, in XML we can let the data structure flow from the data itself, and use XML-related standards like Cascading Style Sheets (CSS) or Extensible Stylesheet Language (XSL) to format the page. Also, the XML version allows us to retain information about the type of data entered in every field. HTML allows us to identify only a half-dozen or so datatypes: abbreviations, acronyms, addresses, block quotes, citations, and variables. And even these are most often (mis)used to affect formatting rather than to identify a logical field.

UNDERSTANDING HTML LIMITATIONS

As the Web has grown over the past 10 years, users have discovered more and more ways of communicating with each other. The foundation of that interchange has been HTML, the Hypertext Markup Language. HTML has been used to present everything from scholarly papers to online catalogs and poetry. However, the structure of Web pages based in HTML says little about the actual information content. The example of a definition list shown previously illustrates the fact that most of the tags offered by HTML affect only the crude layout and presentation of the text on the page, and even that layout information is inflexible. Tags are often used to present information in ways that stretch or violate the meaning of the tags themselves. The XTML definition list coded previously had no definitions listed, for example, but was used only to line up fruits and prices in a particular way.

So, there have been many workarounds to try and impose some sort of flexible order on the data contained on the page. Many of these ad hoc solutions, such as ASP or Cold Fusion, have been moderately successful. For the most part, however, they represent proprietary approaches that have to be reinvented for each new problem domain or require the use of specific server software and hardware that may not fit into your purchasing plans.

By now, you've probably run into the limitations of HTML. You've experienced the frustration of not being able to describe *exactly* what you want to do using the structures available to you as a Web designer or author. You've probably been forced to use inaccessible mechanisms, such as frames or tables, to coerce your page into an unreliable typographical layout, or you've used ugly `<pre>` preformatted and/or `<tt>` typewriter text tags to align data properly. XML is a new standard that allows you to extend the descriptive power of your document almost at will and alter it to suit different purposes as needed. XML makes a lot of things possible that were only vague yearnings before.

IMPROVING PRECISION WITH XML

XML enables you to describe your document exactly in a way that can be "understood" by a machine. Although humans have no trouble looking at a page and deducing what certain layouts mean, such as an invoice, for example, computers aren't quite that smart. They need help. Descriptive XML tags such as `<seller>` and `<price>` make far more sense to machines than the anonymous layout tags that HTML currently provides. XML provides a mechanism, the Document Type Definition (DTD), which lets you share knowledge about the structure of your data with anyone you choose.

VALIDATING DOCUMENT STRUCTURE WITH XML

XML enables you to force validation of the structure of your document. You can enforce the presence of certain items, while making others optional, and link one structure with another. In other words, if you choose to include Item ABC, you can force an instance of Item XYZ to go with it. Alternatively, if ABC is present, then XYZ can be excluded.

INTRODUCING LAYOUT FLEXIBILITY WITH XML

XML makes it possible to truly vary the presentation of documents according to their intended use. Instead of compelling you to decide whether a data set is better presented as a list or as a table, you can present it in different ways for different purposes. On the printed page, a table is useful and hyperlinks are worthless, but in an audio browser for the blind, a hyper-link-navigable set of lists might be more accessible. Entering the same data into a database might require normalization and other transformations that would be superfluous elsewhere. A single XML source can support all these uses.

ACHIEVING PLATFORM INDEPENDENCE WITH XML

XML is completely platform-independent and extremely robust. No other data transport or distributed processing mechanism can make this claim. XML is text-based. You can look at the raw data and make perfect sense of it. Because XML describes a simple flat-file database, every application using any sort of database access can use XML as a lowest common denominator for transport, generating and translating from XML for transfer while using normalized or proprietary formats internally. Almost all database applications already have the capability to create a comma-delimited flat-file equivalent of database records, so expanding the commas into XML tags is almost trivial.

DESIGNING OBJECT-ORIENTED DOCUMENTS WITH XML

Although the long-term success of object-oriented techniques is still debatable, XML is developing in ways that will eventually support object-oriented programming and design methods as an option. Although the current standard is slightly improved over the standard block sequential model, initiatives such as SOX, the Schema for Object-oriented XML, or equivalents will provide fully object-oriented access to database-like and other elements of XML structures.

REDEFINING THE POSSIBILITIES OF WEB DEVELOPMENT

HTML currently operates as an elaborate and sophisticated virtual fax machine originally designed to allow scholars to share copies of academic papers with each other on request. HTML layout tags mirror the physical structure of such a paper, primarily a simple outline with associated text and graphics. One labels headers, paragraphs, lists, tables, and illustrations. The default layout is linear, with text proceeding in an orderly fashion down the page.

The few meaningful tags, <CITE>, <ADDRESS>, and so on, are designed to highlight such things as article and book citations, a scholarly concern, and the address of the author. Everything else that goes into the make up a research paper, the 3×5 cards, the calculations and categorizations, the deep understanding of the subject matter structure, is just dumped in the trash on the way to the hyperlinked faux paper. It's not much to work with really. Everything else, the entire structure of the current Web, has been piled on top of that early design. It's a tribute to the original designers that everything still works as well as it does.

However, the difference between text and data is that data has structure and context. Human beings can recognize or extrapolate structure and context from visual cues, so for purely human interaction HTML is sufficient. But computers don't think that way. Or think at all for that matter.

DATA GRANULARITY AND STRUCTURE

XML is designed to allow every meaningful division of a document to be unambiguously identified as part of a coherent tree structure that either a human or a computer can use. So an entire car can be described as a complete parts list, with everything from the engine to nuts and bolts broken down into lists of components. Or a book can be described as a collection of the chapters, paragraphs, footnotes, illustrations, and so on that make it up. It's a stunning concept, although it can't yet capture data structures that are not tree-like.

Many abstractions cannot be represented as trees. The meaning of "honor" may be clear to a Marine but you can't disassemble it into component parts like a car, although there are clearly related concepts that inform the concept of honor. So "honor" is undoubtedly related to "fidelity" in some way, but the exact relationship disappears into the sort of vague cloud that network designers are fond of and philosophers can extrapolate into lengthy books.

Likewise, the Web itself is not a tree, but an enormously complex network of independent nodes linked in a directed graph with no particular starting point or root. (Figures 2.1 and 2.2 in the next chapter may make this clearer.) A tree has a single root and every branch is separate.

The database-like applications of XML, such as describing the component parts of a car, are usually more straightforward than describing complex objects such as a book. It may seem odd to think that a book is more complicated than a car, but it's true. The problem is one of *exclusion*, making sure that an object can't appear inappropriately as one of its own descendents. So a car usually has only one engine, and a second engine is not usually a component part of the first engine.

However, a book may contain references to other books, or be part of a series, or be one book in multiple volumes. Those books may in turn refer to the original book. The typographical design of a book may contribute to the text in subtle ways. The individual structures that make up a book may be related to each other in complex aesthetic or conventional formations that are interleaved in the typographical rendering in a non-linear fashion. Footnotes and endnotes are only one example.

A medical text might contain transparent overlay pages, for instance, meant to be both individually and simultaneously viewed. A project book for children might have parts meant to be cut out and manipulated either two- or three-dimensionally by the reader. A book might contain illustrations that can be easily viewed only with a separate stereographic viewer of some sort.

A table of contents or an index is not, strictly speaking, part of the linear text of a book but rather an attached tool for linking into the body of the book in a useful way. A glossary may be necessary for a full understanding of the text but is rarely if ever read sequentially. A bibliography or in-text reference may refer to almost any sort of document or object, including film, sound recordings, newspaper articles, or magazines, as well as books, none of which are contained in the text itself but may be packaged with it.

A book, in short, is more like a directed graph than a tree in actual use, although it may be barely possible to describe it sequentially for the purpose of printing it. There is no definite starting point when you read it; you can flip around from page to page in no particular order and with no particular object in mind if you want. It's part of a Web of other books and requires a metaphysical addition, that of literacy, to the physical object for it to make any sense. You couldn't create a database that corresponded to Marcel Proust's *Remembrance of Things Past* without losing quite a lot in the conversion.

A car, on the other hand, is pretty much the sum of its parts and subassemblies, and its behavior is entirely defined by the linkages and components built into it.

UNDERSTANDING THE CONCEPT OF DESCENDENTS

A descendent is a subassembly or part, if you're more comfortable with concrete objects than abstract examples. A car is made up of a frame, an engine, wheels, a transmission, and a bunch of other parts that are all connected in strict order, many of which are in turn constructed of other parts. An engine has a block, pistons, and many other gadgets such as carburetors and distributors attached to it. Any describable section or component of the entire assembly is a descendent of the physical object, "car." Each may or may not have descendents. A bolt, for example, is a terminal leaf of the car tree.

In a book, on the other hand, a paragraph may not have a paragraph as a direct descendent, but it *may* have a footnote, and that footnote may be so large that it has paragraphs inside it. But should footnotes be allowed inside footnote paragraphs? Probably not. Is a footnote paragraph a different sort of animal than a paragraph in running text? XML has unavoidable difficulty with exclusion because it was specifically dropped from the definition of the language.

XML must rely on careful construction of the DTD to avoid putting child elements where they don't belong, but this strategy fails in some instances. At times, you must rely on the common sense of the user to avoid problems.

Note
Although you might think of exclusion problems as an XML weakness, some balance had to be struck between the expressive power of the language and the ease with which it could be used and implemented. Recursive exclusion is a *difficult* problem. Descriptive perfection is probably theoretically impossible in any case (Goedel's Theorem), so choosing one level of imperfection over another is a matter of engineering judgment. XML was designed to be both useful and inexpensive, sound engineering criteria both, and like any human construct is a compromise between the desire for luxury features and economic reality.

UNDERSTANDING THE RELATIONSHIP BETWEEN SGML, XML, AND XHTML

XML is a *meta-language*, a special language that allows you to completely describe a class of other languages, which in turn describe documents. It's like an island in the sea of SGML, another and more powerful meta-language. XML is defined as a "proper subset" of SGML, which means no pieces are added to SGML to make XML, but pieces are taken away to make the language easier to parse, understand, and use. XHTML is a production of XML, as HTML is a production of SGML.

Because XML is designed to be *extensible*, the languages created with XML are extensible as well. As in SGML, the language descriptions created by XML are called DTDs, Document Type Definitions. You'll find out much more about them later. But first, take a look at SGML, the mother of XML and its related standards.

SGML

SGML, the Standard Generalized Markup Language, is a more powerful ancestor of XML and also a meta-language used to describe application languages. Although it has many useful features, the complexity of the language makes it extremely hard to use and learn. It's also not quite true that nothing was added to SGML to make XML. For example, when multiple ATTLIST declarations defining the same ELEMENT were needed in XML, they were added to SGML and then worked back into XML so that you could still call XML a proper subset. Language designers are devious sometimes.

Although used by many major corporations and government organizations, the expense and difficulty of learning and using SGML, Hy-Time, Text Encoding Initiative (TEI), and other complex document description languages made it difficult for laypersons and smaller organizations to access the tremendous power of these languages to format structured data. XML is an attempt to make most of the power of SGML and the rest accessible to non-specialists. Another goal is to make stable implementations of a structured document language easy to create so that the cost of editors, validators, and other tools comes within reach of ordinary people.

Tip from

LeeAnne.com
Words to weave by

If your XML project relates to a major industry, asking major firms and associations questions that address the needs of that industry may reveal existing SGML DTDs. If so, these may be able to be used as a basis for XML DTDs and enable your project to address a larger audience than if you just started from scratch. It pays to investigate your target market thoroughly.

IBM, one of the largest publishers in the world, with hundreds of millions of pages of documentation required for its computers and other systems, has used SGML from the earliest days as a data repository and prepress layout engine.

The Federal government uses SGML for parts procurement, manuals, automating bids on government contracts, inventory control, and many more sophisticated database systems. The armed services, the space program, and the U.S. Government Printing Office all use SGML to ensure interoperability and data accessibility.

Because XML is a subset of SGML, many applications originally coded in SGML are being ported to XML. For the most part, the changes required are more-or-less mechanical in nature, although some difficulties exist. For technical reasons, many of these problems will be resolved by simplifying the descriptions and making them more exact. As an XML designer, you may find yourself working with SGML DTDs, so gaining an understanding SGML DTDs will help you successfully modify and use them.

Remember that SGML has been around for a long time, at least in computer lifetimes. Many problems have already been solved and have huge installed user bases. Being able to communicate with these existing systems and users may mean the difference between success and failure for startups looking for a market. Although XML can be used to access SGML databases, it takes some DTD design work.

Tip from	
LeeAnne.com Words to weave by	If your target market includes government agencies or contractors, there are probably existing SGML DTDs exactly suited to at least part of their problem space. If so, there are probably industry groups already translating those DTDs to XML. So it pays to do your homework before undertaking XML DTD development. An appropriate DTD may already be available.

Although you don't have to know SGML to learn and use XML, it is fairly common to modify existing or legacy SGML DTDs into XML DTDs in the course of daily life as an XML expert. You will learn enough about this process to be able to do it with some confidence.

Caution	A caution is in order here. Many SGML DTDs are huge because the problems they address are large. You can't expect to waltz up to a 900-page SGML DTD that took a team of 20 experts five years to develop and convert it to XML in an afternoon. It might take a wee bit longer than that. It might take a year or more.

XHTML

XHTML, Extensible Hypertext Markup Language, is an HTML-like markup language defined as an XML DTD. HTML is defined as an SGML DTD, so redefining as an XML application makes it more useful in an XML world. In particular, this means that the XHTML language is extensible, allowing users and groups of users to extend the language in powerful ways. Implications of this extensibility include

- Single edit cycle documents that encapsulate databases, printed user manuals, and Web display functionalities in one file.
- Tremendous opportunities for extended e-commerce transactions and information exchange automation using standardized XML vocabularies.

- An easy way to reuse or convert many of the millions of HTML Web pages in existence today, retaining compatibility with existing browsers while enabling new features for those using XML-enabled agents.

- Allowing XML Web pages to be automatically validated, completely eliminating many common coding errors while retaining compatibility with legacy browsers.

- Providing simple mechanisms that enable the Web to evolve to meet the needs of the diverse communities it encompasses without requiring proprietary or non-standard additions that make life difficult.

Like the current HTML definitions, there are strict, transitional, and frames versions of the XHTML DTDs. XHTML is designed to address a particular problem space: how to create XML Web pages that can be viewed with ordinary HTML browsers while not giving up the advantages that XML provides.

However, XHTML is only one of many XML languages designed to address particular problem domains. Throughout this book you'll examine other examples, languages designed to simplify the production of multimedia documents, for example, or texts incorporating mathematics.

XML in Theory and Practice

XML is so logical you may wonder why it took so long to be invented. Part of the answer is that the basic concepts have been around for a long time but were only recently applied to computer data files. A component-based parts list, for example, is a trivial requirement for putting together any complex mechanical device. But the idea of extending this paper tool to the electronic one, and generalizing the concept so it could be used for anything made up of component parts, including non-physical objects, was a flash of insight very typical of human progress over the centuries.

People organize almost everything into hierarchies. It's the only way to handle truly complex tasks, from buying supplies for the Department of Defense to building space shuttles. Any hierarchical structure can be described with XML, from the parts list that makes up an airliner to the corporate structure of IBM. But XML has limitations. It's not truly object-oriented, for example, so users with problem sets requiring a fully object-oriented (O-O) approach will have some trouble applying XML to their tasks. Initiatives are underway, however, to extend the domain of XML in object-oriented ways, so this limitation may be resolved eventually.

As an example of their non-object-orientedness, XML documents can't really inherit from their ancestors and are not truly encapsulated because their internals are fully exposed. They do exhibit polymorphism and other object-oriented behaviors, so they're a step in the right direction as far as the O-O world is concerned.

In the meantime, there's much that can be done with XML. Look at a few simple ones to start.

In one way, you've been coding XML for a long time already. HTML is so close to an XML application that many well-coded Web pages will read into an XML processor without problem or complaint. The XHTML 1.0 standard from W3C reformats the existing HTML 4.0 DTDs, SGML constructs all, into valid XML DTDs. This will allow many existing HTML documents to be viewed as XHTML documents. So, your existing pages may need no work at all to turn them into XML. Many of those pages that do require some minor rework can be reliably converted in batch by simple conversion programs such as Tidy, from Dave Raggett at W3C.

> **Note**
>
> Markup tags aren't the only mechanisms that can affect the context and representation of text. There are various pointer mechanisms used to create a database of characteristics and then point to each instance of it in your document. Microsoft Word uses this technique, as do Tagged Image Format Files (TIFF). The weakness of these schemes is that they are not robust. If any part of the header that contains the pointers becomes corrupt, the entire document is destroyed. One of the reasons for the rapid growth and success of the Web is the robust behavior of text-based markup.

PRACTICAL EXAMPLES OF XML

So, applying your existing knowledge of HTML is one good way to start learning about XML. It's a language of tags and attributes, just like HTML, and uses many of the same conventions. In HTML, matching pairs of tags surround most content, an opening tag and a closing tag, like this:

```
HTML: <H1>Headline</H1>
```

XML works the same way. XML encourages, but doesn't enforce, slightly more verbosity than HTML does, so the preceding code in a real XML application might look like this:

```
XML: <headline1>Headline</headline1>
```

In XHTML, the same code would look like this:

```
XHTML: <h1>Headline</h1>
```

which is exactly the same except that XHTML uses lowercase tags only. HTML is case-insensitive, so using the XHTML convention makes your tags acceptable in both environments.

Now might be the time to point out that, unlike HTML, all XML languages are case sensitive. How the tag is defined, casewise, is the way you have to use it. So, many XML applications use all lowercase and none can accept different capitalizations of their keywords or attributes.

Attributes are used in exactly the same way except that they must be quoted every time. So although you can get away with this in HTML

```
<IMG height=20 width=20 src="myimage.gif">
```

in any XML-based language you would use this:

```
<image height="20" width="20" source="myimage.gif />
```

Did you notice the slash at the right end of the <image> tag? That points out another XML difference. Although HTML allows certain tags to be used without closing tags, XML doesn't. Every tag has to be closed, even when it's an empty tag such as the HTML <IMG> tag or the XHTML <img> tag. The best way to do this is to put a slash at the end of the tag, separated by a space from the rest of the attributes and content. This doesn't seem to break any HTML browsers and tells XML that the tag is closed.

```
XML/HTML-compliant examples: <br />  <img src=" ... />
```

This syntax may appear odd at first, but it makes perfect sense when you think about it. HTML DTD information, or what passes for it in most browsers, is contained internally in the browser itself. XML allows a parser to be validating or non-validating, in which case it can't access the DTD to be able to tell the difference between tags with content and empty tags. So, you have to tell the parser directly using this simple format.

XML TAG ORDER

XML isn't as loose about the order of tags either. Tags must be closed in the context in which they were opened. Always. So putting tags in the wrong order, allowed by most HTML browsers in spite of the fact that it's officially disallowed, is forbidden in XML. The first tag opened is always the last one closed:

```
Wrong: <i><b>Italics Bold Text<i><b>
Right: <i><b>Italics Bold Text<b><i>
```

Tip from

Words to weave by

Tag order is important! *Context* is another term for scope, so if you think of tags like plates in the push down stack of plates in a cafeteria you can't go wrong. If you open an <i> tag within the scope or context of a <b> tag, it has to be closed within the same scope or context. You can't do it after you close the <b> tag. It has to be closed before.

It doesn't matter how far away the tags are from each other. The tag context acts like a pushdown stack of plates in a serve-yourself restaurant. The tags have to come off the stack in the exact reverse order as when they were pushed down. Alternatively, you can't traverse the document structure tree by swinging from limb to limb like an ape. You have to walk it like an ant.

Tip from

Words to weave by

First in, last out. This simple rule is easy to follow and, if your source is pretty printed, easy to see. Every nesting level has to close all its tags before exiting. And, all these metaphors are implied by the tree structure of XML documents.

Speaking of trees, most of the things you use every day have component parts that are more or less invariant and can be organized into a tree-like hierarchy. A bottle of aspirin, for example, has component bits, a body, a lid or top of some sort, one or more labels that describe the contents, and the contents themselves. If you were given the job of assembling aspirin bottles from their components, you would find that there is an order you have to do things in to avoid spilling the pills. Labels go on first, then tablets, then top. Top, label, tablets won't work at all. Tablets, label, top *might* work but you do risk spilling tablets if the bottle goes on its side. So an XML description might go as shown in Listing 1.1.

LISTING 1.1   AN ASPIRIN BOTTLE BROKEN DOWN TO COMPONENTS

```
<bottle>
  <top>
    type 3 childsafe
  </top>
  <body>
    <body-type>
      100 count plastic
    </body-type>
    <contents>
      <count>
        100
      </count>
      <content-type>
        aspirin
      </content-type>
    </contents>
  </body>
  <labeling>
    <frontlabel>
      XYZ brand generic
    </frontlabel>
    <rearlabel>
      XYZ directions and warning
    </rearlabel>
  </labeling>
</bottle>
```

Every sub-element is properly nested inside its container element and there is exactly one root element, the bottle. This is most of what's truly necessary for an XML file to be considered well formed. Of course there are many ways of describing an aspirin bottle and every description is more-or-less arbitrary. A particular bottle might come in a box, for example, and have a printed package insert. Or it might be blister-packed for a different market. Or it might have many different labels for different languages. The possibilities are as endless as the world of goods and services. However, the bottle as a whole is made up of a container body, the labeling, the top, and the aspirin contained within it. One can easily understand that aspirin tablets are nested within the bottle. It may be slightly less obvious that the bottle itself is made up of parts which are logically nested within the concept of "bottle" used here. But overall, because it's a container, an aspirin bottle is about the most intuitive and accessible example of nesting commonly available.

Tip from
LeeAnne.com
Words to weave by

If aspirin bottles aren't clear, try thinking of any other object or idea with a hierarchy. People do this kind of classification all the time, from the organization chart for your firm (absent dotted lines) to the scientific classifications of plants and animals. Anything with a parts list is a hierarchy. Those little nested Russian Easter dolls are also a good example, or a set of nested mixing bowls.

Taxonomy is the difficult science of dividing up the analog world into digital classifications. Various trade groups have come together to decide how to create standard names and structures for their products and component pieces. That way a bottle manufacturer can tell an aspirin maker what sorts of bottles are available in the catalog and how much they cost. Or an aspirin maker can tell a pharmacy what sorts of packaging are available. User-friendly tools will make it easy to author documents described in this way and as shown in Figure 1.1.

Figure 1.1
A view of Multidoc Pro Publisher editing our hypothetical XML aspirin bottle document with the XML data structure displayed.

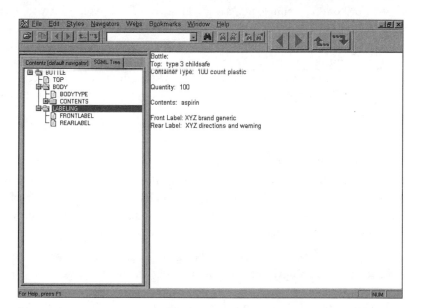

DOCUMENT TYPE DEFINITIONS

An XML DTD, (*Document Type Definition*), is at one level merely a record of how XML is used in a particular document. It's not necessary to have a DTD to do interesting things. But to access the full power of XML a DTD is a necessary step.

Tip from
LeeAnne.com
Words to weave by

Think of a DTD as a Project Plan. It forms the organizational framework for larger projects. You don't need them for a one-time effort, but if you expect to share information with anyone else, or if the project is large, you should have one.

Without a DTD, you can't use extended character sets or encodings easily. Nor can you use the most powerful authoring tools, which validate and enforce proper document structure as you write. Parameter entities, a powerful macro facility that makes life easier for XML developers, are also out of reach. And finally, you'll have to supply values for every attribute because a DTD is needed to set default values.

With all those reasons to have a DTD, about the only reason not to have one is the difficulty of making one, admittedly an intricate task for complex document systems. But it doesn't have to be *all* that difficult. XML was designed to be simple to use and understand. There are only a handful or two of keywords to memorize and the structure of the language is straightforward. It's not rocket science. DTDs are discussed more thoroughly in Chapter 3, "Understanding XML Document Type Definitions."

In this book, you'll learn how to modify existing DTDs and even construct a DTD from scratch, or convert a simple SGML DTD into an XML one. After you have a DTD that works, you can use programmatic tools to automatically manipulate the data in your documents in almost any way you can think of. You'll explore applications that rewrite your XML code into ordinary HTML so that any browser can see it the way you intend. You'll experiment with parsing your own document structure to demonstrate how easy it is to access your data with Java, Perl, JavaScript, or other programming language. What you do with this extraordinary capability is really up to you.

FUTURE DEVELOPMENTS

XML is a standard on the move, although the designers at W3C wisely broke up the entirety of what might be called XML into many component parts. This ensures that smallish parts can be released as W3C Recommendations when agreement is reached by the various W3C Working Groups instead of waiting for an accord on the whole thing.

Even as we speak, final comments are being taken on a variety of extensions to the basic XML Recommendation and vigorous debate is going on about others. It may be that several competing solutions co-exist for a while, as they often do in the inharmonious and quasi-anarchic environment of the Web. Commercial vendors propose solutions they already have in their pockets, hoping to capitalize on being the first to market, although user groups propose others, which they see as being bigger, better, faster, or more in some way. It's quite a circus.

XLINK AND XPOINTER

Among the most interesting developments are the two related proposals first described as XML Linking Language (XLL) but now broken into smaller components called XLink and XPointer.

XLink and XPointer solve an important problem on the Web. Current HTML hyperlinks are strictly one-way affairs with little selectivity. Achieving fine granularity in linking to a document requires write access to its source code. This is hardly satisfactory in a dynamic and less-than-benign environment like the Web where access is carefully guarded against evildoers and idiots. As an example, in an ordinary HTML document one can only link to the top or to named locations within the document at which there happens to be a tag like this:

```
<a name="someName"></a>
```

If that tag doesn't exist and you can't persuade the author of the document to put it where you want it, you can't link to it using HTML. If it's there, it's a simple matter to link to it like this:

```
<a href="documentURL#someName">Link</a>
```

If not, you need to find someone with write access to the document or do without.

Caution	Depending on HTML-style write access, even within your own company, is rarely wise although needed with our present toolset. There are many departments who will not be happy giving write access to outside users, human resources and payroll or accounting for common examples, and as more departmental applications become Web-enabled, maintaining a site with embedded links will become a nightmare. But with XLink and XPointer, documents can be accessed without regard to existing named locations, although that mechanism is still available.

XLink extends this primitive capability with sophisticated capabilities to *transclude*, or include remote copies of portions of several documents into host documents, vary the presentation and destination of links according to user-defined criteria, and do other fun stuff with distributed data. With the addition of XPointer, you can even access the object model of the document itself to allow virtual targets to be defined almost anywhere in a remote document. In the near future, it may be possible to implement dynamic rendering of custom pages based merely on linking criteria. It's getting to the point where no two people will see the same Web page without deliberately choosing to do so.

XSL—STYLE SHEETS ON STEROIDS

XSL, the Extensible Stylesheet Language, is another initiative that's very close to bearing fruit. Current CSS, Cascading Style Sheet, and CSS2 Recommendations are limited to cosmetic touching up of the appearance of an existing document based on HTML or XML tags and attributes. The only way to alter the document radically was with Dynamic HTML, with its attendant compatibility problems and headaches. But XSL allows write and rewrite access to the entire document using XPath, a standard description of document struction, including transcluded parts brought in by Xlink, and based on the entire object model of the document. You'll look at XLink and XPointer in detail in Chapter 9, "XLink and XPointer."

You could, for example, code an XSL style sheet to generate a table of contents automatically by traversing the document tree, prefixing the document with the generated table of contents, and then displaying the document itself. Or you could rearrange the page itself, deleting sports news and bringing in abstracts of new astronomical discoveries instead, or eliminating national news in favor of local coverage. Two of the three subparts of XSL, XSL Transformations and XPath, are already released as Recommendations. The final piece is XSL proper, the formatting language. Look out DHTML and goodbye to (most) scripts! You'll look at these more closely in Chapter 12, "CSS1, CSS2, DSSSL, XSL."

All in all, a lot of things you now depend on Internet home ports to do for you will be possible at home. Vendors will sell or give away style sheets that can be customized to access the information you want to know about and toss random intrusions into the bit bucket.

XML Signatures will allow Web pages to be signed by the author in a manner that cannot be repudiated, allowing some measure of trust to be built over a network whose information seems highly suspect at times.

A CONCISE DESCRIPTION OF XML ORIGINS

Markup has been with us almost since the beginning of written language. The Egyptians, who used one of the most ancient writing systems in the world—hieroglyphic symbols—marked personal names with an oval cartouche to distinguish them from ordinary words. They also used color to highlight important phrases, sort of an Egyptian boldface. Because Egyptian could be written either from left to right or from right to left, depending on context, they faced the pictures of animals and people toward the start of the line as an antique bi-directional attribute and markup. They thought it was more polite to have the figures greet you as you read along the line. It would be rude if the figures faced away. Figure 1.2 shows a portion of the Rosetta Stone, one of the important milestones in our understanding of communications and the past.

Figure 1.2
Egyptian hieroglyphics
c. 196 BCE illustrating
the use of cartouche
markup for names
and of rtl bi-di
markup.

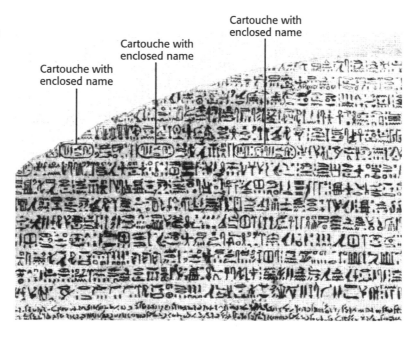

Cartouche with enclosed name

Cartouche with enclosed name

Cartouche with enclosed name

ANCIENT HEBREW MARKUP CONVENTIONS

Ancient Hebrew, as written in the Torah, has almost no markup at all except for decorative "crowns" over seven letters and two final letter forms. Like many writing systems, ancient Hebrew came late to the idea of putting spaces between words, one of the earliest markup schemes, but the present Torah is usually seen with those newfangled inventions in place.

> **Note**
>
> Although these quick language hints are brief, it's important to remember that XML is designed to support all human languages. So, Hebrew is merely a simple example of a large class of language problems an XML designer may face.

A passage in Torah Hebrew would look something like this:

THIS IS A SENTENCE OF TORAH STYLE WRITING THIS IS THE NEXT SENTENCE THIS IS THE THIRD SENTENCE AND SO ON

Except that ancient Hebrew didn't use any indication of vowels, preferring to supply them by a process of sheer reason, so the above four sentences would actually look more like this:

THS S SNTNC F TRH STL WRTNG THS S TH NXT SNTNC THS S TH THRD SNTNC ND S N

It's a somewhat daunting task, even when you know the words by heart. The text is usually read with the aid of a pointer so you don't get lost on the page.

Remember, one person's markup is another's essential aid to understanding. It's quite common to make special reader's versions of Torah with vowel markings and indications of the melody to use while chanting to make up for poor memories and lack of skill.

ANCIENT ROMAN MARKUP CONVENTIONS

The history of our own Roman lettering is similar, with word spacing, rhetorical punctuation, the introduction of lowercase letters to make the difference between ordinary words and important ones more obvious, and similar innovations designed to make writing easier to understand and use. Along about the Renaissance the semicolon was introduced to mark a certain subtle relationship between thoughts, but we've been lumbering along with a markup system many hundreds, even thousands of years old for quite some time now.

We use it daily, underlining words, punctuating sentences, capitalizing proper names and the starting character of every sentence to make our thoughts clear on paper.

It wasn't quite good enough for formatting printed books, however. Through sheer human ingenuity printers and typographers developed a clever system of markup to identify and call for formatting changes to parts of books and other printed matter. The printer's markup is actually called markup, and our name comes from their use of it because it was added by hand, "marked up," on typewritten or manuscript pages. All the tricks of the printer's trade have special marks, boldface, italic, small caps, indentations and spaces of various sorts, font changes, special treatments of titles, chapter headings, running footers, headers, colophons, page numbering, and a host of others. Figure 1.3 shows a typewritten page marked up as an editor might see it, with callouts for typographical style and text treatments.

Figure 1.3
A typewritten sample document marked up with a copyeditor's notations to the type-setter.

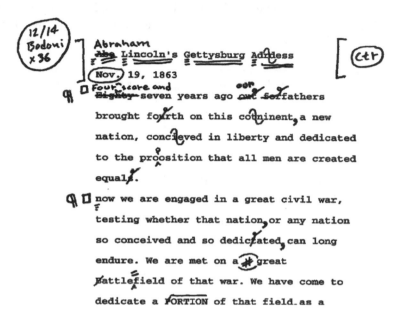

MARKUP IN RECENT HISTORY

With the advent of the computer age a new paradigm was needed to allow production of formatted documentation and papers. One of the earliest, Runoff, was coded by Jerry Saltzer for the CTSS operating system on the IBM 7094 in the early 60s and later ported to Multics, another early operating system. Runoff was the first important tool ported to the newly invented UNIX (one of whatever Multics was many of) operating system from Bell Labs. Runoff and all its descendents use special markup tags to control the formatted appearance of the text, just as we do today. In many ways it can be regarded as the ancestor of both HTML and XML, although modern applications have gone far beyond what these early programs were designed for.

A Canadian named William Tunnicliffe called for the separation of formatting information from information content in electronic media in 1967. Almost simultaneously, Stanley Rice, a New York book designer, proposed a system of universal editorial structure tags. A great idea was coalescing and gathering momentum.

Out of these threads came the Generic Coding concept and from this came in turn GML, the Generalized Markup Language created by Charles Goldfarb, Edward Mosher, and Raymond Lorie of IBM in 1969 to successfully encode and publish millions of pages of IBM documentation.

After a bit more development, GML and Generic Coding came together again in 1978 in the form of a committee to develop a new language, based on GML but extended with new ideas contributed by many people. In 1980, SGML, the Standard Generalized Markup Language was released in draft. By 1983 the new draft standard had been issued as an industry standard, GCA 101-1983, and adopted by the Internal Revenue Service and the U.S. Military.

Between 1983 and 1987, work was being done on an SGML publishing standard for books, serial publications, and articles with optional components for mathematics, scientific papers, and complex tables. It was adopted as an ANSI standard, Z39.59, in 1988 and later in revised form as an international standard, ISO 12083.

In 1986, the international SGML standard, ISO 8879:1986, was published and things started heating up. In 1988, the U.S. Department of Defense issued the CALS (Computer-aided Acquisition and Logistical Support) SGML standard as MIL-M-28001.

Since that time, many large projects based on SGML have flourished in relative obscurity outside scholarly and industry circles, the Text Encoding Initiative (TEI), HyTime, ISO 10744, the Hypermedia Time-based Structuring Language, a vastly complex standard supporting synchronized multimedia of all types, and many others.

All these projects have been huge with large amounts of study required just to become familiar enough with the language and facilities to become productive in their vast expanse of possibilities. Which brings us right around to XML.

CHAPTER

2

UNDERSTANDING XML SYNTAX

In this chapter

UNDERSTANDING XML STRUCTURE

XML is actually two languages, or meta-languages really, both described in the same document. The first is a set of rules for producing well-formed XML documents whereas the second is a set of rules for producing an XML *Document Type Definition*, or DTD, which allows the structure of the XML document to be constrained and validated against those constraints. The distinction between these two languages is often blurred, because a complete XML document includes at least the optional presence of a DTD, whether it's actually present or not. To complicate things further, the DTD may consist of two parts, an *internal subset* and an *external subset*.

This chapter looks at the XML document without dwelling too much on the DTD, because it's possible to create an XML document without reference to a DTD. For performance reasons, many XML documents will be used without ever validating against the DTD, even if the DTD is available. Over slow connections, reading in a DTD located external to your local machine may be tediously slow, and because DTDs may contain references to other documents, resolving all the external references may take an inordinate amount of time even with a high speed connection. Users are accustomed to seeing HTML documents load incrementally, so they can be read before the document finishes loading, but validating XML parsers aren't allowed to display the document unless it's valid, so the document won't appear on the user's screen until everything is loaded. This can be disconcerting.

However, every document is created with a DTD in mind, whether the DTD is explicit or not. Even when creating documents without a DTD, a tentative sort of DTD has to be floating around in your mind as you create the document, because a DTD describes a data structure.

GETTING TECHNICAL WITH XML

Appendix A, "XML/XHTML Reference," describes (in part) the basic XML syntax by listing the Extended Backus-Naur Form (EBNF) notation that the W3C XML 1.0 standard itself uses to define it. Selected EBNF production rules are supplemented by terse descriptions of the explicit validity and/or well-formedness constraints with which W3C has modified or extended particular EBNF rules. Although EBNF is wonderfully compact, allowing legal productions in a programming language to be succinctly defined as a series of grammatical transformation rules, W3C has left quite a bit out of the EBNF description of the language for simplicity. Most of the missing bits are in the form of constraints, verbal descriptions of additional criteria that a given production must obey, but some are actually found in the text of the standard.

EBNF is just a shorthand way of saying things about programming languages, and you could just as easily describe XML in a slightly more accessible way using words, although the EBNF is concise by comparison with the plain English equivalent. However, some things are difficult (or tedious) to express in EBNF, and EBNF itself is terse to the point of obscurity for most people, so W3C has chosen to mix the two styles of language description in its recommendation. Some production rules are described fully in the EBNF notation and the accompanying text is only an explanation of what the EBNF actually says. Some production rules are described fully only by a combination of the EBNF rule and its accompanying commentary in the text, so the EBNF rule serves as a sort of overall framework to which the textual comments must be added to characterize the actual rule.

In practice, the EBNF in the XML 1.0 Recommendation from W3C is and must be supplemented by various textual constraint additions contained in the body of the document to really understand it. But after you understand how it all fits together, the EBNF rules are useful as a quick crib sheet to jog your memory of how the language works.

Note

> Although there is an EBNF syntax for XML, that description is not complete. Without taking into account the various constraints listed in the Recommendation and carefully reading the text, an incorrect understanding and implementation is almost inevitable.

That's why the EBNF listing is available for you in the appendix, not to learn how to use XML, but to remind you of how it's used when you don't want to search through the entire specification looking for a particular construction. Because the XML 1.0 Recommendation is fairly concise, you might also want to keep a bookmark pointing to Tim Bray's Annotated XML 1.0 Recommendation at `http://www.xml.com/axml/testaxml.htm` because it more plainly explains some of the thinking that went into the specification. Note also that you have to read the errata section of the specification carefully. Many substantive changes have been made and, although these changes are reflected in this book, more changes may be made in future.

Now this may all sound complicated but it's really not. You are probably familiar with following rules that may change in context. For example, the rule that says you have to stop at a red light when driving a car is a simple rule and universally applicable, so when you learned to drive, you learned that rule quickly. But in some states, a special modification of the red light rule allows you to turn right after stopping unless otherwise posted. That sounds like a simple rule as well, but that rule would have to have a validity constraint attached to it because not all states allow this. A footnote would suffice for most purposes. The alternative would be to make lots of similar rules about red lights with special conditions built in to handle exceptions. This sort of thing is tedious to do in EBNF so W3C stuck with a simple rule and added constraints, which are more or less like footnotes, to the rules that needed them.

Describing New Vocabularies with XML

XML is dual-natured; a meta-language which allows you to describe new document structures and vocabularies as well as the language used to express that structure and vocabulary in a document instance. There is a clear difference between an XML document, which may or may not be associated with a DTD expressed in the XML meta-language, and an XML DTD. They use completely different syntaxes to describe an XML document, the one by example and the other prescriptive.

XML Document Type Definitions (DTDs) describe instances of XML languages, which are sometimes called XML vocabularies. XML documents are created using those languages. Unfortunately, that distinction is sometimes lost in casual speech, and particular XML vocabularies and associated DTDs are described loosely as "XML."

Although you need to know both to fully master XML, it's actually not necessary to define a DTD to create and use an XML vocabulary as long as you obey the rules. A user of an XML language or vocabulary may never see nor care about the DTD used to describe her particular application anymore than the thousands of individuals working in Web design using HTML may know or care about the W3C HTML 4.0 SGML DTD used to describe HTML. In fact, a DTD might not even exist. It just doesn't matter all that much at the application level. Because you're reading this book, however, it's assumed that you will be called upon to design or work with DTDs in some way, and a truly deep knowledge of XML requires that you understand how and why a DTD is constructed and used.

UNDERSTANDING DOCUMENT TYPE DEFINITION ADVANTAGES

Although DTDs are optional because an XML processor can infer a reasonable DTD from an instance of XML, having a DTD available offers many advantages:

- A DTD describes the organization of a document in a way that can be easily shared.

- A DTD allows a designer to create a *robust* transformation between a given type of XML document and another format for display or transfer. Because you know everything possible about documents with a DTD, you'll know how to handle structures that may not exist in a particular sample but are allowed by the document type, even if you've never seen them.

- A DTD allows a *validating* parser to determine whether a particular document is constructed according to the rules set up by the originators of the specification. This is extremely important for EDI and other applications in which documents will be shared and used by other processes.

- Without a DTD, an XML authoring environment cannot give hints about which elements are required or optional at a given point and which attributes the current element can take. Context-sensitive menus or hints are an enormous help in speeding document development and preventing errors.

- Without a DTD, the creator of an authoring manual or style document has no way of knowing how the defined document should be constructed. An authoring manual is an embodiment of the knowledge expressed in a DTD, although not a DTD in itself.

- Specifying the DTD used in a document identifies the revision level of the standard used to create it. When documents evolve in functionality and syntax, this can be an important clue about how to display or transform a document in new situations.

Having a DTD available conveys significant information and benefits, *if* you need those benefits. But like everything else in life, there's a cost involved.

Coping with Document Type Definition Disadvantages

For all their advantages, DTDs are not without problems. They use a different syntax than the rest of XML, so it requires a slightly different skill set to construct one. In addition, like any technical description, getting involved in the DTD design before thinking about the way you want your data structures to look in the document itself can bog you down in detail when you should be looking at the overall structure. Many people design the XML document using the intended XML vocabulary and then use an automatic DTD extraction tool to generate a DTD from the document itself. After this is done, the DTD can be fine-tuned by adding to or tweaking the source code.

PART
I
CH
2

The following disadvantages of DTDs exist as well:

- With a DTD, a validating XML user agent requires at *least* one extra read operation to access the location where the DTD is available. Although caching may lessen the performance hit for some network users, many foreseeable uses of XML documents will preclude the use of cache storage.

- A DTD greatly increases the complexity of the parser required to determine whether a document should be displayed. For some devices, this may not be feasible.

- Some *validating* authoring environments that use a DTD make it difficult to save your workspace at the end of the day or restore it the next day unless the document is in a valid state. This can be annoying if you have a lot of work left to do and need to leave it for a while.

- A DTD is theoretically capable of continuing external reads without limit because a DTD can incorporate other DTDs and entity sets. It's possible that some complex documents may take unacceptable amounts of time before they render on the display device when using a validating parser.

The basic tradeoff in deciding whether to use a DTD is between the free-wheeling ability you're used to with HTML—being able to do pretty much whatever you want and patch things up on-the-fly—and a much more structured environment in which every "i" must be dotted and every "t" crossed. In many situations, such as when you are creating documents meant for general availability and distributed creation, you need that strict enforcement of rules and will want a DTD. In others, such as when you are developing a new XML document type, you won't need or want strict enforcement and can do without a DTD, at least during initial design.

But after development has led to a stable product, you'll want to formalize your design so it can be easily distributed. Although you might also want to create a user's manual, a DTD is a simple way of letting users test their document to be sure that they truly follow the guidelines they read in the manual. At that point, you might even regret that DTDs allow so much flexibility. If you intend a field to contain a phone number, defining the field as CDATA leaves a lot to be desired.

In fact, XML Schema allows even stricter rule-making capabilities, which can be useful in situations that demand very strict control over field content, as you'll see in Chapter 7, "XML Schemas."

IS XML JUST HTML ALL OVER AGAIN?

XML is a language of tags and attributes much like HTML, but an HTML mutated almost beyond recognition. XML is HTML on steroids.

XML is far more structured than HTML. Whereas HTML processors routinely accept wildly inaccurate and malformed code and attempt to make sense of it on the screen, XML is *required* to abort when it encounters a fatal error, which is almost any error at all. This is a throwback to the early days of data processing in some ways, when any error in code was punished with a core dump that you could spend hours deciphering. Expect to spend a bit more time debugging XML than you have previously spent on HTML.

Along with this unforgiving behavior, however, XML is far more powerful. Whereas HTML contented itself with 77 tags or so, depending on who was counting, XML has a potentially infinite number of tags, structured in almost any way you choose.

The basics are still the same, however, and your experience with HTML will make it easy to accept the evolutionary step that XML and its associated standards represent. Using XML is not quite as easy as rolling off a log but it's not like climbing Mount Everest either. With a little discipline and knowledge, which this book will help you gain, you'll be coding XML before you know it.

In fact, in a way you've been coding XML all along with your previous use of HTML. Not only is well-made HTML awfully close to XHTML—the XML-compliant replacement for HTML—but *clean* HTML 4.0 code is quite readable as XHTML 1.0. Because HTML 4.0 was structured as an SGML application and XML is a subset of SGML, this makes a lot of sense. The minor syntactic differences between XHTML, an XML vocabulary, and HTML, an SGML vocabulary, can be automatically adjusted if desired.

An XML document author is usually issued an authoring or coding manual (or sheet, for small DTDs) describing the tags used in the XML application, their attributes and possible values, and how they nest within each other. Following such a coding manual is no more difficult than remembering that a table row <tr> has to nest inside a table <table> and has, or should have, no meaning outside that context.

For most purposes, this is enough. XML authors are no more likely to be technical gurus who can instantly extrapolate the structure and use of an application from a glance at the DTD than are freeway commuters likely to be expert automobile mechanics. XML is able to give authors quite a bit of help in learning how to use a particular application, because they're encouraged to give tags meaningful names that are easy to remember. The creator of an application *should* provide an authoring manual that explains how to use it in simple terms. The theory is that any future data analyst could look at your XML code and figure out what it is and how it's structured without recourse to the original design documentation (presumably lost in the dust of history) based on structure and element names alone.

PART

I

CH

2

Tip from

Words to weave by

> Although any XML processor can tell you whether your code is well-formed and a manual can help you construct a valid document, the DTD lets you check your work unambiguously. This can be a separate step from the writing process, however, depending on the type of authoring tool used.

Whether your code fulfills that ideal is largely up to your use of tag names within some tiny limits:

- Tag names starting with the string "xml" in any case combination are reserved; that is, you're not permitted to create them no matter what the provocation. Don't invent them on your own. If you feel you *must* have one, submit it to W3C as part of a Member Submission (assuming, of course, that you are a member) and see what happens.

- Tag names containing a colon are apt to be interpreted as identifiers with an associated namespace, so using colons in tag names is strongly discouraged and may eventually be forbidden. Why take a chance? Avoid them.

- A tag name has to start with a "letter," which in this context is any Unicode/ISO/IEC 10646 letter or ideograph, or an underscore (or a colon, which you already know to avoid to prevent confusion with namespaces).

After that, a tag name can include any Unicode/ISO/IEC 10646 "letter," ideograph, or digit, plus the combining characters, extenders, periods, hyphens, spaces, or colons. A few human languages have otherwise legal characters that cannot begin a legal name in that language. These characters are excluded from the list of characters if they're in a position which could be viewed as "first" after a hyphen or other logical word break. But if you know the language, that will be obvious.

The Thai character *mai yamok (looks like a backward f without a crossbar)*, for example, looks like a letter but can't be used to begin a word because it signifies repetition of the previous letter.

The combining characters are special characters used to add an accent to another character, many of which normalize to a single accented character. This is a convenience for keyboard entry, because many languages that include accented characters allow you to enter them using special "zero-width" accent characters, which can attach themselves to any other character.

The extenders are various special punctuation marks such as (in European languages) middle dot, triangular colon, and half-triangular colon. The extended characters are similar in other world scripts, not alphabetic exactly, but fitting in there somehow. If you need to use one in a language other than English, you'll probably know what they are so they're easy to find. But if you don't speak or write Arabic, using an Arabic "tatweel" in your tag name is probably an affectation, although strictly allowed.

STARTING WITH XML

In a sense you already know how to code in XML if you have become used to writing clean, well-made HTML 4 code. You may need only to eliminate some bad habits to become a competent XML coder, so here you will concentrate on the differences between XML and HTML. This focus highlights the skill sets required for XML and makes clear the many similarities between XML and HTML:

- **XML is case sensitive because capital letters are not a universal concept**—If you were to accommodate capital letters as equivalents, you would have to do the same for thousands of other letter variations in other languages, an onerous task. Some languages don't even have cases. There's no such thing as lowercase Hebrew, for instance, and Arabic distinguishes between initial, medial, and final forms of letters. For those who like to put their tags in uppercase and attributes in lowercase to make them stand out, this is terrible news. But modern coding editors make this less of an issue than it might have been previously. It's common to define special colors to mark tags, for example, so using uppercase is somewhat of an historical anachronism, like line numbers in COBOL.

- **XML is very sensitive to the proper nesting of tags**—Tags cannot end in a different context from which they started. So if you want `<bold><italics>`, you have to close your emphasized phrase with `</italics></bold>` to avoid a fatal error. Because XML can reference and include XML documents and document fragments anywhere on the Web that you have no control over, every XML document has to obey the same rules so you don't break one another's documents.

- **XML is not well protected against recursion**—Although it's possible to set up explicit exclusions at a given level, with a complex document structure it's difficult to maintain those exclusions at lower levels, especially when using tags that may apply at any level. So, the HTML prohibition of including an anchor `<a>` tag within another anchor tag is there in XHTML, but not enforced beyond direct inclusion.

- **XML requires you to close every tag, even empty tags**—Because it's possible to create an XML document that doesn't use a DTD, an XML processor has no way of knowing whether a tag is empty. Because all XML documents have to be *well-formed*, you have to mark empty tags with a special syntax that tells an XML processor the tag is empty and closed. You do that by placing a space and a slash mark at the end of the tag like this:

```
<break />
```

There's an alternate syntax which works just as well for real XML processors but often breaks HTML Web browsers when used with XHTML, which is to close an empty tag such as <br> with </br> like this:

```
<br></br>
```

Unfortunately it's too dangerous to use safely. Many current and most legacy browsers don't recognize the non-HTML closing tag and do odd things with it. Navigator 4.7, for example, may trash the display when it stumbles across a closing break tag. The exact behavior may vary by position in the code and the exact empty tag being closed. In short, it's error prone and should be avoided.

- **XML requires the use of either single or double quotes around attribute values**—Where HTML is lax about numbers especially and almost anything without included spaces, XML treats everything as character strings and lets the application figure everything out.

- **XML supports multiple languages**—It doesn't really support the extended character sets used in many European languages by default, as does HTML. There's an easy mechanism for including these, as well as the entire Unicode (also known as ISO/IEC 10646) character set of more than a million characters, so support for Chinese, Arabic, and many of the more exotic languages of the world is a piece of cake.

Other than the differences noted in this list, XML is very similar to HTML in the way tags are marked, attributes are argued, and content is placed between tag pairs. If you write *clean* HTML, the conversion of your HTML to XML-based XHTML is so trivial that it's possible to let a machine do it for you. Of course, XML is not limited to languages that look like HTML, so your document structure is limited only by the necessary tree structure and by your own imagination.

Tip from

LeeAnne.com
Words to weave by

For Windows machines, it's hard to beat the power and functionality of the HTML-Kit program from Chami.com (`http://www.chami.com/`), which uses Dave Raggett's excellent Tidy program to clean up and optionally convert your code to clean XML. It inserts all those pesky closing tags and the special EMPTY closing tag syntax, tweaks tags that don't nest properly, and much more. Tidy is available on the Mac with a port from Terry Teague at `http://www.geocities.com/SiliconValley/1057/tidy.html` and there are several UNIX flavors hanging around the Web. There's also a Java port for O-O enthusiasts. See Dave Raggett's Web page at W3C for up-to-date details on these and other versions at `http://www.w3.org/People/Raggett/tidy/`.

Using skills you probably have today, you could start producing simple XML documents within a few hours of practice. The language was designed to be transparent in use, so it could be easily understood and used. The terse or obscure descriptions of XML in most documents are hard to understand in an effort to be precise in a way that programmers can translate easily into applications that work. There's a bit more to learn before real mastery is obtained, but it's not all that difficult.

Before you begin dismembering the language, you should look at the XML document as a whole.

DEFINING THE XML DOCUMENT AS A WHOLE

An XML document is a collection of entities, which can be either parsed or unparsed. *Unparsed data* is anything that the XML processor can't understand, binary data or data that is only meaningful to other applications. *Parsed data* is anything that XML can understand, either as characters or markup.

An XML document must be well-formed. In the W3C XML 1.0 Recommendation, quoted here precisely, this status is laconically described as meeting these requirements:

- Taken as a whole, it matches the production labeled *document*.
- It meets all the well-formedness constraints given in this specification (the XML 1.0 Recommendation).
- Each of the parsed entities referenced directly or indirectly within the document is well-formed.

The first constraint says that to be well-formed, an XML document has to obey all the rules that describe a document in the XML 1.0 Recommendation. Those rules essentially say that an XML document has to contain a prolog and a single element which forms the root element of the document together with optional comments and processing instructions. They also say that you can tack on comments and processing instructions to the end of the document but, unfortunately, the XML parser has no way of telling whether these tacked on comments and processing instructions are associated with the document. Since they can follow the closing tag, an XML parser can't even tell whether all tacked on processing instructions and comments were received. This violates the general rule in XML that the parser must be able to tell whether a document is complete. If you use processing instructions or comments, put them in the prolog where they are far safer and can't get lost.

The second constraint says that the document follows the well-formedness constraints described in the document. These constraints are examined in the following "Understanding the Well-Formedness Constraints" section. One of the well-formedness constraints is that recursive parsed entities are forbidden. Recursion in this prohibition refers to the formation of an entity loop, in which one entity incorporates itself or another entity which incorporates itself to whatever level of indirection. This also means that a document cannot refer to itself, even indirectly through an external entity. It can't refer to an external entity unless that too doesn't refer to itself, even indirectly. Non-validating parsers may not catch this error, but it's still an error. Logically, it's apparent that if document A includes document B, defining B as containing A leads to an endless loop. It's the endless loop that's forbidden.

Note

In XML terms, being well-formed is another way of saying that an XML document forms a tree, or a branch of a tree, that is complete in and of itself. This is necessary because XML allows you to build larger documents from smaller ones and is a key to being able to use XML over the Web. You'll discover more formal rules later in this chapter.

Although being well-formed might be considered enough because a well-formed document has a DTD that describes it, an infinitely large number of DTDs can be constructed that also describe it. So for full validity, an associated DTD is required. You'll learn more about DTDs in Chapter 3, "Understanding XML Document Type Definitions."

The document production is defined in only two statements, again quoting from the XML 1.0 Recommendation:

- It contains one or more elements.

- There is exactly one element, called the *root* or *document element*, no part of which appears in the content of any other element. For all other elements, if the start-tag is in the content of another element, the end-tag is in the content of the same element. More simply stated, the elements, delimited by start and end tags, nest properly within each other.

The first statement says that there has to be at least one element in a document or, alternatively, that a well-formed document can't be empty.

The second statement says that the document has to be a tree in the narrow sense. It can't be an arbitrary connected network or have any other topology that doesn't reduce to a simple tree. It has to be complete so you can tell the difference between a successful download and a partial one.

Note

> Technically, a *tree* is a connected graph that contains no circuits. In other words a tree branches from its root without connecting back to itself and therefore doesn't contain multiple edges or loops. Anything that contains loops or multiple edges isn't a tree but something else and you can't do that in XML. An interesting side effect of this is that you can pick any arbitrary point on a tree, shake it a bit, and convert a node into a root, rearranging the tree into another with a different order of traversal. This illustrates the whimsical nature of classification schemes.

A partial download is possible in HTML, because HTML doesn't require a closing `</html>` tag, or indeed almost any closing tags. Sometimes the browser can detect the interruption but it's not guaranteed. This means that a partial document can masquerade as complete and the user has no way of knowing unless there's some obvious fault in the text. XML prevents these problems, which may be important if a user later claims that a license agreement, for example, wasn't displayed in total. Insisting on a complete tree, an example of which is shown in Figure 2.1, eliminates these potential problems.

A graph that doesn't form a tree, on the other hand, cannot be made into an XML document unless the graph can be pruned to eliminate any non-tree features. In Figure 2.2, for example, the graph on the left could be pruned by eliminating one path from the topmost leaf to either node. In the same figure, the graph on the upper right would have to have one root eliminated, because an XML document can have only one root.

Figure 2.1
This depicts a well-formed tree. You could make an XML document out of the structure represented by this tree.

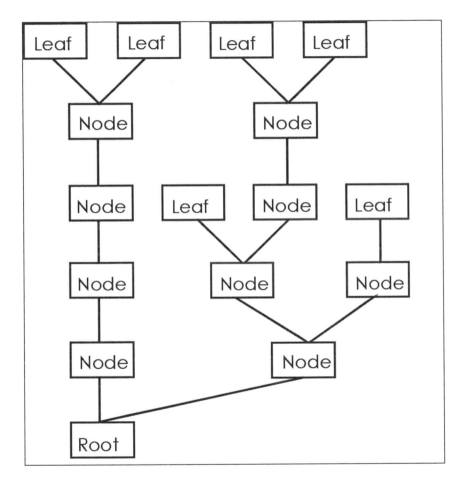

You should also be aware that trees are often depicted growing upside down, with the root at the top and the branches growing downward. This is done to accommodate our habit of reading pages from top to bottom, so the first thing we encounter on this upside down tree is the root, just as an XML parser would, and scanning down the page brings us deeper into the foliage of the tree.

Figure 2.2
This illustration depicts two graphs that are not trees. They are not capable of being turned into XML documents.

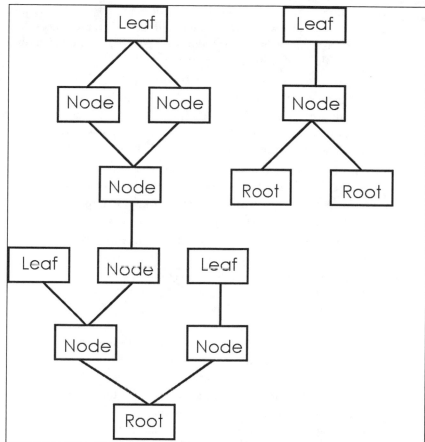

UNDERSTANDING THE WELL-FORMEDNESS CONSTRAINTS

Besides the basic properties required in an XML document as listed in the previous "Defining the XML document As a Whole," section, an XML document must meet certain extra criteria called constraints. The following list describes the well-formedness constraints:

- Parameter entities in the internal subset can only occur where markup can occur. They can't occur inside markup. This is a completely arbitrary rule and was done to simplify the task of parsing internal DTDs (see Chapter 3).

- The name in an element's end-tag must match the name in the start-tag. This is almost trivial. Few of us would expect to be able to close a `<cite>` tag with a `</citation>` tag.

- An attribute name cannot appear more than once in the same start-tag or empty-element tag. Again, this is fairly obvious. What are you supposed to do with a mal-formed line of code like this?

```
<image src="one.gif" src="two.gif" />
```

- Attribute values cannot contain direct or indirect references to external entities. This is more subtle and was done to simplify life for XML processors. In an environment in which arbitrary character encodings are possible in external entities, it would be hard to handle them all correctly in an attribute.

- The replacement text of an entity referred to directly or indirectly in an attribute value (other than `"&lt;"`) must not contain a <. This is for simplicity and error handling. If you allowed an un-escaped < inside an attribute, it would be hard to catch a missing final quote mark. Also, because you have to escape < in running text anyway, treating it differently inside an attribute value would be inconsistent.

- Characters referred to using character references must be legal characters. In other words, you can't hide characters that would otherwise be illegal by indirection or by defining them as numeric equivalents. So, for example, `&#x0000;` is not a legal character no matter how you refer to it.

- In a document without a DTD, a document with only an internal DTD subset containing no parameter entity references or a document with a value of `"standalone='yes'"` on the XML declaration, the name given in the entity reference must match that in an entity declaration. One exception is that well-formed documents need not declare any of the following entities: `&amp;`, `&lt;`, `&gt;`, `&apos;`, or `&quot;`.

  Basically, the declaration of a parameter entity must precede any reference to it, but there are some situations in which a non-validating XML processor stops processing entity declarations. So if the non-validating processor is confident that all declarations have been read and processed, then it can declare a well-formedness error and abort processing if it finds an undeclared entity. On the other hand, if any of the ways in which the non-validating XML processor stops processing entities have occurred, then it's not an error to encounter an undeclared entity. This is a complicated way of saying that non-validating XML processors may or may not catch undeclared entities, depending on the situation.

- An entity reference must not contain the name of an unparsed entity. In short, you can't plunk binary data into the middle of text without some sort of handling mechanism declared. So, the following code is permitted and the value passed on to the user agent or browser if and only if it represented an external unparsed entity which had already been declared as a notation:

  ```
  <image &myimage; />
  ```

- A parsed entity must not contain a recursive reference to itself, either directly or indirectly. Although dictionary makers may like to declare that a hat is a chapeau and a chapeau is a hat as if this means something, XML won't let you get away with it.

- Parameter-entity references may only appear in the DTD. In other words, you can't carry over processing data into the final document and expect it to mean anything. You might as well expect that you could insert a C statement, say `printf("Hello, world"\n);`, onto your typewritten page and expect it to be replaced with some value and have the carriage returned for you. On the other hand, although it's a logical error if you *expect* it to happen, such text wouldn't actually break anything either, any more than printing the above line of C code in your text generates an error. Because % is only a character and doesn't have to be escaped inside your document, it's hard to see how such an "error" would be found out. Although factually interesting, this is a null statement as far as error processing goes.

THE PROLOG: THE XML DECLARATION

Every XML document should begin with an XML declaration that identifies the file as an XML file and also identifies the version of XML being used in this particular document. The fact that this is not mandatory is due only to the fact that there are many HTML and SGML files lying about on the Web that were perfectly well-formed XML as well. Why break what's already working? The XML declaration is also the place you declare your encoding and whether the document is standalone. The order shown in the following snippet is mandatory, although the encoding and standalone attributes are both optional:

```
<?xml version="1.0" encoding=" ISO-8859-1" standalone="yes">
```

Encodings let you identify which of many character sets you plan to use in the document. This is important because, unlike HTML, which presupposes ASCII and forces you to use ASCII names, XML allows speakers of Hindi, for example, to use a Devanagari encoding and make their text and editing environment readable to ordinary citizens who happen to be XML authors. Or a Chinese author might prefer Chinese characters in tags and content. With few limitations based on the rules for the languages themselves, you can use scripts and ideographs in element names as well as content.

As a simple example of the sorts of limitations which exist based on language rules, consider the superscript letters "st" in the quasi-abbreviation "1st." The letters really modify the "1" so that you know it's supposed to be pronounced "first." There is no legal situation in English (or any European language) in which you are free to use this construction at the beginning of a "word." So "stwhile" doesn't legally expand into the word "erstwhile."

Similarly, "St Ives" should be pronounced "Saint Ives." In XML, you could define an element named <St> according to the rules, but because the superscript letters aren't legal at the beginning of words in any European language, you can't define an element named <tmisbehaving> (to be pronounced "ain't misbehaving") because it would violate the rules of our language. Interestingly, although you can't use ordinary numeric digits at the beginning of a name, you can use Roman numerals, even though the Roman numeral "3" is defined as a single character, "III." This handles relatively uncommon constructions like "XIVth Century."

The standalone attribute allows you to turn off an external DTD if you want to. It may have other effects as well but it's difficult to say exactly what in a few words. You'll learn more about this attribute in the "Standalone Documents" section later in this chapter.

CHARACTER ENCODINGS

The most likely character encoding for American English (and any other language) is probably UTF-8, which is the default. This is the Unicode extended character set often used on UNIX systems. It's a variable-length encoding, using anywhere from 1 to 5 bytes of data for each character, which may cause problems in Java and other environments. If your system demands a fixed byte length, UTF-16, which uses two bytes per character like Java, is a good choice because XML processors must be able to detect either encoding without any declaration at all. UTF-8 and UTF-16 are the only encodings which XML parsers are *required* to recognize and are sufficient to handle any world language in common use.

On the other hand, most Windows systems don't produce UTF-8 but rather ISO-8859-1, which is the ISO-Latin-1 character set used for British and American English and most other Western European languages. This is not a default value, so it should be specified in your encoding declaration like this:

```
<?xml version="1.0" encoding="ISO-8859-1">
```

Otherwise, certain characters may not map to UTF-8 correctly and may cause readability problems in your document. In general, if you plan to produce primarily English text with an occasional word or phrase in another European language, that's all you need to know about character encodings.

The following information is of primary interest to those whose primary language is something other than English and who will probably recognize the encodings their word processing applications produce or infer it from context. If you don't plan to produce documents using these encodings, you can skip the "Other Encodings" section entirely.

OTHER ENCODINGS

Other common encodings are ISO-10646-UCS-2 and ISO-10646-UCS-4, which should be used for two of the various encodings of Unicode / ISO/IEC 10646 used most often for some European languages.

The values ISO-8859-1, ISO-8859-2, and so on through ISO-8859-10 should be used for the various parts of ISO 8859 (8-bit fonts) used for Latin-1 (West European), Latin-2 (East European), Latin-3 (South European), Latin-4 (North European), Cyrillic, Arabic, Greek, Hebrew, Latin-5 (Turkish), and Latin-6 (Nordic), in that order. The values ISO-2022-JP, Shift_JIS, and EUC-JP should be used for the Japanese language encoding forms of JIS X-0208-1997. Every XML processor should, but might not, recognize at least these encodings. XML processors may recognize other encoding names as well, such as ASCII, US-ASCII, or EBCDIC-US. It's suggested by the W3C XML 1.0 Recommendation that character encodings registered with the Internet Assigned Numbers Authority (IANA), other than those just listed, should be referred to using their registered names.

Tip from

Words to weave by

These registered names are defined to be case insensitive, so processors wanting to match against them should do so in a case-insensitive way.

If you choose a particular character encoding, other than the defaults, UTF-8 or UTF-16, which potentially address the entire Unicode/ISO character space of more than a million characters, you should also ensure that the relevant entity sets are imported into your document for clarity and ease of use (if you're using an English word processor or authoring environment). You would do this most commonly for ISO-8859-1 and the special characters defined for HTML and XHTML. For most MS-Windows machines in Western Europe and the Americas, you should choose a character encoding of ISO-8859-1, the Latin-1 character set that Windows uses, mostly. You'll use ENTITY declarations that look like this:

```
<!-- Latin-1 characters for XHTML -->
<!ENTITY % HTMLlat1 PUBLIC "-//W3C//ENTITIES Latin1//EN//HTML"
    "http://www.w3.org/TR/xhtml1/DTD/HTMLlat1x.ent">
  %HTMLlat1;
<!-- Special characters for XHTML -->
<!ENTITY % HTMLspecial PUBLIC "-//W3C//ENTITIES Special//EN//HTML"
     "http://www.w3.org/TR/xhtml1/DTD/xhtml-special.ent">
   %HTMLspecial;
<!-- Mathematical, Greek and Symbolic characters for XHTML -->
<!ENTITY % HTMLsymbol PUBLIC
     "-//W3C//ENTITIES Symbols//EN//HTML"
     "http://www.w3.org/TR/xhtml1/DTD/HTMLsymbolx.ent">
   %HTMLsymbol;
```

You'll learn more about character declarations later in this chapter, but you should take away from this discussion that for ordinary documents in English using Windows-based authoring software, you'll probably want to explicitly declare the ISO-8859-1 character set to ensure that the ISO-Latin-1 character set is properly interpreted. Although the ordinary English typewriter keyboard letters are equivalent in UTF-8 and ISO-8859-1, certain accented and special characters are different and the ISO-8859-1 character set is much smaller.

If you're using non-English word processing or authoring software, especially if you're using a non-European operating system, you should ascertain which encodings are being generated so you call upon the appropriate encoding in your declaration.

There's probably more information here than most people want to know about character encodings, but when you need the information to produce a readable document in, say, Russian, you need it badly. The Roman Czyborra Web site has links to a lot more information, including images of some common character sets: http://czyborra.com/charsets/iso8859.html.

STANDALONE DOCUMENTS

According to the W3C XML 1.0 Recommendation, "Standalone documents have no external markup declarations which affect XML information passed from the XML processor to an application."

This is a stunningly terse and obscure way of saying that `standalone="yes"` means that

- There are no default attribute values declared in an external DTD which aren't explicitly set in the document.
- There are no entities other than &, <, >, ', and " used which have not been declared locally or possibly read in from a file by reference.
- There are no elements with only element content containing whitespace in any form.
- There are no external attributes subject to normalization, which means that the contents of attributes cannot have whitespace in them, or character or entity references.

It *doesn't* mean there is nothing external to the document. There might be. It mainly means that at whatever point the non-validating XML processor stops reading external documents, the processing of *all* declarations stops.

You can do all these things if and only if you put them into the internal DTD subset.

External data which are not markup are not within the scope of this statement. So, you can still have graphics files, included text files, and anything else as long as they aren't markup and as long as you declare them in the internal DTD subset.

After all that, the XML processor isn't required to notify the application as to whether the document is standalone. In fact, the processor isn't required to do much of anything with this information or behave in any particular way when it encounters this information.

Basically, the designer of the DTD has to figure out whether documents authored using that DTD can be standalone and tell people, including authors. Authors who know that the DTD has been designed to be standalone or who have converted a document not designed to be standalone into the alternative format, can insert `standalone="yes"` into their XML declaration as documentation of that fact:

```
<?xml version="1.0" standalone="yes" ?>
```

Documents which are not standalone can be automatically converted, assuming that a facility to do this is available, or manually if otherwise, into standalone documents algorithmically.

CONSTRUCTING THE XML DOCUMENT PROLOG: THE DOCUMENT TYPE DECLARATION

The prolog of an XML document contains several statements. The first, the XML declaration, declares that the following document is XML. The second, the Document Type Declaration, is the method you use to identify the Document Type Definition (DTD) used by a particular document. The fact that the acronym DTD might apply to the Document Type Declaration is an unfortunate coincidence. DTD refers only to the latter, not the former. There can be only one Document Type Declaration in an XML document, so it's entered on the document instance itself. Because multiple DTDs can be combined to make a single document, this allows control of DTD loading to reside in each individual document.

The Document Type Declaration (DOCTYPE) has two parts, both optional. The first references an external DTD and uses the keywords PUBLIC or SYSTEM to identify a catalog entry or a URI, respectively. If catalogs aren't implemented in your XML processor, you can specify both parts at once without the second keyword:

```
<!DOCTYPE your-doc-name PUBLIC "{catalog id}">
<!DOCTYPE your-doc-name PUBLIC "{catalog id}" "{uri}">
<!DOCTYPE your-doc-name SYSTEM "{uri}"
```

PART

I

CH

2

The second optional part of the DOCTYPE declaration allows you to enter an internal DTD subset directly into your document. There are severe restrictions on the sort of information that you can put into the internal DTD, but you can do quite a lot anyway. The internal DTD subset is surrounded by square brackets like this:

```
<!DOCTYPE your-doc-name [ {internal DTD declarations} ]>
```

You can also combine the two, allowing you to add certain types of declarations and entities almost at will:

```
<!DOCTYPE your-doc-name PUBLIC "{catalog id}" "{uri}" [ {internal DTD
[ccc]declarations} ]>
```

For clarity, the internal subset is usually set off with carriage returns like this:

```
<!DOCTYPE your-doc-name PUBLIC "{catalog id}" "{uri}" [
 {internal DTD declarations}
 ]>
```

The DOCTYPE declaration must use the name of the root ELEMENT of the DTD, whether internal or external, as the field labeled your-doc-name in the previous examples. So if the name of the root element of your DTD is Dave, your DOCTYPE declaration should start like this:

```
<!DOCTYPE Dave … >
```

Your coding manual or sheet tells you what to say on the DOCTYPE if you are an author. If you are a DTD designer, you should supply such a coding manual or sheet to every author.

You might also create one master DTD that calls in the DTD parts you need, much like ordering from a menu. When you have a mix of functionality that allows you to create the document structure you need, you can publish the resulting DTD and save the trouble of doing it again and again for each new document. You can find out more about DTDs in Chapter 3.

CONSTRUCTING THE DOCUMENT BODY

An XML document consists of text, which usually consists of mingled markup and character data. The prolog contains markup only, but that isn't the interesting part, because you need data to go with your markup before it's anything other than empty boxes to put things in. The body of your document contains almost everything that counts from an application (and human) perspective, sprinkled liberally within your markup.

CHARACTER DATA

A DTD can declare many types of data that might be used in your document, but the default data type is always CDATA, for ordinary character data. The coding sheet or manual tells you what sort of data can be entered into each attribute or element content field.

Assuming that the type is CDATA, you can put pretty much anything you want into the field as long as it doesn't contain unescaped markup.

It's entirely possible to construct a DTD that contains no text within elements. Instead, one can put the significant data inside attributes associated with each element, which can all be declared as empty or containing element content only. This is sometimes done to convert a document using an encoding standard such as MARC, which is basically a binary format, to XML.

MARKUP

Markup consists of the entirety of the non-character data content of an XML file. The various forms that markup can take are shown in Table 2.1.

TABLE 2.1 XML MARKUP SYNTAX

Markup Type	Markup Syntax
start-tags	`<elementName [attributes] > …`
end-tags	`… </elementName>`
empty-element tags	`<elementName [attributes] />`
entity references	`&entityName; or %parameterEntityName;`
character references	`&#decimalNumber; or &#xhexNumber;`
comments	`<!-- comment -->`
CDATA section delimiters	`<![CDATA[ cdata stuff ]]>`
document type declarations	`<!DOCTYPE name externalID? [DTDstuff]>`
processing instructions	`<?processorID data ?>`
XML declaration	`<?xml version encoding standalone ?>`

Everything else is character data.

Markup always starts with either the < character, in which case it always ends with the > character, or with the & character, in which case it always ends with the ; character. The rest of this chapter explores different kinds of markup.

UNDERSTANDING HOW XML FORMS LOGICAL STRUCTURES

The nesting of elements is the only mechanism used to indicate logical structure in an XML document. The start and end tags in the text stream tell the XML processor that a node has been encountered.

If the XML processor encounters another start tag before the matching end tag, the processor knows that it's either on a new node in the tree or a leaf. If no new start tag is encountered and the end tag is found, the processor knows that this is a leaf and can proceed iteratively at that level of the tree until another start or end tag is encountered. Processing proceeds stepwise based on this simple rule. If the processor is validating the document, each node can be associated with a rule governing what sorts of content can appear within it. An empty tag is, by definition, a leaf because it can contain no further content.

PART

I

CH

2

> **Note**
>
> Most of the data structure contained in an XML document can be accessed sequentially and without building the structure in memory. A start tag starts a node or leaf and the matching end tag ends it. Any tags encountered between a start tag and its matching end tag start a new node or leaf. This principle is the basis of SAX and other event-driven XML processors (see Chapter 11, "SAX–The Simple API for XML").

The rest of the logical structure of the document is defined by the attributes associated with each element. In addition, the logical structure can vary based on the contents of conditional sections contained within the document or its subparts.

HOW XML FORMS PHYSICAL STRUCTURES

The nesting of entities is the only mechanism used to indicate physical structure in an XML document. The entity definitions encountered in the text stream tell the XML processor that a separate entity has been encountered.

There are many types of entities, from the tiny entities that form individual characters like this: (space) or &sp; (space), to the external entities that allow you to incorporate portions of other XML documents into your own or include references to unparsed data, such as multimedia files in a document for later rendering by a user agent.

An XML document is a collection of such entities. Each of those subentities must be complete in and of itself. This means that because the structure of the document as a whole must be a simple tree, each subentity must be a single node or must also be a simple tree. You build larger structures by grafting on subentity nodes or trees as portions of your larger tree.

If you look at Figure 2.1, shown previously, you could partition that diagram into sub-trees only as long as you could take a pencil and circle all the elements of your proposed tree and only cross one line, the branch that joins your group of elements to the main tree. If you cross more than one line, you can't form a legal sub-tree. This means that you have to include a single lowest node which will form the root of your new sub-tree.

If your documents contain multiple sub-trees in different files, every sub-tree file must be a complete XML document tree in and of itself.

Look at the two connected graphs shown previously in Figure 2.2. You see that either there are two roots, which you'll remember is forbidden in XML, or a simple circuit (a loop) in the graph, which prevents it from being an XML structure in the first place. There are, in fact, substructures of that tree that seem to be simple trees; however, the one loop is a fatal flaw. As a whole, these structures cannot be made into XML documents. In the first case, by rearranging the structure, you could probably turn it into a simple tree, but one root would become a leaf in the new structure.

In the second case, you could isolate a large portion of the structure as a simple tree and make that part into an XML structure. But you would have to find some other way of representing that part which is not a tree unless you cut one of the circular paths and transform it into a simple tree.

Tip from

LeeAnne.com
Words to weave by

A connected graph with a circuit can be trimmed by cutting any part of the circuit that leaves a complete tree.

As one possible solution, the looping structure could be declared as a notation and passed on to some other application to handle.

Alternatively, as a primitive and almost trivial idea, a hyperlink might solve your problem, depending on what you're trying to say with this structure. At a hyperlink, you jump from the document to somewhere else, metaphorically above the plane of the paper your document is printed on. You can land anywhere, including the document itself, thereby performing the otherwise impossible feat of leaping from leaf to leaf or even to another tree entirely.

A hyperlink thus represents meta-information about the structure of the tree, or about the structure of other trees, that stands to some extent outside the tree itself.

START TAGS AND END TAGS

There are two types of tags used in XML, tags with content and empty tags. Tags with content must have a start tag and an end tag. The start tag contains the name of the element inside angle brackets with optional attribute arguments. The end tag contains the name of the element preceded by a slash and all within angle brackets. You can't argue attributes in an end tag. The following code represents a tag with content:

```
<title subtitle="A Journey Home">There and Back Again</title>
```

They look very much like standard HTML tags and shouldn't cause any problems other than that of well-formedness, which demands that they truly nest within each other. You can't have tags that alternate with each other like this malformed example:

```
<bold><italic>EMPHASIZED TEXT</bold></italic>
```

Although it's a common error in HTML, XML is far more finicky and won't permit this construct. You have to nest the tags properly as shown here:

```
<bold><italic>EMPHASIZED TEXT</italic></bold>
```

Notice that the tags now nest properly within each other.

Caution

You *must* close every tag that starts in the context of a given tag (or tags) before the context of that tag is closed.

Empty tags have a special format available, although the same start tag/end tag scheme can be used for them as long as you remember not to put content of any sort between the start tag of the empty element and its immediately following end tag. Also, you might be concerned if it's possible that your XML document will be seen by an ordinary Web browser because end tags for elements that look like empty HTML tags may cause the browser to crash or behave in strange ways. For general use, however, the special format is mnemonic in itself, an advantage because you can *see* that the tag is empty, and it doesn't break most browsers.

Ordinarily, you start and end empty tags within the same angle brackets by following the name of the element and all its potential attributes with a space, a forward slash, and then the closing angle bracket:

```
<image source="myphoto.jpeg" type="JPEG" />
```

Of course the type must be declared as a notation, but that will be discussed in the "Unparsed Entities" section.

NORMALIZATION

Normalization is a fancy word for bringing things down to the lowest common denominator and putting them into a sort of canonical form. In the context of XML, it refers to the process of resolving entity references in locations in which such references can occur, regularizing linefeeds to account for the several different ways of treating them in different operating systems, and tidying up a few more things that need doing in certain cases.

Tip from

LeeAnne.com
Words to weave by

The designer rarely has to worry about normalization except in a negative way. The XML parser should perform all needed normalizations, so the only thing the document architect need think about is whether normalization will affect his data when making a round trip from un-normalized form to normalized and back again.

It turns out that there are two places where whitespace might be encountered: in character data within the document and in character data argued in element attributes.

In the first case, it's difficult to distinguish "significant" whitespace from insignificant whitespace in parsed entities. It seemed best to the designers to pass on all whitespace to the application along with the processor's best guess, based on the DTD, about which data is definitely insignificant and which might or might not be. This passing of the buck makes sense because the application is in the best position to know what to do with extra white-space.

Caution

> The XML processor can only make a guess about what's significant whitespace and what's not based on whatever has been defined in the DTD or any other schema language used. Your application must be prepared to handle erroneous guesses.

With end-of-line handling, also a form of whitespace, there's another problem. Newlines are treated differently on different systems. The common alternatives are a linefeed (UNIX), a carriage return (MacOS), and both carriage return and linefeed characters (MS Windows). It's also common for applications to insert anomalous sequences of any of these in any order when they encounter a file from a foreign system. W3C decided they couldn't do everything and chose a set of reasonable rules. If the parser sees either `;#x0D;&#x0A;` (carriage return, linefeed) or `&#x0D;` (carriage return) it replaces it with `&#x0A;` (linefeed), the UNIX newline character. A few Microsoft Windows programmers were somewhat less than pleased.

Note

> Microsoft and Apple chose differing mechanisms to separate lines, with Microsoft choosing the "belt and suspenders" technique common with teletypes and using a carriage return and then a line feed character to indicate a newline. Apple decided that the line feed was redundant and felt that a solitary carriage return would do, modeled presumably after the way an ordinary typewriter behaves. UNIX had been using a solitary line feed character to accomplish the same thing all along, and that was the standard agreed upon for XML. So both Microsoft and Apple have to use special logic to handle carriage returns in XML and HTML documents.

In attributes, there is a standard transformation sequence and then special added processing for everything except CDATA:

- Character references are processed by appending the referenced character to the output attribute value.
- Entity references are processed by recursively processing the replacement text of the entity.
- Whitespace characters, #x20 (space), #x0D (carriage return), #x0A (linefeed), #x09 (horizontal tab), are processed by appending #x20 (space) to the normalized output value, except that only a single #x20 (space) is appended for a "#x0D#x0A" (carriage return, linefeed) sequence that is part of an external parsed entity or the literal entity value of an internal parsed entity.
- Other characters are processed by appending them to the normalized output value.
- Yet another transformation is applied if the attribute datatype is *not* CDATA, the default. Leading and trailing spaces are stripped and multiple spaces are collapsed into one space.

The distinction between the two types of normalization lies in that you can conveniently pass long strings in an attribute, folding lines to fit the page, although element content remains relatively pristine.

ELEMENT TYPES

Surprisingly, if you're validating, it's not an error to use an element type that hasn't been declared although the parser may issue a warning. In fact, allowing undeclared element types within other elements, no matter what their content model says, is the basis of being able to supplement a document's DTD with elements from other namespaces. So all you have to do is use the undeclared element in a correct, well-formed manner while possibly identifying the namespace it comes from. Because you've already explored what well-formed means, take a look at the more interesting case, a valid document.

PART

I

CH

2

> **Note**
>
> In XML terms, being well-formed is another way of saying that it forms a tree, or a branch of a tree, that is complete in and of itself. This is necessary because XML allows you to build larger documents from smaller ones and is a key to being able to use XML over the Web. Other more formal rules are discussed elsewhere in this chapter.

Every element in a valid XML document has been defined in the DTD associated with that document by the DOCTYPE declaration. The DTD declares the following:

- Actual names of the elements
- Rules used to determine which elements can nest within other elements and in what order
- Possible attributes and their default or constant values
- Character values of enumeration types
- Unparsed entities used in the document and how they are referenced by name
- Language encodings used in the document
- Character entities used in the document
- Other information important for the processing and rendering of the document

Following those rules, you're able to create documents according to the template the document designer had in mind when she created the DTD. In a non-validating environment, you can just make up tags and attributes as you go along.

The coding sheet or manual lays all this out in an easy-to-read and understand format, *if* your DTD author has done her job. When authoring an XML document or correcting an error, you may not have the luxury of a full authoring environment. You may be using vi over telnet from a thousand miles away. It's always important to keep the coding documentation handy in case you're called up in the middle of the night and asked if you wouldn't mind fixing your million dollar database access system, please?

Figure 2.3, later in this chapter, shows a validating authoring environment that can save a lot of time and make life easier for you by automatically encapsulating the DTD information that might otherwise have to be presented in a coding document in programmatic form. However, such tools are neither infallible nor available on every platform. Although they may generate "helpful" error messages when they stop processing your file, the actual message may have little or nothing to do with the error you actually made. You'll have to use your head, not a tool, in many cases.

ENTITY NAMING RULES

Entity names must start with a character, which is any character glyph within a given writing system that corresponds to our usual idea of a Latin character plus the ASCII characters underscore and colon. The first character can be followed by characters, digits, and a selection of accents and extenders representing glyph combinations of one sort or another. Processing instructions must not start with the ASCII letters XML, xml, or any mixed-case variations of those three characters. It's a very bad idea to use the ASCII colon character except when using namespaces, although it's possible to do so legally, since the presence of a string followed by a colon in a name *looks* like it refers to a namespace even when it doesn't.

> **Note**
>
> Surprisingly, many explanations of XML get this part wrong. Although everyone agrees that you can use encodings in content, the fact that this freedom extends to markup as well is harder to grasp. Everyone is so used to the limitations of HTML that it's difficult to remember to embrace this freedom.

The only place that *some* ASCII is mandatory is in a DTD, which is a behind-the-scenes document that ordinary authors might never actually see. Literals that name public identifiers—the characters that fill the literal parts of a `<!DOCTYPE PUBLIC "-//public identifier" "uri">` declaration—must be ASCII characters because that's an Internet standard. Numeric character references such as `&#x0D;` must be entered using a very limited ASCII number set. The ISO 639 language codes and the ISO 3166 country codes used in the `XML:lang` amd XHTML `lang` attributes must also be in ASCII, again because these are Internet standards. There are a few other places such as quote marks, which must be ASCII quotes, special markup characters like `&gt;`, keywords, like `<!ELEMENT … >` and `IDREF`, and so on, where ASCII is required, but in general you don't have to worry about using equivalent characters from the national language character sets defined in the Unicode/ISO/IEC 10646 standards.

The rest of XML is friendly to speakers of languages other than English. Even what Unicode and ISO call "combining characters" and "extenders" are allowed in tags as well as content. These are essentially the accent marks that can be placed in names to signal to display engines that an accent should be combined with the previous character, however that may be performed. So the French, Germans, and many others who use a Latin alphabet can see tags that are spelled correctly in their own language with proper accents and umlauts, as can speakers of Hindi, Hebrew, Arabic, and the many other languages that use such characters.

> **Caution**
>
> Although it's great that XML allows Chinese characters in markup and content, that doesn't mean your system actually supports the display and entry of Chinese characters, or any other of the many ideographic, syllabic, and alphabetic writing systems in use around the world. You'll need a character set as well as keyboard and operating system support for full functionality.

After years of Eurocentric, even Anglocentric, dependence on ASCII and extended ASCII on the Web, XML has evened the playing field somewhat for all players at the Web level, including the myriad of users who will be able to access information in their native languages and scripts. Having a single standard means of communicating in, say, Chinese, in which there are three main "standards" and a number of variations, is sure to improve the availability of rendering engines as well as reduce their cost.

Attribute Lists and Types

In your XML coding sheet, you'll find a list of attributes for each element. If you're using a validating editor such as XML Pro 2.0, you'll probably have a menu of available attributes whenever you place the working cursor on an element in the document tree view. There is also a menu of elements that can be inserted at this point in the file.

Such an editor can be a tremendous timesaver because it takes away some of the burden of learning a coding sheet or manual. However, a good coding sheet can give a far more accessible general overview and explain the rationale behind the document structure, something even a validating editor cannot do.

Figure 2.3 shows some of the strengths of this sort of editor. The tree structure of the document is clearly displayed although a large or complex document can quickly overwhelm the limits of readability on a small screen. The highlighted cursor shows where you are in the document at any given time. A list of available attributes for the element you've highlighted is visible on the screen as well. You can scroll down through them and pick the ones you want to employ for this particular element.

There is very little checking of your attribute values that can be done at the processor level. XML by itself doesn't offer facilities to validate attributes and element content in detail beyond checking that enumerated choices have been entered correctly, which a validating editor does automatically, and a few other minor details. XML Pro and other authoring environments may offer you a pull-down list of enumerated values so you can't make a mistake, but that's about it. The solution to this dilemma is XML schemas, which you'll learn about in Chapter 7.

Even the little field checking provided may not be reasonable in actual use. If you think telephone numbers have to be numeric, for example, you're flying in the face of various language-dependent conventions which may use periods, hyphens, commas, slashes, parentheses, or even spelled-out words on the telephone keypad to represent numbers. For some purposes, the U.S. military uses a hexadecimal telephone keypad which adds the "digits" A,

B, C, and D to the usual 0–9 plus * and #. Telephone TouchTone™ standards, officially called DTMF (Dual Tone Multi-Frequency) tones, allow for this, so you should too. Postal (ZIP) codes in many countries include letters as well as digits. And large numbers and decimal fractions may have punctuation marks inside them that vary from country to country, often a comma and period respectively but quite often a period and comma in an exact reversal of meaning. In general, everything is more complicated than you think, and adding silly restrictions on input is almost guaranteed to cause problems and make you look bad.

Figure 2.3
XML Pro 2.0 is being used to edit an XHTML file. Note the list of available attributes for an anchor element based on the position of the element cursor.

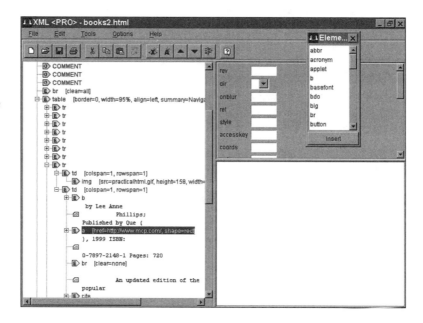

Caution

In a global environment, it pays to be really careful about what is allowed and what is not in any data field. Although many schemes are on their way to allowing fine detail in field constraints, the examples given should give you pause. Telephone numbers might look like this: 011 41 09 23 44 23 in France or like this in a small island in the Pacific: 011 8524 99 99 22 33. You have to come to some happy compromise between what the user demands and what you're prepared to accept. In many cases, the capability to override range checking at user demand can help alleviate frustration. You could remind U.S. customers about the "correct" number of digits in a phone number while allowing anyone to type in whatever they want if they insist.

Although an XML application may only be enforcing constraints in an underlying database, before finalizing your analysis, consider the fact that the database may be designed in an insular or shortsighted manner that doesn't meet the real demands of a global marketplace. Some data is inherently regional in nature, and a mature individual is cognizant of that fact. Whether one eats with the fork in the right hand or the left is a matter of taste, not error checking. In the case of cosmetic differences, consider normalizing the data before error checking or storage. There's no earthly reason a British user has to guess that we often surround area codes with parentheses in the U.S. and Canada before her input is accepted.

UNPARSED ENTITIES

An unparsed entity is anything the XML processor can't recognize, whether it be binary data such as an image or audio file, or text that should be passed to an application without being processed in any way. HTML uses comments to hide such text from the HTML browser, but XML has several mechanisms that work more reliably. In fact, XML is not required to pass comments onto the application at all, so they can't be used as freely as they are in HTML. This was, I think, a bit of pique on the part of some of the designers, who hated the idea of using comments for real data. In HTML, the contents of a <SCRIPT> tag are defined to be PCDATA, which can contain anything at all.

Be that as it may, you should follow the new rules with XML.

An unparsed entity must first be declared as a NOTATION, a special declaration that names a helper application that knows how to deal with entities of a particular type. You give the notation a name, an optional public identifier, and then the less optional name of the helper application, like one of these options:

```
<!NOTATION mnemonic-name PUBLIC "public-identifier">
<!NOTATION mnemonic-name PUBLIC "public-identifier" "application-name.exe ">
<!NOTATION mnemonic-name SYSTEM "application-name.exe ">
```

The first option works only if you have a catalog. The second and third work whether you have a catalog or not. You can't count on a catalog because it's an SGML tool that many current XML processors have tacitly inherited from their SGML predecessors. Catalog lookup isn't specified in the W3C recommendation and it can never be counted on. Use the last two versions if you possibly can. On the other hand, hard-coding knowledge of the location and identity of a helper application into each and every DTD is an error-prone anachronism on the Web.

Caution
By redefining the way scripts behave in the presence of comments, the designers of XML have introduced an incompatibility problem between XML and HTML. In all likelihood, XML processors will continue to pass on comments to the application because many pages will break without that behavior. Also, the processors are *permitted* to pass on the commented information by the same language by which they're *permitted* not to.

After you've defined an unparsed entity notation, it has to be declared as an entity like this

```
<!ENTITY mnemonic-name NDATA mnemonic-name>
```

and then listed as an attribute in an element so you can actually use it:

```
<!ELEMENT name EMPTY>
<!ATTLIST name type NOTATION "mnemonicname"
      … >
```

The mnemonic names don't share the same namespace so it doesn't matter whether they duplicate each other, which I encourage if only for the sake of keeping things clear.

At this point, you're back on the coding sheet and can use the datatype so defined. The datatype can only be used as an attribute of an element declared to be of that type or have that type available to it in an enumeration. Other attributes collect the information that the external helper application needs to be able to process the data.

A typical application might be an image file which could be argued like this:

```
<image source="uri" alt="graphic description" type="gif89a">
```

This element would require the following declarations in the DTD:

```
<!NOTATION gif89a    PUBLIC "-//CompuServe//NOTATION Graphics Interchange Format
89a//EN" "explorer.exe ">
<!ENTITY gif89a NDATA gif89a>
<!ELEMENT image EMPTY>
<!ATTLIST image source CDATA #REQUIRED
                alt   CDATA #IMPLIED
                type  NDATA gif89a >
```

With most tools, it won't matter whether you specify the format as gif87a or gif89a, because the same tools handle both formats. It's unreasonable to expect the person coding the file to know the difference between the two anyway.

Notations will be much improved with the addition of the facilities of XLink/XPointer to help keep track of helper locations. With the overall instability of the Web at its present level and the wide variety of facilities and architectures on user machines, any help the poor user can get will make configuring XML tools easier. The DTD as it exists now requires far too much UNIX-style tweaking of files for ordinary users to have much fun with it.

Note

> XLink and XPointer are trying to overcome the limitations of current pointer technology. They allow all sorts of relationships, including reverse pointers to be generated on-the-fly in documents without write access, performing their magic on the display copy itself rather than crude physical insertion of tags in content.

XML requirements for notations as they now exist are exacting in the extreme. Being able to point out the location of a helper application may be handy for notations that are uncommon or highly specialized. However, the user agent can be expected to know how to display many of the more common types such as GIFs, JPEGs, PNGs, WAVs and other more or less standard binary file types used on the Web. Here's a list of common notations:

```
<!NOTATION eps       PUBLIC "+//ISBN 0-201-18127-4::Adobe//NOTATION
     ➥Postscript Language Reference Manual//EN" >
<!NOTATION tex       PUBLIC "+//ISBN 0-201-13448-9::Knuth//NOTATION The
     ➥TeXbook//EN" >
<!NOTATION cgmchar   PUBLIC "ISO 8632/2//NOTATION Character encoding//EN" >
<!NOTATION cgmbinary PUBLIC "ISO 8632/3//NOTATION Binary encoding//EN" >
<!NOTATION cgmclear  PUBLIC "ISO 8632/4//NOTATION Clear text encoding//EN" >
<!NOTATION tiff      PUBLIC "ISO 12083:1994//NOTATION TIFF-1//EN" >
```

```
<!NOTATION jpeg      PUBLIC "ISO/IEC 10918:1983//NOTATION Digital
   ➥Compression and Encoding of Continuous-tone Still Images (JPEG)//EN" >
<!NOTATION gif87a    PUBLIC "-//CompuServe//NOTATION Graphics Interchange
   ➥Format 87a//EN" >
<!NOTATION gif89a    PUBLIC "-//CompuServe//NOTATION Graphics Interchange
   ➥Format 89a//EN" >
<!NOTATION fax       PUBLIC "-//USA-DOD//NOTATION CCITT Group 4 Facsimile
   ➥Type 1 Untiled Raster//EN" >
```

Of course, you'll have to add a system ID to actually use these, either as a pointer to a local helper application or in the catalog file, if available for your tools, that centralizes the locations of these helpers.

REAL-WORLD APPLICATIONS

You've already seen some of the tools you might use to author an XML document above but where do you find DTDs to author against? Well, you can read further in this book and write your own or you can use one already in existence.

Many DTDs are in the public domain or are available as standards from ISO, ANSI, or other standards body. An extensive list appears at the back of this book, but here are a few of the more important applications of XML that are making waves in the world today:

- Health Level-7 (HL7), the Health Informatics Standard was founded in 1987 to develop standards for the electronic interchange of clinical, financial, and administrative information among health care computer systems. The HL7 focus is on using SGML and XML as a transport mechanism between differing health care information systems.

- Real Estate Transaction Standard (RETS) is an XML-based method of exchanging real estate transaction information. A competing standard is Real Estate Markup Language (RELML) which uses XML DTDs to describe residential, commercial, and open land listings for posting on the Web.

- RosettaNet, the Lingua Franca for Business, is an EDI/E-Commerce initiative aimed at procurement for the computer industry.

- MathML and ChemML are two scientific XML standards that allow mathematicians to publish equations and chemists to present chemical formulae.

- SMIL, the Synchronized Multimedia Markup Language, is HyTime for Everyman, a multimedia markup language that lets content providers produce sophisticated visual and audio presentations.

- ICE, Information and Content Exchange, although not strictly an XML application being a transport mechanism, allows the exchange of online assets and personal information over the Web.

- SAE J2008 is an XML-based ordering and inventory system for the automotive industry; MISTI, the Missile Industry Supply-chain Transaction Infrastructures, does the same for the space industry.

- Chinese DTDs provide the specialized structure needed for Chinese language publishing. Similar DTDs exist for Japanese, Korean, Vietnamese, and many other human languages.

- GedML, a genealogy XML standard, encourages the free flow of genealogical data over the Web. Software already exists to convert standard GEnealogical Data COMmunication (GEDCOM) files to GedML.

The list goes on and on. As you can see, the range of applications is immense, touching almost every field of human endeavor. Few businesses can safely ignore XML, although there are so many existing and proposed standards in many fields that there's bound to be some sort of shakeout as major contenders jockey for pole position in a fracas of dueling proposals.

Tip from

LeeAnne.com
Words to weave by

With so many proprietary proposals on the table, you might wonder what the differences are between them. For the most part, you'll have to ask potential vendors to disclose their DTD as there are comparatively few DTDs available on the Web. There are two repositories that may give you a start. On Microsoft platforms, the BizTalk consortium at `http://www.biztalk.org/` has a searchable list, although it's not easy to use and requires you to guess what the appropriate keywords might be that describe the sort of DTD you're looking for. The Organization for the Advancement of Structured Information Standards (OASIS), at `http://www.oasis-open.org/` plans another but only has the DocBook DTD and a subset of the CALS table model DTD called Exchange Table Model up for public view right now. Many vendors are treating their DTDs as if they were state secrets.

Each browser maker has proposed standards which the others cry are slanted toward themselves. Just as the browser wars led to the development of proprietary "extensions" to HTML, which tended (or tried) to lock out other browsers creating a Babel of incompatible methods that still plague us today, XML is going to be in flux for some time to come.

The basics are already there, however, and a user community increasingly demanding of open standards is driving the various proposals toward convergence. Many of the major successes have been with standards from ISO and ANSII, which sell documentation to support their standards-making efforts but provide neutral ground for all partners. For the price of the documentation, usually a few hundred dollars, anyone can play on the same level ground.

GETTING DOWN TO CASES

Now that you know something about the basics of XML, you need to decide how to use it. You've already learned that DTDs are a way of precisely describing the format and layout conventions of an XML document and why they should be used in some situations but not in others. You've also learned some of the differences between XML and XHTML, and how they make a world of difference for the Web as a whole through the internationalization of character sets and tagging languages. In later chapters, you'll learn about some of the security and privacy facilities built in to XML that make it suitable for business to business (B2B) communications.

Some of these security facilities have already been implemented in hardware implementing transaction dispatching, digital signature, and Secure Sockets Layer (SSL) in silicon, the XML equivalent of a graphics accelerator chip. This means the infrastructure required to support high-volume XML transaction processing is becoming readily available.

Defining a B2B transaction processing system requires the ability to communicate very clearly what the records to be passed between systems look like, because those systems may be on different platforms and implemented in different programming languages. An XML DTD is ideal for communicating this information, because it can be guaranteed to be unambiguous and platform independent. After the transaction is implemented in an application, neither system involved in a transaction will need access to the DTD, because all knowledge about the DTD required for any particular processing requirement will be captured in the program code that handles the transaction on either end.

This scenario is common for any interprocess communications application using XML; the initial stages require a mutually agreed upon DTD that serves as part of the system documentation and testing facilities, but the need for a DTD goes away after the system is up and running. This is in contrast to documents that may be served to anyone without a pre-arranged and transaction-aware process on the other end. When a document is viewed in a general-purpose browser, the information contained in the DTD may be required for proper presentation and handling of the information contained therein. So DTDs are potentially more important for casual users than they are for communications between prearranged partners in an ongoing relationship.

UNDERSTANDING XML DOCUMENT TYPE DEFINITIONS

In this chapter

Dissecting an XML Document Type Definition

A DTD (Document Type Definition) defines the form and syntax of XML language constructs. You create DTDs using simple rules that can seem far more complex than they really are. By creating or altering a DTD and making it available on the Web, you can effectively make a new or extended language understandable and usable by anyone whose browser supports XML. Most XML pages use public DTDs, which allow them to exchange data with other users in a standard format. Local extensions to a standard DTD allow the use of in-house structure extensions that are not relevant to other users.

A DTD is not needed to make a well-formed XML document. In fact, if your XML code is being generated automatically, you might reasonably opt to skip this step. To gain the benefits of being able to check your XML document for validity, however, you will need a DTD. And, to share your data easily over the Web, a DTD is a necessary step toward universality. A DTD allows you to capture and validate the full possibilities of your data structure instead of off the cuff improvisations when you want to slip in an optional field.

In a complex document, any particular document may use only a subset of the full possibilities defined by the document design. By identifying optional parts in a DTD, you retain control over their location in the structure even though they're not used in every case. At the same time, with the help of a DTD you can ensure that mandatory parts are always there, even though the document is well-formed without. A DTD allows you to share your document structure and the information that structure embodies across a wider audience than was previously possible.

You don't have to use proprietary data formats that require both parties to possess the same software, an enormous expense if you deal with many collaborators, customers, or vendors. Instead, you can publish your data structure where it can be freely viewed and used, or exchange one file with each vendor/customer, which furnishes a key to understanding how each field relates to the document as a whole.

> **Note**
>
> A DTD is a precise data structure description that can be passed on to an automated tool. This raises the possibility of mechanizing the conversion of data from one form to another, or from one language to another, with minimal human intervention.

XML was designed in a way that allows XML processors and applications to view and use XML documents without access to a DTD, even if one exists. If a link goes down you don't want the data in a document to become worthless, after all. So a DTD is only a part of the picture—an important part, but a part nonetheless.

Using Document Type Definition Notation and Syntax

In general, most professional DTDs group their declarations by type and in a logical order, which makes them much easier to read and understand. The exact order is critical in some cases, but not in others, depending on whether the information is needed at the time a lookup table entry is made. Some expansions of entities are made only when used. Parameter entities are almost always needed, so they should usually come first.

Tip from	To avoid having to think about what's needed and what isn't, it's a good habit to declare everything before using it. This makes it a little easier to find things as well, because you can usually look toward the top of the DTD to find an antecedent declaration.
 LeeAnne.com Words to weave by	

You should make the root of your document tree the first ELEMENT, because many processors assume that the first element is the root. This mirrors the structure of well-formed XML to some extent, because the first tag encountered is always the root.

As a rule of thumb and for ease of use, ENTITY declarations should be made before ELEMENT and ATTLIST declarations that use them. ELEMENT declarations should be made before ATTLIST declarations that modify them. NOTATION declarations must be located prior to any use of the notation. Figure 3.1 shows an example of good XML coding practice.

PART
I
CH
3

Figure 3.1
This is a short example of well-organized XML DTD code.

```
--------------- Top of File ---------------
<!-- Memo DTD -->
<!-- Notations -->
<!NOTATION jpeg PUBLIC "ISO/IEC 0918:1983//NOTATION
                Digital Compression and Encoding of
                Continuous-tone Still Images (JPEG)//EN">
<!-- Predefined Entities -->
<!ENTITY lt     "&#38;#60;">
<!ENTITY gt     "&#62;">
<!ENTITY amp    "&#38;#38;">
<!ENTITY apos   "&#39;">
<!ENTITY quot   "&#34;">
<!-- Element names -->
<!ENTITY % Doctype   "memo">
<!ENTITY % Logo      "logo">
<!ENTITY % Block     "block">
<!ENTITY % Regarding "regarding">
<!ENTITY % Author    "author">
<!ENTITY % Body      "body">
<!ENTITY % Paragraph "paragraph">
<!-- Content substitutions -->
<!ENTITY % %Body;    "(%Paragraph;+)">
<!ENTITY % %Block;   "(%Logo;, %Author;, %Regarding;, %Body;)">
<!-- Document Root -->
<!ELEMENT %Doctype; ( %Block; )>
<!-- Document Body -->
<!ELEMENT %Author; (CDATA)>
<!ELEMENT %Logo; EMPTY>
<!ATTLIST %Logo;
```

Note that each section lists the different DTD declarations in a logical group, with each ATTLIST immediately following the ELEMENT it modifies and the rest arranged by type. This makes it easy to find each piece when you go looking for it.

UNDERSTANDING LITERALS

Literal data is any quoted string not containing the quotation mark used as a delimiter for that string. The quotation mark can be either a single quote or a double quote at the convenience of the coder. If you want to make a literal of a string containing both single and double quotes, you can escape whichever one you use to quote the string. Literals are used for specifying the content of internal entities, the values of attributes, and external identifiers. The following are some examples of literal data:

- Literal data: `"The quick brown fox jumps over the lazy dogs."`

- Alternate form: `'The lazy hen clucked "merrily" over her jumbled nest.'`

- Escaped form: `'Now is the time for George&apos;s "good guy" quote:'`

The first example uses simple quotes, as they would be entered in the U.S. The second uses initial single quotes as they do in the U.K. and many other parts of the English-speaking world. The third example contains both single and double quotes, so the single quote used as an apostrophe is escaped using a character entity.

DECLARING A NOTATION

A *notation* is anything that the XML processor can't understand and parse (notations are also called *unparsed entities*). Although this conjures up the idea of binary data, it can also be text that XML doesn't understand. A chunk of JavaScript, for example, could be kept in an external file and referred to as a notation.

> **Caution**
>
> Notations only can refer to external files. There's no way to hide information inside a document and pass it on to a user agent for special processing unless you put it inside an XML tag and instruct the agent to do something with the contents of the tag. If you want to include text data containing special characters inside the document, you should escape it inside a CDATA element as described in the later section, "Escaping a Text Block in a CDATA Section."

The problem with notations is that they require access to the DTD to use the notation. Although you might use the internal subset of the DTD to make notation information available locally to the document, non-validating parsers are not required to read the internal DTD subset.

NOTATION syntax is simple:

```
<!NOTATION name identifier "helper" >
```

The identifier is a catalog entry, as used in SGML. Many XML processors are recycled SGML processors, so they support a catalog by default. This is slightly safer than pointing to a helper application that may or may not be there, but XML requires the helper application to be referenced in any case, which can lead to anomalous behavior. You might reference Adobe Photoshop, for example, as the helper application for viewing a GIF image, but the browser is likely to know how to display GIFs on its own. The browser is also far more likely to be able to integrate the image properly into the rendered document on a display device or printer, a task that Adobe Photoshop is quite incapable of. Using both the identifier and the "name" of the helper allows you to compromise between just telling the user agent what sort of file is being passed and telling it explicitly how to display it while knowing nothing whatsoever about the environment the document is being displayed in.

Although some people may encourage you to behave as if Microsoft Windows is the center of the universe and do something like this

```
<!NOTATION gif SYSTEM "gif" >
```

which actually works on Windows systems, I'm not one of them. Use this syntax at your peril. The above example assumes the presence of the Windows system Registry to resolve the reference, which registry is not exactly universally available and short-circuits the standard system identifier completely.

A safer course is to enter the entire catalog entry and identifier sequence. This method gives a stronger hint to the eventual application that will deal with the processed XML file about what might be done with it but doesn't actually process the notation reference. The bare system identifier, `"gif"`, works on Windows systems because Windows knows about GIFs already. But a handheld device or even a computer using another operating system may not have the knowledge of how to handle GIF images at its beck and call.

So it would be best to recast the previously shown reference as

```
<!NOTATION gif89a PUBLIC "-//CompuServe//NOTATION Graphics Interchange Format
89a//EN" "gif">
```

Notations can't be used in isolation. They have to be declared in an entity as well. A complete declaration sequence might look like this:

```
<!NOTATION gif89a    PUBLIC "-//CompuServe//NOTATION Graphics Interchange Format
89a//EN" "gif">
<!ENTITY gif89a SYSTEM "gif89a.gif" NDATA gif89a>
<!ELEMENT image EMPTY>
<!ATTLIST image source CDATA #REQUIRED
              alt    CDATA #IMPLIED
              type   NDATA gif89a >
```

In your document, your tag would look like this

```
<image source=uri"
      alt=[image of something]>
```

You can also create an enumerated list of notation types, which uses a slightly different syntax to describe the notation type:

```
<!NOTATION gif87a    PUBLIC "-//CompuServe//NOTATION Graphics Interchange Format
87a//EN" "gif">
<!NOTATION gif89a    PUBLIC "-//CompuServe//NOTATION Graphics Interchange Format
89a//EN" "gif">
<!ENTITY gif87a SYSTEM "gif87a.gif" NDATA gif87a>
<!ENTITY gif89a NDATA SYSTEM "gif89a.gif" NDATA gif89a>
<!ELEMENT image EMPTY>
<!ATTLIST image source CDATA #REQUIRED
              alt    CDATA #IMPLIED
              type   NOTATION (gif87a | gif89a) "gif89a" >
```

In your document, your tag would look like this

```
<image source=uri"
        alt=[image of something]>
```

but you could override the default type given in the attribute list like this:

```
<image source=uri"
        alt=[image of something]
        type="gif87a" >
```

This lets the user agent know that the image is in GIF87a format, if that matters at all.

NOTATIONS ARE AWKWARD SOLUTIONS

NOTATIONs are interesting devices because they allow you to isolate binary data as well as character-ish data, such as scripts or interpreted source code, which you don't want the XML processor to have to deal with. In that sense, they're a good thing. But the specificity required becomes quickly tiresome. XML is being used here as a dispatcher to choose among alternatives that quickly become obsolescent as new binary technologies emerge.

The NOTATION syntax is somewhat of an anachronism left over from SGML, which uses them extensively. It's possible that they had to be included for compatibility with the older standard, but on the Web it's almost inconceivable that you would know the *permanent* location of anything, even on your own system. File systems evolve and change; nothing is constant. NOTATION declarations tacitly assume an unchanging environment that never alters, or alters so glacially that tweaking a catalog entry isn't a chore.

The Web is different. Changes propagate overnight. Before you can wink an eye someone has a new multimedia widget out there and *everybody* is using it. The plug-in mechanism already used by browsers might have been a better way of doing this. Or maybe we could just declare a plug-in NOTATION. Even better would be to let the browser and the server negotiate the best format for a particular situation.

Unfortunately, the better way has yet to emerge. So until it does, using the official method is an interim solution. Hopefully, whatever new mechanism supplants this awkward hack will be able to use the older method to extrapolate from the hard-coded location to where an appropriate processor might be found. In any case, you should think long and hard before including notations in an XML document and be prepared for something better to take the place of notations in the near future.

ENTITY DECLARATION

The ENTITY declaration is one of the most simple, in spite of the fact that there are so many different types of entities. The list of restrictions placed on entities is confusing, however, and so tersely described in the XML 1.0 Recommendation that it takes a thorough reading or two before you get it. You'll learn more about entities and have the opportunity to compare and contrast their various uses in the "Understanding the W3C Entity Table" section later in this chapter.

If you think of an XML document as a collection of entities, which are, roughly speaking, objects in the object-oriented sense, the entity declaration is a way of pointing at one instance of a particular object. There aren't that many options and it's not that hard to learn. Following is the basic format:

```
<!ENTITY name value >
```

The name part has two options, one with no modifier as you see it here and one with a preceding percent sign (%) followed by a space that marks a parameter entity. The value part has three basic options: either some form of quoted string, an identifier that points to a catalog entry or location external to the file, or a notation reference. The following are some variations for parsed entities:

```
<!ENTITY name PUBLIC "catalog entry" >
<!ENTITY name PUBLIC "catalog entry" "uri" >
<!ENTITY name SYSTEM "uri" > <!-- External ID -->
<!ENTITY name "&#0000;" > <!-- General entity mnemonic for character entity -->
```

The following is how you reference parameter entities:

```
<!ENTITY % name PUBLIC "catalog entry" >
<!ENTITY % name PUBLIC "catalog entry" "uri" >
<!ENTITY % name SYSTEM "uri" > <!-- External ID -->
<!ENTITY % name "&#0000;" > <!-- Parameter entity mnemonic for character entity -->
```

Parameter entities behave differently than general entities because they were designed for different purposes. The difference in their declarations is designed to be obvious when you, or the XML processor, sees one.

The way you refer to them is different as well. A general entity is referred to like this:

```
&name;
```

Although a parameter entity is referred to like this:

```
%name;
```

This is a relatively trivial difference that masks a huge difference in usage.

PARAMETER ENTITIES

The parameter entity is a bit like a C macro designed for use in the DTD itself, so that you can identify objects—collections of data—for use during the process of building the DTD. After this is done, parameter entities have no meaning anywhere else. So if your document happens to contain a string that looks like the name of a parameter entity, it will be ignored, or rather, treated as the simple text that it is.

Inside the DTD however, a parameter entity has great utility. You can use it to store chunks of markup text for later use, or point to external collections of markup text for convenience.

In the internal DTD subset, parameter entities can only be used to insert complete markup. So, the following declaration and use is legal:

```
<!DOCTYPE name [
<!ENTITY % myname "<!ELEMENT e1 ANY>">
```

```
%myname;
...
]
```

The following example, using external references pointed to by a URI and, in the second entity, a public ID (or catalog entry), is also legal:

```
<!DOCTYPE name [
<!ENTITY % myname SYSTEM "uri">
%myname;
<!ENTITY % myname2 PUBLIC "catalog entry" "uri">
%myname2;
  ...
]
```

However, this example, which tries to define parts of markup that will be resolved later, is not legal in the internal DTD subset:

```
<!DOCTYPE name [
<!ENTITY % mypart "ANY">
<!ENTITY % myname "<!ELEMENT e1 %mypart;>">
%myname;
...
]
```

Note that this code *would* be legal in the external DTD subset or an external entity.

In a non-validating XML processor, the external references may or may not be fetched and incorporated into the document, but this is not an error whichever way it goes.

<table>
<tr><td>Note</td><td>The distinction between validating and non-validating XML processors may seem trivial but almost all browsers are and will be non-validating. On the Web, it will be possible for a DTD to reference dozens of locations, any of which may reference dozens more. A validating browser must read in *everything*, potentially the entire Web, before it displays *anything*. The wait can become tiresome.</td></tr>
</table>

This brings up a subtle point. If the internal DTD subset contains a mixture of internal and external parameter entity references, a non-validating processor must stop processing them as soon as it doesn't interpret one, which it is permitted to do. The reason for this is that the reference may become undefined:

```
<!DOCTYPE name [
<!ENTITY % myname "<!ELEMENT element1 ANY>">
%myname1;
<!ENTITY % myname2 SYSTEM "uri"> <!--external file contains <!ELEMENT element2
ANY>
%myname2;
<!ENTITY % myname3 "<!ELEMENT3 e1 ANY>">
%myname3;
  ...
]
```

If the non-validating XML processor reads the external parameter entities, which it is permitted to do, all three elements are declared. If it doesn't read any external parameter entities, which it is also allowed to do, then only `element1` is declared. The reason is that the processor doesn't know whether the external reference contained a declaration of `element3` among its text, in which case the value of `element3` would have been whatever that value was, because the processor *would* have seen that first *if* it had read it. Because it doesn't know for sure, it *must* ignore all succeeding entity and attribute list references. To make matters even more complicated, a non-validating XML processor is permitted to skip *all* parameter entities, in which case none of the elements are defined.

Up to that point, however, a non-validating XML processor is required to read and process the internal subset of the DTD, if any such DTD subset exists. So any other declarations inside the internal subset, including setting the replacement text of internal general entities, setting default attribute values, and normalizing attributes must be processed and performed. Figure 3.2 shows a metaphorical representation of the difference between the views seen by validating and non-validating XML parsers.

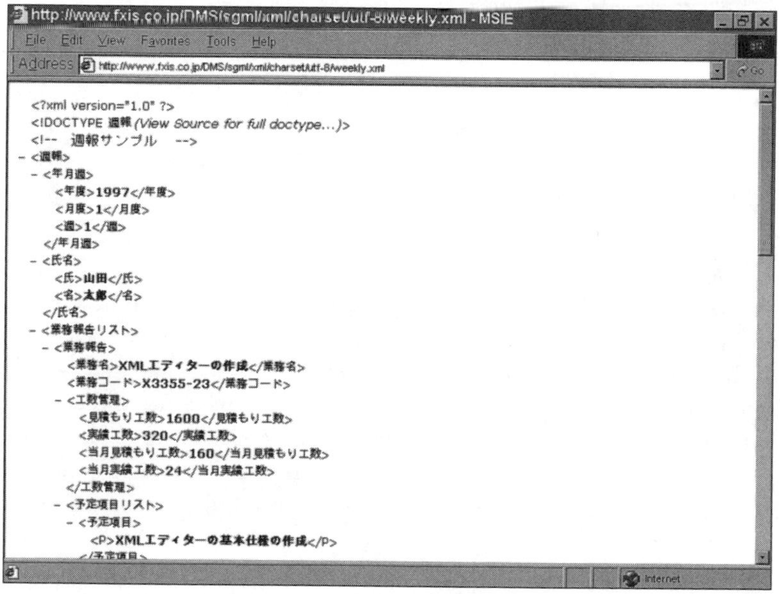

Figure 3.2
The difference is shown between the view of an XML document seen by a validating parser and a non-validating parser.

The validating parser sees everything clearly. The non-validating parser may or may not be able to see the entities and definitely doesn't see the DTD although it knows that the DTD exists.

Even though the non-validating XML processor must read and process the internal subset of the DTD until, and if, it's required to stop processing, it can't validate the document on that basis. If it did, it would be a validating processor and would be required to read everything.

Note

It's surprising how many people get parameter entities wrong and it's one of the problems with the EBNF that forms a part of the XML 1.0 standard. Programmers are familiar with EBNF and think it must define everything, but a large part of the specification is actually contained in the often-obscure accompanying text. You have to read both the EBNF and the text to fully capture the meaning of the W3C Recommendation.

GENERAL ENTITIES

A *general entity* can occur in the document itself, at least potentially. They're identified by a particular syntax in the declaration:

```
<!ENTITY name {stuff} >
```

The big distinction in general entities is whether they're internal, in which case stuff is a quoted string, or external, when it's a catalog entry or a URL.

```
<-- General Internal Entity -->
<!ENTITY name "text of some sort" >
<-- General Internal Entities -->
<!ENTITY name  PUBLIC "-//LeeAnne.com//My XML Stuff//EN" >
<!ENTITY name  PUBLIC "-//LeeAnne.com//My XML Stuff//EN" "my-dtd=stuff.dtd" >
<!ENTITY name  SYSTEM "http://www.leeanne.com/xml/my-xml-stuff.dtd" >
```

External entities may not be included in the document if the XML processor is not validating. Internal general entities *may* appear in the DTD, but only as the values in an attribute list or an entity. Basically this means that they have to appear with quoted strings.

UNPARSED ENTITIES

The unparsed entity has already been treated earlier in the explanation of NOTATIONs. Unparsed entities can only be external, but the externality of the entity is taken care of by the notation declaration referred to in an NDATA attribute. Their use, like that of notations in general, is somewhat controversial. There's no particular reason that the designer of a DTD has to know what particular sort of multimedia file is going to sit inside a document and then dispatch it to the proper handler sight unseen. Instead of being a generic document template, then, the DTD is limited by the types of unparsed files foreseen from the beginning and accounted for.

This is unlike the existing case with HTML. Within limits, you just point to a binary file and the application figures out what it is and how to display it. It's unlike the case in the UNIX environment that many of the designers of XML came from. Within limits, in UNIX you just use a file. Executable files are self-identifying and behave properly on their own. That would have seemed a much more robust approach, in my humble opinion.

Be that as it may, you're stuck with the difficult necessity of updating your DTDs whenever a new graphics or audio format is invented. Your alternative is to leave the DTD alone and fall by the wayside as video supplants still images, as interactive video supplants spectator video, and 3D virtual reality supplants mere 2D interaction.

The ENTITY declaration for an unparsed entity works hand in hand with the notation entity. The NOTATION *must* be declared before using it in an ENTITY.

Here's what a declaration for an unparsed entity would look like in your DTD along with the element declaration that is necessary to actually instantiate a particular example:

```
<!ENTITY gif89a SYSTEM "gif89a.gif" NDATA gif89a>
<!ELEMENT image EMPTY>
<!ATTLIST image source CDATA #REQUIRED
                alt    CDATA #IMPLIED
                type   NDATA gif89a >
```

In your document, your tag would look like:

```
<image source=uri"
       alt=[image of something]>
```

You can also create an enumerated list of notation types, which uses a slightly different syntax to describe the notation type, as you learned in the discussion about NOTATION declarations:

```
<!NOTATION gif87a    PUBLIC "-//CompuServe//NOTATION Graphics
Interchange Format 87a//EN" "gif">
<!NOTATION gif89a    PUBLIC "-//CompuServe//NOTATION Graphics
Interchange Format 89a//EN" "gif">
<!ENTITY gif87a NDATA gif87a>
<!ENTITY gif89a NDATA gif89a>
<!ELEMENT image EMPTY>
<!ATTLIST image source CDATA #REQUIRED
                alt    CDATA #IMPLIED
                type   NOTATION (gif87a | gif89a) "gif89a" >
```

In your document, your tag would look like this:

```
<image source=uri"
       alt=[image of something]>
```

but you could override the default type given in the attribute list like this if your gif was in the older gif87a format:

```
<image source=uri"
       alt=[image of something]
       type="gif87a" >
```

This tiny example points out the folly of this approach. How many people know offhand which of the two formats their gif files adhere to? How many care? Yet XML as it exists today makes this and many other trivialities a matter of pressing import. In the immortal words of Tim Bray, one of the XML 1.0 design team, "This is completely bogus."

ELEMENT DECLARATION

The element declaration is the part of XML you see most clearly in the final product. It represents the actual tags you'll use in your documents, and you have to have at least one or your document isn't valid XML. A non-validating XML processor will never see your DTD, but the tags and attributes contained in your document will describe it fairly completely anyway. Along with an associated style sheet, you can display the document correctly without any DTD at all.

If you don't care what the document looks like, you may not even need a style sheet. This might be the case for a document that was essentially a database, or was designed as a transport mechanism to transfer structured data between two applications.

The ELEMENT declaration looks like this:

```
<!ELEMENT name content-model >
```

The *name* is the name of your tag in use. The content model is where things start to get interesting.

The content model can contain an arbitrary mixture of terminal and non-terminal elements. Non-terminal elements are the names of other elements while terminal elements are text or other content. This is the syntax that forms nodes in your document. There are two general content models. The first model describes sequential—or ordered—content which uses a comma-separated list to indicate that one element has to follow another to the end of the ordered list. The second model uses a vertical "or" bar as a list separator to indicate a selection between alternatives. With these two mechanisms, you can construct almost anything.

ORDERED CONTENT

Entity names separated by commas are sequentially ordered. The first in the list is first, the second second, and so on. The items on the list should be surrounded by parentheses for clarity, although it's not strictly necessary for a pure ordered list:

```
<!ELEMENT name ( sub-element1, sub-element2, sub-element3, … ) >
```

SELECTION CONTENT

Entity names are separated by "or" bars (|), the vertical bars that should be available on your national-language–specific keyboard, often above the backslash (\). They should and must be surrounded by parentheses. In use, they look like this:

```
<!ELEMENT name ( sub-element1 | sub-element2 | sub-element3 | … ) >
```

REPEATING XML CONTENT ELEMENTS

Content names, or groups of content names surrounded by parentheses, can be followed by a question mark (?), a plus sign (+), or an asterisk (*) to indicate a repetition factor, sometimes called an *occurrence indicator*. No repetition mark means that the element must appear once and once only. A question mark means that the item can appear zero or one time. A plus sign means that the element appears at least one time and repeats as needed. An asterisk means that the element repeats as needed but is optional. In other words, an asterisk means zero or more. These signs can be combined with parentheses and the previous sequence or alternation to form structures of arbitrary complexity.

Content models are so important to XML that it might pay to write these down somewhere until you have them memorized. Table 3.1 lists the symbols used to indicate repetition factors and the two types of content model.

TABLE 3.1   OCCURRENCE INDICATORS USED IN XML DTDs

Syntax	Meaning
?	Zero or one occurrence
+	One or more occurrences
*	Zero or more occurrences
(a | b)	Either a or b but not both
(a , b)	A followed by b

If you're familiar with Regular Expressions in Vi, Emacs, and other UNIX-style editors, the syntax will be fairly familiar. The following example shows several uses:

```
<!ELEMENT name (( sub-element1 | sub-element2)? , (sub-element-3))+ >
```

This says that the element contains one or more substructures containing either `sub-element1` or `sub-element2` followed by one instance of `sub-element3` or it contains one instance of `sub-element3`. So, the following are all valid productions:

```
<name><sub-element3></sub-element3></name>
<name><sub-element3></sub-element3><sub-element3></sub-element3></name>
<name><sub-element1></sub-element1><sub-element3></sub-element3></name>
<name><sub-element2></sub-element2><sub-element3></sub-element3></name>
```

Even this simple example can generate an infinite number of productions, although it might become boring to list them. The ways in which these simple elements can combine can become confusing quickly. One of the user-friendliest uses of parameter entities is to encapsulate subsets of these behaviors so you can think about them separately.

PART

I

Ch

3

Note

> *Look-ahead* is a term from the compiler/parser world that simply means the parser can look ahead in the input stream and backtrack to resolve ambiguities. Because this implies the ability to buffer the entire document in memory if necessary, anything more than the one-character look-ahead—so common that it's not usually dignified with the name look-ahead—needed to resolve tokens was dropped from the language definition. Avoiding arbitrary levels of look-ahead means that an XML parser can be small and lightweight, suitable for handheld and other devices with limited memory and power.

Because XML processors don't do look-ahead, you have to guarantee that your content model can be successfully parsed without backtracking before handing it over. A good strategy is to structure a content model with a lot of optional elements as an alternative between cascading models with optional elements dropped off the beginning of the model subset:

```
(a,b,c,d) | (b,c,d) | (c,d) | (d)
```

You can't drop off elements from the end or put alternatives in the middle because then the parser would have to backtrack to parse them. So content models that look anything like the following ambiguous examples probably don't do what the designer intends them to do:

```
(a,b,c,d) | (a,b,c) | (a,b) | (a)
(a,b,c,d) | (a,b,d) | (a,d) | (a)
```

In both these examples, when the parser encounters element a, the first alternative, (a,b,c,d), is chosen. None of the other alternatives can be considered and may be ignored. Some XML parsers may generate an error when encountering a non-deterministic content model, however, so you're required to ensure that all content models are unambiguous.

> **Note**
>
> Technically, the ambiguous content models shown here are non-deterministic, which means it's not possible to construct a finite state automaton to process them. It may be possible to convert a non-deterministic content model to one that is deterministic algorithmically, but this is not guaranteed.

By nesting known bits of combining logic into larger ones, what might be daunting when viewed in its entirety can be broken down into component parts. Unfortunately, because of limitations on the internal DTD subset, this facility is only available in the external DTD.

TERMINAL CONTENT

The leaves of our document tree are represented by terminal content, of which there is one type: #PCDATA. *Parsed Character Data* is mixed content that can contain both text and markup. This is the most general type of leaf. When you use a mixed content model you cannot control the order or occurrence of elements, although you can constrain the elements to be of a certain type.

It would be used in an element like

```
<!ELEMENT name (#PCDATA | el1 | el2 | el3 | … )* >
```

or like this with no control over element type:

```
<!ELEMENT name (#PCDATA)* >
```

It's fairly straightforward.

> **Tip from**
>
>  LeeAnne.com
> Words to weave by
>
> You could use this type of element content to contain XML tags from another namespace, for example, in an XML document without violating the DTD of the base document. Although the document DTD would have no idea what the inserted tags meant, the governing DTD of the namespace and the designer of the page presumably would.

EMPTY CONTENT

If the element is declared as EMPTY, there is no content. So if you use the start and end tag convention, you have to guarantee that the end tag immediately follows the start tag like

```
DTD declaration: <!ELEMENT anyname EMPTY>
XML document instance: <anyname></anyname>
```

or you'll generate a validation error.

You'll also probably break any browser that runs into it if the name happens to look like an HTML empty tag. So this is unsafe although perfectly legal in XML:

```
<img></img>
```

All in all, it's probably better to use the special empty tag syntax like this:

```
<anyname />
```

Notice there is a space between the element name and the forward slash, and the slash is followed immediately by the closing angle bracket.

Note

> Because empty elements are, by definition, empty, the only possible content they can carry is in the attributes associated with each empty element. In general, any text content can easily be included in an attribute. The only real limitation is that you can't typically extend the document itself by means of an attribute. There are two important exceptions: A notation could theoretically call a process that inserted more content, much as one can do using Dynamic HTML, and it is possible to transclude content from an external file using attributes on an XLink anchor element. See Chapter 8, "XPath," and Chapter 9, "XLink and XPointer," for more information on XLink, XPath, and XPointer. Indirectly, it would also be possible to use XSLT to transform a document based on the value contained in an attribute, but that will have to wait until we discover XSL in Chapter 13, "Cascading Style Sheets and XML/XHTML."

ANY CONTENT

This is the ultimate in loose declarations and means exactly what it says. An element so defined can contain anything at all:

```
<!ELEMENT anyname ANY>
```

It's the equivalent of listing every element in your DTD in any order but saves a lot of typing time.

ANY content is handy primarily for developing a DTD or for debugging a broken DTD if you have an example document but no DTD. If you have validity errors in your first cut you can try changing the content model to ANY in likely spots until the DTD is valid so you can load it into a DTD design tool. At that point, you can start tightening up your content model until it just begins to pinch. Then you have a valid DTD. With a large document model, this can be tedious but it's the DTD designer equivalent of knitting, after a while the process becomes so mechanical you hardly think about it.

CREATING ATTLIST DECLARATIONS

ATTLIST is a container for the attributes associated with an ELEMENT. It has a straightforward syntax but complex alternatives that make it challenging to know every one:

```
<!ATTLIST element-name attribute-name-1 datatype default-data
                       attribute-name-2 datatype default-data
          … >
```

The following subsections define which datatypes can be used in an attribute list. For non-validating parsers, these datatypes are somewhat beside the point because the parser won't know anything about them. If your interest lies in downstream processing of XML documents using non-validating parsers, you can skip this whole section without much loss.

XML Datatypes

There are many more datatypes allowed in attributes than there are in content models. Where a content model allows only for PCDATA, attributes can take fairly specific datatypes. The XML attribute datatype defines in general terms what sort of information an entity can contain and how it will be structured. The attribute datatype is taken from the following list:

- **CDATA**—Character Data is a string.

- **ID**—A tokenized unique ID within a document. Although you're permitted to declare a default value, there's really no point in doing so. Also, because you need access to the DTD to determine whether there is an ID contained in the element, it's worthless to non-validating processors. Most tools that depend on IDs posit a theoretical ID with the name "id" that exists within every element and uses it whether it's been declared or not.

- **IDREF**—A tokenized reference to a unique ID. See ID.

- **IDREFS**—A tokenized list of references to unique IDs within a document. See ID.

- **ENTITY**—A tokenized reference to an entity which refers to a notation. This is another way of referring to unparsed data.

- **ENTITIES**—A tokenized list of references to entities which refer to notations. This is another way of referring to unparsed data.

- **NMTOKEN**—A tokenized reference to a NAME token.

- **NMTOKENS**—A tokenized reference to a list of NAME tokens.

- **NOTATION**—An enumerated reference to a list of notation datatypes. This is an exception to the rule that all unparsed entities must be external. If you define an attribute of type NOTATION for an element, you can actually put your notation data inline within your document. Assuming that you would defined the attribute type as a NOTATION in the following XML example, you would be able to include JavaScript without an external reference, if and only if you're using a validating parser.

  ```
  <Script type="JavaScript"> … JavaScript Code … </Script>
  ```

  To say that you would have to be careful when you do this is an understatement. Note that it's not an error for an external user agent to fail to understand a notation, so the JavaScript may be rendered as simple text or ignored completely depending on the combination of parser and user agent.

- **(attr1 | attr2 | …)**—An enumerated list of possible attribute values. Many XML authoring environments display these as a drop-down or pop-up selection list for ease of use.

Because multiple attributes can exist in a single element, an ATTLIST can get complex. They all obey the same set of rules, however, so careful study should set you right after any initial confusion.

The following subsections go into greater detail about the contents of attributes, starting with the default value syntax.

SPECIFYING DEFAULT DATA IN AN ATTRIBUTE

The default-data placeholder in the attribute list template earlier in this section can be either #REQUIRED, #IMPLIED, or a default value; or #FIXED and a constant value.

These are working examples:

```
<!ATTLIST elementname attr1 #REQUIRED
                      attr2 #IMPLIED
                      attr3 "default-value"
                      attr4 #FIXED "constant-value">
```

Both #REQUIRED and #IMPLIED don't take a default value because they would be meaningless in context. If the attribute is #REQUIRED, it has to be there whether there's a default value or not. If the attribute is #IMPLIED, the attribute is not necessary and need not be present.

PART

I

CH

3

> **Note**
>
> If ever there was a confusing term, #IMPLIED is it. It sounds almost like "default." You might naively think that the "implied" value was the default. But it isn't. *Implied* is there to tell the processor that it needn't bother looking for an attribute because it might not be there. The choice of words was an unfortunate lapse from clarity, nothing more.

IMPLIED is a holdover from the days of SGML, when straightforward description was sometimes sacrificed for a precise "logical" term whose origins lie hidden in the dusty mind of a programmer from the ancient days. In my opinion, the word is a simple malapropism because a somewhat related and often confused term, "inferred," describes precisely what the processor should do with an "implied" attribute, which is to infer the attribute's existence or non-existence based on the presentation of the element in the XML document itself.

ATTRIBUTES OF TYPE CDATA

This is *really* simple. It's a character string. The following example defines an attribute named string whose value is CDATA and a default value for that string:

```
<!ATTLIST name string CDATA "string stuff">
```

Note that, as always, non-validating parsers won't read the definition or default value of external DTDs.

ATTRIBUTES OF TYPE ID

These refer to unique IDs within your document and furnish an easy way to ensure that there is an available name to form the other end of a link. Although this is a clever thing to do, in practice most browsers are probably not going to validate and will never see the ID definition. Most current pointer tools impute the presence of an attribute of type ID named id or name whether it's in the DTD or not, thereby letting them generate links without tears.

The following code defines an ID attribute named node and then shows how the attribute might be used in an XML document.

```
DTD declaration: <!ATTLIST name node ID #REQUIRED>
XML document instance: <name node="A1234"
```

A safer course would be to define the ID attribute with the name id, so non-validating parsers can infer its intent just as HTML browsers do the name attribute. In the following section, you'll see two ways to do this.

ATTRIBUTES OF TYPE IDREF

This is a way to refer to the other end of an id/idref pair. The IDREF points to the id.

```
DTD declaration: <!ATTLIST anyname pointer IDREF #REQUIRED>
XML document instance: <anyname pointer="A1234"
```

In HTML terms, this is the rough equivalent of the href attribute that points to a named anchor.

Note

IDs are so handy it's a shame to have to plug them in everywhere, especially when you don't have write permissions on the source document. The next generation of linking mechanisms, XML XLinks and XPointers, will allow you to automatically use the document structure itself to obtain nearly the same result in the display document.

In an ideal world, IDs are the most likely artifacts to remain stationary, or relatively so, in a document. For this reason, they make good targets for pointers. The URL#namevalue fragment syntax used in HTML to point to locations within the document also works in XML, except that the target must be an ID.

The corollary to this is that both ID and name attributes should be declared for every possible target, because legacy user agents will find the element containing the indicated name attribute and XML-aware user agents will find the ID. You could, theoretically, collapse the two into one attribute by declaring a name attribute to be of type ID if you knew that the document would be viewed using validating XML parsers only. Unfortunately, the ID tag is also used in HTML, in a type of schizophrenia resulting from trying to keep the old syntax and create a new one that seemed more self-explanatory. So, it's best to declare two attributes with the same value. ID-type attributes must be unique within a document and name attributes should duplicate the ID-type attribute.

So ideally, one would define the following attributes in any element that might be used as the target of a hyperlink:

```
<!ATTLIST anylink id    ID      #IMPLIED
                  name NMTOKEN #IMPLIED
                  other-attributes… >
```

If you wanted to enforce the presence of the two link attributes on an element, you could define them as required like this:

```
<!ATTLIST anylink id   ID       #REQUIRED
                   name NMTOKEN #REQUIRED
                   other-attributes… >
```

Please note that the name attribute can't be of type ID, although it should duplicate the content of the id attribute, since the parser would enforce ID attribute uniqueness, preventing you from declaring a second instance of an attribute of type ID. In use, you could instantiate the target of a hyperlink like this:

```
<anylink id="A1234" name="A1234">anytargetcontent</anylink>
```

If the name of the anylink element were chosen to be a, both HTML-only browsers and XML-aware browsers would find the same location.

```
<a id="A1234" name="A1234">anytargetcontent</a>
```

This is the strategy used by XHTML, since it's designed in part to be accessible to as many legacy HTML browsers as possible as well as providing the benefits of extensibility for XML-aware browsers.

PART

I

CH

3

ATTRIBUTES OF TYPE ENTITY

This is how you would use an attribute of type ENTITY to refer to a notation:

```
<!NOTATION gif PUBLIC "…">
<!ENTITY gifpicture SYSTEM "mypicture.gif" NDATA gif>
<!ELEMENT picture EMPTY>
<!ATTLIST picture src ENTITY #REQUIRED>
```

In an XML document proper you would use the picture tag defined in the DTD like this:

```
<picture src='gifpicture'>
```

This is one more way that XML requires you to be a multimedia guru. Although I'm sure there's an important distinction between the many ways available to do this, the real question is whether it should be done at all. See my comments on notations in general earlier in this chapter.

Note

I hate to harp on this and I promise not to do it after this chapter, but forcing the XML processor to know about all the possible multimedia types is not a robust way of doing things. In the first place, it means that you can't insert an image or multimedia file within a document unless you can guarantee that all your users will be using validating XML parsers. This seems excessively limiting. The W3C XML working group seems to have ignored the example of browser plug-ins and server-side redirection, which would have made it possible to negotiate with the user agent to ascertain its capabilities and supply an appropriate multimedia file if possible. If not, the user agent would know that it had to find an appropriate helper on its own, just as most now do with unrecognized MIME content types. A better mechanism should have been provided. Content negotiation between the browser and the server would have been the modern method of providing this flexibility, because different user environments might require entirely different file formats.

That said, the convention *does* work, even if it's awkward, and it may be replaced in the future with a simple mechanism that ignores the existing machinations in favor of some other method of identifying content type. The W3C standards for persistent URIs strongly discourage tying locations to data type and access methods, which the existing notation syntax violates.

Because the datatype might change in future, W3C currently recommends that content negotiation take place between the server and the user agent to determine what data types are supported and what types are available. In that case, you should refer to a notation as a bare name, like "myimage", and let the server figure out what kind of image is available for that particular agent and supply it, telling the agent what it supplied so there can be no mistake. It will all come out in the wash, as they say, so rest assured that this will undoubtedly change sometime in future.

ATTRIBUTES OF TYPE NMTOKEN

The contents of an attribute are constrained to look like a name token as defined in the XML Recommendation. In other words, it consists of one Unicode/ISO letter, ideograph, underscore, or colon followed by letters, ideographs, digits, periods, hyphens, underscores, or colons repeated as often as you like in any combination. This means simply that a name can't start with a digit, period, or hyphen, although it may contain any of these plus underscores or colons after the initial character but no other typographical symbols like asterisks, slashes, strokes, ampersands, or the like. The phrase "letters and ideographs" includes the characters one would ordinarily use to indicate words in a given language. For example, in Chinese these might be single characters indicating complete words; in Japanese, characters indicating complete syllables; and in many languages, individual letters indicating consonants and vowels which are combined to form words. The potential combinations of these extend the meaningfulness of names to include almost the entire population of the world literate in any human language.

> **Caution**
>
> As stated previously, using colons is strongly discouraged because they're easily mistaken for a namespace prefix. Also, the string `"xml"` in any case combination is reserved.

These are NMTOKENS:

```
name
new_name
_name.name-suffix
name.suffix
:name
luftballoons99
name1.suffix_part
```

and these are not:

```
name&more
99luftballoons
.name
$value
name(function)
```

Although few texts on XML, in English at least, demonstrate the use of ideographs and non-Roman scripts in an element name due to the difficulty of typesetting them, among other reasons, the capability exists and will be used extensively in those areas that need this capability. Figure 3.3 shows an example of a Japanese language XML document available on the Web from the FujiXerox site at `http://www.fxis.co.jp/DMS/sgml/xml/charset/utf-8/weekly.xml`.

Figure 3.3
An example of a Japanese language document marked up with meaningful Japanese XML tags.

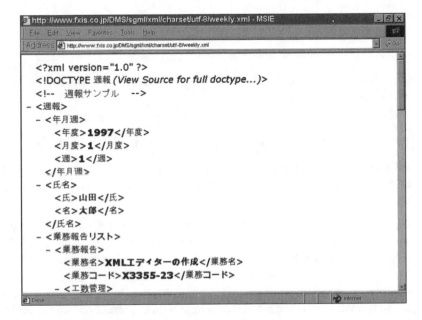

The link to this example was kindly supplied by the *Chinese XML Now!* site of Academia Sinica at `http://www.ascc.net/xml/`. The site contains numerous links to information of interest to developers of Chinese XML documents, test suites to confirm the capability to handle Chinese input properly, and examples of Chinese language XML documents.

ATTRIBUTES OF TYPE NOTATION

These have to match the NMTOKEN definition and are given in a simple alternation list that defines the enumeration of possible types. One of these can be chosen but not more than one. A default value can be specified but need not be. They look like this in use:

```
<!ATTLIST name type (gif87a|gif89a) >
```

The same NOTATION enumeration would look like this when defined with a default value:

```
<!ATTLIST name type (gif87a|gif89a) "gif89a" >
```

All notations must be declared before they're used in an attribute list.

ENUMERATED ATTRIBUTES

Enumerated attributes look just like the previous examples and are defined using an alternation list, but don't refer to notations. They're handy for creating lists of choices. Most XML editing environments give you a little drop-down list for choosing which value you want out of the list. The following code demonstrates a simple enumerated attribute as defined in a DTD:

```
<!ATTLIST name choice (yes|no) >
```

Like NOTATION attributes, enumerated attribute values can take a default value:

```
<!ATTLIST name choice (yes|no) "yes" >
```

The above DTD snippet defines an attribute, choice, that can take the values "yes" or "no" and whose default value is "yes".

USING SPECIAL XML DATATYPE CONSTRUCTIONS

Although the constructions in the following subsections appear in the document rather than in the DTD, the functions they serve are closely related to concepts already discussed in this chapter.

Processing instructions allow the document author to include text in the document that shouldn't be parsed or displayed by the XML parser or user agent. Instead, they should be passed to a special helper application defined in the processing instruction itself. They include what you might use a <script> element for in HTML but are much more general. Note especially that they don't use SGML comment tags to hide text. This is not advisable in XML because XML parsers are not required to pass on the text of comments to the user agent.

CDATA sections are a shorthand way of escaping an entire block of text, so any included markup characters are treated as text instead of markup. Like a CDATA content description in the DTD, they tell the parser that it shouldn't attempt to parse any of the text contained within the element.

PROCESSING INSTRUCTIONS

A processing instruction is passed on directly to the application with no attempt to evaluate it. It begins with <? and ends with ?> and cannot contain the characters xml in any case combination.

Tip from

LeeAnne.com
Words to weave by

Many people have longed for a mechanism to include binary data directly in their XML file. No more waiting around for external references to load, no more wondering if the data is still where you left it last. The whole file is one big glob of data. In theory, this is a nice idea, but guaranteeing that the closing strings don't appear in binary data is a difficult problem, and is probably too much to ask an XML processor to handle.

Using a processing instruction, you can pass data directly to a particular interpreter:

```
<?javascript {javascript stuff} ?>
<?Tcl {Tcl stuff} ?>
…
```

The advantage of this is that you can freely pass things along to an interpreter or program runtime without going through the process of adding a notation to your DTD. Of course, your processor data mustn't contain the string ?> without escaping it.

ESCAPING A TEXT BLOCK IN A CDATA SECTION

A CDATA section is a convenience that allows you to put a bunch of character data into your document without having to tediously escape every single markup character—or what might look at first glance to be markup characters—contained in it.

In use it looks like this:

```
<![CDATA[Any old text at all including < and & signs or
even examples of XML tags <!ENTITY list … >]]>
```

A CDATA tag is a convenience. You could have done the same thing by escaping all the special characters like

```
Any old text at all including &lt; and &amp; signs or
even examples of XML tags &lt;!ENTITY list … >
```

but possibly spent a lot longer at it and with more possibility of getting it wrong.

The only constraint is that your data can't contain the sequence]]> ending the section. Figure 3.4 shows the CDATA section in use.

PART
I

CH
3

Figure 3.4
An XML page showing a CDATA section in use to avoid having to escape a section of markup in the MultiDoc Pro SGML/XML browser.

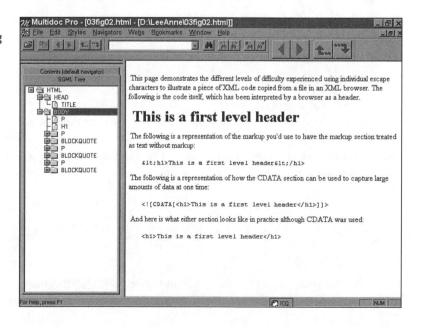

UNDERSTANDING THE DIFFERENCE BETWEEN WELL-FORMED AND VALID XML

The difference between well-formed and valid XML is simple: Valid XML has a DTD associated with it and has been verified against all the rules contained in the DTD in addition to being well-formed. Merely well-formed XML, on the other hand, is not *necessarily* valid, although it may be.

Well-formed XML follows a these rules:

- Tags must nest properly. Every beginning and ending tag pair must fully contain any tag pair that begins inside it. In other words, no start-tag, end-tag, empty-element tag, element, comment, processing instruction, character reference, or entity reference can begin in one entity and end in another.

- In the internal DTD subset, parameter entity references can occur only at the top level, where markup declarations can occur, and not within markup declarations. Parameter entities are not restricted in the external DTD subset.

- The name in an element's end-tag must match the element type in the start-tag.

- No attribute name may appear more than once in the same start-tag or empty-element.

- Attribute values cannot contain direct or indirect entity references to external entities.

- The replacement text of any entity referred to directly or indirectly in an attribute value (other than <) must not contain a <.

- Characters referred to using character references must be legal characters.

- The declaration of a parameter entity must precede any reference to it.

- The declaration of a general entity must precede any reference to it that appears in a default value in an attribute-list declaration.

- Parameter-entity references may only appear in the DTD and have restrictions in the internal DTD subset.

The only practical way to tell whether you have a valid XML document is to use an automated tool to read in the document itself, including its DTD, and let the tool parse it. Hand-checking can help but is notoriously error prone, even when you're careful. It typically takes two, three, or even more attempts to get a new DTD and document type to load for the first time. Sometimes it takes many more attempts, so be patient and persevere because you *will* succeed.

LEARNING HOW TO USE EXTERNAL DTDS AND DTD FRAGMENTS

One of the strengths of XML is that you can use or reuse the document types defined for one document for as many others as you like. DTDs can reside in a central repository and can even be combined to make larger DTDs by choosing modular sections.

The following subsections describe how DTDs can be accessed in XML documents or in the DTDs that define them.

POINTING TO AN EXTERNAL DTD

Non-local external DTDs can be pointed to using the DOCTYPE declaration like this if the DTD is on the Web:

```
<!DOCTYPE article PUBLIC "-//LeeAnne.com//Article DTD//EN"
"http://www.leeanne.com/XML/article.dtd">
```

Or, a series of DTD fragments can be pointed to using parameter entity references like this:

```
<!DOCTYPE  article PUBLIC "-//LeeAnne.com//Article DTD//EN"
"http://www.leeanne.com/XML/article.dtd"> [
<!ENTITY % header PUBLIC "-//LeeAnne.com//Header DTD//EN"
"http://www.leeanne.com/XML/header.dtd">>
%header;
<!ENTITY % footer PUBLIC "-//LeeAnne.com//Footer DTD//EN"
"http://www.looanno.oom/XML/footer.dtd">>
%footer;
…
]>
```

This mechanism is widely used to call in files of character entity references but can also be used for other purposes. Be aware, however, that non-validating processors are forbidden to interpret any parsed entity following an external parameter entity reference it doesn't read.

The reason is that the state of every parsed entity is undefined after any external reference not incorporated into the document. In fact, it's legal for a non-validating processor to ignore external entities entirely.

POINTING TO A LOCAL DTD

Although a local DTD is also an external DTD, there is a slightly different syntax used to reference local DTDs because one doesn't ordinarily include a catalog reference. Local DTDs can be pointed to using the DOCTYPE declaration like this if the DTD is on your local hard drive:

```
<!DOCTYPE article SYSTEM "article.dtd">
```

A series of DTD fragments can be pointed to using parameter entity references like this:

```
<!DOCTYPE  article SYSTEM "article.dtd"> [
<!ENTITY % header SYSTEM  "header.dtd">>
%header;
<!ENTITY % footer SYSTEM  "footer.dtd">>
%footer;
…
]>
```

This mechanism is widely used to call in files of character entity references but can also be used for other purposes. Be aware, however, that non-validating processors are not allowed

PART

I

CH

3

to interpret any parsed entity following an external parameter entity reference, including a DTD, it doesn't read.

The reason for this is that the state of every parsed entity is undefined after any external reference not incorporated into the document because a value might or might not have been set for it in the unread external entity. A non-validating parser has no way of knowing one way or another. In fact, it's legal for a non-validating processor to ignore external entities entirely.

Tip from	
 LeeAnne.com Words to weave by	Why do we bother with non-validating processors anyway? Wouldn't it be better to validate *everything*? In a word, no. Imagine how difficult it would be to load a page if browsers required every link to be traversed and verified before it would highlight a hyperlink. XML browsers can *transclude*, include as actual content, documents from anywhere on the Web. So you have no control over how pages are structured. If a page you transclude includes extensive and recursive access to other pages or DTDs, you may have a long wait before the page loads. XML browsers are likely to mark the place where an external reference is made and let the user choose whether to load it, much as the user has control over taking a hyperlink.

It's likely that most actual user agents (browsers) used on the Web are non-validating. The potential overhead of validation, visiting every referenced location, is so great that the most sensible plan for any browser is to wait to visit external documents until requested to do so by the user.

USING DTD FRAGMENTS

The preceding two examples both used DTD fragments to extend the article DTD. If you think of a document as a tree, then a DTD fragment is a way to graft on another limb to the tree. The DTD must be structured in a way that this can be done with careful attention to namespaces until the XML namespace initiative comes to fruition.

The most common use of DTD fragments is to reference the long lists of general entities used to refer to character entities by mnemonic name. So you can use the more understandable ‘ instead of ‘ when referring to a left single quotation mark. Few people have memorized the table of ISO and Unicode character by number. It's just too hard for most people. The easiest way to use the mnemonics is to call in a predefined set of them by name. There are a lot of these, of course, but the ordinary ones you'll see are Latin-1, Special Symbols, and Mathematics and Greek Symbols.

Here's how to point to Latin-1 for XHTML:

```
<!ENTITY % ISOlat1 PUBLIC "-//W3C//ENTITIES Latin1//EN//XML"
                "http://www.w3.org/TR/xhtml1/DTD/HTMLlat1x.ent">
%ISOlat1;
```

The one we just looked at is defined as

```
<!ENTITY lsquo   "&#8216;"> <!-- left single quotation mark, U+2018
ISOnum -->
```

inside the special characters set and invoked like this:

```
<!ENTITY % HTMLspecial PUBLIC "-//W3C//ENTITIES Special//EN//HTML"
        "http://www.w3.org/TR/xhtml1/DTD/HTMLspecialx.ent">
%HTMLspecial;
```

If you're going to do any math at all you might need this one as well:

```
<!ENTITY % HTMLsymbol PUBLIC "-//W3C//ENTITIES Symbols//EN//HTML"
        "http://www.w3.org/TR/xhtml1/DTD/HTMLsymbolx.ent">
%HTMLsymbol;
which contains things like <!ENTITY cong       "&#8773;"> <!--
approximately equal to, U+2245 ISOtech -->
<!ENTITY asymp    "&#8776;"> <!-- almost equal to = asymptotic to,
U+2248 ISOamsr -->
<!ENTITY ne       "&#8800;"> <!-- not equal to, U+2260 ISOtech -->
<!ENTITY equiv    "&#8801;"> <!-- identical to, U+2261 ISOtech -->
<!ENTITY le       "&#8804;"> <!-- less-than or equal to, U+2264 ISOtech -->
<!ENTITY ge       "&#8805;"> <!-- greater-than or equal to, U+2265 ISOtech -->
<!ENTITY sub      "&#8834;"> <!-- subset of, U+2282 ISOtech -->
<!ENTITY sup      "&#8835;"> <!-- superset of, U+2283 ISOtech -->
```

These symbols are commonly used in mathematics and scientific fields. This symbol set also contains Greek letters and other goodies to make it easier to type simple mathematics into your pages.

A good way to allow easy use of modular DTDs is to provide stubs within the document, which can be used to expand on DTD capabilities when needed and ignored

As an example, a DTD might start out with some entities that point to null files like this:

```
<!ENTITY % header SYSTEM  "nullfile.dtd">>
%header;
<!ENTITY % footer SYSTEM  "nullfile.dtd">>
%footer;
…
]>
```

When you wanted to actually *use* the header and footer information you could override these values with ones that actually do something like this:

```
<!DOCTYPE  article SYSTEM "article.dtd"> [
<!ENTITY % header SYSTEM  "header.dtd">>
<!ENTITY % footer SYSTEM  "footer.dtd">>
 …
]>
```

In the next chapter, you'll explore another way to insert new tags, or entire branches

PARAMETER ENTITIES

A *parameter entity* is a way to store data (or point to it for later retrieval) for later use. Parameter entities are valid only within a DTD and have different behaviors in the internal subset of the DTD and the external subset. This asymmetric behavior was decided upon to make it easier to parse an internal DTD for a non-validating XML processor.

Note

After spending so much time clarifying the different ways in which you can use parameter entities to make life easy, it's somewhat ironic that most of the XML schema proposals pretty much scrap parameter entities in favor of an XML-like, as opposed to DTD-like, syntax. And so it goes....

You can put any number of things into a parameter entity and use them at your convenience. A typical use is to read in external files within a DTD, either in the external or internal subset. Another common use is to store integral bits of markup parts so that they can be used in a mnemonic way as shorthand for complex expressions. For bits of markup that are used over and over again, the gain in clarity can be enormous.

You may want to refer to Chapter 4, "Extending a Document Type Definition with Local Modifications," for a complete example of working with and around parameter entities. The following expands an element defined using parameter entities because a a copy of it was made in the internal DTD subset:

```
<!ELEMENT blink %Flow;>
<!ATTLIST blink
  %attrs;
>
```

The previous code, with two parameter entities in two locations, expanded through a series of indirection to this:

```
<!ELEMENT blink (#PCDATA | p | h1 | h2 | h3 | h4 | h5 | h6 | div | ul | ol | dl |
menu | dir | pre | hr | blockquote | address | center | noframes | isindex |
fieldset | table | form | a | br | span | bdo | object | applet | img | map |
iframe | tt | i | b | big | small | u | s | strike |font | basefont | em | strong
| dfn | code | q | sub | sup | samp | kbd | var | cite | abbr | acronym | input |
select | textarea | label | button | ins | del | script | noscript)* >
<!ATTLIST blink
    id            ID            #IMPLIED
    class         CDATA         #IMPLIED
    style         CDATA         #IMPLIED
    title         CDATA         #IMPLIED
    lang          NMTOKEN       #IMPLIED
    xml:lang      NMTOKEN       #IMPLIED
    dir           (ltr|rtl)     #IMPLIED
    onclick       CDATA         #IMPLIED
    ondblclick    CDATA         #IMPLIED
    onmousedown   CDATA         #IMPLIED
    onmouseup     CDATA         #IMPLIED
    onmouseover   CDATA         #IMPLIED
    onmousemove   CDATA         #IMPLIED
    onmouseout    CDATA         #IMPLIED
    onkeypress    CDATA         #IMPLIED
    onkeydown     CDATA         #IMPLIED
    onkeyup       CDATA         #IMPLIED
>
```

This expansion is obviously somewhat harder to read than the parameter entity equivalent, especially if the construct is used in many locations.

UNDERSTANDING THE W3C ENTITY TABLE

Table 3.2 explains where everything can go in a nutshell. Although it really isn't all that clear, a similar table is used in the W3C XML 1.0 Recommendation to attempt to clarify the rules that entities obey in various contexts and is reproduced or paraphrased almost everywhere:

TABLE 3.2   XML 1.0 ENTITY TYPE BEHAVIORS

Entity Type	Parameter	Internal General	External Parsed General	Unparsed	Character
Reference in Content	Not recognized	Included	Included if validating	Forbidden	Included
Reference in Attribute Value	Not recognized	Included in literal	Forbidden	Forbidden	Included
Occurs as Attribute Value	Not recognized	Forbidden	Forbidden	Notify	Not recognized
Reference in Entity Value	Included in literal	Bypassed	Bypassed	Forbidden	Included
Reference in DTD	Included as PE	Forbidden	Forbidden	Forbidden	Forbidden

Let's try to clarify this blob of information. The first row of the table refers to locations in the document itself. The second and third rows refer to locations in either the document or its DTD. The final two rows refer to locations in the DTD only. The table starts to make sense only when you realize that the information content depicted is sparse. There are quite a number of entries that tell you only that a given entity type can only appear in one location. I question whether the table is all that valuable, although people *will* duplicate or paraphrase it. In the actual XML 1.0 Recommendation, almost all the real information about the table lies in the text that references it.

Let's list the few bits of information the table contains in seven simplified rules:

- Parameter entities can be used only in the DTD. Outside the DTD, their calling sequence, %name;, is treated as plain text.
- Inside a declaration, parameter entities are expanded but only in the external subset.
- Outside of a declaration, parameter entities can only be used to insert complete markup declarations and surround all insertions with a leading and trailing space.
- Internal general entities can only be used to insert text and are *bypassed* in the DTD. Bypassed means that they are recognized and their name is entered into a lookup table with no current value. When they are declared, the lookup entry has a value associated with it. It's an obscure way of saying you can use them before they are declared.

- External parsed general entities are treated just like internal general entities except that you can't refer to them in an attribute value. This is on account of the difficulty of handling character encodings in the context of an attribute.

- Unparsed entities can only be used as a name in an entity declaration. Nothing else is recognized in that context, including character entities. The only responsibility of the XML processor is to notify the helper application declared in a notation declaration that the unparsed entity needs processing.

- Character entities are treated like general entities except that they are included immediately in all cases. Although they are universal, in most cases they should be used as general entities from one of the predefined sets. The raw numeric references, although legal, are almost impossible to read and understand. So, the mnemonic `&ne;` is easier to identify than the decidedly hard to remember `&#8800;` equivalent, although both refer to the "not equal to" (≠) symbol.

Parameter entities are so powerful, in fact, that the XML 1.0 standard takes care to curb their power by restricting them first to the DTD and then further restricting the most complex uses to the external subset of the DTD, where non-validating XML processors never (well, rarely) look.

Tip from LeeAnne.com Words to weave by	If you're using parameter entities to store text, be aware that XML processors insert one leading and one trailing space when expanding them. This is to discourage people from using them to store small pieces of text and building words (or especially markup!) out of them.

The need for parameter entities probably will eventually disappear when one or more of the XML schema proposals gains market share in the minds of users. But this will be a while as the dueling standards have a lot to reconcile yet.

ALTERING AN XML DTD

Several mechanisms are built into the XML DTD to allow you to alter an existing DTD. The first of these, conditional markup, has to be built into the DTD when it's created but, after that, you can change how it behaves on-the-fly by overriding the value of one or more parameter entities. The other mechanisms described in the following sections, adding new attributes or elements, require less planning but their effects are invisible to other users of the DTD. The appropriate mechanism in each case is a design decision.

CONDITIONAL MARKUP

Many people can't see the use for conditional markup. However, this facility gives the DTD designer the ability to create "debugging" or alternative versions of the DTD that reside in the file itself, where they can't be lost and where you can encourage people who change anything to make sure to handle the conditional parts as well.

Conditional markup uses the familiar parameter entity mechanism to declare particular items as having the value IGNORE or INCLUDE. They look quite a bit like a CDATA section except that the contents must be markup surrounded by the special conditional begin and end sequences:

```
<!DOCTYPE book PUBLIC … [
<!ENTITY % debug 'INCLUDE' >
<!ENTITY % release 'IGNORE' >
]>
  <!ENTITY % debug 'IGNORE' >
  <!ENTITY % release 'INCLUDE' >
  <![%debug;[
  <!ELEMENT book (comments*, front, body, back?)>
  ]]>
  <![%release;[
  <!ELEMENT book (front, body, back?)>
  ]]>
```

To swap back and forth between versions that allow comments to be prepended to the book and those that don't, just override the debug and release entity values somewhere in the internal DTD subset. Note that the strings DEBUG and IGNORE are XML keywords and have to be in uppercase as shown, however, you can use any appropriate name for the parameters. Also note that DEBUG is just a value. You can use this mechanism to construct arbitrarily complex DTD variants by judicious choice of sections to be selectively included or skipped, and by creating parameter entities that select or ignore them. Few DTD designers on small projects are ever likely to have to use this tool as it was designed in SGML for environments with scores of coders working over months and years. When your DTD is thousands of lines long, you don't want to fool around with ad hoc debugging changes. The fact that you can use the mechanism in other ways is a bonus.

USING NEW ATTRIBUTES

An attribute can be added to an element at any time because attribute lists are concatenated with the first declaration of any particular attribute name taking precedence over any following declaration. If there are no duplicates, the attribute is added to the list of existing attributes, or creates a new one if attributes had not been previously declared. Chapter 4 covers this topic in detail.

You just add an ATTLIST declaration to the internal DTD subset or equivalently an external DTD file which reads in your new attribute declaration before reading in the DTD proper. Here we add a required field to the alt attribute for an image to encourage people to use it as the WAI recommends:

```
<DOCTYPE book [
<!ATTLIST image alt CDATA #REQUIRED>
]>
```

USING NEW ELEMENTS

Elements are a little harder, although easily done. You have to find a place for them in the existing DTD and go through a sometimes lengthy process to fit them in, but it's largely a piece of cake. Chapter 4 goes into great detail on this subject. This oversimplified example uses the internal DTD subset to add a new element, postit, with a simple content model to the book DTD:

```
<DOCTYPE book [
<!ELEMENT postit #PCDATA >
]>
```

It doesn't define a place for it in the content models of the DTD nor define attributes the element might take but you'll see how to do both these things in Chapter 4.

UNDERSTANDING THE XHTML DTDS

XHTML is an attempt to duplicate, within the limits of XML, the functionality of HTML 4.0. Although there are subtle differences, it is largely a success. Validated HTML documents can be fairly easily converted into valid XHTML documents.

In Chapter 4, you'll explore the idea of changing the XHTML DTD to suit yourself, which allows you an opportunity to study the DTD in detail. The transitional XHTML DTD is located at the back of this book as well as on the CD-ROM that accompanies it with the filename, xhtml1-transitional.dtd. The frameset and strict DTDs are also provided as xhtml1-frameset.dtd and xhtml1-strict.dtd respectively for the sake of comparison and completeness.

GETTING DOWN TO CASES

In this chapter you've examined the XML DTD in detail. You should understand how they're constructed in whole and in part. Every declaration with the DTD has an exact syntax with rules that must be followed, and the XML macro facility—parameter entities—has an even stricter set of rules, which limit its use to the external DTD subset.

However, the whole issue of defining and using DTDs is a thorny one in XML. Most of the really useful things you might like to do, such as including graphical illustrations in a document, or defining IDs within a document so stable references to particular locations can be pointed to using XPointer and XPath, require that the DTD be parsed by a validating parser.

Validating parsers have problems of their own. Because they require that the entire document be read in completely before displaying any part, they slow down page loading to the point that it's irritating to look at unless the document is sitting on the hard drive of the machine you're using to view it. Because the DTD itself may not be available on demand, or might require waiting through a lengthy dialup sequence, load time can be expected to be highly variable on that account alone.

Certain XML browsers may try to finesse the problem by incorporating knowledge of particular DTDs within their code, but this raises the issue of latency when and if a DTD changes for any reason. Although DTDs should probably be invariant over geologic time, there's no way to ensure that this is so rather than the goodwill of the author. The possibility of "validating" against an incorrect local copy of the DTD then exists for any such scheme to improve document load time by hiding knowledge in the browser.

CHAPTER 4

EXTENDING A DOCUMENT TYPE DEFINITION WITH LOCAL MODIFICATIONS

In this chapter

EXTENDING A DTD

In Chapter 3, "Understanding XML Document Type Definitions," you discovered what a DTD was and learned about the possibility of extending it. Because an XML DTD is the basis of document interchange between many document authors or automated document creators, and because the actual DTD might be archived in a location over which you have no control, it's often impossible to change the DTD without consensus among all the users of the DTD. But sometimes there are local communities or interest groups for which the DTD lacks some feature that would facilitate communication although others see no reason to change, so no one can agree on what the changes should look like. The following are three ways a DTD can be extended locally without touching the external DTD subset:

- You can override external subset ENTITY values in the internal subset of an XML document; this method is subject to rather severe constraints.

- You can freely override or extend external subset ATTLIST declarations in the internal subset of an XML document.

- You can add ELEMENT and any other declarations as long as they don't already exist in the XML external subset, which in most cases is the DTD itself. This can be very useful if the external DTD allows for it.

Caution

If you use any external parameter entity that is not read by a nonvalidating processor, all following entity and attribute list declarations are ignored. Although proper, this behavior can be disconcerting.

In many cases, these three options give you considerable flexibility and allow you to extend a DTD quite handily, provided the DTD designer allowed for it. It helps considerably if the DTD was designed for easy extensibility, and there are several techniques you can use to control exactly which parts of the DTD are modifiable and which are not if you have the luxury of designing your own DTD.

ADDING A NEW ATTRIBUTE TO AN EXISTING ELEMENT

The simplest way to add new information capacity is to place it in an attribute. Because an ATTLIST can be easily overridden or extended in the local DTD subset, you can add an attribute to an ELEMENT or change its definition simply by redefining the ATTLIST associated with it. XML merges the values in ATTLISTs that reference the same ELEMENT to avoid conflict. If an attribute has exactly the same name, the first reference (that is, the one in the internal DTD subset) holds, even if a later ATTLIST uses a different definition. This is a problem with older SGML-only tools because SGML did not allow redefining an ATTLIST until XML forced the issue. But all modern SGML/XML tools should support this usage.

As an example, let's begin with the following fragment of a DTD called book.dtd:

```
<!ELEMENT book (title, … ) >
<!ELEMENT title (#PCDATA) >
```

```
<ATTLIST title author CDATA #REQUIRED
              titletype #CDATA "Fiction"
         …
         >
…
```

This needs to be modified by adding a language attribute to the formal description of the book title and changing the default `titletype` category from Fiction to NonFiction. Usually, only one statement needs to be added to the internal subset, the new `ATTLIST`. This would be added to the XML document itself in the internal subset of the DTD like this:

```
<!DOCTYPE book [
<!ATTLIST title language #CDATA "German"
     titletype #CDATA "NonFiction" >
]>
```

Tip from

Words to weave by

XML enables an `ATTLIST` to be redefined as many times as you want, but the first instance of any particular attribute defines that attribute permanently. SGML was only recently redefined to conform with this behavior, so older SGML tools might raise an exception when these multiple redefintions are encountered.

In use, the new attribute and default values are added to the title `ELEMENT`. Because roughly anything you can do with `ELEMENT` content can also be done with an attribute within an `ELEMENT`, you can make quite extensive additions to a DTD with this method as long as there is an existing element to which you want to add your data.

ADDING A NEW ELEMENT

Adding new elements is trickier. Simply because you can define a new `ELEMENT` doesn't necessarily mean that there is a proper place to put it in the document structure as a whole. And to make matters worse, the mechanism whereby it might be possible to easily modify or extend an external DTD—the internal subset—was specifically hobbled by the designers of XML, preventing you from using parameter entities at anything other than the top level. In other words,

```
<!ENTITY % junk "garbage">
%junk;
```

is legal in the internal subset, whereas the much more valuable

```
<!ENTITY % useful "handy stuff">
<!ELEMENT %useful; >
```

is not. This means that you can't simplify life by using the same sort of shorthand notations you can use in the external DTD subset. You have to expand everything to eliminate any parameter reference inside other elements. This makes programming a little easier for people wanting to parse the internal subset and a little more difficult for people who just want to work with it.

USING EXISTING PARAMETER ENTITIES TO MODIFY THE DTD

This is a situation that cries out for object-oriented behavior, and XML has a mechanism that allows for limited inheritance—the parameter ENTITY. The DTD has to have existing parameter entities available to override before you can extend it in this manner.

The example for this process uses the XHTML 1.0 Transitional DTD Draft developed by W3C because it was specifically designed to be easily extensible. The first thing to notice is that almost everything is defined as an ENTITY before use as ELEMENT content. This enables maximum flexibility to treat the external subset more or less like an object.

Insertion points must be moved into the internal DTD subset and all parameter ENTITY references must be expanded into their equivalents, which might be tedious, but it can usually be done without excessive effort. With sufficient care, it can be done even in the most complex instances, assuming that the entity is used in a modular manner to begin with. If the entity is used in several places, every use must be carefully scanned to make sure that the intended modifications don't unintentionally break something else.

As a practical example we'll imagine that, while reading the XHTML 1.0 Transitional DTD, you discover that the W3C seems to have left out your favorite HTML tag—the fabled <BLINK>. Quickly realizing that the very foundations of civilization will rock and business prosperity decline precipitously unless you rectify this situation for your local files, which use <BLINK> extensively, you begin to inspect the DTD, the entirety of which can be found in Appendix A, "XML/XHTML Reference."

> **Note**
>
> Before you write harsh letters you'll regret sending the next day, I'm well aware that no sane person would want to do this. The <BLINK> tag was chosen as an example simply because everyone is familiar with the intended behavior and it's a fairly complex problem. It illustrates the actual difficulty of inserting a tag that does more than add a little trivial CDATA in a parameterized environment.

Because <BLINK> can occur both inline and as a block tag, a logical place to begin looking is in a location that supports similar tags, such as <ins> and <del>. The fact that both these tags are not limited to any type can be seen from inspection of the DTD itself, which is admirably well-documented. The following code is the actual source code of the XHTML 1.0 DTD, which is used as an example of a DTD that cannot be changed at its source:

```
<!--==================== Inserted/Deleted Text ============================-->
<!--
  ins/del are allowed in block and inline content, but it's
  inappropriate to include block content within an ins element
  occurring in inline content.
-->
<!ELEMENT ins %Flow;>
<!ATTLIST ins
  %attrs;
  cite          %URI;         #IMPLIED
  datetime      %Datetime;    #IMPLIED
  >
```

```
<!ELEMENT del %Flow;>
<!ATTLIST del
  %attrs;
  cite          %URI;              #IMPLIED
  datetime      %Datetime;         #IMPLIED
  >
```

The caveat about including block content within this sort of ELEMENT used inline reflects a weakness of both XHTML 1.0 and XML; it's awkward to exclude content in XML without tedious workarounds. The authors of the XHTML DTD made a judgment call here to allow XHTML authors to do their own monitoring and allow this particular ambiguity in spite of the danger.

The most common way to work around exclusions is to create a special content model for a particular element. But to extend the exclusion through all child elements requires that each child element be redefined with its own name. This quickly becomes burdensome and error prone except in the most trivial cases.

Caution

Exclusions are particularly difficult when converting an SGML DTD to an XML version. They're used with wild abandon in most SGML DTDs, and getting rid of them or working around them can be fiendishly infuriating. In the worst cases, you're better off recreating the XML DTD from scratch.

Using the ELEMENT and ATTLIST definitions for <ins> as a model, a model definition can be created for <BLINK> that eventually can be placed in the internal XML DTD subset like this:

```
<!--==================== Blinking Text ==============================-->
<!--
  blink is allowed in block and inline content, but it's
  inappropriate to include block content within a blink element
  occurring in inline content.
-->
<!ELEMENT blink %Flow;>
<!ATTLIST blink
  %attrs;
>
```

The <ins> is defined using an entity called Flow, so hopefully it will be possible to slip in the new element because entities are the key to easy extensibility. First, the Flow entity must be expanded cleanly. Referring back to the code sample, %Flow is defined as a combination of several parameter entity types and one element type like this:

Tip from

Words to weave by

Although tedious, expanding parameter entities is a very mechanical process. In fact, it could be profitably automated using a simple Java or even a Perl program.

```
<!-- %Flow; mixes Block and Inline and is used for list items etc. -->
<!ENTITY % Flow "(#PCDATA | %block; | form | %inline; | %misc;)*">
```

As you can see, the Flow entity uses a series of parameter entities to define its content model.

EXPANDING PARAMETER ENTITIES   The presence of parameter entities in our Flow content model is a very small fly in our ointment because the newly revealed parameter entities must be expanded before we can continue. Drat! Remember, parameter entities must be defined *before* they can be used. On the other hand, the fine granularity this reveals also means that there are more chances of finding an ideal location for any desired modification. We'll try to avoid noticing the fact that each of the now-visible parameter entities must also be expanded, including the one in the ATTLIST, each having more antecedents, before we're finished. Sigh. Sisyphus endlessly rolling his rock up the mountain only to see it topple over and down the other side never had a more disheartening task. But we can only try.

After tracing back through the DTD and expanding all the entities that appear along the way, eventually a proper internal subset version of the new DTD entries is reached. The following code lists the DTD with all entities fully expanded:

```
<!--==================== Blinking Text ============================-->
<!--
   blink is allowed in block and inline content, but it's
   inappropriate to include block content within a blink element
   occurring in inline content.
-->
<!ELEMENT blink (#PCDATA | p | h1 | h2 | h3 | h4 | h5 | h6 | div | ul | ol |
dl | menu | dir | pre | hr | blockquote | address | center | noframes |
isindex | fieldset | table | form | a | br | span | bdo | object | applet |
img | map | iframe | tt | i | b | big | small | u | s | strike |font |
basefont | em | strong | dfn | code | q | sub | sup | samp | kbd | var |
cite | abbr | acronym | input | select | textarea | label | button | ins |
del | script | noscript)* >
<!ATTLIST blink
   id           ID            #IMPLIED
   class        CDATA         #IMPLIED
   style        CDATA         #IMPLIED
   title        CDATA         #IMPLIED
   lang         NMTOKEN       #IMPLIED
   xml:lang     NMTOKEN       #IMPLIED
   dir          (ltr|rtl)     #IMPLIED
   onclick      CDATA         #IMPLIED
   ondblclick   CDATA         #IMPLIED
   onmousedown  CDATA         #IMPLIED
   onmouseup    CDATA         #IMPLIED
   onmouseover  CDATA         #IMPLIED
   onmousemove  CDATA         #IMPLIED
   onmouseout   CDATA         #IMPLIED
   onkeypress   CDATA         #IMPLIED
   onkeydown    CDATA         #IMPLIED
   onkeyup      CDATA         #IMPLIED
>
```

The fully-expanded code looks like it contains most of the elements of XHTML inside the new blink tag content model, which seems appropriate because almost anything can sit inside the tag. The huge list of ELEMENTs seems to be a tribute to the amount of compression and improvement in readability that can be achieved with an ENTITY or two. However, it's a little tedious to create and daunting to read. But for this example, it will work.

Tip from
LeeAnne.com
Words to weave by

> If your particular validating XML parser doesn't read the internal DTD subset as it should, you can test your tentative solution by inserting it at the very beginning of a local copy of the external DTD itself. Because the internal subset is read before the external one, the single combined file will approximate the behavior of the XML 1.0 standard behavior.

At this point, the new element can be tested for syntax using a any XML validator. Because the new `blink` element hasn't been inserted into a content model, it won't actually do anything, but validating right now can be a useful check on your progress so far.

FINDING AN APPROPRIATE PLACE FOR THE NEW ELEMENT   With the new code, it is easier to look for the best place to make the second modification, finding a place to insert the new tag into an existing content model. The tag is defined and it looks like it can contain all the correct elements, but there is no place to put it. It must be inserted where all the correct elements can contain it. PCDATA won't do. Although `block`, `form`, and `inline` seem intuitively inappropriate, they could also be dismissed by inspection. The best place to look is at `misc`, which is exactly where `ins` and `del` are located:

```
<!FNTTTY % mico "ins | del | script | noscript">
```

This seems to be where the `ins` and `del` elements find their place in the XHTML content models, and we know *a priori* that they behave similarly to how we want the `blink` element to operate in that they affect the appearance of all the text between the start and end tags of the element.

Tip from
LeeAnne.com
Words to weave by

> In fact, if your extension is even distantly similar to an existing element in the DTD, it almost always pays to explore the complete antecedents of that element before casting about randomly for a place to put your new element.

This congruence makes the choice of the `misc` element as the location to place our new `blink` element seem both logical and compelling.

INCORPORATING THE NEW ELEMENT INTO THE XHTML DTD   To fully incorporate the new ELEMENT into the XHTML 1.0 Transitional DTD, the existing value must be overridden with the new one in the internal DTD subset:

```
<!ENTITY % misc "ins | del | blink | script | noscript">
```

The expanded definition of the blink ELEMENT and ATTLIST should also be added. This creates a valid DTD override that can be tucked into the lookup table and should work fine when combined with the public XHTML DTD.

But before combining the DTDs, there is one more task to complete. Every DTD requires a unique `xmlns` namespace identifier to allow user agents (browsers) to identify specific

PART

I

CH

4

DTDs. Because the XHTML DTD is required to define the xmlns parameter, this must also be added. But because the XHTML DTD is being used as a base, an entity called XHTML-transitional-blink.ns can be added to indicate where the blinking DTD is located:

```
<!ENTITY % XHTML-transitional-blink.ns "http://www.leeanne.com/XML/blink.dtd">
```

Unfortunately, the XHTML transitional DTD doesn't have a default namespace defined by that entity name, so it doesn't do much good other than documenting our intentions. But there is a lot to be said for good documentation.

Here is the complete code:

```
<!DOCTYPE html PUBLIC "-//W3C//DTD XHTML 1.0 Transitional//EN"
"http://www.w3.org/TR/xhtml1/DTD/transitional.dtd" [
<!ENTITY % XHTML-transitional-blink.ns "http://www.leeanne.com/XML/blink.dtd">
<!ENTITY % misc "ins | del | blink | script | noscript">
<!--==================== Blinking Text ============================-->
<!--
   blink is allowed in block and inline content, but it's
   inappropriate to include block content within a blink element
   occurring in inline content.
-->
<!ELEMENT blink (#PCDATA | p | h1 | h2 | h3 | h4 | h5 | h6 | div | ul | ol |
dl | menu | dir | pre | hr | blockquote | address | center | noframes |
isindex | fieldset | table | form | a | br | span | bdo | object | applet |
img | map | iframe | tt | i | b | big | small | u | s | strike |font |
basefont | em | strong | dfn | code | q | sub | sup | samp | kbd | var |
cite | abbr | acronym | input | select | textarea | label | button | ins |
del | script | noscript)* >
<!ATTLIST blink
   id            ID              #IMPLIED
   class         CDATA           #IMPLIED
   style         CDATA           #IMPLIED
   title         CDATA           #IMPLIED
   lang          NMTOKEN         #IMPLIED
   xml:lang      NMTOKEN         #IMPLIED
   dir           (ltr|rtl)       #IMPLIED
   onclick       CDATA           #IMPLIED
   ondblclick    CDATA           #IMPLIED
   onmousedown   CDATA           #IMPLIED
   onmouseup     CDATA           #IMPLIED
   onmouseover   CDATA           #IMPLIED
   onmousemove   CDATA           #IMPLIED
   onmouseout    CDATA           #IMPLIED
   onkeypress    CDATA           #IMPLIED
   onkeydown     CDATA           #IMPLIED
   onkeyup       CDATA           #IMPLIED
>
]>
...
```

In the previous listing the modified misc ENTITY is on line 4. The start of the new blink ELEMENT is on line 11 and the new blink ATTLIST starts on line 18.

And here is how the complete code looks in an external DTD:

```
<!ENTITY % XHTML-transitional-blink.ns "http://www.leeanne.com/XML/blink.dtd">
<!ENTITY % misc "ins | del | blink | script | noscript">
<!--==================== Blinking Text ============================-->
<!--
   blink is allowed in block and inline content, but it's
   inappropriate to include block content within a blink element
   occurring in inline content.
-->
<!ELEMENT blink (#PCDATA | p | h1 | h2 | h3 | h4 | h5 | h6 | div | ul | ol | dl |
menu | dir | pre | hr | blockquote | address | center | noframes | isindex |
fieldset | table | form | a | br | span | bdo | object | applet | img | map |
iframe | tt | i | b | big | small | u | s | strike |font | basefont | em | strong
| dfn | code | q | sub | sup | samp | kbd | var | cite | abbr | acronym | input |
select | textarea | label | button | ins | del | script | noscript)* >
<!ATTLIST blink
     id           ID              #IMPLIED
     class        CDATA           #IMPLIED
     style        CDATA           #IMPLIED
     title        CDATA           #IMPLIED
     lang         NMTOKEN         #IMPLIED
     xml:lang     NMTOKEN         #IMPLIED
     dir          (ltr|rtl)       #IMPLIED
     onclick      CDATA           #IMPLIED
     ondblclick   CDATA           #IMPLIED
     onmousedown  CDATA           #IMPLIED
     onmouseup    CDATA           #IMPLIED
     onmouseover  CDATA           #IMPLIED
     onmousemove  CDATA           #IMPLIED
     onmouseout   CDATA           #IMPLIED
     onkeypress   CDATA           #IMPLIED
     onkeydown    CDATA           #IMPLIED
     onkeyup      CDATA           #IMPLIED
>

<!ENTITY % XHTML-Blink " PUBLIC "-//W3C//DTD XHTML 1.0 Transitional//EN"
                   "http://www.w3.org/TR/xhtml1/DTD/transitional.dtd" [
%XHTML-Blink;
```

PART

I

CH

4

TESTING FOR VALIDITY

The complete code can be tested to see whether it validates as long as there is a connection to the Web. If there is no connection, it can be tested with local files—but that somewhat misses the point of avoiding creating local versions of public standards. The advantage of all this is that the blinking files can be distributed to anyone without persuading W3C (or anyone else) that <blink> is a good thing to do. It is clear to all that the standard is extended, not changed, and the isolation of the extended elements makes it equally clear what changes were made. This technique allows new elements to be added to almost any DTD. Figure 4.1 shows the validated code.

Figure 4.1
This is the DTD validated using Near & Far Designer™ from Microstar Software, Ltd. Because this product is a stand-alone DTD designer and not an XML processor, I've used the testing strategy from the note in the earlier "Expanding Parameter Entities" section to test the concept by approximation.

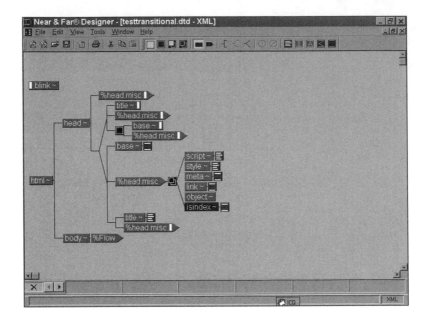

Note

There are dozens of validation tools—some better than others. But the XML 1.0 Specification states that anything claiming to accept XML must accept the internal subset and do something sensible with it. Any tool that doesn't do this can't really claim to process XML files. Appendix B contains an extensive list of validation tools. These tools are constantly being extended to meet competition, so you should investigate the current capabilities of a validation tool before choosing it.

CREATING A DTD EXTENSION

The process of extending a DTD by modifying the internal subset has the advantage of being portable and has few ongoing maintenance issues. The following section summarizes the steps of the process in an easy-to-remember list. Although every task is slightly different, there's enough similarity that a general list of steps makes sense.

Extending a DTD is primarily a strategic exercise because the exact sequence of steps changes with every target DTD. Studying a specific sequence of steps, as done in the previous example, can only demonstrate the overall process involved. The real test of strategic ability is performing the task in an unknown situation.

The same general sequence of activities should be followed for every element or attribute addition to an existing DTD. The following list succinctly describes these steps although a given situation might persuade you to vary their order or spend more or less time on each.

1. Inspect the external DTD for parameter entities that can be modified in the internal DTD subset.

2. Inspect attribute lists for locations in which new or modified attributes might add needed information or improve convenience.

3. Work out an approach, choosing either or both methods to include your needed structure.

4. If your method involves parameter entities, work backward through the external DTD, expanding all parameter references as you go, when inserting ENTITY override declarations. The internal subset doesn't allow free use of parameter entities.

5. Be sure that you cover both requirements for new elements. They need a definition of their inclusions and a place in the overall document structure. In other words, they must be part of an existing element or you won't be able to use them. Because they are brand new, you have to declare them as ELEMENTs as well.

6. If a new ELEMENT, ATTLIST, or ENTITY uses a NOTATION, that notation must be declared before use.

This exercise has actually covered two lessons. First, a DTD can be easily modified using a strategy in detail, and second, a DTD contains design elements enabling it to grow and evolve over time. The XHTML DTD was carefully crafted by DTD experts with many years of experience among them. It's worth studying as a source of good technique and as an example of good workmanship.

ADDING A NEW ELEMENT REVISITED

Adding an element does not work in every case. Sometimes there aren't any ENTITY definitions to override or existing elements located in the right place that you can add attributes to. The only possible solution in that case is make a local copy and modify it directly. Of course, if the functionality and structure to be added is that far removed from the existing DTD, it might be better to construct a new DTD—one designed to fit the specific needs instead of trying to twist an unsuitable one into a jury-rigged pretzel.

To illustrate this, assume that in the previous example, the existing ENTITY declarations aren't there and that there are no elements to which attributes can be added. Logically, a blink attribute can be added to every displayable tag to solve the problem by brute force. But that doesn't fulfill the requirement of the `<blink>` tag being available for general use.

Instead, the entire DTD must be copied using any text editor. The changes should be made directly, substituting the modified misc ENTITY for the original and inserting the blink ELEMENT in an appropriate spot—directly after the ins and del elements. For example

```
<!ENTITY % misc "ins | del | blink | script | noscript">
```

and

```
<!--=================== Blinking Text =============================-->
<!--
```

```
    blink is allowed in block and inline content, but it's
    inappropriate to include block content within a blink element
    occurring in inline content.
  -->
<!ELEMENT blink %Flow;>
<!ATTLIST blink
  %attrs;
>
```

Thus, the complete external subset looks something like this:

```
...
<!-- these can occur at block or inline level -->
<!ENTITY % misc "ins | del | blink | script | noscript">
<!ENTITY % inline "a | %special; | %fontstyle; | %phrase; | %inline.forms;">
<!-- %Inline; covers inline or "text-level" elements -->
<!ENTITY % Inline "(#PCDATA | %inline; | %misc;)*">

...
<!--==================== Inserted/Deleted Text ==========================-->
<!--
    ins/del are allowed in block and inline content, but it's
    inappropriate to include block content within an ins element
    occurring in inline content.
  -->
<!ELEMENT ins %Flow;>
<!ATTLIST ins
  %attrs;
  cite        %URI;          #IMPLIED
  datetime    %Datetime;     #IMPLIED
  >
<!ELEMENT del %Flow;>
<!ATTLIST del
  %attrs;
  cite        %URI;          #IMPLIED
  datetime    %Datetime;     #IMPLIED
  >

<!--==================== Blinking Text ============================-->
<!--
    blink is allowed in block and inline content, but it's
    inappropriate to include block content within a blink element
    occurring in inline content.
  -->
<!ELEMENT blink %Flow;>
<!ATTLIST blink
  %attrs;
>
...
```

In the previous listing the modified misc ENTITY is on line 3. The new blink ELEMENT is on line 33 and the new blink ATTLIST starts on line 34.

Tip from

Although it is undesirable to modify a DTD by brute force for many reasons—not the least of which is the responsibility to publish your modified DTD in some way and then maintain it in perpetuity—in some cases, this is the only option. But brute force does have its compensations. Although there is a maintenance problem with a variant DTD, the relative simplicity of being able to use parameter entities makes this approach cleaner. Instead of a slightly ugly mess of expanded entity references, there is a slick DTD that looks as if it were originally written that way.

SUMMING UP THE DTD CHANGE PROCESS

The previous DTD sample code is shortened by replacing text with ellipses to save space. Although only one statement is modified and two are added, the external DTD is still completely copied and replaced to make the changes. The only problem now is that the modified DTD must be made available separately on the Web so people can use it. Also, every time the original DTD is changed, the modified DTD must be changed as well. The cleaner methods shown here are far preferable if at all possible.

An alternative would be to copy the external DTD subset into the internal DTD subset and resolve all parameter entities by replacing the parameterized text with the literal replacement text by hand. This is too complicated to be viable.

Although any DTD might look terribly complex, it will usually decompose into a number of smaller pieces that are easy to understand and use. The hard part is figuring out how to use the new ELEMENT and how it would best fit into the existing document structure. In this small example, understanding HTML helped speed up the process, but a similar approach works with any DTD.

Part

I

Ch

4

Tip from

It's very difficult to reconcile namespaces in modular DTDs without the added complexity of XML Namespaces. Although namespaces enable you to specify those elements belonging to which DTD, no one claims that they are easily understood or simple to use.

When creating advanced DTDs you might want to use in modular fashion, unique names are highly advisable. They are an easier to understand workaround for the primary mechanism. You might want to use an identifying prefix on every element to enforce uniqueness while retaining legibility through mnemonic suffixes. This way, you can tell where an element came from as well as what it does.

When merging and modifying DTDs, it is common to encounter namespace collisions (which put simply means that the same element or attribute name is used for two or more DTDs). Because DTD names are usually chosen to be mnemonic, telephone numbers are often called telephoneNumber or a close variation. This makes collisions more likely than in languages in which variable names are chosen by other rules. So, it is sometimes necessary to identify the actual source of a name. The official W3C method of identifying namespaces and merging DTDs safely is XML namespaces, discussed in detail in Chapter 6, "XML Namespaces."

This has the advantage of always working, but the constant prefixing required and learning what rules apply in each situation is tedious and error-prone when editing by hand. In fact, XML namespaces were designed to be suitable for machine processing; human usability and readability were secondary requirements.

This de-emphasizing of usability and readability in favor of universality is quite proper, because a page might be read millions of times and created only once, but for throwaway tasks that don't require using preexisting DTDs, ensuring name uniqueness can save considerable editing difficulty.

CREATING AN EXTENSIBLE DTD

Yet a third technique, the one that started out from the opposite end with the `blink` tag, is to define everything in which change is allowed as a parameter entity in the external DTD subset. That way a user can modify the default values by redefining the entity in the local internal DTD subset or in an external DTD that incorporates the base DTD.

If absolute stability is required in any region, simply avoid the use of parameter entities. This is an ideal way to allow extensibility as the DTD reads nicely, has good modularity and granularity, and is always complete in and of itself so it can be independently validated.

Tip from  LeeAnne.com Words to weave by	There are a few design habits that make extending a DTD almost trivial. Extensive use of parameter entities to allow good and accessible granularity at the code level helps a lot, as does good modularity at the design level.

Before you eliminate parameter entities for the sake of stability, though, consider whether the resulting code is equally readable. Sometimes it makes sense to tolerate the possibility that someone might modify a section you would prefer they didn't because parameter entities make code easier to read and maintain internally as well as modify externally.

CREATING A MODULAR DTD

It was mentioned previously that it's possible to use unique prefixes to avoid conflicts in namespaces, but this is only an interim solution until XML namespaces are fully implemented in XML user agents. Creating a DTD that can be used by anyone as a part of their own DTD snippets—regardless of agent support—is only possible when the writer controls all parts of the DTD creation process. In any arbitrary case, one has no guaranteed control over the entire process and XML namespaces are required to support arbitrary DTD combinations.

To implement unique names, a number of strategies might be employed, of which the following is only one. Let's say I wanted to create a DTD that accessed a particular kind of datafile, such as Tandem SQL. One good approach might be to prefix every element with the letters "TSQL-" so the likelihood of collision with another namespace is fairly small, even if the namespace is later used by another designer. When namespace support is universal, this step will be unnecessary, but in the meantime it is an excellent workaround.

It also gives people a hint when a DTD breaks because of someone modifying external DTD declarations. Instead of trying to track down an obscurely named element, of which nobody seems to remember anything, the `<TSQL-access-method>` tag gives a broad hint about its origins every time. To be fair, XML namespaces allow precisely disambiguated elements as well.

In general, any clearly-defined subset of functionality is a candidate to be isolated from the rest of the structure if the sub-tree is well-defined within the entire document. Modularity also means that different teams can be set to work on different parts of the task. This also ensures more hope of accomplishing everything as needed and on time.

UNDERSTANDING MODULAR DTDs

The current generation of XML DTDs has largely been developed in isolation, with each vendor and each industry creating so-called "standards" with no particular thought given to how those DTDs might interact with other DTDs or whether the new DTD is even necessary. Although this helps satisfy the egos of the parties involved, it leads to enormous duplication of effort on every new project.

Tip from

LeeAnne.com
Words to weave by

The "Not Invented Here" (NIH) syndrome has caused more needless work for more designers than you can shake two sticks at. It means that software designers, and even companies, are reluctant to use anyone else's modules in their code, even when the "foreign" code has been tested and improved upon for years. Even an untried kludge one cobbles together on the spot is better than trusting another programmer.

PART

I

CH

4

XML itself is being used on more platforms that were originally contemplated by the designers of HTML. The typical proliferation of specialized DTDs to address every type of device has made it almost impossible to keep up with even the range of available DTDs. In many cases, the "new" DTDs for specialized devices are merely subsets, or logical subsets, of existing DTDs, although the names might have been changed beyond recognition.

W3C is cognizant of this trend and is trying to encourage the development of modular DTDs that can be economically abstracted for different types of application and target media. By modularizing DTDs, designers can work like real engineers, specifying parts from a catalog instead of building everything from scratch.

By concentrating on functionality and application requirements rather than reinventing every wheel and bolt in every application, development is increased and the boring low-level details of implementation might possibly be avoided or curtailed.

Modular XHTML, a standard currently under development by W3C, will address the low-level presentation and layout capabilities of many devices and physical media. Modular content DTDs will allow content developers to use similar functional components to build larger DTDs addressing particular data-storage and transfer needs. Because XHTML is designed to be extensible, the DTD can be easily extended to implement new capabilities as new devices are developed.

A modular DTD might consist of element sets, attribute sets, and content model sets, all of which might be implemented using external documents that can be combined to create hybrid XML DTDs. Parameter or other substitution entities might (and probably should) be a part of any modular DTD to make it easy to manage the complexity of even the most modular DTDs.

The following are the steps for creating a modular DTD:

1. Identify what parts of your document model are truly independent of one another and might be useful to others in isolation. The CALS table model from SGML was used as the basis for both HTML and XHTML tables, and the presentation elements in XHTML might be useful separately.

2. If modular portions are discovered, ensure that the modular section is written independently, including being sure that parameter entities and external documents shared between other modular DTDs are used in a controlled manner.

3. Define all element content models, logical attribute groupings, and major document groupings in parameter entities, because these structure are easily accessed and redefined from outside the DTD, making it easier to extend the DTD later. Examples of good attribute groupings include the internationalization (i18n) group of attributes in XHTML, the interactive events attributes, and common collections of events used in many elements.

4. Experiment with the modularity of the DTD, refining it as necessary to extend its usefulness and power.

Like any strategic approach to design, it is important to be flexible and respond to the situation of the moment rather than taking a cookbook approach to design.

Supplying Local Values to an External DTD

Another approach to extending a DTD is to allow for it from the beginning. One could insert placeholders into an external DTD that would be filled by the internal subset. Because XML does not allow ELEMENT or NOTATION entities to be overridden by values in the internal DTD subset, this means that they have to be left out of the external subset. In turn, this means that defining them in the internal subset is mandatory.

Caution

Both of the following approaches have risks and are a little messy. For simplicity, I prefer to make DTDs more elegant and extend them with subtlety, but these are variants of brute force with just a little more finesse that can be very valuable in selected cases.

Alternatively, conditional markup can be used to allow the external subset to suppress an ELEMENT inclusion. That way a DTD can be created that is valid by itself and still allows users to add local modifications.

As an example of the first approach, consider the following fragmentary external DTD subset:

```
<!ELEMENT whitepaper (companylogo, companyinfo, text, …)
<!ELEMENT text (#PCDATA) >
…
```

and then the following internal DTD subset:

```
<!DOCTYPE whitepaper [
<!NOTATION jpeg      PUBLIC    "ISO/IEC 0918:1983//NOTATION
                              Digital Compression and
                              Encoding of Continuous-tone
                              Still Images (JPEG)//EN">
<!ELEMENT companylogo SYSTEM "companylogo.jpeg" NDATA jpeg>
<!ELEMENT companyinfo CDATA #REQUIRED>
]>
```

The local information would be available to the document but could be redefined at will for different companies. Rather nice, but messy if you forget to add the required information and you can't validate the external DTD by itself. The second approach would be safer, making the markup conditional and allowing users to suppress default values and supply them in the internal DTD. The following snippets implement this approach, first in the external DTD subset:

```
<!ELEMENT whitepaper (companylogo, companyinfo, text, …)
<!ENTITY supressdefault "INCLUDE">
<![supressdefault[NOTATION jpeg  PUBLIC "ISO/IEC 0918:1983//NOTATION
                              Digital Compression and
                              Encoding of Continuous-tone
                              Still Images (JPEG)//EN">]]>
<![supressdefault[ELEMENT companylogo SYSTEM "defaultlogo.jpeg" NDATA jpeg>]]>
<![supressdefault[ELEMENT companyinfo CDATA #REQUIRED>]]>
<!ELEMENT text (#PCDATA) >
…
```

and then the following internal DTD subset:

```
<!DOCTYPE whitepaper [
<!ENTITY supressdefault "IGNORE">
<!NOTATION jpeg      PUBLIC    "ISO/IEC 0918:1983//NOTATION
                              Digital Compression and
                              Encoding of Continuous-tone
                              Still Images (JPEG)//EN">
<!ELEMENT companylogo SYSTEM "companylogo.jpeg" NDATA jpeg>
<!ELEMENT companyinfo CDATA #REQUIRED>
]>
```

Both of these techniques are less than elegant, although they might be useful in certain situations.

USING XHTML DTDS TO RENDER XML DOCUMENTS IN LEGACY BROWSERS

XML documents viewed in most legacy browsers are not terribly readable. The text might or might not flow into a solid mass of run-on text, and the XML tags mean nothing to most legacy HTML browsers.

PART

I

CH

4

Until XML becomes widely supported, one approach to XML support is to interweave content-rich namespace-qualified XML tags with XHTML tags that describe the physical layout. Theoretically, this allows an application to strip out either, to ignore either, or to process both. Exactly how this might be accomplished is a part of the XML Schema proposal discussed in Chapter 7, "XML Schemas." CSS, XSL, or an ad hoc (and dangerous) "fiddling" with proprietary methods of particular browsers might also allow XML documents to be displayed in a legacy browser.

As an example of a relatively safe way to embed XML content in XHTML tags, consider the following fragment:

```
<html xmlns:wa="URI">
<head><title>Worth Ambition</title></head>
<body>
<wa:book>
<h1><wa:title>Worth Ambition</wa:title></h1>
<h2><wa:author>Lee Anne Phillips</wa:author></h2>
…
</wa:book>
</body>
</html>
```

Notice that the formatting performed is minimal, just enough to make the fragment legible, and the document can be rendered far more elegantly if the browser supports XML, but at least a minimal formatting is provided in legacy browsers. This way, users aren't presented with a mishmash of run-on text.

GETTING DOWN TO CASES

Making local modifications to a DTD allows a subset of DTD users to alter a DTD to suit their needs without going through the process of persuading all users of the DTD to make changes and without foregoing some of the benefits of a shared DTD.

As an example of a real world need that might encourage the development of a local DTD variant, consider a vendor who makes available the entire catalogs of multiple wholesalers.

That vendor might have available extensive information about the products in XML format from the wholesaler but also wants to provide a uniform catalog number so users of their online catalog can easily order items without risking the confusion that might result if wholesaler catalog numbers overlap.

By adding a new vendor catalog number field to the DTDs of each wholesaler DTD, the added information can be easily presented to the user without going to the trouble of converting each wholesaler document to a common format. In fact, with transclusion, the vendor may not even have to provide Web space for entire catalogs, but can rely on placeholder documents containing only the vendor catalog number and a link to the item description on the wholesaler site. The transcluded item can be formatted by a local CSS or XSL style sheet to provide a common look and feel to the vendor site.

CHAPTER 5

Building a DTD from Scratch

In this chapter

SPECIFYING A CUSTOM DTD

Building a custom DTD is not an easy task. It's quite common for complex DTDs to require the design and coding services of many people for many months. And there is still ongoing maintenance as you discover errors or design flaws that require fixing or redesign. This is no different, really, from any documentation plan, which is what a DTD amounts to. In defining a DTD, you're setting down exactly what you think your documents are going to look like, and any evolution in the document requires updating the DTD.

As a small example, let's say you're designing a magazine. You know that all articles have a title, but is it possible that one title is used in the table of contents and another at the top of the article itself? Many magazines do, so you want two title fields in that case—one, the longer title for the article head and another, probably shorter, for the contents page. You might also want to provide for subtitles, or maybe not. It depends entirely on what you want the magazine to look like as a whole.

Unlike paper, which is infinitely flexible, a DTD, like a formal documentation plan, is a fixed embodiment of your ideas of what a document looks like, and it requires some effort to change. This is an important protection as well. By ensuring that these issues are thought about during the authoring phase, there is less work to be done in production and rewrite. But if you later discover that there is a situation you hadn't thought of, for example an article with two authors when you had envisioned only one, you have to go back to the DTD and fix it.

All in all, you can expect to spend about the same amount of time designing a DTD as you would defining the layout and style of a magazine, or the coding standards for a programming project, or any organizational effort involving a standards process. You have to interview and account for the ideas and domain knowledge of stakeholders—including management, users, contributors, domain experts, and others involved in whatever activity the XML document is expected to capture.

This chapter focuses on the skills needed to translate that collective domain knowledge into a DTD that enables every needed operation to be performed and that doesn't get in the way (too much) when you add in "oddball" outliers. A huge problem with converting paper records to a machine-readable form is that one discovers that all kinds of information and cross-reference links have been entered between the lines and into the margins of whatever paper form was originally devised. You need domain knowledge to take those marginal notes into account and discern the true structure of the paper database. You need knowledge of DTD principles to avoid recursion and other errors. You also need knowledge of the industry to do process engineering or reengineering based on DTDs or electronic interchange standards that already exist for your industry or profession.

If you do your job well, using modern process and business analysis techniques, you wind up with a robust and stable platform on which later evolution can take place without requiring disrupting upheavals. You might incorporate object-oriented rapid deployment and test strategies such as those advocated by Walker Royce, Grady Booch, Ed Yourdon, and others to iterate through cycles of design, implementation, and evaluation to actively involve stakeholders in the entire process.

BUILDING A DTD

This section shows the steps involved in creating a DTD, starting with design and ending with a completed DTD ready for testing and acceptance.

The following is a typical software project management scenario:

1. **Design**—Marshall knowledge and experience, together with specific data-gathering, to produce a DTD requirements statement and plan.
2. **Implementation**—Proceed stepwise through development to build a modular DTD.
3. **Test**—Test the DTD using various debugging and test tools.
4. **Iterate**—Go back to the design step if necessary to further develop the DTD.
5. **Acceptance**—Accept and deliver a finished DTD product.

As you can see, the same general development plan applies equally well to DTD development, and the same sorts of project management tools can be used to manage both sorts of development.

DESIGNING THE DTD: DATA GATHERING

Every design starts with knowledge of prior art. In the engineering world, prior art doesn't connote paintings by the Old Masters, but rather artifacts already designed and engineered relating to your design criteria.

No matter what your industry, from medicine to publishing, chances are that someone has already thought about what people in that industry need to do their business and embodied that thought into a DTD or another electronic interchange standard. A portion of your design effort should be spent identifying and studying prior art and literature.

Appendix B, "Tools for XHTML Editing and Conversion," provides an extensive list of organizations that create and publish DTDs. Among them might be one that meets your needs and has already been agreed upon by other members of your industry, or one that comes close to meeting your needs. It is foolish to spend time developing something from scratch that might already exist. Real engineers don't fool around.

Even if there is no pre-existing DTD, there might be another type of engineering in existence that can be studied to compare previous design thoughts and decisions. Candidates for this prior art, to use a term current in the intellectual property world, might be books, white papers, programs, database applications, scientific disciplines, or anything representing the human engineering effort to understand and organize the field of endeavor. An example might be looking at the relationship between the Dewey Decimal System and the Library of Congress Call Number before undertaking the creation of a DTD for a library card catalog. In addition, because the MARC system is an important interlibrary data-exchange language, you would want to make sure that your total document system can easily generate and understand binary MARC records.

PART

I

CH

5

This section looks at an area that's well-understood—publishing. In fact, there are many DTDs that address this industry because publishers and authors were very familiar with markup, and the first markup languages were even designed to facilitate publishing. For the purposes of this example, the reservoir of prior art is ignored because the task would then be a trivial matter of picking the already-existing DTD to use.

This example is based on a magazine-type article, both because the task seems small, and because it serves to demonstrate how to fit the created DTD into an enclosing one— a magazine—to demonstrate modularity.

DESIGNING THE DTD: COLLECTING DOMAIN KNOWLEDGE

Begin by marshalling the domain knowledge, in no particular order:

- An article has a title.
- An article might have a dedication.
- An article might have an abstract.
- An article has a body of text.
- An article might have an appendix or notes section following the body of text.
- An article might have bibliographic information associated with it, publication date, copyright holder, subject classification, author, and so on.
- An author has a name, an address, possibly a university or work affiliation, a title of some sort, probably optional in this country as we tend to be informal, and other stuff.
- A body of text might have footnotes or endnotes.
- A body of text might have illustrations or tables.
- A body of text might have sections.

The list could go on; as you can see, the sum of our domain knowledge starts to get rather imposing even for so simple a thing as a magazine article. There are many more topics that haven't even been mentioned yet, such as language, character set used, various kinds of emphasis or special text treatments, strikeout text, and so on. This example uses a minimum subset of everything that might make up an article to keep the example compact and readable.

The end of the design process should produce a clear idea of what the design goals are. For simplicity, assume that the following three goals (in no particular order) :

- The DTD should be able to create a simple magazine article, incorporating as much of the domain knowledge as possible.
- The DTD should be modular and easily extensible.
- The DTD should have element names that are easily translatable into other languages for the sake of portability among authors of differing nationalities.

Now consider what a DTD contains—the document structure, storage conventions, and descriptive parts to start with, but also shorthand conventions for naming and using collections of information as if they were one thing, external processing required for certain data types, and other critical information about every aspect of a document instance.

IMPLEMENTING THE DTD: STARTING WITH THE DATA

Start by defining the element names—the equivalent of defining the data dictionary in a procedural programming project or an object list in the object-oriented equivalent.

For now, assume this DTD will be called an article, but by putting that information into a parameter entity, it leaves open the possibility to override in the future. In fact, this should be done with every element name. It would be handy if all tag names could be translated into other languages, for example, by overriding these entity declarations without disturbing the DTD itself. This method enables authors to see meaningful descriptive fields when they edit a document. For example, "publisher" in German is *Verleger*, and a German author might be more comfortable filling in a data field labeled in German rather than English.

Tip from

Words to weave by

By putting all visible names in parameter entities, you enable authors who use languages other than English to use your DTD easily by overriding them in the internal subset—replacing them with equivalent translations. The resulting document can be used either as-is in other publishing applications or easily converted back to the English version of the DTD using XSLT, an XML-related document transformation language discussed in Chapters 11, "SAX—The Simple API for XML," and 13, "Cascading Style Sheets and XML/XHTML."

Gathering all the element names in one place makes it easy to pick and choose from them as the elements are being designed. At the end of the process, you should have a list of names at one level of redirection—the parameter entities—which collect every element to be designed in one spot. As in any modern programming project, you also implement a *naming convention*, with parameter entities (placeholders for element names) capitalized and their replacement text left in lowercase. You might want to choose a different and more elaborate scheme, but it is important to be able to tell by looking at it whether you are dealing with a tag name through indirection. That way, it is harder to make mistakes.

The following listing shows the element names we want to use in our DTD defined as parameter entities so they can be easily changed:

```
<!-- Element names -->
<!ENTITY % Doctype    "article">
<!ENTITY % Front      "front">
<!ENTITY % Body       "body">
<!ENTITY % Back       "back">
<!ENTITY % Title      "title">
<!ENTITY % Author     "author">
<!ENTITY % Date       "date">
<!ENTITY % Publisher  "publisher">
<!ENTITY % Copyright  "copyright">
<!ENTITY % Part       "part">
<!ENTITY % Paragraph  "paragraph">
<!ENTITY % Number     "number">
<!ENTITY % Notes      "notes">
<!ENTITY % Appendix   "appendix">
```

For the most part we've used the convention that the parameter entity names are simply the names we want to call the elements with the addition of capitalized first letters. For English speakers, at least, this will make it easy to call up the correct entity name when coding the DTD.

IMPLEMENTING THE DTD: DEFINING THE ROOT

Now that the element names are defined, you can start defining the content models of the elements themselves, beginning at the root and filling in the branches of the document tree as you go along. This takes care of the major architecture first and then fills in around the edges to refine and extend the model. It would be equally correct to start at a small and easy-to-understand branch, fill in other branches, and join them all at the root. It all depends on how your mind works, big picture first versus fine detail.

While exploring the root, also think about ways to make this DTD robust and extensible, incorporating as many of the ideas as possible with each element in turn.

In the root, the highest level view of the document, insist on some sort of front matter, the body of the article, and then add optional back matter. Put these three elements in parameter entities as well, both to retain some flexibility as you write and because that makes it easy to reuse this basic format if you create another type of written document with similar properties. Because you haven't decided how the elements are structured yet, leave them as parameter entity placeholders for now—the equivalent here of a program stub—and fill them in later.

The following code snippet shows how the basic block structure is parameterized and then used:

```
<!ENTITY % block     "(%front;, %body;, %back;)">

<!-- Document Root -->
<!ELEMENT %Doctype; ( %block; )>
```

Notice that the list of elements called block is inside a pair of parentheses. Because this is an ordered list, you don't strictly need them. In fact, because parentheses are around the block entity itself in the root, these parentheses are redundant. But if a selection list is added at a future time, or a pair of parentheses is mistakenly eliminated some day, you might be grateful for the "redundant" parentheses later. They don't hurt and might help.

Tip from

LeeAnne.com
Words to weave by

You should almost always add parentheses around every content model list of elements, even if you don't really need them. Absent parentheses around a selection list is a potent and common source of hard-to-locate errors.

Also note that the "block" name cannot be modified. Although you might be sorry later, it seems unlikely that you would ever want to change so simple a declaration of the root. You have to draw the line somewhere in every DTD. Extensibility is a noble goal and localization is a fine thing to offer. But that little thing is held back in this example as a symbolic placeholder for all the possible improvements that could be made but won't be for the sake of simplicity and getting the product finished on time. Chapter 4, "Extending a Document Type Definition with Local Modifications," shows how convenient it is for later test and modification if most of the structure of the DTD is carried in parameter entities, a special macro construct that enables one to modularize DTD component parts into compact representations of complex parts.

Now you can start filling in more of your knowledge by breaking down the front and back matter into component pieces. Label the sections before going too far, so you can keep track of where you are. While we're at it, the breakdown into sections ought to be referenced by indirection anyway, so we'll make a new block declaration to hold the whole thing. As always, put all the tentative definitions into parameter entities, because you might want to change them someday. It's easier to do this as you're coding the DTD than it is to go back and catch every instance of every name.

Although this can be done in steps, the following code shows the finished product to save time. Notice that the component parts of the block are labeled with an identifying comment and set off in sections. Again, as seen when modifying the DTD in Chapter 4, this makes it easy to find the sections you want if you later want to extend or modify the document in some way.

```
<!-- Element names -->
<!ENTITY % Doctype    "article">
<!ENTITY % Front      "front">
<!ENTITY % Body       "body">
<!ENTITY % Back       "back">
<!ENTITY % Title      "title">
<!ENTITY % Author     "author">
<!ENTITY % Date       "date">
<!ENTITY % Publisher  "publisher">
<!ENTITY % Copyright  "copyright">
<!ENTITY % Part       "part">
<!ENTITY % Paragraph  "paragraph">
<!ENTITY % Number     "number">
<!ENTITY % Notes      "notes">
<!ENTITY % Appendix   "appendix">
<!-- Content substitutions -->
<!ENTITY % %Front;    "(%Title;, %Author;, %Date;, %Publisher;?, %Copyright;?)">
<!ENTITY % %Body;     "(%Part;+|%Paragraph;+)">
<!ENTITY % %Part;     "(%Number;?,%Title;?,%Paragraph;+)">
<!ENTITY % %Back;     "(%Notes;, %Appendix;*) | (%Appendix;*)">
<!ENTITY % block      "(%front;, %body;, %back;)">
<!-- Document Root -->
<!ELEMENT %Doctype; ( %block; )>
<!-- Document Front Matter -->
<!ELEMENT %Title; (#PCDATA)>
<!ELEMENT %Author; (#PCDATA)>
<!ELEMENT %Date; (#PCDATA)>
<!ELEMENT %Publisher; (#PCDATA)>
<!ELEMENT %Copyright; (#PCDATA)>
<!-- Document Body -->
<!ELEMENT %Part; (%part;)>
<!ELEMENT %Number; (#PCDATA)>
<!ELEMENT %Paragraph; (#PCDATA)>
```

```
<!-- Document Back Matter -->
<!ELEMENT %Notes; (%Paragraph;)+>
<!ELEMENT %Appendix; (%part;)>
```

When adding occurrence indicators, defined in Chapter 3, "Understanding XML Document Type Definitions," always add them as close to the terminal definition as possible to make them easier to understand.

Although not perfect—there's no way to make a boldface element inside a paragraph, for example—this seems sufficient to start testing. We deliberately inserted an error on line 20 so you will have something to catch when you later test the code.

TESTING THE DTD

To test the DTD, try opening it in Near & Far Designer, a DTD designer that validates as it loads.

When loading the DTD, it produces an error message—as seen in Figure 5.1. The following code represents the resulting error message:

```
Opening XML file: "d:\w3c\myarticle.dtd"
ERROR   line 23 , column 22 :delimiter "|" invalid: only delimiter ",", delimiter
")" and token separators are allowed
File read unsuccessfully.
```

Figure 5.1
Near & Far Designer™
doesn't like the
new DTD.

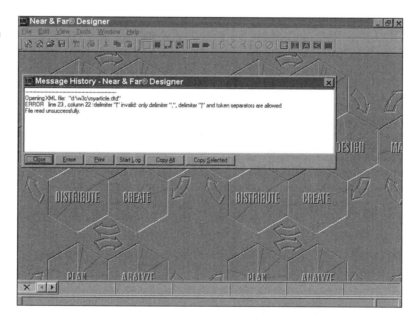

This doesn't really give us much help, because line 23 looks like this and *appears* to be perfect or at least so simple that it would be hard to make a mistake:

```
<!ELEMENT %Doctype; ( %block; )>
```

But remember that the block entity is going to be expanded into all those parameter entities before that line is processed. There must be something wrong with one of them.

Try looking at the list of expansions to see which one has some sort of error. There is a clue in the words `delimiter "|" invalid`. Look at those lines containing a "|" first. Luckily, there are only two:

```
<!ENTITY % %Body;      "(%Part;+|%Paragraph;+)">
<!ENTITY % %Back;      "(%Notes;, %Appendix;*) | (%Appendix;*)">
```

Take a minute to look at the rest of the message. `Only delimiter ",", delimiter ")" and token separators are allowed`. These are the delimiters of an ordered list when not in parentheses. If you still can't see it, and in a complex DTD it might be much harder, you can start expanding the parameter entities by hand, inserting them one by one into line 23 until something makes sense. In the end, you are left with the same message, but it refers to whichever of the previous two statements is in error and points a little closer to where the problem lies.

As in Chapter 4, expanding entities is a very tedious process, so to make a long story short, when you have a selection you must put the selection inside parentheses, which was forgotten here:

```
<!ENTITY % %Back;      "(%Notes;, %Appendix;*) | (%Appendix;*)">
```

Fix it here where it can be seen:

```
<!ENTITY % %Back;      "((%Notes;, %Appendix;*) | (%Appendix;*))">
```

Also fix it in the test DTD so you can test it again. Now the code looks like this:

```
<!-- Element names -->
<!ENTITY % Doctype    "article">
<!ENTITY % Front      "front">
<!ENTITY % Body       "body">
<!ENTITY % Back       "back">
<!ENTITY % Title      "title">
<!ENTITY % Author     "author">
<!ENTITY % Date       "date">
<!ENTITY % Publisher  "publisher">
<!ENTITY % Copyright  "copyright">
<!ENTITY % Part       "part">
<!ENTITY % Paragraph  "paragraph">
<!ENTITY % Number     "number">
<!ENTITY % Notes      "notes">
<!ENTITY % Appendix   "appendix">
<!-- Content substitutions -->
<!ENTITY % %Front;    "(%Title;, %Author;, %Date;, %Publisher;?, %Copyright;?)">
<!ENTITY % %Body;     "(%Part;+|%Paragraph;+)">
<!ENTITY % %Part;     "(%Number;?,%Title;?,%Paragraph;+)">
<!ENTITY % %Back;     "((%Notes;, %Appendix;*) | (%Appendix;*))">
<!ENTITY % block      "(%front;, %body;, %back;)">
<!-- Document Root -->
<!ELEMENT %Doctype; ( %block; )>
<!-- Document Front Matter -->
<!ELEMENT %Title; (#PCDATA)>
<!ELEMENT %Author; (#PCDATA)>
```

```
<!ELEMENT %Date; (#PCDATA)>
<!ELEMENT %Publisher; (#PCDATA)>
<!ELEMENT %Copyright; (#PCDATA)>
<!-- Document Body -->
<!ELEMENT %Part; (%part;)>
<!ELEMENT %Number; (#PCDATA)>
<!ELEMENT %Paragraph; (#PCDATA)>
<!-- Document Back Matter -->
<!ELEMENT %Notes; (%Paragraph;)+>
<!ELEMENT %Appendix; (%part;)>
```

Now when the test DTD is read into Near & Far Designer, you see something completely different. Expand all the groups to make it slightly more interesting. When it comes up, it has just the root element and the block group visible. Figure 5.2 shows the DTD fully expanded.

Figure 5.2
Now you can see why people like automated tools. Here is a graphic view of the structure of the DTD in Near & Far Designer. It's hard to see how it could be improved.

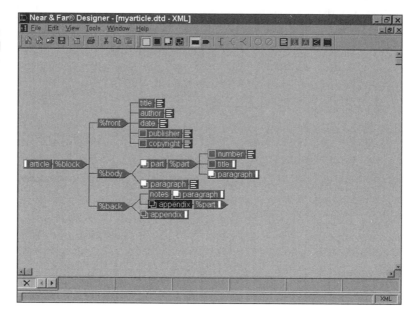

The DTD says that you must have a title, author, and date followed by an optional publisher and an optional copyright date. Then you must either have one or more parts, which have an optional number and an optional title followed by one or more paragraphs. This seems to make sense because an article has to have something besides a title or nobody reads it. In the back matter, you have either notes and appendixes, no notes and just appendixes, or simply no back matter at all.

As mentioned previously, the DTD still lacks a many things that would be necessary in a complete DTD—such as emphasis of various sorts, the possibility of footnotes, and on and on—but this actually produces a result that looks like a real article as it is. You can now write a coding sheet, which shouldn't be too hard, and hand off the task of writing articles to authors. The authors need know nothing at all about the DTD itself, only what tags are available and where they can go.

This fulfills our design goals, which were to make the DTD capable of capturing a simple magazine article, be as flexible and extensible as possible, and allow each tag name to be overridden for the convenience of authors using a foreign language. As in Chapter 4, parameter entities make it easy to add a new element anywhere in the existing tree. If you wanted to add a colophon to the back matter, for example, just plug in a new element, exactly as was done with the `blink` element in Chapter 4, fiddle with a few entity declarations, and you are done.

UNDERSTANDING DTD DESIGN PRINCIPLES

A DTD represents a tree with a single root and no logic loops or ambiguities. At any point, that tree can be traversed using a simple logic. The first activity of your design effort must be to identify and document any pre-existing logical structure that might be in your target document and that you want defined in the XML equivalent. If this structure can't be transformed into a tree of some sort, you might have to look further, but chances are you will find some such structure if you examine it enough. It's a rare discipline that resists this transformation because it is human nature to arrange things into neat categories.

It might help to write down your tentative categories, thoughts, relationships, data fields, and whatever else on 3x5 cards, or maybe 4x6 cards if you have a lot to write, and start arranging them on a table or the floor. If you use sticky notes you could use a wall if you don't want to crawl around on the floor and if the project is extensive. You might see a pattern emerge, or maybe not.

Caution

You should resist the temptation to fire up an automated design tool and start tweaking until you have a paper design laid out where you can make sense of it. Automated tools are fantastic things and very valuable for speeding the final stages of DTD development, but you have to know where you're going with them first or you can get carried away and lose sight of the initial goal.

PART

I

CH

5

Everyone has the problem of displaying a project on a relatively tiny computer screen. Even with the capability to collapse portions of the tree and expand others, you can't see the forest all at once, only little icons representing parts of it.

You saw that even with the tiny DTD, the expanded view took half the page in Near & Far Designer. As the view shifts to tinier and tinier icons as the DTD is expanded, you quickly lose the capability to visualize its entirety.

There are some concerns about extensibility and the possibility of localization when designing this DTD. You might not have the same set of problems and could avoid one layer of indirection if forcing authors to use English—or French, and so on—tags is acceptable.

This points out the fact you started with previously: Design has to come first or you don't know what you're doing and are just thrashing about.

HANDLING PROBLEMS WITH EXCLUSIONS

Some documents might define structures that should not be nested. An HTML example would be a paragraph `<p>` element, which can't be directly contained in another paragraph element. A paragraph can be nested within another block-level element though, so you only have to make sure that the content model for a paragraph doesn't include itself, and the problem is solved.

But some elements can't nest however indirectly. A simple exclusion based on the content model might not work in that case, because legitimate parts of the content model might be able to carry the element in other contexts. An example would be the HTML anchor `<a>` element, which can't be nested at any level. A simple content model can't protect against this. In fact, short of defining duplicate names for the affected content, there's no way to state, in XML, that an element may not have itself as a descendent.

You must tell the author whether there are any such restrictions; XML has no way of enforcing compliance.

HANDLING PROBLEMS WITH RECURSION

XML doesn't allow parsed entities to have themselves as their own descendents. It creates an endless loop if such entities are allowed. Recursive parsed entities are like dictionaries that define a word in terms of another and then define the second word in terms of the first.

Imagine finding a pair of definitions that look like this: Zarf; the small metallic object held in a finjan. Finjan; the often decorative stand or holder for a zarf. Dictionaries are infamous for recursive definitions—productions that depend on one another for meaning in a circular fashion. If you know what a zarf is, the meaning of finjan becomes clear and vice versa.

Note

> To eliminate any possible frustration, *zarf* is a rather obscure word referring to a small round-bottomed Turkish coffee cup with no handle. *Finjan* is also a Turkish word and refers to the stand or holder for the cup that enables you to put it down without it tipping over. The exact Western equivalent is those conical white disposable coffee cups that fit into a brown plastic holder. The word ZARF is rather famous in computing circles because it was the code name of the Air Force "tiger team" that cracked the Multics security system. They drank a *lot* of coffee.

A DTD cannot use circular logic to define a tree structure. So the following code produces an error:

```
<!ENTITY % zarf %finjan;>
<!ENTITY % finjan %zarf;>
```

And the equivalent, using external parsed entities, is in error too. The first file is named `zarf.xml`:

```
<!ENTITY zarf SYSTEM "http://www.leeanne.com/usingxml/finjan.xml">
&zarf;
```

and the second is named `finjan.xml`:

```
<!ENTITY % finjan  SYSTEM "http://www.leeanne.com/usingxml/zarf.xml">
&finjan;
```

In a validating parser, these should cause a fatal error. But in a non-validating parser they might not.

XML doesn't have reliable facilities for preventing recursion. Whereas a validating parser might detect simple recursions in external parsed entities, a non-validating parser won't. Even some validating parsers might have limits to the depth of external parsed entities they're willing to visit to ensure the validity of a local file. It's theoretically possible to create a DTD using indirect recursion that would take forever (or nearly so) to determine that the DTD will not validate.

TROUBLESHOOTING A BROKEN DTD

Finding an error in a DTD can be a tedious business. Finding multiple errors is even worse. Most editing and display environments refuse to load such a misshapen thing and exit with a single error message that might or might not identify the line number on which the processor realized that it had found an error. The point of realization might not be the actual point at which the mistake was made.

Careful inspection of the source and comparison with the error message might help isolate the error. Many tools have bugs, however, which prevent any trivial error identification. It's best to use a variety of tools and try them all in sequence. Some are better than others at particular errors. Some have a more informative error message in a particular case. But none are perfect.

Things to look out for are missing quotes, missing parentheses (as in the previous example), using a parameter entity in the internal subset (it's so tempting), misspelled declarations (another reason to use real names instead of arbitrary codes), and forgetting that notations and entities have to be declared before you can use them.

MAKING YOUR DTD BULLETPROOF

DTDs are pretty robust things on their own. With so few elements it's hard to get really confused when you're editing one. There are quite a number of things you can do to make it harder to make mistakes though.

Start with comments. Although the previous code was minimally commented, in a production DTD you want to add a design overview and some hints about how the DTD was constructed and how to make common changes. The sample DTD was designed so you could change element names easily, so you ought to explain how it is done. Many shops ask you to identify yourself in your code as well. Not only should you be proud of your designs but, if anything needs changing, you might want to have the opportunity to take first crack at it. The following code shows how the addition of comments can include information about how the document fits into a corporate structure, what its overall structure looks like, and who created it.

```
<!-- This is the article DTD and forms part   -->
<!-- The XYZ corporation document standards    -->
<!-- Typical invocation:                        -->
<!--     <!DOCTYPE article                      -->
<!--       PUBLIC "-//XYZ//Simple Article//EN"  -->
<!--            "article.dtd">                   -->
<!-- This DTD coded by Lee Anne Phillips 1999   -->
<!-- Element names                               -->
<!-- For easy localization, all Element names   -->
<!-- have been collected below as parameter      -->
<!-- entities. To localize this DTD, override    -->
<!-- each Name with a local equivalent name.     -->
<!-- All name containers are capitalized so      -->
<!-- they're easy to spot in the DTD but you     -->
<!-- don't have to touch them anywhere but       -->
<!-- here.                                        -->
<!ENTITY % Doctype   "article">
<!ENTITY % Front     "front">
<!ENTITY % Body      "body">
<!ENTITY % Back      "back">
<!ENTITY % Title     "title">
<!ENTITY % Author    "author">
<!ENTITY % Date      "date">
<!ENTITY % Publisher "publisher">
<!ENTITY % Copyright "copyright">
<!ENTITY % Part      "part">
<!ENTITY % Paragraph "paragraph">
<!ENTITY % Number    "number">
<!ENTITY % Notes     "notes">
<!ENTITY % Appendix  "appendix">
```

Every section should be expanded on to make it clear, as in the following:

```
<!-- Content substitutions -->
<!-- For easy modification, all content names -->
<!-- have been collected below as parameter    -->
<!-- entities. To customize this DTD,           -->
<!-- override content values here.  -->
<!ENTITY % %Front;  "(%Title;, %Author;, %Date;, %Publisher;?, %Copyright;?)">
<!ENTITY % %Body;   "(%Part;+|%Paragraph;+)">
<!ENTITY % %Part;   "(%Number;?,%Title;?,%Paragraph;+)">
<!ENTITY % %Back;   "(%Notes;, %Appendix;*) | (%Appendix;*)">
<!ENTITY % block    "(%front;, %body;, %back;)">
<!-- Document Root                              -->
<!ELEMENT %Doctype; ( %block; )>
<!-- Document Front Matter -->
<!ELEMENT %Title; (#PCDATA)>
<!ELEMENT %Author; (#PCDATA)>
<!ELEMENT %Date; (#PCDATA)>
<!ELEMENT %Publisher; (#PCDATA)>
<!ELEMENT %Copyright; (#PCDATA)>
<!-- Document Body -->
<!ELEMENT %Part; (%part;)>
<!ELEMENT %Number; (#PCDATA)>
<!ELEMENT %Paragraph; (#PCDATA)>
```

```
<!-- Document Back Matter -->
<!ELEMENT %Notes; (%Paragraph;)+>
<!ELEMENT %Appendix; (%part;)>
```

The comments could be expanded with some whitespace to make them stand out more, but in the interest of saving space for more important things this isn't done here.

Next, make sure your element and entity names make sense when you see them in isolation. Although it might be tempting to save some keystrokes by using goofy techno-names, such as "p" and "n" instead of "paragraph" and "notes," that can become confusing. The ideal XML document self-describes itself. You shouldn't need a scorecard to tell who the players are. If your names don't make sense to a random person off the street, it's certain that some author will put the wrong words in the wrong part of the document someday soon. And it won't be their fault. It will be yours. Everyone will know.

Also, the physical DTD structure is arranged so all the things that are likely to need changing are collected in two locations and separated by the type of change likely to be made. Whereas no technique of arranging code is truly foolproof, this is the best that can be done.

The following are the steps to making a bulletproof DTD:

1. Spend time on design before coding anything.

2. Use a naming convention to make the intended use of element names and parameter entities clear.

3. Use comments to explain significant detail. Don't waste time noting the obvious, but if anything might not be clear, let people know what your reasoning was when you created it.

4. Tend toward verbosity. Element names don't have to look like a computer geek escaped from the glass castle and got into your document. Label things the way you might like to see file drawers labeled if you had to find the records of the blood donor who was going to save your life.

5. Arrange everything logically. Group similar elements together and follow elements by their attribute declarations immediately. You should never have to spend much time searching for an entity of any sort anywhere in your DTD.

Although troubleshooting DTDs can be difficult, with good design and precise coding habits, the possible errors are minimized and the problems easier to find than if the DTD is a jumble of unrelated layers of indirection with no easy way to identify how element names are used.

AVOIDING TRICKY CODING TECHNIQUES

Notice that there is a level of indirection used in the element names. This adds a little complexity, but because this is an isolated technique and used for a very limited purpose—storing and using element names—it's safe enough.

PART

I

CH

5

You can get a little wild with this technique, though, and with arbitrary text it isn't really safe. The following code shows why:

```
<?xml version='1.0'?>
<!DOCTYPE trickycode [
<!ELEMENT trickycode (#PCDATA) >
<!ENTITY % trickyline '&#37;trickytext;'>
<!ENTITY % trickytext '&#60;!ENTITY trickyword "flaky" >' >
%trickyline;
]>
<trickycode>This sentence demonstrates &trickyword; code.</trickycode>
```

In general, using parameter entities to build arbitrary text is dangerous, especially when the text contains markup. If you get it wrong, or more importantly if the person who maintains the DTD at oh-dark-hundred in the wee small hours two years from now gets it wrong, it can be amazingly hard to find an error with so many dependencies.

In line 4 we define a tricky line of code with the percent sign signifying a parameter entity escaped. The parameter entity, `%trickytext;`, hasn't been declared yet so it isn't expanded when the escaped percent sign is replaced with the percent character. This is okay because you haven't used the line yet either. The XML processor recognizes that the percent sign signifies a parameter entity but doesn't yet know what to do with it. An entry is made in a symbol table somewhere and the XML processor expects everything to be made clear eventually—and it is.

Next, we define the tricky text in line 5. Notice that the greater than symbol is escaped. When the processor reads this line it performs the substitution immediately. Nothing much happens besides that yet, except that the parameter entity `%trickyline;` now has a value, `<!ENTITY trickyword "flaky" >`, that happens to be a well-formed bit of markup.

Now invoke the parameter entity `%trickyline;` in line 6. The tricky line is expanded and the XML processor recognizes that it must now look at the symbol table and fetch the definition of the equally tricky text, which happens to be the little bit of markup hidden inside the parameter entity `%trickyline;`. Everything is expanded and the hidden markup now sits in the DTD code disguised as parameter entity, where it is very hard to see, and defines a general entity named `&trickyword;`, which can then be used in the body of the text at line 8.

So somewhere in the document the tricky word is used as a general entity. It works, as shown in the following code snippet, but is really flaky.

```
This sentence demonstrates flaky code.
```

Just try to figure out where it comes from if you don't already know. Anything you have to scratch your head over when you see it done is unlikely to be safe. You might forget what you did. You might be retired in Maui. Some guy fresh off the street might be assigned to modify your elegant code with crude hacks. Anything can happen, so it is best to plan for the worst.

ENSURING DTD COMPATIBILITY

XML namespaces, as fully discussed in Chapter 6, "XML Namespaces," make life a lot easier for DTD designers who want to combine DTDs to make a bigger and better version that handles two things at once. They are not fully supported by all user agents yet, however. In the meantime, the only other way to guarantee DTD compatibility is to make sure that no names are shared between the two namespaces without depending on the availability of namespaces to distinguish name collisions.

There are several ways to do this but the easiest is to use the localization entity declarations you so cleverly inserted in your code as a courtesy for speakers of languages other than English to alter the names of any conflicting elements. For that matter, you could alter them all with a self-explanatory prefix and save everybody time that would otherwise be spent figuring out what came from where.

In our example, this could be done like this:

```
<!DOCTYPE XYZ-article
     PUBLIC "-//XYZ//Simple Article//EN"
            "article.dtd" [
<!ENTITY % Doctype    "XYZ-article">
<!ENTITY % Front      "XYZ-front">
<!ENTITY % Body       "XYZ-body">
<!ENTITY % Back       "XYZ-back">
<!ENTITY % Title      "XYZ-title">
<!ENTITY % Author     "XYZ-author">
<!ENTITY % Date       "XYZ-date">
<!ENTITY % Publisher "XYZ-publisher">
<!ENTITY % Copyright "XYZ-copyright">
<!ENTITY % Part       "XYZ-part">
<!ENTITY % Paragraph "XYZ-paragraph">
<!ENTITY % Number     "XYZ-number">
<!ENTITY % Notes      "XYZ-notes">
<!ENTITY % Appendix  "XYZ-appendix">
<!ENTITY % their-dtd SYSTEM "their-dtd.dtd">
%their-dtd;
]>
```

You don't much care what names the other DTD uses, even if it also has meaningful names for paragraphs, titles, and the like, even if another DTD element is named "article," because all element names are now prefixed with a meaningful identifier of your own choosing and can be changed at will. This DTD is fairly safe even without using namespaces because you thoughtfully made life easy for other people who might want to change the names for their own reasons.

Of course you might not be able to pull in another external DTD into this internal DTD subset, so you might have to go to a single external DTD that pulls in both DTDs. Just be sure to rename your elements before you call in the other DTD.

With XML namespaces, you have to declare them and then identify them by their name-space everywhere they're used. This seems slightly more straightforward and easier, because you can make your application changes globally and automatically with a simple edit command.

It has the added advantage that you don't have to wait for XML namespaces to garner full support.

GETTING DOWN TO CASES

Building a DTD from scratch is the route being taken by most DTD creators right now. They plan on funding their development efforts by selling access to the DTD for the most part, so the applicability of these proprietary DTDs will likely remain in the business-to-business (B2B) for some time to come. For the general public to be able to use a DTD, which is where the true value of XML lies in most cases, the DTD will have to be publicly available.

Although building a DTD is theoretically only worthwhile if no existing DTD fulfills the requirements of a given task, the existence of proprietary DTD strategies has encouraged the proliferation of multiple variants on the same theme. It's an especially confusing and hard-to-comprehend mess because you can't even compare competing proprietary DTDs in many cases without purchasing them. In the case of DTDs supplied by industry membership organizations, where the members of a particular consortium have the power to influence DTD development to suit a common purpose, this may be satisfactory. But for the general public, a different model is needed.

Although there are existing DTD archives that purport to collect DTDs so they can be made generally available, this rather begs the question of where DTDs should be located. In the case of truly public DTDs, a central location might be the only sensible solution, but in many cases the best location for a DTD is at the location of the document which uses it. It's possible, although unwise, for a DTD to evolve over time. Given our experience with the overall level of maintenance of the Web it seems likely that pages which depend on an "evolved" DTD may break and it might be years before anyone notices besides occasional users.

So keeping your own copies of "public" DTDs might be a reasonable solution to the chaos and flux in existence on the current Web. And of course keeping local copies encourages the proliferation of multiple versions of the "same" DTD, because the temptation to tweak a DTD "just a little" may prove to be too much to bear for some designers. Latency too, which on the Web may be measured in years, will prevent many documents from evolving to meet new standards as common public DTDs change over time.

The only solution is to allow for infinite variety in your view of the Web. You will probably never be able to depend on invariant and unchanging Web structure, so any Web documentation architecture has to be flexible as well. The Persistent URL (PURL) technology seen at `http://purl.oclc.org/` may help to provide some measure of continuity in some cases. But it will probably be necessary for some Web equivalent of the Library of Congress, or major university libraries, which will archive copies of documents and their associated DTDs commonly referred to by others, to satisfy the requirements of scholarship and stable reference.

Project Gutenburg (http://www.promo.com/) and Bibliomania (http://www.bibliomania.com) are initial (non-XML) attempts to fill this need but there are countless others with similar missions, including many based firmly in SGML or XML such as the Text Encoding Intiative (TEI) at http://www.tei.uic.edu/orgs/tei/ and the Women Writers Project at Brown University (http://www.wwp.brown.edu/).

These latter projects are committed to archiving both XML documents and their DTDs so that scholars and others who wish to use classic texts have a central (or at least stable) repository where they can be found. A stable library makes it possible to incorporate linked or transcluded XML documents and DTDs without risking the loss of continuity that would result from losing the location of the reference.

PART

I

CH

5

CHAPTER 6

XML NAMESPACES

In this chapter

USING MULTIPLE DTDS WITH NAMESPACES

XML namespaces provide a method of reusing markup in documents even though collisions between element names and attributes used in any particular markup might exist. A collision means that an element or element/attribute combination defined in one DTD has the same name as an element defined in another. By explicitly referring to the namespace in which a given piece of markup is defined, multiple instances of external namespaces can be used and accounted for in a single document. Namespaces exist for the purpose of making element and attribute names unique. The specification that defines them mentions no other reason for their existence. As you see in the section entitled "Using Namespaces in Nonstandard Ways" later in this chapter, that hasn't prevented their use in many other contexts.

Note

A *namespace* simply means the context in which a given name is used with some guarantee of uniqueness. In XML, a namespace may be related to the DTD used to define a set of tags and attributes by using its URL as a unique identifier, because a DTD guarantees naming uniqueness. But any unique identifier can be used to define a namespace, not just the URL of a DTD. In other contexts, such as when using an ISBN number as a namespace identifier there might or might not be a guarantee of uniqueness since the naming authority that allocates unique ISBN numbers doesn't define a DTD associated with them.

When multiple DTDs are in use in the same document, which can easily happen when you try to use DTDs from different environments, there is no way for the XML processor to decide *a priori* that the particular `<table>` tag in use comes from the XHTML namespace and not from the MathML namespace. Confusion often reigns. Although XML namespaces are a recommendation of the W3C, they are not yet universal but are valuable enough that you can count on them being implemented in most contexts soon.

As an example, examine the namespace of XML itself:

```
xmlns:xml="http://www.w3.org/XML/1998/namespace"
```

Because W3C has complete control of its own namespace, the namespace can be, and is, guaranteed by W3C to be unique. Any future XML specification can easily be assigned a different namespace to mark the difference between them. Note, however, that the XML namespace has been assigned the prefix `xml:` by the preceding code. This is its default value for, and only for, XML itself. No other namespace can be assigned this prefix, and trying to do this would be an error in any case combination. So it's unclear exactly how the namespace prefix `xml:` could be associated with a newer version of XML and exactly what a namespace-aware user agent might make of it. The proper syntax required to declare and use namespace prefixes is explored in the next section, "Declaring a Namespace."

You should also be aware that there is an RFC-2611 referring to URN (Uniform Resource Name) Namespace Definition Mechanisms. This is not directly related to XML Namespaces, although the XML Namespace specification refers to RFC 2141, *URN Syntax*, which is in turn related to this one. Namespaces in these other contexts are discussed in the section, "Namespaces in Other Contexts" later in this chapter. A URN is an alternate mechanism for identifying a namespace discussed in that section.

DECLARING A NAMESPACE

Namespaces are declared using a universal XML attribute named xmlns. This attribute is available in every XML element even if it has not been declared in a DTD and is recognized even in a validating parser without that declaration. It is part of the XML language itself.

Create a namespace by including an xmlns attribute in the start tag or root element of the document or fragment. The scope of the namespace is that single element and all its children. As an example, look at a simple XHTML document. XHTML is particularly interesting because it was designed to be easily extended using other XML DTDs and requires a namespace to be declared in every XHTML document to be considered valid:

1. The namespace for XHTML 1.0 is http://www.w3.org/1999/xhtml, so the root element `<html>` must declare that namespace as a minimum:

```
…
<html xmlns="http://www.w3.org/1999/xhtml">
  …
</html>
```

   If there are no other namespaces used, or if it is the primary namespace, it can be declared as the default namespace and no prefix is needed.

2. Using another document DTD within XHTML is quite simple as well. In this case, you need at least one of the namespaces to be explicitly called out with a prefix, like this:

```
…
<html xmlns="http://www.w3.org/1999/xhtml"
      xmlns:doc="http://www.oasis-open.org/docbook/">
  …
</html>
```

> **Note**
> DocBook doesn't have an official namespace declared so declare one for it. The prefix declared for the DocBook DTD is "doc" and is actually *suffixed* to the xmlns declaration using a special syntax associated with the xmlns attribute alone:
> ```
> xmlns:doc="…"
> ```

3. After you've declared the DocBook Namespace, you can use DocBook tags with the declared prefix within your XHTML document, like this:

```
…
<html xmlns="http://www.w3.org/1999/xhtml"
      xmlns:doc="http://www.oasis-open.org/docbook/">
  <head>
    <title>DocumentTitle</title>
  </head>
  <body>
    …
    <doc:title>BookTitle</doc:title>
    …
  </body>
</html>
```

Alternatively, you could use DocBook tags without declaring them first by including the DocBook namespace on each DocBook tag, like this:

```
...
<html xmlns="http://www.w3.org/1999/xhtml">
  <head>
    <title>DocumentTitle</title>
  </head>
  <body>
    ...
    <title xmlns:doc="http://www.oasis-open.org/docbook/">BookTitle</title>
    ...
  </body>
</html>
```

This has the same effect as declaring a prefixed namespace and then using the prefix because, by definition, the namespace prefix is only a shorthand placeholder for the actual namespace. Internally, the namespace-aware user agent should use the actual namespace, not the prefix, to guarantee uniqueness. But using namespaces with less than global scope might cause problems for CSS and other mechanisms with less than perfect understanding of namespaces. Most current implementations only understand the prefix syntax, so attribute-level namespaces are not equivalent to global namespaces in practice, even though they should be theoretically.

4. After a prefixed namespace is declared, you can address attributes within that namespace using the namespace prefix on the attribute name, but this can lead to complex, confusing, and ultimately undefined interactions between the user agent and the DTD unless great care is taken. For example, because XML namespaces are case-sensitive whereas URIs on the Web are not, the following code is legal in the context of XML namespaces but not in the context of XML or XHTML:

```
...
<html xmlns:xhtml="http://www.w3.org/1999/xhtml"
      xmlns:xht="HTTP://WWW.W3.ORG/1999/XHTML">
  ...
  <body xhtml:title="FirstTitle" xht:title="SecondTitle">
    ...
  </body>
</html>
```

XML namespaces do not recognize the fact that the two namespaces in the preceding example are equivalent with the only difference between them being case. So the illegal double assignment of values to the same XML attribute goes unnoticed.

At the start of every XHTML document, there is a mandatory declaration of the xmlns attribute that declares it to be a part of the XHTML namespace such as the following:

```
<html xmlns="http://www.w3.org/1999/xhtml">
```

This declaration also sets it up as the default namespace because there is no namespace prefix associated with the namespace. The namespace prefix is part of the extended syntax of the xmlns attribute that enables you to set a mnemonic prefix associated with a namespace that can be used in element names so you can easily track which element you're using at any given time. As an example, the following code declares the namespace for HTML 4.0 and associates a prefix to it so it can be used in combination with the XHTML namespace:

```
<html xmlns="http://www.w3.org/1999/xhtml"
      xmlns:htm="http://www.w3.org/TR/REC-html40">
```

The preceding fragment declares the XHTML namespace as a default, so any name without a prefix is assumed to be in that namespace. It then declares a prefix, `htm`, using a special colon-separated syntax on the `xmlns` attribute, and associates a URI with it, the official namespace of HTML 4.0.

Tip from
LeeAnne.com
Words to weave by

> Using a default namespace enables you to skip adding those ugly prefixes to every tag. You should think about which tags you use most commonly and set those as the default, thereby enabling you to save a lot of typing and make your code easier to read. It might also allow you to recycle most of any style sheet you use with your pages, adding style sheet properties and values only for the new tags.

Not only did you associate a namespace prefix with the namespace when you opened it, you were able to use that prefix to label the html tag itself. This happens to be the root element for this document tree, so you've set the scope of the default namespace to cover the entire document. The two `xmlns` attributes are not really the same, which would be illegal in either HTML or XML, because they are in different namespaces as indicated by suffixing the second `xmlns` attribute with a namespace prefix, even though they share the same tag. This gets a little confusing.

Tip from
LeeAnne.com
Words to weave by

> In the preceding examples, although both namespaces are URLs, a subset of URIs, there's currently nothing sitting at either location that can be read to discover what the namespace is. You could call a namespace Fred (a relative URL and therefore a URI) as long as you were consistent. The prefix is just a placeholder for the full namespace name and can always be replaced by it using the `xmlns` attribute.

Now there are two namespaces that are almost identical. Each has a `<p>` tag, an `<h1>` tag, and so on. But you can tell them apart through a simple addressing mechanism:

The `<p>` tag from the XHTML namespace is simply the `<p>` tag. All unqualified tags are in this namespace by default. The `<p>` tag from the HTML 4 namespace can be addressed as

```
<htm:p>This is some text in the HTML 4 namespace.</htm:p>
```

The same principle applies to attributes.

You can even access attributes from both namespaces inside the same tag. Here it is in action:

```
<img src="image.gif" htm:src="picture.gif"
     alt="[Image]"  htm:alt="[Image]" >
```

PART

I

CH

6

Exactly what a namespace-enabled browser would do with this odd declaration is left as an exercise for the lively imagination of the reader and the vagaries of browser development.

This is the entirety of XML Namespaces in a nutshell. Using namespaces simply enables a user agent or browser to distinguish between otherwise ambiguous tags and attributes. Because namespaces are so important, and because non-standard uses of namespaces have become common, you explore them in greater detail in the following sections, but almost everything you'd want to do is contained within this section.

USING QUALIFIED NAMES

A *qualified name* is simply the local part of the name, whether it is the element itself or one of its attributes, plus the prefix that serves as a placeholder for the full namespace name. At all times it's possible to use the full namespace name instead of or in addition to the prefix shorthand, and this should be done for elements whose scope might extend beyond the current document.

So the following <p> tags are equivalent, assuming we've declared the htm namespace prefix as previously stated:

```
<html xmlns="http://www.w3.org/1999/xhtml"
      xmlns:htm="http://www.w3.org/TR/REC-html40">
<htm:p>Some text in the HTML 4.0 namespace.</htm:p>
<p xmlns="http://www.w3.org/TR/REC-html40"> Some text in the HTML 4.0
namespace.</htm:p>
```

You can think of the prefix as a shorthand way of entering the entire xmlns attribute on each tag.

Because attributes cannot be associated with other attributes, using a namespace prefix is the only way to associate a namespace with an attribute.

IDENTIFYING NAMESPACES IN ELEMENTS AND ATTRIBUTES

Here is an example Web page snippet using two namespaces, one experimental version from my book review pages at http://www.cybergrrl.com/review/ and the XHTML spec itself:

```
<html xmlns="http://www.w3.org/1999/xhtml"
      xmlns:wbo="http://www.leeanne.org/bookreview">
   ...
<wbo:entry>
   <dt>
      <img src="wbfiction.gif" alt="Fiction" height="11"
           width="25" align="BOTTOM" />
      <wbo:link><a href="q1-2_1999.html#Saturday">
        <wbo:name>Dodici Azpadu's</wbo:name>
        <wbo:title><cite>Saturday Night in the Prime of
Life</cite></wbo:title></a>
      </wbo:link><br />
   </dt>
      <dd>
```

```
        Reviewed by
        <wbo:reviewer>Lee Anne Phillips</wbo:reviewer>
        <wbo:issue>(Q1-2, 1999)</wbo:issue>
        <wbo:category>(F)</wbo:category>
    </dd>
</wbo:entry>
```

The XHTML namespace is the default, so you don't need qualified names for the XHTML 1.0 tags throughout that give this document an unambiguous display structure. The namespace from the review page forms an XML data structure specifically designed for the index of reviews. By interleaving the XML tags with the XHTML tags, you get a page that displays correctly in almost any browser and still enables easy access to the data fields.

Figure 6.1 shows the book review page code in an editing environment with no awareness of XML, which might in fact be the ordinary means of editing small snippets of XML within larger files if XML-aware browsers fail to achieve universal presence on the desktop. Figure 6.2 shows the same document displayed in a browser with no knowledge of XML whatsoever. As you can see, the embedded tags from the XHTML namespace allow the legacy browser to behave reasonably. Given the fact that most users upgrade browsers only when purchasing a new machine, it seems likely that it will be many years before XML-enabled browsers even approach universality. XML-editing environments are also unlikely to exist on every desktop, so many mixed HTML/XML pages will be created using the tools most familiar to the user.

Figure 6.1
You can use the Visual SlickEdit programmer's editor to view the structure of an XML Web page using XML namespaces to interleave the tags.

This is a common use for namespaces, using HTML or XHTML to "beautify" or "pretty print" the page to make up for the fact that most of the world can't do any form of style sheets for XML tags.

Editing XML

Although there are many specialized tools around for editing XML files, this author is more comfortable with a real programmer's editor for most purposes. Visual SlickEdit emulates Vi, Emacs, and the much-lamented Brief, all nerdish editors deluxe. Although it's very nice having drop down menus for attributes, regular expressions are nicer. Plus, you can write your own macros if you don't like the way it works.

Concern for accessibility becomes more important as the Web becomes saturated by graphic displays of everything. Using namespaces and CSS or XSL, you can selectively display text content in accessible form while making flashy graphics available to those who want them and can use them.

Figure 6.2
The same page displayed in Netscape Navigator 4.7. The XML tags have no effect on the display in this model because it's targeted at accessible browsers, and this edition of Navigator knows nothing of XML.

Because XML namespaces are really just arbitrary names, you can tag almost anything with them for purposes other than sharing a few tags in common. In a business setting, you could tag different categories of merchandise with their own namespace but using the same database record structure. This allows you to treat hammers differently than hammocks and hemlocks for display, for example, even though they're all just similar entries in an inventory and purchasing system. In fact, any situation in which you want to distinguish between instances of the same record are amenable to identification with namespaces.

You could define those separate namespaces like this:

```
<html xmlns="http://www.w3.org/1999/xhtml"
      xmlns:hammer="http://www.leeanne.org/hammers"
      xmlns:hammock="http://www.leeanne.org/hammocks"
      xmlns:hemlock="http://www.leeanne.org/hemlocks">
```

Then you could do something like this:

```
<hammer:price>$29.95</hammer:price>
<hammock:price>$29.95</hammock:price>
<hemlock:price>$29.95</hemlock:price>
```

and use a style sheet to render tools in black, lawn furniture in green, and horticultural items in brown. Or you could set up an XSL transformation to generate three different catalogs listing all the hammers in one place, all the hammocks in another, and all the hemlocks in a third.

Contrariwise, you can tag multiple instances of totally different record structures to enable your applications to tell them apart and to avoid conflict in namespaces. This is what namespaces were designed to do, and they are handy at it as seen in the previous HTML 4.0 and XHTML 1.0 examples.

DOING WITHOUT NAMESPACES

In Chapter 4, "Extending a Document Type Definition with Local Modifications," you saw the possibility of simply overriding the names of elements instead of using namespaces when you're trying to use modular DTDs. Because XML namespaces don't really address the problem of modular DTDs, in that you can't merge the DTDs themselves but merely keep track of what tag came from where, that might be a more appropriate mechanism while we wait for XML Schemas.

Overriding names has the side effect of making documents written using the overridden element names unrecognizable by any style sheets that were set up for the original document namespace. It also makes the tags into a form that is unrecognizable without access to both the internal and external DTD subsets. But using XML namespaces is almost as difficult. You either have to add qualified names to your style sheet to be able to use them or wait for some future namespace alias system to allow style sheets to refer to actual namespaces rather than prefixes. This is such a common problem, because document authors pick their own prefixes whereas the namespace is theoretically assigned, that the XML namespace working group is looking into just such an automatic namespace prefix reconciliation system.

The same problem exists when overriding names into a foreign (non-English) language. The clarity that results for authors speaking languages other than English might well be worth the inconvenience of using some translation tool to convert finished documents back into the standard DTD terminology for worldwide publication. Although in XSL you can potentially rewrite tag descriptions on the fly, sober experience has shown that it is sometimes necessary to delve into XML and even SGML code without the benefit of fancy editing environments.

Namespaces are merely a stable workaround that enable useful work to get done until XML Schema comes to pass. Although namespaces enable you to use element names from different namespaces, XML namespaces say nothing about what the names mean or what sort of data they contain. They aren't a replacement for SGML's Architectural Forms or anything else.

PART

I

CH

6

Using namespaces in a document amounts to creating a new document type. Almost everything changes to some extent. You'd expect to have to create a style sheet to go with it and to spend some time getting everything right. Although you can save considerable work by careful choice of your default namespace, so that your style sheet remains largely the same, you're going to have to do some work. But the best thing about namespaces is that they do work, even in their limited domain, and let you work until everything settles down.

DECLARING NAMESPACES IN NON-EUROPEAN LANGUAGES

The current definition of namespaces has serious internationalization problems, because their restriction to URI syntax carries with it a dependence on US-ASCII, which for historical reasons is the *lingua franca* of the Internet. Although this is very convenient for some users—readers of this book in English for example—another class of users is significantly disadvantaged—that is every speaker of any language not based on a Roman alphabet. Most current European languages use characters or digraphs consisting of a base character and an accent or other distinguishing mark to extend the Roman alphabet to cover the needs of the actual language. Because US-ASCII is so ubiquitous, certain standards have developed for more or less automatically transforming actual words in an equivalent form that can be represented in US-ASCII, such as German ü (u-umlaut) can be written as "ue" in Bücher.

But some non-English keyboards might not contain US-ASCII characters because they aren't used in the language spoken by the keyboard user. A Russian keyboard, for example, might not have any Roman characters on it at all, although there might be a superficial resemblance between certain Cyrillic characters and Roman letters. Likewise, an Arabic keyboard might lack anything even approximating Roman characters, so a site named www.zebra.com might not be terribly convenient to type for anyone using either keyboard. When you add the fact that the existing URI standard supports only left to right text, whereas Arabic and many other languages use right to left order, the difficulty is compounded.

And regardless of convenience, a URI using a Roman alphabet isn't at all mnemonic for anyone not used to such an alphabet. And mnemonics matter. Companies spend millions of dollars for Internet domains that are easy to remember and type. Although the Web has been dominated by English, or at least European languages, for many years, the surge of interest in the Internet on the part of the Chinese, Japanese, and other non-Western economic powers means that accommodations eventually have to be made for them.

Proposals have been made to extend URIs to include support for UTF-8 ISO-10646 character sets, but these all have significant disadvantages as well, including the transmission of intermediate gibberish such as http://www.أليس.om/ that is difficult to comprehend and use if native support for these sorts of translations is not built into the user agent. It should be noted that similar problems exist for EBCIDIC character encodings used in the IBM mainframe world.

In the short run, it seems quite likely that nothing at all will be done to make Internet domains more convenient and mnemonic for international users because so much of the network infrastructure would have to be updated. But the pressure for change grows as what are now "developing" nations become economic powerhouses. India, for example, is reported to have more Internet bandwidth available per capita than the United States, and companies based in India are growing in strength and reach into the marketplace. Although India uses English in part, there are also many regional or national scripts in daily use.

USING NAMESPACES IN OTHER CONTEXTS

Namespaces are used in other than XML contexts, because unique identifiers have many uses in the field of computing, but unique identifiers are also valuable commodities and might be hinged about with proprietary restrictions and, when they refer to people, privacy and legal concerns. In these contexts a namespace is usually identified by a Uniform Resource Name (URN). The same URN mechanism can identify a namespace in XML, however, so you should be aware of the limitations of URN identifiers.

RFC-2611, *URN Namespace Definition Mechanisms*, refers to another method of defining namespaces based on recognized central authorities responsible for administering URN identifiers. RFC-2169, *A Trivial Convention for Using HTTP in URN Resolution*, sketches a hypothetical URN resolution mechanism. But in practice, none of these methods and protocols are likely to do much good. The collators or issuing authorities in charge of this information are not likely to give it away, and casual users of the information are not likely to be willing to pay to resolve or verify random URN references.

International Standard Serial Numbers (ISSNs), for example, are administered by the ISSN International Centre in Paris, `http://www.issn.org/`. They actually have a database one can search (for a fee) to identify a serial based on an ISSN, which is rare among "authorities." including Serials, in this context, refers to magazines and other periodical publications.

By way of contrast, ISBN numbers are assigned by a bewildering array of agencies and sub-agencies, including publishers themselves, so that identifying any particular item might not, in fact, be possible if the publisher has gone out of business and you can't find it referenced anywhere else. There is a more-or-less central authority maintained by the publisher R.R. Bowker, but even that authority is split between the US (Bowker) and individual agencies in each country, with a few countries with historic and linguistic ties sharing a common agency.

Because Bowker publishes books, including Books in Print, containing the keys to discovering which numbers have been assigned to large subsets of all published books, some resolution of an arbitrary ISBN number may be possible using a paper reference. And because Bowker also publishes guides for discovering which prefixes are assigned to which publishers, it's theoretically possible to resolve any ISBN number. But there is no online method of resolving all references and probably never will be. Some sub-agencies and publishers might not even have email addresses, much less Web sites, so the only possible universal resolution mechanism is very slow. One has ultimately to rely on the physical post offices of each country for this purpose, not a satisfactory solution for most real-time requests, although the format of an ISBN-based namespace seems to imply some sort of on-line timeliness: `xmlns="URN:ISBN:0789719967"`. Information on ISBNs can be found at `http://www.isbn.org/`.

Similarly, a U.S. social security number fulfills certain requirements of a namespace; it is theoretically unique and is assigned by a central authority. But for privacy reasons a social security number is not resolvable to an identity for most inquirers and not verifiable either. And social security fraud is so rampant that some numbers might be in use by hundreds of individuals, or the actual person referenced "officially" by that number might be dead and the social security people don't know it, or there might never have been anyone referenced officially by a completely fraudulent number. But that doesn't mean that there are no records containing these numbers. The whole point of Social Security fraud is to enter these numbers into databases, so they're all over the place.

The whole idea of a namespace in this sense is a little unsettling, because it implies universally accessible databases with extensive information available to anyone who enquires. When applied to people, the problem is apparent, but even when applied to physical objects there are philosophical and practical problems.

It seems doubtful that there *should* be a truly universal product code for books. That would mean that you'd have to pay some authority such as `ISBN.org` for the privilege of publishing a book. In many cases it might be impossible or inadvisable to register a book at all since the responsible authority might be a totalitarian or repressive regime that wants certain subjects suppressed. And even that doesn't take into account art and other singular works. If we require the Mona Lisa to have a UPC (Uniform Product Code) number and be bar-coded on the back, we might have to rethink our whole concept of what art is, possibly destroying it in the process. If everything has to be defined in advance, or defined at all, then free speech and art are in peril.

There might even be an existential paradox. There might not be any such thing as a unique and universal identifier when applied to actual persons or objects. A person with dual citizenship and two passports is probably not two different people simply because two different jurisdictions have assigned that person a different unique identifier. But the same individual with two passports fraudulently obtained from the same jurisdiction might be a different story. The purpose of the latter fraud would presumably have been to *pretend* to be two people, and the success of the fraud implies that everyone of official significance assumes that there *are* two separate people. So in that limited sense, pretense approaches reality. And a person who's managed not to be identified by any state or agency at all is presumably still real, even though there's no official record that says so.

So if the best that we can do only *approximates* this ideal state of unique identifiability, we're probably not justified in behaving as if we can, in fact, depend on a perfection that does not exist. Most of us have experienced the ineffectual attempts of bureaucrats to recover from rulebook failure, which can send them into a tizzy of incoherent thrashing or obstinate refusal to acknowledge reality; we should design systems that are considerably less fragile.

USING NAMESPACES IN NONSTANDARD WAYS

After W3C XMLNamespaces defined a universal attribute guaranteed to be available across every DTD, a few enterprising programmers decided to overload namespaces with other contexts. The most notorious example is Microsoft, which has used the otherwise nonstandard `xmlns:HTML="http://www.w3.org/Profiles/XHTML-transitional"` as a special namespace and reserved namespace prefix coerced into a switch to turn on special style sheet processing for XHTML elements in Internet Explorer 5. Likewise, `<xsl:stylesheet xmlns:xsl="http://www.w3.org/TR/WD-xsl">` is used as a switch to turn on XSL style sheet processing in Internet Explorer.

But similar uses abound, including within W3C itself. SMIL, for example, plans eventually to use an XML namespace to identify extensions to SMIL using a `system-required` attribute whose value is a namespace. In other words, the namespace is used as a switch to identify whether a particular implementation of SMIL supports an extension implied by that namespace.

These uses go far beyond the mere need to unambiguously identify tags and their attributes and extend namespaces into a metalinguistic role as arbiter of syntax and primitive control structure rather than a simple mechanism for making names unique.

Whether this is wise remains to be seen, but you can note that the XSL namespace pointed to by Microsoft's "`http://www.w3.org/TR/WD-xsl`" has no relationship to the current W3C namespace defined for the XSL standard. Placing existential or syntactical knowledge about particular implementations of any standard in code seems fraught with peril because timely updates are impossible. It seems far more likely that some future mechanism will allow this information to be encoded in a file of some sort available from the namespace URI and retrieved dynamically, allowing standards to be updated at a central location without requiring hard-coded knowledge to be encapsulated and fossilized in every application.

GETTING DOWN TO CASES

In this chapter we've explored the concept of namespaces, a method of allowing XML DTDs to be safely combined in a single document. We've explored alternatives to namespaces to account for the occasions in which namespace support is not available, such as when using legacy user agents that don't support the concept. Examples of this might include SGML browsers, that don't know anything about namespaces, or legacy HTML browsers, which can support XML only with the addition or substitution of HTML or XHTML tags to supplement or replace the native XML document.

Although we've seen that XML namespaces are a universal solution in many cases, they're not an ideal solution. They're complex, hard-to-read, and poorly suited for dynamic page construction using multiple XML sources at the present time, although dynamic transclusion of multiple XML documents is implied by the XLink and XPointer facilities discussed in Chapter 9.

PART

I

CH

6

It seems clear that eventually namespaces will be automatically accounted for when multiple documents are read from the Web into a single host document, although no current XML-aware user agent supports such behavior. The pressure to accommodate dynamic transclusion and the display of random documents will ensure that such facilities are supplied eventually, although the vast scope of XML and the XML-related standards will probably make full support for all possible features difficult for vendors to offer except incrementally.

We've also discussed some of the difficulties inherent in both URL-based and URN-based namespace identifiers. Neither is without flaws and both may require a paradigm shift in the way Web designers think about locating things on the Web. One possible technology that might help alleviate both problems is that of Persistent URLs, PURLs, which interpose an agent or server between the user and the ultimate location of a resource so that resource location changes can be accommodated at one or more central (and unchanging) sites. Read about PURLs at `http://purl.oclc.org/`.

But full use of namespaces may also require an unprecedented change in the way naming authorities are funded. When a naming authority becomes a part of the XML common carrier system by being used as the source of URN authority, some method of automatic allocation of financial incentive will be needed, either by a general (and very small) "tax" on Internet traffic, or by other means. The present-day ASCAP and other recording societies' model, in which the authors of music are automatically paid for the use of their music on the "free" radio broadcasting system, argues that this wouldn't be difficult, just complex to implement without parties feeling unfairly taken advantage of.

The development of the XML-based Web may take many forms—indeed all possible forms may battle for market dominance for quite some time—but we can see the direction that development will probably take by analogy with current broadcasting systems. Both pay-per-view and advertiser-supported systems will probably flourish, while many popular subscription services will probably be bundled in the Web equivalent of cable TV by vendors willing to negotiate bulk purchases and pass savings on to consumers.

XML SCHEMAS

In this chapter

UNDERSTANDING XML SCHEMAS

Schemas are the next generation of structure definition languages, replacing or extending the crude schema and data-typing mechanisms built into the XML 1.0 DTD itself. Typical database requirements for structured input data are much more rigorous than XML 1.0 alone can guarantee. Where XML will allow almost any information of any length in any alphabet in the world to be entered into a CDATA field, a database might accept only 20 ASCII characters in the internal field which corresponds to it. Without the capability to define the length and nature of information entered into XML data fields, the application has to send the data to its destination and rely on error and bounds checking there to catch mistakes. Of course that would generate extra traffic over the network and, if the information is meant to be delivered in batch mode, impose an unacceptable delay between entering the data and finding out that some portion of it is in error.

XML Schemas are the radical solution. Schemas allow real boundary and error checking so that potential XML structured records can be parsed and checked not only for well-formedness but also internal validity. Unfortunately, the XML Schema specifications are currently numbered among the most difficult and obscure of all the XML specifications. Although this will probably change somewhat when the final recommendations emerge, things haven't started out all that well. The Working Group has issued a schema primer along with the recommendations to help ease the process of learning how to use schemas somewhat but this chapter explains what's going on even more simply.

In this chapter, you'll look at and implement samples from the current last call working draft of XML Schema at the time this book went to press. Although there are no actual implementations available to test our code, you can simulate sample outputs from hypothetical XML-aware versions of existing browsers to make it clear what the technology may look like in practice.

RATIONALE FOR A NEW SCHEMA LANGUAGE

Because XML is designed to be the universal format for structured documents and data on the Web, it follows that one of the requirements for a schema facility is that it use XML as its medium of expression. This is an effort by W3C to constrain the endless proliferation of languages and syntax mechanisms on the Web that has allowed ad hoc constructs such as inline scripting languages and the various flavors of Cascading Style Sheets to use completely different syntax and information formats from HTML itself. Indirectly, this has led to such questionable practices as commenting out the script or style sheet to avoid breaking many browsers.

The capability to comment out a style sheet or script is theoretically absent in HTML, because the content of style and script elements is supposed to be #CDATA, that is, text not containing markup of any sort, including comments. Browsers that know the content of both these elements is #CDATA, which forbids the browser from parsing the enclosed data looking for markup, will read the enclosed text, including the comment, as significant text.

This means that the script language or style sheet processor has to ignore the begin SGML/XML comment string (<!--) to avoid breaking the script. But the end SGML/XML comment string (-->))>)>) SGML/XML comment strings> might confuse the script or style sheet processor, so you have to comment out the end SGML comment string with the appropriate style sheet or script language comment syntax in turn.

Still older browsers, which don't recognize the script and style elements at all, will view their contents as #PCDATA by default. In parsing the contents these older browsers will see the comment and ignore all the enclosed text. It's quite clever really.

So by a process of interlocking circular logic, legacy browsers that don't recognize scripts treat the content of the style and script tags as #PCDATA because they don't know any better and authors can enclose the content in comments to prevent the browser from rendering it. Browsers that happen to know what style and script elements actually mean *must* treat the content as #CDATA, because *everyone* comments out the script and style sheet content to account for those that don't, so they're forced to ignore the comment and do, in fact, see the enclosed code. It's messy even though it works. But the untidiness of it all drives language designers crazy.

The official line is that you're supposed to use browser sniffing at the server and serve up appropriate pages for each browser. This allows you to leave out the script or style sheet completely for browsers with no support and neatly include the script or style sheet with enclosed code for browsers that support them. Of course, the elaborate comment scheme is redundant if you do it that way. But there are hundreds of browsers and soon to be more. Handling all of them sensibly is impossible for many and very difficult for all. Not everyone with a Web site has access to the server.

The only way to sniff the browser if you can't control the server behavior is with a client-side script, but you have to comment out the script to avoid breaking legacy browsers. It's a Catch 22. So, inline CSS and scripts are likely to remain very useful within XML and it seems likely that the tension between legacy browsers and the desires of language designers is not going to go away soon. And whether comments can contain useful data will remain a sticking point for quite a while yet.

Note

The XML 1.0 Recommendations makes it clear that XML parsers are not required to pass comments along to the application. Inline scripts and style sheets are supposedly obsolescent, at the very least, when viewed by an XML parser. The typical script sequence in HTML actually uses two distinct commenting mechanisms to hide each set of comments from the other, first an SGML <!-- --> comment to hide the script code from legacy browsers, and then a JavaScript // comment to prevent the script from reading the SGML comment end:

```
<SCRIPT><!-- script data // --></SCRIPT>
```

The fact that scripts and style sheets contain #CDATA means those supposed comments really shouldn't be parsed as comments in the first place. Except XML parses almost *everything*; the presence of markup in #CDATA means only that the XML parser may generate a fatal error.

If it weren't for the fact that scripts and external programming languages don't really fit all that well into the XML universe, they'd be perfectly capable of handling the type of input validation that XML Schema is designed to do. In fact, because general-purpose programming languages are inherently more powerful than predefined schema mechanisms, however versatile, you give something up by using XML Schema instead of a custom program.

In return for somewhat less power, you gain wide accessibility of input-checking features for all. Not everyone has the knack of learning and using the more powerful programming languages, nor wants to spend the time required to master those skills. By using XML Schema, quite handy things can be done almost by template. Because it uses XML as its base, the learning curve isn't terribly steep, and because most of the common tasks and data types are built in, you can quickly use it to get the job done without too many tears.

COPING WITH CHANGES IN XML SCHEMA

Although the existing last call draft of XML Schemas is still a work in progress, no substantive changes are planned before the proposed recommendation is released. The W3C is scheduled to release a Proposed Recommendation *sometime* in 2000 and changes may be made at that time or at any point on its way to full Recommendation status. Periodic updates will be made on the Web site associated with this book, `http://www.leeanne.com/usingxml/`, to reflect recent developments and extend the useful life of this reference.

> **Caution**
>
> Any technical reference to a standard as much in flux as XML Schema runs the risk of losing currency. There is a Web site associated with this book that will track changes and update examples from the book to reflect the latest standards throughout the useful life of the book at `http://www.leeanne.com/usingxml/`.

In the meantime, some useful things can be done with the XML Schema already, assuming a browser that supports it is available on your platform of choice. The final Recommendation will only improve the power and expressiveness of a tool already far beyond the facilities easily available now. In this chapter you look at ways to limit the sorts of things that can be entered into data and attribute fields using the preliminary tools that exist now. By the time you read this, the evolution of the W3C working draft may force rethinking of some portions of this discussion, but the groundwork for those thoughts will be clear. As always, the W3C web site at `http://www.w3.org/` is the final arbiter of current recommended practice.

DISSECTING XML SCHEMAS

There have been a number of proposals to W3C addressing the issues of schemas in one form or another. In fact, the existing XML DTD mechanism is a schema of sorts. In the "Understanding Previous XML Schema Proposals" section later in this chapter, you learn a little about the various submissions.

The W3C working group trying to resolve all these conflicting proposals has developed it's own compromise, XML Schema. XML Schema is an XML 1.0 compliant extension of the basic XML 1.0 language that allows the limited constraint capabilities inherent in the XML 1.0 DTD to be extended almost arbitrarily. Instead of the elementary XML 1.0 DTD content types of character, element, or mixed, XML Schema allows content to be limited to a character string of a certain length, for example, or to an integer of a specified range as well as allowing much finer tuning of the content model. It also has the potential to eliminate the need to use a special DTD language because it uses XML itself to define the data type.

UNDERSTANDING SCHEMA STRENGTHS

Even in its present form, XML Schema shows enormous promise. There is a flexible attribute grouping mechanism, analogous to but far more versatile than the XML DTD parameter entity declaration, the capability to declare new datatypes, an archetyping facility that allows you to create structures that visibly share their common components, and much more.

Minimum and maximum values for data items can be declared, multiple schemas can be used in a single document, and the concept of schema-validity is developing rapidly.

The current working draft also allows you to specify a *pattern* on elements and attributes which uses the familiar *regular expression* syntax to describe the sorts of things that are allowed in a given field. The target regular expression model is that of Unicode, which has a few minor extensions to the regular expression as used in the UNIX shell, many professional editors and mail readers, and elsewhere. To specify an element with a pattern, for example, you would create a new type based on an existing type and define the pattern like this:

```
<simpleType name='ZipCode' base='string'>

  <pattern value='\d{5}'/>

</simpleType>
```

This pattern would define a five-digit ZIP Code, as used by the U.S. Postal Service to help presort mail.

Tip from

LeeAnne.com
Words to weave by

There's a good reference to Unicode-style regular expressions at http://www.unicode. org/unicode/reports/tr18/.Unicode requires major extensions to Unix-style regular expressions to handle multiple character sequences when they behave as a single character in some languages. Examples include Spanish "ch" or "ll," which behave as single letters when alphabetized. Extensions were also required to enable specifying characters by mnemonic names instead of numeric values.

PART

I

CH

7

In combination with other XML facilities, even now in the process of development, XML Schemas address a significant chunk of our problem space, leaving less for the beleaguered Web designer or programmer to solve on her own.

IDENTIFYING SCHEMA COMPROMISES

On the other hand, the existing working draft of XML Schema (as of this writing) represents a step away from internationalization toward a U.S.-centric, English-only, ASCII-style orientation. Numbers use European glyphs only at the present time and there is no support for other Unicode glyphs, even though they are included in the XML 1.0 specification.

The only supported calendar system is the secular European Gregorian calendar, although they've expanded on the ISO-8601 standard the XML Schema calendar and time system is based on to allow both negative years and years greater than 9999. So, the ancient and far future worlds can be represented (at least approximately and in Gregorian form only) but everything else must be supported algorithmically, including Julian and other non-Gregorian calendar dates. Christian moveable feasts (for example, Easter), most non-Christian holidays, many of which use a lunar (Islamic) or lunisolar (Chinese/Hebrew) calendar, and even the division of the cycle of the year into weeks and named days are not available in the current draft. Of course, well-known algorithms exist for handling all these conversions, but there are so many that I can understand the difficulty of including them all in one standard.

The decimal point required in at least part of the specification is the Roman period universally used in the United States, although a comma is used for the same purpose in many European countries. The convenient and customary ability to mark off thousands with a division marker (either a comma or a period in Western usage) is also absent.

None of these limitations may last through the Working Draft stage. They've already added Unicode-style regular expressions, which allows much in the way of error checking and solves the two immediately previous problems completely. XSL and XSLT could possibly handle many more. So it's premature to say that this or that is a terrible idea. In fact, the standard is being continually impacted by decisions made in other working groups, on whose work they depend. It's a difficult and thankless task and I, for one, won't burden them with any blame.

I do wish that the attributes and other syntactic mechanisms that XML Schema is based on weren't expressed quite so much in a technical sort of English that owes perhaps too much to programmer's jargon.

It seems likely, however , that construction of Schemas, even more than DTDs, will remain the province of domain specialists worldwide. Although this may mirror the concentration of power and technology in the world, it seems a shame that a neutral method of Schema specification could not have been created that made the technology more accessible to those who use and are most familiar with non-European writing systems. But the W3C standards are intended to be practical rather than ideal. Inventing a Universal Babel Fish may be just barely beyond the capabilities of even these dedicated servants of the common good.

PULLING SCHEMA CAPABILITIES AND POSSIBILITIES TOGETHER

For the time being at least, the XML Schema working draft is divided into two main components, *XML Schema Part 1: Structures* and *XML Schema Part 2: Datatypes*, plus an *XML Schema Part 0: Primer* to help you put everything together. They are addressed in combination here because in practice both parts are needed to do useful work. The evolution of the product is proceeding rapidly so this section talks about needs that W3C is aware of and take some educated guesses about the direction they may take as well.

USING SCHEMA NAMESPACES

XML Schema uses namespaces slightly differently than the rest of the XML suite of standards do and developments there will inevitably percolate through the rest of the related XML standards. Although the namespace part of the specification may change slightly on the way to final recommendation status, at the present time the intention is clear. They plan to offer alternative resolution mechanisms, any or all of which a designer of XML Schema-aware applications can use to find appropriate schema files based on namespaces. In all cases, the application is expected to *dereference* (a programmer's precise term for processing and transcluding a pointer or hyperlink) one or more special XML namespace URIs to yield, however indirectly, one or more schemas referring to appropriate schemas for every namespace in the document. There are several means defined for finding the appropriate schema, which are listed here in no defined order. The XML Schema specification doesn't require an application to implement any particular search strategy to find an appropriate schema nor, indeed, to search for an XML Schema at all if not necessary:

- One option is to do nothing. If the application already knows where the schema is located, it doesn't have to apply heuristics to find it. Likewise, if the application knows there is no schema to be found because the information is warranted to be schema-compliant on entry, neither location nor schema-validity need be tested. Alternatively, the application may have internal knowledge of the relevant schema and can test validity without reference to an external schema.

- Another option allows the application to look for a schema based on the location of the document itself. It might be found as an actual local schema file, an item in a local schema repository or cache, or as an indirect reference in a local catalog file.

- The application can search for a schema based on the namespace of the document and any namespaces associated with document elements and attributes for a schema file. A schema might be found as a local schema file, an item in a local schema repository or cache, or as an indirect reference in a local catalog file.

- The application could search the actual location of the document on the Web, as opposed to using the location as a parameter in a local search algorithm. From there the search strategy could proceed as if it were local.

PART

I

CH

7

- The application can search the actual namespace of the document and any namespaces associated with document elements and attributes for a schema file, as opposed to using these locations as parameters in a local search algorithm. From there the search strategy could proceed as if it were local.

- Because the preceding heuristics may discover multiple schemas, those schemas may find it advisable to incorporate nsi:targetNamespace attributes in their declarations to help the application determine which schemas would be appropriate.

The Schema namespaces may also be found by server indirection, because the server associated with either the document itself or its namespace may have knowledge of the location of the relevant schema predefined within it. Because locations and namespaces may include URNs with an associated location known only to a central authority, the actual location may take quite some time to find. For this reason, the schema specification currently states that dereferencing might be skipped on user request or by design in embedded systems where it's known that all documents conform to the schema before hand.

Use one or more of the following procedures to create one or more XML Schema references for each namespace associated with the document:

Because XML can incorporate parts of many documents and document namespaces into one document, XML Schema can explicitly associate a schema with each namespace to speed up the search process. To do this, you have to declare the namespace as usual, declare the special XML Schema namespace, and then restate the namespace URIs paired with the location of the schema document which refers to it like this:

```
<documentname xmlns:doc="http://www.leeanne.com/usingxml/"
              xmlns:htm="http://www.w3.org/1999/XHTML"
              xmlns:xsi="http://www.w3.org/1999/XMLSchema/instance"
     xsi:schemaLocation="http://www.leeanne.com/usingxml/
                         http://www.leeanne.com/doc.xsd
                         http://www.w3.org/1999/XHTML
                         http://www.leeanne.com/usingxml/xhtml.xsd">
```

If you need to locate a schema with no xsi:targetNamespace predefined, you can use the xsi:noNamespaceSchemaLocation attribute to identify a particular location like this:

```
xsi:noNamespaceSchemaLocation="http://www.leeanne.com/usingxml/">
```

At that point, any of the heuristics listed earlier could be used to locate the actual schema except that the last item regarding the xsi:targetNamespace attribute would not apply.

The schema documents themselves can be made up of parts. To include another schema or portion within a single namespace, include it like this:

```
<include schemaLocation = uri-reference />
```

To include a schema relating to a particular namespace, import it with a namespace and namespace schema pair like this:

```
<import namespace="URI" schemaLocation="URI" />
```

There are still a few problems with namespaces in XML Schema. CSS and many other XML applications have different (or no) mechanisms for resolving multiple namespaces in included documents, especially when the same style sheet may be used to refer to multiple namespaces. The syntax used for multiple namespaces in XML Schema doesn't extend to the documents which use it, so CSS or XSL style sheets applied to an XML document using XML Schema may not work correctly unless the many uses now being made of namespaces are regularized and made consistent across all XML standards.

Note

Namespaces in schemas are still changing. It now seems likely that there will be a physical schema file at the URI pointed to by each namespace declaration, if a URI is present. On the other hand, a non-accessible or abstract namespace identified by a Uniform Resource Name (URN), such as a unique ISBN number, will have no physical location, so a schema will have to be discovered by other means.

Because this in turn implies that access to the Internet may be needed, it would seem to go hand in hand with DTD validation of the XML code itself. It may require access through the namespace to other forms of external data as well, perhaps the DTD, although XML Schemas can do almost everything (and more) associated with a DTD by themselves. To say that this opens the way to greater complications would not be hyperbole although it makes a great deal of sense in principle.

If you validate schema-defined fields within an XML document, it doesn't make a great deal of sense not to validate the document as a whole. If those fields and that document are being used to validate a data entry screen, it doesn't make any sense at all to let a non-validating parser display the fields for entry. But XML doesn't currently define a way to force validation of an XML document. Further, a non-validating processor is currently defined only in relationship to a DTD, but an XML Schema completely replaces a DTD. A parser could legitimately be termed "non-validating," because it didn't validate against the DTD while at the same time permitting the document to be validated against an XML Schema. Given the existence of an XML Schema which can theoretically replace the DTD, the concept of a non-validating parser becomes fuzzy and hard to pin down.

It doesn't seem worthwhile to go to the trouble of validating input if users can avoid the necessity of subjecting their input to scrutiny by simply choosing a different piece of software. There may be security issues as well. Because multiple namespaces are available, any of which might redefine a namespace-qualified schema entirely, the question of how they interact within the same document is not easily answered. There are a lot of issues to be resolved before XML Schemas, namespaces in particular, are ready for prime time.

In the meantime, as you see in Chapter 14, "Using Next Generation Extensible Style Sheets—XSL," it seems possible to use Extensible Style Sheet Language Transformations (XSLT) to affect many of the issues remaining to be resolved by W3C right now, instead of waiting for W3C to solve all our problems.

CODING A SIMPLE XML SCHEMA EXAMPLE

Listing 7.1 provides a truncated example of an XML document using XML Schema to validate element structure and data fields.

LISTING 7.1 A SAMPLE XML CUSTOMER RECORD

```
<?xml version="1.0"?>
<!-- Customer Record -->
<customer xmlns="http://www.leeanne.com/aristotelian/"
          xmlns:xsi="http://www.w3.org/1999/XMLSchema-instance"

xsi:noNamespaceSchemaLocation="http://www.leeanne.com/aristotelian/schemas"

"http://www.leeanne.com/aristotelian/schemas/07xmp01.xsd">
  <customerName>Aristotelian Logic Systems</customerName>
  <customerID>112344-0897</customerID>
  <credit-status>Net-30</credit-status>
  <customer-contact locale="USA">
    <honorific>Ms.</honorific>
    <given-name1>George</given-name1>
    <given-name2>Evelyn</given-name2>
    <family-name>Fayne</family-name>
    <degrees>LLD, PhD</degrees>
    <title>Contracts Director</title>
    <department>Purchasing</department>
    <telephone locale=NANP">+1 101 555.1234</telephone>
    <extension>3456</extension>
  </customer-contact>
  <comment>ALS buys over $300K per year, primarily our Mark IV WKS</comment>
  <shipping-address locale="USA">
    <attention>Attn:</attention>
    <attention-name>Receiving Clerk</attention-name>
    <reference>Ref:</reference>
    <street-address1>987 Technology Pkwy</street-address1>
    <street-address2>Unit 200 - Receiving</street-address2>
    <city>Riverdale</city>
    <territorial-division>Ohio</territorial-division>
    <territorial-abbreviation>OH</territorial-abbreviation>
    <postal-code>31089</postal-code>
    <country>USA</country>
  </shipping-address>
  <billing-address locale="USA">
    <attention>Attn:</attention>
    <attention-name>Accounts Payable</attention-name>
    <reference>Ref:</reference>
    <street-address1>987 Technology Pkwy</street-address1>
    <street-address2>Unit 300 - Accounting</street-address2>
    <city>Riverdale</city>
    <territorial-division>Ohio</territorial-division>
    <territorial-abbreviation>OH</territorial-abbreviation>
    <postal-code>31089</postal-code>
    <country>USA</country>
  </billing-address>
  <creation-date>1995-07-11</creation-date>
  <last-updated>1999-10-11</last-updated>
</customer>
```

In Listing 7.1, there are locale attributes on lines 10, 18, 22, and 34 which allow the schema to validate these fields according to different criteria depending on the location entered into this attribute.

Note particularly the use of the XML Schema `noNamespaceSchemaLocation` facility to point to the actual schema used to schema-validate this document as opposed to validating it to a DTD. This location, which can actually contain a list of locations listed either as directories or actual filenames, will be dereferenced to yield an actual schema if a schema can't be found at the namespace of the document itself. In all cases, build the XML document tree and then traverse the tree in pre-order looking for elements or attributes with accessible schema definitions based on their namespaces. When such elements or attributes are found, schema-validate and transform the document tree accordingly. This sort of ad hoc recursive searching of external Web sites presents much difficulty for real-time browsing.

THE SCHEMA DEFINITION

In this example, several fields are marked with a `locale` attribute that identifies them in terms of their locality so that some sort of special processing can be performed until and if the W3C XML Schema specification catches up to real-world needs. Although this could be done with the Document Object Model (DOM) and any language capable of parsing and acting on the document tree, you would have to handle the validation on your own. Because XML Schema has these facilities built-in, there's no need to reinvent that particular wheel. In Chapter 14, you'll see how you can use Extensible Style Sheet Language (XSL) to transform a basic XML document into a localized version that can be validated easily by one schema.

locale ATTRIBUTES

Most of the `locale` attributes in this example are of type USA, because that's where this customer is located, but the telephone number is marked as belonging to the North American Numbering Plan (NANP) which covers the United States, Canada, and parts of the Caribbean.

This last is done because these nations are all accessed with a common telephone dialing pattern, unlike the rest of the world which uses "special" access codes and "weird-looking" telephone numbers from the North American viewpoint. To allow validation and perhaps use of this record with an automated dialing system, you need some way of distinguishing telephone numbers from different countries.

You also identify the contact type as being from the United States, because the use of titles and organization of names differs from country to country and the telephone number may not reflect the nationality and name formatting preferences of the subscriber. Many of Chinese nationality, for example, prefer that the family name occur first, followed by given names. This can't be done algorithmically from a simple name field because some Chinese surnames have two characters and you can't really trust people to enter names in the right order without help.

As an example of how fields might be processed differently based on locale (or any other attribute), the USA type in the addresses allows you to validate the format of ZIP codes, for example, which are either five digits or five digits, a hyphen, and then four digits. A Canadian postal code uses a letter, a digit, a letter, a space, a digit, a letter, and then a digit—something like this: M5A 4N7—so a U.S. validation scheme won't work. In the United Kingdom, you run into similar (but not quite) postal codes that might look like this: E17 4DZ (a letter followed by two digits, a space, and then a digit followed by two letters).

Tip from

Words to weave by

> Validating human conventions is difficult for a computer. The fallback position, not validating at all, should always be considered for fields that don't really matter. If a person enters an invalid phone number, who really cares? Many people don't have phones at all. But if the Social Security number is invalid, it may have legal repercussions.

As you can see, validation of data types requires a lot of thought in the international marketplace. In the underlying database, there may be no restriction on the type of data that many of these fields may contain, because the proper validation can only be ascertained in context.

In the example, the `locale` attributes provide that context, indicating particular variant versions of the same data field, although you can't do it yet. In the meantime, all the fields are defined in their most general terms, as strings, with the variant versions waiting in the wings, as it were.

Look at the schema shown in Listing 7.2, which is associated with Listing 7.1 from the previous section, taking into account the pitfalls you might fall into if you don't tread warily. This shows the whole thing before breaking it into component parts. For simplicity, this schema is shown as a monolithic record made up of a collection of complex types. The listing shows the type of customer record that might be a part of a firm's database of clients, showing all the data that might be needed by the shipping, accounting, and sales departments.

LISTING 7.2   A SAMPLE SCHEMA FOR AN XML CUSTOMER RECORD

```
<schema name=http://www.leeanne.com/aristotelian/schema/
      xmlns="http://www.w3.org/1999/XMLSchema">
  <element name="customer">
    <complexType>
      <sequence>
        <element name="customerName" type="string" />
        <element name="customerID" type="string" />
        <element name="credit-status" type="string" />
        <element name="customer-contact">
          <complexType>
            <sequence>
              <element name="honorific" type="string" />
              <element name="given-name1" type="string" />
              <element name="given-name2" type="string" />
              <element name="family-name" type="string" />
              <element name="degrees" type="string" />
```

```
                    <element name="title" type="string" />
                    <element name="department" type="string" />
                    <element name="telephone">
                      <complexType base="string" derivedBy="extension">
                      <attribute name="locale" type="string" />
                      </complexType>
                    </element>
                    <element name="extension" type="string" />
                  </sequence>
                  <attribute name="locale" type="string" />
                </complexType>
              </element>
              <element name="comment" type="string" />
              <element name="shipping-address">
                <complexType>
                  <sequence>
                    <element name="attention" type="string" />
                    <element name="attention-name" type="string" />
                    <element name="reference" type="string" />
                    <element name="street-address1" type="string" />
                    <element name="street-address2" type="string" />
                    <element name="city" type="string" />
                    <element name="territorial-division" type="string" />
                    <element name="territorial-abbreviation" type="string" />
                    <element name="postal-code" type="string" />
                    <element name="country" type="string" />
                  </sequence>
                  <attribute name="locale" type="string" />
                </complexType>
              </element>
              <element name="billing-address">
                <complexType>
                  <sequence>
                    <element name="attention" type="string" />
                    <element name="attention-name" type="string" />
                    <element name="reference" type="string" />
                    <element name="street-address1" type="string" />
                    <element name="street-address2" type="string" />
                    <element name="city" type="string" />
                    <element name="territorial-division" type="string" />
                    <element name="territorial-abbreviation" type="string" />
                    <element name="postal-code" type="string" />
                    <element name="country" type="string" />
                  </sequence>
                  <attribute name="locale" type="string" />
                </complexType>
              </element>
              <element name="creation-date" type="date" />
              <element name="last-updated" type="date" />
          </sequence>
          <attribute name="locale" type="string" />
        </complexType>
      </element>
</schema>
```

PART

I

CH

7

Figure 7.1 shows the result of validating this schema with XML Spy from Icon Systems at http://www.xmlspy.com/, an XML authoring environment that supports assisted schema construction and editing as well as the same for XSL and standard DTDs.

Figure 7.1
The customer record is displayed as XML code in XML Spy.

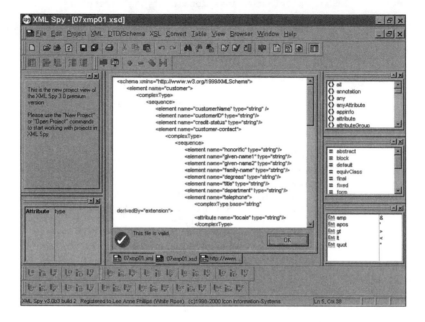

Now you can create an example of a customer record using the schema as a prototype. Listing 7.3 shows the completed code file.

LISTING 7.3   AN XML CUSTOMER RECORD WITH AN ASSOCIATED SCHEMA

```xml
<?xml version="1.0"?>
<!-- Customer Record -->
<customer xmlns:xsi=http://www.w3.org/1999/XMLSchema-instance

xsi:noNamespaceSchemaLocation="http://www.leeanne.com/aristotelian/schemas/07xmp01
.xsd">
  <customerName>Aristotelian Logic Systems</customerName>
  <customerID>112344-0897</customerID>
  <credit-status>Net-30</credit-status>
  <customer-contact locale="USA">
    <honorific>Ms.</honorific>
    <given-name1>George</given-name1>
    <given-name2>Evelyn</given-name2>
    <family-name>Fayne</family-name>
    <degrees>LLD, PhD</degrees>
    <title>Contracts Director</title>
    <department>Purchasing</department>
    <telephone locale=NANP">+1 101 555.1234</telephone>
    <extension>3456</extension>
  </customer-contact>
```

```
    <comment>ALS buys over $300K per year, primarily our Mark IV WKS</comment>
    <shipping-address locale="USA">
      <attention>Attn:</attention>
      <attention-name>Receiving Clerk</attention-name>
      <reference>Ref:</reference>
      <street-address1>987 Technology Pkwy</street-address1>
      <street-address2>Unit 200 - Receiving</street-address2>
      <city>Riverdale</city>
      <territorial-division>Ohio</territorial-division>
      <territorial-abbreviation>OH</territorial-abbreviation>
      <postal-code>31089</postal-code>
      <country>USA</country>
    </shipping-address>
    <billing-address locale="USA">
      <attention>Attn:</attention>
      <attention-name>Accounts Payable</attention-name>
      <reference>Ref:</reference>
      <street-address1>987 Technology Pkwy</street-address1>
      <street-address2>Unit 300 - Accounting</street-address2>
      <city>Riverdale</city>
      <territorial-division>Ohio</territorial-division>
      <territorial-abbreviation>OH</territorial-abbreviation>
      <postal-code>31089</postal-code>
      <country>USA</country>
    </billing-address>
    <creation-date>1995-07-11</creation-date>
    <last-updated>1999-10-11</last-updated>
</customer>
```

All the elements of the record in the schema shown in Listing 7.3 are defined with a sequential order. This ensures that the schema enforces the correct order of element occurrence when used in an authoring environment such as XML Spy or when validated by a validating parser. Other than the elements of type="date" which use and enforce an ISO 8601 date format, this example uses only minimal validation for simplicity. In use, both dates will probably be generated automatically but you never know.

Figure 7.2 shows the result of validating the XML document itself using the schema as the equivalent of a DTD.

It may be that some of the workarounds you'll learn about will be superseded by later developments from W3C, but the general principles will always hold: With enough thought, you can perform almost any arbitrary task using tools that come to hand.

Defining Elements

An element is defined in terms of base types, which may include rich (mixed) content, data types, or elements alone, just as in XML 1.0. Although the syntax looks something like an XML DTD definition, it actually uses ordinary XML syntax rather than the special DTD language. Data types can be extended or restricted by referring to a base type in a sort of object-oriented inheritance. Because this recommendation is still subject to change, the code in Listing 7.4 only suggests the sorts of attributes available in an element and the general sorts of content model attributes can contain. You won't explore this in any detail, because it's all still a bit up in the air.

Figure 7.2
The schema-validated customer record is displayed as XML code in XML Spy.

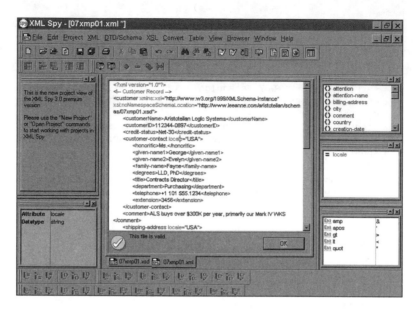

LISTING 7.4   XML SCHEMA ELEMENT SKELETON

```
<element name="elementname"
         id="ID"
         ref="typeReference"
         type="typeName"
         minOccurs= 'Integer' | '1'
         maxOccurs= 'Integer' | '*'
         nullable= 'true' | 'false'
         equivClass="className"
         abstract= 'true' | 'false'
         final="setValue" | ''
         block="setValue" | ''
         default="value"
         fixed="value"
         form="formValues">
  <!-- Content: (( annotation )?,
               ( complexType | simpleType )?,
               ( unique | key | keyref ) -->
</element>
```

Listing 7.4 represents current thinking only and is subject to change. The most authoritative information is always found on the W3C Web site and will be tracked for the useful life of the book on my own Web site at http://www.leeanne.com/usingxml/.

In use, you could create complex or simple structures, just as you can in an XML DTD, by including content elements or complex datatypes in an element schema definition as shown in the following code:

```
<element name="anything">
  <complexType>
    <sequence>
      <element name="One" type="string">
      <element name="Two" type="string">
```

```
    </sequence>
  </complexType>
</element>
```

You could also use a `choice` element to define alternative selections from a list of elements.

DEFINING ATTRIBUTES

Attributes are defined in much the same way as are elements as shown in Listing 7.5.

LISTING 7.5   XML SCHEMA ATTRIBUTE SKELETON

```
<attribute name="name"
           id="ID"
           ref="typeName"
           type="typeName"
           use= 'prohibited' | 'optional' | 'required' | 'fixed' | 'default'
           value="value"
           form="formValues">
<-- Content: (( annotation )?, ( simpleType )?)  -->
</attribute>
```

Listing 7.5 represents current thinking only and is subject to extensive change. The most authoritative information is always found on the W3C Web site and will be tracked for the useful life of the book on my own Web site at `http://www.leeanne.com/usingxml/`.

DEFINING DATA TYPES

Part of the power of XML Schemas lie in their capability to extend the basic datatypes predefined in XML Schema with constraints and extensions. In fact, it's pretty much the whole point. The ability to define fields as predefined primitive types such as numeric, Boolean, or character isn't all that much of an improvement on the basic XML DTD but by extending or limiting those basic types, templates of almost arbitrary complexity can be imposed on your data fields. Extended datatypes can be complex, having many parts, or simple.

The level of complexity allowed by the `datatype` facilities of XML Schemas is formidable. Each datatype has *facets* defined that allow the base datatype to be easily modified. Here's an example of a number in scientific notation, theoretically infinite but with the range constrained to values that can be represented in IEEE 32 bit floating point format:

```
<datatype name="ieee32">
  <basetype name="float"/>
  <minInclusive>
      1.40239846e-4
  </minInclusive>
  <maxInclusive>
      3.40282347e3
  </maxInclusive>
</datatype>
```

The facets for this example are the `minInclusive` and `maxInclusive` elements contained within the `datatype` element but all the constraining facets work the same way. So if you know you're going to be loading this into a database with this as the limits of the field, this particular constraint will prevent overflow or underflow.

The following list contains base data types and facets as currently defined by the W3C XML Schema Working Group. The list is subject to change.

- **string**—A string of characters as defined by ISO 10646 and Unicode. It has constraining facets: pattern, length, enumeration, minlength, maxlength, maxInclusive, maxExclusive, minInclusive, and minExclusive. The latter four facets depend on collating order, which is an enormously complex subject in almost every language.

- **boolean**—A boolean value, either true or false. It has the single constraining facet pattern.

- **float**—A real number. It has constraining facets: maxInclusive, maxExclusive, minInclusive, minExclusive, pattern, and enumeration.

- **double**—A double precision real number. It has constraining facets: maxInclusive, maxExclusive, minInclusive, minExclusive, pattern, and enumeration.

- **decimal**—It has the same constraining facets as float, maxInclusive, maxExclusive, minInclusive, minExclusive, pattern, and enumeration plus the following additional facets: scale and precision. precision is the number of digits following the decimal point. scale is the total number of digits allocated to the datatype.

- **integer**—An obvious subtype of decimal with scale and precision facets set to 0. In other words, the useful constraining facets maxInclusive, maxExclusive, minInclusive, minExclusive, pattern, and enumeration.

- **long**—A IEEE-style subtype of integer with maxInclusive set to be 9223372036854775807 and minInclusive set to be -9223372036854775808.

- **int**—A IEEE-style subtype of long with maxInclusive set to be 2147483647 and minInclusive set to be -2147483648.

- **short**—A IEEE-style subtype of int with maxInclusive set to be 32767 and minInclusive set to be -32768.

- **byte**—A IEEE-style subtype of short with maxInclusive set to be 127 and minInclusive set to be -128.

- **nonNegativeInteger**—An obvious subset of integer with the scale, precision, and minInclusive facets set to 0. In other words, useful constraining facets maxInclusive, maxExclusive, maxInclusive, minExclusive, pattern, and enumeration.

- **unsignedLong**—A IEEE-style subtype of nonNegativeInteger with maxInclusive set to be 18446744073709551615.

- **unsignedInt**—An IEEE-style subtype of unsignedLong with maxInclusive set to be 4294967295.

- **unsignedShort**—An IEEE-style subtype of unsignedInt with maxInclusive set to be 65535.

- **unsignedByte**—An IEEE-style subtype of unsignedShort with maxInclusive set to be 255.

- **positiveInteger**—An obvious subset of nonNegativeInteger with the scale and precision facets set to 0 and minInclusive set to 1. In other words, useful constraining facets maxInclusive, maxExclusive, maxInclusive, minExclusive, pattern, and enumeration.

- **nonPositiveInteger**—An obvious subset of `integer` with the `scale`, `precision`, and maxInclusive facets set to 0. In other words, useful constraining facets `maxExclusive`, `minInclusive`, `minExclusive`, `pattern`, and `enumeration`.

- **negativeInteger**—An obvious subset of `nonPositiveInteger` with the `scale` and `precision` facets set to 0 and `maxInclusive` facet set to -1. In other words, useful constraining facets `maxInclusive`, `maxExclusive`, `minInclusive`, `minExclusive`, `pattern`, and `enumeration`.

- **timeInstant**—An ISO 8601 formatted date and time but with the addition of support for negative years (but not 0) and arbitrarily huge year values based on the proposed revision to ISO 8601. It has the `maxInclusive`, `maxExclusive`, `minInclusive`, `minExclusive`, `pattern`, and `enumeration` constraining facets.

- **timeDuration**—An ISO 8601 formatted time interval. It has the `maxInclusive`, `maxExclusive`, `minInclusive`, `minExclusive`, `pattern`, and `enumeration` constraining facets.

- **recurringDuration**—An ISO 8601 formatted recurring time interval. It has the `maxInclusive`, `maxExclusive`, `minInclusive`, `minExclusive`, `duration`, `period`, `pattern`, and enumeration constraining facets.

- **recurringDate**—A subtype of `recurringDuration`. It has the `maxInclusive`, `maxExclusive`, `minInclusive`, `minExclusive`, `duration`, `period`, `pattern`, and `enumeration` constraining facets.

- **recurringDay**—A subtype of `recurringDuration`. It has the `maxInclusive`, `maxExclusive`, `minInclusive`, `minExclusive`, `duration`, `period`, `pattern`, and `enumeration` constraining facets.

- **time**—A subtype of `recurringDuration`. It has the `maxInclusive`, `maxExclusive`, `minInclusive`, `minExclusive`, `duration`, `period`, `pattern`, and `enumeration` constraining facets.

- **timePeriod**—A subtype of `recurringDuration`. It has the `maxInclusive`, `maxExclusive`, `minInclusive`, `minExclusive`, `duration`, `period`, `pattern`, and `enumeration` constraining facets.

- **date**—A subtype of `timePeriod`. It has the `maxInclusive`, `maxExclusive`, `minInclusive`, `minExclusive`, `duration`, `period`, `pattern`, and `enumeration` constraining facets.

- **month**—A subtype of `timePeriod`. It has the `maxInclusive`, `maxExclusive`, `minInclusive`, `minExclusive`, `duration`, `period`, `pattern`, and `enumeration` constraining facets.

- **year**—A subtype of `timePeriod`. It has the `maxInclusive`, `maxExclusive`, `minInclusive`, `minExclusive`, `duration`, `period`, `pattern`, and `enumeration` constraining facets.

- **century**—A subtype of `timePeriod`. It has the `maxInclusive`, `maxExclusive`, `minInclusive`, `minExclusive`, `duration`, `period`, `pattern`, and `enumeration` constraining facets.

- **binary**—Binary data. It has the constraining facets `length`, `pattern`, `enumeration`, `minlength`, `maxlength`, and `encoding`. Encoding can be either `hex` or `base64`.

PART

I

CH

7

- **uri-reference**—A URI. It the constraining facets `length`, `minLength`, `maxLength`, `pattern`, and `enumeration`.

- **language**—An RFC-1766 language code. It has the `length`, `minLength`, `maxLength`, `pattern`, `enumeration`, `maxInclusive`, `maxExclusive`, `minInclusive`, and `minExclusive` constraining facets.

- **id**—The ID attribute type from the XML 1.0 Recommendation. It has the constraining facets `length`, `minLength`, `maxLength`, `pattern`, `enumeration`, `maxInclusive`, `maxExclusive`, `minInclusive`, and `minExclusive`.

- **idref**—The IDREF attribute type from the XML 1.0 Recommendation. It has the constraining facets `length`, `minLength`, `maxLength`, `pattern`, `enumeration`, `maxInclusive`, `maxExclusive`, `minInclusive`, and `minExclusive`.

- **idrefs**—The IDREFS attribute type from the XML 1.0 Recommendation. An obvious derivation of `idref`. It has the constraining facets `length`, `minLength`, `maxLength`, `pattern`, `enumeration`, `maxInclusive`, `maxExclusive`, `minInclusive`, and `minExclusive`.

- **entity**—The ENTITY attribute type from the XML 1.0 Recommendation. It has the constraining facets `length`, `minLength`, `maxLength`, `pattern`, `enumeration`, `maxInclusive`, `maxExclusive`, `minInclusive`, and `minExclusive`.

- **entities**—The ENTITIES attribute type from the XML 1.0 Recommendation. An obvious derivation of `entity`. It has the constraining facets `length`, `minLength`, `maxLength`, `pattern`, `enumeration`, `maxInclusive`, `maxExclusive`, `minInclusive`, and `minExclusive`.

- **notation**—The NOTATION attribute type from the XML 1.0 Recommendation. It has the constraining facets `length`, `minLength`, `maxLength`, `pattern`, `enumeration`, `maxInclusive`, `maxExclusive`, `minInclusive`, and `minExclusive`.

- **notations**—The NOTATIONS attribute type from the XML 1.0 Recommendation. An obvious derivation of `notation`. It has the constraining facets `length`, `minLength`, `maxLength`, `pattern`, `enumeration`, `maxInclusive`, `maxExclusive`, `minInclusive`, and `minExclusive`.

- **qname**—A *qualified name* from the XML 1.0 Recommendation. It has the constraining facets `length`, `minLength`, `maxLength`, `pattern`, `enumeration`, `maxInclusive`, `maxExclusive`, `minInclusive`, and `minExclusive`.

- **nmtoken**—The NMTOKEN attribute type from the XML 1.0 Recommendation. It has the constraining facets `length`, `minLength`, `maxLength`, `pattern`, `enumeration`, `maxInclusive`, `maxExclusive`, `minInclusive`, and `minExclusive`.

- **nmtokens**—The NMTOKENS attribute type from the XML 1.0 Recommendation. An obvious derivation of `nmtoken`. It has the constraining facets `length`, `minLength`, `maxLength`, `pattern`, `enumeration`, `maxInclusive`, `maxExclusive`, `minInclusive`, and `minExclusive`.

- **name**—A *name* from the XML 1.0 Recommendation. An obvious derivation of entity. It has the constraining facets `length`, `minLength`, `maxLength`, `pattern`, `enumeration`, `maxInclusive`, `maxExclusive`, `minInclusive`, and `minExclusive`.

- **ncname**—The *name* with no included colon from the XML 1.0 Recommendation. An obvious derivation of name. It has the constraining facets length, minLength, maxLength, pattern, enumeration, maxInclusive, maxExclusive, minInclusive, and minExclusive.

Defining and Extending Base Data Types

Schema datatypes can be used as a base to construct other datatypes by inheritance in an object-oriented manner in the latest draft of XML Schemas. New datatypes can be constructed either by extension or restriction of existing datatypes and any datatype can be used as an archetype to build other datatypes.

The following element definition invokes a previously defined archetype, which might contain a number of elements, as a sort of macro facility:

```
<element name="element-name" type="ArchetypeName" />
```

The same thing can be done with attributes:

```
<attribute name="attribute-name" type="ArchetypeName" />
```

Defining Content Models

The basic XML Schema content model mirrors the XML 1.0 DTD. In other words, content can be choice, which is an alternating selection from a list, the equivalent of the "|" separator; seq, which is a sequential list, the equivalent of the "," separator; or many, which is anything, the equivalent of XML 1.0 "mixed" content indicated by (content elements)*. In addition, XML Schema allows the specification of a set of elements that must appear but may appear in any order, *all*. The most common method of specifying a content model is with a group element:

```
<complexType name="TypeName">
  <group name="groupName"
         id="ID"
         maxOccurs="number"
         minOccurs="1"
         ref="name">
<-- Content:  ( annotation? , ( element | group | all | choice |
             sequence | any )* ) -->
  </group>
</complexType>
```

Constraining Element and Attribute Content

Regular expressions are a concept first developed and made widely available in UNIX, basically, and refer to a pattern matching language useful for many purposes, from searching for particular types of strings to character by character translation, other editing, and string comparison.

Regular expressions can be used for a great many attribute and element content constraints. You could, for example, only restrict input to ASCII alphanumeric characters and space by using the following regular expression to eliminate the possibility of allowing arbitrary Unicode or ASCII punctuation characters to be inserted in a database:

```
[a-z,A-Z,0-9, ]*
```

In this example, the commas are only used to make the complex expression easier to understand. They can be omitted without affecting the meaning of the expression in any way.

A regular expression to limit input to a five-digit ZIP code might look like this:

```
[0-9][0-9][0-9][0-9][0-9]
```

In some cases, there are other ways to achieve the same limitation on input. For example, a five-digit ZIP code could also be expressed as a five-digit integer. This is less definitive than the congruent regular expression however, because five-digit ZIP codes can have leading zeros and must be exactly five digits in length. Expressed as an integer, 12 is equivalent to 00012, but only 00012 is a properly formatted ZIP code.

Regular expressions can become complex, and it's beyond the scope of this chapter to explain exactly how they can be used to create precise descriptions of target strings. For a complete explanation, see the appendix in the XML Schema Part 2: Data Types specification itself. For extensive examples of regular expressions in use, see any good UNIX textbook on the vi and/or ed text editors or a dedicated book such as *Mastering Regular Expressions: Powerful Techniques for Perl and Other Tools* by Jeffrey E. F. Friedl, O'Reilly, 1997. A good Vi reference might be *Learning the vi Editor, 6th Edition* by Linda Lamb & Arnold Robbins, O'Reilly, 1998.

VALIDATING ELEMENT CONTENT

Although the current set of validation tools are minimal, they're very powerful. You're able to declare minimum and maximum values for numeric fields, for example, or use regular expressions to validate the format of a string entry field. The following regular expression would validate the format of a telephone number as generally seen in North America, (999) 999-9999:

```
(\(\d{3}\) )?\d{3}-\d{4}
```

VERIFYING RECORD COMPLETENESS

Other than the basic capability to use Unicode regular expressions to validate included data, there is no built-in way to ensure that a field is populated in the general case. For numbers, the minimum and maximum values might also signal an empty field, at least logically. Here's an example that would suffice for a string and prevent passing empty whitespace back to the application. Other data checking might have to be included, of course, in a real-world example:

```
<element name="element-name"
  type="string"
  pattern="[^\t, ,\u000a,\u000d,\u0085,\u000b,\u000c,\u2029,\u2028]*" />
```

Depending on the implementation, the following code might also work but it should be tested first. Many programmers think there are only three or four whitespace characters. Also note the use of the \u metacharacter sequence used in the previous example to signal the start of a Unicode hexadecimal value:

```
<element name="element-name"
  type="string"
  pattern="[^\s]*" />
```

The preceding fragments would return an error if any of an assortment of the many characters that define whitespace appeared in the field and nothing else. These include space, HT, CR, LF, VT, FF, NL, LS, and PS. Other languages might have different ideas about what whitespace looks like, so it might be necessary to add to this set. The other ambiguity is in dealing with unused or control characters within the target character set. Because the ordinary whitespace characters have been excluded, including some that are rarely seen, should the rest of the control set be excluded as well? How about the sets of non alphabetic symbols? Chinese characters? These are decisions that may mean different things in different applications; consider them before committing to a particular test.

LIMITATIONS OF ERROR AND VALIDITY CHECKING

When a database is designed, people look at the information already contained in existing records and attempt to design a system that captures everything without redundancy or omission. Even the best efforts can sometimes fail when converting paper or even digital records because of a natural human propensity to draw outside the lines when an existing structure fails to capture evolving and unforeseen needs. Marginal notes can be placed on paper records, rarely used or partially empty fields can be overloaded with new categories of information. Without exhaustive analysis of the existing records, it can be difficult to guarantee completeness or accuracy.

Error checking compounds this problem and has the potential to deny access to fields that people have been using "unofficially" to do things that were never in the original design specifications. When doing error and bounds checking in an XML document, it's rarely a good idea to go beyond any existing error or bounds checking built into the native application the XML document is meant to reflect. Without analyzing every record and interviewing every user, you can't guarantee that a clearly labeled "bin-number" field hasn't been used to contain parking lot and/or warehouse identifiers for items that can't fit into bins.

Another problem is the growth of unforeseen needs that impact existing fields with a clear but narrow purpose.

THROTTLING AN XML APPLICATION ACCIDENTALLY

For example, it's common for the designers of databases to place unrealistic or over-restrictive limitations on the format of information within their purview that cause unnecessary difficulties for their users in future.

Trivially, telephone numbers in this country are usually seven or eleven digits in length, depending on whether they are local or long distance. The format of area codes in this country at one time prohibited numbers without a 1 or a 0 in the middle position.

Very many data entry fields have been created which demand that these numbers be entered in an exact format like 1 (909) 999-9999 or 999-9999 with a restrictive set of traditional area code limitations.

With the advent of mandatory eleven digit dialing in many localities and the changes in the area code format which now allow any digit in the central position, many of these schemes have had to be replaced at the cost of many hours of programming effort.

Further, the world is a bigger place than our limited experience in Canada and the United States might lead us to believe. Multinational corporations might have a customer in Bordeaux, France whose number may look like +33 (0)556 99 99 99 99, 14 digits instead of 11, and which happens to follow an international standard for the presentation format of telephone numbers, which uses parentheses for an entirely different purpose than we customarily do in the United States.

Internationally, local numbers may vary in their number of digits, even within one city. City codes, which we call area codes, can vary in length as well. Country codes, which happen to be invisible to us as our own country code of "1" is the long distance access number as well, vary from country to country. Our own "1" contrasts with England's "44," Ireland's "353," and the possibility of four digit country codes as the roster of independent states seems to grow yearly. The U.S. military and other military services use private branch exchanges that may use the hexadecimal "numbers" "A," "B," "C," and "D" in addition to 0 through 9.

The naïve telephone number validation schemes of thousands of applications newly confronting an international or military community must be updated at tremendous cost before they can address those markets. If restrictive area code validation was used, that has to been eliminated just to handle the expanding U.S. and Canadian markets. Before constructing a telephone number data field and validating the digits, make sure you really know what sort of data may be presented to it over the long haul and make your expectations clearly known in the form of an onscreen instruction or template. Consider not validating at all.

Likewise, the position and form of titles, postal codes, postal addressing methods, honors, degrees, numbers, and a host of others varies from country to country worldwide.

Using Procrustean schemes too often imposed upon the world by programmers whose idea of universality is limited to allowing for hamburgers with or without onions is a guaranteed way to alienate and annoy potential customers.

FREEFORM INPUT FIELDS

In many cases, the only way to accommodate everyone is to allow freeform input fields, just as street names are allowed to be arbitrary strings. 100 Main Street in Pocatello, Idaho may be 100 Avenida de las Ramblas in San Clemente, California or 100 East 500 North in Salt Lake City, Utah. In some parts of Japan, an address might look like this: Shokado, Nishi-iru,

Nishitoin, Shimodachiura, Kamigyo-ku, Kyoto, Japan. In the Japanese example, which is the street address? Is there a postal code at all? How do you squeeze this record into an Address, City, State, ZIP code field set? Do your database records even allow entering a country name?

Postal codes can precede the city as well as follow it, and may even precede the street address. In a freeform world, our databases may need to be somewhat freeform as well. Although XML 1.0 itself allows data to be defined as being present in any order, the same fields may have a required order in their presentation that may differ from country to country. Be sure that any underlying database or database transformation doesn't scramble or destroy the ordering information, lest you be unable to put it back. These are not unimportant issues. Properly formatted addresses may qualify your company for substantial postage discounts. Improper addresses may send your letters and parcels fluttering gently into the abyss.

UNDERSTANDING PREVIOUS XML SCHEMA PROPOSALS

There have been a series of proposals to W3C attempting to solve parts of the error-checking and validity problem.

The grandmother of all advanced schema proposals is the Hy-Time architectural form, which is part of the SGML world. Like most of SGML and especially Hy-Time, architectural forms have tremendous power. Architectural forms are a collection of rules for extending and altering elements at will. Instead of tweaking the DTD with meta-descriptions encapsulating the XML elements themselves, as do the three following proposals, architectural forms allow you to alter the very structure of existing elements, performing essentially any processing of the element you can imagine without changing the way the DTD behaves at all. Unfortunately, architectural forms simultaneously possess, like Lamont Cranston (The Shadow), the power to cloud men's minds. Implementation of an extraordinarily complex processing language on top of XML, which is supposed to be simple and easy to use, is not likely to occur in the near (or even far) future. It's up against the entire philosophy behind XML, simplicity, and will undoubtedly remain in the Hy-Time world for good.

XML-DATA

Microsoft's proposal was XML-Data, which has excellent data facilities, a namespace mechanism which some felt was too closely tied to a Windows Registry type of resolution facility, and many features that programmers loved. It's highly adapted to the sorts of things Windows programmers do and slightly less friendly toward other environments, so a small outcry arose, as usual. A major weakness is that it uses a unique syntax to describe the schema, and has to be commented, like CSS statements, to avoid improper rendering. Because the XML 1.0 Recommendation makes passing comments on to the application optional, and deprecates the very idea of using comments for code, this seems to be a fatal flaw.

THE RESOURCE DESCRIPTION FRAMEWORK (RDF)

The Netscape contribution was the Resource Description Framework, RDF, which is a generalization of other resource description tools such as the Platform for Internet Content Selection, PICS, and the Dublin Core. It doesn't really address the same data space or even the same issues but was seen as a rival to Microsoft's submission anyway. Like Microsoft's proposal, RDF uses an XML namespace to identify the metadata descriptions of data items in an XML DTD. Unlike XML-Data, the syntax is that of ordinary XML element and attribute declarations, so nothing has to be changed in XML to make it all work. Development of RDF is continuing but it was not and is not designed to address the whole schema problem space.

IBM attempted to pull together parts of each proposal as the Document Content Description, DCD. Like both the Microsoft and Netscape proposals, it uses the XML DTD and extends it with special declarations. DCD combines some of the best features of each of the previously explained proposals. Like XML-Data, DCD has strong data typing facilities. Like RDF, it's very flexible and doesn't go too far outside the XML DTD structure to enable full descriptions of XML elements.

XSCHEMA

The XML-DEV mailing list put forth its own proposal, XSchema, which evolved into the Document Definition Markup Language, DDML. DDML is more object-oriented and, instead of using DTD-like declarations to encode metadata, it uses an ordinary XML structured document to describe the schema. All constraints placed upon the document data are encoded using element nesting and attributes. DDML is slightly more ambitious than any of the three proposals described previously in that it aims to replace the XML DTD entirely. It proposes tools to automatically convert XML DTDs into DDML documents and vice versa. Although this may yet come to pass, and it would certainly have advantages, I suspect that XML and XML Schema has too much of a head start and has enormous commitment from a large number of vendors, so it's probably an also-ran in the context of this book.

THE SCHEMA FOR OBJECT-ORIENTED XML (SOX)

Finally, SOX, the Schema for Object-Oriented XML (which should really be the dysphonious SOOX I suppose), attempts to extend XML into the realm of full object orientation. I strongly suspect that elements of SOX and even DDML will eventually be incorporated into XML Schema. But the W3C has historically set the initial bar rather low when standards are recommended so as not to leave too many companies in the dust. Most proposals that make it to recommendation stage are both practical and doable in a reasonable period of time, so the relative competitive advantages enjoyed by the individual companies that propose standards are minimized.

TROUBLESHOOTING XML SCHEMAS

SETTING DEFAULT VALUES

You want to provide default values for certain fields without altering the document DTD.

This is easily done for attributes and, because the XML Schema duplicates so many features of the DTD, this is unlikely to change. The current W3C thinking seems to be tending towards allowing defaults in element content as well, but this is not set in stone by any means. For setting either a default or fixed value on an attribute, use this format:

```
<attribute name="attribute-name"
  default="value" | fixed="value"
  type="string" />
```

To set the same sort of values on an element, the same general format is used but can be set on the archetype that defines the element as well as the element itself

```
<element name="element-name"
  default="value" | fixed="value"
  type="string" />
```

or

```
<archetype name="ArchetypeName"
  default="value" | fixed="value"
  type="string" />
```

Both of these mechanisms may change but these and all other examples will be posted in updated form on my Web site at http://www.leeanne.com/usingxml/ unless the capability disappears entirely which will also be noted.

PART

I

CH

7

XPATH

In this chapter

IDENTIFYING DOCUMENT LOCATIONS WITH XPATH

XPath is an enabling technology used to identify parts of an XML document. This functionality is shared between XSL, XSLT, XPointer, and other standards that require the ability to locate positions within documents. The notion of addressing the parts of a document with an unambiguous language but without delving into the complexities of the Document Object Model (DOM) is just too good to keep to yourself. As the standards themselves point out, additional pointer and fragment identifier languages might eventually be defined for SMIL or SVG, among many other candidates, as a large part of the whole thrust of current standards development. W3C is modularizing and extending existing standards to make them usable in as many contexts as possible with minimum overhead.

XPath is a special language that lets you describe the location of a particular point in an XML document using stepwise traversal of the document tree using any node as a starting point. As mentioned previously, it forms the common ground between XSL, XSL Transformations, XLink (XLL), and XPointer. Together, they enable flexible and extensible mechanisms for linking structured documents together and a host of other applications. Previous pointer mechanisms have required that physical anchor elements be placed in the linked-to files if anything other than top-level access is required. Current needs make this impossible, because the number of ways others might desire to link into a document is unknown, and the document itself might change dynamically.

Because XPath defines a canonical document structure that any external or internal link can access to identify particular nodes on a document tree and is part of both XLink and XSL, XPath is discussed in this chapter, and XLink and XPointer are discussed in Chapter 9, "XLink and XPointer."

As are many of the XML-related standards, XPath is designed to work with other W3C standards, so it should be just as handy pointing out the parts of a (well-formed) HTML document, RDF, or any well-formed XML-like document.

An XPath has three main parts, a traversal direction called an *axis*, a node test which selects nodes along that traversal, and an algorithmic predicate, which can be used to further refine the exact node selected. We'll examine each part in detail in the reminder of the chapter.

UNDERSTANDING XPATH AXES

Because you can start an XPath from any node, some word had to be chosen to describe the direction of traversal. Lamentably, the word chosen was not inherently comprehensible nor indicative of the fact that it represents a relative direction on an ordered tree.

Axes is one of those needlessly technical words that means the directional keywords enabling you to navigate to places within a document based on your current location. They're more like driving instructions than a grid coordinate or the axle of a wheel. Although everyone can be impressed with people who've studied finite math and predicate logic, the need to impress others with the marvelous and scientific precision of these words is one computer scientists should guard against lest they be perceived as hapless dweebs by the public at large.

XPath uses the metaphorical perspective of an ant sauntering about on the tree itself rather than an arbitrary location scheme. You, the programmer, are the temporary inhabitant of each node as you walk about, traversing the tree by proxy. So you navigate by landmarks and relationships between the nodes, just as many do in real life. The simplicity and economy of this scheme, as opposed to locating nodes by x,y coordinates as the word *axis* naively implies, seems to lend itself more to a warm word such as "relationship" than the clinical "axes." So think of XPath relationships and pretend axes is a scientific word.

The following are some points to remember to help you understand XPath relationships (axes):

- XPath treats the XML document as a tree of nodes, some that have names (the elements, attributes, and namespaces) and some that do not (attribute values and text). Only elements fully participate in relationships. Neither attributes nor text can possess child descendent nodes, and attributes are not ordinarily encountered as nodes at all.

- Because element nodes are the only things with names, XPath always uses a specific node name as the basis for location descriptions, called the *context* in the specification. A minor exception exists in the root node, which has the name "/" but none other. The root node, or any named node, can be used as a basis for a relative path, thereby changing the location of the context node. But although the name of the current, or context node might not be known, that name is always available using the `local-name()` and `namespace-uri()` functions.

- XPath supports XML Namespaces, so a node name might be qualified by a namespace, which is itself an axis.

- XPath supports two types of location paths, relative location paths and absolute location paths. Relative location paths proceed by relationship from a context node other than the root. Absolute location paths proceed from the root. The first example in this sample code is relative and the second is absolute:

```
child::division/child::paragraph
/child::book/child::div/child::para
```

  The first example selects all the paragraph children of the division children of wherever the current, or context node happens to be. Whereas the second selects the same elements but only if they are the immediate children of a book document.

- Because the full XPath syntax is so verbose, there are many abbreviations to simplify location descriptions and make them easier to understand. For the exact locations given in the last bullet, for example, the abbreviated syntax would be

```
division/paragraph
/book/division/paragraph
```

  Although this might not seem like too much of a savings, when the location expression gets complicated, significant numbers of keystrokes can be saved. There is a list of abbreviations in the following "Abbreviations" section.

- XPath also enables you to select elements by the content of their attributes, so in abbreviated syntax

```
division/paragraph[@type="firstParagraph"]
```

selects all the paragraph children of the division children of wherever the current, or context node happens to be, but only if they contain an attribute named type with a value of "firstParagraph". When using XPath in combination with XSLT, for example, this capability enables you to treat first paragraphs differently than following paragraphs if you want to insert drop caps or other special text treatment.

These items comprise the XPath axes in a nutshell, although the ways in which they can be combined and interact are almost infinite.

UNDERSTANDING XPATH NODES

In the preceding section, the word *node* was used quite frequently. But *node* is yet another unfortunate choice of names on the part of the working group, and reflects an attempt to stretch graph terminology beyond the capacity of mere mortals to grasp without advanced degrees in mathematics.

Attribute nodes exist in a kind of third dimension and are not really part of the two-dimensional document tree. They are defined, in fact, as having no parent and and no children, despite the fact that a clear parallel exists between the content (value) of an attribute and the text content of an element.

The only way to make sense of this is to realize that attributes exist inside elements—which are true nodes with descendents and ancestors. Attributes, on the other hand, in some sense are the actual node, and have a much more intimate relationship to it than mere descendency. They are created with the node and die with it. You can think of them more like internal organs than children. Your heart and lungs are not your children, although they have an obvious and intimate connection. Nor are you their parent, because they come into being at the same moment as you, being inherent in your DNA. So using the word *node* to describe them only contributes to confusion and chaos.

Text nodes also have a special relationship to their parent node. First, they are sterile and can have neither descendents nor attributes themselves. This is an important distinction, so it makes little sense to label them with the same name, no matter how it satisfies the logical preconceptions of graph theorists. Because they are children of their immediate parent, it makes some sense to allow traversal of large sections of text as an ordered series of sibling semi-nodes, making them part of the document tree.

However, they behave far differently than do true document nodes, because the XML parser itself is allowed to create and destroy them, gobbling line feed sequences, for example, replacing them with carriage returns or a single space, and replacing Unicode character sequences by *normalized* equivalents. An XML parser can do nothing even remotely similar to a true node.

This duality is inherent in text because it's really a string as well as an ordered series of nodes, but it flip-flops back and forth between its node-nature and its string-nature. Arguing about which nature is "real" is a question more like quantum mechanics, perhaps even metaphysics, than finite math.

In a mixed content model, text can have actual elements embedded within it like plums in a pudding, but these elements are children of the parent, not children of the text. The text, in fact, continues through the enclosed element like a tunneling electron through a quantum potential barrier or the starship Enterprise through hyperspace. Without this behavior, string matching is nearly impossible, because "this *string*" (with italics) would not be equivalent to "this **string**" (with bold). In operation, you might have to force this behavior with a whatToShow flag in the DOM. See Chapter 10, "DOM—The Document Object Model," for details.

→ For more information about the logical view, **see** "Controlling the Logical View of the Document Tree" **p. 223**.

KEEPING TRACK OF YOUR POSITION IN A DOCUMENT

The phrase *context node* is used later in this chapter, only because that's what the specification calls it, so you might as well learn to recognize the term. This really means the current node, the one you are working on at any given moment. The equivalent in a word processing document is the location of the cursor.

The following list describes the basic relationships between nodes in terms of the current, or context, node. Portions of the following descriptions are taken from or expand on the W3C XPath Recommendation, which can be viewed in its entirety at http://www.w3.org/TR/:

- **child**—This relationship contains the children of the current, or context node, by which is meant the location of the node "cursor" as currently placed.

- **descendent**—This relationship contains the descendents of the current, or context node. A descendent is a child or a child of a child and so on. The descendent axis never contains attribute or namespace nodes for a reason explained later in the items involving siblings.

- **parent**—This relationship contains the parent of the current, or context node. Although the current specification implies that the parent of an attribute is the node that bears it, this raises an important question of asymmetry: How can an attribute have a node as its parent when the node doesn't have a child that is an attribute. Attributes don't really participate in the parent, child, or sibling relationship in that way and are more like personal qualities in people. Just as your intelligence or enthusiasm couldn't be described as related to one another except metaphorically, nor your mother be the parent of your honesty, except (again) metaphorically, attributes have no *real* parents or siblings.

- **ancestor**—This relationship contains the ancestors of the current, or context node. An ancestor is a parent or the parent's parent and so on. The same caveats about attribute and namespace nodes apply.

- **following-sibling**—This relationship contains all the following siblings of the context node. If the current, or context node is an attribute node or namespace node, the following-sibling axis is empty. That is a fancy way of saying you can't navigate anywhere from an attribute leaf without first going back to the parent node containing it. Because attributes can be added to an element at any time by changing the DTD in either the external or internal DTD subset, you can't depend on them for gross navigation.

- **preceding-sibling**—This relationship contains all the preceding siblings of the current, or context node. If the context node is an attribute node or namespace node, the preceding-sibling axis is empty, as mentioned previously.

- **following**—This relationship contains all nodes in the same document as the current, or context node that are after the context node in document order, excluding any descendents and excluding attribute nodes and namespace nodes.

- **preceding**—This relationship contains all nodes in the same document as the current, or context node that are before the context node in document order, excluding any ancestors and excluding attribute nodes and namespace nodes.

- **attribute**—This relationship contains the attributes of the current, or context node. The axis is empty unless the context node is an element. Although attributes participate in the usual representations of the directed graph that is a document tree, the arc between a node and the attributes it bears is more like a metaphysical dotted line sort of *aura* than true descendency. If you think of them as being on a higher plane than the physical relationships a node has with its parents, children, and siblings, you won't be far wrong.

- **namespace**—This relationship contains the namespace nodes of the current, or context node. The axis is empty unless the context node is an element. Because as stated in Chapter 6, "XML Namespaces," a namespace is a sort of shorthand for an `xmlns` attribute, this should be crystal clear by now. And because the namespace is really an attribute, either directly or as the namespace prefix shorthand for the same thing, the same caveats apply to them as apply to other attributes. This also raises an interesting point about namespace prefixes on attributes. Because a namespace prefix is exactly equivalent to an `xmlns` attribute when used on an element name, what exactly does it mean when you affix a namespace prefix to an attribute? This serves to underscore the metaphysical nature of namespaces and attributes in general.

- **self**—This relationship contains just the current, or context node itself, your ant-like self.

- **descendent-or-self**—This relationship contains the current, or context node and all the descendents of the context node. This enables the designer to address the contents of an element regardless of whether sub elements exist or are added later.

- **ancestor-or-self**—This relationship contains the current, or context node and all the ancestors of the context node. This enables the designer to address the entire branch of a document an element resides on regardless of whether additional layers of ancestor elements exist or are added later.

Note that between them, ancestor, descendent, following, preceding, and self account for the entire accessible document space centered on a single element. In other words, a document consists precisely of a single element and all its ancestors and descendents plus all preceding nodes excluding ancestors and all following nodes excluding descendents. This analysis excludes attribute "nodes" and namespace "nodes," all in a metaphysical relationship to the document proper and so, difficult to capture in terms of human relationships.

All these relationships could theoretically be expressed as equivalent ordered child relationships off the root, but for reasons of convenience are explicitly named relative to any location. This enables not only economy of expression but also a certain measure of robustness if the document changes in any way that affects the relationship of its various nodes.

> **Note**
>
> Sequentially numbered child relationships are, in fact, the basis of the tumbler or stepwise addressing notation described in the "Understanding XPointer" section of Chapter 9.

USING XPATH ABBREVIATIONS

Because XPath locations are expected to be used manually as well as automatically generated, there are a lot of abbreviations meant to save keystrokes and increase the legibility of complex location directions.

This short example shows how abbreviations can be used to save keystrokes. In the following document fragment, pretend you have navigated through the document and are now at the node named "chapter," which thereby becomes the context node. A location has the following three parts:

1. A relationship or axis followed by two immediately consecutive colons.
2. A node name or test, which can include namespace information. A node name or test can be followed by a further relationship or axis and a second node name or test, and so on.
3. A predicate, which is an expression that can be evaluated to yield further information about the intended location. Predicates can include functions and Boolean logical relationships. A predicate can also include a relationship or axis, to determine how the expression is to be applied.

The only mandatory part is the node name or test, because the other parts have default values. The following code snippet is used in the examples:

```
<chapter>
  <title>Now and Again</title>
  <paragraph lang="en-UK">
    <quote>
      This is the colour of darkness, that civilisation not be
      obscured by grey detail.
    </quote>
  </paragraph>
```

```
<paragraph>
  The above quote is from Prufrock, 1947…
</paragraph>
</chapter>
```

In the preceding document fragment, you might select all the child elements of chapter like this, assuming that chapter is the current node:

```
child::*
```

But because the child relationship is the default relationship in XPath, the same result could be achieved with

```
*
```

If you wanted to select the first paragraph element contained in the chapter, you could write

```
child::parargraph[position()= 1]
```

which includes all three parts of an XPath location, but again, it might be more expedient to save a few keystrokes and use an abbreviation

```
paragraph[1]
```

that is allowed by the abbreviation rules. Child is the default relationship and position() is the default expression in a predicate.

There are many other common abbreviations, and the possible permutations are very large, but the manner in which you can select a node by the value of an attribute warrants special consideration. The full syntax for selecting a paragraph element base on the value of the included lang attribute is

```
child::paragraph[attribute::lang="en-UK"]
```

but the abbreviated form would be

```
paragraph[@lang="en-UK"]
```

This makes the relationship slightly easier to grasp without puzzling out which colons are attached to what.

In the following list, italic names are arbitrary and can be replaced with any valid name. First listed is the unabbreviated syntax, then an equals sign, followed by the abbreviated syntax, if any, an N/A otherwise, an em-dash, and an explanation. The possible combinations of abbreviations and unabbreviated syntax are theoretically infinite, so this list is somewhat abbreviated:

> **child::*element-name* = *element-name***—selects the *element-name* element children of the current, or context node.
>
> **child::* = ***—selects all element children of the current, or context node.
>
> **child::text() = text()**—selects all text node children of the current, or context node.
>
> **attribute::*name* = @*name***—selects the *name* attribute of the current, or context node.

`attribute::*` = `@*`—selects all the attributes of the current, or context node.

`child::`*`element-name`*`[position()=1]` = *`element-name`*`[1]`—selects the first *element-name* child of the current, or context node.

`child::`*`element-name`*`[position()=last()]` = *`element-name`*`[last()]`—selects the last *element-name* child of the current, or context node.

`child::*/child::`*`element-name`* = `*/`*`element-name`*—selects all *element-name* grand-children of the current, or context node.

`/child::`*`document`*`/child::`*`chapter`*`[position()=5]/child::`*`section`*`[position()=2]` = `/`*`document`*`/`*`chapter`*`[5]/`*`section`*`[2]`—selects the second *section* of the fifth *chapter* of the *document*, which lies at the root and that arbitrary names can be replaced by anything of course.

`child::`*`chapter`*`/descendent::`*`element-name`* = *`chapter`*`//`*`element-name`*—selects the *element-name* element descendents of the *chapter* element children of the current, or context node.

`/descendent-or-self::node()/child::`*`element-name`* = `//`*`element-name`*—selects all the *element-name* descendents of the document root and thus selects all *element-name* elements in the same document as the current, or context node.

`/descendent-or-self::node()/child::`*`list-name`*`/child::`*`item`* = `//`*`list-name`*`/`*`item`*—selects all the *item* elements in the same document as the current, or context node that have a *list-name* parent.

`self::node()` = `.`—selects the current, or context node.

`self::`*`element-name`* — `N/A`—selects the current, or context node only if it is an *element-name*.

`/` = `/`—selects the document root.

`self::node()/descendent-or-self::node()/child::`*`chapter`*`[position()=8]` = `.//`*`chapter`*`[8]`—selects the eighth chapter element descendent of the current node.

`/descendent-or-self::node()/child::`*`element-name`* = `.//`*`element-name`*—selects the *element-name* element descendents of the current, or context node.

`parent::node()` = `..`—selects the parent of the current, or context node

`ancestor::*` = `N/A`—selects all the ancestors of the current, or context node

`parent::node()[attribute::`*`language`*`]` = `../@`*`language`*—selects the *language* attribute of the parent of the current, or context node.

`child::`*`element-name`*`[attribute::`*`language`*`="en-UK"]` = *`element-name`*`[@`*`language`*`="en-UK"]`—selects all *element-name* children of the current, or context node that have a *language* attribute with value "*en-UK.*"

`child::`*`element-name`*`[attribute::`*`language`*`="en-UK"][position()=5]` = *`element-name`*`[@`*`language`*`="en-UK"][5]`—selects the fifth *element-name* child of the current, or context node that has a *language* attribute with value "*en-UK.*"

`child::element-name[position()=5][attribute::language="en-UK"]` = *element-name*`[5][@language="en-UK"]`—selects the fifth *element-name* child of the current, or context node if that child has a *language* attribute with value "*en-UK.*"

`child::chapter[child::title="Introduction"]` = *chapter*`[title="Introduction"]`—selects the *chapter* children of the current, or context node that have one or more *title* children with string-value equal to "*Introduction.*"

`child::chapter[attribute::title]` = *chapter*`[@title]`—selects the *chapter* children of the current, or context node that have a *title* attribute.

`child::chapter[attribute::title and attribute::subtitle]` = *chapter*`[@title and @subtitle]`—selects all the *chapter* children of the current, or context node that have both a *title* attribute and a *subtitle* attribute.

`child::chapter[attribute::title or attribute::subtitle]` = *chapter*`[@title or @subtitle]`—selects all the *chapter* children of the current, or context node that have either a *title* attribute or a *subtitle* attribute.

XPATH CORE FUNCTIONS

Each function in the XPath function library is specified using a function prototype, which gives the return type, the name of the function, and the type of the arguments. If an argument type is followed by a question mark, then the argument is optional; otherwise, the argument is required.

NODE SET FUNCTIONS

The node set functions return information related in some way to individual nodes or node sets:

- *number* `last()`—The `last` function returns a number equal to the context size from the expression evaluation context. This is an obscure but precise way of saying that, if the current, or context node contains a string, `last()` is the rough equivalent of `size-of(string)`. But if the position of the context is offset into the node by means of a predicate from the location of the containing element, `last()` might better be thought of as `sizeof(substring)`.

- *number* `position()`—The `position` function returns a number equal to the context position from the expression evaluation context. This is an obscure but precise way of saying that, if the current, or context node contains a string, `position()` is the rough equivalent of current position of the character cursor within that string. This position can be offset by means of a predicate from the location of the current, or context node.

- *number* `count(node-set)`—The `count` function returns the number of nodes in the argument node-set. This is pretty straightforward. If you've selected a group of nodes by any of the node selection mechanisms, this tells you how many nodes were selected.

- *node-set* `id(object)`—The `id` function selects elements by their unique ID and returns a node-set list. This is one more way of selecting a set of nodes.

- *string* `local-name(`*node-set?*`)`—The `local-name` function returns the local part of the expanded-name of the node in the argument node-set that is first in document order. If the argument is missing, the node-set is the current, or context node.

- *string* `namespace-uri(`*node-set?*`)`—The `namespace-uri` function returns the namespace URI of the expanded-name of the node in the argument node-set that is first in document order. If the argument is missing, the node-set is the current, or context node.

- *string* `name(node-set?)`—The `name` function returns a string containing a namespace-qualified name representing the expanded-name of the node in the argument node-set that is first in document order. A namespace-qualified name is the node name plus the namespace prefix associated with the expanded namespace URI. If the argument is missing, the node-set is the current, or context node.

STRING FUNCTIONS

The string functions allow string manipulations of the contents of nodes and attributes:

- *string* `string(`*object?*`)`—The `string` function converts an object to a string. If a node object contains a number, it is converted to a roughly equivalent string, but this function is not meant to convert numbers for presentation to a user. If the object is a node list, the string value of the first node in the list in document order is returned. If the object parameter is missing, the string value of the current, or context node is returned. If the node is empty, the null string is returned.

- *string* `concat(`*string*`, `*string*`, `*string**`)`—The `concat` function returns the concatenation of its arguments. This is one of the most basic of string operations, allowing individual parts of a string to be picked up from any number of places and assembled one or more pieces at a time.

- *boolean* `starts-with(`*string*`, `*string*`)`—The `starts-with` function returns true if the first argument string starts with the second argument string, and otherwise returns false.

- *boolean* `contains(`*string*`, `*string*`)`—The `contains` function returns true if the first argument string contains the second argument string, and otherwise returns false.

- *string* `substring-before(`*string*`, `*string*`)`—The `substring-before` function returns the substring of the first argument string that precedes the first occurrence of the second argument string in the first argument string, or the empty string if the first argument string does not contain the second argument string. This enables you to edit the source string to trim an unwanted tail from the string before grabbing it.

- *string* `substring-after(`*string*`, `*string*`)`—The `substring-after` function returns the substring of the first argument string that follows the first occurrence of the second argument string in the first argument string, or the empty string if the first argument string does not contain the second argument string. This enables you to edit the source string to trim an unwanted head from the string before grabbing it.

- *string* `substring(string, number, number?)`—The `substring` function returns the substring of the first argument starting at the position specified in the second argument with length specified in the third argument. This enables you to edit the source string to select a substring of known length from the string before grabbing it.

- *number* `string-length(string?)`—The `string-length` returns the number of characters in the string. If the argument is omitted, it defaults to the context node converted to a string, in other words the string-value of the context node.

- *string* `normalize-space(string?)`—The `normalize-space` function returns the argument string with whitespace normalized by stripping leading and trailing whitespace and replacing sequences of whitespace characters by a single space. Whitespace characters are the same as those allowed by the XML 1.0 Recommendation.

- *string* `translate(string, string, string)`—The `translate` function returns the first argument string with occurrences of characters in the second argument string replaced by the character at the corresponding position in the third argument string. This enables you to edit the source string to translate uppercase letters to lowercase or any similar transformation.

BOOLEAN FUNCTIONS

The Boolean functions perform various Boolean tests or operations on their arguments and returns a value based on the test or operation:

- *boolean* `boolean(object)`—The `boolean` function converts its argument to a Boolean value. If the object is zero, empty, or zero length, the Boolean value is false, but true otherwise.

- *boolean* `not(boolean)`—The `not` function returns true if its argument is false, and false otherwise. In other words, this function returns the negation of its Boolean value.

- *boolean* `true()`—The `true` function returns true.

- *boolean* `false()`—The `false` function returns false.

- *boolean* `lang(string)`—The `lang` function returns true or false depending on whether the language of the context node as specified by xml:lang attributes is the same as or is a sub-language of the language specified by the argument string.

NUMBER FUNCTIONS

The number functions perform various numeric operations on their arguments, performing conversions as needed:

- *number* `number(object?)`—The `number` function converts its argument to a number.

- *number* `sum(node-set)`—The `sum` function returns the sum, for each node in the argument node-set, of the result of converting the string-values of the node to a number.

- *number* `floor(number)`—The `floor` function returns the largest (closest to positive infinity) number that is not greater than the argument and that is an integer.

- *number* `ceiling(`*number*`)`—The `ceiling` function returns the smallest (closest to negative infinity) number that is not less than the argument and that is an integer.

- *number* `round(`*number*`)`—The `round` function returns the number that is closest to the argument and that is an integer.

USING XPATH PREDICATES

Like any programming API, even though the area of applicability is deliberately curtailed, the XPath functions can be combined and used in almost infinite ways. In addition, many of the more complex functions are most useful in combinations with other APIs or with XSLT or other application that actually manipulates the document. Although it's very handy to be able to address sub-strings within a text node, for example, unless you are going to use that information to alter the document, or another document using that sub-string, it's little more than an academic exercise.

So an active imagination is a large part of deciding how to use the predicate capabilities. Without first deciding what you want to do, knowing what you can do is of little use. But at the same time, knowing what you can do is a spur to the imaginary faculty, and can be of great help when deciding whether a thing is possible or not.

Look at the following simple example to illustrate the general principles. The string functions can be used to perform simple manipulation of text nodes in an XML document. Assuming you had a document fragment that looked like this:

```
<purchase-date id="pd123">04/17/2000</purchase-date>
```

You could use the following command combination to extract the year:

```
substring-after(substring-after(string(id("pd123")),"/"),"/")
```

That would yields the string "2000." What you want to do with the information is entirely up to you. The `id()` function is used to extract the node with the value of "pd123" and then used the `string()` function to convert the contents of that node to a string. Then the `string-after()` function was used twice to clip first the "04/" and then the "17/" from the resulting string, yielding the year "2000" in string format. Of course, at that point, you could have wrapped the whole thing up in

```
string(number("2000") div 2)
```

if you preferred the last millennium to this one.

PROBLEMS WITH HTML ANCHORS AND LINKS

Traditional links and pointers are, on the one hand, far too simple to accommodate the ways people can imagine using them. On the other, they are way too complex. In HTML and carried over into XHTML there are quite a few ways to link to an object or location using a large number of attribute names to describe the actual hyperlink. These ways are as follows:

- As a hyperlink within an anchor, or `<a>` tag, which can be used as both linking element and target, a confusing merging of functions, with an *href* attribute when used as a link and a name, or id reference, when used as the target of a link.

- As a hyperlink within an image, or `<img>` tag, which actually has three possible links built in, the *src*, *usemap*, and *longdesc* attributes. This sort of link indicates a primitive form of transclusion, which has been subsumed by the more general XML features described in XLink.

- As a hyperlink within a link, or `<link>` tag, with an *href* attribute. These links can indicate relationships between HTML documents and may, or might not, be presented by a user agent in some way. The manner in which these links are used is not terribly uniform and very much browser dependent.

- As a hyperlink fragment within a path, or `<base>` tag, with an *href* attribute. The fragment identified by the *href* attribute is used to construct a complete URL.

- As a hyperlink within an area, or `<area>` tag, with an *href* attribute. This is a very primitive form of indirect, or out-of-line linking, which has been subsumed by the more general XML features described in XLink.

- As a hyperlink within a frame, or `<frame>` tag, with *src* and *longdesc* attributes. This sort of link indicates a primitive form of transclusions, which have been subsumed by the more general XML features described in XLink.

- As a hyperlink within an inline frame, or `<iframe>` tag, with *src* and *longdesc* attributes. This sort of link indicates a primitive form of transclusion, which has been subsumed by the more general XML features described in XLink.

- As a hyperlink within an applet, or `<applet>` tag, with *codebase* and *archive* attributes. Both of these represent the source of resources used in a manner similar to what can now be more uniformly done by XML-style transclusion, which has been subsumed by the more general XML features described in XLink.

- As a hyperlink within an object, or `<object>` tag, with *classid*, *codebase*, *data*, *archive*, and *usemap* attributes. All these are primitive forms of transclusion, which have been subsumed by the more general XML features described in XLink.

- As a hyperlink within a parameter, or `<param>` tag, with a *ref* attribute. Again, this is a primitive form of transclusion.

- As a hyperlink within a quote or block quote, or the `<q>` and `<blockquote>` tags, each with a *cite* attribute. This link may or may not be implemented by the HTML user agent.

- As a hyperlink within an insertion or deletion, or the `<ins>` and `<del>` tags, each with a *cite* attribute. This link may or may not be implemented by the HTML user agent.

- As a hyperlink within a head, or `<head>` tag, with a *profile* attribute. This link may or may not be implemented by the HTML user agent.

- As a hyperlink within a body, or `<body>` tag, with a *background* attribute that implements a transclusion-style incorporation of an image within a document.
- As a hyperlink within a script, or `<script>` tag, with an *input* attribute.
- As a hyperlink within an input, or `<input>` tag, with a *usemap* attribute.
- As a hyperlink within a form, or `<form>` tag, which has the *action* attribute.

There is little consistency of the syntax used to link to the external source, other than the sometime use of href attributes to imply some sort of hypertext link with the src attribute relegated to implying some sort of transclusion. But the bewildering array of attribute names referring to linked locations is both error-prone and overly complex.

For example, an external link in an HTML anchor (`<a>`) element looks like

```
<a href="URI"></a>
```

but a similar link in an image map is referenced indirectly as

```
<img src="URI-1" usemap="URI-2" ismap>
```

The distinctions between the names of attributes used for transclusion, in the manner of an HTML img tag, and those used for traversable hyperlinks might have made sense in a pre-XLink world. But there's little reason for these artificial attempts to predefine behavior now, because XLink completely generalizes link syntax and separates different types of links by specific attributes describing the actual type of link being made. Instead of a toolbox of specialized links with specific purposes, the new linking toolkit enables a handful of tools to perform multiple tasks.

Many of the special attribute names were an attempt to identify the exact nature of the link, or to tell the processor what sort of thing should (or could) be done with it. Many of the *special* link names also contributed to redundancy, so error recovery was easier. Many of the linking attributes have never been implemented in a commercial browser. The *cite* attribute for quotes and textual change markup for example, or the *longdesc* attribute.

A uniform method of describing links, and a way in which choices could be presented, would go a long way toward ensuring that browser creators actually implemented the entire recommendation, not just the parts they liked or found easy to do.

GETTING DOWN TO CASES

Because you can't actually do much of anything with an XPath relationship or predicate except point at something with it, there's little you can say about them other than that simple fact. The various functions XPath defines are used merely as ways of obtaining the indices and determine the conditions that allow you to point more precisely.

XLINK AND XPOINTER

In this chapter

UNDERSTANDING THE NEW XML LINKING TOOLKIT

This chapter examines the two linking mechanisms used by XML, Xlink, and XPointer. The first addresses how links are actually created and traversed, whereas the second is used to address XML document fragments used to build up new documents from parts of old ones by extending the addressing capabilities of XPath. XPointer adds string matching and absolute cursor and range positioning within elements, so one can surgically address and excise a single word as easily as a range that encompasses a major portion of an external document.

> **Caution**
>
> The XLink specification is still in working draft but is proceeding toward Recommendation status rapidly. We'll treat the current draft as if it were the final version but please be aware that some details may change. Please reference the current version of XLink at `http://w3.org/tr/`.

XLink extends the familiar HTML linking anchor tag (and other tags with linking functionality) with extensive additions to that basic technology that, it must be remembered, is the foundation and heart of the hyperlinked World Wide Web. To the basic HTML anchor repertoire of links, anchors, and URLs, XLink adds

- Links to multiple destinations
- Bi-directional links
- Links that point to read-only documents (using XPath)
- Links that are labeled with descriptive titles clarifying how the link is used
- Links that expand in place (a process called *transclusion*) to embed external content in an XML document as images are embedded now
- Links that are automatically traversed when a document is loaded. This can allow the inclusion of external content or the substitution of one page for another.

Whereas HTML supports limited transclusion in the form of the `<img>` and `<object>` tags, XLink enables any external entity to be used in the same way.

> **Note**
>
> The current W3C specification for the XPath/XPointer/XLink trio is actually less powerful in some ways than defined in the current XSL specification. Although this will surely change, be aware that there's more than one way to link documents in the growing XML suite of standards.

XPointer is the working edge of XLink, based on XPath but adding a few enhancements of its own. XPointer can address spans within a document as well as single locations, even down to strings within the document and even without any special tags in the document provided by the author. Where XPath is based on *nodes*, special locations within the document identified by tags, XPointer enables shifting the exact location of the pointer off center, to enable the addressing of individual characters, strings, and even spans that cross element boundaries.

Together with XPath, XPointer ensures that pointers are readable and usable by human beings, as opposed to machine-readable byte counts or hashed indices that a human couldn't use without help. XPointer even has a special syntax called *bare name addressing* designed to enable pointing into HTML documents using the simple `URI#anchor-name` syntax instead of the `URI#xpointer(id("anchor-name"))`, to support the vast amount of legacy text available on the Web.

USING XLINK, THE EXTENSIBLE LINKING LANGUAGE

Enter XLink. Because XML has no fixed set of tags, a means of declaring links associated with any element is needed. Because you can't depend on contextual information to tell you what to do with the link, all the subtle differences in treatment seen in the HTML examples of link types above had to be accounted for with explicit descriptions. And because everyone was agreed that extra features were needed, a variety of link types beyond what HTML had used were added to the mix. Examples include links that can be traversed in either direction and links offering multiple destinations, which can be selected by the user when the link is selected. So a single link can behave like a pull-down or pop-up window.

And although it might seem complex, in some ways it's actually a simplification of the current status quo. Instead of a long list of specific elements and associated attributes with link or link-like behavior, there is now one mechanism that can be used either to duplicate existing practices, or to expand the possibilities for linking behavior in ways difficult to imagine (unless you hail from the HyTime world, the original model and impetus behind the XML linking standards).

On the other hand, XLink doesn't begin to cover the complex relationships between linked objects that HTML attributes like `archive` or `usemap` do. More work is needed.

The following sections investigate specific XLink features that are substantially different from previous HTML linking technologies.

ACCESSING THE ENTIRE DOCUMENT

Using XPath and XPointer, XLink is able to access any part of the document, not just the root and sundry named and anchored parts. This means that a quote, for example, could be inserted into a document through *transclusion*, logically copying the content of an external file into a host document, and attributed at the same time. So if you want to find the source of the quote, you simply follow a link, perhaps one of many with each link descriptively labeled, to the actual text corpus from which the quote was abstracted. Or, alternatively, a researcher or scholar, even without write access to the text that uses the quote, could insert such a link from the outside, as the technological equivalent of sticky notes when an external document is viewed from a host document. Because multiple links are permitted, any number of notes could refer to the same location or item, and different scholars could use their own local host documents to annotate the same source document with their own research and conclusions.

> **Caution**
>
> XLink, like frames, permits uncontrolled transclusion of the copyrighted contents of other sites or authors if improperly used. Using other people's copyrighted images or words without permission is theft, even if you attribute the source to avoid the stigma of plagiarism. There have been several successful lawsuits against sites that appropriated content illegally, so be sure to obtain permission in advance or seek the advice of a copyright attorney before incorporating outside content into your own site.

Although *transclusion* may be a new word to you, the concept is very simple. It means that an external file is included within a document as if it actually existed within it, although it remains separate in reality.

XLink makes this sort of thing possible with almost any content, not just images. If a text file is transcluded into a host document, you can search for the text within the host document as if it were present in the host document all along. Although this more inclusive virtual document is put together on the fly, exists only for the moment, and will disappear when you're done viewing and interacting with it, it behaves just as if it were real.

> **Note**
>
> Given the existence of a large text corpus on the Internet such as the Gutenberg Project—as well as more specialized collections of documents and graphical replicas of incunabula and medieval manuscripts—the opportunities for online scholarship are multiplying without limit. Existing guidelines for electronic scholarship can be found at the Text Encoding Initiative Consortium home page at `http://www.tei-c.org/`.

One of the more interesting advantages of XLink is its capability to create links into multimedia non-text files. So you can link to more than text and with far more granularity than existing HTML links can provide.

Of course, there's more to XLink than scholarship, and the possibilities for new types of interactive documents without the complexities of proprietary implementations of Dynamic HTML expand the potential of the Web and offer ample scope for the XML document designer to explore the frontiers of creativity and power.

XLINK LINKING TYPES

XLink makes a somewhat artificial and redundant distinction between simple links and extended links, with simple links being the equivalent of simple HTML-style anchor (`<a href="URI" attributes >locator</a>`) and image (`<img src="URI" attributes />`) links. The extended links offer the full power of XLink to the designer, although they're not immediately understandable by legacy HTML browsers—but neither are the new simple links.

Other than a dubious sort of backward compatibility and the capability to use the familiar `href=URI` attribute on an anchor look-alike to construct a link, there seems to be little or no reason to use the simple syntax. And the difficulty of migrating a link from the old simple syntax to the new extended version would seem to argue for starting out clean with the new syntax so that links can easily evolve as a site does. The following sections provide a quick overview of the two main link types, simple and extended. and

SIMPLE LINKS

A *simple link* involves one local and one remote resource, and the link can only be traversed in one direction and is always inline. *Inline* means only that there is a local resource that participates in the link.

Caution

> In the following example, the DTD might or might not be read to determine default attribute values, so in most documents you should explicitly set each and every attribute. This example skips that precaution to simplify the XML involved.

A simple link can be constructed using some variation of the following DTD definition and XML statements:

```
<!ELEMENT simpleLink ANY>
<!ATTLIST simpleLink
  xlink:type    (simple)           #FIXED "simple"
  xlink:href    CDATA              #REQUIRED
  xlink:role    NMTOKEN            #FIXED "anyPredefinedRole"
  xlink:title   CDATA              #IMPLIED
  xlink:show    (new
                |replace
                |embed
                |undefined)        #FIXED "replace"
  xlink:actuate (onLoad
                |onRequest
                |undefined)        #FIXED "onRequest" >
```

This particular definition works as the equivalent of an HTML anchor element. For behavior that mimics an HTML image element, redefine the `xlink:actuate` attribute as `onLoad` and the `xlink:show` attribute as `embed`. You might want to declare the content model as `EMPTY` as well.

You could use the simple link like this for typical hypertext link behavior:

```
<simplelink href="URI">Some content</simplelink>
```

Or, if you defined the simple link as an empty element with `show="embed"` source and `actuate="onLoad"` behavior, that is, automatically transclude the referenced content when the host document is loaded, you could use it like this:

```
<simplelink href="URI" />
```

Of course the appropriate attributes, `show` and `actuate`, would have to be defined in the `simplelink` ATTLIST, as defined in the XLink Element Skeletons section below.

EXTENDED LINKS

Extended links can include any number of resources, none of which have to be local. If there are no local resources, the link is also out-of-line, in other words, uses external documents and locations only and is located there rather than in the host document. Otherwise, the link is inline.

Caution

As with the previous example of a simple link, the DTD for the following example might or might not be read to determine default attribute values. In the interest of simplicity, attributes are not explicitly set in this example.

An extended link is more complex to construct. However, the capability to include more than one resource in a single link, offer more than trivial link functionality, and extend the link at will makes it far more versatile. although a simple link requires no particular content, an extended link contains several content elements that contribute to the total functionality of the link. The following DTD could be used to define an extended link content profile equivalent to the simple link in the previous section:

```
<!ELEMENT extendedlink (locatorElement, arcElement, resourceElement)>
<!ATTLIST extendedlink
  xlink:type      (extended)              #FIXED "extended" >

<!ELEMENT locatorElement EMPTY>
<!ATTLIST locatorElement
  xlink:type      (locator)              #FIXED "locator"
  xlink:href      CDATA                  #REQUIRED
  xlink:role      (remote)               #FIXED "remoteRoleType"
  xlink:title     CDATA                  #IMPLIED

<!ELEMENT arcElement EMPTY>
<!ATTLIST arcElement
  xlink:type      (arc)                  #FIXED "arc"
  xlink:from      (local)                #FIXED "local"
  xlink:to        (remote)               #FIXED "remote"
  xlink:show      (new
                  |replace
                  |embed
                  |undefined)            #IMPLIED
  xlink:actuate (onLoad
                  |onRequest
                  |undefined)            #IMPLIED >

<!ELEMENT resourceElement ANY>
<!ATTLIST resourceElement
  xlink:role      (local)                #FIXED "local" >
```

In this example, the arc element uses predefined xlink:to and xlink:from attributes. You could use this extended link like this:

```
<extendedlink>
  <locatorElement xlink:href="URI" />
  <arcElement />
  <resourceElement>click here</resourceElement>
</extendedlink>
```

Far more complex link types are possible but this really isn't much more complicated then the simple link above. The possibility of extending the link still further makes this syntax far more versatile. The content model of the extended link can be made more general and the fixed to and fixed from points of the arc made definable, so multiple resources can be included in the same link:

```
<!ELEMENT extendedlink (locatorElement | arcElement | resourceElement)*>
<!ATTLIST extendedlink
  xlink:type     (extended)              #FIXED "extended" >

<!ELEMENT locatorElement EMPTY>
<!ATTLIST locatorElement
  xlink:type     (locator)               #FIXED "locator"
  xlink:href     CDATA                   #REQUIRED
  xlink:role     NMTOKEN                 #IMPLIED
  xlink:title    CDATA                   #IMPLIED>

<!ELEMENT arcElement EMPTY>
<!ATTLIST arcElement
  xlink:from     NMTOKEN                 #IMPLIED
  xlink:to       NMTOKEN                 #IMPLIED
  xlink:type     (arc)                   #FIXED "arc"
  xlink:show     (new
                 |replace
                 |embed
                 |undefined)             #IMPLIED
  xlink:actuate (onLoad
                 |onRequest
                 |undefined)             #IMPLIED >

<!ELEMENT resourceElement ANY>
<!ATTLIST resourceElement
  xlink:role     (local)                 #FIXED "local" >
```

In this example, the arc element uses a predefined xlink:type of "arc" to identify what kind of XLink element it is but leaves the values for xlink:to and xlink:from undefined so that they can have values associated with them in the XML document itself. You could use the extended link like this:

```
<extendedlink>
  <locatorElement xlink:role="parent" xlink:href="URI-1" xlink:title="Doc-1" />
  <locatorElement xlink:role="child" xlink:href="URI-2"  xlink:title="Doc-2" />
  <locatorElement xlink:role="child" xlink:href="URI-3"  xlink:title="Doc-3" />
  <arcElement xlink:from="parent" xlink:to="child" />
  <arcElement xlink:from="child" xlink:to="parent" />
  <resourceElement>Link to related file here.</resourceElement>
</extendedlink>
```

There is no pre-defined behavior associated with this sort of link, which presents a potential choice of a link between the parent resource and either of two children, or between either of two children and a parent resource. A user agent might offer a pop-up menu of choices or any other presentation with similar end results.

DECIPHERING XLINK SYNTAX

An XLink is usually defined in an XML DTD by a series of attributes, most of which are optional. The value of the first attribute in the following list, type, is also carried by a corresponding set of predefined elements with the same names as the type attribute values in the

XLink namespace. This means that you can use XLinks in your documents without defining linking elements in your own DTD by using the predefined XLink tags, a handy simplification.

XLink elements can be either any XML element with an included XLink `type` attribute in its `ATTLIST` or an XLink element proper, as defined by the XLink DTD in the XLink namespace. When we refer to an XLink element in this chapter, we mean both possibilities interchangeably unless specifically limited to one or another. Other than `type`, all the attributes listed below can be associated with either the XLink elements proper or with elements from your own DTD that have been defined as XLink elements by the addition of an XLink `type` attribute. The XLink attributes are illustrated in the following list:

- `type`—Takes one of the seven following values:
  - `simple` acts much as does an HTML anchor element, the `<a href="URI"></a>` tag pair. The `simple` attribute corresponds to the tag of the same name in the XLink namespace. Although an `extended` link is capable of exactly the same behavior, the special `simple` type allows a syntax that looks quite a bit like an HTML link for the sake of ease of use and familiarity.
  - `extended` enables you to include multiple linking elements within a containing extended link element. The `extended` attribute corresponds to the tag of the same name in the XLink namespace.
  - `locator` elements, those which contain a locator attribute, are meant to be contained within an extended link element. They are the equivalent of the content of a hyperlink in HTML that lets you see where the link is located in the document and select it. The `locator` attribute value corresponds to the tag of the same name in the XLink namespace.
  - `arc` defines traversal behavior within extended links. The `arc` attribute value corresponds to the tag of the same name in the XLink namespace.
  - `resource` defines a visible link part that participates in any XLink link. The `resource` attribute value corresponds to the tag of the same name in the XLink namespace.
  - `title` defines a readable string associated with the link that can be displayed by a user agent. The `title` attribute value corresponds to the tag of the same name in the XLink namespace.
  - `none` indicates that the element has no XLink significance. The `none` attribute value corresponds to the tag of the same name in the XLink namespace.

  Within the XLink namespace, these seven values are also defined as elements and can be used directly, for example:
  ```
  <xlink:simple href="URI" attributes />
  ```
  The behavior of these seven link types is explored in more detail later in this chapter. A `type` attribute is required on all XLink element types.

- `href`—The attribute that defines where the target resource is located. The `href` attribute is not allowed on `extended`, `arc`, `resource`, and `title` type elements and is required on `locator` elements.

- `to`—One end of an arc, or link connecting two resources. The value should be an `IDREF` which refers to the resource `role`. The to attribute is not allowed on `simple`, `extended`, `locator`, `resource`, and `title` type elements.

- `from`—The other end of the arc, or link connecting two resources. The value should be an `IDREF` which refers to the resource `role`. The from attribute is not allowed on `simple`, `extended`, `locator`, `resource`, and `title` type elements.

> **Note**
>
> The syntax of `to` and `from` seems a little fuzzy to me, because the specification allows a single `from` or `to` value to describe the link between multiple instances of documents with the same `role` name. So although the role is not an `id`, within the typical XML meaning implying uniqueness, the reference to these multiple role instances implies that they're singular.

- `show`—Takes three values in simple links:
  - `new` creates a new window in which to display the content. This should be done with caution, if at all.
  - `replace` does what a hyperlink typically does now, replaces the browser window contents with new content
  - `parse` is intended to grab the content of the remote resource and insert it into a document as if it were originally included there.

  The `show` attribute is not allowed on `locator`, `resource`, and `title` type elements.

- `actuate`—Can take two values in simple links:
  - `user`—enables the user choose when to activate a link.
  - `auto`—automatically activates the link.

  The `actuate` attribute is not allowed on `locator`, `resource`, and `title` type elements.

> **Caution**
>
> Links that are followed or updated automatically—as can be done even now in HTML by client pull or server push (to force a page update from the user agent or the server, respectively)—are quite often pernicious and evil. Automatic replacement of entire pages is hostile to persons who might become confused by the change or cannot easily use the back function quickly enough to escape the clutches of such ill-conceived schemes. Screen readers often start reading from the top of the page every time a page is refreshed, although this aural "flicker" might be invisible to a sighted user. Likewise, automatic invocation of `new` pages is an execrable habit when used by Web designers to make their sites "sticky" at the expense of users with limited vision, memory, or dexterity. Using automatic links to replace content entirely or create a new window is contrary to the spirit of the WAI; the only legitimate use would be to parse and insert transcluded content such as the XLink equivalents of HTML `img` tags.

- `role`—Contains a string meant to describe the link's purpose to process the link in some way. Although the string should be human readable, it's not meant for display. An `arc` element can use the `role` attributes associated with a resource to identify the end points of the arc and the direction taken to traverse the arc. The `role` attribute is not allowed on `title` type elements.

- `title`—Contains a string meant to display a human-readable description of the purpose of the link. Although the WAI suggests that link content itself contain human-readable text describing the link rather than non-informative phrases such as "click here," the fact that any element might be used as an XLink means that alternative means of conveying this information should be available. The `title` attribute is a uniform mechanism for supplying explanatory text in any situation.

The preceding attributes are used in elements, as are any XML attributes, and the `xlink:type` attribute is the key to the functionality of the element. For ease of use, XLink also predefines elements with names identical to each type so you don't have to define XLink mechanisms in your DTD, but can use XLink elements directly from the XLink namespace. The next subsection covers skeleton element definitions for XLink elements in a DTD.

XLINK ELEMENT SKELETONS

This section explicitly shows the attributes taken by each type of XLink element. Not every attribute is necessary and the `type` attribute might be replaced by explicit elements predefined within the XLink namespace. In that case, you can use them in your documents directly, and needn't define XLinks in your DTD. But for internationalization and localization, the capability to define XLinks with meaningful names might simplify life for XML authors whose native language is other than English. The DTD syntax should always be considered primary, with a handy shortcut provided for English speakers in the form of the predefined elements.

SIMPLE ELEMENTS

A simple link with any name can be defined with the following syntax in your XML DTD:

```
<!ELEMENT simpleElement ANY>
<!ATTLIST simpleElement
  xlink:type    (simple)           #FIXED "simple"
  xlink:href    CDATA              #REQUIRED
  xlink:role    NMTOKEN            #IMPLIED
  xlink:title   CDATA              #IMPLIED
  xlink:show    (new
                |replace
                |embed
                |undefined)        #IMPLIED
  xlink:actuate (onLoad
                |onRequest
                |undefined)        #IMPLIED >
```

The most significant attributes in the previous skeleton are `show` and `actuate`, which together describe how the link will behave.

PART

I

CH

9

Tip from

 LeeAnne.com
Words to weave by

The only things that actually exist in the XLink namespace are the attributes themselves, together with their corresponding predefined elements, so your DTD must declare explicit XLinks if you want to use your own names.

An equivalent link is predefined within the XLink namespace with the name `simple`. You can use it directly in your code if you declare the XLink namespace like this:

```
<mydocument xmlns:xlink="http://www.w3.org/XML/XLink/" >
  …
  <xlink:simple href="URI" actuate="onRequest" attributes >
  …
  </xlink:simple>
  …
</mydocument>
```

Using the predefined XLink links offers some hope that the link might be understood by your user agent even without access to the document DTD, and save the trouble of declaring XLink mechanisms in your DTD—which is not nearly as convenient as simply using the predefined elements. A simple element has no significant child elements within the XLink namespace so it cannot be modified by other XLink elements.

EXTENDED ELEMENTS

An extended element enables the full range of XLink linking mechanisms to be used, allowing multidirectional links with multiple destinations to be created either in or out of line:

```
<!ELEMENT extendedElement ANY>
<!ATTLIST extendedElement
  xlink:type    (simple)              #FIXED "simple"
  xlink:role    NMTOKEN               #IMPLIED
  xlink:title   CDATA                 #IMPLIED
  xlink:show    (new
                |replace
                |embed
                |undefined)           #IMPLIED
  xlink:actuate (onLoad
                |onRequest
                |undefined)           #IMPLIED >
```

Extended elements can include multiple destinations and are the real heart of XLink because they implement the extended functionality required to go beyond the mere one-way hyper-link defined in HTML and XHTML. An extended element can have significant `locator`, `arc`, `resource`, and `title` XLink children, which is to say these children actually *do* something.

LOCATOR ELEMENTS

A locator element enables you to identify the end points of an XLink linking arc:

```
    <!ELEMENT locatorElement EMPTY>
    <!ATTLIST locatorElement
      xlink:type    (locator)             #FIXED "locator"
      xlink:href    CDATA                 #REQUIRED
      xlink:role    NMTOKEN               #IMPLIED
      xlink:title   CDATA                 #IMPLIED>
```

A locator element can have a `title` XLink child.

ARC ELEMENTS

An arc element describes the actual linking arc between XLink locations, providing traversal rules that enable the user agent to know in what direction the arc points and by what display mechanism the resource at the end of the arc should be displayed:

```
<!ELEMENT arcElement EMPTY>
<!ATTLIST arcElement
  xlink:type     (arc)                #FIXED "arc"
  xlink:role     NMTOKEN              #IMPLIED
  xlink:title    CDATA                #IMPLIED
  xlink:show     (new
                 |replace
                 |embed
                 |undefined)          #IMPLIED
  xlink:actuate  (onLoad
                 |onRequest
                 |undefined)          #IMPLIED >
  xlink:from     NMTOKEN              #IMPLIED
  xlink:to       NMTOKEN              #IMPLIED
```

An arc element can have a `title` XLink child.

RESOURCE ELEMENTS

Resource elements identify resources that participate in the link, the visible text or other element that can be selected in some way to actuate the link or call up a branching mechanism to choose from a list of possible actions.

```
<!ELEMENT resourceElement ANY>
<!ATTLIST resourceElement
  xlink:type     (resource)           #FIXED "resource"
  xlink:role     NMTOKEN              #IMPLIED
  xlink:title    CDATA                #IMPLIED>
```

A resource element has no significant XLink children.

TITLE ELEMENTS

Title elements contain human-readable text that the user agent or browser can present to the user when needed for understanding.

```
<!ELEMENT titleElement ANY>
<!ATTLIST titleElement
  xlink:type     (title)              #FIXED "title"
  xlink:title    CDATA                #IMPLIED
```

A title element has no significant XLink children.

SIMPLE LINKS REVISITED

A simple link is more or less what HTML does now, combining the functions of locator and link in a single element. Because this is XML, the link has to have a namespace. Because this is XLink, there are several new attributes that describe the behavior of the link. You should define the names and namespace of the special XLink attributes in the DTD, because it makes the resulting code cleaner to look at. Here are two examples of what your XML linking element might first look like with the XML namespace declared in the DTD, and then second without the XLink namespace declared in the DTD

```
<anchor href="pricelist.xml"
  type="simple"
  role="price list"
  title="Price List"
  show="replace"
  actuate="user">Price List</anchor>
```

PART

I

CH

9

compared with no DTD declaration:

```
<anchor xmlns:xlink="http://www.w3.org/XML/XLink/"
  xlink:type="simple"
  xlink:href="pricelist.xml"
  xlink:role="price list"
  xlink:title="Price List"
  xlink:show="replace"
  xlink:actuate="user">Price List</anchor>
```

Although XML, in general, is more verbose than HTML, the excessive use of namespaces makes it marginally harder to use. Taking the opportunity to define XLink attributes in the elements more commonly used as links might make the resulting code easier to read especially if your native language is not English. And of course this assumes that your target XML has access to and validates against the document DTD. If not, you'll have to use the XML namespace always and depend on the possibility that the XLink namespace value will be implemented as a switch in the user agent.

Contrast both of the preceding examples with the roughly equivalent but very terse XHTML tag, which takes advantage of the XHTML DTD but doesn't enable you to take advantage of quite the flexibility inherent in XLink method:

```
<a href="pricelist.xml">Price List</a>
```

Another alternative, which would combine some of the advantages of both methods, is to coerce the element into the XLink namespace like this:

```
<xlink:a href="pricelist.xml"
  type="simple"
  role="price list"
  title="Price List"
  show="replace"
  actuate="user">Price List</xlink:a>
```

Of course, you must have previously declared the XLink namespace.

The following is an example using presentation MathML, showing a simple link that you can view in Figure 9.1:

```
<math>
 <mrow>
  <mi>y</mi>
   <mo>=</mo>
```

```
<mi></mi>
<mfrac href="URI" xml:link="simple">
  <mn>1</mn>
  <msqrt>
  <mrow>
  <msup>
    <mi>x</mi>
    <mn>2</mn>
  </msup>
  <mo>+</mo>
  <mn>1</mn>
  </mrow>
  </msqrt>
  </mfrac>
 </mrow>
</math>
```

Figure 9.1
A link is present but not indicated on the entirety of a mathematical statement as viewed in Amaya, the W3C browser.

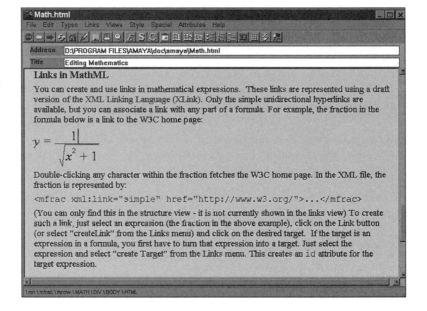

EXTENDED LINKS REVISITED

Extended links are where all the fun is. They enable you to place outgoing virtual links in documents you can't actually modify and other fancy stuff. In addition, an extended link is far easier to update if the type of link changes during the existence of the document—to include other resources, for example, or to enable the link to be traversed in both directions.

The following is an example that creates a two-way link in an arbitrary document:

```
<xlink:extended href="URI"
  type="extended"
  role="price list"
  title="Price List"
  showdefault="replace"
```

```
      actuatedefault="user">
Price List
</xlink:extended>
```

INLINE LINKS

An *inline link* is one in which the content of the link serves as a participating element of the link. More simply, an inline link behaves like the HTML `<a href="URI">`*Selection Text*`</a>` where *Selection Text* activates the link.

The following code snippet is an example of an inline link:

```
<anchor xlink:href="URI" attributes >Selection Text</anchor>
```

As with all links, the elided attributes should include `xlink:role=` and `xlink:title=` values to ensure human readability. Because not every browser supports these attributes on links, the selection text should also be descriptive. Although you can include links that look like `click here`, those sorts of links are singularly uninformative to blind and visually disabled users.

As technology advances, this unimaginative style might also prevent accurately using the links in outline-driven audio browsers such as might be used in automobiles. A compressed link list that reads `here`, `click here`, `this`, `here`, `link`, `click here`, `here`, `here`, is unlikely to be of any utility whatsoever. Do your users a favor by including that descriptive text within the selection text. So in the following listing offering links to various airport Web pages, the first example is better than the second:

```
<airports>
  <anchor href="sf.xml">San Francisco Airport</anchor>
  <anchor href="chigago.xml">Chicago O'Hare Airport</anchor>
  <anchor href="newyork.xml">New York Kennedy Airport</anchor>
  <anchor href="oakland.xml">Oakland Airport</anchor>
</airports>
```

The second example uses essentially meaningless and indistinguishable link resource descriptions so, although the same information appears to be available at first glance, it won't be presented correctly in many browsers:

```
<airports>
  San Francisco Airport <anchor href="sf.xml">here</anchor>
  Chicago O'Hare Airport <anchor href="chigago.xml">here</anchor>
  New York Kennedy Airport <anchor href="newyork.xml">here</anchor>
  Oakland Airport <anchor href="oakland.xml">here</anchor>
</airports>
```

Always use meaningful link resource descriptions to ensure maximum flexibility in link presentation.

OUT-OF-LINE LINKS

An *out-of-line link* is one in which the link is defined separately from the activation and location elements. As you learned previously in this chapter, this is the good stuff. With an out-of-line link you can create links between two documents that have no authorial relationship with one another or with your own pages. You can create links in external documents that link back to your own and vice versa, so you can send people off to foreign parts with the promise of a return ticket at least.

The following is an extended one-way link between a hypothetical catalog item and an associated price list. Both ends of the link are external to the document that defines the links, although this is not required in the general case:

```
<xlink:extended
  type="extended"
  role="price list"
  title="Price List"
  showdefault="replace"
  actuatedefault="user">
  <xlink:locator href="URL#lpl142" id="lci9872" />
  <xlink:locator href="URL#lci9872" id="lpl142" />
  <xlink:arc from="lci9872" to="lpl142" show="parsed"/>
</xlink:extended>
```

If you wanted a two-way link, simply add another arc like this:

```
<xlink:arc from="lpl142" to="lci9872" show="parsed"/>
```

It's surprisingly straightforward. Figure 9.2 shows the relationship between the documents. Note that there's no direct relationship between the document A from which the link is made and the two documents B and C in which the link is created. The link is only visible when the documents are accessed from document A. Another document could create similar links without either ever stepping on one another's toes. The only requirement is that ID attributes with the names shown in the example exist in the document. If not, alternative navigation must be provided.

Figure 9.2
Here is a one-way
extended XLink from
an external document.

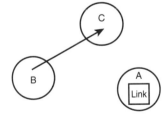

LINK BEHAVIOR

Link behavior is basically what happens when you follow a link. There are currently three actions, replace, new, and parse, which, respectively, replace the contents of the current window, create a new window, and parse the external file, rendering it within the current window as if it were part of the base document.

Creating new windows should never be done as a matter of course. It's confusing to many persons with visual or cognitive disabilities and might burn enough resources on low-end computers to crash them. If people want to surf on out of your site, let them. You won't gain many friends (or customers) by clinging to their ankles as they try to haul themselves out the door. The following code shows, against better judgment, the extended link appearing in a new window:

```
<xlink:extended
  type="extended"
  role="price list"
  title="Price List"
  showdefault="replace"
  actuatedefault="user">
  <xlink:locator href="URL#lpl142" id="lci9872" />
  <xlink:locator href="URL#lci9872" id="lpl142" />
  <xlink:arc from="lpl142" to="lci9872" show="new"/>
</xlink:extended>
```

SUMMING UP XLINKS

There are many ways to use XLink capabilities to link to other documents, inline and out-of-line, `simple`, and `extended`. Although the `simple` syntax has some advantage in terms of economy there seems little reason to use it in practice. It doesn't gain significantly in compatibility with existing browsers and gives rise to two alternative link choices with no real benefit to outweigh the added complexity.

Note

An obvious area of future development in XLink might be some way of cleanly supporting frames and converting them into something reasonable at the same time. They're not going to go away soon in XHTML, although their behavior can be precisely duplicated using XLink and either CSS or XSL style sheets. Using frames in the first place is nonetheless strongly discouraged.

XLink enables the Web designer to insert elements into an XML page to create and document links between documents, including links between resources contained in a remote document to another remote document, neither of which need have read access. The next section examines XPointer.

UNDERSTANDING XPOINTER

XPointer provides extended methods of pointing at specific locations or ranges (*spans*) inside documents. It uses the XPath language as a base, which is closely related to the TEI pointer language and in turn related to the HyTime pointer language. As described in the previous chapter, XPath offers the aspiring link creator an extensive and expressive syntax for describing exact locations within documents based on document structure as well as the more traditional IDs and anchors.

Note

TEI pointers use a dotted notation to separate nodes rather than the slash notation used by XLink. Other than that, the two linking languages are similar.

XPointers typically occur as URI fragments (sometimes called *selectors*), that is, the string following the # at the end of a URI. There are three ways to write an Xpointer:

- As a bare `idname` shorthand for `xpointer(id("idname"))`, a facility intended to help ensure some backwards-compatibility with HTML
- As a series of "/" delimited numbers, sometimes called *stepwise addresses* or *tumblers*
- As the full form, which can be based on XPointer or on another pointer scheme such as SMIL and might use any abbreviated forms defined in that scheme

Note that the bare `idname` syntax doesn't address the very common use of the `name=` attribute on an HTML `<a>` anchor, although `id=` and `name=` values, according to the HTML standard, should be identical if both attributes are present in an HTML anchor. Because this is so, it should be trivial to add appropriate `id=` values to the older `name=` model when converting from HTML to XHTML.

The use of *idnames* is encouraged by this syntax because it's likely to be the most stable form of reference within documents. This has several corollaries: Because XML can transclude parts of other documents within a document, `id=` values should, if possible, be unique not only within documents but across documents as well. Because it's very likely that your own documents will be linked to others, the best way to ensure that links to your documents are stable is to use `id=` values often and wisely. It wouldn't be inappropriate to use an `id=` field in every heading, and possibly even at every paragraph. If later editing changes the order of your exposition, the id values help ensure that the reference itself retains its utility even when you don't know who has linked to your document or exactly how or where.

Tip from

LeeAnne.com
Words to weave by

Tumbler sequences are simply a numbered series of integers separated by slashes. Each integer represents the nth child element of the element before it. Although the word tumbler has disappeared from the specifications, you still see the word in use. They can be used from any arbitrary element node in a document or from the root.

Although tumblers might be tempting, because they are simply a series of child selections proceeding down the document tree from the root, they're also the most fragile. If you decide to collapse the first two paragraphs of your document into one, every link to the rest of the document is instantly broken.

This is a bad example of an XPointer using tumblers:

```
<xlinklocator href="URL#xpointer(/2/3/2/7)"  attributes >
```

This is a better example using element names:

```
<xlinklocator href="URL#xpointer(/chap[3]/para[2])" attributes >
```

This is the best example using an XPointer id:

```
<xlinklocator href="URL#lpl2341" attributes >
```

Although these all might address the same location, only the last is likely to survive an extensive edit. The first is very fragile because adding or deleting a single element anywhere along the path will alter the reference, the second less so but not ideal because inserting or deleting a chap element in any of the first three positions will change the reference, as will adding or deleting a para element in any of the first two positions.

The following sections explore how to use links to extend the concept of hyperlinks to read-only documents, starting with the most trivial, a one-way link to such a document. We then extend that basic functionality with more complex ways to enable linking *from* read-only documents and multiple links.

MAKING LINKS TO READ-ONLY DOCUMENTS

There is no difference between creating an extended link to a read-only document and any other document. The same syntax is used for each, except that you can't base the link in the read-only document, but must use an external referrer page to maintain the links. The following creates a two-way link between two documents, in which you can imagine you have no write permissions:

```
<xlink:extended
  type="extended"
  role="price list"
  title="Price List"
  showdefault="replace"
  actuatedefault="user">
  <xlink:locator href="URL#lpl142" role="lci9872" />
  <xlink:locator href="URL#lci9872" role="lpl142" />
  <xlink:arc from="lci9872" to="lpl142" show="new"/>
  <xlink:arc from="lpl142" to="lci9872" show="new"/>
</xlink:extended>
```

The role names in the above references are deliberately arbitrary, because we don't actually have to know what relationship the documents have with each other. The references to the role and arc directions could, in fact, be programmatically generated and inserted in the source document.

RELATIVE ADDRESSING

The previous examples have shown absolute addressing by means of an ID contained within each document, much as can be done now with simple HTML anchor elements. But the entire syntax of XPath plus the XPointer extensions is available for navigating through the document. As you learned previously in this chapter, always choose to navigate from an internal ID if possible, as close to your target as possible. The following example shows pure relative navigation from the root, from the third child of the eighth child from the root, and from the fifth child of the fourth child from the root. Each location is given an ID so that both end points of the XLink arc between them can be easily located, but the underlying navigation is very insecure, because any change in the number of elements before the selection elements irrevocably alters the location:

```
<xlink:extended
  role="price list"
```

```
        title="Price List"
        showdefault="replace"
        actuatedefault="user">
<xlink:locator href="URL#xpointer(/8/3)" id="lci9872" />
<xlink:locator href="URL#xpointer(/5/4)" id="lpl142" />
<xlink:arc from="lci9872" to="lpl142" show="new"/>
<xlink:arc from="lpl142" to="lci9872" show="new"/>
    </xlink:extended>
```

Both URI fragments address unnamed child elements relative to the root. Note that both ends of the arc are relatively insecure, although they themselves have been given ID values to facilitate reference by the arc elements, because the document could be edited in such a way that the intended location is no longer referenced by the above expression.

ABSOLUTE ADDRESSING

You have already seen absolute addressing, which depends on finding an element with an ID exactly where you want to go. In your own documents, you can help this process for your own links, as well as those that might be made by others, by including unique IDs for every significant element. Here's still another example using absolute addressing:

```
<xlink:extended
  role="price list"
  title="Price List"
  showdefault="replace"
  actuatedefault="user">
  <xlink:locator href="URL#lpl142" id="lci9872" />
  <xlink:locator href="URL#lci9872" id="lpl142" />
  <xlink:arc from="lci9872" to="lpl142" show="new"/>
  <xlink:arc from="lpl142" to="lci9872" show="new"/>
</xlink:extended>
```

Both ends of the arc in this example use IDs with no relative addressing from that base. This is the most stable form of addressing because authors know that a location with an ID is likely to be referenced from outside the document, and will sensibly avoid changing or deleting the ID when editing or updating the document.

SELECTING BY NAME

Selecting by element name is less robust than selecting by ID but far better than pure relative addressing. Even the tiniest change in a document can alter a relative path whereas an element change might or might not affect a selection based on element name, depending on whether the change affects elements of the same name as the selection. It's even possible to combine the two styles, using addressing by ID to locate a place near your final destination and navigating by element name from there. The following example uses this element name syntax:

```
<xlink:extended
  type="extended"
  role="price list"
  title="Price List"
  showdefault="replace"
  actuatedefault="user">
```

```
<xlink:locator href="URL#xpointer(/chap[8]/para[3])" id="lci9872" />
<xlink:locator href="URL#xpointer(id("lcp21")/para[3])" id="lpl142" />
    <xlink:arc from="lci9872" to="lpl142" show="new"/>
    <xlink:arc from="lpl142" to="lci9872" show="new"/>
</xlink:extended>
```

The preceding example uses both a series of element names from the root, and a single element name from an element identified by an ID. Neither is completely secure, but more secure in the event of a simple edit to a location preceding it than a pure relative address would be. Bolding the first word of a chapter, for example, would change the number of child elements but not the number of a chapter or paragraph.

XPOINTER EXTENSIONS

XPointer uses all the functions defined in XPath, but with quite a few extensions to improve applicability to XPointer's primary task, addressing parts of a document in a link. Although the simple XPath constructs offer quite a bit of power, XPointer also made several extensions to the XPath set to extend the possible uses that might be made of other documents. Although the following constructs look similar to node locators, they cannot be used except as the initial and only locator fragment in a URI and return values that are not nodes at all and might not even contain nodes. The semantics of what user agents are to do with this information is still very much up in the air:

- `range::`*XPath-node-locator* `to` *XPath-nodelocator*—Takes a pair of XPath node locators separated by "to" as arguments and returns the string containing the first location and continuing to the last location, including any contained markup, to the user agent. This is an example:

```
xpointer(id("sec2.1")/descendant::P[last()] to
        id("sec2.2")/descendant::P[last()])
```

Because XPointer also enables you to select down to the character level, this enables you to select any contiguous portion of an XML document.

- `string-range::"`*literal*`"?,`*integerposition*`?,`*integerlength*`?,`*predicate*`?`—Takes a comma-separated list consisting of a quoted *literal* string followed by a numeric *integerposition*, a numeric *integerlength*, and an optional XPath `predicate` and searches the text of the document only, ignoring markup and collapsing extra whitespace into a single space for the literal if included, otherwise operates from the character before the numeric position, and returns `length` characters of the instance selected by the XPath `predicate` if present.

Multiple matches can occur but are non-overlapping. So `string::"hope",,9,[position()=2]` operating on the text `"hope hope hope hope"` returns a string containing the last two `hope` strings in one string, `"hope hope"`, not the middle two.

An omitted *integerposition* is assumed to be 1 and cannot take the value zero. If negative, counting proceeds from the end of the string toward the front whereas, if positive, counting proceeds from the point before the first character selected by the *literal* and toward the end of the string. It is not an error for the *integerposition* to lie outside the string itself.

An omitted `length` is assumed to be zero and negative values are not allowed so `length` always has a positive direction. It is not an error for the length to overshoot the end of the document but in that case only the string up to the end of the document is returned.

XPOINTER ABSOLUTE LOCATION FUNCTIONS

The absolute location functions are simply those that return an actual location, free from context. So the `id()` function is context-free, because an ID must be unique within the document and the function returns one location or none.

- *location-set* `id(IDliteral)`—The `id(IDliteral)` function returns the location of the node that contains the ID, "*IDliteral*".
- *location-set* `here()`— The `here()` function returns the inline node location of the XPointer itself in the document where the document cursor is located. It takes no arguments.

The root path, /, an absolute location path in XPointer, is as described in Chapter 8, XPath, located before any other markup in the document. So it will never be returned as a location from `here()`.

- *location-set* `origin()`—The `origin()` function returns the out-of-line node location of the point at which a user initiated a node traversal. It takes no arguments.
- *location-set* `start-point(location-set)`—The start-point(*location-set*) function returns the start point of each location in the argument *location-set*.
- *location-set* `end-point(location-set)`—The end-point(*location-set*) function returns the end point of each location in the argument *location-set*.

XPOINTER BOOLEAN FUNCTIONS

There's only one extension to the XPath Boolean functions, a shorthand method of telling whether an operation has returned a single node that saves a comparison. The function is `boolean unique()`. The unique function returns true if and only if the context node list contains exactly one node.

SELECTING A RANGE

Using a range requires using the XPointer range extension syntax:

```
<xlink:simple
  type="simple"
  role="price list"
  title="Price List"
  show="parse"
  actuate="user"
  href='URL#xpointer(id("lap1248") to id("lap28")'>Select this link for Price
➥List</xlink:simple>
```

SELECTING STRINGS

Using a range within a string requires using the XPointer extension `string-range`:

```
<xlink:simple
  href='URI#xpointer(id("lap234")/string-range(/,"text",1,10)'
  type="simple"
  role="code"
  title="Code"
  showdefault="replace"
  actuatedefault="user">
</xlink:simple>
```

Assuming that codes were identified by ID, this would return a 10 character string containing the code.

TROUBLESHOOTING XLINK AND XPOINTER

The range of potential errors in XLink and XPointer isn't really all that large. Because they can be checked as you go about creating them in the first place, and it would be fairly trivial to add the capability to visually select a location or range to a graphical XML document editor, it will probably be fairly easy to ensure that links work initially. But many pages change on a daily basis, so trying to find a stable point of reference or a uniform structure might tax the ingenuity of the cleverest designer.

HANDLING BROKEN LINKS

Shortly after linking to a document, you notice that your links don't work anymore.

On the Web, links are among the most fragile of human artifacts. With XLinks, however, there's even more chance for error because you might depend not only on the URL address, but on the URI fragment that identifies a location in the document. There are strategies that minimize the chance of a link going south, however, although it depends on careful inspection of the source document. First, relative links off the root are more delicate than links that navigate from internal landmarks. Almost any change in the document might alter the path sufficiently to send your users into left field.

Links that use an internal ID are usually the most robust, because document authors tend to conserve IDs because their own links might depend on them. So finding an existing anchor point near your selected starting point might help keep the link working correctly.

If the document has no internal anchor points, then try to key off the basic structure, headings, sections, whatever makes sense in the document itself. Instead of saying that you link points to the 144th child element from the root, see if identifying it as the second paragraph in section 8 makes for a more stable link over time.

Identifying the element type of your destination also makes the path slightly more robust, because you bypass changes in other element types. Always choose named element types over child or sibling relationships if possible.

CHECKING THE SYNTAX OF LINKS

After coding an XML document using XLink, you want to make sure that the links work correctly but your existing and favoriate browser doesn't support XLinks yet.

You have to use a tool that supports XLinks to test your links. InDelv is one option. Or parse the source yourself with a parser that understands XLinks. If your XLinks can be modified to follow the supported syntax, there is a link tester at W. Eliot (Dr. Macro) Kimber's, home page: `http://www.drmacro.com/hyprlink/xlink/xptrtest.html`. This tool has certain syntax limitations as described on the page itself.

PART II

MANIPULATING XML

DOM—THE DOCUMENT OBJECT MODEL

In this chapter

UNDERSTANDING DOM

The Document Object Model is a way of interfacing with an XML document in terms of its deep structure using an application programming interface (API). The DOM is not terribly interesting unless you are prepared to program to the API, using a scripting language at least, although most present work seems to be in Java or other object-oriented language. But if you're willing to do a little programming, accessing the DOM allows you total control over the document, allowing you to search and alter it in almost any way you can think of.

DOM objects are accessed through *methods*, a precisely defined way of talking to the object that is explored more fully in the section devoted to methods later in this chapter. Methods are fundamental to the object-oriented worldview; if an API doesn't hide information and force interaction through methods, it isn't truly object-oriented. The XML DOM fulfills both these conditions.

The DOM hides the underlying physical structure of an XML document completely. Although internally it can be thought of as a tree, an XML document is most often stored as a sequential flat file. There is, however, nothing to prevent an XML document from being stored as a relational database, or any other storage technology you can think of, as long as an interface is written to present the DOM structures and methods to the outside world.

The DOM enforces access through methods. Although it might look like you can access the entire document, in fact you are only accessing its representation. The actual tags used in a sequential flat file are invisible to DOM, and the pointers and queries required to access an equivalent relational database representation of an XML document are likewise invisible.

DOM defines two levels of structure: a fully object-oriented view of the document as an object and collection of objects (as implied by the name of the specification), and a node-level view that is less expensive to process but nonetheless inherently object-oriented because the simpler interface is accessed through methods as well.

In tiny applications, the processing expense of creating and using the full object-oriented view is too great to be practical. Having an alternative method of addressing the document means that it's possible to do significant processing of the document on small, perhaps even hand-held, devices.

| Note | To simplify greatly, *object-oriented* is a technical term for a programming technology that enables program modules to act as if they were alive in some ways, or at least separate entities. An object is able to initialize itself, a potent source of error in older paradigms, and inherit characteristics from its "parent." Like a living thing, an object has an inside and an outside. The insides are more or less hidden from view. You access and manipulate the object by talking to it in a very controlled vocabulary called a *method*, just as you could teach a dog to do a simple trick by saying "Sit!" When you say something is object-oriented, you say that it has properties that enable you to treat it like a similar black box. |

The node-level view shares something with SAX, the Simple API for XML, which the next chapter covers, and other event-driven XML parsers because they all deal with nodes and logically perform their functions by traversing the document tree. Unlike event-driven parsers however, DOM enables you to move around the tree at will. You can traverse the tree in pre- or post-order, for example, or query and transform the document itself on the fly. This is something that would be possible in SAX only with multiple passes over the document and is covered in Chapter 11, "SAX—The Simple API for XML."

> **Note**
>
> At the present moment, XML contains no mechanism for associating dynamic events with a document other than working within the XHTML namespace. DOM Level 2 contains such a tool and should be available by the time you read this or shortly thereafter. Another possibility for including dynamic behavior in a document is expanding CSS with behavioral extensions to enable scripts, or the equivalent, to be called from within a style sheet at CSS level 3 or above but this is in a very initial stage at W3C.

In fact, when you look at the node-level interface, you notice that it looks a bit like the other primary node-level XML standard, XPath. You see the same parent, child, and sibling relationships although DOM uses quite a different syntax.

It should be noted that DOM is an API, not a description of document structure. Although it's often convenient to look at an XML document as a tree, DOM itself makes no such assumptions about the underlying representation of an XML document. This is very consistent with an object-oriented approach; there's no reason one has to know what the document looks like in storage. You could implement DOM on top of a document database that used relational, flat-file, tree, object-oriented, or even associative processing techniques and the result would, by definition, be exactly the same.

DYNAMIC HTML IN NETSCAPE AND MSIE

Dynamic HTML processing is what led to DOM, because both Netscape and Microsoft came up with object models of the HTML document to perform their own proprietary magic on the HTML page. Both were submitted to W3C in due course, and W3C basically liked Microsoft's idea better. So Netscape was caught short in DOM support and tried to finesse the problem by concentrating on the clever things one could do with layers. But the W3C DOM gives access to the entire document, whereas the Netscape version is decidedly more limited.

With that head start, Microsoft benefited from early partial compliance with W3C DOM, whereas Netscape has lagged badly in DOM support. When Mozilla comes out, Netscape promises to be fully DOM compliant, perhaps even more so than Microsoft because they don't carry the full legacy of partial compliance and proprietary extensions.

Microsoft had its own problems with DOM as well, because what W3C standardized wasn't quite what Microsoft had proposed. So the Microsoft DOM is strewn with traps for the unwary, proprietary enhancements that causes pages coded to the Microsoft version of

DOM to break in every other browser. The path toward full standardization from the status quo for both of the Big Two browser-makers is a thorny one, and fraught with peril because of their huge, installed base of users. Luckily, most people haven't used DOM all that much.

WHAT'S MISSING IN DOM

From some of the complaints, you might think everything was missing or inadequate, but DOM Level 1 was always meant to be superseded, and it probably will be by the time you read this. DOM Level 2 is a Candidate Recommendation now, just before turning into a Proposed Recommendation and from there to full Recommendation. Of course the Netscape 4.x Document Object Model is completely strange and is being replaced completely in Mozilla.

DOM was designed to support HTML, and DOM Level 1 is really an HTML creature. The minimum requirements for HTML still form the core of DOM Level 2 but much has been added to support XML and its related standards specifically. Because DOM Level 2 is needed to truly support XML, it is covered here for the most part as though it were already a standard, because toolsets are already available that enable experimenting with the interface—albeit not fully compliant with a standard that is still very much on the move.

IDENTIFYING CHANGES BETWEEN DOM LEVELS 1 AND 2

The existing DOM Level 1 does not support all the features of XML 1.0 as it currently stands. Many features required for CSS support, especially CSS2 features, aren't there, and huge amounts of XML-specific behavior are likewise missing. In this chapter DOM is treated as an organic whole, with early mention of differences so that you know which topics might not be fully implemented until somewhat after this book goes to press.

Tip from	
LeeAnne.com Words to weave by	You are encouraged to use the margins of this book to add your own notes to this and other sections, to remind yourself of changed features or just to memorialize your own reactions to the information. The only time the pages of a book should remain pristine is when it's in the store.

Although DOM-2 is in Candidate Recommendation status at the time of this writing, feedback from implementers might still cause the working group to alter the final document substantially. This means that specific features mentioned might change or be deleted and new features might be added, although the overall direction of DOM-2 is clear.

NEW ATTRIBUTES AND METHODS

These represent changes to existing interfaces to extend their functionality in various ways. In many cases, they are there to support the added requirements of XML-related standards as they come online. These requirements might change, probably in the direction of added features, before the DOM-2 Recommendation now in candidate stage is finalized because many of the XML-related standards are still in flux. The following list represents added features of DOM Level 2 as presently conceived:

- The `Attr` interface has one new attribute: `ownerElement`. This enables convenient access to the owner element of an ID in particular, or any attribute, and is a key component of CSS, XLink, XPath, and other XML-related standards.

- The `Document` interface has five new methods: `importNode`, `createElementNS`, `createAttributeNS`, `getElementsByTagNameNS`, and `getElementByID`. The first of these supports XLink, whereas the middle three support XML namespaces and the last CSS for the most part, but other standards as well.

- The `NamedNodeMap` interface has three new methods: `getNamedItemNS`, `setNamedItemNS`, and `removeNamedItemNS`. These all support XML namespaces.

- The `Node` interface has two new methods: `supports` and `normalize`. These are XML specific and enable the programmer to determine whether the DOM implementation supports a particular string feature and collapses adjacent text nodes into one.

- The `Node` interface has three new attributes: `namespaceURI`, `prefix`, and `localName`. All these are intended to support XML Namespaces.

- The `ownerDocument` attribute was specified to be null when the node is a Document. It is now also null when the node is a `DocumentType` that is not used with any Document yet. This is to support XML transclusion and other document transformations.

- The `DocumentType` interface has two new attributes: `publicID`, `systemID`, and `internalSubset`. These support XML features associated with the XML Document Declaration.

- The `DOMImplementation` interface has two new methods: `createDocumentType` and `createDocument`.

- The `Element` interface has six new methods: `getAttributeNS`, `setAttributeNS`, `removeAttributeNS`, `getAttributeNodeNS`, `setAttributeNodeNS`, and `getElementsByTagNameNS`. They all support XML namespaces.

- The `DOMException` has five new exception codes: `INVALID_STATE_ERR`, `SYNTAX_ERR`, `INVALID_MODIFICATION_ERR`, `NAMESPACE_ERR`, and `INVALID_ACCESS_ERR`.

NEW INTERFACES

The new interfaces fully described in the following sections represent entirely new functionality added to DOM-2.

HTML

The HTML features are designed to support HTML documents, which differ from generic XML documents in having a pre-defined DTD that might be implemented entirely within the user agent.

Many of the interfaces and attributes are really for convenience and offer an alternative way of accessing information available in other ways, but some are designed to address specific HTML elements. The HTMLDOMImplementation interface was added to the existing HTML module. It's designed to enable applications to determine the support level of the current DOM implementation, optionally by specific feature, so that implementation independence can be assured.

VIEWS

A *document view* is one of multiple possible presentations associated with a document as mediated by a style sheet or other mechanism for choosing one out of many potential views. A view might be determined by a media type, user agent capabilities, or even changed dynamically by user interaction. This new module defines the interfaces AbstractView and DocumentView. These provide a basic means of associating different views, either computed or after applying a style sheet, of a document in an application.

STYLE SHEETS

This new module defines the following interfaces designed to supply the basic interfaces required to support any style sheet language, including but not limited to CSS. The StyleSheet, StyleSheetList, MediaList, DocumentStyle, and LinkStyle interfaces support both CSS, XSL, and other style sheet languages.

CSS

This new module defines the following interfaces designed to support Cascading Style Sheets, exposing the actual style sheet constructs to the programmer:

CSS2Azimuth	CSS2BackgroundPosition	CSS2BorderSpacing
CSS2CounterIncrement	CSS2CounterReset	CSS2Cursor
CSS2FontFaceSrc	CSS2FontFaceWidths	CSS2PageSize
CSS2PlayDuring	CSS2Properties	CSS2TextShadow
CSSCharsetRule	CSSFontFaceRule	CSSImportRule
CSSMediaRule	CSSPageRule	CSSPrimitiveValue
CSSRule	CSSRuleList	CSSStyleDeclaration
CSSStyleRule	CSSStyleSheet	CSSUnknownRule
CSSValue	CSSValueList	Counter
RGBColor	Rect	ViewCSS
DocumentCSS	DOMImplementationCSS	HTMLElementCSS

As you can tell from the name of the module and interfaces, all these additions were made to support CSS and CSS2 features. CSS2Azumith, for example, is needed for CSS2 Aural Style Sheets.

Note

It is not appropriate to access a user style sheet, and no means of exposing the user's style decisions is or will be provided.

EVENTS

Events are associated with a document during the time it is being rendered or displayed. They provide the concrete means whereby an application can dynamically perform processing other than that defined by hyperlinks and other mechanisms built in to the language itself. Examples of events include mouse or keyboard actions, focus change, or actions that modify the structure of the document in any way. They are similar but far richer than the primitive attribute-level events associated with documents by HTML.

In the new model, events can be captured by an ancestor of the target element, thereby altering the bubble-up behavior defined by HTML to enable event processing to proceed downward. An event can also be cancelled by any handler to prevent default actions from taking place.

This new module defines the following interfaces: `Event`, `EventListener`, `EventTarget`, `MutationEvent`, `UIEvent`, `MouseEvent`, and `KeyEvent`. These new interfaces enable the programmer to access mouse actions and other interactive events associated with an XML document.

PART

II

CH

10

TRAVERSAL

The Traversal feature enables the programmer to easily move about the logical tree, either in a flattened one-dimensional sequence of nodes in document order, or a two-dimensional, full-tree structure. A `NodeIterator` enables moving backward or forward along the flattened representation whereas a `TreeWalker` traverses a two-dimensional tree. Either view of the tree can be modified by built-in filters called *whatToShow flags* or by a custom filter written for the occasion.

The filters are very powerful mechanisms for simplifying the processing of the tree, because any extraneous details can be easily banished from view, allowing the application to concentrate its processing on just those parts of the document that are of interest.

This new module defines the following interfaces: `NodeIterator`, `TreeWalker`, `NodeFilter`, and `DocumentTraversal`. These new interfaces define methods of traversing the document tree.

RANGE

A range is a contiguous subset of a document bounded by a pair of boundary locations. Because of processing by the user agent or otherwise, a range might not actually appear to be contiguous when displayed.

This new module defines two new interfaces: `Range` and `DocumentRange`, with an associated exception, `RangeException`. This was added to support the XLink standards, allowing you to specify sub-trees within an XML document by range.

SUMMING UP THE DIFFERENCES BETWEEN DOM-1 AND DOM-2

As you can see, the majority of the changes involve support for interactivity, style sheets or XML requirements. But there are a few tidbits that profoundly affect every document. In particular the new Traversal interfaces enable differing tree views of the document tree to be constructed using node exclusions, which corresponds roughly to a grove plan in SGML/ HyTime/DSSSL. This enables you to trim the document tree to suit your own purposes, ignoring tags you are not going to render.

Note Many of the new modules are optional. Before using them you have to test whether your version of DOM supports them using either the DOM Level 2 `supports()` method or the DOM Level 1 and 2 `hasFeature()` method.

Still missing are uniform ways to instantiate a DOM object, access controls and security, access to the XML DTD, and validation. The Working Draft of DOM Level 3 was due out in April of the year 2000, so you should be able to see what W3C has planned just about now—or if not now, soon.

SEEING FORESTS IN TREES

Because XML enables you to link to other documents by means of processing instructions, notations, and attributes that are not children of the node that bears them (an unfortunate oxymoron), or transclude documents outside the base document dynamically, there are many logical trees that can be theoretically constructed with the same document as a base. In addition, you might not need to view or render the entire tree in many applications, defining yet another logical tree consisting of a subset of the complete XML document tree. There might literally be hundreds of trees with their roots in a single document. For convenience, the collection of all these trees is sometimes called a forest or grove.

Although there is currently no easy way to handle groves, DOM Level 2 extends the DOM 1 specification with traversal tools that make navigating through groves simple and easy. DOM Level 2 and above will eventually provide a clear view of the forest through the trees by letting you take any perspective on the document you can imagine. The primary tools for manipulating the document view are the `whatToShow` flags and user-written filters that enable any conceivable view to be imposed on the document.

There are two methods of traversing the DOM Level 2 document tree: with an `Iterator` or with a `TreeWalker`.

An `Iterator` views the document as a simple ordered list of nodes. Because the document tree might be modified during a list traversal, the position of the `iterator` is always between nodes or before the start and after the end respectively. This means that `nextNode()` and `previousNode()` always return something, either a null if attempting to go beyond the terminal locations of the tree or the node currently after or behind it. So traversals might find a different node when reversing direction from the one they saw last. This is not an error.

A `TreeWalker` views the document as a tree, so navigating the tree can employ parent, sibling, and child relationships as well as basic node order traversal. The previous comments about what happens when the underlying document is changed also apply to `TreeWalkers`.

Controlling the Logical View of the Document Tree

Both the Iterator and TreeWalker methods employ whatToShow flags and filters to determine which parts of the tree to display. By selectively allowing different parts of the tree to appear using whatToShow flags and filters, non-essential portions can be skipped over as though they didn't exist. This simplifies things like searching text, because the document can be presented as a flat sequential text file by turning off all flags except the SHOW_TEXT flag. Likewise, if you need to view all the processing instructions for some reason, turn off all the flags except SHOW_PROCESSING_INSTRUCTION. If your particular processing need requires a filter not already supplied by a whatToShow flag, you have to write a filter.

whatToShow Flags

A whatToShow flag is zero or more flags chosen from the following list, taken from the DOM Level 2 Candidate Recommendation. The complete version can be viewed at http://www.w3.org/tr/. The following list describes what the various whatToShow flags do:

- SHOW_ALL—Show all nodes. This value tells an Iterator or TreeWalker to traverse all the nodes of the document except attributes, entities, and notations that are never seen by traversal because they are not part of the document tree.
- SHOW_ELEMENT—Show element nodes. This value tells an Iterator or TreeWalker to traverse the element nodes of the tree, skipping processing instructions and other node types as though they weren't there.
- SHOW_ATTRIBUTE—Show attribute nodes. This value is meaningful only when creating an Iterator with an attribute node as its root. Having an attribute node as its root implies that the attribute node appears in the first position of the iteration list. Because attributes aren't really part of the document tree, they won't otherwise appear when iterating over the document tree.
- SHOW_TEXT—Show text nodes. This value tells an Iterator or TreeWalker to traverse the text nodes of the tree, skipping element, and other nodes as though they weren't there unless they are selected by another flag.
- SHOW_CDATA_SECTION—Show CDATASection nodes. This value tells an Iterator or TreeWalker to traverse the CDATA nodes of the tree, skipping element, and other nodes as though they weren't there unless they are selected by another flag.
- SHOW_ENTITY_REFERENCE—Show Entity Reference nodes. This value tells an Iterator or TreeWalker to traverse the entity reference nodes of the tree, skipping element, and other nodes as though they weren't there unless they are selected by another flag.
- SHOW_ENTITY—Show Entity nodes. This value is meaningful only when creating an Iterator with a single Entity node as its root. Having the Entity node as its root implies that the Entity node appears in the first position of the iteration list. Because entities aren't really part of the document tree, they won't otherwise appear when iterating over the document tree.
- SHOW_PROCESSING_INSTRUCTION—Show ProcessingInstruction nodes. This value tells an Iterator or TreeWalker to traverse the processing instruction nodes of the tree, skipping element, and other nodes as though they weren't there unless they are selected by another flag.

- SHOW_COMMENT—Show `Comment` nodes. This value tells an `Iterator` or `TreeWalker` to traverse the comment nodes of the tree, skipping element, and other nodes as though they weren't there unless they are selected by another flag.

- SHOW_DOCUMENT—Show `Document` nodes. This value tells an `Iterator` or `TreeWalker` to traverse the document nodes of the tree, skipping element, and other nodes as though they weren't there unless they are selected by another flag.

- SHOW_DOCUMENT_TYPE—Show `DocumentType` nodes. This value tells an `Iterator` or `TreeWalker` to traverse the document type nodes of the tree, skipping element, and other nodes as though they weren't there unless they are selected by another flag.

- SHOW_DOCUMENT_FRAGMENT—Show `DocumentFragment` nodes. This value tells an `Iterator` or `TreeWalker` to traverse the document fragment nodes of the tree, skipping element, and other nodes as though they weren't there unless they are selected by another flag.

- SHOW_NOTATION—Show `Notation` nodes. This value is meaningful only when creating an Iterator with a single `Notation` node as its root. Having the `Notation` node as its root implies that the `Notation` node appears in the first position of the iteration list. Because notations are external references and aren't really part of the document tree, they won't otherwise appear when iterating over the document tree.

If a node fails the `whatToShow` test, its children are nonetheless evaluated for inclusion in the view by both `Iterators` and `TreeWalkers`.

FILTERS

Filters are enabled by a simple hook that calls a user-defined function. There are no built-in filters in DOM Level 2 other than the `whatToShow` flags, which use an entirely different mechanism to alter the logical document view. There's only one method associated with a filter, `acceptNode()`, which returns one of three values:

- FILTER_ACCEPT—This value tells the `Iterator` or `TreeWalker` to accept the node. This means that it appears in the logical view of the tree. If this value is not returned, the node does not appear and the behavior of a `TreeWalker` is determined by the actual value returned of the two remaining values.

- FILTER_SKIP—This value tells the `Iterator` or `TreeWalker` to skip the node but process its children if using a `TreeWalker`. Iterators always process the next node seen so FILTER_SKIP and FILTER_REJECT are equivalent for iterators. Because iterators have no concept of child nodes possible in their one-dimensional view, this should make sense when you think about it.

- FILTER_REJECT—This value tells the `Iterator` or `TreeWalker` to reject the node and ignore its children if using a `TreeWalker`. Iterators always process the next node seen so FILTER_SKIP and FILTER_REJECT are equivalent for iterators. Because iterators have no concept of child nodes in their one-dimensional view of the document, this should make sense when you think about it.

In general, FILTER_SKIP is safer to use when a node is to be ignored, because this enables both Iterators and TreeWalkers to use the same filter and behave in a similar manner. In special cases you might want to use FILTER_REJECT, but you should be aware that the filter yields different results if used in both Iterators and TreeWalkers. But for the case in which it's necessary to trim an entire branch of a tree based on the state of a particular node, FILTER_REJECT is the best choice.

The following Java snippet instantiates a NodeFilter() that skips Image elements for any reason you can imagine:

```
class ImageFilter implements NodeFilter {
  short acceptNode(Node nodevalue) {
    if (nodeValue instanceof Element) {
      Element elementvalue = (element)nodevalue;
    if (! elemantvalue.getNodeName().equals("Image"))
      return FILTER_SKIP;
    if (elementvalue.getAttributeNode("NAME") != null) {
      return FILTER_ACCEPT;
      }
    }
  return FILTER_SKIP;
  }
}
```

Note

This section (and other sections) relies on a Candidate Recommendation DOM Level 2 that might change slightly on its way to becoming a Recommendation. As always, the current document as posted at http://www.w3.org/TR/ is authoritative.

Filters are an extremely powerful way to transform the document tree. With a well-designed document, an appropriate filter could modify the document to fit almost any display device or document interactivity need. A lesson plan, for example, could include optional tests with answers that would be displayed based on external criteria, additional reading for those interested in following up on the lesson, and even alternate languages for a bilingual classroom, all in a single document.

USING NODE-LEVEL DOM

The DOM maintains two views of an XML document. First, a flattened view in which everything is a node and can be operated on in terms of position in the document tree. These methods of accessing the document object are associated with the *node* interface and, in DOM Level 2, the *traversal* interfaces. The second uses the methods associated with all the other available interfaces and is discussed in the next section.

Tip from

Words to weave by

Node-level DOM is more frugal in its use processing cycles than the full object-oriented view of the document possible in DOM Level 2 and above, so it might be more appropriate for environments in which performance is critical.

PART

II

CH

10

Many of the node-level and full object-oriented interfaces partially duplicate one another but both versions are retained for the sake of maintaining the overall satisfaction level of the many different constituencies for DOM.

NODE ATTRIBUTES

Node attributes enable evaluation of the current, or context node and certain related nodes.

The node interfaces include the following attributes:

- `nodeName`—Returns the name of the context node.
- `nodeValue`—Returns the value or content of the current, or context node.
- `nodeType`—Returns a numeric code indicating the type of the current, or context node.
- `parentNode`—Returns the closest visible parent of the context node or null if the current node has no parent. Visibility is affected by the `WhatToShow` flags.
- `childNodes`—Returns a `NodeList` containing the names of all child nodes of the current, or context node or null if the current node has no parent.
- `firstChild`—Returns the first child of the context node or null if the current node has no parent.
- `lastChild`—Returns the last child of the context node or null if the current node has no parent.
- `previousSibling`—Returns the previous sibling of the context node or null if the current node has no parent.
- `nextSibling`—Returns the next sibling of the context node or null if the current node has no parent.
- `attributes`—Returns a `NamedNodeMap` containing a list of the attributes born by the current, or context node.
- `ownerDocument`—Returns the document object that contains the context node or null if the current node has no parent.
- *namespaceURI*—Returns the namespace URI associated with the context node or null if the current node has no parent.
- *prefix*—Returns the namespace prefix associated with the current, or context node or null if the current node has no parent.
- *localName*—Returns the local part of the name of the current, context node, that is the name stripped of any namespace prefix. If there is no namespace prefix, this is exactly equivalent to `nodeName`.

The node interfaces have the following methods, interfaces used to manipulate the Document Object Model:

- `insertBefore(newChild, namedChild)`—Inserts a child before a named child node.
- `replaceChild(newChild, namedChild)`—Replaces a named child node with another.
- `removeChild(namedChild)`—Removes a named child node.

- appendChild(newChild)—Appends a new child node to the list of children.
- hasChildNodes()—A Boolean test to determine whether the current, or context node has any children.
- cloneNode(deep)—Copy the current, or context node, optionally including child nodes recursively if the parameter deep is set.
- *supports(featureName)*—A Boolean test to determine whether a DOM implementation supports a particular feature.

Items in *italics* are defined in DOM Level 2.

To the previous list should be added the following attribute and method from the NodeList interface:

- length—Returns the length of the NodeList or null.

There's one additional method to the NodeList interface

- item(indexNumber)—Returns an indexed item from a NodeList.

and the following attribute and methods from the NamedNodeMap interface

- length—Returns the length of the NamedNodeMap or null.

and methods:

- getNamedItem(name)—Returns a named item from the map.
- setNamedItem(nodeArgument)—Adds a named item to the map.
- removeNamedItem(name)—Removes a named item from the map.
- item(index)—Returns an indexed item from the map.
- *getNamedItemNS(nameSpaceURI, localName)*—Returns a namespace-qualified named item from the map.
- *setNamedItem(nameSpaceURI, nodeArgument)*—Adds a namespace-qualified named item to the map.
- *removeNamedItemNS(nameSpaceURI, localName)*—Removes a namespace-qualified named item from the map.

Items in *italics* are defined in DOM Level 2.

DOM Level 2 adds the following traversal interfaces to this basic feature set:

- NodeIterator—With attributes whatToShow, filter, and expandEntityReferences. With methods nextNode and previousNode.
- TreeWalker—With attributes whatToShow, filter, expandEntityReferences, and currentNode. With methods parentNode, firstChild, lastChild, previousSibling, nextSibling, previousNode, and nextNode.
- NodeFilter—With method acceptNode.
- DocumentTraversal—With methods createNodeIterator and createTreeWalker.

The traversal interfaces listed here are defined more thoroughly in the "Forests and Trees" section immediately preceding and are listed here for completeness.

USING OBJECT-ORIENTED DOM

Other than the node interfaces, every DOM interface is fully object-oriented. Because many of these methods are fairly expensive, requiring casts and other processing extravagances, the node-level interfaces enable relatively cheap access to the document without the overhead of full object-orientedness.

Most of the commonly used DOM classes inherit from the node class. So elements, attributes, notations, entities, even the document itself, are nodes. This is a truly trivial but illuminating statement when you recall that an XML document is tree-structured and can therefore be represented as a tree. Because everything that appears on the tree is either a node or the arc spanning two nodes, it follows that everything tangible in an XML document is a node on that tree. This enables the entire document to be accessed and manipulated using DOM methods.

The exceptions to this general rule are classes that are generated and used internally by DOM. So NodeList and NamedNodeMap are not really nodes, because they represent meta-information about nodes that DOM uses for processing and not the nodes themselves. So also DOMException and DOMImplementation are meta-information about the state of the DOM process itself and are not nodes in themselves. When the DOM process exits, these abstractions disappear without a trace, leaving the nodes themselves behind embodied in the various elements, attributes, and miscellaneous parts that make up an XML document.

FUNDAMENTAL INTERFACES

The so-called fundamental interfaces are those required to handle HTML. Although they are also necessary for XML or any structured document, XML requires extended capabilities found, naturally enough, in the section on Extended Interfaces that follows in the next section.

HTML can be processed differently than can a generic XML document, because the DTD is predefined and can be implemented directly in the user agent. In fact, this is the most common method of implementing an HTML user agent. Because this subset of DOM functionality addresses the same problem space as HTML, the fundamental or core interfaces are not covered in depth.

Tip from

LeeAnne.com
Words to weave by

Although the DOM interfaces and methods are defined in an object-oriented manner, an interface is not necessarily a class. The interface is required only to expose methods that correspond to those named, but need not implement a corresponding class. This enables thin implementations of the DOM on top of legacy applications if desired.

The fundamental interfaces include:

- DOMException(code)—Provides a standard interface to a list of error messages that a user module can throw. Some languages don't support exceptions, and the same list of errors can be processed using whatever standard error mechanism exists in that language.
- ExceptionCode—A list of integer constants used by DOMException.
- DOMImplementation()—Provides a method that enables a user application to test DOM implementation capabilities. In DOM Level 2 this also provides implementation-independent methods for creating XML documents.
- DocumentFragment—Provides a lightweight holder for relative small parts of a document that makes it easy to move parts of the document around or to create document fragments to be inserted in the document tree after completing processing.
- Document—Provides methods for addressing the entire document and creating elements, text nodes, comments, processing instructions, and so on that can't exist outside the context of a document.
- Node—Provides methods of manipulating nodes.
- NodeList—Provides a holder for a list of nodes and a method for returning a single item from that list.
- NamedNodeMap—Provides methods of using and maintaining named lists of nodes.
- CharacterData—Provides methods that extend Node with means of handling character data within a node.
- Attr—Provides an attribute abstraction.
- Element—Provides an element abstraction and a number of methods for manipulating attributes.
- Text—Provides a method of breaking text data into smaller parts.
- Comment—Provides an abstraction of comment text.

DOM Level 2 adds a few methods to the roster of core interface modules, but they are otherwise unchanged.

EXTENDED INTERFACES

The extended interfaces are those required to handle XML and XML-like documents and are never encountered when processing HTML documents. All these interfaces are new because they are used to access XML and other document languages. And just as the core interfaces need not be implemented using actual classes, the extended interfaces can expose only the defined methods is so desired. The extended interfaces include

- CDATASection—Provides an abstraction of a CDATA section.
- DocumentType—Provides an abstraction of a document type.
- Notation—Provides an abstraction of a notation.
- Entity—Provides an abstraction of an entity.

■ `EntityReference`—Provides an abstraction of an entity reference.

■ `ProcessingInstruction`—Provides an abstraction of a processing instruction.

DOM Level 2 adds a few new attributes to a couple of interface modules, but the extended interfaces are otherwise unchanged. I heartily recommend reading the specifications themselves, although they are somewhat obscure in parts. They have code snippets and full Java and ECMAScript bindings for the edification of programmers and are always the most authoritative source of information.

Using the explanations in this book combined with the terse descriptions in the W3C specifications should allow a good compromise between utility and excessive parroting of the W3C standards.

DOM Methods

Whereas a full discussion of object-orientation is beyond the scope of this book, you should know that DOM methods (and any object-oriented methods) are very controlled ways to access or modify the information contained in an object.

Object-orientation had its beginnings in process simulation so it should come as only a small surprise (if any) that the document structure objects accessed by DOM methods are dynamic. So if a node contained in an existing `NodeList` is deleted or a new node is added, the `NodeList` reflects that fact without effort on your part. Likewise, adding or deleting nodes in the document tree is transparent to navigation and traversal methods.

This is sometimes hard for procedural language programmers to grasp, because their data structures are static, requiring explicit updates to remain current.

Another object-oriented feature is inheritance, so the node class (a class is more-or-less an object but viewed as a template for creating other objects) has certain methods associated with it. Because elements, for example, are instantiations of class node, they inherit all the node methods and attributes and only have to add a few methods specific to element nodes.

This can also be a source of error, however. A text node cannot be a parent to any child node, although the node methods that relate to children exist in the text node because it inherits these methods from its parent class. Trying to create a child under a text node throws an exception. When reading the W3C specifications, you won't see this prominently mentioned in every interface description but be aware that most document nodes inherit from somewhere. Unfortunately, the DOM recommendation shows the inheritance, if any, of nodes scattered through the separate parts. Whereas the formal interface descriptions in the recommendation itself tell you whether an object inherits or not, for convenient reference here follows a series of subsections containing simple lists showing from where objects inherit, if they do:

DOM Core Inheritance

Inheritance is an object-oriented term that refers to letting one object inherit attributes and methods from an ancestor class from which it is derived. Because DOM need not actually implement most interfaces using classes, inheritance might need to be simulated by other means. These objects form part of the DOM core module:

- `DocumentFragment` inherits from `Node`
- `Document` inherits from `Node`
- `CharacterData` inherits from `Node`
- `Attr` inherits from `Node`
- `Element` inherits from `Node`
- `Text` inherits from `CharacterData`
- `Comment` inherits from `CharacterData`
- `CDATASection` inherits from `Text`
- `DocumentType` inherits from `Node`
- `Notation` inherits from `Node`
- `Entity` inherits from `Node`
- `EntityReference` inherits from `Node`
- `ProcessingInstruction` inherits from `Node`

DOM CSS INHERITANCE

These objects form part of the DOM CSS module:

- `CSSStyleSheet` inherits from `stylesheets::style sheet`
- `CSSStyleRule` inherits from `CSSRule`
- `CSSMediaRule` inherits from `CSSRule`
- `CSSFontFaceRule` inherits from `CSSRule`
- `CSSPageRule` inherits from `CSSRule`
- `CSSImportRule` inherits from `CSSRule`
- `CSSCharsetRule` inherits from `CSSRule`
- `CSSUnknownRule` inherits from `CSSRule`
- `CSSPrimitiveValue` inherits from `CSSValue`
- `CSSValueList` inherits from `CSSValue`
- `ViewCSS` inherits from `views::AbstractView`
- `DocumentCSS` inherits from `stylesheets::DocumentStyle`
- `DOMImplementationCSS` inherits from `DOMImplementation`
- `CSS2Azimuth` inherits from `CSSValue`
- `CSS2BackgroundPosition` inherits from `CSSValue`
- `CSS2BorderSpacing` inherits from `CSSValue`
- `CSS2CounterReset` inherits from `CSSValue`

- CSS2CounterIncrement inherits from CSSValue
- CSS2Cursor inherits from CSSValue
- CSS2PlayDuring inherits from CSSValue
- CSS2PageSize inherits from CSSValue
- HTMLElementCSS inherits from html::HTMLElement

DOM Event Inheritance

These objects form part of the DOM event module:

- UIEvent inherits from Event
- MouseEvent inherits from UIEvent
- KeyEvent inherits from UIEvent
- MutationEvent inherits from Event

DOM HTML Inheritance

These objects form part of the DOM HTML module:

- HTMLDOMImplementation inherits from DOMImplementation
- HTMLDocument inherits from Document
- HTMLElement inherits from Element
- HTMLHtmlElement inherits from HTMLElement
- HTMLHeadElement inherits from HTMLElement
- HTMLLinkElement inherits from HTMLElement
- TMLTitleElement inherits from HTMLElement
- HTMLMetaElement inherits from HTMLElement
- HTMLBaseElement inherits from HTMLElement
- HTMLIsIndexElement inherits from HTMLElement
- HTMLStyleElement inherits from HTMLElement
- HTMLBodyElement inherits from HTMLElement
- HTMLFormElement inherits from HTMLElement
- HTMLSelectElement inherits from HTMLElement
- HTMLOptGroupElement inherits from HTMLElement
- HTMLOptionElement inherits from HTMLElement
- HTMLInputElement inherits from HTMLElement
- HTMLTextAreaElement inherits from HTMLElement
- HTMLButtonElement inherits from HTMLElement
- HTMLLabelElement inherits from HTMLElement

- `HTMLFieldSetElement` inherits from `HTMLElement`
- `HTMLLegendElement` inherits from `HTMLElement`
- `HTMLUListElement` inherits from `HTMLElement`
- `HTMLOListElement` inherits from `HTMLElement`
- `HTMLDListElement` inherits from `HTMLElement`
- `HTMLDirectoryElement` inherits from `HTMLElement`
- `HTMLMenuElement` inherits from `HTMLElement`
- `HTMLLIElement` inherits from `HTMLElement`
- `HTMLDivElement` inherits from `HTMLElement`
- `HTMLParagraphElement` inherits from `HTMLElement`
- `HTMLHeadingElement` inherits from `HTMLElement`
- `HTMLQuoteElement` inherits from `HTMLElement`
- `HTMLPreElement` inherits from `HTMLElement`
- `HTMLBRElement` inherits from `HTMLElement`
- `HTMLBaseFontElement` inherits from `HTMLElement`
- `HTMLFontElement` inherits from `HTMLElement`
- `HTMLHRElement` inherits from `HTMLElement`
- `HTMLModElement` inherits from `HTMLElement`
- `HTMLAnchorElement` inherits from `HTMLElement`
- `HTMLImageElement` inherits from `HTMLElement`
- `HTMLObjectElement` inherits from `HTMLElement`
- `HTMLParamElement` inherits from `HTMLElement`
- `HTMLAppletElement` inherits from `HTMLElement`
- `HTMLMapElement` inherits from `HTMLElement`
- `HTMLAreaElement` inherits from `HTMLElement`
- `HTMLScriptElement` inherits from `HTMLElement`
- `HTMLTableElement` inherits from `HTMLElement`
- `HTMLTableCaptionElement` inherits from `HTMLElement`
- `HTMLTableColElement` inherits from `HTMLElement`
- `HTMLTableSectionElement` inherits from `HTMLElement`
- `HTMLTableRowElement` inherits from `HTMLElement`
- `HTMLTableCellElement` inherits from `HTMLElement`
- `HTMLFrameSetElement` inherits from `HTMLElement`
- `HTMLFrameElement` inherits from `HTMLElement`
- `HTMLIFrameElement` inherits from `HTMLElement`

DOM STRUCTURE

DOM has no actual structure, although it's based on an object-oriented, tree-structured view of the XML document. That is to say the interfaces return values that would be true if they referred to a document that was actually a tree. But DOM doesn't actually assume that the document *is* a tree, it only insists on treating it like one.

This is not an idle distinction. Many applications of XML undoubtedly reify an underlying database or knowledge structure that might have nothing whatsoever to do with trees of any sort.

DOM enables an XML developer to wrap this underlying structure, whatever it is, with a thin veneer of methods that translate that structure into a tree for public consumption, even though the underlying structure and mechanisms are left unchanged.

This is the basis for XML's utility as a transfer medium, allowing XML data streams to be used to transfer data to and from disparate database systems. It's also the basis of XML's value as a display format, because multiple databases can be displayed and manipulated with a single mechanism.

LOOKING AT DOM QUIRKS

There are many features of DOM that duplicate one another or were added at the insistence of a particular vendor, reflecting that vendor's view of what XML was good for. Microsoft, for example, asked for and got an ID attribute to support Data Islands—a way of embedding XML fragments into an HTML document using yet another MS proprietary HTML tag, <XML>.

Microsoft's XML parser has a nonstandard way of loading an XML document for the fairly understandable reason that the original DOM specification didn't address this issue. Because other XML parsers have kept up with the evolving standard whereas Microsoft has committed to stay with their older implementation until DOM Level 2 becomes a Recommendation, this creates a problem when writing to both standards.

Microsoft created a standard method of persisting the XML tree to the XML document, which is deliberately avoided even in the W3C Working Draft DOM Level 2 specification. It's probably a good idea not to cache document structure in this way, but it's tempting because of the gain in performance. A more sophisticated caching mechanism would handle this without programmer intervention.

Microsoft created a method of catching common parsing errors. The list goes on but you get the idea. Unfortunately, using the Microsoft extensions in your code causes the code to break when used on any other platform, a destructive behavior that wins few friends in the long run.

To avoid the tedious business of testing browsers and varying code to suit the environment, you have to code to a subset of DOM capabilities supported alike on many platforms. It's been estimated that handling browser differences accounts for 25% or more of the Web design budget so you can easily see the cost driver for moving as rapidly as possible toward common standards.

EXCEPTION HANDLING

Being object-oriented, DOM throws exceptions of course. Exceptions must be caught in user code so it would behoove you to avoid code tricks that can generate exceptions if at all possible. In particular, filters are not prevented from altering the document tree, although this is unwise in most cases because returning from a filter might find the document in an undefined or ambiguous state. Exactly how to handle exceptions is beyond the scope of this book. You have to handle exceptions according to the conventions of the language being used to access the DOM. In Java, the general syntax is

```
try {
  myRoutine();
  }
  catch (myException exceptionVariable) {
    System.out.println("Error Message:" + exceptionVariable.data);
    }
```

Your own experience might vary depending on the language used and exactly what you want to do with the type of exception uncovered by your handler. It's possible to recover from or ignore many exceptions, or try alternative strategies until something works. Because exception handling is generally cheaper in terms of processing time than trying to code guardian code around every routine to handle every possible source of error, many of which might never occur in actual experience, an exception handler gives you a backup plan when things go wrong. Using exception handlers also enables you to centralize common error routines, allowing your application to remain lean and elegant while recovering from uncommon errors.

GETTING DOWN TO CASES

Because DOM is a programmatic interface, the theory is that a program designed to operate on an XML document on one platform will operate in exactly the same way on any platform. This begs the question of programming language support, because it's quite common for a given language to be implemented in slightly different ways on different platforms, and we've already seen that DOM is currently fragmented to some extent across the Microsoft/Everyone else boundary.

But this last problem should at least partially resolve itself when and if Microsoft implements their promised support of W3C-defined DOM rather than their own. Given the existence of large numbers of existing pages and tools designed to support their non-standard past product, however, this may be difficult to do without breaking large numbers of legacy pages and alienating users who've depended on them in the past. They're on the horns of a dilemma, therefore, and it will be interesting to see how they (and we) cope.

It seems likely that, in practical terms, we will all have to take this history of incompatibility into account for the foreseeable future, unless we restrict our browsing to the most current and regularly updated sites.

And if it's truly necessary to change programming languages to support multiple platforms and take into account multiple versions of the "standard," much of the value of DOM is lost. So DOM cries out for a truly neutral programming language to complement its own platform-neutral design, and the history of Java is an instructive one. Once touted as universal, at least one vendor mentioned in this section "enhanced" it to the point where Java code written for their particular platform wouldn't run anywhere else. In turn, real Java wouldn't run on their platform without severely restricting the sorts of things that one did. In a word, fie on the proprietary machinations of vendors.

XML promises to succeed where other attempts at standardization have failed, because the weight of history is behind eventual standardization when a technology becomes important enough. Some portions of XML have already been moved to silicon, as XML accelerator chips promise to do for XML document exchange what graphics accelerators did for computer gaming. So we can reasonably look to the future with hope despite a long history of bitter disappointment.

SAX—The Simple API for XML

In this chapter

USING SAX INSTEAD OF DOM

Given the complexities of DOM, some sort of tool was needed to let ordinary people process XML files without building a rigorous document tree and brachiating around it like an extraordinarily talented ape, as does DOM. It turns out that there are other ways of looking at an XML file. Although the DOM ape may have an excellent overview of the entire structure, it needs copious resources in memory and processing power to build and retain this information. An ant methodically walking on the branches of the same tree can do a lot of useful work without nearly the effort.

That's exactly what the Simple API for XML (SAX) does. If you walk a tree, not paying much attention to the structure as a whole, you can view it as a sequence of events. First, you find the root. Then you find the first node. By using a simple strategy, you can visit each node in turn, acting on whatever it is you find there. After you've visited every node, you're done.

Most programmers know how to handle this sort of task. It's so common it has a name, an event handler. By walking the tree, which you do by just sequentially reading the file due to the way XML is structured, you convert a complex series of relationships into a simple data stream.

Well, data streams are what any programmer worth her salt eats for breakfast.

> **Note**
>
> SAX comes in two flavors, the older version still used by many applications and a newer version 2.0 that supports namespaces and other fancy stuff introduced by XML. New development should almost always use SAX 2 because namespaces are ubiquitous in the XML paradigm, but you should be able to accommodate older versions of SAX when you encounter them. For the latest information from the author, visit David Megginson's utilitarian Web site at http://www.megginson.com/.

TREE VIEWS VERSUS EVENT VIEWS

When you construct the whole tree before doing anything, you have the advantage of omniscience. You can answer questions such as "Who is the second cousin of this node, twice removed?" On the other hand, it takes a while before you can start grinding out results. First, you have to get everything lined up. If the tree uses a different object model, you can be thrown for a complete loop. And as you've seen with DOM, there are enough holes in the DOM specification and enough temptations to do things *your* way instead of the standard way that you can't really depend on finding the same object model wherever you go. So you have to write variations for every browser's vision of what DOM is, if any. It's a major pain.

Tip from

LeeAnne.com
Words to weave by

> Although DOM is far more powerful, event-driven tools like SAX are more universal and appropriate in some situations. When manipulating a very large file, or when using hand-held devices, the overhead of DOM can be prohibitive. And until the browser makers agree on a common set of functionality, it can be far easier to use SAX or its ilk than juggle the many differences between DOM implementations.

SAX allows you to take an ant's eye view so you don't have to worry about the big picture. You only see your immediate neighborhood. You know who your parent is and that's often enough. If you glance at Chapters 12, "CSS, CSS2, DSSSL, XSL" and 13, "Cascading Style Sheets and XML/XHTML," which deal with cascading style sheets, you'll see that quite a few CSS constructs deal with just that simple relationship. You can improve your ability to handle certain kinds of tasks by retaining more memory of what you found before, but you really don't need much. What you can't do (at least easily) is look ahead to see what comes next, although there are techniques that will allow a limited look-ahead without seriously compromising simplicity. In Figure 11.1, you see the representation of a small tree the way an ant might see it. The fuzzy parts are what you don't know. The clear parts are what you do know. The shaded node is where you are right now.

Figure 11.1
A tree as seen by an ant, secure in the knowledge of its ancestral line and immediate surroundings but blissfully unaware of other branches of the family tree.

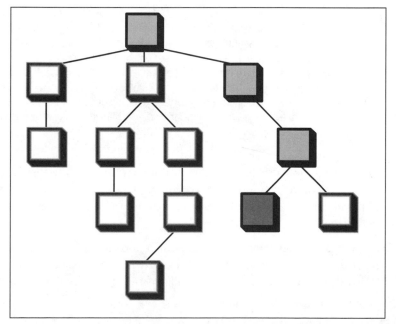

You might be tempted to retain knowledge of siblings while you traverse the tree, but this is folly with an event-driven approach. When you've visited every node, you've collected enough information to construct the entire tree but can only use it as you process the last leaf of the last branch. Like a deathbed revelation, you can't do much with it. Retaining more than direct ancestral knowledge actually makes processing uneven and dependent on a node's exact position in the tree. If you know the previous siblings, you can alter your behavior based on that knowledge but you can't do the same for later siblings because you haven't been there yet.

If you need complete knowledge to do a task, you'll need to use a tree-driven approach, and DOM, however flawed in its current implementations, has at least the blessing and *imprimatur* of the W3C so you can be sure that it will eventually settle down to useful uniformity. The major deviations from W3C DOM exist in the Internet Explorer browser from Microsoft, which also happens to be a major supporter of the standard, albeit loosely, so it's fairly easy to write to that platform exclusively. This may not be a good idea but it's often done.

The next release of Netscape, slated to incorporate the current Mozilla.org open-source rewrite of Navigator functionality, will implement W3C-standard DOM as opposed to the completely different document model of the same name implemented in the current Netscape 4.7 browser. For historical reasons, Netscape went its own merry way with a completely different document object model scheme while W3C was working on the standard. So they had to grit their collective teeth and scrap their model entirely to go to W3C DOM. Luckily, it never achieved much in the way of market penetration so they don't have a huge user base to mollify.

Note

The old paradigm of developing proprietary systems with a relatively low initial cost of ownership and high maintenance costs is fading in favor of standards-based systems with both low initial and maintenance costs. Companies can compete at a much lower market level by maintaining a continuous relationship with their customer than they can by trying to lock them in with proprietary solutions. With standard toolkits such as SAX available free or at low cost, a company no longer has to recoup quite as much development expense in licenses and renewals and can be far quicker to market. This enables them to compete much closer to the bone.

Microsoft has a more difficult problem, because it's closer to the standard but has millions of users who depend on its proprietary version of DOM. Microsoft's migration to a standards-based paradigm will have to take that user base into account, so DOM incompatibilities will likely persist into the foreseeable future.

If you just want to get some work done, with a minimum of fuss and a maximum of speed, an event-driven approach might be best because the grandiose data structures contemplated by DOM don't even exist. An ant can walk any sort of tree and do something useful with it.

→ **See** "Understanding XPath Axes" **p. 174**.
→ **See** "Using XPath Abbreviations" **p. 179**.

UNDERSTANDING SAX PARSERS

SAX is not actually a parser at all, but an Application Programming Interface (API) that provides a set of common controlling mechanisms for a large number of parsers, freeing the programmer to use whichever parser he is most comfortable with. You might think of it as a hotrod. You can put any engine under the hood you care to, deriving whatever benefits that engine may have, without changing the body type or how it steers. It's not the only event-driven XML processor out there in the world. There are quite a few more and they're listed in Appendix B, "Tools for XML/XHTML Editing and Conversion," but one is enough to look at to get the general idea.

→ **See** "XML Parsing Engines" **p. 721**.

Tip from
LeeAnne.com
Words to weave by

There's still a strong free software movement all around the world. You can find free tools to do almost anything connected with programming, including entire operating systems, compilers, debuggers, and XML parsers.

You can find SAX in several forms, depending on what languages you're most familiar with. Java and Python versions are both easily obtained and *free*, so this section takes a look at both.

A Python implementation lives at `http://www.stud.ifi.uio.no/~lmariusg/download/python/xml/saxlib.html` and is kindly maintained by Lars Marius Garshol at the University of Oslo in Norway. The XML community is worldwide, and it's very easy to become quite familiar with people you'll likely never meet in person when you start to work in this field. SAX for Python requires access to Python itself, which has an XML parser bundled with the distribution. Try the Python Web site at `http://www.python.org/` to download the latest version. It's available for a large number of platforms, including a certified 100% Pure Java version that should allow you to run it anywhere with a Java port.

If you need the Java SDK (Software Development Kit) please visit Sun's main site at `http://www.sun.com/` and follow the Java SDK link. The current version is Java 2, version 1.2, which lives at `http://java.sun.com/products/jdk/1.2/` but this may change. The SDK is free.

The Java version lives in several locations, but here is one at the Microstar site, which also offers (for sale) other XML tools: `http://www.microstar.com/products.html`. Scroll down the page to see entries for Ælfred, the parser engine, and SAX itself. Ælfred, for those who don't get the in-joke, was king of the West-Saxons of Wessex (a part of what became England) in the latter part of the ninth century of the common era. Get it? *SAXon*?

You'll want to download both, filling out a form so Microstar knows who you are, which is a small price to pay for a great and useful product you'll be able to use and make money with.

Tip from
LeeAnne.com
Words to weave by

Many of these sites have extensive software examples on them, free for your perusal. There are few better ways to learn the coding tricks of any language than to study existing code created by experts.

You should also tuck away this Web address for future reference: David Megginson's SAX site at http://www.megginson.com/SAX/. Here you'll find the SAX2 engine in Java, quite a bit of information about SAX, and other handy things. There are other parsing engines, Lark from Tim Bray of XML fame, MSXML from Microsoft of Microsoft fame, XML Library from Sun Microsystems of Bill Joy fame, and SXP from Silfide. The XML Software Site at http://www.xmlsoftware.com/ will have links to all of them.

But enough theory, let's *do* something!

EVENT HANDLING IN SAX

This chapter is too small to delve deeply into the mysteries of SAX and XML processing, and you'll do more in later chapters, but for now you can run a variation on the Java code found on David Meginnson's site at http://www.megginson.com/SAX/ that prints out messages when it finds nodes and leaves them. First, you need to replace a few of the default handlers for HandlerBase, one of the subhandlers in DocumentHandler, the handler which receives start- and end-element events, processing instructions, character data, and quite a bit more basic XML stuff:

```
import org.xml.sax.HandlerBase;
import org.xml.sax.AttributeList;
  public class MyTreeTracer extends HandlerBase {
    public void startElement (String name, AttributeList atts) {
      System.out.println("Entering element: " + name);}
    public void endElement (String name) {
      System.out.println("Leaving element: " + name);}
  }
```

Now you have to invoke our new handlers:

```
import org.xml.sax.Parser;
import org.xml.sax.DocumentHandler;
import org.xml.sax.helpers.ParserFactory;
  public class SAXApp {
    static final String parserClass = "com.microstar.xml.SAXDriver";
    public static void main (String args[])
      throws Exception {
      Parser parser = ParserFactory.makeParser(parserClass);
      DocumentHandler handler = new MyTreeTracer();
      parser.setDocumentHandler(handler);
      for (int i = 0; i < args.length; i++) {
        parser.parse(args[i]);}
    }
  }
```

The value "com.microstar.xml.SAXDriver" is for Ælfred, the SAX driver from Microstar. If you use another version you'll have to change this string to match your driver. This code isn't very useful, as you might guess, but with surprisingly little work you can turn it into an actual application tool.

Say you wanted to turn XML code into XHTML. You'll need a few more extensions to the DocumentHandler class, StartDocument (to output our XHTML Prolog and the start of the XHTML document), EndDocument (to wind up our output), and characters, to pass on characters as you see them. You'll also need a bit more I/O capability:

```
import org.xml.sax.HandlerBase;
import org.xml.sax.AttributeList;
import java.io.*;
  public class MyTreeTracer extends HandlerBase {
    private PrintWriter fout;
    public MyTreeTracer() throws IOException {
      fout = new PrintWriter(new FileWriter("aout.html")); }
    public void startDocument() {
      fout.println("<?xml version='1.0'?>");
      fout.println("<!DOCTYPE html PUBLIC '-//W3C//DTD XHTML 1.0 Strict//EN'");
      fout.println("'http://www.w3.org/TR/xhtml1/DTD/strict.dtd'>");
      fout.println("<html xmlns='http://www.w3.org/TR/xhtml1' />");
      fout.println("<head>");
      fout.println("<title>MyTreeTracer Test</title>");
      fout.println("</head>");
      fout.println("<body>"); }
    public void endDocument() {
      fout.println("</body>");
      fout.println("</html>");
      fout.close(); }
    public void startElement (String name, AttributeList atts) {
      fout.println("<p>");
      fout.print(name + ": "); }
    public void endElement (String name) {
      fout.println(" :" + name);
      fout.println("</p>"); }
    public void characters (char ch[], int start, int length) {
      for (int i=start; i < start+length; i++) {
        fout.print(ch[i]); }
      }
  }
```

This doesn't actually do much either, just takes all the character data and prints it on a line by itself bracketed by the name of the element the data is contained in. But the result is pure XHTML 1.0, and with appropriate tests of the element name and processing, you could turn XML code into anything you want.

Tip from

 LeeAnne.com
Words to weave by

Finding existing templates in the public domain that do *almost* exactly what you want may speed your learning and development time until you memorize the languages' idioms and conventions. While you should feel free to experiment with any code before committing to actual production using any code as a base, make sure that it's truly available for use as you intend it by reading the terms of the license very carefully and asking the author or copyright holder if there is any doubt in your mind.

WRITING EVENT HANDLERS

In section "Event Handling in SAX" above, you've written a practical event handler using the facilities of a real system, SAX. This section talks about it a bit more in a theoretical way.

The hard parts of writing event handlers have already been done for you by the people (or person, in the case of SAX) who made the parser/event handler you use. They provide a series of class templates, many of which are mere stubs, that do the hard work of actually walking the document tree and noticing events. The public classes don't usually do much, but serve the useful purpose of keeping the structure in running order until you fill in the blanks with your code. So until you extend those classes with useful methods, they do nothing but spin their wheels while the parser runs merrily over the code doing nothing but walking up and down the branches, but doing it very well.

Whenever the classes find anything interesting, such as a node or tag, some characters, a processing instruction, or the like, they fire off a message to the class responsible for that interesting state. So `startDocument()`, a subclass of `handlerBase()`, is notified when the parser finds the start of the document; `endDocument()`, also a subclass of `handlerBase`, is notified when it finds the end; and others are notified for everything in between. Because that class is extended with your own, your instantiations retain all those messages so you can use them as you see fit. That's just what occurred in the example. Because the base subclass doesn't do anything except keep its place in the parser, when you extended the methods available to its new subclass, you made sure that it did something useful.

Although there are a lot more classes available in Java, all of which do interesting things, the concept is not that hard after you break out of the procedural mindset that sequential programming languages tend to enforce. Instead of micro-managing every detail, you tell new recruits how you do things in your program and let them loose on the task. Like busy little ants, they'll take on their portion of the task without requiring more attention from you until they're done. They'll get up in the morning, come to work, and go home at night, all without supervision.

Looking at SAX in Detail

There is no monolithic SAX that can be described in a nutshell or generated by rotc from a menu of predefined tools. SAX is a programming interface designed to be easily extensible so that you can create new classes and new methods to suit the task at hand precisely and efficiently. SAX implements a core set of functions likely to be useful in any situation using XML and leaves the design and implementation of the program to you, the programmer. There's no getting around the fact that to use it, you really do have to know how to write programs.

It nonetheless seems appropriate to list the core features and properties that SAX makes available so you know what you have to work with before setting out.

SAX Features

SAX comes bundled in two package classes, `org.xml.sax` and `org.xml.sax.helpers`. The first contains the basic functionality required to handle XML documents and the second contains various helper classes.

Interfaces in `org.xml.sax`

Table 11.1 contains a list of the interfaces in `org.xml.sax` together with a short description of their purpose.

TABLE 11.1   INTERFACES IN PACKAGE `org.xml.sax`

Interface	Purpose
Attribute List	Deprecated. This interface is included for compatibility with earlier versions of SAX. It's been replaced by the SAX2 Attributes interface, which includes Namespace support.
Attributes	An interface for listing XML attributes.
ContentHandler	An interface for obtaining the logical content of a document.
DocumentHandler	Deprecated. This interface is included for compatibility with earlier versions of SAX. It's been replaced by the SAX2 ContentHandler interface, which includes Namespace support.
DTDHandler	An interface for intercepting basic DTD-related events.
EntityResolver	An interface for resolving XML entities.
ErrorHandler	An interface for implementing SAX error handlers.
Locator	An interface for associating a SAX event with a document location.
Parser	Deprecated. This interface is included for compatibility with earlier versions of SAX. It's been replaced by the SAX2 XMLReader interface, which includes Namespace support.
XMLFilter	An interface for XML filters.
XMLReader	An interface for reading XML documents.

CLASSES IN `org.xml.sax`

Table 11.2 contains a list of the basic classes in `org.xml.sax` together with a short description of their purpose.

TABLE 11.2   CLASSES IN PACKAGE `org.xml.sax`

Class	Purpose
HandlerBase	Deprecated. This class is included for compatibility with earlier versions of SAX. It's been replaced by the SAX2 DocumentHandler interface.
InputSource	This class identifies a single input source for an XML entity.

EXCEPTIONS IN `org.xml.sax`

Table 11.3 contains a list of the exceptions in `org.xml.sax` together with a short description of their purpose.

TABLE 11.3 EXCEPTIONS IN PACKAGE org.xml.sax

Exception	Purpose
SAXException	Exception class for catching general SAX errors and warnings
SAXNotRecognizedException	Exception class for catching unrecognized identifiers
SAXNotSupportedException	Exception class for catching unsupported operations
SAXParseException	Exception class for catching XML parse errors and warnings

CLASSES IN org.xml.sax.helpers

Table 11.4 contains a list of the classes in org.xml.sax.helpers together with a short description of their purpose.

TABLE 11.4 CLASSES IN PACKAGE org.xml.sax.helpers

Class	Purpose
AttributeListImpl	Deprecated. This class is included for compatibility with earlier versions of SAX. It's been replaced by the SAX2 Attributes, which is implemented in the AttributesImpl helper class.
AttributesImpl	This class implements a default version of the Attributes interface, which can be extended as necessary.
DefaultHandler	This class is a default base for constructing SAX2 event handlers by extension.
LocatorImpl	This class implements a default version of Locator, which can be extended as necessary.
NamespaceSupport	This class implements default Namespace logic for use by SAX drivers.
ParserAdapter	This class allows you to use a SAX1 Parser as a SAX2 XMLReader.
ParserFactory	Deprecated. This interface is included for compatibility with earlier versions of SAX. It's been replaced by the SAX2 Parser interface.
XMLFilterImpl	This class is a base class for deriving XML filters by extension.
XMLReaderAdapter	This class allows you to use a SAX2 XMLReader as a SAX1 Parser.
XMLReaderFactory	This class is a Factory for creating an XMLReader.

ALPHABETICAL LIST OF SAX CLASSES AND METHODS

Table 11.5 contains an alphabetical list of all the features in SAX2 together with a terse syntax hint and short description of their purpose.

TABLE 11.5   FEATURES IN SAX2

Feature	Purpose
addAttribute(*String*, *String*, *String*)	Deprecated—A method in class org.xml.sax.helpers. AttributeListImpl. Adds an attribute to an attribute list.
addAttribute(*String*, *String*, *String*, *String*, *String*)	A method in class org.xml.sax.helpers. AttributesImpl. Adds an attribute to the end of an attribute list.
AttributeList	Deprecated—The interface org.xml.sax. AttributeList. This interface has been replaced by the SAX2 Attributes interface, which includes Namespace support.
AttributeListImpl	Deprecated—The class org.xml.sax.helpers. AttributeListImpl. This class implements a deprecated interface, AttributeList, which has been replaced by SAX2 Attributes, which is implemented in the AttributesImpl helper class.
AttributeListImpl()	Deprecated—The constructor for class org.xml.sax. helpers.AttributeListImpl. Creates an empty attribute list.
AttributeListImpl(AttributeList)	Deprecated—The constructor for class org.xml.sax. helpers.AttributeListImpl. Constructs a persistent copy of an existing attribute list.
Attributes	The interface org.xml.sax.Attributes.Interface. This interface provides methods that return a list of XML attributes.
AttributesImpl	The class org.xml.sax.helpers.AttributesImpl. This class is the default implementation of the Attributes interface.
AttributesImpl()	The constructor for class org.xml.sax.helpers. AttributesImpl. This constructor creates a new, empty AttributesImpl object.
AttributesImpl(Attributes)	The constructor for class org.xml.sax.helpers. AttributesImpl. Creates a copy of an existing Attributes object.
characters(char[], int, int)	A method in interface org.xml.sax.ContentHandler. Catches notifications of character data.
characters(char[], int, int)	Deprecated—A method in class org.xml.sax. HandlerBase. Catches notifications of character data inside an element.
characters(char[], int, int)	Deprecated—A method in interface org.xml.sax. DocumentHandler. Catches notifications of character data.

PART
II
CH
11

TABLE 11.5   CONTINUED

Feature	Purpose
characters(char[], int, int)	A method in class org.xml.sax.helpers. XMLReaderAdapter. Adapts a SAX2 characters event to SAX1.
characters(char[], int, int)	A method in class org.xml.sax.helpers. XMLFilterImpl. Filters a character data event.
characters(char[], int, int)	A method in class org.xml.sax.helpers. DefaultHandler. Catches notifications of character data inside an element.
characters(char[], int, int)	A method in class org.xml.sax.helpers. ParserAdapter. Adapts a SAX1 characters event to SAX2.
clear()	Deprecated—A method in class org.xml.sax.helpers. AttributeListImpl. Clears an attribute list.
clear()	A method in class org.xml.sax.helpers. AttributesImpl. Clears an attribute list for reuse.
ContentHandler	The interface org.xml.sax.ContentHandler. Catches notifications of the logical content of a document.
createXMLReader()	A static method in class org.xml.sax.helpers. XMLReaderFactory. Attempts to create an XML reader from a system property.
createXMLReader(String)	A static method in class org.xml.sax.helpers. XMLReaderFactory. Attempts to create an XML reader from a class name.
declarePrefix(String, String)	A method in class org.xml.sax.helpers. NamespaceSupport. Declares a Namespace prefix.
DefaultHandler	The class org.xml.sax.helpers.DefaultHandler. The default base class for SAX2 event handlers.
DefaultHandler()	The constructor for class org.xml.sax.helpers. DefaultHandler.
DocumentHandler	Deprecated—The interface org.xml.sax. DocumentHandler. This interface has been replaced by the SAX2 ContentHandler interface, which includes Namespace support.
DTDHandler	The interface org.xml.sax.DTDHandler. Catches notifications of basic DTD-related events.
endDocument()	A method in interface org.xml.sax.ContentHandler. Catches notifications of the end of a document.
endDocument()	Deprecated—A method in class org.xml.sax. HandlerBase. Catches notifications of the end of the document.

TABLE 11.5 CONTINUED

Feature	Purpose
endDocument()	Deprecated—A method in interface org.xml.sax. DocumentHandler. Catches notifications of the end of a document.
endDocument()	A method in class org.xml.sax.helpers. XMLReaderAdapter. The end document event.
endDocument()	A method in class org.xml.sax.helpers. XMLFilterImpl. Filters an end document event.
endDocument()	A method in class org.xml.sax.helpers. DefaultHandler. Catches notifications of the end of the document.
endDocument()	A method in class org.xml.sax.helpers. ParserAdapter. Adapts a SAX1 end document event to SAX2.
endElement(String)	A method in class org.xml.sax.HandlerBase Deprecated. Catches notifications of the end of an element.
endElement(String)	Deprecated—A method in interface org.xml.sax. DocumentHandler. Catches notifications of the end of an element.
endElement(String)	A method in class org.xml.sax.helpers. ParserAdapter. Adapts a SAX1 end element event.
endElement(String, String, String)	A method in interface org.xml.sax.ContentHandler. Catches notifications of the end of an element.
endElement(String, String, String)	A method in class org.xml.sax.helpers. XMLReaderAdapter. Adapts a SAX2 end element event.
endElement(String, String, String)	A method in class org.xml.sax.helpers. XMLFilterImpl. Filters an end element event.
endElement(String, String, String)	A method in class org.xml.sax.helpers. DefaultHandler. Catches notifications of the end of an element.
endPrefixMapping(String)	A method in interface org.xml.sax.ContentHandler. Ends the scope of a prefix-URI mapping.
endPrefixMapping(String)	A method in class org.xml.sax.helpers. XMLReaderAdapter. Adapts a SAX2 end prefix mapping event.
endPrefixMapping(String)	A method in class org.xml.sax.helpers. XMLFilterImpl. Filters an end Namespace prefix mapping event.
endPrefixMapping(String)	A method in class org.xml.sax.helpers. DefaultHandler. Catches notifications of the end of a Namespace mapping.

PART
II

CH
11

TABLE 11.5   CONTINUED

Feature	Purpose
EntityResolver	The interface `org.xml.sax.EntityResolver`. Basic interface for resolving entities.
error(SAXParseException)	Deprecated—A method in `class org.xml.sax.HandlerBase`. Catches notifications of a recoverable parser error.
error(SAXParseException)	A method in interface `org.xml.sax.ErrorHandler`. Catches notifications of a recoverable error.
error(SAXParseException)	A method in class `org.xml.sax.helpers.XMLFilterImpl`. Filters an error event.
error(SAXParseException)	A method in class `org.xml.sax.helpers.DefaultHandler`. Catches notifications of a recoverable parser error.
ErrorHandler	The interface `org.xml.sax.ErrorHandler`. Basic interface for SAX error handlers.
fatalError(SAXParseException)	Deprecated—A method in class `org.xml.sax.HandlerBase`. Reports a fatal XML parsing error.
fatalError(SAXParseException)	A method in interface `org.xml.sax.ErrorHandler`. Catches notifications of a non-recoverable error.
fatalError(SAXParseException)	A method in class `org.xml.sax.helpers.XMLFilterImpl`. Filters a fatal error event.
fatalError(SAXParseException)	A method in class `org.xml.sax.helpers.DefaultHandler`. Reports a fatal XML parsing error.
getByteStream()	A method in class `org.xml.sax.InputSource`. Gets the byte stream for this input source.
getCharacterStream()	A method in class `org.xml.sax.InputSource`. Gets the character stream for this input source.
getColumnNumber()	A method in interface `org.xml.sax.Locator`. Returns the column number where the current document event ends.
getColumnNumber()	A method in class `org.xml.sax.SAXParseException`. The column number of the end of the text where the exception occurred.
getColumnNumber()	A method in class `org.xml.sax.helpers.LocatorImpl`. Returns the saved column number (1-based).
getDeclaredPrefixes()	A method in class `org.xml.sax.helpers.NamespaceSupport`. Returns an enumeration of all prefixes declared in this context.
getDTDHandler()	A method in interface `org.xml.sax.XMLReader`. Returns the current DTD handler.
getDTDHandler()	A method in class `org.xml.sax.helpers.XMLFilterImpl`. Gets the current DTD event handler.

TABLE 11.5 CONTINUED

Feature	Purpose
getDTDHandler()	A method in class `org.xml.sax.helpers.ParserAdapter`. Returns the current DTD handler.
getEncoding()	A method in class `org.xml.sax.InputSource`. Gets the character encoding for a byte stream or URI.
getEntityResolver()	A method in interface `org.xml.sax.XMLReader`. Returns the current entity resolver.
getEntityResolver()	A method in class `org.xml.sax.helpers.XMLFilterImpl`. Gets the current entity resolver.
getEntityResolver()	A method in class `org.xml.sax.helpers.ParserAdapter`. Returns the current entity resolver.
getErrorHandler()	A method in interface `org.xml.sax.XMLReader`. Returns the current error handler.
getErrorHandler()	A method in class `org.xml.sax.helpers.XMLFilterImpl`. Gets the current error event handler.
getErrorHandler()	A method in class `org.xml.sax.helpers.ParserAdapter`. Returns the current error handler.
getException()	A method in class `org.xml.sax.SAXException`. Returns the embedded exception, if any.
getFeature(String)	A method in interface `org.xml.sax.XMLReader`. Looks up the value of a feature.
getFeature(String)	A method in class `org.xml.sax.helpers.XMLFilterImpl`. Looks up the state of a feature.
getFeature(String)	A method in class `org.xml.sax.helpers.ParserAdapter`. Checks a parser feature.
getIndex(String)	A method in interface `org.xml.sax.Attributes`. Looks up the index of an attribute by XML 1.0 qualified name.
getIndex(String)	A method in class `org.xml.sax.helpers.AttributesImpl`. Looks up an attribute's index by namespace-qualified name.
getIndex(String, String)	A method in interface `org.xml.sax.Attributes`. Looks up the index of an attribute by `Namespace` name.
getIndex(String, String)	A method in class `org.xml.sax.helpers.AttributesImpl`. Looks up an attribute's index by Namespace name.
getLength()	A method in interface `org.xml.sax.Attributes`. Returns the number of attributes in the list.
getLength()	Deprecated—A method in interface `org.xml.sax.AttributeList`. Returns the number of attributes in this list.

TABLE 11.5   CONTINUED

Feature	Purpose
getLength()	Deprecated—A method in class `org.xml.sax.helpers.AttributeListImpl`. Returns the number of attributes in the list.
getLength()	A method in class `org.xml.sax.helpers.AttributesImpl`. Returns the number of attributes in the list.
getLineNumber()	A method in interface `org.xml.sax.Locator`. Returns the line number where the current document event ends.
getLineNumber()	A method in class `org.xml.sax.SAXParseException`. The line number of the end of the text where the exception occurred.
getLineNumber()	A method in class `org.xml.sax.helpers.LocatorImpl`. Returns the saved line number (1-based).
getLocalName(int)	A method in interface `org.xml.sax.Attributes`. Looks up an attribute's local name by index.
getLocalName(int)	A method in class `org.xml.sax.helpers.AttributesImpl`. Returns an attribute's local name.
getMessage()	A method in class `org.xml.sax.SAXException`. Returns a detailed message for this exception.
getName(int)	Deprecated—A method in interface `org.xml.sax.AttributeList`. Returns the name of an attribute in this list by position.
getName(int)	Deprecated—A method in class `org.xml.sax.helpers.AttributeListImpl`. Gets the name of an attribute by position.
getParent()	A method in interface `org.xml.sax.XMLFilter`. Gets the parent `XMLReader`.
getParent()	A method in class `org.xml.sax.helpers.XMLFilterImpl`. Gets the parent `XMLReader`.
getPrefix(String)	A method in class `org.xml.sax.helpers.NamespaceSupport`. Returns one of the prefixes mapped to a `Namespace` URI.
getPrefixes()	A method in class `org.xml.sax.helpers.NamespaceSupport`. Returns an enumeration of all prefixes currently declared.
getPrefixes(String)	A method in class `org.xml.sax.helpers.NamespaceSupport`. Returns an enumeration of all prefixes currently declared for a URI.
getProperty(String)	A method in interface `org.xml.sax.XMLReader`. Looks up the value of a property.

TABLE 11.5   CONTINUED

Feature	Purpose
getProperty(String)	A method in class `org.xml.sax.helpers.XMLFilterImpl`. Looks up the value of a property.
getProperty(String)	A method in class `org.xml.sax.helpers.ParserAdapter`. Gets a parser property.
getPublicId()	A method in interface `org.xml.sax.Locator`. Returns the public identifier for the current document event.
getPublicId()	A method in class `org.xml.sax.SAXParseException`. Gets the public identifier of the entity where the exception occurred.
getPublicId()	A method in class `org.xml.sax.InputSource`. Gets the public identifier for this input source.
getPublicId()	A method in class `org.xml.sax.helpers.LocatorImpl`. Returns the saved public identifier.
getQName(int)	A method in interface `org.xml.sax.Attributes`. Looks up an attribute's XML 1.0 qualified name by index.
getQName(int)	A method in class `org.xml.sax.helpers.AttributesImpl`. Returns an attribute's qualified (prefixed) name.
getSystemId()	A method in interface `org.xml.sax.Locator`. Returns the system identifier for the current document event.
getSystemId()	A method in class `org.xml.sax.SAXParseException`. Gets the system identifier of the entity where the exception occurred.
getSystemId()	A method in class `org.xml.sax.InputSource`. Gets the system identifier for this input source.
getSystemId()	A method in class `org.xml.sax.helpers.LocatorImpl`. Returns the saved system identifier.
getType(int)	A method in interface `org.xml.sax.Attributes`. Looks up an attribute's type by index.
getType(int)	Deprecated—A method in interface `org.xml.sax.AttributeList`. Returns the type of an attribute in the list (by position).
getType(int)	Deprecated—A method in class `org.xml.sax.helpers.AttributeListImpl`. Gets the type of an attribute (by position).
getType(int)	A method in class `org.xml.sax.helpers.AttributesImpl`. Returns an attribute's type by index.
getType(String)	A method in interface `org.xml.sax.Attributes`. Looks up an attribute's type by XML 1.0 namespace-qualified name.

PART

II

CH

11

TABLE 11.5   CONTINUED

Feature	Purpose
getType(String)	Deprecated—A method in interface `org.xml.sax.AttributeList`. Returns the type of an attribute in the list by name.
getType(String)	Deprecated—A method in class `org.xml.sax.helpers.AttributeListImpl`. Gets the type of an attribute by name.
getType(String)	A method in class `org.xml.sax.helpers.AttributesImpl`. Looks up an attribute's type by qualified (prefixed) name.
getType(String, String)	A method in interface `org.xml.sax.Attributes`. Looks up an attribute's type by Namespace name.
getType(String, String)	A method in class `org.xml.sax.helpers.AttributesImpl`. Looks up an attribute's type by Namespace-qualified name.
getURI(int)	A method in interface `org.xml.sax.Attributes`. Looks up an attribute's `Namespace URI` by index.
getURI(int)	A method in class `org.xml.sax.helpers.AttributesImpl`. Return an attribute's `Namespace URI`.
getURI(String)	A method in class `org.xml.sax.helpers.NamespaceSupport`. Looks up a prefix and obtains the currently mapped `Namespace URI`.
getValue(int)	A method in interface `org.xml.sax.Attributes`. Looks up an attribute's value by index.
getValue(int)	Deprecated—A method in interface `org.xml.sax.AttributeList`. Returns the value of an attribute in the list (by position).
getValue(int)	Deprecated—A method in class `org.xml.sax.helpers.AttributeListImpl`. Gets the value of an attribute (by position).
getValue(int)	A method in class `org.xml.sax.helpers.AttributesImpl`. Returns an attribute's value by index.
getValue(String)	A method in interface `org.xml.sax.Attributes`. Looks up an attribute's value by XML 1.0 qualified name.
getValue(String)	Deprecated—A method in interface `org.xml.sax.AttributeList`. Returns the value of an attribute in the list (by name).
getValue(String)	Deprecated—A method in class org.xml.sax.helpers. `AttributeListImpl`. Gets the value of an attribute (by name).
getValue(String)	A method in class `org.xml.sax.helpers.AttributesImpl`. Looks up an attribute's value by qualified (prefixed) name.

TABLE 11.5   CONTINUED

Feature	Purpose
getValue(String, String)	A method in interface org.xml.sax.Attributes. Looks up an attribute's value by Namespace name.
getValue(String, String)	A method in class org.xml.sax.helpers. AttributesImpl. Looks up an attribute's value by Namespace-qualified name.
HandlerBase	Deprecated—The class org.xml.sax.HandlerBase. This class works with the deprecated DocumentHandler interface. It's been replaced by the SAX2 DefaultHandler class.
HandlerBase()	Deprecated—The constructor for class org.xml.sax. HandlerBase.
ignorableWhitespace(char[], int, int)	A method in interface org.xml.sax.ContentHandler. Catches notifications of ignorable whitespace in element content.
ignorableWhitespace(char[], int, int)	Deprecated—A method in class org.xml.sax. HandlerBase. Catches notifications of ignorable whitespace in element content.
ignorableWhitespace(char[], int, int)	Deprecated—A method in interface org.xml.sax. DocumentHandler. Catches notifications of ignorable whitespace in element content.
ignorableWhitespace(char[], int, int)	A method in class org.xml.sax.helpers. XMLReaderAdapter. Adapts a SAX2 ignorable whitespace event to SAX1.
ignorableWhitespace(char[], int, int)	A method in class org.xml.sax.helpers. XMLFilterImpl. Filters an ignorable whitespace event.
ignorableWhitespace(char[], int, int)	A method in class org.xml.sax.helpers. DefaultHandler. Catches notifications of ignorable whitespace in element content.
ignorableWhitespace(char[], int, int)	A method in class org.xml.sax.helpers. ParserAdapter. Adapts a SAX1 ignorable whitespace event to SAX2.
InputSource	The class org.xml.sax.InputSource. Identifies a single input source for an XML entity.
InputSource()	Constructor for class org.xml.sax.InputSource. The zero-argument default constructor for an input source.
InputSource(InputStream)	Constructor for class org.xml.sax.InputSource. Creates a new input source with an associated byte stream.
InputSource(Reader)	Constructor for class org.xml.sax.InputSource. Creates a new input source with an associated character stream.

PART II
CH 11

TABLE 11.5   CONTINUED

Feature	Purpose
InputSource(String)	Constructor for class `org.xml.sax.InputSource`. Creates a new input source with an associated system identifier.
Locator	The interface `org.xml.sax.Locator`. Interface for associating a SAX event with a document location.
LocatorImpl	The class `org.xml.sax.helpers.LocatorImpl`. Provide an optional convenience implementation of Locator.
LocatorImpl()	Constructor for class `org.xml.sax.helpers.LocatorImpl`. Zero-argument constructor.
LocatorImpl(Locator)	Constructor for class `org.xml.sax.helpers.LocatorImpl`. Copy constructor.
makeParser()	Deprecated—A static method in class `org.xml.sax.helpers.ParserFactory`. Creates a new SAX parser using the 'org.xml.sax.parser' system property.
makeParser(String)	Deprecated—A static method in class `org.xml.sax.helpers.ParserFactory`. Creates a new SAX parser object using the class name provided.
NamespaceSupport	The class `org.xml.sax.helpers.NamespaceSupport`. Encapsulates `Namespace` logic for use by SAX drivers.
NamespaceSupport()	Constructor for class `org.xml.sax.helpers.NamespaceSupport`. Creates a new Namespace support object.
notationDecl(String, String, String)	Deprecated—A method in class `org.xml.sax.HandlerBase`. Catches notifications of a notation declaration.
notationDecl(String, String, String)	A method in interface `org.xml.sax.DTDHandler`. Catches notifications of a notation declaration event.
notationDecl(String, String, String)	A method in class. `org.xml.sax.helpers.XMLFilterImpl`. Filters a notation declaration event.
notationDecl(String, String, String)	A method in class `org.xml.sax.helpers.DefaultHandler`. Catches notifications of a notation declaration.
org.xml.sax	package `org.xml.sax`.
org.xml.sax.helpers	package `org.xml.sax.helpers`.
parse(InputSource)	Deprecated—A method in interface `org.xml.sax.Parser`. Parses an XML document.
parse(InputSource)	A method in interface `org.xml.sax.XMLReader`. Parses an XML document.
parse(InputSource)	A method in class `org.xml.sax.helpers.XMLReaderAdapter`. Parses the document.

TABLE 11.5   CONTINUED

Feature	Purpose
parse(InputSource)	A method in class org.xml.sax.helpers. XMLFilterImpl. Parses a document.
parse(InputSource)	A method in class org.xml.sax.helpers. ParserAdapter. Parses an XML document.
parse(String)	Deprecated—A method in interface org.xml.sax. Parser. Parses an XML document from a system identifier (URI).
parse(String)	A method in interface org.xml.sax.XMLReader. Parses an XML document from a system identifier (URI).
parse(String)	A method in class org.xml.sax.helpers. XMLReaderAdapter. Parses the document.
parse(String)	A method in class org.xml.sax.helpers. XMLFilterImpl. Parses a document.
parse(String)	A method in class org.xml.sax.helpers. ParserAdapter. Parses an XML document.
Parser	Deprecated—The interface org.xml.sax.Parser. This interface has been replaced by the SAX2 XMLReader interface, which includes Namespace support.
ParserAdapter	The class org.xml.sax.helpers.ParserAdapter. Adapts a SAX1 Parser as a SAX2 XMLReader.
ParserAdapter()	Constructor for class org.xml.sax.helpers. ParserAdapter. Constructs a new parser adapter.
ParserAdapter(Parser)	Constructor for class org.xml.sax.helpers. ParserAdapter. Constructs a new parser adapter.
ParserFactory	Deprecated—The class org.xml.sax.helpers. ParserFactory. This class works with the deprecated Parser interface.
popContext()	A method in class org.xml.sax.helpers. NamespaceSupport. Reverts to the previous Namespace context.
processingInstruction(String, String)	A method in interface org.xml.sax.ContentHandler. Catches notifications of a processing instruction.
processingInstruction(String, String)	Deprecated—A method in class org.xml.sax. HandlerBase. Catches notifications of a processing instruction.
processingInstruction(String, String)	Deprecated—A method in interface org.xml.sax. DocumentHandler. Catches notifications of a processing instruction.
processingInstruction(String, String)	A method in class org.xml.sax.helpers. XMLReaderAdapter. Adapts a SAX2 processing instruction event.

TABLE 11.5   CONTINUED

Feature	Purpose
processingInstruction(String, String)	A method in class org.xml.sax.helpers. XMLFilterImpl. Filters a processing instruction event.
processingInstruction(String, String)	A method in class org.xml.sax.helpers. DefaultHandler. Catches notifications of a processing instruction.
processingInstruction(String, String)	A method in class org.xml.sax.helpers. ParserAdapter. Adapts a SAX1 processing instruction event.
processName(String, String[], boolean)	A method in class org.xml.sax.helpers. NamespaceSupport. Processes a raw XML 1.0 name.
pushContext()	A method in class org.xml.sax.helpers. NamespaceSupport. Starts a new Namespace context.
removeAttribute(int)	A method in class org.xml.sax.helpers. AttributesImpl. Removes an attribute from the list.
removeAttribute(String)	Deprecated—A method in class org.xml.sax.helpers. AttributeListImpl. Removes an attribute from the list.
reset()	A method in class org.xml.sax.helpers. NamespaceSupport. Resets this Namespace support object for reuse.
resolveEntity(String, String)	A method in interface org.xml.sax.EntityResolver. Allows the application to resolve external entities.
resolveEntity(String, String)	Deprecated—A method in class org.xml.sax. HandlerBase. Resolves an external entity.
resolveEntity(String, String)	A method in class org.xml.sax.helpers. XMLFilterImpl. Filters an external entity resolution.
resolveEntity(String, String)	A method in class org.xml.sax.helpers. DefaultHandler. Resolves an external entity.
SAXException	The exception org.xml.sax.SAXException. Encapsulates a general SAX error or warning.
SAXException(Exception)	Constructor for class org.xml.sax.SAXException. Creates a new SAXException wrapping an existing exception.
SAXException(String)	The constructor for class org.xml.sax.SAXException. Creates a new SAXException.
SAXException(String, Exception)	The constructor for class org.xml.sax.SAXException. Creates a new SAXException from an existing exception.
SAXNotRecognizedException	The exception org.xml.sax. SAXNotRecognizedException. Exception class for an unrecognized identifier.

TABLE 11.5   CONTINUED

Feature	Purpose
`SAXNotRecognizedException (String)`	The constructor for class `org.xml.sax.SAXNotRecognizedException`. Constructs a new exception with the given message.
`SAXNotSupportedException`	The exception `org.xml.sax.SAXNotSupportedException`. Exception class for an unsupported operation.
`SAXNotSupportedException(String)`	The constructor for class `org.xml.sax.SAXNotSupportedException`. Constructs a new exception with the given message.
`SAXParseException`	The exception `org.xml.sax.SAXParseException`. Encapsulate an XML parse error or warning.
`SAXParseException(String, Locator)`	The constructor for class `org.xml.sax.SAXParseException`. Creates a new `SAXParseException` from a message and a Locator.
`SAXParseException(String, Locator, Exception)`	The constructor for class `org.xml.sax.SAXParseException`. Wraps an existing exception in a `SAXParseException`.
`SAXParseException(String, String, String, int, int)`	The constructor for class `org.xml.sax.SAXParseException`. Creates a new `SAXParseException`.
`SAXParseException(String, String, String, int, int, Exception)`	The constructor for class `org.xml.sax.SAXParseException`. Creates a new `SAXParseException` with an embedded exception.
`setAttribute(int, String, String, String, String, String)`	A method in class `org.xml.sax.helpers.AttributesImpl`. Sets an attribute in an attribute list.
`setAttributeList(AttributeList)`	Deprecated—A method in class `org.xml.sax.helpers.AttributeListImpl`. Sets an entire attribute list, discarding previous contents.
`setAttributes(Attributes)`	A method in class `org.xml.sax.helpers.AttributesImpl`. Copies an entire `Attributes` object.
`setByteStream(InputStream)`	A method in class `org.xml.sax.InputSource`. Sets the byte stream for this input source.
`setCharacterStream(Reader)`	A method in class `org.xml.sax.InputSource`. Sets the character stream for this input source.
`setColumnNumber(int)`	A method in class `org.xml.sax.helpers.LocatorImpl`. Sets the column number for this locator (1-based).
`setContentHandler (ContentHandler)`	A method in interface `org.xml.sax.XMLReader`. Allows an application to register a content event handler.
`setContentHandler (ContentHandler)`	A method in class `org.xml.sax.helpers.XMLFilterImpl`. Set the content event handler.

TABLE 11.5   CONTINUED

Feature	Purpose
setContentHandler (ContentHandler)	A method in class `org.xml.sax.helpers.ParserAdapter`. Sets the content handler.
setDocumentHandler (DocumentHandler)	Deprecated—A method in interface `org.xml.sax.Parser`. Allows an application to register a document event handler.
setDocumentHandler (DocumentHandler)	A method in class `org.xml.sax.helpers.XMLReaderAdapter`. Registers the SAX1 document event handler.
setDocumentLocator(Locator)	A method in interface `org.xml.sax.ContentHandler`. Catches an object which locates the origin of SAX document events.
setDocumentLocator(Locator)	Deprecated—A method in class `org.xml.sax.HandlerBase`. Catches a `Locator` object for document events.
setDocumentLocator(Locator)	Deprecated—A method in interface `org.xml.sax.DocumentHandler`. Catches an object for locating the origin of SAX document events.
setDocumentLocator(Locator)	A method in class `org.xml.sax.helpers.XMLReaderAdapter`. Sets a document locator.
setDocumentLocator(Locator)	A method in class `org.xml.sax.helpers.XMLFilterImpl`. Filters a new document locator event.
setDocumentLocator(Locator)	A method in class `org.xml.sax.helpers.DefaultHandler`. Catches a `Locator` object for document events.
setDocumentLocator(Locator)	A method in class `org.xml.sax.helpers.ParserAdapter`. Adapts a SAX1 document locator event to SAX2.
setDTDHandler(DTDHandler)	Deprecated—A method in interface `org.xml.sax.Parser`. Allows an application to register a DTD event handler.
setDTDHandler(DTDHandler)	A method in interface `org.xml.sax.XMLReader`. Allows an application to register a DTD event handler.
setDTDHandler(DTDHandler)	A method in class `org.xml.sax.helpers.XMLReaderAdapter`. Registers a DTD event handler.
setDTDHandler(DTDHandler)	A method in class `org.xml.sax.helpers.XMLFilterImpl`. Sets a DTD event handler.
setDTDHandler(DTDHandler)	A method in class `org.xml.sax.helpers.ParserAdapter`. Sets a DTD handler.
setEncoding(String)	A method in class `org.xml.sax.InputSource`. Sets the character encoding, if known.

TABLE 11.5 CONTINUED

Feature	Purpose
`setEntityResolver` `(EntityResolver)` resolver.	Deprecated—A method in interface `org.xml.sax.` `Parser`. Allows an application to register a custom entity
`setEntityResolver` `(EntityResolver)`	A method in interface `org.xml.sax.XMLReader`. Allows an application to register an entity resolver.
`setEntityResolver` `(EntityResolver)`	A method in class `org.xml.sax.helpers.` `XMLReaderAdapter`. Registers an entity resolver.
`setEntityResolver` `(EntityResolver)`	A method in class `org.xml.sax.helpers.` `XMLFilterImpl`. Sets an entity resolver.
`setEntityResolver` `(EntityResolver)`	A method in class `org.xml.sax.helpers.` `ParserAdapter`. Sets an entity resolver.
`setErrorHandler(ErrorHandler)`	Deprecated—A method in interface `org.xml.sax.` `Parser`. Allows an application to register an error event handler.
`setErrorHandler(ErrorHandler)`	A method in interface `org.xml.sax.XMLReader`. Allows an application to register an error event handler.
`setErrorHandler(ErrorHandler)`	A method in class `org.xml.sax.helpers.` `XMLReaderAdapter`. Registers an error event handler.
`setErrorHandler(ErrorHandler)`	A method in class `org.xml.sax.helpers.` `XMLFilterImpl`. Sets an error event handler.
`setErrorHandler(ErrorHandler)`	A method in class `org.xml.sax.helpers.` `ParserAdapter`. Sets an error handler.
`setFeature(String, boolean)`	A method in interface `org.xml.sax.XMLReader`. Sets the state of a feature.
`setFeature(String, boolean)`	A method in class `org.xml.sax.helpers.` `XMLFilterImpl`. Sets the state of a feature.
`setFeature(String, boolean)`	A method in class `org.xml.sax.helpers.` `ParserAdapter`. Sets a feature for the parser.
`setLineNumber(int)`	A method in class `org.xml.sax.helpers.LocatorImpl`. Sets the line number for this locator (1-based).
`setLocale(Locale)`	Deprecated—A method in interface `org.xml.sax.` `Parser`. Allows an application to request a locale for errors and warnings.
`setLocale(Locale)`	A method in class `org.xml.sax.helpers.` `XMLReaderAdapter`. Sets the locale for error reporting.
`setLocalName(int, String)`	A method in class `org.xml.sax.helpers.` `AttributesImpl`. Sets the local name of a specific attribute.
`setParent(XMLReader)`	A method in interface `org.xml.sax.XMLFilter`. Sets the parent reader.

TABLE 11.5   CONTINUED

Feature	Purpose
`setParent(XMLReader)`	A method in class `org.xml.sax.helpers.` `XMLFilterImpl`. Sets the parent reader.
`setProperty(String, Object)`	A method in interface `org.xml.sax.XMLReader`. Sets the value of a property.
`setProperty(String, Object)`	A method in class `org.xml.sax.helpers.` `XMLFilterImpl`. Sets the value of a property.
`setProperty(String, Object)`	A method in class `org.xml.sax.helpers.` `ParserAdapter`. Sets a parser property.
`setPublicId(String)`	A method in class `org.xml.sax.InputSource`. Sets the public identifier for this input source.
`setPublicId(String)`	A method in class `org.xml.sax.helpers.LocatorImpl`. Sets the public identifier for this locator.
setQName(int, String)	A method in class `org.xml.sax.helpers.` `AttributesImpl`. Sets the qualified name of a specific attribute.
`setSystemId(String)`	A method in class `org.xml.sax.InputSource`. Sets the system identifier for this input source.
`setSystemId(String)`	A method in class `org.xml.sax.helpers.LocatorImpl`. Sets the system identifier for this locator.
`setType(int, String)`	A method in class `org.xml.sax.helpers.` `AttributesImpl`. Sets the type of a specific attribute.
`setURI(int, String)`	A method in class `org.xml.sax.helpers.` `AttributesImpl`. Sets the `Namespace` URI of a specific attribute.
`setValue(int, String)`	A method in class `org.xml.sax.helpers.` `AttributesImpl`. Sets the value of a specific attribute.
`skippedEntity(String)`	A method in interface `org.xml.sax.ContentHandler`. Catches notifications of a skipped entity.
`skippedEntity(String)`	A method in class `org.xml.sax.helpers.` `XMLReaderAdapter`. Adapts a SAX2 skipped entity event.
`skippedEntity(String)`	A method in class `org.xml.sax.helpers.` `XMLFilterImpl`. Filters a skipped entity event.
`skippedEntity(String)`	A method in class `org.xml.sax.helpers.` `DefaultHandler`. Catches notifications of a skipped entity.
`startDocument()`	A method in interface `org.xml.sax.ContentHandler`. Catches notifications of the beginning of a document.
`startDocument()`	Deprecated—A method in class `org.xml.sax.` `HandlerBase`. Catches notifications of the beginning of the document.

TABLE 11.5   CONTINUED

Feature	Purpose
startDocument()	Deprecated—A method in interface org.xml.sax. DocumentHandler. Catches notifications of the beginning of a document.
startDocument()	A method in class org.xml.sax.helpers. XMLReaderAdapter. Starts document event.
startDocument()	A method in class org.xml.sax.helpers. XMLFilterImpl. Filters a start document event.
startDocument()	A method in class org.xml.sax.helpers. DefaultHandler. Catches notifications of the beginning of the document.
startDocument()	A method in class org.xml.sax.helpers. ParserAdapter. Adapts a SAX1 start document event.
startElement(String, AttributeList)	Deprecated—A method in class org.xml.sax. HandlerBase. Catches notifications of the start of an element.
startElement(String, AttributeList)	Deprecated—A method in interface org.xml.sax. DocumentHandler. Catches notifications of the beginning of an element.
startElement(String, AttributeList)	A method in class org.xml.sax.helpers. ParserAdapter. Adapts a SAX1 startElement event.
startElement(String, String, String, Attributes)	A method in interface org.xml.sax.ContentHandler. Catches notifications of the beginning of an element.
startElement(String, String, String, Attributes)	A method in class org.xml.sax.helpers. XMLReaderAdapter. Adapts a SAX2 start element event.
startElement(String, String, String, Attributes)	A method in class org.xml.sax.helpers. XMLFilterImpl. Filters a start element event.
startElement(String, String, String, Attributes)	A method in class org.xml.sax.helpers. DefaultHandler. Catches notifications of the start of an element.
startPrefixMapping(String, String)	A method in interface org.xml.sax.ContentHandler. Begins the scope of a prefix-URI Namespace mapping.
startPrefixMapping(String, String)	A method in class org.xml.sax.helpers. XMLReaderAdapter. Adapts a SAX2 start prefix mapping event.
startPrefixMapping(String, String)	A method in class org.xml.sax.helpers. XMLFilterImpl. Filters a start Namespace prefix mapping event.
startPrefixMapping(String, String)	A method in class org.xml.sax.helpers. DefaultHandler. Catches notifications of the start of a Namespace mapping.

PART

II

CH

11

TABLE 11.5   CONTINUED

Feature	Purpose
`toString()`	A method in class `org.xml.sax.SAXException`. Overrides toString to pick up any embedded exception.
`unparsedEntityDecl(String, String, String, String)`	Deprecated—A method in class `org.xml.sax.HandlerBase`. Catches notifications of an unparsed entity declaration.
`unparsedEntityDecl(String, String, String, String)`	A method in interface `org.xml.sax.DTDHandler`. Catches notifications of an unparsed entity declaration event.
`unparsedEntityDecl(String, String, String, String)`	A method in class `org.xml.sax.helpers.XMLFilterImpl`. Filters an unparsed entity declaration event.
`unparsedEntityDecl(String, String, String, String)`	A method in class `org.xml.sax.helpers.DefaultHandler`. Catches notifications of an unparsed entity declaration.
`warning(SAXParseException)`	Deprecated—A method in class `org.xml.sax.HandlerBase`. Catches notifications of a parser warning.
`warning(SAXParseException)`	A method in interface `org.xml.sax.ErrorHandler`. Catches notifications of a warning or error.
`warning(SAXParseException)`	A method in class `org.xml.sax.helpers.XMLFilterImpl`. Filters a warning event.
`warning(SAXParseException)`	A method in class `org.xml.sax.helpers.DefaultHandler`. Catches notifications of a parser warning.
`XMLFilter`	The interface `org.xml.sax.XMLFilter`. The interface for an XML filter.
`XMLFilterImpl`	The class `org.xml.sax.helpers.XMLFilterImpl`. The base class for deriving an XML filter by extension.
`XMLFilterImpl()`	The constructor for class `org.xml.sax.helpers.XMLFilterImpl`. Constructs an empty XML filter with no parent.
`XMLFilterImpl(XMLReader)`	The constructor for class `org.xml.sax.helpers.XMLFilterImpl`. Constructs an XML filter with the specified parent.
`XMLNS`	The static namespace variable in class `org.xml.sax.helpers.NamespaceSupport`. The XML Namespace is a constant.
`XMLReader`	The interface `org.xml.sax.XMLReader`. The interface for reading an XML document.
`XMLReaderAdapter`	The class `org.xml.sax.helpers.XMLReaderAdapter`. Adapts a SAX2 XMLReader as a SAX1 Parser.

TABLE 11.5 CONTINUED	
Feature	**Purpose**
`XMLReaderAdapter()`	The constructor for class `org.xml.sax.helpers.` `XMLReaderAdapter`. Create a new adapter.
`XMLReaderAdapter(XMLReader)`	The constructor for class `org.xml.sax.helpers.` `XMLReaderAdapter`. Create a new adapter associated with a particular input stream.
`XMLReaderFactory`	The class `org.xml.sax.helpers.XMLReaderFactory`. A factory for creating an XML reader.

UNDERSTANDING OBJECT-ORIENTED TECHNIQUES

What you did in section "Event Handling in SAX" was object-oriented programming. You didn't have to know much of anything about how the stuff works because the internal processing was hidden from you by the classes you used. You could take just the pieces you needed and tweak them around a little bit, depending on the class itself to hand you everything else you needed on a platter. In the O-O world, they call that *inheritance*. The word is very appropriate because you didn't have to work for it.

Of course, knowing which pieces to take is the real trick. There are piles of documentation on Java, SAX, various and sundry Java add-ons that let you do even *more* interesting things, and SAXON, which adds useful bits and pieces to the SAX API. Nobody knows them all, just the parts they use often. After you start doing real work you'll want to study them and abstract from the great mass the ones that seem most useful for the sorts of things you want to do. If you want to make a visual XML tool, you might look into Swing, the Java GUI library. And don't forget SAXON at `http://home.iclweb.com/icl2/mhkay/`.

Python is also object-oriented, and if you already know it, is a fine tool for processing text, faster than Perl and slightly friendlier in my opinion. Exposing Python to your perusal is all that can be done here. If you have an interest, the Python site mentioned previously has links to Python enthusiasts and resources, not necessarily in that order.

An *object* is a metaphor for some real thing (at least theoretically) and is a container for knowledge about that thing and the methods that expose that knowledge to the world. It exposes just enough of its knowledge to allow you to access what you need from it and hides all the rest. This means you're not tempted to fiddle with bits and pointers and do other dangerous things, which will save a lot of debugging time.

The best part about objects is that they also contain knowledge about how to set themselves up when they're started up and how to put everything away neatly when they're done. In object-oriented terminology, they call this the object's *constructor* and *destructor*. In assembly language terms, it's called saving and restoring the registers. Whatever, it's a very handy thing to have done for you. Many, many mistakes are made at just that point in programming. In Java, a destructor is called a *finalizer*.

Tip from

 LeeAnne.com
Words to weave by

Although constructors and destructors are usually invisible, they can be inherited and extended like anything else. Although this might not be important right now, as you go deeper into Java you'll discover the need to add items that must be allocated or initialized on entry and freed on exit.

This is not a text on object-oriented programming but it's not really all that difficult. Humans are very good at understanding metaphors and O-O programming has as its metaphor a cooperative group of individuals, all of whom specialize in certain tasks and stay out of each other's way otherwise.

To build a house, you need concrete workers for the foundation, carpenters for the framework and exterior walls, plumbers and electricians for interior utilities, drywall handlers for the interior, and roofers to top it all off. In addition, you need a general contractor to manage all the task assignments. None of these individuals need to know anything about how to do the other's job but know everything about their own; they just get their own job to the point where they can pass off responsibility to someone else. The contractor schedules the jobs but doesn't do any of them.

Where object-oriented programming improves on this metaphor is that you can figuratively clone a carpenter, say, and add some knowledge about bricklaying, and have the carpenter handle that task as well without forgetting how to be a carpenter so he won't need help with setting up forms and scaffolding. Even better, you can have a carpenter marry an electrician, producing offspring who know both trades. Although this stretches the metaphor a bit, that's what multiple inheritance does. The former is simple inheritance.

CLASSES

Simply put, a *class* is an archetype that allows you to construct objects as they are needed. When you create a new object, you actually define its class. In turn, you instantiate an instance of the class by creating an object using that class as an archetype. You can't actually use a class at all without instantiating it. Classes are very powerful concepts because they allow the creation and use of any number of objects without allocating storage or handling other mechanics.

In Java, to instantiate an instance of a class, you type in the following code with the names replaced appropriately:

```
classname name;
name = new classname();
```

All the messy details are hidden from your sight and you can concentrate on using your new object rather than figuring out how to make it from scratch.

INHERITANCE

As we hinted in the earlier metaphor, inheritance is a way that classes can be created with most of their capabilities handed to them right off so they can get on with figuring out how to do their new tasks. All you have to do is decide what sort of additional methods you want the object to know and code the new methods. All the old methods, whatever they were, will still work but the new methods will be available as well.

> **Note**
>
> In the most general Object-Oriented paradigm, it's possible for an object to inherit properties from multiple ancestors, so one could theoretically specify an object with `clock` and `radioReceiver` ancestor classes and create a new class, `clockRadio`, with the properties of both. However, problems arise when attempting to combine related classes in this way, so `analogClock` and `digitalClock` might have different methods with the same name which overlap or identical methods with different names. A new class, `dualModeClock`, the descendent of `analogClock` and `digitalClock`, would have to have these problems resolved for it automatically by the environment. Java implements single inheritance only, because that's the simplest way to do it and causes the least problems overall. Keeping track of included methods in an object with multiple ancestors is just too difficult for those with less than god-like powers.

The code to do this in Java is equally simple:

```
class newclassname extends classname {
  public void newMethod() {
    whatever stuff we want the new method to do...;
    }
  }
```

Because you're extending a preexisting class, everything the old class did is still available and all you have to supply is the new functionality. This ensures that your new code has a strong base of well-understood behavior to make supporting it far simpler. Classes that already communicate with the base class can be extended to incorporate the new method without risking the creation of an entirely new interface.

UNDERSTANDING JAVA AND PYTHON

Java is one of the most successful object-oriented languages. Previous to Java, there were many attempts to create an object-oriented language that would be useful in the real world. But they were so slow and inefficient that they never really succeeded in breaking into the mainstream. Who now remembers Eiffel? Or Simula? Okay, maybe SmallTalk, but that was mainly a Xerox toy. C++ was one of the first successes, because it capitalized on the huge base of C programmers available, but C++ isn't really an O-O language, because it doesn't enforce O-O techniques. You can use C++ to code just plain C with no trouble at all, and use just plain C to bust in on anything you choose. Although this may be an ego boost to seat-of-their-pants programmers, it is not Object Orientation.

Java is part hype and part reality, like most things in the commercial world. Universal languages have come and gone before. But Java had the power of an extremely popular compa-

PART
II
CH
11

ny behind it and the time was ripe. The Internet had made the desktop seem far too narrow a place to hold your interest long. With the Internet came a host of problems with proprietary interfaces that it was possible to ignore before because we rarely ventured outside the desktop.

Python is also object-oriented, but is a true interpreted language meant for scripting. For developers, the advantage of scripting languages is that there's no compile step. You just write the code and run it. This speeds up the development process by quite a bit. There are other scripting languages besides Python. You probably already know JavaScript (ECMAScript) and may have run into Perl, which is much used as a CGI handler on the Web. Tcl is another scripting language with a number of adherents. I couldn't say that any of them were better or worse than any other within their limits.

Even JavaScript, which is pretty much limited to Web pages, lets you write quick programs without much trouble. For serious work, Python, Tcl, and Perl are probably best, however. Python is the most object oriented of these three, however, so that's the one I like best. Purely personal.

TROUBLESHOOTING SAX

MY CODE DOESN'T WORK!

You've created a wonderful utility to translate your XML text into French but it ignores all the text and produces a series of blank lines.

You're probably not reading and processing the characters, which uses a different event handler. Because you do see blank lines, you're probably processing elements correctly, assuming you output end of lines somewhere within that part of the code.

MY CODE THREW AN EXCEPTION

Your code runs for a while and then throws an exception, which messes up the screen with a tacky message.

Try reading the exception for a clue as to where it came from. If that doesn't work, try stepping through the code to associate a particular event with the error. This may not work. If all else fails, document the code with output messages in likely spots and see if that helps you narrow it down.

CSS1, CSS2, DSSSL, XSL

In this chapter

STYLE LANGUAGES

The simple layout and formatting facilities built in to the HTML (and XHTML) standard won't suffice for the international environment. They're user hostile because they can't be overridden by users who have particular needs, and because they are limited in their scope. They're also inflexible, forcing document users to maintain multiple copies of each document for different output media. Although many, if not most, pages still use user-hostile tools such as tables, "invisible" gif spacers, and <font> commands to achieve a certain look, this usage is unwise. Although some people point at the number of sites using these tools as proof that the tools are still important, it's equally easy to point at the pathetic load times and complete inaccessibility of many, if not most, Web pages as proof that it's time for a change.

It's now possible to format a page using simple HTML commands that allow it to remain visible and usable in all browsers, including those used by persons with visual disabilities and existing personal digital assistants with Web capabilities while not forgoing the use of interesting font changes and graphic design. The features of CSS, although not well supported in older browsers, can be used, albeit requiring considerable care, to do everything tables and font tags did without breaking the sessions of a significant number of users.

Tip from

LeeAnne.com
Words to weave by

For further information on this topic, see the "<FONT FACE> Considered Harmful "article at http://isoc.bilkent.edu.tr/web_ml/html/fontface.html and the less-than-completely repentant articles by David Siegel at http://www.dsiegel.com/balkanization/ and http://www.xml.com/pub/w3j/s1.people.html.

Laying aside DSSSL (*Document Style Semantics and Specification Language*), FOSIs (*Formatting Output Specification Instance*), and other SGML tools, *Cascading Style Sheets Level 1* (CSS1) was the first practical method of separating the data from the way that data is presented on the Web. CSS offered a balance of power between the author of a Web site and the user and was at least a start on making documents versatile enough to support multiple output media. Many of the effects now moderately common on the Web, *safe* tinted text boxes, *safe* font changes, absolute positioning of text and graphics *without* kludgey one pixel gifs, and much more were made possible by Level 1 style sheets.

However, as designers worked with CSS1, more possibilities were seen and CSS2 (Level 2) soon followed, adding more support for traditional typographical and print publishing traditions, supporting more formatting pseudo-classes, and adding some internationalization options and support for aural browsers as well.

This is the current state of CSS and it promises to improve even further as time goes on. So for relatively simple formatting tasks that don't require complex transformations of the source document, CSS is still the tool of choice for Web designers.

Tip from

Words to weave by

Although CSS can be hard to use in the current browser environment, it is the most flexible and powerful mechanism available to style your documents. With care and the judicious use of scripts, even current browser implementations can be made to do very clever things. See http://www.aegis.com/ for an exemplary nonprofit site that uses BrowserHawk, a script equivalent on the server side, to sniff the user's browser and dynamically serve different content based on what it finds.

In practice, however, CSS doesn't reach an entire class of problems. If a document requires a table of contents, if a list should be sorted before output, or if the language being used requires more than simple layout techniques, CSS currently doesn't handle it. And CSS uses an entirely different language and syntax from HTML, so when a style sheet was placed inline, it had to be rigorously escaped by comments to avoid breaking many older browsers. This is a violation of XML philosophy.

In addition to all these things, the current implementations of both levels of CSS are buggy and inconsistent in scope. CSS is an efficient and robust mechanism for performing limited display formatting tasks, and as the implementations mature it will become even more valuable. However, there is a real need for more than CSS can deliver.

XSL, the *Extensible Stylesheet Language*, is a style language recast in the XML mold and duplicating the functionality of CSS2 as well as adding even more powerful formatting and transformation capabilities. XSL and XSLT, *XSL Transformations*, the related document transformation language, are the culmination of a lengthy evolution by Web standards. Because XSL has a DTD, there is little excuse for failure to implement portions of the specification. XSL is tag-based like XML, so the same skills used to create XML documents are used in XSL, speeding the learning curve. The heart of XSL is transformation and document processing for different media, so XSL is capable of managing complex multimedia document systems.

PART
II

CH
12

Tip from

Words to weave by

Task complexity is the major criterion for choosing between CSS and XSL. If you want to perform extensive rework on the document before presentation, XSL is the tool of choice. But if you want to add a little pizzazz to a page while leaving the basic structure alone, CSS is probably the better choice.

Succinctly, XSL is designed to format and transform XML documents into particular *instances* of the underlying document. The complete XSL specification is broken into two main parts: XSL proper and XSLT. XPath, the XML Path Language, is an integral part of the total specification but external to it in form, because this module is shared by many other standards. XPath was covered in Chapter 8, "XPath."

You'll learn basic concepts in this chapter. You'll further explore applications of CSS in Chapter 13, "Cascading Style Sheets and XML/XHTML," and XSL in Chapter 14, "Using Next-Generation Extensible Style Sheets—XSL."

CASCADING STYLE SHEETS—CSS

By now, you are probably familiar with CSS1 and may have used CSS2 as well. This chapter is not an introduction to CSS nor is it a tutorial that covers the language in its entirety. This chapter looks at the narrow issue of how CSS can be used to format XML documents. Many browsers don't support arbitrary XML code so there are only a few choices.

The XML code in Listing 12.1 describes the data record used in Chapter 7, "XML Schemas," to tag a customer record:

LISTING 12.1   AN XML CUSTOMER RECORD

```
<?xml version="1.0"?>
<?xml-stylesheet href="11xmp01.css" type="text/css" ?>
<!-- Customer Record -->
  <customer xmlns="http://www.leeanne.com/aristotelian/schemas/">
    <customer-name>Aristotelian Logic Systems</customer-name>
    <customerID>112344-0897</customerID>
    <credit-status>Net-30</credit-status>
    <customer-contact locale="USA">
      <honorific>Ms.</honorific>
      <given-name1>George</given-name1>
      <given-name2>Evelyn</given-name2>
      <family-name>Fayne</family-name>
      <degrees>LLD, PhD</degrees>
      <title>Contracts Director</title>
      <department>Purchasing</department>
      <telephone locale="NANP">=1 101 555.1234</telephone>
      <extension>3456</extension>
    </customer-contact>
    <comment>ALS buys over $300K per year, primarily our Mark IV WKS</comment>
    <shipping-address locale="USA">
      <attention>Attn:</attention>
      <attention-name>Receiving Clerk</attention-name>
      <reference>Ref:</reference>
      <street-address1>987 Technology Pkwy</street-address1>
      <street-address2>Unit 200 - Receiving</street-address2>
      <city>Riverdale</city>
      <territorial-division>Ohio</territorial-division>
      <territorial-abbreviation>OH</territorial-abbreviation>
      <postal-code>31089</postal-code>
      <country>USA</country>
    </shipping-address>
    <billing-address locale="USA">
      <attention>Attn:</attention>
      <attention-name>Accounts Payable</attention-name>
      <reference>Ref:</reference>
      <street-address1>987 Technology Pkwy</street-address1>
      <street-address2>Unit 300 - Accounting</street-address2>
      <city>Riverdale</city>
      <territorial-division>Ohio</territorial-division>
      <territorial-abbreviation>OH</territorial-abbreviation>
      <postal-code>31089</postal-code>
      <country>USA</country>
```

```
      </billing-address>
      <creation-date>19950711T034233-8</creation-date>
      <last-updated>19991011T112542-8</last-updated>
   </customer>
```

Remembering that the element names can be any XML tag names, we can use a CSS1 style sheet to perform basic formatting of this data as shown in Listing 12.2.

LISTING 12.2   AN EXAMPLE CSS1 STYLE SHEET FOR THE XML CUSTOMER RECORD

```
// Customer Record
  customer { float: left; clear: left; margin-left: 1pc; color: #000000; }
    customer-name { float: left; clear: left; }
    customerID { float: left; clear: left; margin-left: 1pc; }
    credit-status { float: left; clear: left; margin-left: 1pc; }
    customer-contact { float: left; clear: left; margin-left: 2pc; background:
#ffddff; }
      honorific { float: left; clear: left; }
      given-name1 { float: left; clear: left; }
      given-name2 { float: left; clear: left; }
      family-name { float: left; clear: left; }
      degrees { float: left; clear: left; }
      title { float: left; clear: left; }
      department { float: left; clear: left; }
      telephone { float: left; clear: left; }
      extension { float: left; clear: left; }
      comment { float: left; clear: left; margin-left: 1pc; }
    shipping-address { float: left; clear: left; margin-left: 2pc; background:
#ddffff; }
      attention { float: left; clear: left; }
      attention-name { float: left; clear: left; }
      reference { float: left; clear: left; }
      street-address1 { float: left; clear: left; }
      street-address2 { float: left; clear: left; }
      city { float: left; clear: left; }
      territorial-division { float: left; clear: left; }
      territorial-abbreviation { float: left; clear: left; }
      postal-code { float: left; clear: left; }
      country { float: left; clear: left; }
    billing-address { float: left; clear: left; margin-left: 2pc; background:
#ffffdd; }
      attention { float: left; clear: left; }
      attention-name { float: left; clear: left; }
      reference { float: left; clear: left; }
      street-address1 { float: left; clear: left; }
      street-address2 { float: left; clear: left; }
      city { float: left; clear: left; }
      territorial-division { float: left; clear: left; }
      territorial-abbreviation { float: left; clear: left; }
      postal-code { float: left; clear: left; }
      country { float: left; clear: left; }
    creation-date { float: left; clear: left; margin-left: 1pc; }
    last-updated { float: left; clear: left; margin-left: 1pc; }
```

PART

II

CH

12

Figure 12.1 shows the Opera Browser displaying the formatted customer record. Of course, we could do far more extensive formatting of the output but this is enough to give you the idea.

Figure 12.1
The Opera Browser displaying an XML document using supported CSS2 properties.

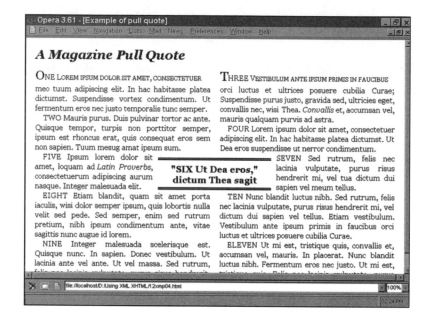

Because many browsers don't implement all the CSS1 features, you can't really count on the `display` property to enable you to force an element to be treated as a block, which is what we really want. However, this can be simulated by setting the `float` and `clear` properties, which are supported more widely, on each list item. Note that this is only one of many alternative presentations of the data. By varying the style sheet, you can format the same document in multiple ways and, even better, style sheets allow users to replace your style sheet with their own custom style sheet more appropriate to their individual needs. The Opera browser from Opera Software in Norway makes this particularly convenient in the form of a Swap Style Sheets button on their Web location bar. Check it out at `http://www.operasoftware.com/`.

Tip from

LeeAnne.com
Words to weave by

With so many alternatives, choosing which features to use can be a problem. A list of CSS features which are relatively safe as well as those which are dangerous appear at Web Review's Style Sheets subsite at `http://webreview.com/pub/Style_Sheets`.

In CSS2, you have much more control, although currently no browsers support the complete CSS2 functionality. Using CSS2, you can perform a primitive transformation on the text by specifying a string that will be inserted before or after an element using a pseudo-class. The style sheet shown in Listing 12.3 improves on the CSS1 version by adding more formatting commands, especially the ability to label the fields. Be aware, however, that CSS2 support of any particular feature is spotty in all the mainstream browsers.

Note

Even if the latest browsers support a feature, that doesn't mean much unless you know your audience really well. At the time of this writing, there were nearly twice as many users of Microsoft's version 4 browser or below as there were MSIE version 5. You can't depend on upgrades even if they're free. For many people, they're too much trouble.

LISTING 12.3   AN EXAMPLE CSS2 STYLE SHEET FOR THE XML CUSTOMER RECORD

```
customer { display: block; margin-left: 1pc; margin-right: 3pc; color: #000000; }
   customer-name:before { content: "Customer Name: "; font-weight: bold; }
   customer-name { display: block; }
   customerID:before { content: "Customer ID: "; }
   customerID { display: block; margin-left: 1pc; }
   credit-status:before { content: "Credit Status: "; }
   credit-status { display: block; margin-left: 1pc; }
   customer-contact:before { content: "Customer Contact: ";  font-weight: bold; }
   customer-contact { display: block; margin-left: 2pc; background: #ffddff; }
     honorific:before { content: "Honorific: "; }
     honorific { display: block; }
     given-name1:before { content: "Given Name 1: "; }
     given-name1 { display: block; }
     given-name2:before { content: "Given Name 2: "; }
     given-name2 { display: block; }
     family-name:before { content: "Family Name: "; }
     family-name { display: block; }
     degrees:before { content: "Degrees: "; }
     degrees { display: block; }
     title:before { content: "Title: "; }
     title { display: block; }
     department:before { content: "Department: "; }
     department { display: block; }
     telephone:before { content: "Telephone: "; }
     telephone { display: block; }
     extension:before { content: "Extension: "; }
     extension { display: block; }
     comment:before { content: "Comment: "; }
     comment { display: block; margin-left: 1pc; }
   shipping-address:before { content: "Shipping Address: ";  font-weight: bold; }
   shipping-address { display: block; margin-left: 2pc; background: #ddffff; }
     attention:before { content: "Attention: "; }
     attention { display: block; }
     attention-name:before { content: "Attention Name: "; }
     attention-name { display: block; }
     reference:before { content: "Reference: "; }
     reference { display: block; }
     street-address1:before { content: "Street Address 1: "; }
     street-address1 { display: block; }
     street-address2:before { content: "Street Address 2: "; }
     street-address2 { display: block; }
     city:before { content: "City: "; }
     city { display: block; }
     territorial-division:before { content: "Territorial Division: "; }
     territorial-division { display: block; }
     territorial-abbreviation:before { content: "Territorial Abbreviation: "; }
```

PART

II

CH

12

LISTING 12.3   CONTINUED

```
    territorial-abbreviation { display: block; }
    postal-code:before { content: "Postal Code: "; }
    postal-code { display: block; }
    country:before { content: "Country: "; }
    country { display: block; }
billing-address:before { content: "Billing Address: ";  font-weight: bold; }
billing-address { display: block; margin-left: 2pc; background: #ffffdd; }
    attention:before { content: "Attention: "; }
    attention { display: block; }
    attention-name:before { content: "Attention Name: "; }
    attention-name { display: block; }
    reference:before { content: "Reference: "; }
    reference { display: block; }
    street-address1:before { content: "Street Address 1: "; }
    street-address1 { display: block; }
    street-address2:before { content: "Street Address 2: "; }
    street-address2 { display: block; }
    city:before { content: "City: "; }
    city { display: block; }
    territorial-division:before { content: "Territorial Division: "; }
    territorial-division { display: block; }
    territorial-abbreviation:before { content: "Territorial Abbreviation: "; }
    territorial-abbreviation { display: block; }
    postal-code:before { content: "Postal Code: "; }
    postal-code { display: block; }
    country:before { content: "Country: "; }
    country { display: block; }
creation-date:before { content: "Creation Date: "; }
creation-date { display: block; margin-left: 1pc; }
last-updated:before { content: "Last Updated: "; }
last-updated { display: block; margin-left: 1pc; }
```

Figure 12.2 shows how this style sheet affects the display in Mozilla, the open-source browser platform created by Netscape and the user community. Look for news about Mozilla on their Web site at http://www.mozilla.org/.

Note

The Mozilla browser, currently in a sort of pre-beta development state, is not recommended for the faint of heart. It's slow but fairly stable, crashes every once in a while, and is still in a state of flux. However, it's a very interesting concept. It remains to be seen whether the open software movement can sustain such a huge undertaking. Let's all wish them luck.

They update the browser about every two or three weeks, so in testing Mozilla, it's difficult to step in the same river twice. However, they're constantly improving and closing in on an actual release date, when Mozilla is slated to become Netscape 5.0 at last.

Figure 12.2
The Mozilla screen shows their coverage of the CSS2 properties.

Even this isn't enough. Coverage of CSS at any level is so wildly inconsistent that trying to code a complex style sheet is an exercise in frustration and hidden display problems that surface only after exhaustive testing. Subtle dependency bugs in the browser implementations can mean that problems may surface on a page after months of successful display when some unrelated item is added or changed.

EXTENSIBLE STYLE LANGUAGE—XSL

The Web design community agreed that something more was needed to support complex styling tasks—that something was XSL, the Extensible Style-sheet Language. *Complex* means documents that require extensive processing before they can be displayed, like a newspaper or magazine with articles continued on a following page. It also means documents in languages (such as Chinese) that don't necessarily follow the horizontal text direction conventions used by most alphabetic scripts. Top to bottom (or bottom to top) line direction, methods of constructing words out of characters that are non-linear (as is Korean), and other display tricks were needed. XSL is the result.

As an example, XSL and XSLT might be used to automatically generate a table of contents and an index from an XML document. Formatting objects means that multiple pages can now be formatted on-the-fly from a single base document. Columns and editorial boxes can be laid out separately from content, as they are in any modern newspaper or magazine, and the content flowed into pre-positioned "holes." An article on page 1 can be continued on page 10, for instance. Chinese newspaper-style top to bottom line formatting can be handled by the user's browser instead of being laboriously hard-coded and placed by hand. Because the concepts left, right, top, and bottom are inextricably associated with the direction you write, XSL extended these concepts with before, after, start, and end. The latter concepts are language-neutral, so one style sheet can be used (theoretically) to generate both English and Chinese text styles.

PART

II

CH

12

Tip from

Words to weave by

This styling flexibility is another reason to choose XSL for at least one stage of your document creation process. No other widely supported technology handles top to bottom printing or combines the separate characters of the Korean alphabet into the stacked blocks that constitute words.

But there's more. Instead of learning a completely new language to impose style on a page, XSL looks much like the familiar XML and HTML tags. Like XML, XSL has a DTD so that it can be validated, and a browser that claims to conform to the specification can be tested for real compliance. On the other hand, like other XML-related standards, XSL depends on the structure of the base document or documents. Using XSL and XSLT to style documents that are not well-formed may yield unexpected results.

Tip from

Words to weave by

XSL incorporates almost all of CSS1 and CSS2 and adds significant features from CSS3 as well. Using XSL, you can perform almost any formatting task that could be accomplished with CSS and more. XSLT, the related transformation language, allows you to literally transform the XML document into something else entirely. It's often used to "translate" XML into HTML for display using legacy browsers.

The following code illustrates the simplicity (and relative verbosity) of using XSL to specify the document sections to receive each style treatment on the XML text of Shakespeare's *The Comedy of Errors* placed in the public domain by Jon Bosak:

Here is the short section used in this example without the root and lower portions of the XML document.

LISTING 12.3A   AN XML SNIPPET FROM SHAKESPEARE'S *THE COMEDY OF ERRORS*

```
<?xml version="1.0"?>
<!DOCTYPE PLAY SYSTEM "play.dtd">
<PLAY>
<TITLE>The Comedy of Errors</TITLE>
<SCENE>
<TITLE>SCENE I.  The house of ANTIPHOLUS of Ephesus.</TITLE>
<STAGEDIR>Enter ADRIANA and LUCIANA</STAGEDIR>

<SPEECH>
<SPEAKER>ADRIANA</SPEAKER>
<LINE>Neither my husband nor the slave return'd,</LINE>
<LINE>That in such haste I sent to seek his master!</LINE>
<LINE>Sure, Luciana, it is two o'clock.</LINE>
</SPEECH>

<SPEECH>
<SPEAKER>LUCIANA</SPEAKER>
<LINE>Perhaps some merchant hath invited him,</LINE>
<LINE>And from the mart he's somewhere gone to dinner.</LINE>
<LINE>Good sister, let us dine and never fret:</LINE>
```

```
<LINE>A man is master of his liberty:</LINE>
<LINE>Time is their master, and, when they see time,</LINE>
<LINE>They'll go or come: if so, be patient, sister.</LINE>
</SPEECH>

<SPEECH>
<SPEAKER>ADRIANA</SPEAKER>
<LINE>Why should their liberty than ours be more?</LINE>
</SPEECH>

<SPEECH>
<SPEAKER>LUCIANA</SPEAKER>
<LINE>Because their business still lies out o' door.</LINE>
</SPEECH>

<SPEECH>
<SPEAKER>ADRIANA</SPEAKER>
<LINE>Look, when I serve him so, he takes it ill.</LINE>
</SPEECH>
<SPEECH>
<SPEAKER>LUCIANA</SPEAKER>
<LINE>O, know he is the bridle of your will.</LINE>
</SPEECH>

<SPEECH>
<SPEAKER>ADRIANA</SPEAKER>
<LINE>There's none but asses will be bridled so.</LINE>
</SPEECH>
</SCENE>
</PLAY>
```

And here is the actual XSL Style Sheet that displays the output shown in Figure 12.3.

LISTING 12.3B   AN XSL STYLE SHEET FOR THE PLAY

```
<xsl:stylesheet
    xmlns:xsl='http://www.w3.org/XSL/Transform/1.0'
    xmlns:fo='http://www.w3.org/XSL/Format/1.0'
    result-ns="fo">

  <xsl:template match='/'>
    <fo:display-sequence
                start-indent='6pt'
                end-indent='6pt'
                font-size='12pt'>
      <xsl:apply-templates/>
    </fo:display-sequence>
  </xsl:template>

  <xsl:template match="TITLE">
    <fo:block   font-size="18pt"
                background-color="#ffff00"
                start-indent="24pt">
      <xsl:apply-templates/>
    </fo:block>
  </xsl:template>
```

LISTING 12.3B   CONTINUED

```
<xsl:template match="LINE">
  <fo:block    start-indent="32pt">
    <xsl:apply-templates/>
  </fo:block>
</xsl:template>

<xsl:template match="SPEAKER">
  <fo:block    space-before="12pt">
    <xsl:apply-templates/>
  </fo:block>
</xsl:template>

</xsl:stylesheet>
```

Please note that none of the mainstream browsers currently support formatting objects, which are necessary to view these XSL styles. Use the powerful InDelv Browser from InDelv at `http://www.indelv.com/` (now in beta but shortly to be released) to show the sorts of formatting that can be accomplished as shown in Figure 12.3.

Figure 12.3
The InDelv browser showing an XSL-formatted page.

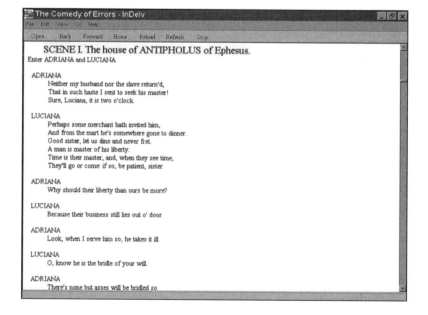

Note

The InDelv XML/XSL editor/browser is one of the best-designed and easiest to use XML editor/browsers still in beta. You can swap views of the document to inspect the XSL style sheet, look at the source code, and even import random Web pages with an automatic Tidy cleanup and error report. It's quite impressive even in its pre-release form. You can find it at `http://www.indelv.com`.

The production version of the InDelv editor will likely be released in the summer of 2000, so it should be available in complete form by the time you read this. The pre-release InDelv browser works now and is available for download from their site.

DOCUMENT STYLE SEMANTICS AND SPECIFICATION LANGUAGE—DSSSL

DSSSL is an ancestor of XSL, and is still used by many document specialists. From DSSSL came the formatting objects used by XSL, although in DSSSL they are called flow objects. DSSSL is extremely complex, requiring more programming skills than XSL, but it is correspondingly powerful. Many user communities use DSSSL routinely to perform the many document transformations needed at different points in a publishing process, for instance, or to transform data into canonical forms for storage or exchange.

Tip from

LeeAnne.com
Words to weave by

Like SGML, if your organization needs to use DSSSL you probably already do. For most, DSSSL is far too esoteric to use easily. XSL is a good compromise between power and ease of use, with usability the most important consideration for many organizations.

CHOOSING A STYLE LANGUAGE

The choice between CSS, XSL, DSSSL, and scripting languages may be forced upon you by your environment or the needs of your project. Every style mechanism has both strengths and weaknesses. You might want to consider two- or even three-step processes, performing an initial style format with XSL, then using XSLT to generate an XHTML page with attached CSS style sheet to ensure wide support during the transition between quirky CSS support and wide support of the fixed XSL standard.

Tip from

LeeAnne.com
Words to weave by

This step-by-step process is the exact process used by many large publishing houses. An author turns in a document marked up with a simple set of tags, the tags are then augmented with more complex tags by a trained editor for an internal editing process, and finally the augmented tags and text are turned by yet another editor or typesetter into the specialized typesetting language used by the target press.

STYLE LANGUAGE SUPPORT

I've talked about this in passing but it can't be overemphasized; style language support is not universal. The current version of Microsoft's Internet Explorer browser uses an outmoded XSL model that amounts to a language of its own. Although it may be recognizable as XSL, it's also different enough that many features either don't work or don't work as planned. Netscape has no support at all except in the loosely related Mozilla open-source testbed. Opera won't be including XSL support until sometime after the W3C working draft becomes a recommendation.

Previously Figure 12.2 showed that Mozilla has fairly good support for XML and CSS2 built in, but the page fails to display properly in any current version of Internet Explorer, Netscape, or Opera. The following paragraphs take a look at a simple CSS1 task and how Netscape and Microsoft handle it, as well as Opera because this browser is widely used by persons with visual disabilities and internationally.

The example is a very simple page with a floating element. It exists in the real world, so you'll see the compromises that had to be made to make it all work without using tables. As a reminder, tables are difficult to navigate or understand for persons with visual disabilities so they should be avoided as layout elements if possible. Unfortunately, the careless implementations of floating elements by many browser makers have made tables much easier to use than float, although float would be by far the better way to do it if only it were possible. div elements are used to duplicate the effect of an outer container element as if this were another type of XML file, but it's still XHTML so any browser can render it in *some* way.

Listing 12.4 shows the style sheet and code for a simple page using CSS.

LISTING 12.4   AN EXAMPLE WEB PAGE USING XHTML AND INLINE CSS

```
<?xml version="1.0"?>
<!DOCTYPE html PUBLIC "-//W3C//DTD XHTML 1.0 Strict//EN"
    "http://www.w3.org/TR/xhtml1/DTD/strict.dtd">
<html
 xmlns="http://www.w3.org/TR/xhtml1">
  <head>
    <title>
      Tabor Sarah Books
    </title>
<style
 type="text/css">
    <!--
      body { font-family: serif; font-size: 18pt; margin: 10pt; }
      h1 { font-size: 32pt; }
      img { float: left; margin-right: 10pt; }
      div.ritual { margin: 10pt; }
      div.origin { margin-left: 20pt; }
      div.publisher { margin-left: 20pt; }
      div.order { margin: 20pt; }
      div.address { margin: 20pt; }
      div.price { margin-left: 20pt; }
      div.title { margin: 10pt; clear: left;  }
      div.telephone { margin: 10pt; }
      div.fineprint { margin: 10pt; font-size: 10pt; }
      div.linkout { margin: 20pt; }
    // -->
</style>
</head>
  <body>
    <h1>Tabor Sarah Books</h1>
    <img src="splash.gif" height="365" width="54"
     alt="[Image: A stream of water splashes into an open hand]" />
```

```
<div class="ritual">
  <a href="ritual.html"><cite>A Ritual of Drowning - Poems of
  Love and Mourning</cite></a><br />
  <div class="origin">
    by Teya Schaffer<br />
    <div class="publisher">
      Tabor Sarah Books, 1999, Oakland and Palo Alto<br />
      ISBN: 0-935079-18-1<br />
    </div>
  </div>
  <div class="order">
    This book can be ordered from:
    <div class="address">
      Tabor Sarah Books<br />
      367 50th Street<br />
      Oakland CA 94609<br />
    </div>
    <div class="price">
      The current price is $10.95 US domestic postage paid.
    </div>
  </div>
</div>
<div class="title">
  <cite>Chag Sameach! a Jewish holiday book for
  children</cite><br />
  <div
   class="origin">
    by Patricia Schaffer<br />
    <div class="publisher">
      Tabor Sarah Books, 1985, Oakland and Palo Alto<br />
    </div>
  </div>
  <div class="order">
    This book can be ordered from:
    <div
     class="address">
      Tabor Sarah Books<br />
       3345 Stockton Place<br />
       Palo Alto, CA 94303
    </div>
    <div class="price">
      The current price is $$7.70 US domestic postage paid.
    </div>
  </div>
</div>
<div class="title">
  <cite>How Babies and Families Are Made - There is more than
  one way!</cite><br />
  <div class="origin">
    by Patricia Schaffer<br />
     illustrated by Suzanne Corbett<br />
    <div class="publisher">
      Tabor Sarah Books, 1988, Oakland and Palo Alto
    </div>
```

LISTING 12.4   CONTINUED

```
      </div>
      <div class="order">
        This book can be ordered from:
        <div class="address">
          Tabor Sarah Books<br />
          3345 Stockton Place<br />
          Palo Alto, CA 94303
        </div>
        <div class="price">
          The current price is $$9.70 US domestic postage paid.
        </div>
      </div>
    </div>
    <div class="telephone">
      Phone inquiries for all titles: +1 650 494-7846<br />
      Titles are also available through women's bookstores.
    </div>
    <div class="fineprint">
      <hr />
      Page Copyright &#169; 1999, by Lee Anne Phillips
      <a href=
      "mailto:Lee%20Anne%20Phillips%20&lt;leeanne@leeanne.com&gt;">
      &lt;leeanne@leeanne.com&gt;</a> - All Rights Reserved
      Worldwide
      <p>
          Illustration is from <cite>A Ritual of Drowning - Poems of
        Love and Mourning</cite> Copyright &#169; 1999 by Teya
        Schaffer - All Rights Reserved Worldwide
      </p>
    </div>
    <div class="linkout">
      <p>
        For more reviews of outstanding books by women, please
        visit the <a
        href="http://www.cybergrrl.com/review/">Women's Books
        Online</a> pages kindly hosted by <a
        href="http://www.cybergrrl.com/">Cybergrrl!</a>
      </p>
    </div>
  </body>
</html>
```

In Figure 12.4, we show how the page looks in the current Netscape browser. It's pretty darned bad. This code can be viewed on the CD-ROM as 12xmp03.html as well as on the Web at http://www.leeanne.com/usingxml/index1.html to see how your current browser handles the code.

Figure 12.4
Netscape delivers a
CSS display with
serious legibility
problems.

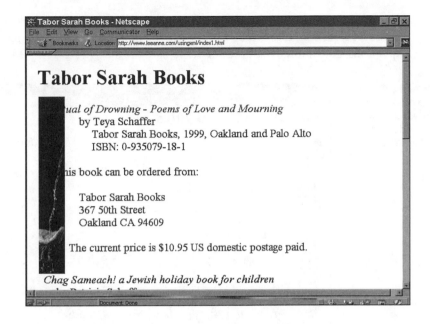

Look at the MSIE version in Figure 12.5. Although it's readable, it still doesn't do what it's supposed to.

Figure 12.5
Microsoft Internet
Explorer is more legi-
ble, but ignores the
insets while process-
ing the floated image,
a serious formatting
error. Although less
irritating, it makes for
an ugly display.

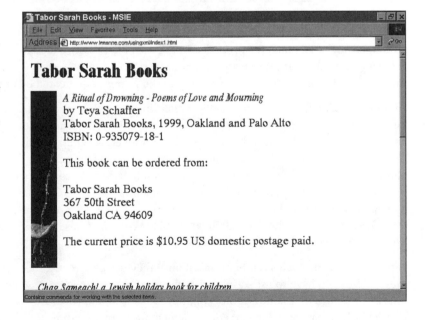

Figure 12.6 shows the page in the current version of Opera. It's almost the same as the Microsoft IE version, except that it messes up the line of text that was supposed to have a 10 point margin almost as badly as Netscape does the lines preceding.

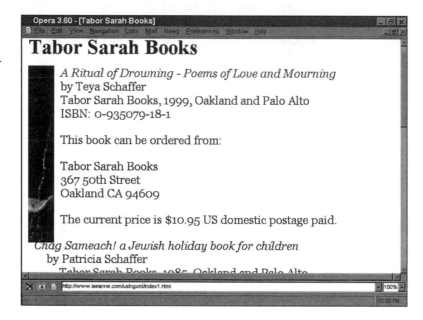

Figure 12.6
Opera delivers the page with formatting errors and minor legibility problems.

None of these implementations are clean and all mess up the display in one way or another, although they're all "mature" products. In the example chosen, Netscape fares worst but it's easy to pick a different set of features that leave the other browsers at a disadvantage. All three browsers handle margins improperly in the vicinity of a floated element.

In Figure 12.7, you can see the results of checking the style sheet with TopStyle, a tool designed to identify problems with style sheets and even perform a number of cross-browser checks. Unfortunately, the style sheet passes with no errors at all so this is something TopStyle doesn't catch. This isn't the fault of the tool, which is an excellent value, but of the complexity involved in testing every possible combination of properties in every possible way. There are 13 properties in the code out of a total of 55 available choices with an average of 10 values each. That's only 9.4×10 to the 34th or, to put it simply, roughly 90,365,466,692,518,617,600,000,000,000,000,000 combinations, give or take a few gazillions. That's an awful lot of tests to make.

Although these problems can be tweaked until they work correctly, the resulting code is messy. Also, you have to use scripts to implement browser-specific code or avoid using margins at all, replacing them with blockquotes, which is an improper but very common use of that XHTML feature. With current implementations of cascading style sheets, you're often in trouble no matter what you do. Almost every CSS feature has similar problems when you consider cross-browser support. In Appendix E, "CSS1, CSS2 Reference," property and value pairs that are relatively safe to use are shown in boldface type. You'll notice that the amount of boldface isn't overwhelming.

Figure 12.7
TopStyle reports on many style sheet problems but doesn't find any in this style sheet. Oh, well.

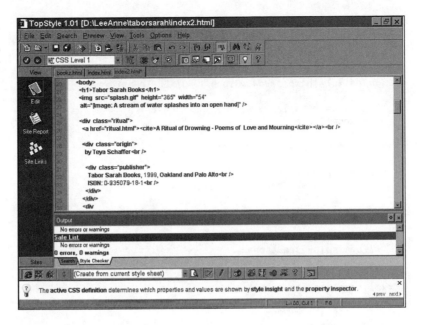

The code that works is tweaked to reduce cross-browser problems to a manageable level and can be seen on the Web at http://www.leeanne.com/usingxml/11xmp04.html as well as on the CD-ROM as 12xmp04.html. Many real sites find it necessary to employ a special server-side routing tool like BrowserHawk to "sniff" the user's browser and deliver different pages based on which browser is in use. Or they use inline scripting to choose different inline code based on the browser. To put it mildly, it's a pain in the neck but at least it works. Sort of.

Tip from

LeeAnne.com
Words to weave by

W3C has a set of CSS testing tools available on their site at http://jigsaw.w3.org/css-validator/ and http://www.w3.org/Style/css/Test/. You can also use a commercial validation tool such as TopStyle, at http://www.bradsoft.com/topstyle/.

For the last example, the CSS2 style sheet is translated directly into XSL, as shown in Listing 12.5. Because XSL implements most of CSS2 more or less directly, it's usually easy to translate one language into another after you know the proper syntax. Again note that XSL has extended the concepts of margin left, right, top, and bottom with before, after, start, and end to reduce invidious language-dependent assumptions (although the older model is still available). The margin properties retained for compatibility with CSS are used just to make the style sheets easier to compare. Also style definitions are added for a few XHTML elements because you can't depend on a true XML browser to display these in any particular way.

Listing 12.5   An XSL Style Sheet for an XML Document

```xml
<?xml version='1.0'?>

<xsl:stylesheet
    xmlns:xsl='http://www.w3.org/1999/XSL/Transform'
''
    xmlns:fo='http://www.w3.org/XSL/Format/1.0'
    version='1.0'>
''
<xsl:output method='fo'/>

  <xsl:template match='/'>
    <fo:display-sequence
        margin='10pt'
        font-family='serif'
        font-size='18pt'>
      <xsl:apply-templates/>
    </fo:display-sequence>
  </xsl:template>

  <xsl:template match="h1">
    <fo:display-sequence
        font-size='32pt'>
      <xsl:apply-templates/>
    </fo:display-sequence>
  </xsl:template>

  <xsl:template match="div[@class='ritual']">
    <fo:block
        margin='10pt'>
      <xsl:apply-templates/>
    </fo:block>
  </xsl:template>

  <xsl:template match="div[@class='origin']">
    <fo:block
        margin-left='20pt'>
      <xsl:apply-templates/>
    </fo:block>
  </xsl:template>

  <xsl:template match="div[@class='publisher']">
    <fo:block
        margin-left='20pt'>
      <xsl:apply-templates/>
    </fo:block>
  </xsl:template>

<xsl:template match="div[@class='order']">
    <fo:block
        margin='20pt'>
      <xsl:apply-templates/>
    </fo:block>
  </xsl:template>

  <xsl:template match="div[@class='address']">
```

```
    <fo:block
        margin='20pt'>
     <xsl:apply-templates/>
    </fo:block>
  </xsl:template>

  <xsl:template match="div[@class='price']">
    <fo:block
        margin-left='20pt'>
     <xsl:apply-templates/>
    </fo:block>
  </xsl:template>

  <xsl:template match="div[@class='title']">
    <fo:block
        clear='left'
        margin='10pt'>
     <xsl:apply-templates/>
    </fo:block>
  </xsl:template>

<xsl:template match="div[@class='telephone']">
    <fo:block
        margin='10pt'>
     <xsl:apply-templates/>
    </fo:block>
  </xsl:template>

  <xsl:template match="div[@class='fineprint']">
    <fo:block
        margin='10pt'>
        font-size='10pt'>
     <xsl:apply-templates/>
    </fo:block>
  </xsl:template>

  <xsl:template match="div[@class='linkout']">
    <fo:block
        margin='20pt'>
     <xsl:apply-templates/>
    </fo:block>
  </xsl:template>

  <xsl:template match='p'>
    <fo:block
        space-end='6pt'
        space-before='6pt'
        space-after='6pt'>
     <xsl:apply-templates/>
    </fo:block>
  </xsl:template>

  <xsl:template match='cite'>
    <fo:inline-sequence font-style='italic'>
      <xsl:apply-templates/>
    </fo:inline-sequence>
  </xsl:template>
```

LISTING 12.5   CONTINUED

```
<xsl:template match='hr'>
  <fo:display-rule
      margin='10pt'
      rule-thickness='1.5pt'>
    <xsl:apply-templates/>
  </fo:display-rule>
</xsl:template>

<xsl:template match='a'>
  <fo:simple-link
      external-destination='{@href}'
      color='rgb(0,0,255)'>
    <xsl:apply-templates/>
  </fo:simple-link>
</xsl:template>

</xsl:stylesheet>
```

XSL is far more verbose than CSS, as you can easily see, because the equivalent CSS2 style sheet takes up a mere 13 lines!

COMBINING XHTML AND XML FOR STYLE PROCESSING

Because older browsers often don't support XML at all, much less XSL, applications that want to reach the widest audience while retaining some of the advantages of XML mix XML content in with their XHTML tags. This allows the XHTML tags to handle the lowest level of formatting possible while retaining the flexibility of XML for data tagging and searches. Of course, the document has to be well-formed, but this is hardly a disadvantage because error-free HTML code tends to be valid according to the HTML DTD anyway. In the examples used in the last section, instead of the laborious div sections you could tag your data with XML tags, using an XML namespace, as well as the basic XHTML layout tags. That way you can easily perform searches and XSL-style transformations on the document while allowing the document to be viewed by the millions of legacy browsers still in use on the Web. Please note that those include many browsers used by persons with special accessibility needs, so you can't just wish them away with a tacky "best viewed in browser X" logo and download link.

Tip from

LeeAnne.com
Words to weave by

Not everyone uses the same browser any more than everyone wears the same perfume or cologne. Some people use text-based or aural browsers, sometimes because they must and sometimes because they're handy. The ubiquitous nature of Web-surfing PDAs and the possible inclusion of aural browsers in everything from your cell phone to your car makes it imperative to take all possible users into account when designing your pages. A Palm Pilot is not a WebTV and a WebTV is not a Power Mac G4.

Taking this approach, Listing 12.6 shows this code fragment with XML tags mixed in with the XHTML lookalikes.

LISTING 12.6   AN EXAMPLE OF AN XHTML DOCUMENT WITH XML INCLUSIONS AND A DEFAULT INLINE STYLESHEET

```
<?xml version="1.0"?>
<?xml-stylesheet type="text/xml" href="taborsarah.xsl"?>
<!DOCTYPE html PUBLIC "-//W3C//DTD XHTML 1.0 Strict//EN"
    " http://www.w3.org/1999/xhtml ">
<html
  xmlns="http://www.w3.org/1999/xhtml"
  xmlns:tabor="http://www.leeanne.com/taborsarah/">
  <head>
    <title>Tabor Sarah Books</title>
<style
 type="text/css">
    <!--
    body { font-family: serif; font-size: 18pt; }
    h1 { font-size: 32pt; }
    img { float: left; }
    div.fineprint { font-size: 10pt; }
    div.origin { margin-left: 20px; }
    div.title { clear: left; font-size: 18pt; }
    // -->
</style>
    <meta http-equiv="PICS-Label"
      content='(PICS-1.1 "http://www.rsac.org/ratingsv01.html" l
    gen true r (n 0 s 0 v 0 l 0)' />
    <meta http-equiv="PICS-Label"
      content='(PICS-1.1 "http://www.classify.org/safesurf/" l gen
    true r (SS~~000 1))' />
  </head>
  <body>
    <blockquote>
      <tabor:page-header><h1>Tabor Sarah Books</h1></tabor:page-header>
      <tabor:image><img src="splash.gif" height="365" width="54"
       alt="[Image: A stream of water splashes into an open
          hand]" /><tabor:image>
      <div class="ritual">
        <blockquote>
          <blockquote>
            <tabor:link><a href="ritual.html"><cite>A Ritual of Drowning
               - Poems of Love and Mourning</cite></a></tabor:link><br />
            <blockquote>
              by <tabor:author>Teya Schaffer</tabor:author><br />
              <tabor:publisher>Tabor Sarah Books</tabor:publisher>,
              <tabor:publish-date>1999<tabor:publish-date>,
              <tabor:publish-city>Oakland and Palo Alto<tabor:publish-city>
              ISBN: <tabor:ISBN>0-935079-18-1</tabor:ISBN><br />
              <br />
            </blockquote>
            <blockquote>
              This book can be ordered from:
              <blockquote>
                <tabor:order-address>Tabor Sarah Books<br />
```

LISTING 12.6   CONTINUED

```
              367 50th Street<br />
              Oakland CA 94609<br /></tabor:order-address>
            </blockquote>
            The current price is <tabor:price>$10.95</tabor:price>
            US domestic postage paid.
          </blockquote>
        </blockquote>
      </blockquote>
    </div>
  </blockquote>
  </body>
</html>
```

Notice that a lot of XHTML text appears outside of the XML tags. Using XSLT (or CSS2), you can generate these extraneous text inclusions from within your style sheet so you don't really need them to perform document rendering. If you store this data in an external database, you probably don't want redundant information kept in more than one place.

Tip from

LeeAnne.com
Words to weave by

> For repetitive information such as a catalog display, XSL can cut down on the amount of coding enormously, even if users never see the XML directly. With XSL's capability to manipulate and transform documents on-the-fly, it can be ideal for generating many pages from one database using a shared template.

Although it may be some time before true XML browsers become widely used, they do exist in the form of SGML browsers, which can easily make the transition to XML and, in many cases, already have. With support for XSL added to complement existing support for DSSSL and proprietary style sheets, it's possible to get a feel for what XML browsing will be like in the near future. Mozilla already supports some of the new standards, and promises to support more as the Recommendations roll out the door at W3C, and there are companies working on the same exploratory basis even as we speak. CiTEC (`http://www.citec.fi/`) of Finland, for example, already has an XML/SGML browser available, MultiDoc Pro, and will be releasing a Doczilla-based product in the near future.

Much of the enthusiasm and support for XML exists outside the United States, Canada, and the United Kingdom, because we are already well-served by existing browsers. Finland has strong ties to Russia and other parts of the former Soviet Union, so support for Cyrillic national scripts and multiple language support make XML far more attractive than it might be to a random user in the English-speaking world.

USING CSS AND XSL IN TANDEM

Also notice that the preceding example uses both CSS style sheets inline and an external XSL style sheet. This allows support for many legacy browsers while preserving maximum functionality for users with XML/XSL-aware browsers.

As mentioned in several places earlier, XML-aware browsers such as MultiDoc Pro and InDelv already exist. Mozilla and CiTEC are jointly working on Doczilla, which is the XML version or module of the full Mozilla product. Although InDelv is the only current true XML browser that supports XSL, the rest will likely be caught up by the time you read this or shortly thereafter. Far too much is riding on this to let XML languish for lack of browser support, and many companies are lining up and getting ready to take your money for the real thing in XML-enabled browsers.

Note

> Responsible and reasoned disagreement exists about the level of XML support that can be expected in the immediate future, with the current text taking an optimistic view. Some see fully XML-compliant browsers as being slow to penetrate the user market, in part because of competition from the many free and time-tested HTML browsers currently available and on the desktop. However, we think the advantages of XML support will outweigh this inertia.

On the other hand, the initial support for XSL and XSLT may be invisible to the user and located on the server, because an interim solution to serving XML pages to HTML users is performing the translation on the server and delivering plain HTML to the desktop. Of course this forgoes most of the power of XML, so the people who gladly pay hundreds of dollars for computer output speakers with subwoofers and surround sound may be reluctant to defer full XML support for the sake of a few dollars.

SUMMING UP

All style languages share a common goal: to allow the separation of content from display. XML/XSL extends that basic goal with extraordinary flexibility and power. You've already seen how mixing in XML tags allows you to easily format different chunks of code in different ways, even though they may basically be running text. If you have Word 2000, try saving a document as a Web page and then look at it in a text editor. Everything is a `<p>` tag followed by a `class`. The classes are then used to let a huge style sheet format the code. It works, but it makes for an ugly and hard-to-read source.

Tip from

Words to weave by

> On the other hand, creating Word 2000-generated Web pages and then using XSL to transform them into standard XML, or even XHTML, including a style sheet, might be a good way to capture legacy data for a Web-enabled application.

However, XML enables you to tag those sections with meaningful names and still allows you to format those sections with CSS. Or anything else. That last part is important. For an author, this means that all I have to do is put in a tag that tells my publisher what I mean by a particular line of text. I can let a typographical designer decide how to display it in the best and most attractive way. So I don't have to know how to design books, just write the text that goes into them. My publisher doesn't have to know anything about XML, just how to interpret the codes I write in the typographical context.

As you've seen in this chapter, existing support for CSS and XSL is problematic. The next generation of browsers from Netscape, Opera Software, and other vendors promises to improve the situation greatly. But the problem of legacy browser support will be around for some time to come.

TROUBLESHOOTING CSS

STYLE COMMANDS DON'T WORK AS EXPECTED

I adjusted some text property and it doesn't work or doesn't work as it should. Sometimes, my browser crashes when I use a particular command.

Welcome to the exciting world of style sheets. First, try validating the style sheet using the W3C (http://jigsaw.w3.org/css-validator/) or other validation tool. Then validate your browser using the W3C test suite at http://www.w3.org/Style/css/Test/. You may have to ask someone for advice if you get tired of beating your head against the wall. Try the CSS Pointers Group at http://css.nu/.

YOU'RE SICK OF STYLE SHEETS

Why won't my style sheets behave when I test them in different browsers?

If you don't mind your document looking remarkably like thousands of other sites on the Web, the first thing to try is using someone else's style sheet. The W3C kindly keeps a selection of tested style sheets handy at its Web site. They test for the browser you use and feed you the right version with no effort at all on your part. Look here: http://www.w3.org/StyleSheets/Core/. Do be careful not to choose any of the several with dark backgrounds if you care about whether people can read your pages without strain. The Web heads at Verso (http://www.verso.com) who designed these styles obviously like this effect because it appears on their splash page, but it makes pages hard to read unless the font size is increased.

A second alternative is to use a scripting language to select from several variations on your style sheet that work for different browsers. Although it's still a lot of work to make three or four style sheets for every page, at least it's a manageable task.

→ For information about validation and other tools, **see** Appendix B, "Tools for XML/XHTML Editing and Conversion," **p. 717**.

Eventually, XSL itself will be able to serve up differing style sheets based on content negotiation with your XML-aware browser. But that capability will have to wait for the next version of XSL.

TROUBLESHOOTING XSL STYLE SHEETS

STYLE SHEETS DON'T DO WHAT THEY SHOULD

I created a fabulous style sheet that doesn't work. I've tried tweaking it and still nothing clicks.

At the present state of the art, don't jump to the conclusion that you've goofed up. Assuming you've validated your style sheet for simple errors with a tool such as Stylus[tm], it may be that your XML browser doesn't support the particular function you're using. The best course is to ask someone. There are a number of mailing lists whose members support each other with advice and even short code samples. For XSL, you might try the XSL-list hosted by Mulberry Technologies. See their Web site for details on signing up: `http://www.mulberrytech.com/`.

SELECTIONS DON'T WORK

I want to select a paticular node on the document tree and I can't get it to work.

The Document Object Model can be difficult to use and understand without careful study. It may help to use a graphical XML tool so you have a bit of help visualizing the tree structure. Remember, too, that if two XSL templates address the same node, the more specific match is used, not the less specific one.

CASCADING STYLE SHEETS AND XML/XHTML

In this chapter

WORKING WITH CASCADING STYLE SHEETS

In this chapter, assume that style sheets actually work the way they're supposed to, because the alternative is to conclude that they're so poorly supported as to be essentially worthless on the Web. Although this may seem whimsical, it makes sense. If you're careful, you can create style sheets that don't break. At the least, you can use scripting to choose style sheets based on known problems.

Cascading Style Sheets (CSS) is the W3C's original attempt to separate content from display considerations. It does this by allowing the author to choose what sort of "decoration" to hang on every single branch of the document tree. Like decorating a tree for the winter holidays, the amount and type of decoration is up to you. By allowing the decisions on presentation to be made separately from the content of the material, the designer is free to create a uniform "look and feel" for a site while freeing authors from worrying about how the information will look after it's on the page. There are two levels of CSS so far, with level 3 well on the way. CSS1 doesn't explicitly allow itself to be used to style XML, but CSS2 does, so I think we can assume that even CSS1 engines are going to allow themselves to refer to XML tags for the sake of uniformity and compatibility.

You will be using CSS at some level in the foreseeable future because, as you discover later in this chapter, XSL is much more complex and more likely to be the tool of specialists. XSL and XSLT, on the other hand, have enormous power and can be used to effect transformations of the display and complex renderings beyond the capability of CSS to deliver on its own.

Many people who are familiar with the Web and even the design of entire Web sites know little of CSS, because it doesn't really work with the mix of browsers actually used on the Web. Many sites have made a conscious decision not to use CSS at all to avoid the complexity and extra work that trying to account for all the many compatibility issues requires. So, CSS is addressed in more detail than this series normally would, covering some of the basics as well as the fine points.

Style sheets also make it possible for a designer to accommodate persons with special needs. Accessibility isn't just limited to persons with visual or other disabilities. The same techniques used to enable users with physical or mental disabilities are also useful and even necessary for the entire population in selected circumstances. So the driver of an automobile in traffic needs aural browsing as much as does a person with a vision disability, and an auto mechanic working under a car needs hands-free navigation as much as does a person with a motor disability.

UNDERSTANDING HOW STYLE SHEETS WORK

Style sheets work by identifying a tag, class (in HTML only), attribute, ID, or other identifiable structural feature of the document tree, called in CSS a *selector*, and associating the selector with a *declaration* containing one or more *property and value* pairs.

XML and XHTML style sheets should always be stored externally, because CSS uses different language syntax than both XML and XHTML and would be misinterpreted if not wrapped in a CDATA section or processing instruction. The proper mechanism is to use a processing instruction for an arbitrary XML document. Six non-exclusive choices exist for XHTML documents:

- Using a `link` element
- Using an `xml-stylesheet` processing instruction
- Using an XHTML `style` element with an external link
- Using the `style` element with inline commented-out code
- Using `style` attributes on individual elements
- Using inline `style` selector/declaration pairs wrapped in a CDATA element.

However, passing style sheet commands to a display agent using a processing command will break many existing HTML user agents. Some will incorrectly display the content of the command, but almost all the rest will ignore it. Likewise, existing HTML user agents will ignore CDATA content, so that doesn't do us much good either. The two external alternatives, external links from a `link` or `style` element are nonstandard for XML but *should* work for XHTML. However, external style sheets are not supported by many older browsers. HTML 4.0 defined `style` content as CDATA, so the entire content was available for use even though it was enclosed in comments. XHTML 1.0 also defines the `style` content as CDATA, so it *should* behave in the same way except that XML parsers are not required to pass on comments to the user agent, so comments containing style information may be stripped from the output and therefore invisible to the browser.

In fact, unless the parser makers ignore the option to discard comments and allow commented style content to be seen by the browser, XHTML will not be terribly useful on the Web until all the old user agents in the world magically disappear.

So, the pragmatic strategy seems to be to enclose the content in comments to cover legacy agents, use an external link to cover current and future agents, and hope for the best. That supports the widest number of current users without breaking XML-aware browsers; however, it doesn't strictly obey the XML standard.

Tip from

 LeeAnne.com
Words to weave by

I think throwing away the comment mechanism for the sake of an imagined gain in *logical* behavior was a huge mistake. In the first place, the Web isn't all that logical because it abounds with incompatibilities and inconsistent behavior, of which the XML treatment of comments is yet another. In the second, the *discard comments* behavior is optional. Why go to the trouble of potentially breaking almost every existing HTML page that uses style sheets if you don't have enough courage of conviction to follow through?

COPING WITH BROWSER IMPLEMENTATIONS OF CSS

The implementations of CSS from all the major browser manufacturers have been spotty, to put it charitably. So, putting the style sheet decisions in the hands of a specialist saves enormous amounts of debugging time for authors as well. The only feasible styling strategies at the present time are either to dynamically serve up a different style sheet for every different browser or to simplify the style sheet to the point that every browser displays it more or less properly. Only a handful of properties are safe to use in this manner.

Tip from

 LeeAnne.com
Words to weave by

Most authors should stick to the real tools of their trade: headers, paragraphs, and various types of lists. Style creation is a specialized task; it's hard to learn and should be assigned to an expert in the oddities of CSS implementation on the different browser varieties if possible.

The next generation of browsers may alleviate this problem to some extent, but the upgrade rate for browsers is fairly low, so it won't go away soon. The unfortunate decisions and outright blunders made by CSS implementers from the major browser manufacturers will haunt page layout and formatting designers for many years to come.

The Mozilla and Opera browsers promise to include almost complete support for CSS level 2 soon, although the past Netscape record of CSS compliance is poor and Opera's is only fair to good so far (although Opera is easily the best of the mainstream browsers). Still, the open-source nature of the Mozilla (Netscape) code means at least that the inevitable mistakes and bugs can be found and corrected, and Opera has always been strongly committed to standards compliance. The problem seems to be that CSS is devilishly difficult to do right.

Considering that a Web browser is essentially an on-the-fly formatting engine, such as those found in graphical (WYSIWYG) editors, this should come as no surprise. Everyone seems to have trouble doing graphical formatting right. Even editors who have been around for decades still get into weird modes from time to time in which the display breaks down.

CSS can alter document properties in nonlinear order. So, your tentative page layout has to dynamically account for changes in pseudo-elements, such as first-line, justifying the line (maybe), and calculating which characters actually appear on the first line given the physical characteristics of your particular display device and window size. Then the rendering engine may have to redo the calculations when you change between the document style sheet and a user style sheet while changing the font size of everything. The iterations required to get it all right and the difficulty of the task mean that none of the major browsers has actually implemented *hard* CSS features such as full justification of text.

Microsoft's latest implementation of CSS, although it includes limited support for CSS2 and XML, hasn't really improved on CSS1 support. Lately, Microsoft has been paying more attention to standards—in their publicity at least—but the installed base of buggy or nonstandard

Microsoft implementations, including CSS, is a tremendous liability in trying to move forward. Whether to include "bugwards-compatibility" is an issue that all makers have to address, but Microsoft is especially vulnerable because the majority of browsers in use today are from Microsoft. Many of these are older versions that will probably never be updated until the host PC itself is scrapped and replaced. They're in a tough spot, condemned by some users if they do and condemned by others if they don't.

USING XML ELEMENTS AS SELECTORS

XML elements and attributes can be theoretically used to form *selectors* in CSS1 and CSS2 just as they can in HTML. In fact, CSS2 addresses this issue directly, retaining only the dotted *class* notation as a special HTML case. CSS2 element selection is otherwise exactly the same for HTML, XHTML, and arbitrary XML documents. So if you avoid the dotted notation, the same style sheets should be usable for both XML and HTML documents by merely changing out the element names.

However, many browsers have tried to maintain their special knowledge of HTML so they can make reasonable guesses about how to fix errors in the page on-the-fly. This means most browsers don't actually understand CSS at all in a meaningful way, but *simulate* CSS compliance through a series of special-purpose routines. This makes their so-called CSS engines, as poor as they are for HTML, almost useless for general XML documents because there's no way to create special knowledge for arbitrary element names. Although HTML had a defined DTD from almost the earliest days, actual implementations ignored it except in an advisory sort of way, with hacks and kludges attempting to compensate for the notoriously poor state of Web design and widespread HTML garbage masquerading as usable pages. But of course, after you explicitly allow for malformed syntax and common mistakes, bad coding practices proliferate without limit.

UNDERSTANDING CSS SELECTORS

The large number of CSS properties and values are not really that hard to understand. For the most part they're fairly logical, at least for English speakers, although memorizing the exact words can be daunting. An exhaustive treatment of XHTML appears in Appendix A, "XML/XHTML Reference," and of CSS1 and CSS2 properties in Appendix E, "CSS1, CSS2 Reference," so I won't bother with them here. It's assumed that you probably already have at least some exposure to style sheets in HTML.

Basically, *elements* refer to tags in your document, although the *pseudo-elements* refer to virtual tags that don't *really* exist in the document itself. The browser uses these tags and virtual tags to decide when and where to apply the properties and values argued in the element.

Rules govern how to put style sheets together. Table 13.1 summarizes the way tags, attributes, and values are put together to form a complete selector:

TABLE 13.1   CSS SELECTORS

Pattern	Meaning
*	Matches any element
E	Matches any E element
E F	Matches any F element descendent of an E element
E > F	Matches any F element child of an E element
E:first-child	Matches element E when E is a first child
E:link	Matches element E if E is the source anchor of a hyperlink when the target is not yet visited
E:visited	Matches element E if E is the source anchor of a hyperlink when the target is already visited
E:active	Matches E during certain user actions
E:hover	Matches E during certain user actions
E:focus	Matches E during certain user actions
E:lang(c)	Matches element of type E if it is in (human) language C
E + F	Matches any F element with an E element sibling immediately preceding it
E[foo]	Matches any E element with the foo attribute set (whatever the value)
E[foo="warning"]	Matches any E element whose foo attribute value is exactly equal to "warning"
E[foo~="warning"]	Matches any E element whose foo attribute value is a list of space-separated values, one of which is exactly equal to "warning"
E[lang|="en"]	Matches any E element whose lang attribute has a hyphen-separated list of values beginning (from the left) with "en"
DIV.warning	*For HTML only*—the same as DIV[class~="warning"]
E#myid	Matches any E element ID equal to myid

Note that the dotted class syntax is the only pattern privileged to HTML and that it cannot reliably be used with XML despite assurances to the contrary on the part of some. This is because class is just another attribute to XML. Because you can use the explicit attribute value syntax to do the same thing, nothing is lost but the convenience of a shorthand format.

An XML ID, on the other hand, has a privileged position although it may not have that name. An XML ID must have a tokenized value of "ID" but can have any name although there can be only one "ID" in an element.

In use, one would use selectors to construct style sheet commands as shown in the following section.

Using Selectors to Construct Style Sheet Commands

The following selector selects `linesegment` elements in an XML document, allowing you to define one or more property value pairs to all instances of that element:

```
linesegment { property: value; property: value; … }
```

The following selector selects h1, h2, and h3 elements in an XML or HTML document, allowing you to define one or more property value pairs to all instances of all three elements:

```
h1, h2, h3 { property: value; property: value; … }
```

The following selector selects any paragraph element descended from a chapter element in an XML document, allowing you to define one or more property value pairs to those instances of this element:

```
chapter paragraph { property: value; property: value; … }
```

The following selector selects any paragraph element with a chapter element parent in an XML document, allowing you to define one or more property value pairs to those instances of this element:

```
chapter > paragraph { property: value; property: value; … }
```

The following selector selects the first paragraph element with a chapter element parent in an XML document, allowing you to define one or more property value pairs to those instances of this element. This might be used, for example, to define some special treatment of the first paragraph in a chapter:

```
chapter:first-child paragraph { property: value; property: value; … }
```

The following selector selects the first letter of the first paragraph element with a chapter element parent in an XML document, allowing you to define one or more property value pairs to those instances of this element. This might be used, for example, to define an initial decorative drop cap letter in the first paragraph in a chapter:

```
chapter:first-child paragraph:first-letter { property: value; property: value; … }
```

The range of possible selectors is almost limitless, because they can be combined in almost arbitrary ways. For further reference, see the W3C Recommendations themselves or a text specializing in Cascading Style Sheets.

Using Pseudo-Elements and Pseudo-Classes

A number of pseudo elements and classes have no objective reality in the source code of the page. They are there to make particular typographical treatments of the text possible without special tags. Many of these features require information from the browser rather than the author, because the final decisions can only be made at the moment the page is being rendered.

As an example, the first-line pseudo-element allows the author to treat the first line of text in a paragraph (or other block element) differently from the rest of the body text. Common examples might be indenting the first line; printing the first line in bold, small caps, or other special text treatment; or even varying the font size slightly. Exactly what the first line consists of differs by the font, point size, line length, and other variables. The Web designer has little or no control over any of these things. Nor should she. Most of these decisions should be left to the needs or desires of the user.

It should be noted in Table 13.2 and Table 13.3 that first-line and first-letter can only be attached to block level elements and can only affect certain properties. In addition, the link, active, and visited pseudo-classes can only be attached to the A element in CSS1, although extending this (and other) functionality to XML elements is common but nonstandard. The following tables shows generic examples of selectors where X represents an arbitrary element.

TABLE 13.2 CSS1 PSEUDO-ELEMENTS

Pseudo-Element	Describes
X:link	Unvisited link
X:visited	Visited links
X:active	Active links
X:first-letter	First letter of a block element
X:first-line	First line of a block element

TABLE 13.3 CSS2 PSEUDO-CLASSES

Pseudo-Class	Describes
X:first-child	First child element of an X element
X:link	Unvisited link of an X link element
X:visited	Visited link of an X link element
X:hover	User action
X:active	Active link of an X link element
X:focus	User action
X:lang(lang-code)	Match a human language attribute
X:first-letter	First letter of a block element
X:first-line	First line of a block element
X:before	Access the location immediately before an element so content can be inserted at that point
X:after	Access the location immediately after an element so content can be inserted at that point

We already saw several instances of using pseudo-elements and pseudo-classes in the "Understanding CSS Selectors" section above so we won't duplicate these here.

SETTING CSS PROPERTY/VALUE PAIRS

After an element has been selected, you can apply a property/value pair to it. The list of properties is very large, as a glance at Appendix E will tell you. Many of the interesting effects are only available in CSS2, and the planned CSS3 extensions will allow even more control over the appearance and layout of the document. When these levels are implemented in any XML browser, life should prove interesting.

→ For more information about cascading style sheets, **see** "CSS Quick Reference" **p. 763**.

The following examples describe simple rendering properties that could be associated with XML elements using XML selector and declaration pairs with descriptive text:

```
paragraph { font-size: 14pt; }
```

Set the font size of a paragraph element to 14 points:

```
paragraph + sub-paragraph { text-indent: 0; }
```

If a subparagraph element is immediately preceded by its paragraph sibling, don't indent it:

```
*[status="deleted"] { text-decoration: line-through; }
```

If any element has a status attribute with value equal to "deleted", strike through any enclosed text:

```
 division > paragraph:first-child { text-indent: 5pt; }
```

If a paragraph element is the first child of a division element, set the indent to 5 points.

More than one property/value pair can be set with the same selector by simply including them within the curly braces. The final semicolon acts as a separator and should always be included.

CSS CLASSES

Although the class selector is not used in XML, you should be able to recognize it so that you can easily convert the notation to a safe alternative:

```
div.warning { color: red; }
```

In an HTML document, if a div element has a class attribute with a value equal to "warning", set the text color to "red".

This is illegal in XML, because a class attribute has no special meaning. But you can achieve the same effect like this:

```
div[class="warning"] { color: red; }
```

In any HTML or XML document, if a div element has a class attribute with a value equal to "warning", set the text color to "red".

As conversions go, this is about the simplest in the world. You could easily write a Perl script to do it for you if there were a lot of them, say if you were converting an entire site to be XML compatible and didn't know exactly where such constructs might exist.

PART

II

CH

13

USING XML AND HTML IDs

ID's have a special position in both XML and HTML, although there's a slight incompatibility in why they're special. In HTML and XML, the style syntax

```
x#value { property: value; }
```

where x is any element and value is the value of an attribute named id, sets an arbitrary property to an equally arbitrary value.

Unfortunately, this handy syntax is also used in a URI to identify a position within a document, sometimes called a *fragment*. However, in HTML the target described by the syntax is an element with a name attribute set to that value. In XML, on the other hand, the target is an element with an id attribute with that value. So, in XHTML, indeed in any XML document, the best course is probably to always use both attribute names and set them to the same value. The following is an XHTML example:

```
<paragraph id="target1" name="target1">Stuff</paragraph>
```

That way the target is found no matter what convention is followed by the user agent. In XML, the ID is required to be unique within a document or the document is invalid. In HTML, both the name and id attributes should be unique but are not ordinarily checked.

In XML, the ID can be given any name. So,

```
<paragraph identifier="target1" name="target1">Stuff</paragraph>
```

contains an "ID" if the DTD looks (in part) like this:

```
<!ELEMENT paragraph (#PCDATA)>
<!ATTLIST paragraph identifier ID      #REQUIRED
                    name        NMTOKEN #REQUIRED >
```

So, in XML, if you want an ID actually *named* "id", you'll have to declare it in the DTD, like this:

```
<!ELEMENT paragraph (#PCDATA)>
<!ATTLIST paragraph id      ID      #REQUIRED
                    name    NMTOKEN #REQUIRED >
```

MEDIA TYPES

CSS2 introduced the concept of different media types, that is, target devices which share certain identifiable characteristics. Although they have specific names, it should be noted that any device that shares the same set of characteristics is of that media type. As CSS evolves and as new devices proliferate, new media types may be defined in the future. A CSS media type names a set of CSS properties. A user agent that claims to support a media type by name must implement all the properties that apply to that media type.

Note

Media means the general class of output device when used in CSS, such as "handheld," which refers to small output devices: cellular phones and personal digital assistants, as well as the specialized hand-held computers often used in inventory and data collection applications in industry. Correspondingly, *print* refers to paged media in general, both hardcopy paper output and display devices that emulate a virtual piece of paper by restricting rendering to a non-scrolling window.

The names chosen for CSS media types reflect target devices for which the relevant properties make sense. In the list of CSS media types found in Table 13.4, the parenthetical descriptions are not normative. They only give a sense of what device the media type is meant to refer to.

TABLE 13.4 CSS MEDIA TYPES

Media Type	Target Media
all	Suitable for all devices.
aural	Intended for speech synthesizers. See the "Aural Displays" section for details.
Braille	Intended for Braille tactile display devices.
embossed	Intended for paged Braille printers.
handheld	Intended for handheld devices (typically small screen, monochrome, limited bandwidth).
print	Intended for paged, opaque material and for documents viewed onscreen in print preview mode. Please consult the "CSS3 Hardcopy Support and Emulation" section for information about formatting issues that are specific to paged media.
projection	Intended for projected presentations, for example projectors or print to transparencies. Please consult the "CSS3 Hardcopy Support and Emulation" section for information about formatting issues that are specific to paged media.
screen	Intended primarily for color computer screens.
tty	Intended for media using a fixed-pitch character grid, such as teletypes, terminals, or portable devices with limited display capabilities. Authors should not use pixel units with the tty media type.
tv	Intended for television-type devices (low resolution, color, limited-scrollability screens with sound available).

Media type names are case insensitive.

Media types go hand in hand with the @media rule. An @media rule defines a curly-brace delimited section of a style sheet which applies to that particular media.

PART

II

CH

13

```
@media print {
        BODY { font-size: 10pt }
        }
@media screen {
        BODY { font-size: 12pt }
        }
@media screen, print {
        BODY { line-height: 1.2 }
        }
```

In each of the above examples, multiple selectors and property/value pairs could have been defined within each media rule.

CSS3 HARDCOPY SUPPORT AND EMULATION

Hardcopy output and simulated hardcopy output onscreen is the big innovation in CSS3. Many important text effects only make sense when limited to a single page of known size. The popular use of two-column text with a central "pull quote" box often seen in magazines is an example of this. Although one can simulate this with a lot of hard work using HTML/XHTML, the effect doesn't hold up well under edit or dynamic resizing of the window. Figure 13.1 shows a sample page with a pull quote. Note that the associated code is nonlinear and would require careful reworking if you wanted to add words to one section.

Figure 13.1
Note that this is a tour de force in Opera— with the pull quote simulated by hand rather than simply described. The point is that CSS3 supports paged media and will be able to do this directly using page-based floats.

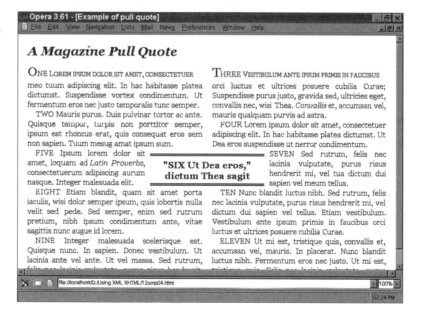

Listing 13.1 shows the style sheet that makes it work. It divides the page into left and right sections, and further subdivides those sections into top, middle, and bottom left and right sections to accommodate the pull quote, which has its own style selectors and properties. In addition, it divides the header into left and right sections, so that everything fits together.

LISTING 13.1 SIMULATED FLOATING TEXT BOX STYLE SHEET

```
EM { font-style: italic; }
BODY { background: none #ffffff; color: #000000; font-size: 1em;
       font-family: Georgia,"Goudy Old Style","Bookman Old Style","Times New
Roman",serif;
       font-weight: normal; margin: 0; border: none; padding: 0;
       width: auto; }
DIV.lefthead { background: #ffffff url(../graph/pmarblet.jpg) top left
               repeat-x;  color: #000000; margin: 0 80px 0 0; border: none;
               padding: 0; height: 50px; width: auto; }
DIV.righthead { background: #ffffff url(../graph/JR-logo.jpg) top right
               no-repeat; color: #000000; float: right; margin: 0;
               border: none; padding: 0; height: 50px; width: 80px; }
DIV.left1 { margin: 0; border: none; padding: 0; float: left; width: 50%; }
DIV.right1 { margin: 0; border: none; padding: 0; float: right; width: 50%; }
DIV.left2 { margin: 0; border: none; padding: 0; float: left; width: 35%; }
DIV.right2 { margin: 0; border: none; padding: 0; float: right; width: 35%; }
DIV.generic { margin: 0; border: none; padding: 0; width: auto; }
DIV.pullquote { margin: 0.6em 0 0 0; border-top: double #000000 5px;
               border-right: none; border-bottom: double #000000 5px;
               border-left: none; padding: 0; float: left; width: 30%; }
H1 { background: transparent; color: #000000; font-size: 1.6em;
        font-family: Georgia,"Goudy Old Style","Bookman Old Style","Times New
Roman",serif;
        font-weight: bold; font-style: italic; margin: 0; border: none;
        padding: 20px 0 0 20px; text-align: left; width: auto; }
H2 { background: #ffffff; color: #000000; font-size: 1.4em;
        font-family: Georgia,"Goudy Old Style","Bookman Old Style","Times
New Roman",serif;
        font-weight: bold; margin: 0; border: none;
        padding: 0.3em; text-align: center; width: auto; }
IMG { float: right; margin: 0.4em 0 0 0; border: none; padding: 0; }
P { margin: 0; border: none; background: #ffffff; color: #000000;
    font-family: Georgia,"Goudy Old Style","Bookman Old Style","Times New
Roman",serif;
    font-size: 1em; font-weight: normal; text-align: justify;
    line-height: 1.3; }
P.firstleft:first-letter { font-size: 1.6em; }
P.firstleft:first-line { font-variant: small-caps; }
P.firstleft { padding: 0.7em 0.6em 0 20px; text-indent: 0; }
P.firstright:first-letter { font-size: 1.6em; }
P.firstright:first-line { font-variant: small-caps; }
P.firstright { padding: 0.7em 20px 0 0.6em; text-indent: 0; }
P.bodyleft { padding: 0 0.6em 0 20px; text-indent: 1em; }
P.bodyright { padding: 0 20px 0 0.6em; text-indent: 1em; }
P.spacer { padding: 0; clear: both; font-size: 0em; width: auto; }
```

PART
II

CH
13

Listing 13.2 shows the XHTML code. Note that the following code separates the text that needs to be placed in the virtual columns into disjointed and out of sequence blocks. This is done so that everything will *appear* to flow naturally, like a magazine or newspaper column, in spite of the fact that current browsers don't support this. It should be noted that the beta version of Opera is aware of paged media, so being able to define this in reality is not all that far off.

LISTING 13.2   XHTML SOURCE CODE FOR SIMULATED FLOATING TEXT BOX

```
<?xml version="1.0"?>
<!DOCTYPE html PUBLIC "-//W3C//DTD XHTML 1.0 Strict//EN"
    "http://www.w3.org/TR/xhtml1/DTD/strict.dtd">
<html
 lang="en-US"
 xmlns="http://www.w3.org/1999/xhtml">
  <head>
    <title>
      Example of pull quote
    </title>
    <link
     rel="StyleSheet"
     href="12xmp04.css"
     type="text/css"
     media="screen" />
  </head>
  <body>
    <div class="righthead">
      <p class="spacer">
      </p>
    </div>
    <div class="lefthead">
      <h1>
        A Magazine Pull Quote
      </h1>
    </div>
    <div class="left1">
      <p class="firstleft">
        ONE Lorem ipsum dolor sit amet, consectetuer meo tuum
        adipiscing elit. In hac habitasse platea dictumst.
        Suspendisse vortex condimentum. Ut fermentum eros nec justo
        temporalis tunc semper.
      </p>
      <p class="bodyleft">
        TWO Mauris purus. Duis pulvinar tortor ac ante. Quisque
        tempor, turpis non porttitor semper, ipsum est rhoncus
        erat, quis consequat eros sem non sapien. Tuum mesug amat
        ipsum sum.
      </p>
    </div>
    <div class="right1">
      <p class="firstright">
        THREE Vestibulum ante ipsum primis in faucibus orci luctus
        et ultrices posuere cubilia Curae; Suspendisse purus justo,
        gravida sed, ultricies eget, convallis nec, wisi Thea. <em>
        Convallis</em> et, accumsan vel, mauris qualquam purvis ad
        astra.
      </p>
      <p class="bodyright">
        FOUR Lorem ipsum dolor sit amet, consectetuer adipiscing
        elit. In hac habitasse platea dictumst. Ut Dea eros
        suspendisse ut nerror condimentum.
      </p>
    </div>
    <p class="spacer">
```

```
    </p>
    <div class="left2">
      <p class="bodyleft">
        FIVE Ipsum lorem dolor sit amet, loquam ad <cite>Latin
        Proverbs</cite>, consectetuerum adipiscing aurum nasque.
        Integer malesuada elit lauditum erat meum sit.
      </p>
    </div>
    <div class="pullquote">
      <h2>
        "SIX Ut Dea eros," dictum Thea sagit
      </h2>
    </div>
    <div class="right2">
      <p class="bodyright">
        SEVEN Sed rutrum, felis nec lacinia vulputate, purus risus
        hendrerit mi, vel tua dictum dui sapien vel meum noventum
        eram nic qua perditat tellus.
      </p>
    </div>
    <p class="spacer">
    </p>
    <div class="left1">
      <p class="bodyleft">
        EIGHT Etiam blandit, quam sit amet porta iaculis, wisi
        dolor semper ipsum, quis lobortis nulla velit sed pede. Sed
        semper, enim sed rutrum pretium, nibh ipsum condimentum
        ante, vitae sagittis nunc augue id lorem.
      </p>
      <p class="bodyleft">
        NINE Integer malesuada scelerisque est. Quisque nunc. In
        sapien. Donec vestibulum. Ut lacinia ante vel ante. Ut vel
        massa. Sed rutrum, felis nec lacinia vulputate, purus risus
        hendrerit. Integer malesuada scelerisque est.
      </p>
    </div>
    <div class="right1">
      <p class="bodyright">
        TEN Nunc blandit luctus nibh. Sed rutrum, felis nec
        lacinia vulputate, purus risus hendrerit mi, vel dictum dui
        sapien vel tellus. Etiam vestibulum. Vestibulum ante ipsum
        primis in faucibus orci luctus et ultrices posuere cubilia
        Curae.
      </p>
      <p class="bodyright">
        ELEVEN Ut mi est, tristique quis, convallis et, accumsan
        vel, mauris. In placerat. Nunc blandit luctus nibh.
        Fermentum eros nec justo. Ut mi est, tristique quis. Felis
        nec lacinia vulputate, purus risus hendrerit mi, vel dictum
        vel tellus.
      </p>
    </div>
  </body>
</html>
```

PART

II

CH

13

A link element was used instead of a processing instruction because that syntax is most widely understood. Despite my own advice, to save space the style sheet was not used inline.

Also, the dotted class notation was used because Opera, the only browser besides Mozilla that understands this style sheet, doesn't currently understand the bracket notation.

Figure 13.2 shows the page in the Mozilla browser.

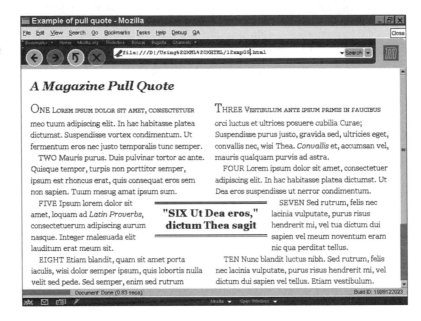

Figure 13.2
Note the slight ugliness of the pull quote margin in Mozilla. It could just as easily have been made to look better in Mozilla and slightly ugly in Opera but everything is a compromise.

The page isn't shown in Microsoft Internet Explorer or Netscape Navigator 4.7 because it just doesn't work at all. This is no surprise, because if the style sheet is run through the TopStyle style sheet validator it warns you about it because of known bugs in major browsers.

AURAL DISPLAYS

One of the greatest strengths of CSS2 is its capability to define different style sheets for different media. Because aural displays have completely different characteristics than do visual ones, the special characteristics of aural browsers can be taken into account without affecting other displays. On the CD-ROM, there is an example of an aural browser reading a small section of a page as a person driving a car, a cell phone user, or an individual with a visual disability might hear it. The product used is the JAWS screen reader from Henter-Joyce at http://www.hj.com/ and the filename is jawsdemo.wav. Alternate formats are provided for persons using other operating systems: jawsdemo.au, and jawsdemo.aiff. On the Henter-Joyce Web site are available multimedia downloads describing the product and demonstration version of the program, as well as an explanation of how JAWS can interact with their screen magnification application, MAGic, to create a versatile working environment for persons with low vision and other special needs.

To distinguish different speakers, an aural browser might place one in a simulated position off to the left and the other to the right. Emphasis can be made by differing volumes, and headings could be distinguished by pitch. Some browsers, or at least their physical hardware, have the capability to set up different voices as well, and use simulated height above or below the speaker's ear level. So, the list of properties designed for these browsers may seem strange at first.

The following style sheet fragment illustrates the use of aural properties to render an XML document. Please refer to the example audio sample on the CD-ROM as mentioned above to hear how these might sound in use.

```
{ volume: <number> | <percentage> | silent |
         x-soft | soft | medium | loud |
         x-loud | inherit ; }
```

Set the volume.

```
{ speak: normal | none | spell-out | inherit ; }
```

Set style of speech.

```
{ pause-before: <time> | <percentage> | inherit ; }
```

Set pause-before speaking value. This gives the listener time to get ready for the aural sound or perform some necessary action, like bringing the hands to a resting position on the keyboard after pressing a control key.

```
{ pause-after: <time> | <percentage> | inherit ; }
```

Set pause-after speaking value. This helps the user to distinguish separate thoughts, so one use might be to pause after sentences and pause for a slightly longer time after paragraphs.

```
{ pause: <time> | <percentage> | inherit ; }
```

Shorthand property to set pause-before and pause-after. Logically, this might be used to bracket speech utterances with a pause at either end, to set off, for example, a phrase in parentheses from the surrounding text.

```
{ cue-before: <url> | none | inherit ; }
```

Set cue-before speaking sound. This might be used to play a bell sound before an answer or warning message.

```
{ cue-after: <url> | none | inherit ; }
```

Set cue-after speaking sound. This might be used, for example, to signal to the user to perform some action, such as stopping another playback device before continuing.

```
{ cue: <url> | none | inherit ; }
```

Shorthand property to set cue-before and cue-after sounds. This property might be used, for example, to introduce and close parenthetical comments in text.

PART
II

CH
13

```
{ play-during: <url> | mix? | repeat? | auto |
         none | inherit{s2]
```

Set a sound to play during another sound, so that a nonlinear aural presentation can be created without the support of SMIL. An example much seen on the Web is the background music on some pages.

```
{ azumith: <angle> | left-side | far-left | left |
         center-left | center | center-right |
         right | far-right | right-side | behind |
         leftwards | rightwards | inherit ; }
```

Set simulated location of a sound source or speaker. Note that achieving the full range of effects possible requires some sort of surround-sound audio system although stereo is adequate for simple left-right placement of a source.

```
{ elevation: <angle> | below | level | above | higher |
         lower | inherit |
```

Set simulated height of a sound source or speaker. Elevation is measured in a positive direction from directly in front of and level with the listener sweeping overhead and behind, then below until front level is reached again. In a negative direction the perceived location moves from front level down and back, then overhead and to front level again. Note that hearing vertical sound placement angles requires more channels and speakers than most home theater systems are capable of. It seems likely that gaming systems will offer this capability before it becomes widely available elsewhere.

```
{ speech-rate: <number> | x-slow | slow | medium |
         fast | x-fast | faster | slower | inherit ; }
```

Set speech rate. Number is words per minute.

```
{ voice-family: <specific voice> | <generic voice> |
         inherit ; }
```

Set voice family. Specific voices are dependent on the user agent.

```
{ pitch: <frequency> | x-low | low | medium | high |
    x-high | inherit ; }
```

Set average speech pitch (frequency). Male=120Hz, Female=210Hz, and Child=300Hz.

```
{ pitch-range: <number> | inherit ; }
```

Set pitch range, the average modulation a speaker uses in a sentence. Female voices tend to use a greater pitch range and male voices tend toward a lower pitch range. Number is 0-100. 50=average.

```
{ stress: <number> | inherit ; }
```

Set intonation pattern. Number is 0-100.

```
{ richness: <number> | inherit ; }
```

Set the overtone pattern of a voice from flat to very rich. Number is 0-100.

```
{ speak-punctuation: code | none | inherit ; }
```

Set spoken punctuation or inferred from pause and tone.

```
{ speak-numeral: digits | continuous | inherit ; }
```

Set digit-by-digit (telephone) or natural (money).

Aural options also exist for other CSS2 constructs, such as tables.

AUDIO RENDERING OF TABLES

```
{ speak-header: once | always | inherit ; }
```

Set behavior of aural table rendering.

ANGLES

The following value measurements describe angles. The first is the familiar degree measurement we usually indicate with a little circle like this: 90°. Angles are measured in a positive direction starting at front center and sweeping around the listener in a continuous arc clockwise. So 90deg indicates a position at the extreme right and 240deg indicates a position at the extreme left. Negative angles are measured counterclockwise in the same manner. So -90deg is equivalent to 240deg.

- **deg degrees**—One 360th of a full circle. 180deg refers to a location directly behind the listener.
- **grad gradians**—Almost a degree: 360deg = 400grad.
- **rad radians**—1deg = π/180rad or 360deg = 2πrad.

Angles may be negative and are measured clockwise from directly in front of the listener. There are certain mathematical calculations in analytic geometry, trigonometry, and calculus which are more conveniently performed when angles are measured in radians or grads but these measurements are not commonly seen or used except in these specialized mathematic and scientific contexts.

TIMES

The following value measurements describe the duration of a sound or other event.

- **ms milliseconds**—Thousandths of a second.
- **s seconds**—An ordinary second—one sixtieth of a minute.

Times may not be negative.

PART

II

CH

13

FREQUENCIES[AURAL][S2]

The following value units describe frequencies, the number of times a sound cycles (which generates the perceived pitch of the sound) in terms of full cycles per second.

- **Hz Hertz**—The number of cycles per second.

- **kHz kiloHertz**—The number of cycles per one thousandth of a second or alternatively, one thousand Hertz.

Frequencies may not be negative.

Full realization of the properties listed here requires the support of three-dimensional surround-sound environments; however, these are becoming more common as ultra-realistic computer games demand more and more of their host systems. Even now, head-phones are available with multiple sound sources that do realistic audio ambiance, so it won't be too long before all these things are available at reasonable cost.

HANDHELD DEVICES

Another common display type, handheld devices typically have low-resolution screens, sometimes with only one bit color depth (B/W), poor or no sound capabilities, and various other limitations. The archetypical handheld device nowadays is one of the various Palm Pilot variations, which has no keyboard and fairly good B/W graphics. Handwriting recognition and touch-sensitive screens replace keyboards and mice. So although the display is very small, you could access an online database over the Web using wireless connectivity. Then you could make an inquiry, perhaps even a purchase, all without leaving the comfort of your beach chair on the Kona side of Hawaii. Figure 13.3 shows a Psion Java-based netBook surfing the Web with full VGA color on a handheld device.

Figure 13.3
A Psion netBook keyboard and display shown with a Web page displayed on a custom browser.

The EPOC-32 standard nonproprietary operating system developed by Psion has been adopted by Ericsson, Nokia, and Motorola for their Web-enabled cellular phones, so software developed for the Psion platform should run without problem on many platforms. Opera Software of Norway already has an initial port of their Opera browser out for the handheld device platforms, with full CSS1 support.

MINIATURE DISPLAYS

The smallest displays so far are those on cell phones and alphanumeric pagers, which usually have 4 lines of 16 characters (or so) and no sound other than beeps while you're looking at them. A phone, of course, has at least the possibility of delivering sound as well, but probably only one activity at a time. While you're looking at the display, you won't be able to hear the phone without an external gadget. Likewise, while you're on the phone, you can't see the display.

Figure 13.4 shows the display screen of a NeoPoint 16000 dual-mode cellular phone, showing its comparatively large display screen—11 lines. It's superimposed on the larger screen displays of the Psion netBook, full-color VGA, and the Psion 5000 series, monochrome half VGA in size to show how these more powerful handheld devices compare to a cell phone. All these displays can use CSS to modify the display dynamically based on the actual display characteristics.

Figure 13.4
The NeoPoint 16000 Web-capable cell phone is compared in size to the displays of VGA-compatible handheld devices with full keyboards.

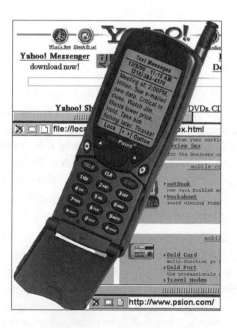

Still, useful information can be and is delivered to such systems every day. From stock quotes to short messages to reminder notes, the pager has become a symbol of our modern age. And the cell phone, of course, is so ubiquitous that people don't even bother looking for public phones anymore; they just ask a random stranger if they could please use her phone to make an emergency call.

XML combined with XSL/XSLT and selective media formatting, using either XSL or CSS, will make far more information available than the typical canned applications available now. As information content becomes more accessible and cheaper to manipulate, there's no reason someone can't make a million bucks with an application, for example, that lets you call on your cell phone to get movie times and, after choosing a show, download to your phone driving directions and a map. It's a brave new world, eh?

OTHER MEDIA TYPES

The possibilities for expanding media types are endless, from three-dimensional displays and virtual reality to adding the ability to feel the motion of a boat or car. These are already available using motion-simulator chairs and position-sensing goggles in some computer gaming systems and have long been available in high-end military and commercial flight- and combat-simulation environments.

CSS3 will be adding behavioral properties as well, making it possible for style sheets to be truly interactive and incorporating most of the functionality of scripting languages into the style sheet. That means in turn that download times and bandwidth requirements for slow connections and small displays can be drastically reduced, because the style sheet will be able to figure out what kind of display and connection you have and tailor its requests to the server accordingly.

TROUBLESHOOTING

NOTHING WORKS THE WAY IT'S SUPPOSED TO!

After hours of effort, all in vain, you've decided that style sheets aren't worth a plugged nickel.

It's true that style sheets are hard to get right. The best advice is to put them in the hands of a real expert. If you insist on struggling with them, start small. Look over the properties in boldface in Appendix E and use only those to start. At the same time, as the example pull quote screen showed, you can actually do interesting things with them, just not in all browsers using the same code. This argues for using scripts to selectively use different style sheets for each of the common browsers. That way, you can concentrate on getting one browser at a time to do exactly what you want it to do and avoid pulling out your hair.

You can also use a style sheet editor and validator like Top Style at http://www.bradsoft.com/topstyle/. It's almost impossible to keep in mind the number and identity of selectors and properties supported from one release of the popular browsers to another. Because many of the CSS1 selectors and properties were labeled "optional," many software developers negligently failed to test style sheets using the optional features and crash ignominiously when they encounter them. Some browsers are not well integrated and implement style sheets using a kludgey "grab bag" approach that mirrors their approach to elements and document structure. These browsers are prone to fail when selectors and properties are used in combinations or in a context not foreseen by the authors. Even with a power assist, it's not an easy task to create a style sheet that doesn't break something somewhere, even if the syntax is perfect.

Although the current state of CSS is chaotic, the new release from Netscape, after Mozilla is turned over, promises an unprecedented level of support for CSS1 and CSS2, and probably CSS3 to follow. With that pressure, Microsoft may be thinking about getting on board as well. Although older browsers always will be with us, simple server-side sniffing can serve a minimal page, although modern browsers can display information-rich content fully and flexibly formatted.

It's also true that CSS support is key to making the Web accessible to everyone from persons with vision disabilities to people in their cars, who had *better* not be able to see a video screen. With CSS3 eliminating *any* need for HTML-style tables, and having the capability to swap in user style sheets as necessary, the designer can concentrate on design—the artful side of the business—and ignore the dull technical details that drag us all down.

USING NEXT-GENERATION EXTENSIBLE STYLE SHEETS—XSL

In this chapter

LOOKING CLOSELY AT XSL

The last chapter compared CSS to decorating a tree. Well, if CSS is like hanging candy canes, XSL is like genetic engineering. Unlike CSS, which uses the document itself as the basic structure on which to hang formatting and display information, XSL starts by reading the document tree and then reconstructs it to its heart's content.

Three main pieces make up XSL: XSL proper, the Extensible Stylesheet Language; XSLT, XSL Transformations; and XPath, the XML Path language. XPath isn't really XML at all, but a way of addressing document fragments within documents. XPath, which is covered in detail in Chapter 8, "XPath," forms a part of many specifications, a trend in W3C specifications as they become more modularized and less monolithic, so it will be handy in many contexts. XLink and XPointer, discussed more thoroughly in Chapter 9, "XLink and XPointer," are the other parts of the XML linking triumvirate.

Both XSLT and XPath have been issued as Recommendations; XSL is the only one still in the Working Draft stage. Part of the reason is that XSL is just plain hard. XSL is where the formatting gets done, and the Working Group seems intent on solving many problems at once. XSL already incorporates most of CSS1 and CSS2, with significant bits of CSS3 added in for good measure. Because CSS3 is in a preliminary stage of development, XSL risks diverging from it if the specification is nailed down too soon. It seems entirely possible that it won't be finalized until CSS3 is.

This chapter explores XSL as it exists now, examining XSL templates, how elements are selected, and the flow of control. You'll also walk through several examples of using XSL to layout XML documents for display in legacy browsers, the most common use today. The same techniques can be used to format and display XML in XML-aware browsers as well.

UNDERSTANDING XSL TEMPLATES

An XSL template describes the way elements are matched and transformed. Because a template can be applied recursively, a single template is sufficient to match an entire tree if properly defined. Of course, if you want to do different things to the different parts of your document tree, you'll need more templates.

Here's an example of a simple recursive template:

```
<xsl:stylesheet xmlns:xsl="http://www.w3.org/XSL/Transform/1.0"
                xmlns:fo="http://www.w3.org/XSL/Format/1.0">
  <xsl:template match="root-document name">
    <!-- processing stuff goes here -->
  <xsl:apply-templates select="node()" />
  </xsl:template>
</xsl:stylesheet>
```

Very roughly, anything that doesn't look like it belongs in the XSL namespace is output to the browser. So you can put as much as you want into the indicated space, even an entire Web page, and it magically appears on the other side. These things really are templates.

Everything inside them is part of the template that will be output *except* those few things that have been labeled as XSL commands by appearing in the XSL namespace. And *they're* invisible, like those guys dressed in black in a Noh play who hurry the action along without us ever noticing. So anything from any other namespace, including the default namespace if that doesn't happen to be the XSL namespace, is simply passed through to the output without any further processing.

ELEMENT MATCHING

An element can be matched in several ways. The most direct way is shown in the previous example; use the following:

```
<xsl:template match="element-name">
```

Just place the actual element name within the quotes and you're ready to go. But there are many ways to go about it, some of them subtle and some not. XSL uses XPath to find nodes, so referring to Chapter 8 may help explain a few things. To jog your memory, here's a little cheat sheet that lists the most common XPath selectors used by XSL to identify document locations for the purpose of initiating the emission of formatted display code:

→ **See** "Using XPath Abbreviations," **p. 179**.

- paragraph selects the paragraph element children of the context node.
- * selects all element children of the context node.
- text() selects all text node children of the context node.
- @name selects the name attribute of the context node.
- @* selects all the attributes of the context node.
- paragraph[1] selects the first paragraph child of the context node.
- paragraph[last()] selects the last paragraph child of the context node.
- */paragraph selects all paragraph grandchildren of the context node.
- /doc/chapter[5]/section[2] selects the second section of the fifth chapter of the doc.
- chapter//paragraph selects the paragraph element descendants of the chapter element children of the context node.
- //paragraph selects all the paragraph descendants of the document root and therefore selects all paragraph elements in the same document as the context node.
- //orderedlist/item selects all the item elements in the same document as the context node that have an orderedlist parent.
- . selects the context node.
- .//paragraph selects the paragraph element descendants of the context node.
- .. selects the parent of the context node.
- ../@lang selects the lang attribute of the parent of the context node.
- paragraph[@type="warning"] selects all paragraph children of the context node that have a type attribute with value warning.

- `paragraph[@type="warning"][5]` selects the fifth `paragraph` child of the context node that has a type attribute with value warning.

- `paragraph[5][@type="warning"]` selects the fifth `paragraph` child of the context node if that child has a type attribute with value warning.

- `chapter[title="Introduction"]` selects the `chapter` children of the context node that have one or more `title` children with string-value equal to Introduction.

- `chapter[title]` selects the `chapter` children of the context node that have one or more `title` children.

- `employee[@secretary and @assistant]` selects all the `employee` children of the context node that have both a `secretary` attribute and an `assistant` attribute.

Although you can ignore most of the complexity if you only plan to do simple things, to really swing through the trees you'll probably need to use the more subtle syntax for finding nodes remote from your present location. In fact, the hardest part about navigating the document tree is keeping track of where you are at any given moment. It helps to have a listing handy so you can draw numbered lines and labels as you brachiate from point to point.

> **Note**
>
> To *brachiate* is simply to swing through trees from branch to branch while dangling by one's hands, as an ape might. When one traverses a tree in this manner, one doesn't have to visit every point.

Listing 14.1 shows a simple XML document. Later in this chapter you'll see how legacy browsers can display this document using XSL to generate an HTML document from the XML original.

LISTING 14.1 A SAMPLE XML PRODUCT LIST

```
<?xml version="1.0"?>
<productList xmlns="http://www.leeanne.com/aristotelian/productlist"
    xmlns:xsi="http://www.w3.org/1999/XMLSchema-instance"

xsi:schemaLocation="http://www.leeanne.com/aristotelian/productlist/03xmp01.xsd">
  <!-- Aristotelian Product List -->
  <listTitle>Aristotelian Logical Systems - Product List</listTitle>
  <product>
    <name>European Translator</name>
    <model>Mark IV</model>
    <languages>de fr es en</languages>
  </product>
  <product>
    <name>Universal Translator</name>
    <model>Mark V</model>
    <languages>de fr es en jp</languages>
  </product>
  <product>
    <name>Universal Translator</name>
    <model>Mark VI</model>
```

```
      <languages>de fr es en jp ch</languages>
    </product>
    <product>
      <name>BabelFish</name>
      <model>Mark VII</model>
      <languages>de fr es en jp ch kl rm fg</languages>
    </product>
    <product>
      <name>BabelFish</name>
      <model>Mark VIII</model>
      <languages>all {by direct thought transference}</languages>
    </product>
</productList>
```

Note that this document contains a list of products. Because there's no obvious reason to think that the number of products is fixed, some sort of control structure is needed that will allow you to iterate through the list. The "Processing and Control Flow" section later in this chapter describes this control structure in detail.

Listing 14.2 contains the XML Schema this XML document conforms to:

LISTING 14.2   AN XML SCHEMA FOR THE PRODUCT LIST

```
<?xml version="1.0" encoding="UTF-8"?>
<!DOCTYPE xsd:schema PUBLIC "-//W3C//DTD XMLSCHEMA 19991216//EN" "" [
        <!ENTITY % p 'xsd:'>
        <!ENTITY % s ':xsd'>
]>
<xsd:schema xmlns:xsd="http://www.w3.org/1999/XMLSchema"
            xmlns="http://www.leeanne.com/aristotelian/productlist"
            targetNamespace="http://www.leeanne.com/aristotelian/productlist">
  <xsd:complexType name="productType" content="elementOnly">
    <xsd:sequence>
      <xsd:element name="name" type="xsd:string" />
      <xsd:element name="model" type="xsd:string" />
      <xsd:element name="languages" type="xsd:string" />
    </xsd:sequence>
  </xsd:complexType>
  <xsd:element name="productList">
    <xsd:complexType content="elementOnly">
      <xsd:sequence>
        <xsd:element name="listTitle" type="xsd:string"/>
        <xsd:element name="product" type="productType" minOccurs="1"
maxOccurs="unbounded"/>
      </xsd:sequence>
      <xsd:attribute name="xmlns:xsi"
                     type="xsd:uriReference"
                     use="default"
                     value="http://www.w3.org/1999/XMLSchema-instance"/>
      <xsd:attribute name="xsi:noNamespaceSchemaLocation"
                     type="xsd:string"/>
      <xsd:attribute name="xsi:schemaLocation"
                     type="xsd:string"/>
    </xsd:complexType>
  </xsd:element>
</xsd:schema>
```

Please see Chapter 7, "XML Schemas," for further explanation of XML Schema.

PART

II

CH

14

PROCESSING AND CONTROL FLOW

XSLT has three, maybe four, control flow mechanisms besides branching using XPath:

- ```
  <xsl:for-each select="node-expression" >
    content
  </xsl:for-each>
  ```

is instantiated for every selected node in the current node list.

- ```
  <xsl:if test="Boolean test" >
    <xsl:template>
      content
    </xsl:template>
  </xsl:if>
  ```

is instantiated every time the test evaluates to true. Otherwise it's not.

- ```
  <xsl:choose>
    <xsl:when test="Boolean">
      <xsl:template>
        content
      </xsl:template>
    </xsl:when>
    <xsl:when test="Boolean">
      <xsl:template>
        content
      </xsl:template>
    </xsl:when>
  </xsl:choose>
  ```

The first in a list of xsl:when tests to evaluate to true is instantiated within an xsl:choose element. Any following xsl:when tests are ignored within the xsl:choose element.

- ```
  <xsl:otherwise>
    <xsl:template>
      content
    </xsl:template>
  </xsl:otherwise>
  ```

is instantiated if control falls through all the previously listed xsl:when tests within an xsl:choose element. The xsl:otherwise element only has meaning within an xsl:choose list. It can be regarded as always evaluating to true and is used like this:

```
<xsl:choose>
  <xsl:when test="Boolean">
    <xsl:template>
      content
    </xsl:template>
  </xsl:when>
  <xsl:when test="Boolean">
    <xsl:template>
      content
    </xsl:template>
  </xsl:when>
  <xsl:otherwise>
    <xsl:template>
      content
    </xsl:template>
  </xsl:otherwise>
</xsl:choose>
```

- `<xsl:sort select="string" lang="??" data-type = "text" | "number" | qname-but-not-ncname order = "ascending" | "descending" case-order = "upper-first" | "lower-first" />` sorts on the listed criteria, ignoring the natural tree order of the document.

Using some combination of these you should be able to do just about anything with the XML tree. For the first working example, the `for-each select="selector"` is used to generate an HTML table from the XML structure using iteration.

ITERATION

There are two methods of iteration in XSLT. The first is to recurse through the tree. By starting at the root, you can recursively visit every node of the tree, although you have no control over what comes next because you're walking the tree in node order. However, XSL also has an `XSL:for-each` construct that allows a template to visit each element descended from the current element and select each in turn. This is what is used to display the product list document, because it seems to fit the structure best.

`<xsl:for-each select="node-expression" >` … is instantiated for every selected node in the current node list. This allows you to iterate through the children of the element selected by `node-expression` to perform some sort of processing on each in turn.

The style sheet code shown in Listing 14.3, which acts on the document defined in Listing 14.1, generates standard HTML code from the XML original and should work in any browser that supports tables.

LISTING 14.3   A STYLE SHEET ACTING ON THE XML PRODUCT LIST

```
<?xml version="1.0" encoding="UTF-8"?>
<xsl:stylesheet xmlns:xsl="http://www.w3.org/TR/WD-xsl">
  <!-- XSL Stylesheet for Aristotelian Product List -->
  <xsl:template match="/">
    <html>
      <head>
        <title>
          <xsl:value-of select="//productList/listTitle"></xsl:value-of>
        </title>
      </head>
      <body>
        <h2><xsl:value-of select="//productList/listTitle"></xsl:value-of></h2>
        <div>
          <table border="1">
            <tr>
              <th>Product</th>
                <th>Model Number</th>
                  <th>Supported Languages</th>
            </tr>
            <xsl:for-each select="//productList/product">
              <tr>
                <td><xsl:value-of select="name"></xsl:value-of></td>
```

LISTING 14.3   CONTINUED

```
                <td><xsl:value-of select="model"></xsl:value-of></td>
                   <td><xsl:value-of select="languages"></xsl:value-of></td>
            </tr>
          </xsl:for-each>
        </table>
      </div>
    </body>
  </html>
 </xsl:template>
</xsl:stylesheet>
```

Figure 14.1 shows how this document looks in browser view after the XSL transformation using Icon Information Systems' XML Spy, which can be found at http://www.xmlspy.com/.

Figure 14.1
The Aristotelian Logical Systems product list is shown in browser view by XML Spy.

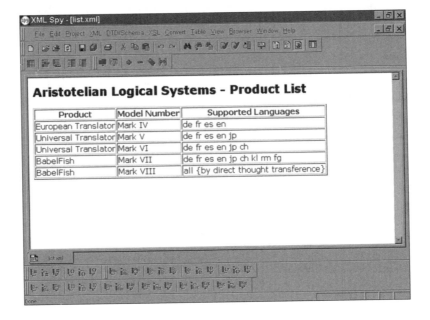

The other control flow mechanisms, the standard if sequence, and the choose...when... otherwise... sequence used to construct a switch behave in a similar and predictable way so they aren't covered here.

Although it's not traditionally thought of as a control-flow mechanism, you can use sort to alter natural visitation order as well, as described in the "Processing and Control Flow" section earlier in this chapter.

UNDERSTANDING XSL FORMATTING OBJECTS

XSL has a huge list of *formatting objects* (fo) which look like CSS properties, although their similarity doesn't extend *too* far. Like CSS properties, an XSL formatting object has a set of properties which can be associated with the object and which depend on the type of object it is. There aren't many rendering engines that actually display XSL formatting objects, because it's time-consuming and difficult to implement error-free handling of many of these objects and the specification is subject to change at any time. You have to be fairly dedicated to even try.

InDelv has a partial implementation, but it's unabashedly beta code and will be in that state until the standard settles down. But to implement even what's there in the Working Draft is far beyond the capabilities of any existing browser, because support for paged media containing languages such as Chinese—written from top to bottom—is built into the specification, but it hasn't really been done before. The W3C is even talking about adding non-rectangular formatting objects, which would require a skilled craftsperson to do by hand in the olden days, using the experience of a lifetime to cut in letters to just the right separation so they looked right. But on the Web, you don't even know what alphabets are available to fulfill the need for words, much less the size of the page. So every page has to be planned and executed anew.

Any company that tries will certainly require native-speaker informants in dozens of languages to be sure of getting the basics right. How do you justify a vertical line, for example? Or justify a line in Arabic, which requires extending the forms of certain letters to take up more space without changing the spacing between words or letters? Arabic uses a cursive script, and it's required to flow. Beauty of form is an integral part of writing Arabic and most computers are rather poor judges of aesthetic merit.

In real life, Arabic type cases contain multiple extenders that allow a typographer to stretch those characters that must be used to justify a line by inserting one or more extended horizontal strokes between the first part of the letter (which has been split in half for just this purpose) and the last part. Typesetting software can do much the same thing, and XML processors will usually pass documents on to external processes to handle typesetting.

Because the XML document itself forms a tree by definition, the formatting object output is also a tree. In fact, it's an XML document although very hard to prove so. XSL uses namespaces to such an extent, including as internal switches, that validating an XSL document against its DTD is almost beyond what machines can be made to do. It promises to be an interesting coming year.

DISPLAYING AN XML PAGE IN ANY BROWSER

One method of laying out XML content, of course, in the absence of real XSL, is to transform it to HTML or XHTML and apply CSS style sheet formatting to display the result as you want it. The limitations of style sheets still hold because you're still using the same old battered browser you used last year, and you haven't really gained much besides the extra steps of putting the document into XML and translating it back out of XML. If that were all that were possible, you might as well not bother except for the fact that you can now serve any browser the correct code using server-side browser sniffing.

The nascent XSL support available in Microsoft's Internet Explorer and the InDelv browser promises a great future because XSL and XSLT can do things CSS can only dream about.

PART

II

CH

14

You could, for example, take a document and automatically generate a table of contents and an index, and then put them all together in a fully paginated and ready to print version in the twinkling of an eye. You've already seen that XSL/XSLT can be used to transform an XML document into a simple HTML document on-the-fly, reusing the same XML field for both the `<title>` field and the initial `<h2>` header. Similar techniques can add formatting objects and more complex transformations at will.

XSL contains all sorts of ways to affect the layout of documents. You can sort them, prune branches, graft others on, and in general tweak the document tree until it's almost unrecognizable. You'll see how this is done in the "Using XSL and XSLT" section toward the end of this chapter.

HANDLING XML CONTENT

The individual characters of the data contained in non-empty elements are also nodes, although it would be tedious to step through them one by one. So XSL kindly supplies a shorthand, the `node()` node-set selector. When used in a select attribute like this

```
<xsl:apply-templates select="node()" />
```

the processor recursively visits every child node until it gets back. Along the way, it automatically seeks out and passes on plain text, as well as finding any XSL commands that may have been missed and causing them to be executed appropriately. If you never needed to change your mind about anything, a nice job could be done by letting the `node()` zombies do their thing untouched by human hands, if the style sheet were only set up right.

UNDERSTANDING XSL FORMATTING PROPERTIES

XSL formatting properties are applied to formatting objects, which are abstract views of the document that define certain areas to which properties can be applied. Formatting objects can be refined by their interaction with the document itself, so a footnote-body formatting object may actually span several pages when displayed, based on maximum footnote area criteria defined for the document by other formatting objects and properties. Multiple footnote bodies, for example, each take up room on the page, so it may be necessary to flow one or more footnotes to a following page, or even break a long footnote across several pages, to accommodate a minimum area of running text on each page.

XSL properties are applied to formatting objects, so you might think of the formatting object as the rough equivalent of a CSS selector, although the XSL property is, by design, the more precise equivalent of a CSS property.

The list of properties for CSS1 and CSS2 is available at the back of the book in Appendix E, "CSS1, CSS2 Reference," as well as on the enclosed CD-ROM. Although there are differences between these values and the "real" XSL capabilities, nobody really knows what the list will look like when it's finally released as a Recommendation. However, with the understanding that these are not quite final, here's a short list of the XSL formatting objects and the CSS-style properties that made it past the XSL Working Group and are now headed more or less toward acceptance in the wider world. Wish them all the luck in the world.

Pagination and layout formatting objects:

```
fo:root
fo:declarations
fo:color-profile
fo:page-sequence
fo:layout-master-set
fo:page-sequence-master
fo:single-page-master-reference
fo:repeatable-page-master-reference
fo:repeatable-page-master-alternatives
fo:conditional-page-master-reference
fo:simple-page-master
fo:region-body
fo:region-before
fo:region-after
fo:region-start
fo:region-end
fo:flow
fo:static-content
fo:title
```

Block formatting objects:

```
fo:block
fo:block-container
```

Inline formatting objects:

```
fo:character
fo:initial-property-set
fo:external-graphic
fo:instream-foreign-object
fo:inline
fo:inline-container
fo:leader
fo:page-number
fo:page-number-citation
```

Formatting objects for tables:

```
fo:table-and-caption
fo:table
fo:table-column
fo:table-caption
fo:table-header
fo:table-footer
fo:table-body
fo:table-row
fo:table-cell
```

Formatting objects for lists:

```
fo:list-block
fo:list-item
fo:list-item-body
fo:list-item-label
```

Link and multi-formatting objects:

```
fo:simple-link
fo:multi-switch
fo:multi-case
fo:multi-toggle
fo:multi-properties
fo:multi-property-set
```

Out-of-line formatting objects:

```
fo:float
fo:footnote
fo:footnote-body
```

Other formatting objects:

```
fo:wrapper
fo:marker
fo:retrieve-marker
```

Accessibility properties:

```
source-document
role
```

Absolute-position properties:

```
absolute-position
top
right
bottom
left
```

Aural properties:

```
azimuth
cue-after
cue-before
elevation
pause-after
pause-before
pitch
pitch-range
play-during
richness
speak
speak-header
speak-numeral
speak-punctuation
speech-rate
stress
voice-family
volume
```

Border, padding, and background properties:

```
background-attachment
background-color
background-image
```

```
background-repeat
background-position-horizontal
background-position-vertical
border-before-color
border-before-style
border-before-width
border-after-color
border-after-style
border-after-width
border-start-color
border-start-style
border-start-width
border-end-color
border-end-style
border-end-width
border-top-color
border-top-style
border-top-width
border-bottom-color
border-bottom-style
border-bottom-width
border-left-color
border-left-style
border-left-width
border-right-color
border-right-style
border-right-width
padding-before
padding-after
padding-start
padding-end
padding-top
padding-bottom
padding-leftpadding-right
```

Font properties:

```
font-family
font-size
font-stretch
font-size-adjust
font-style
font-variant
font-weight
```

Hyphenation properties:

```
country
language
script
hyphenate
hyphenation-character
hyphenation-push-character-count
hyphenation-remain-character-count
```

Margin properties-block:

```
margin-top
margin-bottom
margin-left
```

```
margin-right
space-before
space-after
start-indent
end-indent
```

Margin properties-inline:

```
space-end
space-start
```

Area alignment properties:

```
alignment-adjust
baseline-identifier
baseline-shift
display-align
dominant-baseline
relative-align
```

Area dimension properties:

```
block-progression-dimension
content-height
content-width
height
inline-progression-dimension
max-height
max-width
min-height
min-width
scaling
scaling-method
width
```

Block and line-related properties:

```
hyphenation-keep
hyphenation-ladder-count
last-line-end-indent
line-height
line-height-shift-adjustment
line-stacking-strategy
linefeed-treatment
space-treatment
text-align
text-align-last
text-indent
white-space-collapse
wrap-option
```

Character properties:

```
character
letter-spacing
suppress-at-line-break
text-decoration
text-shadow
text-transform
treat-as-word-space
word-spacing
```

Color-related properties:

```
color
color-profile-name
rendering-intent
```

Float-related properties:

```
float
clear
```

Keeps and breaks properties:

```
break-after
break-before
keep-with-next
keep-with-previous
orphans
widows
```

Layout-related properties:

```
clip
overflow
reference-orientation
relative-position
span
```

Leader and rule properties:

```
leader-alignment
leader-pattern
leader-pattern-width
leader-length
rule-style
rule-thickness
```

Properties for links:

```
active-state
auto-restore
case-name
case-title
destination-placement-offset
external-destination
indicate-destination
internal-destination
show-destination
starting-state
switch-to
```

Properties for markers:

```
marker-class-name
retrieve-class-name
retrieve-position
retrieve-boundary
```

Properties for number-to-string conversion:

```
format
grouping-separator
grouping-size
letter-value
```

Pagination and layout properties:

```
blank-or-not-blank
column-count
column-gap
extent
flow-name
force-page-count
initial-page-number
master-name
maximum-repeats
odd-or-even
page-height
page-position
page-width
precedence
region-name
```

Table properties:

```
border-collapse
border-separation
caption-side
column-number
column-width
empty-cells
ends-row
number-columns-repeated
number-columns-spanned
number-rows-spanned
starts-row
table-layout
table-omit-footer-at-break
table-omit-header-at-break
```

Writing-mode–related properties:

```
direction
font-height-override-after
font-height-override-before
glyph-orientation-horizontal
glyph-orientation-vertical
unicode-bidi
writing-mode
```

Miscellaneous properties:

```
content-type
id
provisional-label-separation
provisional-distance-between-starts
ref-id
```

```
score-spaces
src
visibility
z-index
```

Shorthand properties:

```
background
background-position
border
border-bottom
border-color
border-left
border-right
border-style
border-spacing
border-top
border-width
cue
font
margin
padding
page-break-after
page-break-before
page-break-inside
pause
position
size
vertical-align
white-space
xml:lang
```

UNDERSTANDING GENERATED CONTENT

Pretty much anything you put inside a template gets output when the template is processed, as long as it's not another XSL element. So it's fairly easy to generate content, as you saw in our first example.

In general, the following construct is the minimum required to generate a transformation:

```
<xsl:stylesheet xmlns:xsl="http://www.w3.org/XSL/Transform/1.0"
                xmlns:fo="http://www.w3.org/XSL/Format/1.0">
  <xsl:template match="/">
    <!-- processing stuff goes here -->
    Fiat Lux!
  <xsl:apply-templates />
  </xsl:template>
</xsl:stylesheet>
```

This generates a tiny transformation which, in this case, consists of the UC Berkeley motto, "Fiat Lux!" on the output. Of course that's not a terribly useful thing to do, turning your entire document into two words, but getting some actual output is fun and proves that you're doing *something* right. You can grow your style sheet from there, backing up only when you break something and the darned thing doesn't work all of a sudden.

The `xsl:apply-templates` element on line six recursively processes all the children of the current element, so if further processing is unnecessary, this element can be left out, as was done in the first example. Further processing was skipped then because the entire logic of the transformation was contained in the first template. In the next section, you'll see how to use `xsl:apply-templates` in an actual application.

SORTING IN XSL

Because XSLT operates on the view of the document tree kept in memory, the layout of the tree can be dynamically changed by means of many commands. So, although you might think you would have to alter your program logic extensively to perform operations on a document tree sorted into a non-default order, in actuality all you have to do is perform the sort; all operations within the scope of the sort will act on the tree as if were sorted in that order to begin with. If you want to recover the original order you'll have to exit the scope of the procedure that sorted the list in the first place:

```
<xsl:sort
  select = string-expression
  lang = { nmtoken }
  data-type = { "text" | "number" | qname-but-not-ncname }
  order = { "ascending" | "descending" }
  case-order = { "upper-first" | "lower-first" } />
```

Sort elements are used as children of an `apply-templates` element. The first sort element identifies the primary sort key, the second, the secondary sort key, and so on.

So, the following style sheet fragment would sort the Aristotelian document described previously on the name field only:

```
<xsl:template match="/">
  <html>
    <head>
      <title>
        <xsl:value-of select="//productList/listTitle"></xsl:value-of>
      </title>
    </head>
    <body>
      <h2>
        <xsl:value-of select="//productList/listTitle"></xsl:value-of>
      </h2>
      <div>
        <table border="1">
          <tr>
            <th>Product</th>
              <th>Model Number</th>
                <th>Supported Languages</th>
          </tr>
          <xsl:apply-templates select="//productList/product">
            <xsl:sort select="name" />
          </xsl:apply-templates>
        </table>
      </div>
    </body>
  </html>
</xsl:template>
```

You would then have to define a template to actually iterate through the sorted names and output the sorted items as was done in the first example.

NUMBERING IN XSL

Numbering is an automatic transformation provided to allow you to insert numbers into a document. You might use these to identify the node order of the document, insert sequential line numbers, insert page numbers, identify chapter numbers, generate a table of contents, and the like:

```
<xsl:number
  level = "single" | "multiple" | "any"
  count = pattern
  from = pattern
  value = number-expression
  format = { string }
  lang = { nmtoken }
  letter-value = { "alphabetic" | "traditional" }
  grouping-separator = { char }
  grouping-size = { number } />
```

THE MICROSOFT XSL MODEL

Microsoft has, as usual, gone its own way with XSL style sheets. They use a different DTD and have larded the standard with extensions that can't be used anywhere but on Microsoft processors because they support Microsoft-specific features. Although Microsoft Internet Explorer is the only released major browser that supports something approaching XSL and XSLT, the release is non-standard enough that most conforming style sheets are incorrect when read into MSIE. Contrariwise, going backward from an MSIE file that works in that environment is usually impossible as well. Microsoft has a beta technology release of its new and far more compliant XSL/XSLT engine available on the developer Web site at `http://msdn.microsoft.com/downloads/webtechnology/xml/msxml.asp` but it should be incorporated in the next release of Internet Explorer.

So, unless you're on an internal corporate network with Draconian rules on what computers can be installed and with what software—all of it Intel and Microsoft—you're pretty much out of luck and XML/XSL is just one more tedious Microsoft dialect you have to write special routines for. Unless of course you take the Microsoft view and insist that the rest of the world just doesn't see the advantages of keeping in step with whatever comes out of Redmond.

Hopefully, the coming release of Mozilla as the next generation Netscape browser will put a tiny bit of pressure on Microsoft to conform, but I wouldn't hold my breath. Operating system dialects serve companies in much the same way that slang serves children—it makes them appear cool and hip to their peers and makes adults look foolish when they try to talk to them. But this leaves a bit to be desired when people have serious work to do.

Up until now, most Web sites have been market-driven, and marketeers will do anything to get their message across, including making different versions of their sites to achieve the maximum effect for every different browser. Glitzy marketing campaigns from the likes of

PART

II

CH

14

Coca Cola and that ilk aren't going to let a few obstacles to communication thrown up by browser manufacturers stand in the way. They'll hire some consultants, convene some focus groups, and make the site *look* like it was designed by the latest music video idol even if the owners wear Brooks Bros. suits with starched white shirts and regimental ties.

But nonmarketing business people have better things to do with their time than fiddle with browser dialects, as the tremendous push for XML shows. These same people are relatively intolerant of anything that either costs money or stands in the way of making money, which multiple browser standards do in both instances. Studies have shown that accounting for proprietary differences in browser technology adds between 25% and 50% in development time and costs for the average Web project. Browser dialects are going to converge one way or another because making a negative impact on the bottom line is frowned upon in the best financial circles.

OPERA BROWSER

If you want an idea of what a standards-based browser can do, take a look at the beta version of the Opera 4.0 browser from Opera Software at `http://www.operasoftware.com/` and see how handy it makes so many things. Ever fiddled with copying images from a site? (Not that we're advocating violating anyone's copyright!) Try using Opera, which has a "Copy File and Images" selection on the menu.

Tired of trying to decipher tiny dark blue type on black pages with wavy moirè patterns that give you a headache? Opera has a handy little button at the bottom of the screen that switches between Web site styles and user display options, allowing you to instantly reformat the offensive page as large black text on a pristine white page. There's another button to toggle loading of images, so on days when the network slows to a crawl, you can turn the images off and save enormous amounts of time.

Opera version 4.0, now in beta, adds support for XML and CSS1/2 and looks promising in demonstrations so far, although it won't have full XSL support until some time after the W3C XSL Recommendation is released. Opera's implementation of CSS1/2 style sheets is rivaled only by Mozilla and Emacs/W3, and the browser is small and cheap besides. The whole thing fits nicely on a floppy disk. Remember those? Before gigabyte applications filled up your hard disk?

USING XSL AND XSLT

For an exmaple, take a look at a real XML record from a database of book reviews. Listing 14.4 shows the XML Schema and Listing 14.5 shows the XML document.

LISTING 14.4 AN XML REVIEW DTD

```
<?xml version="1.0" encoding="ISO-8859-1"?>
<!-- document root -->
<!ELEMENT review (page-header, review-body)>
<!-- elements in alphabetical order -->
```

```
<!ELEMENT blurb (blurb-text | web-address | blurb-middle)*>
<!ELEMENT blurb-middle (#PCDATA)>
<!ELEMENT blurb-text (#PCDATA)>
<!ELEMENT body (book-title, book-author, book-publisher, byline, review-text)>
<!ELEMENT book-author (#PCDATA)>
<!ELEMENT book-copyright (book-text, book-title, book-copyright-text)>
<!ELEMENT book-copyright-text (#PCDATA)>
<!ELEMENT book-publisher (web-address, publish-date, publish-location)>
<!ELEMENT book-text (#PCDATA)>
<!ELEMENT book-title (#PCDATA)>
<!ELEMENT byline (byline-text, mail-address)>
<!ELEMENT byline-text (#PCDATA)>
<!ELEMENT citation (#PCDATA)>
<!ELEMENT commentary (plaintext | citation)*>
<!ELEMENT copyright-reserved (#PCDATA)>
<!ELEMENT footer (review-copyright, book-copyright, blurb)>
<!ELEMENT header (prefix, short-title)>
<!ELEMENT host-name (#PCDATA)>
<!ELEMENT mail-address (mail-locator)>
<!ATTLIST mail-address
          refer CDATA #REQUIRED
>
<!ELEMENT mail-locator (#PCDATA)>
<!ELEMENT page-header (page-title)>
<!ELEMENT page-title (#PCDATA)>
<!ELEMENT plaintext (#PCDATA)>
<!ELEMENT prefix (#PCDATA)>
<!ELEMENT publish-date (#PCDATA)>
<!ELEMENT publish-location (#PCDATA)>
<!ELEMENT publisher-name (#PCDATA)>
<!ELEMENT review-body (header, body, rule, footer)>
<!ELEMENT review-copyright (review-text, mail-address, copyright-reserved)>
<!ELEMENT review-text (#PCDATA | commentary)*>
<!ELEMENT rule EMPTY>
<!ELEMENT service-name (#PCDATA)>
<!ELEMENT short-title (#PCDATA)>
<!ELEMENT web-address (web-locator)>
<!ATTLIST web-address
          refer CDATA #REQUIRED
>
<!ELEMENT web-locator (publisher-name | service-name | host-name)>
```

LISTING 14.5 AN XML REVIEW DOCUMENT

```xml
<?xml version="1.0" encoding="UTF-8"?>
<!DOCTYPE review SYSTEM "http://www.leeanne.com/taborsarah/13xmp03.dtd">
<review>
 <page-header>
  <page-title>Review: A Ritual of Drowning</page-title>
 </page-header>
 <review-body>
  <header><prefix>Review: </prefix><short-title>A Ritual of Drowning</short-title>
  </header>
  <body>
   <book-title>A Ritual of Drowning - Poems of Love and Mourning</book-title>
   <book-author>Teya Schaffer</book-author>
```

LISTING 14.5 CONTINUED

```
<book-publisher>
 <web-address refer="http://www.leeanne.com/taborsarah/index.html">
  <web-locator><publisher-name>Tabor Sarah Books</publisher-name></web-locator>
 </web-address>
 <publish-date>1999</publish-date>
 <publish-location>Oakland and Palo Alto</publish-location>
</book-publisher>
<byline>
 <byline-text>Reviewed by Lee Anne Phillips </byline-text>
 <mail-address refer="mailto:Lee Anne Phillips &lt;leeanne@leeanne.com&gt;">
  <mail-locator>&lt;leeanne@leeanne.com&gt;</mail-locator>
 </mail-address>
</byline>
<review-text>
<commentary><plaintext>
 How many ways can a heart break and yet be mended? In this
 heartrending but essential collection by Teya Schaffer,
 grief is examined in raw, searing detail and transformed
 into the highest art. I was reminded of Jane Yolen's <citation>
 Cards of Grief</plaintext></citation><plaintext> by the power and beauty of
➥the whole
 and reduced to helpless tears by many of the individual
 parts. Is this a lamentation? A love story? Or some of
 both? Or perhaps even a paean of praise. It starts,
 thankfully, with a strong statement of reconciliation that
 helps us through the rough spots to come as we prepare to
 follow Teya through her lover's final illness and death.</plaintext>
 </commentary>
 </review-text>
</body>
<rule/>
<footer>
 <review-copyright>
  <review-text>Review Copyright &#169; 1999, by Lee Anne Phillips</review-text>
  <mail-address
  refer="mailto:Lee%20Anne%20Phillips%20&lt;leeanne@leeanne.com&gt;">
   <mail-locator>&lt;leeanne@leeanne.com&gt;</mail-locator>
  </mail-address>
  <copyright-reserved> - All Rights Reserved Worldwide</copyright-reserved>
 </review-copyright>
 <book-copyright>
  <book-text>Poem excerpts are from </book-text>
   <book-title>A Ritual of Drowning - Poems of Love and Mourning</book-title>
   <book-copyright-text>
   Copyright &#169; 1999 by Teya Schaffer - All Rights Reserved Worldwide
   </book-copyright-text>
 </book-copyright>
 <blurb>
  <blurb-text>For more reviews of outstanding books by
             women, please visit the </blurb-text>
   <web-address refer="http://www.cybergrrl.com/review/">
    <web-locator><service-name>Women's Books Online</service-name></web-locator>
   </web-address>
   <blurb-middle>pages kindly hosted by</blurb-middle>
   <web-address refer="http://www.cybergrrl.com/">
```

```
      <web-locator><host-name>Cybergrrl!</host-name></web-locator>
    </web-address>
  </blurb>
  </footer>
 </review-body>
</review>
```

There's only a single record here, but it should be enough. There's nothing in the record you want to ignore, because the whole review should be published, and you've already added a processing instruction that points to the as yet nonexistent style sheet. There are a few things to add between certain of the fields but you can get to that when you start looking at individual fields.

STARTING THE TRANSFORMATION TREE

First, you need to start your transformation tree. Because what you're doing can start with any document, start with a generic root (/) abbreviation as the selector:

```
<xsl:template match="/">
  <!-- processing stuff goes here -->
</xsl:template>
```

This statement selects the root node in any document. All other nodes are children of this node so you're at the right spot anyway. Now you have to figure out what to do with the information in the record. You can turn it into HTML at this point, although that kind of begs the question; however, that's what the vast majority of legacy browsers support, so why fight destiny? Legacy browsers aren't going to go away any time soon, so most XML pages will probably be served as HTML to many users.

It would be nice also to output formatting instructions, however, those don't work very well yet. Eventually, an XML-aware browser will know how to display formatting objects instead of hokey HTML, but that's later. The same techniques can be used to do either task. While you're at it, put in the xsl:stylesheet wrapper and namespace declarations:

```
<xsl:stylesheet xmlns:xsl="http://www.w3.org/XSL/Transform/1.0"
                xmlns:fo="http://www.w3.org/XSL/Format/1.0">
  <xsl:template match="/">
    <!-- processing stuff goes here -->
  </xsl:template>
</xsl:stylesheet>
```

After considerable editing, you wind up with the code shown in Listing 14.6.

LISTING 14.6   AN XSL STYLE SHEET FOR THE REVIEW DOCUMENT

```
<?xml version="1.0" encoding="UTF-8"?>
<xsl:stylesheet xmlns:xsl="http://www.w3.org/TR/WD-xsl">
  <!-- XSL Stylesheet for Aristotelian Product List -->
  <xsl:template match="/">
    <html>
      <head>
        <title>
```

LISTING 14.6 CONTINUED

```
        <xsl:value-of select="//review/page-header/page-title" />
      </title>
    </head>
    <body>
      <h2>
        <xsl:value-of select="//review/page-header/page-title" />
      </h2>
      <blockquote>
        <h3><xsl:value-of
          select="//review/review-body/body/book-title" /></h3>
        <blockquote>
          <h3>by <xsl:value-of
            select="//review/review-body/body/book-author" /></h3>
          <xsl:for-each
            select="//review/review-body/body/book-publisher/web-address">
            <h3><a><xsl:attribute name="href"><xsl:value-of
            select="refer" /></xsl:attribute><xsl:value-of
            select="web-locator/publisher-name" /></a>,
            <xsl:value-of
              select="//review/review-body/body/book-publisher/publish-date" />;
            <xsl:value-of
              select="//review/review-body/body/book-publisher/publish-location"
➥ /></h3>
          </xsl:for-each>
        </blockquote>
      </blockquote>
      <blockquote>
        <h3><xsl:value-of
          select="//review/review-body/body/byline/byline-text" />
        <xsl:for-each
          select="//review/review-body/body/byline/mail-address">
          <a><xsl:attribute name="href"><xsl:value-of
              select="refer" /></xsl:attribute><xsl:value-of
              select="mail-locator" /></a>
        </xsl:for-each>
        </h3>
      </blockquote>
      <xsl:for-each select="//review/review-body/body/review-text/commentary">
        <blockquote>
          <xsl:for-each select="*">
            <xsl:if xsl:test="contains(string(local-name()),'plaintext')">
              <xsl:value-of select="." />
            </xsl:if>
            <xsl:if xsl:test="contains(string(local-name()),'citation')">
              <cite><xsl:value-of select="." /></cite>
            </xsl:if>
          </xsl:for-each>
        </blockquote>
      </xsl:for-each>
      <xsl:for-each select="//review/review-body/rule">
        <blockquote>
          <hr />
```

```
                  </blockquote>
              </xsl:for-each>
              <blockquote>
                <xsl:value-of select="//review/review-body/footer/review-
➥copyright/ review-text" />
                <xsl:for-each
                  select="//review/review-body/footer/review-copyright/mail-address">
                  <a><xsl:attribute name="href"><xsl:value-of
                      select="refer" /></xsl:attribute><xsl:value-of
                      select="mail-locator" /></a><xsl:value-of
                      select="//review/review-body/footer/review-copyright/copyright-
➥reserved" />
                </xsl:for-each>
              </blockquote>
                <br />
              <blockquote>
                <xsl:for-each
                  select="//review/review-body/footer/book-copyright">
                      <xsl:value-of select="book-text" />
                      <cite><xsl:value-of select="book-title" /></cite>
                      <xsl:value-of select="book-copyright-text" />
                </xsl:for-each>
              </blockquote>
                <br />
              <blockquote>
                <xsl:for-each
                  select="//review/review-body/footer/blurb">
                      <xsl:value-of select="blurb-text" />
                  <xsl:for-each
                    select="web-address"><a><xsl:attribute
                      name="href"><xsl:value-of
                      select="refer" /></xsl:attribute><xsl:value-of
                      select="web-locator/service-name" /></a>
                  </xsl:for-each>
                  <xsl:value-of select="blurb-middle" />
                  <xsl:for-each
                    select="web-address[1]"><a><xsl:attribute
                      name="href"><xsl:value-of
                      select="refer" /></xsl:attribute><xsl:value-of
                      select="web-locator/host-name" /></a>
                  </xsl:for-each>
                </xsl:for-each>
              </blockquote>
          </body>
        </html>
      </xsl:template>
    </xsl:stylesheet>
```

TROUBLESHOOTING XSL

XSL STYLE SHEETS AREN'T WORKING EITHER!

You've abandoned CSS in favor of the new and breezy XSL and XSLT. To your great surprise, XSL is not working either.

Well, it's early days yet. The Microsoft Internet Explorer browser is the only readily available commercial browser release to support XML at the time of this writing and it's not really yet conformant with the standard, such as it is. Dozens of document creation packages do support the draft XSL standard, at least in beta, such as the XML Spy and InDelv XML editing environments, as well as SAXON, Jade, and others. Play with them from time to time and they're bound to come out right in the end.

PART III

INTERGRATING XML WITH OTHER TECHNOLOGIES

CHAPTER 15

GETTING INFORMATION ABOUT THE USER

In this chapter

USER PROFILES

As the Web has developed, the information that sites collect about users has exploded into detailed names, addresses, email addresses, credit card information, shopping habits, complete demographics, and even racial data or information about complexion and hair that might allow racial identity to be inferred.

In the United States, there is little limit on what information can be collected and almost no limit on whether that data can be sold to others. It's been observed that there are more restrictions on divulging the names of the videos you rent from a video store than on intimate medical or financial data on the Web. In the meantime, that information is a valuable commodity. Names and data can be sold almost at will and advertisers are willing, indeed anxious, to buy it.

Data collecting is tolerated because, for the most part, people don't know that the data is being sold to third parties. The U.S. government has little interest in protecting this data and allows almost anything to be done with it. They won't even pass legislation to users to control the use of their email addresses, tacitly approving the inundation of American citizens with spam.

But *some* people *are* becoming alarmed. Many countries have rigid restrictions on personal information that passes national boundaries, even if freely given and legal to use within those boundaries. The European Union as a whole has issued privacy directives that control what Web sites can do with information the sites have collected. So, all Web site operators with sufficiently deep pockets must have some sort of comprehensive privacy policy in place lest they find themselves sued in Germany for disclosing information from a transaction initiated by a German citizen. The safest policy for corporations with an international presence is probably never to divulge identifiable personal data to a third party.

With that background, , the World Wide Web Consortium (W3C) began work on an XML-based language they called the Platform for Privacy Preferences (P3P). The W3C is primarily made up of people with large economic stakes in the status quo for the most part, so P3P is a compromise between allowing users to control their information and allowing sites to demand private information before serving the user.

PROFILE TRADEOFFS

In the first place,   many sites won't choose to use P3P. If a popular site doesn't use the platform, there will be strong pressure on users to forgo their privacy for the convenience of accessing the site. Just try browsing the Microsoft Web site with cookies turned off to get a sample of how difficult asserting your right to privacy can be.

Then again, if you access the TV Guide site at `http://www.tvguide.com/` and allow them to collect your cable company's identification information and ZIP code, they offer a localized schedule of TV programs available in your locality in return. They store the information in a cookie so you don't have to enter it again. The intrusion is fairly minimal, although the site could conceivably sell the data they *do* collect, raw numbers of Internet users by ZIP code and whether they subscribe to a cable service. Likewise, local weather information, convenient online shopping, and help with computer problems may demand data from the user before making those services available.

From experience with current offerings from various vendors, anything from money to free access to services that would otherwise have to be paid for may be offered as incentives to disclosing maximum data. In fact, this information is so valuable that some companies are willing to give you a free computer and free Internet access in exchange for letting advertisers flood your screen with targeted ads.

Tip from

LeeAnne.com
Words to weave by

An example of the tradeoff between privacy and benefits is PrivaSeek (`http://www.privaseek.com/`), an online broker of user information. After signing up with the service and disclosing personal information, the service offers to protect your privacy unless you choose to disclose. If you do, you can receive a small payment from advertisers or site owners and PrivaSeek garners a commission.

Unfortunately, after you've turned over your data to any company, the company can pretty much do what they want with the data without notice and almost without recourse in the United States. Because there are few laws regulating the sale of personal data in the United States, the only way you could possibly assert your rights against a company would be to institute a civil suit for breach of contract or fraud, but P3P isn't designed to exchange or guarantee contract information. In fact, the information exchange in P3P is decidedly one-sided. There are many fields facilitating the exchange of personal data from the user to a site that demands the data, although the exact content of those fields is not clearly disclosed. In contrast there are few to none for the reciprocal demand of a user for information about a company.

The only identifying data field that's currently "mandatory" for the Web site itself to fill in is the entity attribute on the policy element, which *should* contain the name of the entity plus physical contact information. But there's no real enforcement mechanism and the field isn't structured, so whatever winds up in the field is left to the imagination of the designer. The browser won't be able to tell you whether anything is missing because the field is unstructured. The only way for a user to ascertain that the entity field actually contains useful contact information is to look at it before proceeding. It seems more like an afterthought in response to bitter criticism than a well thought out feature.

A Web site can demand a user's address and phone number using the P3P protocol, but there's no way for a user to demand the Web site's physical address and telephone contact information before completing a transaction unless they read the entity information before proceeding. To suggest that you shouldn't do business with a site that doesn't trust you enough to tell you where they are might belabor the obvious, but you might be surprised to note that a large number of Web sites make this information extraordinarily difficult or impossible to obtain.

And the awkwardness of the entity contact mechanism rather begs the question: What's the point of an automated system if it requires human interaction to initiate every transaction? And how does one save the contact information for later use without writing it down?

USING COOKIES TO MAINTAIN A PROFILE

In contrast to the XML-based P3P model, which is transparent and interactive, using cookies is a crude answer to the problem of controlling privacy, because they are stored on the user's computer and can be easily deleted by the user if desired. They aren't transparent, however, and you can't usually tell what's inside them by looking. So you have to retain or delete cookies on general principles rather than by any sort of rational choice based on the data they contain. Also, the site that set the cookie already has control of your data, and the decision to store the information on site or sell it is their decision, not yours. In fact, it's perfectly legal in the United States to transfer your cookie information to another firm, so multiple vendors can share a single server-side customer database by passing an index, which can be stored in a cookie, into the database around to their cohorts. It's somewhat like tattooing a barcoded identifying number on your arm so merchants know who you are and how much money is in your billfold as soon as you enter their virtual store.

Even on sites that claim to protect your online privacy, the advertisers that place those ubiquitous "banner ads" are not technically part of the site, so they aren't bound by any such policy. They do, in fact, compile and sell extensive databases of personal information about the browsing habits of individuals. So even a site that claims not to collect *any* information from you can purchase and use the same information from a third party, or even a wholly-owned subsidiary, and then resell it without any hindrance whatsoever.

Cookies aren't portable across browsers. So if you use several browsers, you'll have to re-enter data for each one, losing at least some of the promised convenience. Likewise, if you delete cookies periodically, the information those cookies contain has to be re-entered when next queried by the site that requested it to begin with.

Deleting your cookies could be a source of frustration to site owners as well, because their carefully collected shopping history and demographics can be wiped out with a few user keystrokes, enabling long-time customers to return to a clean slate in the blink of an eye. We should here pause and shed a heartfelt tear.

The Opera browser from http://www.opera.com/ has several features designed to help protect your online privacy, including the ability to automatically delete all new cookies when you exit the browser and the ability to prevent scripting languages from executing or new windows from automatically popping up on your screen. To balance this, it has an internal cache of personal data that can be used to fill out forms quickly when and if you want to.

Cookies are site-dependant as well, so every site that puts a cookie on your machine stores its own. If you surf actively, thousands or even tens of thousands of cookies could pile up on your machine, placing the entire cost of maintaining their databases on you. Because most of the information contained in these thousands of entries is duplicated from site to site and has had to be re-entered over and over again, P3P promises some relief from boring, repetitive data entry even without its minimal privacy benefits.

USING A SERVER-SIDE DATABASE

Absent native P3P support, the alternative to cookies is to store the information in a database on the site's server or a third-party broker such as PrivaSeek, TRUSTe, BBB Online, or PrivacyBank.com. Although this allows information to be stored without costing the user anything, it also raises the issue of how that information can be viewed and managed by the user. Or even deleted if the user wants to recapture his privacy after granting limited access to it.

In the United States, there are currently no methods of recapturing data after someone has acquired access to it, no matter what agreement was made with the person who originally captured it. So although RealNetworks claimed to guarantee your privacy, that agreement didn't extend to RealJukebox, which runs on your machine and is not a Web site. So RealNetworks can and has sold your music listening habits to third parties without your knowledge or consent. TRUSTe has found this to be consistent with their policies, in spite of the fact that ordinary users are highly unlikely to understand how and why exceptions to the stated privacy policies are permissible.

Caution	At least several so-called privacy guarantors have no physical address or telephone number available on their own Web sites. Which leaves the user in the uncomfortable position of trusting a company with no idea where to go to find the company if a dispute arose. This should probably raise a red flag when considering which of the many available services to use.

Tip from  Words to weave by	Privacy brokering services theoretically offer one way of guaranteeing the user's ability to edit or even delete their information. Presumably they will also enforce re-use policies, much like the vendors of mailing lists, to ensure that an advertiser can't capture data once and then maintain their own database. But there's no guarantee that this will be done, and in fact, it's easy for a site to weasel out of their agreements through means that are essentially invisible to the user. There's so much money to be made from selling your private information that the temptation to cheat or mislead is always there, since there are few if any legal remedies available to protect your privacy. The only real solution is strong legal penalties, including jail time for company executives, against firms found guilty of violating online privacy.

On the other hand, if a user accesses the Web from many machines, a server-side database has the potential to simplify the user's life a bit because data doesn't have to be re-entered for every new machine. However, an irritating login and password sequence is interposed before the site can be accessed. We'll discuss this last problem more thoroughly in the next section.

USER IDS AND PASSWORDS

An existing technology that almost everyone hates is user IDs and passwords, which has the advantage of placing the issue of identifying users directly in their own hands. If a user doesn't want to be identified by that user ID any more, he can simply stop using it. And, of course, passwords and user IDs are crucial to certain types of secure systems. In fact, certain levels of security can't be reasonably achieved without requiring user ID/password pairs.

But most existing schemes ignore the requirements of real password security. Although a site may demand a password, it usually offers no means of changing it if the password is known to have been compromised, and makes little or no restriction on the format of passwords. So dictionary words are acceptable to most systems, or re-using a password for years, or laughably short or obvious passwords.

The fatal flaw of every site-specific password system is that they require a separate user ID and password for each new system, so the user quickly collects more IDs and passwords than can be conveniently memorized, or the site recycles its user IDs based on aging criteria. So, a user with what they suppose is a valid password finds herself locked out because the site has rudely given her ID away to someone else because the user hasn't visited often enough to suit the organization.

It's a source of endless frustration to users. Either they post their user IDs and passwords on their walls with little stickies or they try to reuse the same user ID and password on every site, a significant security breach. An unscrupulous administrator on any site that collects user IDs and passwords could conceivably try that user ID and password on other sites with a fair likelihood of succeeding. Whether this is merely bad or extremely bad depends only on what sites the user has visited.

Tip from

Words to weave by

Many sites are now explicitly asking users to use their email address as a user ID. This has the advantage, from the site's perspective, of capturing the email address. The user can easily remember the user ID and can easily use the same ID and password everywhere. From a security viewpoint, it's a miserable strategy, because half of the user ID/password security pair is easily guessed by hackers, defeating part of your protection. And the likelihood of using the same ID and password everywhere means that employees of any site can use your information to log in on your behalf anywhere else.

So, passwords, although they're theoretically capable of ensuring extraordinary levels of security if properly used, have such weaknesses in practice that their safety is doubtful overall. Only the most meticulous and dedicated user could achieve the full measure of security possible with a password scheme, and casual users tend to use passwords with minimal security in favor of ease of use.

P3P—PLATFORM FOR PRIVACY PREFERENCES

P3P is now in last call working draft status and currently scheduled for final Recommendation transition in June of the year 2000. Although this may change, probably in the direction of delay if it does, the standard as it exists is fairly close to what's needed and probably will evolve only slightly if at all.

One thing that will definitely change is the data transfer mechanism, which will be deleted from the specification at the next revision according to the Working Group. It was determined that most vendors were planning to use proprietary or already existing open standards for data transfer, so there seemed to be little need for a separate mechanism.

In fact, the only justification would be convenience for the user, who will have to re-enter data for each and every proprietary scheme. The ubiquity of lengthy telephone queue's and difficult to use automated phone systems may be a reliable indicator of the monomania and lack of real concern for user convenience of most corporations and Internet presences.

The difficulty of specifying a data transfer mechanism without potential security oversights and omissions cannot be overstated. Security and telecommunications experts have spent years designing and verifying such standards. To suggest that a new standard could be defined in a few months boggles the mind. Far better to defer to encryption and security specialists who've had many years of experience and even existing products than to do a slapdash job, compromising the P3P standard as a whole, or delay the issuance of the P3P standard until such a mechanism could be robustly designed.

WHAT HAPPENS WITH P3P

The P3P standard is both a protocol and, indirectly, a data collection standard. The first interaction the user has with a P3P-enabled browser is some sort of request for data. With each piece of data, the browser should also ask how the user will allow the information to be used. P3P doesn't specify how this data is to be collected or stored, so the browser is free to implement an interactive dialog box, present an options screen through user intervention, or even collect each piece of data in response to browser proposals. This is the sequence of events involved in a P3P negotiation.

First, the client makes a GET request:

```
GET /index.html HTTP/1.1
Host: www.leeanne.com
Accept: */*
Accept-Language: en
User-Agent: NewBrowser/6.0
```

At this point, the client doesn't know whether the site has a privacy policy in place or not. It becomes clear only when the server returns a response pointing to a privacy standard and the XML machine-readable description of the privacy policy governing the site:

```
HTTP/1.1 200 OK
Opt: "http://www.w3.org/2000/P3Pv1"; ns=12
12-Policy: http://www.leeanne.com/usingxml/14xmp01.xml
Content-Type: text/html
Content-Length: 1500
Server: NewServwe/2.0
```

The client then can compare the returned policy with the user's preferences, decide whether the site policy is acceptable, and interrupt the exchange if it's not. The agent can then ask the user if lesser degrees of privacy are acceptable, displaying any CONSEQUENCES data to help with the decision and possibly displaying the human-readable site-policy to clarify the issues involved. If the user decides that the lesser privacy is okay, the exchange continues. If not, the exchange is terminated.

If the site has no policy, the client assumes the worst possible privacy policies are in place and asks the user if he wants to continue. We encourage users to immediately vacate the site, because the only way to place pressure on Web site operators to implement P3P policies is to drive down their hit statistics.

Organizations using P3P will send you a similar proposal the first time you visit, describing the information it wants from you and what it plans to do with it. The proposal will explain what happens if you grant access to the data and what happens if you don't. The organization is free to make those policies anything it wants them to be. The user is free to make any decision at all but should cache every policy URI, so she can compare it with the URI returned on the next visit, if any, to determine whether the policy has changed.

If the proposal is accepted, the user probably won't even notice that the transaction has been made. If it's rejected, the browser may present a dialog box asking for a decision about granting more access to the user's privacy data for that particular site. A weakness of the P3P language as it exists now is that the user is presumed to be the only party to the interaction with the ability to be flexible about privacy. The site is allowed little flexibility in negotiating privacy parameters for the visit other than the crude capability to set different policies for different subdirectories.

Because the internal data transfer mechanism has been removed from the P3P specification, an external process undoubtedly will perform the data transfer. This makes a great deal of sense. The full complexity of a protocol which supported internationalization, accessibility, simple and structured data, digital signature, periodic update, expiry, and a myriad of other issues becomes obvious once the problem is investigated in detail.

FORMAT OF PRIVACY POLICY INTERCHANGE

The P3P is still in Working Draft stage, and currently no applications completely support the standard. Last call on the Draft is slated for the end of April, 2000, and it should move toward Candidate Recommendation status somewhat after that date. Until that time, it would be premature to count on anything but the most general outlines of the standard, because it's gone through Last Call status before and gone back for further work.

The final standard probably will look similar to the P3P profile listed in the case study section later in this chapter, "Getting Down to Cases," a POLICY element enclosing both mandatory and optional elements.

The POLICY element itself must contain an xmlns attribute pointing to the version of P3P used and an ENTITY attribute containing the name of the entity describing the privacy policy of the site and contact information describing how to get in touch with them.

The policy should contain a DISCLOSURE element describing the location of the human-readable policy associated with this XML policy and a brief description of who is given access to the information collected.

The policy should also contain a DISPUTES-GROUP element containing DISPUTES elements describing what to do in case of disputes about the privacy of your data. These elements can point to anything from customer service at the site to a privacy assurance organization to the courts for a lawsuit.

Next, the policy should contain one or more STATEMENT elements describing the actual types of data collected and the uses to which they'll be put. The STATEMENT element contains PURPOSE elements, a RECIPIENT element, a DATA-GROUP element (which in turn contains DATA elements), a RETENTION element, and optionally a CONSEQUENCE-GROUP element.

The PURPOSE element describes what the information will be used for. The RECIPIENT element tells the user who may use the information. The DATA-GROUP element contains one or more DATA elements describing the data collected. The RETENTION element tells the user how long the data will be stored. The CONSEQUENCE-GROUP element contains one or more CONSEQUENCE elements, which tell the user what benefits accrue from allowing collection of this data. Because this information may be displayed to the user by default or in response to a privacy dialog box, multiple CONSEQUENCE elements can be given with different xml:lang attributes to allow localization of prompts.

Studying the plain-language privacy policy and equivalent P3P example given in the "Getting Down to Cases" section will make this fairly clear. When the actual standard is released as a Recommendation it will be found at http://www.w3.org/p3p/.

END RESULTS FOR PRIVACY

P3P policies promise quite a bit of control over your privacy if the tension between Web site operators and users can be resolved. But it occurred to the W3C that some operators might promise complete privacy and then fail to follow through or renege after the fact. After all, they could be sitting on a pile of data potentially worth millions of dollars. Even with good intentions, the vagaries of business cycles might tempt them to alter their policies after the fact or even lie outright.

So the assurance element identifies some sort of auditing body which verifies that policies are what the owner says they are, and that they cannot change from one visit to the next without someone noticing.

Tip from

LeeAnne.com
Words to weave by

It's almost impossible for users to determine if their privacy has been violated without obsessive use of different IDs for every site together with painstaking record keeping. Most people will have to rely on privacy brokers, who have a financial incentive to keep some level of control on your information, together with auditing firms such as TRUSTe, located at http://www.truste.org/.

Knowing that policies haven't changed is a vital, if minimal, part of the P3P standard. Otherwise it would be possible to do a "bait and switch" on the users by advertising a strict internal use only privacy policy, collecting names and other identifiers, changing the policy to "published," and selling the names. So P3P declares that the policy URI itself must change if the policy changes. That way, at least your user agent can tell you that the policy has changed if you happen to visit the site again.

But there *will* be lesser players who might not mind pushing the edge of morality if no one is looking over their shoulder, so outside auditing agencies may achieve some level of prominence in the new world of privacy. Current assurance providers include BBBOnline or TRUSTe, all providing seals that can be placed on a site to ostensibly assure users that their privacy concerns are provided for on that site. But we've already seen that even these minimal protections are rather easily circumvented in the current political and business climate in the U.S.A. The privacy situation in Europe is decidedly better, and the European Union has been in the vanguard of privacy legislation worldwide, which may eventually confer a business advantage to European firms if users become seriously concerned about their online privacy.

So privacy brokers and auditors may help prevent, or at least enable you to avoid, the more abusive practices, such as sites that masquerade as something completely different to the search engines and then spontaneously open a dozen windows to other sites to maximize their "clickthrough" revenue. However, no current scheme has the weight of law behind it, so most are essentially without teeth. When micropayment mechanisms become more widespread, the potential exists to defraud users by bouncing their browsers through an endless series of little tiny pay-per-view pages. If the value of each individual transaction is small enough, many users may set their electronic wallets to automatically pay out a penny, let's say, rather than have to individually decide whether this or that page is worth one tenth of a dime.

On the other hand, in spite of somewhat abusive practices on the part of certain sites, the assurance providers have been rather reluctant to pull their trusted seals from sites which have apparently pushed the limits. This illuminates the tension between the assurance agencies' mission statements and their perfectly natural desire to continue being paid.

OPS/P3P—OPEN PROFILING STANDARD

In 1997, Netscape Communications Corporation, Firefly Network, Inc., and Verisign, Inc. proposed the *Open Profiling Standard* (OPS) to the W3C. They envisioned the standard as working with P3P and complementing it and it may yet do so. Microsoft Corporation also submitted a standard, *Privacy and Profiling on the Web*.

W3C took these submissions into account when developing P3P, and incorporated some elements—the bare concepts of user information and server negotiation for the most part—in the P3P protocol. Not all was included, however, and in particular the encryption and signature mechanisms. W3C Digital Signatures may provide part of this lack, filling in the `certificate` placeholder, but the P3P Working Group's decision to eliminate the data transfer mechanism will probably push encryption mechanisms off to third-party providers along with the data transfer itself. They also left out multiple personas from Privacy and Profiling on the Web, which was a significant improvement on privacy for many users because they were permitted to create multiple misleading identities to allow them to surf some sites with no possibility of linking to other personas.

P3P will undoubtedly be altered by the time you read this to incorporate hooks to third party data transfer tools. OPS, or a descendent, may be one of them.

JavaScript and Scripting Languages

There's no theoretical reason that P3P couldn't be implemented with a Java, or even JavaScript, dialog box embedded in a page downloaded from a Web site. From the perspective of the site owner, this frees up resources on the server because the entire protocol dialog, including any negotiation or data collection, can be performed with no server processing required. The only trouble is that there must be a standard way to store the data on the user's machine or the user winds up having to re-enter the same information over and over again.

Right now, no such mechanism is available. Cookies are specific to a given site, and allowing external processes to read and write to user machines is folly on the user's part. Microsoft posts alerts and critical security updates to their update site with great regularity, primarily because of weaknesses in the OLE/ActiveX interface, which allow hackers read or write access to user machines through any of the thousands of holes the programmers overlooked.

In combination with some sort of user process, such as the PrivacyMinder Java program described next, the client-side policy negotiation approach might make some sort of sense, but this scheme would soon be superceded by native browser support in any event, so it's hard to see any real benefit.

Implementations of P3P already exist, albeit in prototype form. AT&T's PrivacyMinder is a client-side Java program that allows the exchange of personal data at user discretion. PrivacyMinder's default security level is very private indeed, allowing no identifiable information to be collected, monitoring requests for information from the user data repository and preventing those requests which violate the user's settings from completing.

Netscape (Mozilla) likely will implement P3P eventually, because P3P is on Netscape's want list and can be mostly implemented as an application of RDF, which will definitely be available. As of today, P3P is not present in the development code. This makes perfect sense because the standard is still in Working Draft.

Microsoft is also planning to support P3P, probably soon after the standard is finalized. The Microsoft Passport electronic wallet product already interfaces to TRUSTe, `http://www.truste.org/`, and BBBOnline, `http://www.bbbonline.com/`, the Better Business Bureau site.

The Opera browser has an innovative approach to filling out forms, one half of the tedious business of supplying or denying user data. Opera maintains an internal database of user information that can be used to fill out forms with a keystroke or two per field. This feature can be used to simplify the entry of manual forms, one way of controlling which information goes where. And Opera also has the ability to prevent scripting languages from running and can delete cookies automatically every time you exit the browser, so a certain level of privacy is enforced at the browser level.

Tip from

LeeAnne.com
Words to weave by

If you're lucky enough to possess your own domain and have postmaster authority, which delivers all mail to you, one way of auditing your own privacy is to fill out the email address with username information identifying the site you gave it to. If that ID later shows up in a spam from another site, you'll know whom to blame when you receive e-mails addressed to *untrustworthy.website@mydomain.com*.

GETTING DOWN TO CASES

Assume that you want to create a privacy statement for my Web site, `http://www.leeanne.com/`.

You don't want to hire a lawyer, because the site actually doesn't collect any information nor does it actually do anything with information, not even glancing at the server logs that are available if we choose to look at them. Microsoft LinkExchange has an online privacy wizard that will give you a good start on a human-readable privacy statement at `http://privacy.linkexchange.com/`. You will answer a series of questions about the use you intend for the information on this site, including the policies of sites we link to and a few other tidbits. We can see the resulting text in Figure 15.1.

Figure 15.1
The Microsoft LinkExchange Privacy Wizard generated this human-readable privacy statement.

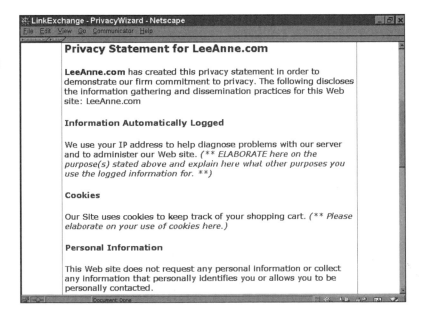

The following privacy information from the wizard is listed in plain-text format so you can view it with ease. The places reserved for user elaboration have been left as is, so you can see where the wizard leaves them:

```
Privacy Statement for LeeAnne.com
LeeAnne.com has created this privacy statement in order to demonstrate our
firm commitment to privacy. The following discloses the information gathering
and dissemination practices for this Web site: LeeAnne.com
Information Automatically Logged
We use your IP address to help diagnose problems with our server and to
administer our Web site. (** ELABORATE here on the purpose(s) stated above and
explain here what other purposes you use the logged information for. **)
Cookies
Our Site uses cookies to keep track of your shopping cart. (** Please
elaborate on your use of cookies here.)
Personal Information
This Web site does not request any personal information or collect any
information that personally identifies you or allows you to be personally
contacted.
Because we do not collect any personal information on this Web site, we do not
share any personal information with any third parties nor do we use any
personal information for any purposes.
External Links
This site contains links to other sites. LeeAnne.com is not responsible for
the privacy practices or the content of such Web sites.
Public Forums
This site makes chat rooms, forums, message boards, and/or newsgroups
available to its users. Please remember that any information disclosed in
these areas becomes public information and you should exercise caution when
deciding to disclose your personal information.
Security
This site has security measures in place to protect the loss, misuse, and
alteration of the information under our control. (** Please elaborate on the
security measures that you have in place. **)
Contacting the Web Site
If you have any questions about this privacy statement, the practices of this
site, or your dealings with this Web site, you can contact:
info@leeanne.com
```

Because no wizard can foresee all possibilities, the wizard generated several placeholders to show where the statement should be expanded. Of course, if you wanted to mention more uses that might be made of the data you *do* collect, essentially IP addresses and certain other technical information, you would add it here. You might assume that an IP address is not identifiable down to a personal level, because most people who surf via an ISP share a pool of addresses. However, more people are using DSL and other advanced connectivity technologies, which often have an individual IP address assigned to an individual user. In those cases, an IP address is a direct line into the user's computer and must be jealously guarded.

So before promising that the site doesn't and won't ever collect identifiable data, you might want to think hard about the full implications of this statement. In the case of this site, no interactivity is planned but one never knows. At some future date it might be desirable to add the capability to purchase books online, for example, or to allow people to post comments to an online bulletin board.

Although this generated privacy policy is a starting point, you should probably try out several iterations with different assumptions before committing a site to a restrictive policy. Don't forget that P3P policies for a given site should remain stable over time if this essentially self-regulatory scheme is to have any meaning whatsoever. Even if you can't ever foresee changing your mind about the policies of your site, your heirs and assigns might have different ideas. If your site is part of a larger enterprise or marketing strategy, you should definitely contact a contract lawyer for advice before posting any such document to the Web.

Here's an example of an XML P3P file generated to more-or-less conform to the previous human-readable privacy policy text:

```
<POLICY xmlns="http://www.w3.org/2000/P3Pv1"
        entity="LeeAnne.com, 4200 Park Boulevard #250,
                Oakland, CA, USA">
  <DISPUTES-GROUP>
    <!-- The following three lines could be inserted to
         point to an assurance organization that would
         audit the privacy policies of this site. Since
         this is only an example, I'll point to an
         organization guaranteed to do nothing. -->
    <DISPUTES resolution-type="independent"
              description="LeeAnne.org"
              service="http://www.leeanne.org"
        image="http://www.leeanne.com/usingxml/14xmp01.gif"/>
  </DISPUTES-GROUP>
  <DISCLOSURE
    discuri="http://www.leeanne.com/usingxml/14xmp01.html"
    access="nonindent" change_agreement="no" />
  <STATEMENT>
    <IDENTIFIABLE><no /></IDENTIFIABLE>
    <CONSEQUENCE-GROUP>
      <CONSEQUENCE>You're able to use our shopping cart
                  to order merchandise</CONSEQUENCE>
      <RECIPIENT><ours /></RECIPIENT>
      <PURPOSE><current /></PURPOSE>
      <!-- The following information is here because we
           may, at some future date, implement a shopping
           cart service for online ordering. At the present
           time we neither set nor read cookies or gather
           any other data. -->
      <DATA-GROUP>
        <DATA name="dynamic.cookies" category="state" />
        <DATA name="dynamic.miscdata" category="state" />
      </DATA-GROUP>
      <RETENTION><indefinitely /></RETENTION>
    <STATEMENT>
    <IDENTIFIABLE><no /></IDENTIFIABLE>
      <RECIPIENT><ours /></RECIPIENT>
      <PURPOSE><admin /><develop /></PURPOSE>
      <!-- The following information is collected
           automatically by the server. Although we
           don't do anything with it at the present
           time we may, at a later date, use this
           data to optimize our server, Web site, or
           ISP connectivity options. -->
```

PART

III

CH

15

```
<DATA-GROUP>
  <DATA name="dynamic.clickstream.server" />
  <DATA name="dynamic.http.useragent" />
  <DATA name="dynamic.http.referrer" />
</DATA-GROUP>
<RETENTION><indefinitely /></RETENTION>
<STATEMENT>
</POLICY>
```

The mapping between human-readable text and machine-readable XML code is necessarily rough, because natural language is an imperfect medium at best. In an actual privacy statement, it might be wise to have both a lawyer and a programmer consult on how these two statements should intersect.

CHAPTER 16

SECURITY AND PRIVACY

In this chapter

VULNERABLE DATA AND DATA SERVERS ON THE WEB

XML is not a secure system of protocols. In fact, it was designed to be perfectly open and transparent to inspection. So if you need security, and almost everyone does, you need to add security features from outside the XML world. Even XML-related security initiatives such as XML Signatures and P3P are plain text meta-descriptions of security, not actual implementations.

Everything in cyberspace is becoming more connected by the minute. More and more private financial, medical, and other personal data is being stored on the Web in accessible formats. The most accessible personal data, of course, is the information on our own computers, because most home and small office computers have no security worth mentioning. After that, comes the information stored on the servers of major financial and health-services organizations.

The information on financial and health-services servers is usually well-protected against even determined hackers, because a vulnerable bank can have its electronic pockets picked of millions of dollars in the wink of an eye. A vulnerable health-services organization can suffer the same eventual result as a consequence of a more protracted lawsuit for disclosing private information at random.

However, most of these firms can legally sell the information they have to certain others without even notifying you. Insurance companies exchange data as a matter of course "To combat fraud," they say. But a similar policy of spying on millions of innocent people in hopes of catching the occasional crook would be clearly unconstitutional if the police did it. Financial institutions do the same thing, posting the credit histories of everyone they run across on virtual bulletin boards where almost anyone can see them if they have enough money to spend. Even pharmacies have been caught selling the names of people who use certain medications to drug companies, who can then market competing products directly to users.

Although this may seem innocent enough to some, there are many medications or combinations of drugs which have clearly defined purposes that might reveal far more than most people want *anyone* else knowing, much less some venal marketeer with an economic axe to grind. Or worse, a political opponent, an employer, or anyone else with the power to harm us given enough knowledge about our secret selves. So a person who has a prescription for an antipsychotic drug used to treat schizophrenia might be discriminated against in employment if it were widely known. One might also be concerned if random strangers knew that one was taking an antiviral drug often prescribed for genital herpes and also for opportunistic cytomegalovirus and herpes infections in AIDS patients, or an antidepressant.

Sponsored health information sites can generate very intimate data for the ad space provider as well, since they are able to capture the user's clickstream and tell their advertisers what sort of page interests that user. Click on information about hair loss and ads for Rogaine may pop up. You may start receiving offers in the mail as well or even by telephone.

In the past, some data has had a minimal level of security attached to it because the formats were highly compressed and, in the case of relational databases, complex to decipher from a dump of the raw records. So, a hospital patient record in a legacy database might look something like this:

```
Jane Doe/789-1234567/047/398 211 734/ …
```

All the information shared between multiple patients is indexed into secondary tables, so deciphering a record requires some level of database sophistication perhaps beyond the capabilities of most of the users of the database.

An XML version of the same information listed cryptically in the previous example is far more accessible to snooping:

```
<patient>
  <name>Jane Doe</name>
  <medical-ID>789-1234567</medical-ID>
  <allergies>penicillin</allergies>
  <medications>
    some combination of very embarrassing
    prescription drugs
  </medications>
  <history>
    <record>
      more embarrassing information
    </record>
    <record>
      secrets even your mother doesnít know
    </record>
  </history>
</patient>
```

In this form, you can see more clearly why one might be concerned. Given enough information about the drugs one takes, anyone could make strong inferences about the other's private life even without looking at clinical notes and other records. Because the records are plainly understandable by anyone, you have to investigate all possible means of accessing the record and shut them down.

The coming availability of endless streams of data over the Internet using XML-based transmissions streams makes control of private information even more critical because, as we saw in the previous record, the meaning of the stream is immediately apparent unless steps are taken to disguise the stream during transmission.

In Chapter 15, "Getting Information About the User," you looked at P3P, the W3C privacy platform, which tries to give users at least some control over their personal data. However, P3P doesn't even begin to cover all the issues of security because it only protects you against people who play by the rules. There are electronic privacy groups like EPIC at http://www. epic.org/ lobbying for more controls on privacy. The U.S. Federal Trade Commission and European Union are both trying to promulgate regulations, in part to help bridge the gap between very restrictive European privacy laws and the relatively unregulated online privacy situation that exists in the U.S. But these only affect actual firms and individuals who pay attention to laws and regulations.

In this chapter, you look at how to handle those who play by no rules at all by learning how this patient record, and similar sensitive data, can be protected during storage, transmission, and update.

Tip from

LeeAnne.com
Words to weave by

For most sites, the primary means of preventing intrusion should be a lock on the computer room door, because many thefts or intercepts of data require nothing more than access to the physical machine and maybe a floppy disk or two.

Physical control of access to the record is the first line of defense, because the physical record is, in some sense, primary and may be far more detailed than a computer record linked to the physical file. X-rays, for example, are rarely digitized in most offices, so an online medical record only points to the physical location of the file that contains them.

An online records system that's connected to the Internet so users of the system can send email, for example, is also vulnerable to electronic intrusion from the outside unless precautions are taken.

UNDERSTANDING HOW ROUTERS PROTECT YOUR DATA

If an internal network is exposed to the Internet, anyone on the outside can access the machines on the local network if he knows the machine's actual network address. In a UNIX environment, for example, one could Telnet to a random physical IP address, such as 193.32.129.20, and treat the machine at the other end (if any) as if it were sitting on your desktop unless pains are taken to make the address inaccessible.

The first logical line of defense for most sites should probably be a *router*, a piece of hardware which takes traffic off the Web and translates that traffic onto an internal network as if it had originated locally while preventing certain types of traffic from passing through. It does the same thing for outgoing requests.

Because the actual IP addresses of individual machines on the secured network are never exposed, a considerable level of security is inherent in any router. If the router has the capability to filter packets selectively based on origination or port destination, an additional level of security is added. Most current commercial routers have this capability. So to protect the hypothetical patient record, you tell your router to allow only certain kinds of controlled access, refusing Telnet in particular, but also FTP, rlogin, rsh, and other dangerous intrusions.

Routers are ubiquitous on the Web. In fact, they're really the hardware incarnation of networking and the Internet itself. Although routers offer a level of security when they're set up to do so, almost every bit of data you've ever seen on the Internet has been delivered through a series of routers, the machines which send packets of data toward their ultimate destinations.

They do this by maintaining routing tables, which list paths to known destinations and the address of a place to send something to when the routers don't know where it goes. If a router collects traffic toward a given destination, they can ask another router for the address and place it into their internal routing table. If the routers know how to deliver a message to a given address, they advertise the fact if anyone asks. The two actions are separate. A router can return information on routing without being willing to carry the traffic, or can carry the traffic without being willing to disclose the final destination.

The following sections delve further into the innards of routers, explaining briefly the basic mechanisms by which traffic is carried on the Internet.

THE TCP/IP PROTOCOL

To understand how a router works, you need to know a little bit about the TCP/IP protocol that makes communication over the Internet possible. The complete protocol makes use of a layered series of idealized protocols called a *stack*. Figure 16.1 shows a typical rendering of the TCP/IP protocol stack. The only actual communication takes place at the physical level, as one might expect, but the message that the various levels pass back and forth between each other make it look to the application as if it's really communicating directly with another application. The dotted line shows this belief, although each of the lower protocols *also* believes that it's communicating to its counterpart on the other system, so Figure 16.1 could show similar dotted lines between every layer.

Figure 16.1
The TCP/IP protocol stack shows communication between applications.

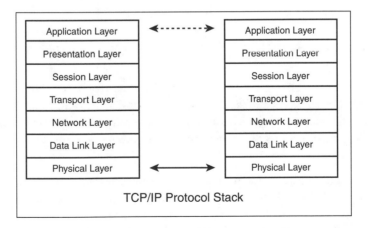

These layers are logical guidelines rather than fixed targets and it's fairly common to see layers combined in particular applications. TCP sits at the transport level and IP is immediately below at the network layer. The two lowest layers, data link and physical, are usually implemented in firmware running on your network card, although they too can be implemented in software. The physical layer actually interfaces to the hardware your particular network runs on, and handles the tasks of generating and deciphering the electrical signals on the wire or electromagnetic radiation in the air.

TCP/IP collectively breaks data into segments called *packets* and then transmits those packets over the Internet. When the packets arrive at their destination, they're reassembled into the complete message and ultimately delivered to the recipient. This task is broken into two parts: the TCP part does the disassembling and reassembling and handles error recovery, whereas IP handles addressing and delivery of packets toward their destination.

UNDERSTANDING IP—THE INTERNET PROTOCOL

Note that IP only tosses packets *toward* their final destination. It uses a *connectionless datagram* protocol with absolutely no control over whether packets arrive. Although packets are addressed with an IP address and a port number, the route those packets take toward their destination is determined heuristically by every intermediate processor. More than one copy of a given packet may arrive at the destination or none at all. It doesn't matter to IP.

Note

> *Connectionless* means there isn't a real path maintained between the origination and the destination. The path a message takes is determined by the network itself, with the actual path varying as network conditions change. A *datagram* is simply a message with a destination address. Routers send the packets along toward their destination but don't know anything about the contents.

There's no way for IP to tell whether a particular packet has arrived or even where a packet came from when it sees it. This makes it vulnerable to subversion by people wanting to gain unauthorized access to other people's machines. Although there are more secure implementations of IP in the works, including versions which use encryption and non-repudiation mechanisms to make attacks far more difficult, little actual network traffic uses these new protocols.

Because there's no error recovery built into IP and no way to tell whether a packet has been delivered, each packet is also labeled with a time-to-live field that allows it to be killed if it overstays its welcome on the network. Also, routers are free to discard packets they're too busy to handle or packets they don't want to carry, and that's how they protect against intrusion.

A router protecting your system advertises its willingness to route traffic toward your internal system without revealing the actual physical address. Contrariwise, when an outgoing packet is queued up, the router advertises itself to the machines on your network as the best way to reach that destination without revealing any information about alternate routes. Because any router is free to discard any IP packets at any time, enabling security on it is a matter of making it more finicky than usual about the packets it sends on to a destination. It's all handled more or less automatically and is part of the real cleverness of the whole Internet protocol. As a whole, it's very robust although the individual pieces may be weak.

UNDERSTANDING TCP—THE TRANSMISSION CONTROL PROTOCOL

Most secure protocols, such as Virtual Private Network (VPN), Secure Sockets Layer (SSL), and Vtun (Virtual Tunneling), rely on TCP, which is responsible for establishing a connection, breaking messages into packets so IP can send them as datagrams, gathering up all the little datagrams arriving for any particular session and bundling them back together, and handling any errors that occur along the way.

TCP uses IP as a transport mechanism but adds a limited number of security features on top of it. The most important is packet numbering, which increments the start of each new session by some largish number and reserves a score of thousands of packets for it on-the-fly. Anything coming in has to carry the right sequence number or it is automatically rejected as not belonging to the same session. In addition, every incoming data packet has to be acknowledged. So if a packet is intercepted, the sending process knows about it. Spoofing the complete transaction is rather difficult for most people.

Although this can be accomplished using expensive hardware, few people have the resources to hijack a session. The most common attacks on security depend on subverting logical behavior. Trying to figure out a password by looking over someone's shoulder or by logical deduction is much easier than trying to intercept and decipher the radio interference signature of individual key presses.

Commonly, medical information systems allow access to other health professionals, often by means of a login screen, so many medical systems are vulnerable to attack using spoofing to take over confidential sessions already in progress. The "Spoofing" section later in this chapter discusses this in greater detail.

A common method of logical attack is to use various "back doors" built into almost all operating systems to make user services possible. Although a site may strictly prohibit uploading data files by individual users, the same site lets an email service upload thousands of files. If a means is found to trick the email service into believing that the email files are actually something else, you've uploaded the very files you're not supposed to be able to upload. In the following two sections, I describe two common methods of attack in general terms to illustrate the sophistication and means used by persons wanting to obtain unauthorized access to your system.

THE INTERNET WORM

A famous example of an Internet attack is the "Internet Worm" created by Robert Morris, a 23-year-old student at Cornell in 1988. Among several other techniques, the worm used the email service and a particular program often left running on Unix machines, which carry most of the traffic on the Internet.

Older versions of this program, written in more trusting times, stored the incoming requests in an internal buffer designed to be large enough to handle any legitimate request. The worm sent a message deliberately larger than the internal buffer, which then overflowed the buffer and wrote the end of the message (which contained executable code) into the code space of the program, where it was immediately executed.

By exploiting yet another serious weakness in the older program implementation, the worm was able to seek out remote users on other systems using the same technique, whereupon it copied itself to those systems and so on in a programmatic pyramid game. Unlike real pyramid schemes, where the perpetrators quickly run out of victims to exploit, computer systems are rather gullible. So, Internet bandwidth was quickly filled with gajillions of copies of the worm redepositing itself everywhere at once. This led to an almost complete shutdown of legitimate Internet traffic for several days as sites discovered what was happening and disconnected themselves from the Internet to prevent swamping local processors.

The sad part is that Morris actually claims to have thought he'd done something clever, and boldly experimented with the entire network without permission on the assumption that, when he proved his concept, he could reveal himself as the genius behind the program to general acclaim and lucrative employment offers. Of course, he also took pains to disguise the real source of the worm by trying to conceal his identity and running it first from a machine at another university, so his protestations of complete innocence seemed slightly disingenuous to the people who prosecuted and sentenced him. For all that, he got off rather light by today's standards, receiving only probation and a fine that had little relationship to the actual costs incurred by the owners of the countless systems he messed with. People who do such things today often go to jail.

There are many other Internet services that have been exploited in the same or similar ways, so keep close track of your "trusted" applications. The Internet Worm could just as easily have been designed to seek out important medical records and transmit them via email to an anonymous account for later pickup by a snooper.

SPOOFING

Spoofing is a technical attack on the security of a machine that relies on exploiting an existing trusted relationship. *Hijacking* is a somewhat similar attack requiring slightly more knowledge and considerably more equipment.

As discussed earlier in this chapter, communications on the Internet take place by means of the TCP/IP protocol, which allows host and client machines to communicate with each other over what amounts to a giant party line. Although many users think of their connection to the Internet as if it were a telephone conversation, with a dedicated wire going from their workstations to the Web sites they want to look at or to the email recipients they want to reach, this idea is incorrect. In actuality, Internet traffic can be "sniffed" by anyone with the right technical equipment and access to some portion of the data stream.

Because the TCP/IP protocol stack is very robust by design, allowing IP packets to be routed almost anywhere, it's actually fairly easy to pretend to be someone you're not as long as you can keep the machine you're impersonating quiet in some way.

I won't go into the messy details of how to do this, to avoid encouraging experimentation which might lead to imprisonment and disgrace, but it's one of the more common attacks on UNIX machines (servers) and should be guarded against by your site administrator. Before entrusting your data to a server on the Web, ask what measures have been taken to prevent spoofing or hijacking user sessions. At the very least, your administrator should include periodic analysis of the server logs as part of the solution. The behavior of TCP can be changed as well, to eliminate the predictability that makes spoofing attacks possible.

> **Note**
>
> IP in its next incarnation will include the capability to encrypt the payload, so breaking into existing connections is going to become *somewhat* harder. Encryption is not a substitute for a complete security policy, however, and a security administrator should consider it only one tool in their necessary toolbox.

Another solution is a firewall or router that filters out incoming messages that appear to come from *within* the secure domain, unlikely in real life. A corollary to this is that outgoing packets from within the secure domain should be filtered to remove packets that appear to originate from outside it, which is also very unlikely to occur in the normal course of events.

The former indicates that your site may be under attack from a spoofer, whereas the latter means that someone on your site might be trying to spoof some other site. Both are bad.

PART

III

CH

16

SHUTTING SECURITY BACK DOORS

Closing the back doors into systems with sensitive data is most of what routers do in the way of security. By hiding the actual addresses of resources on the network, everything has to be done by remote control through the router. Because the router can be set to reject most types of remote control completely, or allow access only by known hosts, most forms of fiddling at the door are severely limited. Most routers and the servers behind them also keep logs. So if you see a lot of failed login attempts, which have their own well-known port, or other unauthorized accesses, you can be fairly sure that somebody is trying to guess a password, and you can take steps to track down the culprit before he succeeds. It often takes longer to hack into a secure installation with an alert system administrator than it does for that administrator to track down the actual identity of the hacker, so repeat offenders are caught fairly often. Hacking a computer is a federal crime in most cases, so the FBI may become involved as well.

> **Note**
>
> Lest you become overly alarmed, the number of actual hacker assaults on security systems has gone down in recent years. The decrease comes from improved security, improved law enforcement, and the fact that many hackers have matured enough to realize they could make big bucks actually *working* in the high-tech world instead of fooling around with it.

Routers are not terribly expensive, with fairly decent machines available for around $400 (U.S.). The more speed and simultaneous connections you need, the more expensive the router will be. Readily available commercial routers go all the way up to T1 and T3 speeds (1,544,000bps and 43,232,000bps respectively, in comparison with the typical dialup modem at 56,000bps) and there are many vendors, although Cisco Systems at http://www.cisco.com/ carries quite a bit of Internet traffic and offers a range of routers suitable for everything from the home office to the high speed backbone provider. There are even routers capable of much higher speeds, up to OC192 (9.6 Gigabits per second), used between major network providers and research universities.

Commonly available routers range from small systems suitable for a home or small office, such as those available from Cisco, Cayman Systems at `http://www.cayman.com/` or Netopia at `http://www.netopia.com/`, as well as those suitable for major Internet backbones, such as those from Juniper Networks at `http://www.juniper.net/`.

ERECTING SECURITY FIREWALLS

A *firewall* is a combination software and hardware barrier between the outside world and your network or computer. It keeps track of attacks on a system using a variety of complex techniques, prevents attacks when it can, logs attacks so you know when your system has been hit, and may even give you real-time notification. The lines between routers and firewalls have blurred in recent years, with many routers offering some level of firewall functionality and many firewalls behaving as virtual routers.

The hypothetical medical record is a tempting target, because this sort of information is actually an item of commerce in certain circles, so you have to close as many entry points as you can while tracking attempts to break in. If you think of your data like money in a bank, a firewall is like the vault, allowing controlled access by a limited group while presenting strong barriers to anyone else who wants to enter. But even strong vaults need security cameras to capture a secure record of unauthorized entry attempts, and the system logs are the computerized equivalent of bank security video cameras.

Using a firewall and/or router can be vital, especially if you use online chat rooms, promiscuous ICQ messaging, and the like, which tend to be frequented by people with time on their hands. Some of these people may be able to spy on your hard drive while talking to you online. Cable modems route your network traffic past everyone on the same cable. They're all sitting at home with no one looking over their shoulder. Some sort of protection is absolutely required.

Archetypically, a firewall is a single computer with two network interface cards, one fronting on the Internet and the other on a secure private network. The firewall machine examines the source address, destination address, and port number contained in the header of each packet seen and filters the packet based on what it finds.

Because most network services listen and send on well known ports, this has the effect of preventing certain types of service request entirely. `finger`, for example, on port 79, is often blocked for incoming traffic by the administrator for security reasons. `finger` shows whether a user is logged in, which may not be safe to let everyone in the world know. By preventing `finger`, they prevent an outsider from determining that a woman is working late at the office, enabling a stalker to lay in wait for her outside the door until she leaves.

`telnet`, on port 23, and `ftp`, on ports 20 and 21, are similarly made unavailable by zealous security managers. They can be worked around using HTTP upload forms and such on the site, although somewhat less convenient for the user, but have grave risks when freely accessible by anyone.

USING PROXY SERVERS

A *proxy server* is the opposite of a firewall in some sense, because it's primarily designed to keep users in. It has a nice security side effect in that it lets users on your internal network access the Internet in a controlled way and disguise them when they do. Proxies do this by monitoring and intercepting user requests and reissuing the request using their own network addresses. When the reply comes back from the network, the proxy passes on the data to the original user.

Because the outside world never sees addresses on the internal network, it's harder for a malicious person on the outside to get inside a well-designed firewall, even if that person has access to HTTP and other server logs and can inspect incoming requests. On the other hand, a clever user on the inside can use any permitted direct service through a proxy to do almost anything he wants, so both firewalls and proxy servers require a solid backup in the form of an aggressive and meticulous security systems administrator.

A primary tool of security systems administration is careful and continuous monitoring of firewall and proxy logs to detect both improper attempts to access the internal network from the outside and improper attempts to avoid detection by the proxy server. Malefactors on the inside looking out are as dangerous as those on the outside looking in and somewhat more likely to be malcontented and knowledgeable about internal security.

Inspection of the proxy logs also allows organizations to monitor all the network activities of their employees, so these logs are often used to discover and discipline employees who violate organizational policies on Internet use.

Proxies often implement an internal cache as well, so common requests to the Internet can be short-circuited by replying directly to the user using the information found in the cache, a significant savings in time and resources.

WELL-KNOWN PORTS AND OTHER SYSTEM SERVICES

One key to protecting your system from unauthorized service requests is knowing which port the request may come in on. The next section provides a list of common services.

WELL-KNOWN PORT ASSIGNMENTS

The well-known ports have been in use since the earliest days and are "well-known" because they exist by common agreement and are standardized across the entire Internet. The well-known ports are in the range 0–1023, although the very oldest assignments are all under 255. RFC-1700, Assigned Numbers, describes the current well-known ports but may be reissued with a different number at any time to update the list. This is illustrated in Table 16.1.

TABLE 16.1   MOST COMMON PORT NUMBERS ON THE INTERNET

Service Name	Port	Service Description
	0	Reserved
ftp-data	20	File Transfer [Default Data]
ftp	21	File Transfer [Control]
ssh	22	SSH Remote Login Protocol
telnet	23	Telnet
smtp	25	Simple Mail Transfer
time	37	Time
nameserver	42	Host Name Server
nicname	43	Whois
domain	53	Domain Name Server
gopher	70	Gopher
finger	79	Finger
http	80	World Wide Web HTTP
kerberos	88	Kerberos
pop2	109	Post Office Protocol - Version 2
pop3	110	Post Office Protocol - Version 3
nntp	119	Network News Transfer Protocol
ntp	123	Network Time Protocol
snmp	161	SNMP
snmptrap	162	SNMPTRAP
send	169	SEND
irc	194	Internet Relay Chat Protocol
https	443	HTTP protocol over TLS/SSL
ph	481	Ph service
uucp	540	uucpd
uucp-rlogin	541	uucp-rlogin
cybercash	551	CyberCash
doom	666	Doom id Software

The previous table contains a few of the most well-known ports, because most of the well-known ports are for protocols and applications software hardly anyone has ever heard of. The game Doom, of course, has its own port number to facilitate networked game sessions by programmers and others with lots of spare time to fool around. Quake, Unreal, and Kali are similarly blessed.

REGISTERED PORT ASSIGNMENTS

Registered ports are primarily those requested by manufacturers and vendors for their particular applications, although a few are in use by HTTP and other network services. It's common for programmers to assign their own port numbers in this range. The Registered Ports are in the range 1024–49151.

TABLE 16.2   REGISTERED PORTS

Service Name	Port	Service Description
	1024	Reserved
socks	1080	Socks
http-alt	8008	HTTP Alternate
http-alt	8080	HTTP Alternate (see port 80)

Only a few of these are listed here because most are used by proprietary applications and services most people never run across.

DYNAMIC PORT ASSIGNMENTS

Dynamic port assignments are used for video and audio streaming, among other things, or any service which may require a dedicated port for any amount of time. Many applications allow their dynamic port requirements to be tuned, so the huge and rather unmanageable theoretical range can be trimmed considerably when they're required to work through proxy servers and firewalls. The only reason you have to be aware of them ordinarily is when setting up your proxy or firewall server, because they'll have to be configured as available for use in secure systems.

The dynamic and/or private ports range from 49152–65535. These aren't listed here because they're free for any special use you can make of them.

HTTP—THE HYPERTEXT TRANSFER PROTOCOL

Ports are often used by an application on a default basis, so an HTTP request from your browser goes out to port 80 unless otherwise specified. They can also be entered directly by using the full HTTP addressing protocol, which lets you enter a port number following an HTTP site address like `http://www.anyname.com:portnumber/` where *portnumber* is any valid port number at which a server process listens.

Commonly, a secure version of HTTP might sit at a different port number from insecure HTTP—often 8080 or 8008, although 443 is also common—so internal secure links might point to `http://www.anyname.com:8080/securepage.html`.

Alternatively, the server itself can be set up to treat `https://www.anyname.com/` differently than `http://www.anyname.com/` and handle the port routing problem on its own. Servers are actually quite clever and can perform a lot of magic behind your back. One of the things they're good at is treating some requests in special ways based on the fistful of information the browser sends along with every request.

Tip from

LeeAnne.com
Words to weave by

Just because a page *looks* simple doesn't mean it *is* simple. The W3C logo on a site is actually called `W3C.html` in the source code for the page. Every request for the file `W3C.html` is automatically translated into an appropriate form, text or graphics, for the browser used to access the splash page.

Many Web designers who use HTML-based redirection and dynamic reconfiguration based on browser sniffing could probably better use server-based features to do the same thing more reliably and with fewer side effects.

REAL WORLD FIREWALL PRODUCTS

In the server world, famous firewall names like Check Point at `http://www.checkpoint.com/`, Trusted Information Systems (now Network Associates) at `http://www.nai.com/`, and Raptor Systems (now AXENT) at `http://www.axent.com/` are expensive but well-suited for large commercial environments.

However, firewalls are not just the concern of large corporate sites. As more individuals and small businesses are connected to the Internet using dedicated IP addresses such as many DSL and cable connections, they're all becoming vulnerable to the same sorts of attacks that can be made on corporate or governmental sites. Although attacks can be made at random to any IP address, individual and small business sites are usually less protected than corporate ones. If you have a machine at home, is it password protected? Is the password a *good* one? Do you change it regularly? Do you have *any* means of detecting whether anyone is trying to break in? Do you have a router instead of a modem?

For most of us, the answer is no. And the ISP's, cable networks, and telco's who sell access to the Internet are not at all forthcoming about the real risks of being online. However, a number of security products are designed for small business and home use, including ConSeal Private Desktop from Signal 9 Solutions at `http://www.signal9.com/` and BlackICE Defender from Network ICE at `http://www.networkice.com/`. AtGuard from WRQ (`http://www.wrq.com/`) has been packaged into Symantec's Norton Internet Security 2000 at `http://www.symantec.com/`, which includes WRQ's AtGuard, parental control, and antivirus software in one package. The cost for most of these products is about $50 (U.S.).

Figure 16.2 shows the control screen for Signal 9's PC Firewall, which incorporates the capability to exchange encrypted messages (at no added cost) as well as protect against most network assaults. A large number of rules are shown and more can be added as needs dictate. The items in the log are actually not attacks, but ICQ trying to advertise my presence on the Internet. This is a significant breach of security, because ICQ and other similar packages let everyone know what your IP address is right this minute and ICQ has, in fact, been used to launch attacks on other people's computers. Always keep such programs updated, because security holes are found and fixed periodically. Even better, consider not using them at all, or restricting the number of people who can access your ICQ information to a small group of friends.

Signal 9 also has Virtual Private Network (VPN) software available, which sets up encrypted communication paths over the Internet, allowing you to treat the Internet as a secure local area network wiring plant and link to remote offices and sites as if they were in the next cubicle.

Note

Easy-to-use applications such as cDc's Back Orifice, L0pht Heavy Industries' L0phtCrack, and Neikter's NetBus mean that even stupid idiots can hack into your unprotected system, just like the clever ones. You don't have to have any special knowledge to hack a system nowadays, just a handy little program on disk. And that doesn't even count Satan, supposedly a system administrator's tool for discovering security weaknesses in their own system but also often used by hackers to infiltrate systems they don't own.

Of course these are not the only firewalls available for home and small office computers, but represent two of the best and most widely available commercially. A little research on the Web will reveal many more.

Caution

Advertising your IP address is like letting people know which picture the wall safe is hidden behind. You have to be fairly confident that the safe itself will hold up to a concerted attack or you're better off hiding it's existence. If you have a Web site, which necessarily discloses its IP address, keep it on a separate machine and network from your personal or business life and make access from it to your internal network very difficult. Many organizations force downloads to the Web server to be made by floppy disks or other physical transport media.

These single machine "firewalls" are so named by analogy. A true firewall is software with a hardware assist, network interfaces that are physically connected to different networks. By extension, you can consider a similar process that sits on a single machine and filters packets before allowing them to access the machine itself a firewall, although there is no real separation between the network access hardware and the vulnerable machine.

When a request comes in off the Internet, the firewall decides whether to let it through or not. Commonly, firewalls allow HTTP requests to pass, although not necessarily, and certain other clearly defined types of information are allowed to pass as well. Everything dangerous is excluded.

Figure 16.2
Signal 9's PC Firewall control screen showing rules in use.

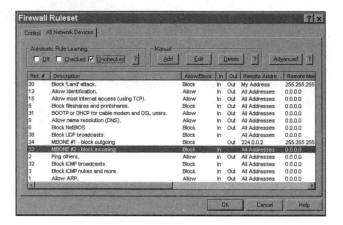

The safest course is to allow nothing in or out. This is the exact security method used by the most highly secure military computers. They have wire cages around them and no cables coming in other than the power cable. Everything is carried in and out on paper or other secure transfer medium. Paper and other media are regularly shredded by expensive machines that turn documents into mush. It does little good to invent security systems if you toss your secrets into the trash for anyone to read. A slightly different approach to firewalls is used by the Private Desktop application from the same Signal 9 company and shown in Figure 16.3. This package actually monitors outgoing traffic by the name of the program which originated it, so even if a worm manages to infiltrate your system undetected, its capability to communicate with the outside world will be sharply curtailed. This package is aimed squarely at the home market, and where PC Firewall requires some level of understanding of the basic protocols to determine what the rules mean, Signal 9's Private Desktop hides unneeded information from the user and lets most traffic through after a simple and easy to understand onscreen query.

The Signal 9 screen was generated by the first use of programs which require network connectivity to function.

Another firewall product for the home and small business market is BlackICE Defender from Network ICE. It has the expected intrusion features plus one that appears unique, a companion ICEcap program that collects and coordinates attempted intrusion information across an entire network so that reporting and analysis can be conveniently performed at a single location for larger environments. Figure 16.4 shows the ICEcap analysis screen.

Figure 16.3
Signal 9's ConSeal Private Desktop control screen shows the activity log.

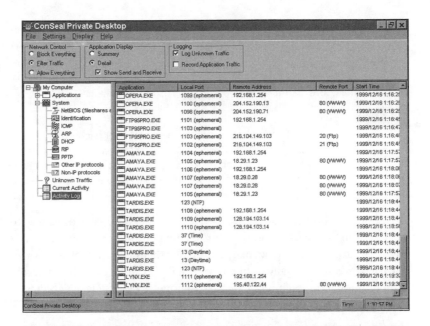

Figure 16.4
Network ICE's ICEcap product shows data collected from several BlackICE-protected systems.

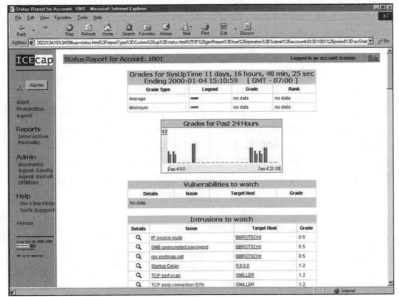

CREATING UNIQUE PASSWORDS

The Hollywood fantasy of some smart-mouth little kid dialing up the neighborhood nuclear weapons center and starting WW III by typing the name of the president's dog as a password is just that, fantasy. But most of us ordinary folk use access passwords similar to that fantasy president. We use our husband or wife's first and middle (or maiden) name (very popular), the name of a favorite movie or game character (also very popular among young unmarried men), a birth date, a pet's name, a trivial pattern of keys on the keyboard, or the like. Many hacking tools exploit this human weakness, so a big part of system security is making sure your users can't set their password to a silly and easily guessed string. Many sites run attempted password changes against a filter which prevents using dictionary words, proper names, and common keyboard patterns as a password.

Caution

Please be aware that using Satan and most other hacker tools on a system that doesn't belong to you is an excellent way to get fired from your job, thrown off your ISP, sent to prison, bankrupted, and either divorced or socially ostracized, not necessarily in that order. Computer security people are not easily amused and often find it difficult to see the joke.

Most home and office systems are extremely vulnerable. Without a way to detect and log security attacks, a hacker can try a list of common women's names, character names (you might be surprised just how many guys fancy themselves JamesBond or Agent007), and dictionary words sequentially until one works. This can be done by an automated daemon without human intervention. Contrary to popular belief, *DukeNukem* isn't a particularly clever password.

One way to make a memorable password is to use the initial or other characters of a unique phrase with unique modifications. "Peter Piper *8* a peck of pickled peppers" would turn into "PP8apopp" (although mention in this book turns this particular password into a well-known one).

For even more security and a longer password you might try a longer phrase like, "I am a pretty little Dutch girl, as pretty as pretty can be, and all the boys on the baseball team are going crazy over me". If you take first letters, the result would be "IaaplDg,apapcb,aatbotbtagcom" and reasonably hard to guess from the outside. This particular phrase is one I personally could hardly forget, after chanting it almost daily while skipping rope and growing up. It would be even better if I'd changed the words around slightly but you get the idea. Of course, if you do alter the base phrase, be sure that it will *remain* memorable even after tweaking.

Tip from

LeeAnne.com
Words to weave by

Even better than a password is a physical authentication scheme that doesn't use reusable passwords. Every time you login to a system over a network there is a significant chance that the password will be sniffed. Many authentication systems exist, from card access systems to retinal scan devices.

Almost anything you already have in your memory store is good, because the fact that it's already there means that you've done the hard part and can concentrate on the algorithm you use to extract letters from it. Individual phrases are better than common ones. "My grandmother's maiden name was Mathilde Pedersen" ("MgmnwMP") is inherently better than "An apple a day keeps doctors away" ("Aaadkda"), because far fewer people share or could guess the former phrase even though they both have eight characters. Never use a password of less than six to eight characters. It's too easy to cycle through every possible combination of characters when you use short passwords.

Use your own longer phrase. Use last letters. Tweak the phrase. Say it backward. Be inventive. But especially, don't use "Batman!" or anything like it.

Tip from  LeeAnne.com Words to weave by	A good password *must* be memorable, so you don't need to paste it on a yellow sticky. It should also be very hard to guess. Mix in numbers, punctuation, and symbols as well as letters. And you *must* change your password regularly and at any time you've had to type it in from a remote location.

ENCRYPTION

Encryption is the process of scrambling data about so that only someone with the secret knowledge of how the data was scrambled can read it. The science of *cryptology* (the study of encryption algorithms) has come a long way since the Double Dutch and Pig Latin we used in the schoolyard. The older word for this mysterious science was *ciphering*, from the Arabic word for zero, *sifr*, which was so mysterious in those ancient days that it seemed like magic. So deciphering a jumble of letters into plain text seemed like conjuring something from nothing, and deciphering ciphers became a state secret entrusted to the military and civil authorities.

Note	The first electronic stored-program computer, Colossus, was developed by Alan Turing and his associates under British government auspices to crack the German Enigma code. The whole project was so secret that they allowed the ENIAC group to claim precedence for many years. In fact, the myth of ENIAC is so pervasive that you still hear it so described.

Modern high-security encryption schemes can beat most assaults on system information, if not necessarily protect system integrity. So while a hacker may have been able to weasel in through a back door or sniff your email, if data files and messages are encrypted and digitally signed, the likelihood of his being able to do anything besides delete files and fling things about is greatly reduced.

There are two main types of encryption techniques: *symmetrical* and *asymmetrical*. With symmetrical techniques, the same password is used to encrypt and then decrypt the message. In asymmetrical systems, one key is used to encrypt the message and another is needed to decrypt it. It's also possible to use a combination of both methods.

SYMMETRIC CODES

The earliest codes were symmetric because they didn't have the computing power available to compute one-way mathematical functions of any complexity. The classic Caesar Cipher is a trivial example, with a one-letter key. You encode a message by counting up through the alphabet the number of letters from A to the chosen key and decode using the opposite process. Caesar reportedly used C as the key (vanity?):

```
THE QUICK BROWN FOX JUMPED OVER THE LAZY DOGS
VJG SWKEM DTQYP HQZ LWORGF QXGT VJG NCBA FQIU
```

In an era in which most people couldn't read, this was actually fairly secure.

The Caesar Cipher was supposedly invented by Julius Caesar, obviously untrue because this sort of cipher predates him by thousands of years and was even used in ancient Egypt. But the Caesar Cipher evidently *was* used by the Roman legions to communicate secretly. It's quick and easy to keep track of in your head so you don't need to keep written materials lying around that might betray your cipher to spys.

Since that time, symmetric ciphers have progressed almost beyond recognition and have become an entire branch of mathematics and computing. But all the symmetric ciphers require some sort of communication to take place between the parties before a secure communication can occur. This means either transporting the key, or information on how to construct the key, in some manner and storing the information somewhere to boot, all of which makes these systems vulnerable to physical or eavesdropping attack.

ASYMMETRIC CODES

Asymmetric encryption schemes solve the problem of communicating keys between the partners in a cryptographic communication by publicly revealing a key, which allows anyone to send a secure message to any recipient with a public key. They operate by means of one-way or trap-door functions. These are mathematical operations which can be easily computed in one direction but which can't be undone with nearly so much ease without a secret key. So, the recipient of the encoded message decrypts the message with his secret key and the plain text is revealed.

The holder of a private key can also encrypt a message that anyone with access to her public key can read, which is not terribly handy for passing secrets; however, it forms the basis of digital signatures, which you will learn more about in the "Digital Signatures" section later in this chapter.

PGP is one of many systems, as mentioned previously, but it's easy and cheap to experiment with and deserves special mention. Here's one of many free distribution sites for PGP: http://web.mit.edu/network/pgp.html.

Asymmetric ciphers allow you to post your encryption key publicly, allowing anyone at all to send encoded messages to you and preventing anyone except yourself from decrypting the cipher.

The other half of this equation is that you can sign a message using your private key and anyone who knows your public key can decipher it and verify that the message comes from you in actual fact. This will eventually allow electronic documents to be signed electronically and make online transactions easily enforceable in court. Several European countries already recognize electronic signatures, and the United States will catch up eventually.

The formidable bit of jumble shown in Listing 16.1 is my own very secure (4096-bits) electronic public key using PGP for my default e-mail ID.

LISTING 16.1 THE AUTHOR'S PGP KEY

```
-----BEGIN PGP SIGNED MESSAGE-----
Hash: SHA1

- -----BEGIN PGP PUBLIC KEY BLOCK-----
Version: PGP for Personal Privacy 5.5.2
```

```
mQGiBDhaiyERBADcSohdD9yGzWIP1QZ9aZImDN9drNyMImxsOmKdP0WmU5VuM7sZ
ptrFEWonNsTFQmBbtYVAQztLpztaapdLiR05vJHv/qnA/150EN3eojUCh6qMmhu3y
Wh/cDqr9N+xC8YI+VoP+/ix4zA+jI9GAHCydJRnvP6opDHFkOYt9IE3BVwCg/7xp
LUEOUOJeGGtq2N6q7qERUuUEAK3ORmTBWS9XvYxNSN1/OZTpKOnZ3tyCOz378Evs
WMriY2y1ngJj1yeFi5a3GJ7KseIsgQUHxLB+unY5X/T9nR7PJGRis0fnjN+sAC0j
W/ik/EXK1G8Y7t/DBjDwlcatj92uCVpEzlfBSFC0FjuglwSQuGQOAUT6xh4qhWEi
eUx9BADH3gmn0DZi8TfHFvPkKeHzxNhLsGY+Os96GbhrzE51EwY7avrbgFLYe4Z3
Yl6AoZzQOcUFBS1U1PYSiOGKse2+JDFbGHcNyKs8FK16tyKy+cwCkVHnbBtDQWtk
LtDFHs9acOcgX3d/Qzv+IQ0pffgV0jUcxaniixz0Dqa3xtKI7bQnTGVlIEFubmUg
UGhpbGxpcHMgPGxlZWFubmVAbGVlYW5uZS5jb20+iQBLBBARAgALBQI4WoshBAsD
AgEACgkQ+e69xICJydp0rQCg7z178bs3JFLNmd5esCRO1tnRXccAoPaCFE7TjV+g
h2AMnbILSAl1AHNxuQQNBDhaiyIQEAD5GKB+WgZhekOQldwFbIeG7GHszUUfDtjg
o3nGydx6C6zkP+NG1LYwSlPXfAIWSIC1FeUpmamfB3TT/+OhxZYgTphluNgN7hBd
q7YXHFHYUMoiV0MpvpXoVis4eFwL2/hMTdXjqkbM+84X6CqdFGHjhKlP0YOEqHm2
74+nQ0YIxswdd1ckOErixPDojhNnl06SE2H22+slDhf99pj3yHx5sHIdOHX79s+z
xIMRJitDYMPj6NYK/aEoJguuqa6zZQ+iAFMBoHzWq6MSHvoPKs4fdIRPyvMX86RA
6dfSd7ZCLQI2wSbLaF6dfJgJCo1+Le3kXXn11JJPmxiO/CqnS3wy9kJXtwh/CBdy
orrWqULzBej5UxE5T7bxbrlLOCDaAadWoxTpj0BV89AHxstDqZSt90xkhkn4DIO9
ZekX1KHTUPj1WV/cdlJPPT2N286Z4VeSWc39uK50T8X8dryDxUcwYc58yWb/Ffm7
/ZFexwGq01uejaClcjrUGvC/RgBYK+X0iP1YTknbzSC0neSRBzZrM2w4DUUdD3yI
sxx8Wy2O9vPJI8BD8KVbGI2Ou1WMuF040zT9fBdXQ6MdGGzeMyEstSr/POGxKUAY
EY18hKcKctaGxAMZyAcpesqVDNmWn6vQClCbAkbTCD1mpF1Bn5x8vYlLIhkmuqui
XsNV6z3WFwACAg//f0YTkdIaae2KgiBhuMrXUo+rhdHy7Rq++gH7bA7KSMKtBsLg
+cRkv4yfV2NdoQArTFdA2dY14BKPPpsF32THU+IVEBzyJG4Ii9jUtmTDElWMzbKw
pt5lC1/FfDmjDmQdLAgcbmtviZ9B5deivfBTwD9zXgu2y8pYONVa89wkdc3lnUTF
8lxBH9t5LJ0NJe7+bKECwbdXsulW0sH0LR6P31mSERAIE430jtz2/3WNOUX7cFqy
/39DdmTr6AesZBwZIUi8BFU533B/ZzS/YWh5FENK5WLuV32Ia4E3IjM3/8O6khI4
HnEnTIj0N74a05ElUbjQzP7RFrIYlxAdG1gU+uVBcE/7t6bObIa7O7sgeBQnzuyK
9aEW0aKwKd9uUN5Vqks3zKCu6MWvShyOEF3bJQKQ48268AGN7hc0lKuLkoRhkxY0
3PI9Wrn+ExW/58pV0pcb5opPo2tSlZIAK3ExXcEq/2DDL6KD2BLfseZa/l/HeZww
VBcKFy0qsIUkYklX7wyHIjNyunwnK6X+lUytwccjUOqHK+hTFCDUn7ZlYpaDhqt6
GxoKY4/AlWIr3K70ozldVF8Dua9gYg1ZMoYS7ElPwcNHjobcwI+IwVlSFDWLZHAq
ncaHkPUSm+EcpIMLZvuamZ9Yl1mlif7PeewZVqqQrkbPgA61+glp5a5wBQuJAEYE
GBECAAYFAjhaiyIACgkQ+e69xICJydpImACdFgr4Lba2LO+htIRrfXanZqKG1h4A
n0iMXY/mlu2Wp80rne53HLvtMhei
=Nb3Y
```

```
- -----END PGP PUBLIC KEY BLOCK-----

-----BEGIN PGP SIGNATURE-----
Version: PGP for Personal Privacy 5.5.2
```

```
iQA/AwUBOFqLufnuvcSAicnaEQJxwwCgsPWRtOmdIyQlIEGg4YrODM18qucAoNeb
pzrhsH4OxTLMfaXGnHGi09Kj
=BEt4
```

```
-----END PGP SIGNATURE-----
```

Note that it's signed, so you can see that I verify that it's really my key. Please don't try to type this in. It's available on my Web site at http://www.leeanne.com/ and on the enclosed CD-ROM if you want to test it.

Combinations of both methods are often used because there are many very fast symmetric encryption algorithms and the asymmetric ones tend to be relatively slow. Essentially, the asymmetric public key method is used to transmit a symmetric encryption key and then the session proceeds using the faster symmetric key.

Be aware that most government-approved encryption systems such as DES were deliberately designed to be easy to crack. The best encryption algorithms, such as the one used by PGP or the strong RSA or Diffie-Hellman methods, are classified as "munitions" by the U.S. government. These algorithms were hazardous to export without running afoul of regulations evidently designed to prevent their domestic use and slow the spread of cryptographic knowledge until the U.S. Department of Commerce finally allowed export of commercial cryptographic products in January, 2000. Although these prior restraints on publication of encryption source code were recently held to be unconstitutional by the Ninth Circuit Court of Appeals, invalidating the entire law, the government has appealed for review and will undoubtedly take the issue to the Supreme Court, thus trying to preserve the right to control such exports even though they're essentially agreeing that the cat's out of the bag already.

Tip from

 LeeAnne.com
Words to weave by

The 56-bit DES algorithm has been cracked by one special purpose microcomputer in two days. So, you can assume that all the export-legal methods would barely cause a hiccup on an NSA or other governmental supercomputer.

In this regard, the U.S. government is being either thick-headed or, more likely, disingenuous. The cryptographic cat is already out of the bag. They can't stuff it back in no matter how hard they try because everyone with any interest in secrecy or privacy is already using existing very secure products, many of which are free or very low cost. The asymmetric PGP is one example. A French company has a symmetric cipher they call CS-Cipher, which allows up to 128-bit encryption, they'll sell to anyone. They're posting a prize of 10,000 Euros (currently about US$9500) to anyone who cracks, it so you might want to take a look if you like solving difficult puzzles. There's a free version with 40-bit security but they do charge for the highest levels.

You should also note that the export restrictions actually do nothing in practice other than create hassles for the manufacturers and users of cryptographic products. For example, Netscape has export and domestic versions, with the domestic version available with strong encryption only at the cost of filling out a lengthy form.

RESTORING STRONG ENCRYPTION

However, there are sites all over the world that restore strong encryption to the crippled export version of Netscape. Fortify is one at http://www.fortify.net/ and Safe Passage is another from C2net at http://www.c2.net/. C2net also supplies a full-strength version of SSL, Stronghold, so strong encryption products are available worldwide in any event. Cryptography is constantly advancing. The latest developments include quantum cryptographic techniques that make interception and decryption of encoded messages theoretically impossible without discovering a new physical reality that allows quantum uncertainties to be resolved without affecting the state of the system.

DO-IT-YOURSELF FILE ENCRYPTION

Many tools are available that can encrypt and decrypt your files online, so company secrets can be kept in a secure fashion even if a physical or logical break-in exposes the contents of your hard disks to inspection by hostile parties. Some are trivial to decode although possibly just beyond the capability of an ordinary twelve-year old, in case you have something you want to keep from your children. Some are extremely difficult, and deciphering them would assure the cryptological fame of the cryptographer who broke them. There are so many cryptography products available that it would be unfair to give the impression that RSA and PGP are the only games in town. A search on "cryptography" or "computer security" will turn up hundreds.

Tip from

Words to weave by

Not all cryptographic products are created equal. Many offer only the illusion of security. Investigate alternatives before choosing one.

TCP/IP ENCRYPTION

Encryption is also a part of the next generation of TCP/IP, at least at the IP level. The Sun implementation of IPv6, sometimes called IPng (IP next generation), includes a protocol called SKIP, Simple Key-management for IP. SKIP uses a rather clever Diffie-Hellman public key system to encrypt and transmit short packet keys, which in turn encrypt the data contained in the packets without adding too much overhead to each packet. It's a secure mechanism whose values change on a regular basis to eliminate the possibility of accumulating enough data to start noticing repetitions.

This level of encryption can float along under the encryption offered by SSL, so the combination of the two can be much greater than the sum of its parts. Because IP is connectionless, including anything other than a very short key is way too much overhead because the key has to appear in each packet. So, SKIP changes the packet key often to avoid giving cryptographers too much text to work with.

Using the Internet to provide private communications in this way is sometimes called *tunneling* and is the basis of Virtual Private Networks, which use the Internet to link portions of a network securely without disclosing the plaintext content of the actual traffic over the net. Unless carefully designed, virtual private networks are susceptible to a method of attack called *traffic analysis*, which involves keeping track of how many messages and how much data is transmitted along the secure path. By observing or manipulating events in the external world and then observing how much data streams between the linked sites, a cryptographer can make good guesses about the content of the messages themselves, which makes decrypting them somewhat easier.

Much as language is learned by observing the exchange of repeated words and actions, a cryptographer can decipher the codes used by observing the back and forth chatter between nodes of the virtual network.

So very secure systems often maintain a constant level of traffic, continuously transmitting random messages when there are no actual messages to send. Although this uses up bandwidth, it also means that there is no pattern of activity to observe, making cryptographic attacks more difficult. Although the rival cryptographer might still observe or manipulate events in the outside world to guess at the content of traffic, he has no way of knowing which of very many messages actually contain that traffic.

SECURITY AND PRIVACY INITIATIVES

The most famous security initiative in the context of this book is, of course, P3P as discussed in the previous chapter, but it didn't spring from nowhere. *Trust marks*, *user-controlled blocking software*, and *authentication services*, each addressing different parts of the problem, have been in existence for years as vendors try through industry groups to forestall government intervention. P3P is only one such group. The electronic privacy service provider eTrust spends millions advertising its internet privacy program, whereas Netscape is fond of the Open Profiling Standard (OPS), which allows users to send encrypted email and create "digital passports" stored on the user's hard drive, which can be used to automatically access shopping Web sites.

The major accounting firms are all getting in on the electronic commerce act as well. Price Waterhouse, Coopers & Lybrand Consulting, Ernst & Young, Arthur Andersen, and others are either forming relationships with vendors such as CyberCash, taking over entire online commerce departments for their customers, or at least thinking about it.

The Coordinating Committee for Intercontinent Research Networking, an international group, is working on a collaboration between research groups in different countries to promote common privacy and security infrastructures and policies.

The problem of intrusive commercial email (sometimes called *spam*, with apologies to Hormel) is being addressed by several organizations, including CAUCE, http://www.cauce.org/ and MAPS, http://mail-abuse.org/.

Even the Internal Revenue Service has jumped on the bandwagon with their Strategies for Growth featuring prominent mention of security and privacy concerns of U.S. taxpayers and ways to ensure these concomitant with their desire to move rapidly toward electronic filing of returns.

CERT, formerly the Computer Emergency Response Team, at http://www.cert.org/, publishes advisories and accepts reports on attempted break-ins. It's an invaluable resource for network and computer security administrators.

The Electronic Frontier Foundation, http://www.eff.org/, keeps track of assaults on our privacy by governmental organizations primarily, although they also track privacy invasions by commercial and other entities. The Electronic Privacy Information Center at `http://www.epic.org/` spreads its attention more evenly across governmental and private intruders on our collective privacy.

Cryptography Research has an extensive list of links to cryptographic resources on the Web at `http://www.cryptography.com/`.

Cookies and other forms of personal data and behavior tracking can be defeated manually or by available software on many platforms. Examples include the free Internet Junkbuster Proxy at `http://www.junkbusters.com/ht/en/ijb.html` for Windows 95/98/NT and UNIX, which blocks both cookies and banner ads under Windows. Another is interMute at `http://www.intermute.com/` which blocks cookies, banner ads, and popup windows but only runs under Windows. A Java-based solution called Muffin at `http://muffin.doit.org/` is available but rather difficult to set up. But then it's free so it's hard (or at least ungrateful) to complain.

Many people don't know that the banner ad providers can trace your movements within a Web site, and even from site to site by placing a cookie on your local machine. Every time you reach a new site served by the same banner ad provider, they may know who you are if the cookie is available to them. Because "data mining" (another word for monitoring clickstreams) is so valuable to advertisers, knowing where you surf as you travel from site to site is a window into your interests and even your thought patterns.

Figure 16.5 shows the log screen from interMute overlain on an Altavista search page. Notice that there are no banner ads on the Altavista page and the log lists 24 ads that would have been displayed without using this tool. In a work environment, the savings in time needed to download the ads, much less the interruption if an employee is enticed into clicking on the ad, might justify the purchase price within a few months.

Part III

Ch 16

Figure 16.5
An interMute log display shows the number of ads blocked in a very short session.

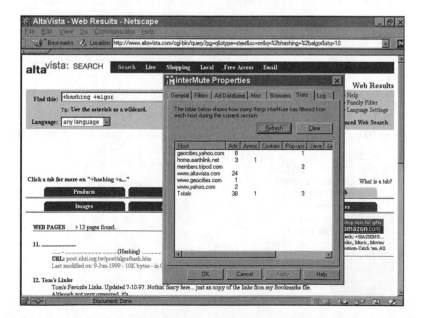

DIGITAL SIGNATURES

A digital signature is a method of affixing a unique identifier that cannot be repudiated at some later date. Like a handwritten signature, a digital signature should be self-identifying to some extent.

The history of digital signatures is made up of many parts. First, hashing offers a way to create an *almost* unique number which throws away almost all the information contained in the document except for its identity. Just as a fingerprint doesn't tell you anything about a person except that he or she is unique among individuals, a hash function condenses the information and structure of a document into a relatively small number that can identify the document among many others with an extremely high degree of probability.

The better the hash function, the more likely the resulting number will be truly unique.

So by hashing a message and including the hash in an encrypted message using a private key, anyone with the public key can decrypt the encoded signature and obtain the hashed condensation of the original message. After applying the hash function again, the results can be compared and the message itself verified as being the same message that was signed.

SIGNED XML

The W3C XML digital signature working group is still in the preliminary stages of defining a standard at the time of this writing, but digital signatures are well-enough understood that the final recommendation likely will look much like the draft.

Because many types of digital objects may need to be signed in an XML context, the working draft places no restrictions on the content of signed documents. XML Signature is designed to ensure the integrity of documents of any sort, whether XML or not, and whether they are located remotely or locally. They also serve to authenticate messages and signatures associated with a document.

Because XML documents can be drastically modified by means of style sheets, filters, included images, and other non-XML content included as notations, XML Signature captures the complete context of a document as it is seen at the time of signing. Parts of the document not seen are not signed and not guaranteed as to integrity by implication.

Although the exact syntax is still up in the air, an XML signature will probably look something like this, taken from the latest working draft syntax document from W3C:

```
<Signature>
  <SignedInfo>
    (CanonicalizationMethod)?
    (SignatureMethod)
    (<Reference (URI=|IDREF=)? Type=?>
      (Transforms)?
      (DigestMethod)
      (DigestValue)
    </Reference>)+
  </SignedInfo>
```

```
  (SignatureValue)
  (KeyInfo)?
  (Object)*
</Signature>
```

where the optional CanonicalizationMethod describes the method used to achieve Canonicalization, that is, expanding all entity references into full forms and performing other transformations intended to ensure that documents which seem to be the same are in fact equivalent. SignatureMethod describes the exact type of signature being generated, for example, and the Reference items point to the actual parts of the documents being signed. The other items describe the actual signature and related data.

Although this all sounds complex, the basic concept is simple; construct a hash value that describes the data, encrypt it in some reversible way using the private key associated with a public key algorithm, and package the lot. Anyone who want to verify the source document can recompute the hash value and then decrypt the signed and encrypted original value using the public key that corresponds to the private key. If the values are the same, the documents are quite probably the same.

SIGNED MARKUP DESCRIPTION LANGUAGES (SMDL)

Digital signatures, as defined a couple sections earlier in this chapter, are hot right now and will soon be applied to everything that moves over the Web. There are already initiatives underway to add digital signatures to HTML, XHTML, and even computer graphics and other multimedia files. This is being done partly to assure that content remains stable and partly to address intellectual property concerns about multimedia content placed on the Web. Although technologies such as RealAudio make some attempt to disguise the actual location of the content, one can nonetheless lift these files from their locations and illegally re-use them for other purposes. However, defacing the music with an audible sound would ruin it, as would scrawling identification across an artwork or photograph.

Steganography is a method of concealing encrypted data in a manner which cannot be detected, even if you suspect that secret communications are being exchanged. It uses unused information space in almost any file, and can be made sufficiently redundant that the secret information will survive being copied, cropped, edited, or otherwise altered along with its shrouding host file.

So steganography, the science of hiding encrypted information in tiny variations of lightness and darkness, or sound levels, or any other variable with statistical properties that can be manipulated, offers musicians, photographers, and others whose work is easily stolen on the Web and hard to find once stolen, a way to prove legal ownership. The preceding sentence illustrates a very primitive form of steganography by encoding the phrase, "hello, world." in **boldface** letters within the plain roman text. In a real steganographic message, the variations in the text would be so small that they could only be detected if you knew what to look for and the message itself might be encrypted.

When steganographic information is used to provide identification and copyright information, it's usually called digital watermarking, or just watermarking for short, and there are many vendors with steganographic products available.

One of the most complete listings of steganographic links and information is on Dr. Eric Milbrandt's Steganography Info and Archive pages at `http://members.tripod.com/steganography/stego.html`, where he maintains a huge collection of information, links to software, and much more. Many steganography packages are either inexpensive shareware or free.

Much more sophisticated methods are possible and steganographic tools have been incorporated into many professional graphics and audio editing and creation environments. Adobe Photoshop, for example, allows you to add robust digital watermarks to your finished artwork from a menu selection using the Digimarc steganographic product. Figure 16.6 shows an exaggerated and greatly enlarged view of what happens when you add a watermark. The base image was a plain white screen, so that the alteration would be clear, but the adjustments in each pixel were so tiny that they couldn't be seen without altering the image itself to magnify the very slight variations in brightness into a black and white image with 100% contrast between pure white and anything else.

Figure 16.6
An actual steganographic embedded code fragment viewed with Adobe Photoshop to allow the alterations to be seen.

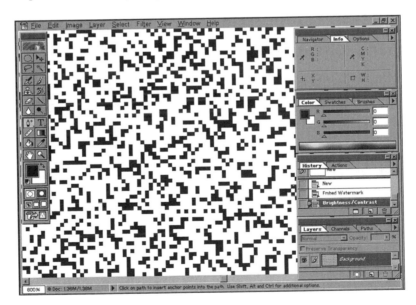

Figure 16.7 shows the splash page of a steganographic product vendor whose enthusiastic claims have outpaced reality slightly, because it's quite obvious that the image can be and has been copied. I assume that there is a digital watermark on the picture and that it may scanned from this page and identified—at least this should be so. The non-copy part of the claim depends entirely on the browser environment and how one goes about copying. In fact, the image on the right doesn't display at all unless scripts are enabled, something many cautious people quite rightly avoid, and the so-called "copy protection" depends on trying to copy the image in a stereotypical way. If one thinks outside the "normal" parameters, copying the image is a trivial task.

Figure 16.7
A steganographic product vendor splash page shows the results of speaking before thinking.

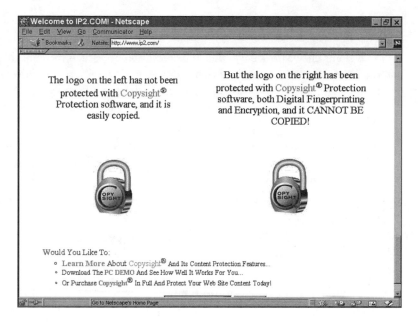

I'm dwelling a little on this image because it illustrates the most important tool in both the cracker's toolkit and the security administrator's first aid bag. Imagination. Going outside the lines is how crackers do things they're not supposed to be able to do. Thinking outside the lines is how an alert security administrator prevents cracker and hacker attacks before the fact and solves the problem quickly when penetrations occur.

Quite frankly, fiddling around with complicated Java scripts to display an image and supposedly prevent copying is a gigantic waste of time and bandwidth, because it's a trivial matter to defeat such schemes. If you can *see* the image, you can capture the image from the display buffer of your machine with a single key press. Why on earth anyone would bother with foolishness like that when, at the very same time, the image is made inaccessible to people who aren't using their browsers in quite the way they are expected to is quite beyond me. Equal parts arrogance, hubris, and thoughtlessness I suspect.

→ For more information about Java and accessibility, **see** "Using JavaScript as a Rendering Engine," **p. 627**.

SSL—SECURE SOCKETS LAYER

Encryption is a large part of the security offered by Netscape's SSL (Secure Sockets Layer), which is supported by most of the major server vendors including Netscape, of course, Microsoft, and Apache. TLS (Transport Layer Security), which is a successor to SSL, is an official standard of the IETF.

The SSL process looks like this:

1. The client sends a request to connect to the secure server like this: `https://servername.domain.com`.

2. The server sends a presigned authenticated and non-reprudiable certificate to the client. Steps 1 and 2 are collectively called the *handshake*.

3. The client checks to see whether the certificate was issued by an authority it trusts. If the client finds a trusted authority, it proceeds to the next step. Otherwise, it either cancels the connection or proceeds insecurely without authentication. Alternatively, the client can ask the user whether the proposed certificate authority should be trusted and the session proceeds appropriately.

4. The client compares the information in the certificate with the information received from the site itself—its domain name and its public key. If the information matches, the site is authenticated.

5. The client tells the server which encryption schemes and types of encryption keys it can use.

6. The server chooses the strongest encryption scheme it shares with the client and tells the client which one will be used.

7. Using the chosen encryption scheme, the client generates a session key (a symmetric encryption key used only for this transaction) and encrypts it using the server's public key.

8. The client sends the encrypted session key to the server.

9. The server receives the encrypted session key and decrypts it using its private key.

10. The client and the server use the same session key to encrypt and decrypt the data they send and receive.

Because unencrypted data is only sent at the very start of the session, during the handshake and encryption negotiation, the method is very secure if the encryption scheme is secure in itself. Unfortunately, DES (56-bit encryption) or worse is a lowest common denominator in many of these systems, so the level of actual security can vary dynamically from server to server and from very good to not very good at all.

Note

Any security scheme that relies on certificates, as this one does, should be aware that certificates are designed to expire at some point. Recently, millions of certificates expired (by design) with the Y2K rollover, so users have had to update their browsers and servers with new certificates to continue using secure transactions.

Not that it's perfect even with strong encryption, however. There is a technique called *hyperlink spoofing* which can be used to attack the transaction, possibly fooling the client into believing that it's communicating directly with the secure server when in fact it's been conned into communicating through a spoofing proxy. The MD5 hash code used to authenticate the messages also has a few security holes, so it's possible to generate replacement messages that hash to the same value.

On the other hand, cracking SSL, even at the 56-bit DES level, is a formidable task. It's not the sort of thing you do during your lunch hour on a whim. It helps to have NSA-sized super-computers at your beck and call. And when the strong RSA algorithms, which permit much higher levels of encryption are used, it's currently impossible. The bit length of encryption schemes is a sort of shorthand way of describing how complex the transformation is by describing the length of the key used to create the cipher text. Cryptographically, this is not a true measure of safety but is sufficient for rough measures, assuming that the cryptanalysts have been doing their jobs.

Tip from

Words to weave by

> The minimum key length required for safety is generally agreed to be on the close order of 128 bits, but there are cynics who believe that 256 bit codes or even more are needed to ensure that this year's big secret doesn't become next year's old news. Science marches on, eh?

As computer power increases, the minimum length of the key required for full security goes up without limit.

HASHING

Hash functions are methods of checking the validity or even identity of a document or mathematical operation. The most familiar is the operation of "casting out nines," which you may have used in school to check whether you added a column of numbers correctly. This particular hash function is basically modulus arithmetic and throws away quite a bit of information about the individual numbers but identifies many common calculation errors.

As hash functions have improved, the amount of data they retain has increased, but they all work by throwing away data in some algorithmic fashion, retaining some sort of overall "fingerprint" of the original data that can be useful in many ways.

One type of hash function is used to check that a data stream hasn't become corrupted in some way. When used to check on the validity of a data stream, the hash value is sometimes called a CRC, or cyclic redundancy check. CRC's work by computing a value on-the-fly based on the values of each character transmitted. At the end of the transmission, the computed value is transmitted as well. The receiving process uses the same function as the data arrives and, by comparing the value the originator calculated to the value it arrived at on its own, any simple error in transmission can be identified.

These primitive types of hashing can be deceived if there are a number of errors, some of which cancel out others. So CRC's are sometimes calculated in several manners, each vulnerable or strong in different ways, so fewer mistakes slip through the net.

Checking a document to ensure that it hasn't been changed is a simple variation on the CRC scheme but with a larger number of more complex hash methods used to ensure that any change to the document is reflected in a different hash value. So although a simple CRC might be one or two bytes in length, allowing many possible transmissions to collapse into a single value, a hash identifying a document as unchanged must be far larger, enough so that every document in the world has a different hash value.

MD5, for example, generates a message digest of 32 hexadecimal digits, or 128 bits in length, roughly 3×10^{38}. This is a large enough number that Scrooge McDuck didn't have that much money. That's more possible documents than there are grains of sand on all the beaches of the world.

The successor to MD5, Secure Hash Algorithm (SHA), generates an 160-bit number, which is quite a bit more secure than MD5.

P3P

P3P is a small part of the entire security puzzle, and we covered it in some detail in Chapter 14, but it's worth reiterating here: Your personal data is a big part of what security is all about. Most people don't keep nuclear secrets lying about on their home computers. Their personal information is all they have worth stealing. But it *is* worth stealing. In fact, it's probably being surreptitiously purloined every time you go online.

TROUBLESHOOTING SECURITY PROBLEMS

AN EXAMPLE OF COMPUTER SECURITY

Let's suppose your computer has been hacked. Either some sort of damage has been done, a taunting message has been left on the console, or you inspect your logs and discover an unauthorized root or administrator login.

First, disconnect your system from the Net. Do this immediately with a fail-safe method, like removing the Ethernet cable from the back of the machine. It's quite possible that the cracker is still on your system or may reconnect or do further damage while you're trying to diagnose and fix your machine. So, give yourself a break from urgency by creating a little breathing space.

Now it's time to start looking about for what happened. This can be surprisingly difficult. One of the first items to be replaced on systems that have been successfully hacked is an assortment of modified versions of the very system tools you'll need to track down potential problems. If there are multiple computers on the network, it pays to monitor and log network traffic from all systems. Analysis of network traffic at or about the time of the break-in may help track down the actual source of the attacks.

On UNIX systems, the `ls` and `ps` commands, as well as many other system tools, are often replaced with versions that have a built-in blind spot for the hacker's files and processes. On Windows systems, the `dir` command and some Windows utilities can be similarly altered. A good virus detection program can often spot those files that have been altered if you take the time to have it make a signature hash of every file on an uncompromised system, but you have to keep the signature file in a safe place, offline, or it may be compromised as well.

So your first step should be to haul out your handy cracker response kit, which has in it safe copies of important files and utilities. For UNIX, at a minimum you should keep `find`, `ps`, `ls`, `cp`, `rm`, `mv`, `gdb`, `nm`, `strings`, `file`, `strip` (gnu)`tar`, `zip`, `grep`, `less` or `more`, your favorite editor, your favorite shell program, your virus detection program and data files, and `mount`. Of course, you'll want secure copies of your distribution and backup media as well, because you may have to repair damage or restore files.

On most Windows machines, you'll primarily want DOS level tools because they are stand-alone programs that you can use in a controlled way. Trying to track down changed files using a Windows session when you can't trust any of the many files that make up the Windows runtime environment is an exercise in futility. You'll need a boot disk, `dir`, `find`, `attrib`, `chkdsk`, an editor (hopefully better than edit), your virus scanner emergency boot disk, the Windows distribution media on CD-ROM, and any other tools that might help. With Windows, you may have to either restore everything from backup, with little assurance that the backup is truly clean, or reinstall everything from its distribution media and carefully restore data files only from the backup.

WINDOWS SYSTEM SECURITY TOOLS

Windows is a particular target for crackers because most of the machines in the world run some version of Windows right now and its weaknesses are widely known. Although the older versions of Windows were relatively insecure and fairly easy to break into, with the development of Windows NT and the recent release of Windows 2000, which is partially based on Windows NT, the security picture has gotten much brighter for Windows users.

The wide range of tools available to the UNIX systems administrator will not be available under either DOS or Windows unless you've purchased a package of add-on tools from a company such as Mortice Kern Systems at `http://www.mks.com/`. Mortice Kern Systems duplicates many UNIX tools, even an X-Windows work-alike that runs under Windows NT, 98, and 2000. Their standard MKS Toolkit contains a large bit of the standard UNIX interface, whereas the MKS Toolkit Select adds the graphical tools including an X Windows server.

Although these tools may not be completely familiar or accessible to administrators who are only used to a Windows environment, the power of the UNIX commands may lead some to consider expanding their horizons.

In both cases, careful inspection of file sizes and listings of all directories on the execution path may reveal programs that shouldn't be there. Especially look for oddities, such as a file or directory named "..." or programs whose sizes have changed. If possible, console logs should be habitually directed to a hardcopy printer via a fork, because the first action of crackers who successfully gain root or administrative access is often to rewrite console and system logs to eliminate as many traces of their attack as they can.

It's not uncommon for successful crackers to leave some sort of signature hidden somewhere on your machine, or for debugging or other information in an executable to reveal clues as to the cracker's identity. It's a good idea to ferret out and save all new or changed files for later inspection and possible prosecution. The files changed and the manner in which the attack was carried out are all very important to know so that you can protect your system against further attacks of this nature. After the system has been compromised, it's very likely that it will be attacked again.

Before you shut down the system, you should look carefully at running processes. It's common to install a sniffer program which attempts to monitor and capture login attempts in hopes of collecting even more passwords. All passwords should be immediately expired. You don't know whether any login attempts have already been captured, and you can't depend on users to change a cherished password on their own.

It may even be appropriate to issue new passwords and communicate them to users via a secure channel. Hardcopy letters and express delivery packages, for instance, are rather difficult to intercept and are entirely suitable for communicating keys and passwords. Any system-level login or rarely used login should definitely receive this treatment, and any guest logins should be carefully inspected to make sure their rights and user groups haven't been altered. In fact, all logins should be regularly checked for mysterious increases in system authority.

CHAPTER 17

USING SERVER-SIDE FACILTIES—JAVA

In this chapter

WHY JAVA ON THE SERVER IS SO USEFUL

Java is a simple language that many people find easier to learn than C++ or Perl. The class library that accompanies all Java compilers includes classes handling network communication, image manipulation, database access, multi-threading, and much more. This makes coding common server tasks go more simply—and more quickly.

Java has gained a lot of attention as a cross-platform language. At first glance, you might think that being cross-platform is less of an advantage for server-side programming. After all, you know what platform your server is using, unlike all those client browsers that might come to your Web site. But choosing a cross-platform server solution means that you never worry about moving your Web site to another platform. Often, Web sites do move from one platform to another for a variety of reasons, such as scalability, costs, or corporate policy. It is nice to know that if an external decision forces you to switch servers, your Java code doesn't have to be recompiled.

For many developers, the reason to use Java on the server is so you can develop servlets. These are a handy replacement for CGI that scale far better than CGI, especially Perl CGI. There is more discussion of servlets later in this chapter.

Java is an object-oriented language, of course, and XML and objects seem to work beautifully together. An object that can construct itself from a stream of XML—or that can emit a stream of XML that describes its contents—fits nicely into a server-side solution written in Java. Such code almost writes itself, as is seen in the case studies in this chapter.

And finally, one of the things that makes writing Java programs for XML attractive is that you can get very nice parsers—efficient, supporting both SAX and DOM, reasonably documented—free. In this chapter, you work with XML4J, a product of the IBM AlphaWorks project, released as open source.

SETTING UP YOUR WEB SERVER AND RELATED SOFTWARE

If you're going to write Java programs that run on the server, the first thing you're going to need is a server. All told, you need to install and configure

A Web server—either Microsoft's Personal Web Server or IIS, or Sun's Java Web Server.

The Java Development Kit—version 1.1.8 or higher.

A reference implementation of the Java Server Web Development Kit, version 1.01.

A Java XML parser—XML4J from IBM.

Some sort of database drivers if you plan to do database work.

WEB SERVER SOFTWARE

You can use any Web server software you like and happen to have installed, of course, but this chapter only presents configuration instructions for some very popular choices. You should be able to extrapolate from these to the server you are using. You should also have the JDK installed, or some alternative Java compiler as long as you're sure it produces JDK-only code.

Many NT and Windows 9x users have access to Microsoft's Internet Information Server (IIS.) If you don't, you can download the Microsoft Personal Web Server (PWS) from `http://www.microsoft.com/Windows/ie/pws/default.htm` and use it for the samples in this chapter. (The Personal Web Server is part of the poorly named NT Option Pack, but works on Windows 95 and Windows 98 as well as Windows NT. You do not have to download the entire Option Pack if you only want the Personal Web Server.) Follow the installation instructions provided by Microsoft, with one exception. By default, the Personal Web Server setup does not install the Internet Service Manager, which you use to make your Java CGI programs execute properly. IIS and PWS are both configured in the same way, and this chapter shows how to configure them to use Java and XML on the server.

Figure 17.1 shows the screen on which you select the portion of the Option Pack you want to install. Highlight Personal Web Server and click Show Subcomponents. This brings up the dialog box shown in Figure 17.2. On this dialog, ensure that Internet Service Manager is selected. Proceed with the installation. If you've already installed Personal Web Server without the Internet Service Manager, choose Start, Programs, Windows NT Option 4.0 Pack, Windows NT Option 4.0 Pack Setup, then install the Internet Service Manager.

PART
III

CH
17

Figure 17.1
When installing the NT Option pack, you need a subcomponent that's not included in the default installation.

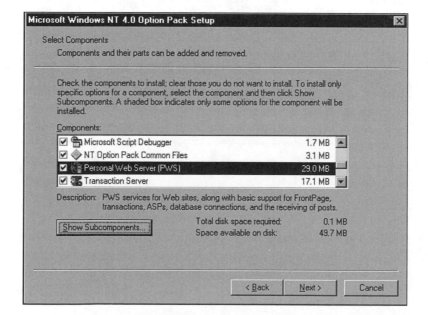

Figure 17.2
Ensure that the
Internet Service
Manager is installed
when installing the
Personal Web Server.

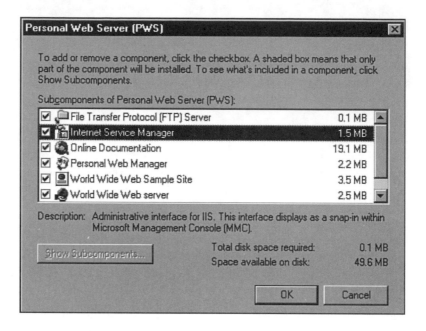

Neither IIS nor the PWS supports Java servlets, so you might prefer to use the Java Web Server instead. The Java Web Server runs on NT, Windows 9x, UNIX, and any other Java-supporting platform. You can download a time-limited trial copy at http://www.sun.com/software/jwebserver/index.html and use it for the samples in this chapter. Follow the installation instructions provided by Sun. This chapter assumes you're working with version 2.0 of the Java Web Server.

Java Web Server Will Be Replaced by iPlanet

As a result of the alliance between Sun and AOL (which owns Netscape,) Sun and Netscape will no longer make separate Web servers. Instead, the Java Web Server and the Netscape Enterprise Server will be replaced by the iPlanet Web Server, Enterprise Edition.

iPlanet supports servlets and a trial version is available. For more information, see http://www.iplanet.com/products/infrastructure/web_servers/.

If you have no Web server installed at all and don't want to test serving out ordinary HTML pages, you can use the tiny Web server that's included in the JWSDK. Read more about that in the section in this chapter on installing the JWSDK.

INSTALLING XML4J—A JAVA XML PARSER

IBM makes its XML4J Java XML parser available as part of its AlphaWorks project. You can download the parser from http://www.alphaworks.ibm.com/tech/xml4j without charge, even if you plan to use it as part of a commercial application. Download XML4J version

3.0.1 (or a slightly later version) to use in this chapter. You are asked to fill in a form to get an "Evaluation License" for the parser. If you plan to incorporate the parser into a commercial product, simply download the commercial license.

After downloading XML4J, install it according to the instructions in readme.html. Be sure to add xml4j.jar to your classpath.

INSTALLING THE JAVA WEB SERVER DEVELOPMENT KIT

The Java Web Server Development Kit is used to write servlets. It's a set of classes that complement the class library in the JDK and some utilities. There have been a number of releases recently, and more scheduled already. This chapter's case studies use version 1.01 of the JSWDK, which implements version 2.1 of the servlet API.

Tip from

Words to weave by

Many developers become confused with the number of similarly named tools available from Sun for Java work. Here's a quick reference:

- JSDK—The Java Servlet Development Kit is a previous name for what is now the JWSDK.
- JWSDK—The Java Web Server Development Kit is a class library and related tools for developing both servlets and Java Server Pages.
- JDK—The Java Development Kit is the basic class library and compiler for Java.

You'll be using both the JDK and the JWSDK to develop servlets.

Download the JWSDK 1.01 from http://java.sun.com/products/jsp/download.html and follow the instructions there for installing it. Make sure you set your path as explained in the file readme.html and that you add the servlets.jar file to your classpath. The instructions in this chapter assume that you do not change the configuration in webserver.xml from the defaults.

That's right, the configuration file for the mini Web server that comes with the JWSDK is an XML file. You're starting to see the prevalence (and usefulness) of XML in the industry.

Java Web Server Development Kit Will Be Replaced by Tomcat

Sun has announced that it will no longer provide reference implementations for the Servlet API. It will retain control of the API, but code that actually implements the API will be written by others. Sun is supporting Apache's Tomcat project and has designated Tomcat as the official reference implementation for version 2.2 of the Servlets specification and version 1.1 of the Java Server Pages specification.

Tomcat is in beta at this writing, so the servlets in this chapter are written with the JWSDK for version 2.1 of the servlet API. You can learn more about the roles of Apache and Sun in the evolution of servlets and JSP at http://java.sun.com/products/jsp/tomcat/. To follow the Tomcat project or download a beta, start at http://jakarta.apache.org/tomcat/index.html.

A SIMPLE CGI PROGRAM THAT EMITS XML

CGI programs are simple to write and to execute from anywhere. They are typically invoked by the Web server when a user submits a form. Although they have some disadvantages that are discussed in the next sections, they are a nice way to start using XML on the server.

EXECUTING A JAVA CGI WITH A PERL WRAPPER

The browser sends requests for CGI programs in a way that looks very similar to requests for plain HTML pages. You can configure the Web server (usually by checking the file extension of the request) so the server knows it should execute a Java application rather than sending back a file. However, there are some issues with environment variables: the information the Web server gets from the browser is put into environment variables, and the Java runner doesn't pass these on to your Java application when it executes. For this reason, and because some developers can't configure their Web server to execute Java directly, it's most convenient to write a simple Perl wrapper for your Java application that sets the variables using Java's -D option and executes the application. Listing 17.1 shows one that works nicely.

LISTING 17.1 A PERL WRAPPER FOR A JAVA CGI APPLICATION

```
#print "Content-type: text/html\n\n";

$ARGV[0] =~ /.*[\\\/](.*?)\..*$/;
$class = $1;

#print "argv is $ARGV[0] - $class\n";

print `java -classpath .;c:/jdk1.1.6/lib/classes.zip;$ENV{'CLASSPATH'}
\"-DSERVER_SOFTWARE=$ENV{'SERVER_SOFTWARE'}\"
\"-DSERVER_NAME=$ENV{'SERVER_NAME'}\"
\"-DGATEWAY_INTERFACE=$ENV{'GATEWAY_INTERFACE'}\"
\"-DSERVER_PROTOCOL=$ENV{'SERVER_PROTOCOL'}\"
\"-DSERVER_PORT=$ENV{'SERVER_PORT'}\"
\"-DREQUEST_METHOD=$ENV{'REQUEST_METHOD'}\"
\"-DPATH_INFO=$ENV{'PATH_INFO'}\"
\"-DPATH_TRANSLATED=$ENV{'PATH_TRANSLATED'}\"
\"-DSCRIPT_NAME=$ENV{'SCRIPT_NAME'}\"
\"-DQUERY_STRING=$ENV{'QUERY_STRING'}\"
\"-DREMOTE_HOST=$ENV{'REMOTE_HOST'}\"
\"-DREMOTE_ADDR=$ENV{'REMOTE_ADDR'}\"
\"-DAUTH_TYPE=$ENV{'AUTH_TYPE'}\"
\"-DREMOTE_USER=$ENV{'REMOTE_USER'}\"
\"-DREMOTE_IDENT=$ENV{'REMOTE_IDENT'}\"
\"-DCONTENT_TYPE=$ENV{'CONTENT_TYPE'}\"
\"-DCONTENT_LENGTH=$ENV{'CONTENT_LENGTH'}\"
\"-DHTTP_ACCEPT=$ENV{'HTTP_ACCEPT'}\"
\"-DHTTP_USER_AGENT=$ENV{'HTTP_USER_AGENT'}\"
\"-DHTTP_REFERER=$ENV{'HTTP_REFERER'}\"
$class`;
```

Tip from  LeeAnne.com Words to weave by	The variables named in this code (SERVER_SOFTWARE, SERVER_NAME, and so on) are all CGI Environment variables, generally accessible from CGI scripts, servlets, and other server-side code that is run at the request of the Web server. If you're not familiar with these particular environment variables, relax: they aren't used in this chapter, which is about XML, not CGI. If you're curious, you can see just what each variable means at http://hoohoo.ncsa.uiuc.edu/cgi/env.html.

The nice thing about this wrapper is that it works for every Java class you might write. You can use this on Web servers that associate file extensions such as .cgi or .class with specific actions. IIS and PWS both work this way. On other servers you might have to write a wrapper for each Java CGI program and hard-code the name of the Java class into the Perl wrapper. These are the lines that make this wrapper generic:

```
$ARGV[0] =~ /.*[\\\/](.*?)\..*$/;
$class = $1;
```

If your Perl regular expressions are a little rusty, here's a translation of those lines. It works with the argument that was passed to the Perl wrapper, and that's going to be a full path to your Java class. It divides that string into three parts: everything up to the last / or \ character, the name of your class, and everything after the last . character. Here are the parts of the regular expression:

> The first .* means "everything up to".
>
> The [\\\/] means "either a \ or a /" (the \ is an escape character because / would normally end the regular expression. \/ means "/" and \\ means "\".
>
> The () in (.*?) instruct Perl to drop whatever matches this part of the expression into $1.
>
> The \..*? means a "." and then anything else to the end of the line.

So if the argument was

```
C:\inetpub\wwwroot\cgi-bin\HelloWorld.class
```

the Perl you've seen would leave HelloWorld in the $1 variable. This gets saved in $class ($1 is an easily overwritten variable) and used on the very last line of the wrapper. Everything else in this wrapper is one very long line spliced together with \ characters. It runs your Java class and passes all the CGI environment variables along in case you need them.

Notice also that this wrapper sets the classpath to the current folder (.), the JDK libraries, and whatever else is already on the classpath.

CONFIGURING THE WEB SERVER

To use this wrapper, first put a copy of it somewhere useful, such as the cgi-bin folder for your Web server. Then configure your Web server to call it whenever a .class resource is requested. For both IIS and PWS, follow these instructions:

PART
III

CH
17

1. Bring up the Microsoft Management Console (see Figure 17.3) by choosing Start, Programs, Windows NT 4.0 Option Pack, Microsoft Personal Web Server (or Microsoft Internet Information Server), Internet Service Manager.

Figure 17.3
Configure IIS or PWS with the Microsoft Management Console.

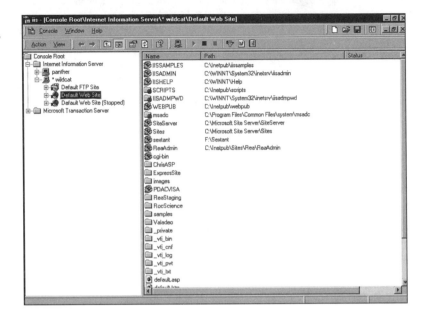

2. Right-click the Default Web Site and choose Properties. Select the Home Directory tab (see Figure 17.4.)

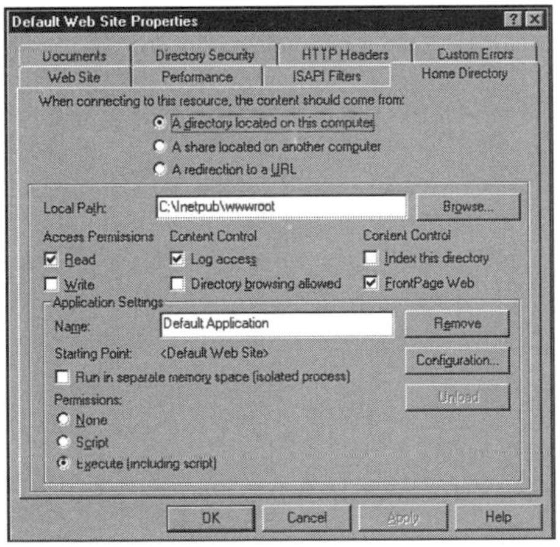

Figure 17.4
The Home Directory tab leads to the file configuration options.

3. Click the Configuration button in the bottom half of the screen. The Application Configuration dialog box appears. Click Add.

4. The Add/Edit Application Extension Mapping dialog appears (see Figure 17.5.) In the Executable box, enter the full path to Perl, followed by the path to the Perl wrapper for Java CGI shown earlier, followed by the string %s %s. For example, on one system, the executable line might read:

```
d:\Perl\5.00502\bin\MSWin32-x86-object\Perl.exe c:\inetpub\java.pl %s %s
```

Figure 17.5
Add a mapping for the .class extension.

5. In the Extension box fill in .class, and in the Method Exclusions box fill in PUT, DELETE. This provides a little extra security, allowing users to execute code on your server but not to upload or remove files.

6. Choose OK on all the dialogs until you return to the configuration console.

It's a good idea to test that your wrapper and your Web server configuration work at this point. Find (or quickly code) a good old Hello World Java application:

```java
class HelloWorld
{
    public static void main(String[] args)
    {
        System.out.println("Content-Type: text/html\n");
        System.out.println("Hello from CGI!");
    }
}
```

Compile this application and copy the .class file to the root of your Web server, probably c:\inetpub\wwwroot. Now, making sure your Web server is started, load it into a browser with a URL such as http://localhost/HelloWorld.class. (If you copy it to somewhere other than the root, adjust this URL accordingly.) You should see something similar to Figure 17.6, proving that the Web server used CGI to call the Perl wrapper, which ran the Java class, which wrote a simple greeting, and that the greeting made it back through the Perl wrapper and Web server to the Web browser. Do not try to code XML CGI in Java until you have the simple Hello World CGI working properly.

PART

III

CH

17

Figure 17.6
Test a simple CGI
written in Java before
moving on to more
complex work.

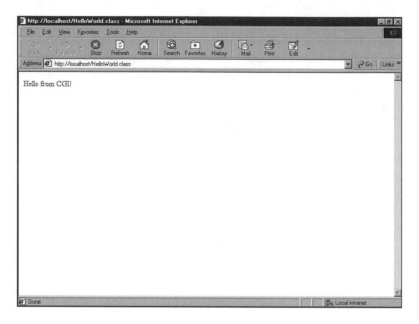

WRITING THE HTML THAT CALLS THE CGI

A typical CGI program is run as the result of the user submitting an HTML form. There are two possible ways a form can be submitted: with an ACTION of GET or of POST. Many CGI programs with just a few parameters use GET, in which case a URL is sent to the Web browser with the parameters embedded in an ordinary URL. If you plan to send many parameters, or one quite long parameter, such as a string of XML, it's better to use the POST method to submit your form. GET ACTION is unsuitable for long strings of data as it truncates after an indeterminate number of characters.

In the sample CGI program for this chapter, the user is prompted to enter a short string of XML that looks something like this:

```
<name>kate</name>
```

A name is extracted from that XML, and slightly different XML is sent back. Of course in a real application the XML would not be typed by the user. It would be generated by some sort of intelligence on the client side, even something as simple as a little JavaScript that wrapped start and end tags around the strings the user entered into a form. Later in this chapter is an applet that provides a more intelligent user interface.

Here is some HTML that produces a form that executes a Java CGI program called ParseXML:

```
<HTML>
<HEAD><TITLE>Using XML</TITLE></HEAD>
<BODY>
<H1>XML from a form and CGI</H1>
<FORM ACTION="ParseXML.class" METHOD=POST>
```

```
Enter some XML in the form &lt;name&gt;Your Name&lt;/name&gt;:
<BR>
<INPUT TYPE=text NAME=XML>
<INPUT TYPE=submit NAME=submit VALUE="Process Request">
</FORM>
</BODY>
</HTML>
```

Notice that the input field on this form has NAME=XML. This name is used when extracting the form fields in the CGI application.

This form can be seen in Figure 17.7, displayed in IE 5. It's very simple—just an input box and a submit button.

Figure 17.7
The form that collects parameters for the CGI application is very simple.

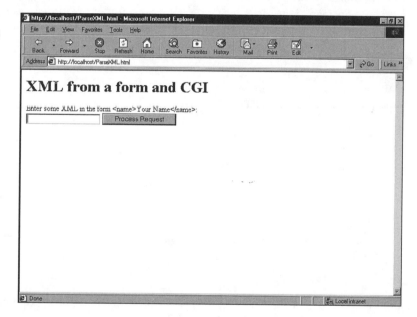

WRITING THE CGI CODE

All CGI programs have the same basic structure:

Write out the content type.

Extract the GET or POST parameters.

Use the parameters to do some processing.

Write some output as a result of the processing.

CONTENT TYPE

The content type is important. For most CGI programs it is text/html, but because this program is going to emit XML, text/plain or text/xml is a better choice. If you would like to write out simple debugging information as you develop, using text/plain eliminates annoying error messages from IE5 if your debugging output doesn't result in well-formed XML. (The consequences of your content type are discussed in more detail in the servlets section of this chapter.)

So the first line of the `main()` method of the `ParseXML` class is

```
System.out.println("Content-Type: text/plain\n");
```

EXTRACTING PARAMETERS

Because the HMTL that called this program specifies `METHOD=POST`, the parameters (the string the user typed into the input text box in this case) are available on standard input. The environment variable `CONTENT_LENGTH`, which was passed along by the Perl wrapper, tells you how many bytes are waiting there for you. You can read them as an array of bytes and convert them to a Java string:

```
String cl = System.getProperty("CONTENT_LENGTH");
System.out.println("got property");
if (cl != null && cl != "")
{
    int length = Integer.parseInt(cl);
    if (length > 0)
    {
        try
        {
            byte x[] = new byte[length];
            System.in.read(x);
            String encodedcontent = new String(x);
        }
        catch (Exception e)
        {
         System.out.println("<br>Error reading and parsing:" + e.toString());
        }
    }
}
```

You might think that the next step is to parse that string, `encodedcontent`. But it's in no state to be parsed. If you opened the HTML shown earlier in a browser and typed `<name>Kate</name>` into the text box, then pressed the Process Request button, the `encodedcontent` variable would contain

```
XML=%3Cname%3EKate%3C%2Fname%3E&submit=Process+Request
```

The string you typed has been URL encoded to hide characters such as < and > from the Web server. To decode it, I wrote a little method based on a utility that comes with the servlet development package discussed later in this chapter.

LISTING 17.2   REVERSING URL ENCODING

```
static private String URLDecode(String s)
    {
      StringBuffer sb = new StringBuffer();
      sb.setLength(0);
```

```
for (int i = 0; i < s.length(); i++)
{
   char c = s.charAt(i);
   switch (c)
   {
      case '+':
         sb.append(' ');
         break;
      case '%':
         try
         {
             sb.append((char) Integer.parseInt(s.substring(i+1, i+3),16));
             i += 2;
         }
         catch (NumberFormatException e)
         {
             throw new IllegalArgumentException();
         }
         catch (StringIndexOutOfBoundsException e)
         {
            String rest  = s.substring(i);
            sb.append(rest);
            if (rest.length()==2)
            i++;
         }

            break;
      default:
         sb.append(c);
         break;
   }
}
return sb.toString();
}
```

Using this method to decode the content is simple:

```
String content = URLDecode(encodedcontent);
```

Assuming the same XML was typed in the text box as before, the content string now holds

```
XML=<name>Kate</name>&submit=Process Request
```

The task that remains is to extract the XML from this, ignoring the information about which button on the form was clicked. Here's a completely non-general approach:

```
int start = content.indexOf("XML=")+4;
int end = content.indexOf("&",start);
xml= content.substring(start,end);
```

In a real CGI application, you would probably use a hash table or some similar structure, parse all the content once, and then extract the parameters you wanted. But as you might be realizing by now, not a lot of real CGI applications are written in Java. This quickie substring approach works for the purposes of this chapter.

USING THE PARAMETERS

To parse the string of XML, create a parser and pass it a `StringReader` made from the string:

```
DOMParser p = new DOMParser();
p.parse(new InputSource(new StringReader(xml)));
Document in = p.getDocument();
```

This code uses a DOM parser—you would do something similar to set up a SAX parser instead. The sample CGI program is expecting to receive a `<name>` element. Here is the code that finds that element and gets the value of its text node:

```
NodeList nodes = in.getElementsByTagName("name");
if(nodes.getLength() > 0)
{
    String submittedname = nodes.item(0).getChildNodes().item(0).getNodeValue();
}
```

Tip from

LeeAnne.com
Words to weave by

If you're not comfortable with this line of DOM code, you might want to re-read Chapter 10, "DOM—The Document Object Model."

The sample CGI program is expected to emit XML that looks something like this:

```
<person>
  <name>
    <first>Kate</first>
    <last>Gregory</last>
  </name>
</person>
```

In a real application, the emitted HTML would be based on values found in a database or calculated from the other input in some way. In this sample application, simple hardcoded XML is enough to demonstrate the techniques. To add a little excitement, one first name gets special treatment:

```
String lastname = "";
if (submittedname.equals("Kate")) lastname = "Gregory";
```

Here's the simple Java code that creates the XML to write out:

```
TXDocument out = new TXDocument();

Element person = out.createElement("person");
out.appendChild(person);

Element name = out.createElement("name");
person.appendChild(name);

Element first = out.createElement("first");
name.appendChild(first);
first.appendChild(out.createTextNode(submittedname));

Element last = out.createElement("last");
name.appendChild(last);
```

```
String lastname = "";
if (submittedname.equals("Kate")) lastname = "Gregory";

last.appendChild(out.createTextNode(lastname));
out.printWithFormat(System.out);
```

This code uses a `TXDocument` because the `printWithFormat()` method call is a very handy way to write out a nicely formatted block of XML. DOM does not provide a method for writing out an entire tree. XML4J comes with a sample called `DOMWriter`, but it writes to `System.out` rather than to the writer of your choice. Using `TXDocument` (which is not in every parser library) makes this a single method call.

PROBLEMS WITH CGI

Almost no one actually writes Java CGI applications. As you've seen, you need to use a Perl wrapper to pass environment variables to your CGI. You also need to decode and extract your parameters yourself. These problems are annoying while you write your first Java CGI, but after that, you can rely on a library of your own work to simplify the tasks.

A bigger problem with CGI is that it doesn't scale well. A CGI approach that involves Perl (and even this simple Java example involves a Perl wrapper) scales even more poorly. To understand why, consider what happens when two or more users are submitting the same form (or in some other manner running the same CGI resource) at the same time.

The Web server starts one entire copy of the CGI program for each user's request. Each program has its own environment variables and memory space. If Perl is involved, each has its own copy of the Perl interpreter running as well. This represents a huge drain on resources. Although a server can easily handle two (or even 10) simultaneous requests for the same CGI resource, there is an unbearable load if there are hundreds or thousands of requests to be met. Also, even with only a handful of requests, there is a delay for the enduser as the CGI application and associated interpreters are started.

A far more efficient (and scalable) approach would be to have a process running all the time, and for each request that comes in to be handled by a new thread within that process. The endusers see quicker responses, and the server uses far less memory and execution time. This is precisely how servlets work.

A SERVLET APPROACH

If you're familiar with applets and with CGI, writing servlets is a snap. (If you're not familiar with CGI, learning servlets is much easier than learning CGI, especially if you intend to work in Java. Doing CGI in Java is actually quite difficult, as you've seen.)

To write a servlet, you write a class that extends a library class called `javax.servlet.http.HttpServlet`. (This class is part of the supplemental class library that comes with the Java Web Server Development Kit.) This is very much like the way an applet is a class that extends `java.applet.Applet`.

When writing an applet, you override methods from the super class, such as paint(). When writing a servlet, you override doGet() and doPost(). These are the methods that are called whenever a browser sends a GET or POST method to the Web server for a servlet. A request that comes from a link, or from the user typing the URL to a servlet, is always a GET request. A request as a result of submitting a form might be GET or POST, according to the METHOD attribute on the <FORM> tag in the HTML.

STRUCTURE OF A SERVLET

A typical servlet looks like this:

```
import javax.servlet.*;
import javax.servlet.http.*;
public class SampleServlet extends HttpServlet
{
  public void doGet(HttpServletRequest req, HttpServletResponse res)
              throws ServletException, IOException
  {
     // write form HTML to res
  }
public void doPost(HttpServletRequest req, HttpServletResponse res)
              throws ServletException, IOException
  {
      // get form fields from req, write output HTML to res
  }
}
```

You follow these steps to develop a servlet:

1. Code the servlet. Because it is a public class, ensure the filename matches the classname.

2. Compile the servlet.

3. Copy the .class file to the folder where the Web server looks for servlets. By default, the Java Web Server looks in the folder servlets under the installation folder.

4. Enter the URL to the servlet into a browser. This tests your doGet() method. For example, if your servlet is called SampleServlet and you have copied it to the folder where Java Web Server looks for servlets, the URL is http://localhost:8080/servlet/SampleServlet.

Tip from

Words to weave by

The string servlet in the URL is mapped to the folder servlets under the installation directory. Don't type servlets in the URL.

5. If your doGet() method emits a form, fill out the fields and submit the form. This tests your doPost() method.

EMITTING A SIMPLE FORM

In the sample servlet for this chapter, the user is prompted to enter a short string of XML that looks something like this:

```
<name>kate</name>
```

A name is extracted from that XML, and slightly different XML is sent back. Here is the code for a doGet() method that emits the form:

```
public void doGet(HttpServletRequest req, HttpServletResponse res)
                 throws ServletException, IOException
  {
    res.setContentType("text/html");
    PrintWriter out = res.getWriter();
    out.println("<HTML><HEAD><TITLE>Using XML</TITLE></HEAD>");
    out.println("<BODY><H1>XML from a form</H1>");
    String Url = req.getServletPath();
    out.println("<FORM METHOD=\"POST\" ACTION=\"" + Url + "\">");
    out.println("Enter some XML in the form &lt;name&gt;Your Name&lt;/name&gt;:");
    out.println("<br> <INPUT TYPE=\"TEXT\" NAME=\"XML\" size=\"50\"><BR>");
    out.println("<INPUT TYPE=submit VALUE=\"Process Request\">");
    out.println("</FORM></BODY></HTML>");
    out.close();
  }
```

This code sets the content type for the emitted document to HTML text, gets a PrintWriter that's associated with the emitted document, and then writes HTML to it. By asking the request object for the path to this servlet, the code ensures that the same servlet class handles the POST request as handled this GET request. Hard-coding your servlet name in the ACTION field leads to hard-to-maintain code and hard-to-catch bugs the first time you copy old code into a new project.

Notice that the input field on this form has NAME=XML. This name is used when extracting the form fields in the doPost() method.

PROCESSING THE FORM

There are two parts to processing a form. One is extracting the fields from the form and the other is doing something with those fields. In the sample servlet, there's only one field of interest. It can be extracted like this:

```
String xml;

String[] vals = req.getParameterValues("XML");
if (vals != null)
{
   xml = vals[0];
}
```

Notice how the string passed to getParameterValues(), "XML", is the name of the INPUT tag in the FORM tag emitted by doGet().

To parse the string, create a parser and pass it a StringReader made from this string:

```
DOMParser p = new DOMParser();
p.parse(new InputSource(new StringReader(xml)));
Document in = p.getDocument();
```

This code is just like the Java in the CGI application shown earlier. So is the code that finds that element and gets the value of its text node:

```
NodeList nodes = in.getElementsByTagName("name");
if(nodes.getLength() > 0)
{
    String submittedname = nodes.item(0).getChildNodes().item(0).getNodeValue();
}
```

The sample servlet is expected to emit the same XML as the CGI sample. It looks something like this:

```
<person>
  <name>
    <first>Kate</first>
    <last>Gregory</last>
  </name>
</person>
```

As mentioned earlier, in a real application, the emitted HTML would be based on values found in a database or calculated from the other input in some way.

Here's the simple Java code that creates the XML to write out:

```
TXDocument out = new TXDocument();

Element person = out.createElement("person");
out.appendChild(person);

Element name = out.createElement("name");
person.appendChild(name);

Element first = out.createElement("first");
name.appendChild(first);
first.appendChild(out.createTextNode(submittedname));

Element last = out.createElement("last");
name.appendChild(last);
String lastname = "";
if (submittedname.equals("Kate")) lastname = "Gregory";

last.appendChild(out.createTextNode(lastname));
out.printWithFormat(pw);
```

This code uses a TXDocument, as the CGI code did, and for the same reasons.

CONTENT TYPE IS IMPORTANT

Figure 17.8 shows the output from this servlet in IE5.

If you've been loading XML into IE 5, you know that it usually is displayed in a tree format. The reason it looks so boring in Figure 17.6 is that the content type was set to text/plain. Changing the content type to text/xml produces the appearance you see in Figure 17.9. IE formats the tags and their content differently, and enables you to expand and collapse tags easily and quickly.

Figure 17.8
The sample servlet in this chapter emits XML. Here IE 5 treats it as plain text.

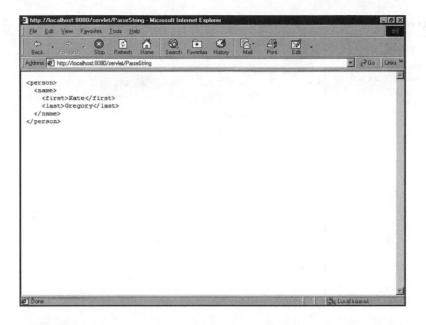

Figure 17.9
When IE 5 knows the servlet output is XML, you get a more useful tree display.

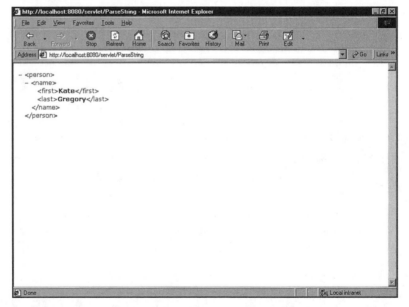

The doGet() method in this servlet set the content type to text/html. Figure 17.10 shows the output in IE 5, along with the View Source window. Do you see what happened? The browser ignored all the tags, under the assumption they were very strange HTML. Always remember to set your content type to the proper value.

Figure 17.10
When IE 5 thinks the servlet output is HTML, all the tags disappear. They are still in the source for the page.

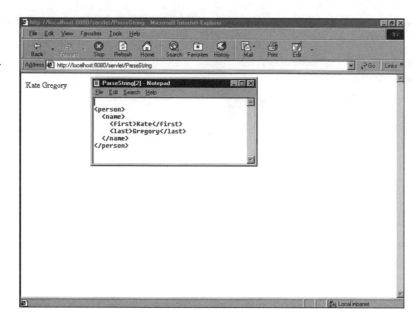

XML displayed in a browser is not a pretty sight. It's a nice way to test that your code is emitting the XML that you think it's emitting, but it's hardly a finished product. The following list explains the three things you can do instead of sending raw XML to an unsuspecting browser:

1. You can assume that the browser is IE 5, and add a style sheet reference so the browser renders the XML document well. As you learned in Chapter 14, "Using Next Generation Extensible Style Sheets—XSL," this is not a simple assumption, and XSL or XSLT that works in IE 5 doesn't always work in other contexts.

2. You can use XSL to transform your XML into HTML on the server and send HTML to the browser. So, no matter what browser the enduser is using, your information is properly displayed.

3. You can write an applet or other client-side intelligence that asks for the XML and uses it in some clever manner to show information to the enduser. This requires a browser that supports applets, a safe assumption by now.

TRANSFORMING XML INTO HMTL ON THE SERVER

You can transform XML on the server into HTML that works in any browser. James Clark's XT is a nice product to use for this purpose. You can get a copy from `http://www.jclark.com/xml/xt.html`. Unzip the file into an appropriate directory, and remember to add `xt.jar` to your classpath, which is probably getting to be quite long about now.

In `xt.jar` are a number of useful Java classes for transforming XML into another kind of XML, or into HTML with the help of a style sheet. The changes to the code presented earlier in this chapter are really quite small, especially if you use the DOM flavor of the transformer and take advantage of the fact you have already created a DOM tree.

It's a little easier to work with the XT classes if the DOM output document that is built as output is an instance of `com.sun.xml.tree.XmlDocument` rather than `TXDocument`. The handy `printWithFormat()` method of `TXDocument` can be replaced with the `write()` method of `XmlDocument`. There's no other consequence within the code presented in this chapter of switching to `XmlDocument`. However, the class doesn't come with any of the packages you've download and installed to this point. To get the `XmlDocument` class, download the Java API for XML Parsing package from `http://java.sun.com/xml/download.html`. (You might have to register and log in to get the package.) Extract the classes and add `jaxp.jar` to your classpath.

Assuming you have an `XmlDocument` called `out` and a `PrintWriter` called `pw`, here's how to transform that document using a pre-written style sheet:

```
XmlDocument transformed = new XmlDocument();
new XSLTransformEngine().

createTransform(XmlDocument.createXmlDocument("http://localhost:8080/name.xsl")).
         transform(out,transformed);
transformed.write(pw);
```

These three rather ungainly lines of code do quite a lot:

> Create a new xml document to hold the transformed tree.
>
> Create a transform engine.
>
> Create a third xml document, passing a URL to a style sheet.
>
> Create a transform based on this style sheet document.
>
> Use the transform to change the original document into the transformed document.
>
> Write out the transformed document.

The middle line is all one single line because there's no need to keep references to the intermediary objects such as the style sheet document or the transform object. Just create it and use it and let it get garbage collected.

Note

The previous code works equally well in a Java CGI application or a servlet.

Here's the XSL that goes with the sample XML used throughout this chapter:

```
<?xml version="1.0" ?>
<xsl:stylesheet xmlns:xsl="http://www.w3.org/1999/XSL/Transform"
                xmlns:xt="http://www.jclark.com/xt"
        version="1.0"
                extension-element-prefixes="xt">
<xsl:template match="/">
```

```
   <HTML><HEAD><TITLE>Name from XML</TITLE></HEAD><BODY>
   <xsl:apply-templates select="person/name" />
   </BODY></HTML>
</xsl:template>
<xsl:template match="name">
  <h1>The name is:</h1>
  <xsl:value-of select="first"/>
  <i><xsl:value-of select="last"/></i>
</xsl:template>
</xsl:stylesheet>
```

I modified this chapter's sample servlet by adding the three lines of code to use `name.xsl` and emit HTML instead of XML. Figure 17.11 shows the way the emitted HTML looks in a browser, along with the source. As you can see, there's no sign of the original XML in the source sent to the browser. The end-user cannot tell that your system uses XML at all.

Figure 17.11
When you transform XML into HTML on the server, the browser never sees the original XML.

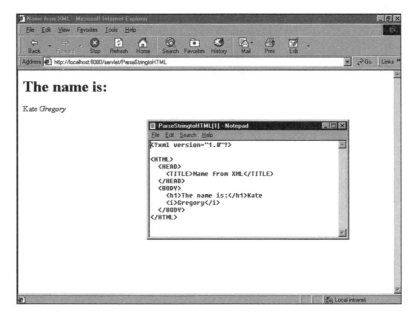

This servlet is taking on more work than it needs to by doing the transformation in every case. Instead, you could use the browser information in the servlet request to detect the browser being used. If it's IE5 or better, send XML with a style sheet tag and let the browser do the work. If not, transform it yourself. You could even use different style sheets for different browsers, so users viewing your site on a cell phone get readable pages, as do developers on 21" screens set to 1600 x 1200 resolutions.

Because servlets can be chained, you could consider writing a chaining servlet that intercepts all XML requests and applies the appropriate style sheet on the fly, returning pure HTML to the browser. This would make your site accessible to users with non-XML-enabled browsers while keeping life simple for those who build pages on your site. If performance is an issue (and sooner or later, performance is always an issue,) keep cached versions of popular transforms of popular files around and just return those quickly. Then you only have to generate new transformations when you get an unusual request.

An Applet Asking for XML

If you can't count on the browser to know what to do with XML, is there ever a time when it makes sense to emit raw XML from server-side code? There certainly is—when you know it's not a browser that's asking for it.

The sample servlet already presented in this chapter had its own user interface: an HTML form that the servlet emitted in response to a GET request. You can make a more attractive user interface by writing an applet that gets the name and having the applet present the output to the user. It can get the XML by running a servlet that generates XML. This servlet is much like the ParseString servlet, but emits XML in response to a GET request. This is partly because there is no need to emit a form in response to a GET request when the applet provides the front end, and partly because sending a POST request from an applet is harder than sending a GET request.

In fact, getting your XML from the server is no extra work at all. On the server, you had a string of XML you wanted to read, so after creating a parser, you called its parse method like this:

```
p.parse(new InputSource(new StringReader(xml)));
```

When the XML you want to read is located at a URL (or is the output of a servlet or CGI program than can be addressed with a URL) you just pass the URL (as a string) to the parse method like this:

```
p.parse(url);
```

It's actually easier than parsing from a string. The parser does all the work of making an HTTP connection, reading all the text that's sent back over the connection, and so on.

With that in mind, the only hard part of writing an intelligent applet is the user interface design. I'm going to skimp on that a little—making good applets isn't the point of this example. A TextField to enter a name, a Button to request that it be sent to the server, and some empty space to write the server's response are all that are needed. The applet's init() method sets things up:

```java
public class GetXML extends Applet implements ActionListener
{
  private String fullname;
  private TextField name;
  private Button button;
  public void init()
  {
    add(new Label("Enter Your Name: "));
    name = new TextField(30);
    add(name);
    button = new Button("Process Request");
    add(button);
    button.addActionListener(this);
  }
  public void actionPerformed(ActionEvent ev)
  {
    // to be shown shortly
```

PART
III

CH
17

```
    }
    public void paint(Graphics g)
    {
        g.drawString(fullname,10,100);
    }
}
```

This code should be familiar to anyone who's written applets with AWT. When the user clicks the button, the `actionPerformed()` method is called. This method builds a URL to the servlet (based on the location of the applet) parses the content of the URL, extracts the first and last name and builds the `fullname` string. Here's how it looks:

```
public void actionPerformed(ActionEvent ev)
    {
        try
        {
        URL xml = new URL(getDocumentBase(),
                          "servlet/ServeXML?XML=<name>" + name.getText() +
"</name>");
            DOMParser p = new DOMParser();
            p.parse(xml.toString());
            Document response = p.getDocument();

        String firstname="";
        String lastname="";
            NodeList nodes = response.getElementsByTagName("first");
            if(nodes.getLength() > 0)
            {
                firstname = nodes.item(0).getChildNodes().item(0).getNodeValue();
        }
            nodes = response.getElementsByTagName("last");
            if(nodes.getLength() > 0)
            {
                lastname = nodes.item(0).getChildNodes().item(0).getNodeValue();
        }
        fullname = firstname + " " + lastname;
        repaint();
        }
        catch (Exception e)
        {
        System.out.println("Exception caught: " +e.toString());
        }
    }
```

All this code should be familiar from the CGI and servlet examples that found the `<name>` element and extracted the value. Figure 17.12 shows the applet after a name is entered and the button is clicked.

The URL names a servlet, ServeXML, which is very like ParseXML except that it returns the XML from its `doGet()` method rather than its `doPost()`. In fact, I made a copy of ParseXML, deleted the `doGet()`, and renamed `doPost()` into `doGet()`. There's no need to show that code here.

The parameters are built right into a URL with a GET request separated from the filename by a ? character. If the name might contain spaces, quotes, or other unusual characters, use a

`URLEncoder` to encode the parameters before sending them to the server. CGI programs have to decode their parameters, and servlets have the work done for them by the `HttpRequest` object.

Figure 17.12
This applet turns ordinary input into XML that it sends to a servlet. The servlet sends XML in response and the applet uses that to draw a string.

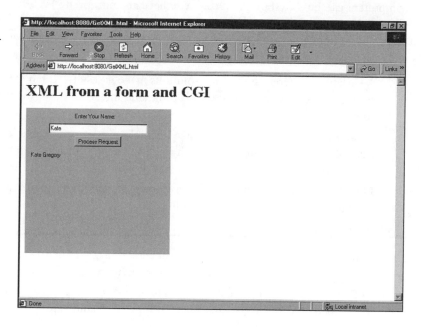

To display the applet, you need to load some HTML into a browser. The browser might be on a computer that doesn't have XML4J installed, so you need to show where it can be retrieved using the ARCHIVE attribute of the APPLET tag. Make sure you copy the jar file to the same directory as the applet. Here's a rather minimal page that works for these purposes:

```
<HTML>
<HEAD><TITLE>Using XML with an applet</TITLE></HEAD>
<BODY>
<H1>XML from a form and CGI</H1>
<APPLET CODE="GetXML.class" HEIGHT=300 WIDTH=300 ARCHIVE="xml4j.jar">
</APPLET>
</BODY>
</HTML>
```

That's all there is to it. The applet and servlet together are forming a nice XML system, communicating with one another using XML. In this example, they both use DOM; in fact they both use XML4J, but there's no requirement that they do so. It would be quite simple to have the server component written in a language other than Java, using a completely different parser, but still writing out XML that the applet knows how to work with. This is the real power of XML.

USING SOCKETS INSTEAD OF HTTP

This chapter has shown you how to use XML on the server over HTTP. The server-side component can be a CGI program or, if you have an appropriate Web server, a servlet. The client-side program can be a Web browser, an applet, or anything else that is able to get a stream of content from a URL. In most situations, using HTTP to exchange information with the server is the right thing to do. The advantages include

A variety of different server-side solutions make it easy to "catch" HTTP requests and route them to executable code. CGI programs and servlets, for example, are quite easy to write.

A variety of client-side libraries make it simple to request information by HTTP. For example the parse() method in both the SAX and COM APIs can be passed a URL, and the parser makes the connection and gets the information.

HTTP traffic is allowed through most firewalls without having to make special arrangements with your system administrators.

Still, HTTP is not always the right solution. Some of the disadvantages are

You can't pass very long strings as parameters to a GET request—and POST requests are harder to send from those client-side libraries.

HTTP is a stateless protocol, so your client and server can't have an ongoing conversation as they could if they used their own protocol and kept the socket between them open all the time.

HTTP requests might be cached by proxy servers between the client and the server, and when caches malfunction "live" data is sometimes stale.

For these reasons, among others, you might prefer to open a socket connection between an applet and an application that runs on the server. If you're familiar with socket programming, adding XML to the mix is no problem at all. You simply exchange strings over that socket—strings of XML. You can read and write those strings as you've already seen in the other sample code in this chapter.

CORBA

CORBA, the Common Object Request Broker Architecture, is a component architecture that simplifies client-server or n-tier development. The components can be on the same machine or distributed across a network. A CORBA client makes a request of a CORBA server through an ORB, or Object Request Broker.

The ORB takes care of the work involved, shown in the following list:

Finding the server (which might be on another machine)

Activating the server

Gathering the parameters that are to be passed to the method (marshalling)

Distributing the return parameters from the method (unmarshalling)

Figure 17.13
An Object Request Broker sits between clients and servers

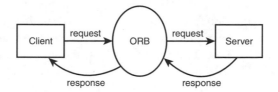

All this work can be done by the ORB after it has an Interoperable Object Reference, or IOR. An IOR generated by one ORB can be used by another ORB—hence the word Interoperable. Most ORBs offer a package of related services to make it simple to get an IOR for a server such as the Naming Service, which identifies servers by name.

CORBA is entirely language-neutral. You define the services your servers offer (the requests they listen to) using a language-neutral notation called Interface Definition Language, or IDL. Utilities that come with the ORB generate Java code, C++ code, or whatever language you need, from this IDL.

PART
III
CH
17

Tip from

LeeAnne.com
Words to weave by

CORBA IDL is not the only IDL around. For example, COM interface definitions are also described as IDL, but the two notations are not identical.

CORBA makes it simple for objects written in different languages to work together. As long as the object requesting services can reach an ORB, and as long as the object providing those services can be reached by an ORB, they can work together. The order they expect their parameters, the primitive types supported by the language, and similar issues simply don't matter to a CORBA developer. The ORB takes care of all that work for you. A client written in Java can make requests of a server written in C without having to worry about JNI or any related technologies. Similarly, your objects can connect across a network without using RMI. The ORB does it all.

CORBA, Java, and XML have a lot in common. Many vendors have developed ORBs that can be accessed as simply as calling any other public Java class. All three are cross-platform solutions. One slogan is "portable data, portable code." XML is the portable data because XML as a format can be understood on any platform. Java is the portable code. And CORBA is the glue that makes it simple to call that code from anywhere, even from a non-Java application running on another platform.

Despite the natural fit between CORBA, XML, and Java, you might have noticed that XML parsers are not CORBA servers, offering parsing services to be requested by a CORBA client. Instead, they are ordinary Java objects. That's because there is some overhead associated with going through CORBA, especially if you are passing long strings of XML back and forth. Because XML parsers are lightweight and readily available, it makes more sense to have an instance of the parser available on the machine that needs the parsing, and to connect that parser directly into your code rather than issuing a remotable request.

426 Chapter 17 Using Server-Side Facilities—Java

There's one other connection between XML and CORBA that might not be readily apparent: the way the XML specifications are written. Official XML specifications, such as the DOM specification, often list function names, parameters, return types, and so on. The specification-writers could have listed these for C++, Java, and so on, but instead they chose a much simpler approach. They defined the interfaces using the CORBA IDL notation. Because agreed-upon mappings exist from CORBA IDL to all the popular programming languages, the specification committee needs only to maintain one list, written in CORBA IDL, and not many different lists written for different programming languages.

Troubleshooting Java and XML

Executing the Java CGI program

It can be difficult to find problems in your CGI program if it won't even execute. The comment at the start of the Perl wrapper is very useful if your Java program is behaving oddly. Just remove the # character from the start of the line and resave your Perl wrapper, then execute your CGI again. Often you can see your Java error messages by doing this. Just remember to replace the comment character again after the Java is working.

Remember also that everything a CGI program writes to standard output appears in the browser. Feel free to add debugging output with calls to System.out.println().

Getting a Servlet Working

If either your doGet() or doPost() is particularly tricky, you might like to get the code working as command-line Java applications first. Servlet error messages can sometimes be rather like Perl error messages: the server just responds 500 Internal Server Error and leaves you guessing. After your application works, copy the code into your servlet and keep testing.

Getting your classpaths correct is vital. On a Windows machine, make sure you set the classpath environment variable with the System tool under Control panel, that you set System rather than User variables, and that you start the Web server after you have set the environment variables. If your Web server is a service that starts whenever the machine is started, you have to stop and start the server (or in the worst case, restart your machine) after updating the classpath. If you're using the Java Web Server, you can stop it by going to the URL http://localhost:9090/, logging in using the ID and password of admin, and clicking the Shut Down button. Then open a fresh system prompt (to get the new environment variables) and restart the server as described in the installation instructions.

CHAPTER 18

Using Server-Side Facilities—ActiveX

In this chapter

ACTIVEX AND COM

ActiveX is a technology built on COM, Microsoft's Component Object Model. COM is the infrastructure that enables executable (binary) programs to communicate with each other, even if they were written in different languages. DCOM, Distributed COM, extends COM to work between different computers, even running different platforms. Work has been underway on COM for Unix for a long time, but at the moment COM is still a Windows world: Windows 95, Windows 98, and Windows NT. COM+ runs only on Windows 2000. A good starting point for learning more about COM is `http://www.microsoft.com/com/tech/com.asp`.

ActiveX controls can be embedded into a Web page just as Java applets can, but only Internet Explorer activates and displays them. They do not work when displayed in Netscape. ActiveX controls are also used within applications, often as part of the user interface. However, it's not necessary for an ActiveX control to have any visible part at all—other programs can still interact with the control and arrange to have the control do some of their work. This kind of control is often simply referred to as "a COM object."

But ActiveX can also be a server-side technology. Microsoft (at `http://www.microsoft.com/NTServer/web/exec/overview/overview.asp`) describes Active Server Pages (ASP) technology as "an open, compile-free application environment in which you can combine HTML, scripts, and reusable ActiveX server components to create dynamic and powerful Web-based business solutions." That's marketing-speak for server-side scripting, with the capability to call ActiveX components to do any heavy lifting your system needs.

ASP is supported on Microsoft's Internet Information Server (IIS) and Microsoft's Personal Web Server (PWS). If you don't have access to an IIS Web server, you can get a copy of PWS at `http://www.microsoft.com/Windows/ie/pws/default.htm`. It is for Windows 95, 98, or NT, despite the fact that it comes with the NT 4.0 Option Pack.

It's a simple matter to interact with an ActiveX control or COM object from an ASP page, as seen later in this chapter. But where do you get the controls? You could write your own, but a large number of COM objects are provided with Windows and other Microsoft products. One COM object that is used in the samples in this chapter is Microsoft's XML parser, MSXML. It's actually part of Internet Explorer 5. Make sure IE 5 is installed on the Web server before continuing. If you don't have it, you can get it from `http://www.microsoft.com/windows/ie/`. Although it might seem strange to install a Web browser on a server, it's the simplest way to get the XML parser COM object installed.

It's worth noting that the original design decisions behind MSXML were made under the assumption that it would be used on the client side, not the server side. Future releases of MSXML will address server-side performance and scalability issues.

Pre-Release Versions of the Microsoft XML Parser

Microsoft moved quickly to include XML in its Internet Explorer Web browser. Unfortunately, some important parts of the specifications, most notably XSL and XSLT, changed after IE 5 was released. The result is that the XML support in IE 5 does not agree with the W3C specifications and recommendations in every way.

Although IE 5 is released and will not change significantly, you can get your hands on more recent versions of the Microsoft XML parser, MSXML2, as long as you understand you are working with pre-release code. Production systems on your public Web server should not use pre-release code. You can get a copy so that when a stable version is released, you're already familiar with using it. In some cases you might choose to accept the risks of work with unfinished material because you need a version of MSXML that supports a specific feature. It's your choice.

You can get beta versions of MS XML from `http://msdn.microsoft.com/downloads/webtechnology/xml/msxml.asp`.

MICROSOFT EVOLUTION TOWARD OPEN STANDARDS

Microsoft hasn't always been seen as committed to open standards developed elsewhere. Plenty of Microsoft developments are *de facto* standards just because they've been adopted by a large number of users. That's not the same as Microsoft deliberately developing a product in accordance with someone else's standard.

If you look back over the history of Microsoft browsers and standards, it's not a pretty sight. Whether it was the various HTML standards, cascading style sheets, JavaScript versus JScript or VBScript, Dynamic HMTL, or early XML drafts, Internet Explorer had a tendency to do things the Microsoft way rather than the standard way. Web sites such as `http://www.webstandards.org/` carry some of the gory details. But as the saying goes, that was then and this is now.

Microsoft has made a significant public commitment to the standards process. That means both helping create the standards and then writing software that meets the standards, whether it is what they would have originally written or not. Although it's still possible to argue that the target amount of compliance is less than it should be, just having a target level of compliance is a big improvement in the view of many observers.

The history of XML support in IE 5 is a good illustration of how Microsoft is adapting its software to standards, even to standards that change after the software has been released.

MICROSOFT DISTRIBUTED INTERNET ARCHITECTURE 2000 (DNA)

Windows DNA is an architecture and a vision built around Windows 2000 for what Microsoft is calling the Business Internet. Microsoft's suite of development tools—Visual Studio—is full of DNA support. COM+, the successor to COM, is how the applications and components communicate and share work. The design decisions behind DNA are based on the reality of networked software: Sometimes connections are slow, sometimes the other machine is down, and performance is always at risk if applications don't scale well.

You can read more about DNA at http://www.microsoft.com/dna/, but the obvious first question is: What does this have to do with XML? The answer is, quite a lot. Here's a description from Microsoft of the sorts of systems DNA is for:

> **Note**
>
> Businesses are rapidly moving to a standard Web-based computing model, characterized by loosely connected tiers of replicated, task-focused systems. A large percentage of business Web sites—collections of servers, applications, and data that offer online services—are built using the Microsoft Windows DNA platform today as the basis for this computing model.

Imagine a system such as the one described in the Microsoft quote for a moment. Loosely connected tiers—that means separated systems share information, but in some standard and portable way, so that one tier can change dramatically without really affecting the code in the other tiers. And when you think of sharing information in a standard, portable way—sharing self-describing information—it's only natural to think of XML.

XML is the key to making Windows DNA work—and I'm not just saying that because this is an XML book. Here's another Microsoft quote: "...you may already be using Windows DNA, or some elements of it. The difference comes in thinking of the parts as an integrated whole flexibly bound by XML." Microsoft has built (or will build) XML support into developer products (Visual Studio), the Web browser (Internet Explorer), database servers (including SQL Server 2000), and the operating system itself (Windows 2000). Not even the initial embrace of the Internet by Microsoft was so pervasive and affected so many different products and teams.

And then there's BizTalk Server 2000, designed to facilitate the exchange of XML documents in a business context. It extends XML, typical of Microsoft's embrace-and-extend policy, to make it more specifically useful to businesses. You can read more about BizTalk in Chapter 19, "Using Common Object Brokers."

Windows DNA 2000 is a large and all-encompassing effort. You might not want to build your entire system the DNA way. Still, it's nice to know that most (or even all) of the Microsoft technologies you use to build your system are XML-aware. That's sure to make your job easier. Just tread carefully to ensure that the XML you produce and read is indeed still standard and portable.

A SIMPLE ASP PAGE

Active Server Pages are, at their simplest, a way to run script on the server. They combine JavaScript or VBScript with HTML that is to be sent to the browser. The script is executed before anything is sent to the browser, and if the user uses View Source, there is no sign of the original scripting code.

> **Tip from**
>
>
> LeeAnne.com
> Words to weave by
>
> You can learn more about Active Server Pages in *Special Edition Using Active Server Pages*, from Que.

The power of ASP is in the objects it provides for you to work with. There are objects that hold application-wide constants, that represent a connection to a database or some records retrieved from that database, and perhaps most importantly, that provide state variables related to the session of a single user who is interacting with your server. ASP uses cookies to tell which session any particular request belongs to.

Here's the structure of a typical ASP page:

```
<%@ Language=jscript%>
<%
Response.ContentType ="text/html";

if(Request("submit").Item == "Process Request")
{

// process the request and emit HTML

}
else
{

// emit HTML for a form

}%>
```

Tip from

LeeAnne.com
Words to weave by

ASP code is ordinary text, rather like HTML. This means that you don't need any special tools to create ASP pages. Because you use a scripting language (JavaScript in these examples) you don't need a tool to compile your code or otherwise prepare it to be run. Just type it in, save it, and load it into your Web browser.

The `Response` object holds the information your code sends back to the browser. This example is just setting the content type. Later in this chapter you see code that writes HTML or other output to the `Response` object.

The `Request` object holds the request headers from the browser. You can determine the value of a form field or, as in this example, determine whether a particular submit button was clicked. More sophisticated ASP pages make heavy use of the `Request` object.

In the sample ASP page for this chapter, the user is prompted to enter a short string of XML that looks something like this:

```
<name>kate</name>
```

A name is extracted from that XML, and slightly different XML is sent back. Here is the code for the part of the ASP page that emits the form:

```
else
{%>
    <HTML><HEAD><TITLE>Using XML</TITLE></HEAD>
    <BODY><H1>XML from a form</H1>
    Enter some XML in the form &lt;name&gt;Your Name&lt;/name&gt;:<BR>
    <FORM action=ParseString.asp method=post id=form1 name=form1>
```

```
        <input name=xmlIn> <BR>
        <input type=submit name=submit value="Process Request">
        </FORM>
        </BODY>
        </HTML>
<%}
```

This is pure HMTL with no variables or calculations in it. ASP enables you to mix HTML with scripting in this way. Note the name of the INPUT field is xmlIn. When the user submits the form, the same ASP page is loaded. This time, the test to see which submit button was clicked executes your request-processing code.

There are two parts to processing a form. One is extracting the fields from the form and the other is doing something with those fields. In the sample ASP page, there's only one field of interest. It can be extracted like this:

```
var xml = Request("xmlIn").Item;
```

Notice how the string passed to Request(), xmlIn, is the name of the INPUT tag in the FORM tag emitted by the other part of this page.

To parse the string, create a parser for the document, set it to synchronous operation, and pass the string to its loadXML() method:

```
var docIn = Server.CreateObject("Microsoft.XMLDOM");
docIn.async = false;
docIn.loadXML(xml);
```

This code uses a DOM parser—the MSXML component only supports DOM. The sample ASP page is expecting to receive a <name> element. Here is the code that finds that element and gets the value of its text node:

```
var nodes = docIn.getElementsByTagName("name");
if(nodes.length > 0)
{
    var submittedName = nodes.item(0).text;
}
```

Tip from

LeeAnne.com
Words to weave by

If you're not comfortable with this line of DOM code, you might want to reread Chapter 10, "DOM—The Document Object Model."

The sample ASP page is expected to emit XML that looks similar to this:

```
<person>
  <name>
    <first>Kate</first>
    <last>Gregory</last>
  </name>
</person>
```

In a real application, the emitted XML would be based on values found in a database or calculated from the other input in some way. In this sample, simple hardcoded XML is enough to demonstrate the techniques. To add a little excitement, one first name gets special treatment:

```
var lastName = "";
if(submittedName == "Kate"){lastName = "Gregory";}
```

Here's the simple JavaScript code that creates the XML to write out:

```
docOut = Server.CreateObject("Microsoft.XMLDOM");

var person = docOut.createElement("person");
docOut.appendChild(person);

var name = docOut.createElement("name");
person.appendChild(name);

var first = docOut.createElement("first");
name.appendChild(first);
first.appendChild(docOut.createTextNode(submittedName));

var last = docOut.createElement("last");
name.appendChild(last);
var lastName = "";
if(submittedName == "Kate"){lastName = "Gregory";}

last.appendChild(docOut.createTextNode(lastName));
```

To write HTML back to the server, an ASP page uses the Response object. In this case, just get the XML from the document object docOut, and write it back to the response:

```
//print out the contents of the tree here
var xmlString = docOut.xml;
Response.Write(xmlString);
```

So far, this code has been very idealistic. What if the parsing doesn't work? Perhaps the XML is not valid against its DTD. Worse, it could be not well-formed. It could be unparseable.

In some programming languages, the parser throws an exception to indicate these sorts of troubles. JavaScript doesn't support exceptions, so instead you have to remember to check the error code of the parser after the parse statement. Here's a typical approach:

```
docIn.loadXML(xml);

if (docIn.parseError.errorCode == 0)
{

    // process the XML as you wish
}
else
{
    Response.Write("<strong>XML Parsing Error</strong><BR>");
    Response.Write("File Position: " + docIn.parseError.filepos + "<BR>")
    Response.Write("Line Number: " + docIn.parseError.line + "<BR>")
    Response.Write("Column Position: " + docIn.parseError.linepos + "<BR>")
    Response.Write("Reason: " + docIn.parseError.reason + "<BR>")
    Response.Write("Error Source: " + docIn.parseError.srcText + "<BR>")
    Response.Write("File URL: " + docIn.parseError.url)
}
```

Notice the use of the `parseError` object from the document into which the XML was loaded. These are generally self-explanatory: for example `line` refers to the line on which the error occurred.

To test your ASP page, just copy it into a folder that's accessible from your Web server. For example, I made a folder called `xml` under `inetpub/wwwroot`. Then start a Web browser and type in the URL to the page: My URL was `http://localhost/xml/ParseString.asp`. Adjust yours accordingly. When you just type in the URL to this page, you see the form in Figure 18.1.

Figure 18.1
The ASP page first displays a simple form.

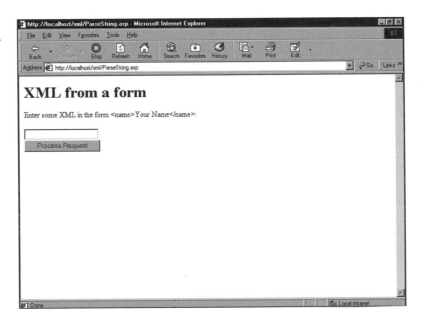

If you were to type the string `<name>Kate</name>` into the text box and press the Process Request button, you'd see XML output such as that in Figure 18.2. This output is XML, displayed as a tree by Internet Explorer 5. IE knows this is XML because the content type is set, such as this:

```
Response.ContentType ="text/xml";
```

Most ASP files set the content type to `text/html`. If you do that, the browser deletes all your tags. If you choose View, Source you see that the tags are still there, but not displayed to you. The browser treats them as strange HTML and ignores them. Figure 18.3 shows the output of the same ASP page with the content type set to `text/html`.

A third possibility for content type is `text/plain`. Some browsers react to this, under certain circumstances, by offering you the chance to download a text file (see Figure 18.4) rather than displaying it in the browser. If you choose to open it from that location, Visual Interdev launches (if it's installed) and the XML is opened in that. For this reason it's wise to avoid a content type of `text/plain` for ASP pages.

Figure 18.2
The output of the ASP
page is XML.

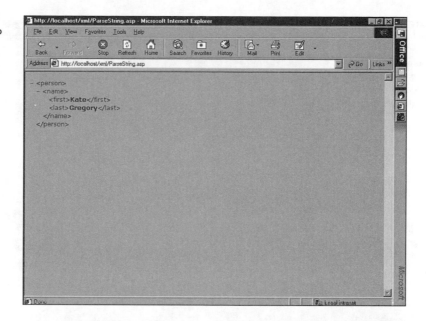

Figure 18.3
When Internet
Explorer has been
told the output is
HTML, none of the
tags are shown,
though they are
in the source.

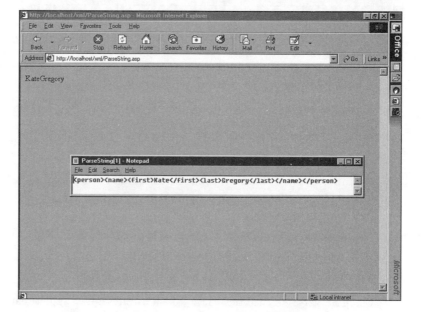

Figure 18.4
When Internet Explorer has been told the output is plain text, you are invited to download the text file rather than viewing it.

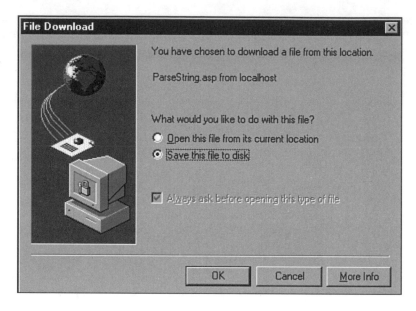

TRANSFORMING TO HTML ON THE SERVER

Writing a page that emits XML is interesting, if not all-encompassing. But XML displayed in a browser is not a pretty sight. It's a nice way to test that your code is emitting the XML that you think it's emitting, but it's hardly a finished product. There are three things you can do instead of sending raw XML to an unsuspecting browser:

1. You can assume that the browser is IE 5, and add a style sheet reference so that the browser renders the XML document well. As you learned in Chapter 14, Using Next Generation Extensible Style Sheets—XSL, this is not a simple assumption, and XSL or XSLT that works in IE 5 doesn't always work in other contexts.

2. You can use XSL to transform your XML into HTML on the server, and send HTML to the browser. This means it doesn't matter what browser the enduser is using, your information is properly displayed.

3. You can write something on the client side that asks for the XML and uses it in some clever manner to show information to the enduser.

There are a number of client-side ways to get that XML and use it. For example, Chapter 17, "Using Server-Side Facilities—Java," demonstrates a Java applet that runs a servlet or CGI on the server and then processes the resulting XML. There's no reason that same applet couldn't get XML from an ASP page on the server.

If you embed a style sheet reference into the XML you emit, you have to count on the browser being XSLT-capable. If it's not, your users see something similar to Figure 18.2: a tree of XML. That's probably not the experience they want from your Web site or intranet application.

Instead of counting on the browser to translate your XML into HTML using XSL, it's a better idea to do it yourself, on the server. And it isn't hard at all—the same component, MSXML, that parses XML for you is also the component that applies XSLT style sheets to XML to produce HTML, assuming that's what you want. Here's how simple it is: When you have a parser instance that holds your output tree, just create another parser instance and load the style sheet into it. Then apply the style sheet and write out the HTML. The code looks like this:

```
// transform the XML into HTML

var xsl = "<?xml version='1.0' ?><xsl:stylesheet
xmlns:xsl='http://www.w3.org/TR/WD-xsl'>";
    xsl += "<xsl:template match='/'>";
    xsl += "<HTML><HEAD><TITLE>Name from XML</TITLE></HEAD><BODY>";
    xsl += "<xsl:apply-templates select='person/name' />";
    xsl += "</BODY></HTML></xsl:template>"
    xsl += "<xsl:template match='name'>";
    xsl += "<h1>The name is:</h1><xsl:value-of select='first'/> ";
    xsl += "<i><xsl:value-of select='last'/></i></xsl:template></xsl:stylesheet>";

var style = Server.CreateObject("Microsoft.XMLDOM");
style.async = false;
style.loadXML(xsl);

if (style.parseError.errorCode != 0)
{
    Response.Write("<strong>XSL Parsing Error</strong><BR>");
      Response.Write("File Position: " + style.parseError.filepos + "<BR>")
    Response.Write("Line Number: " + style.parseError.line + "<BR>")
    Response.Write("Column Position: " + style.parseError.linepos + "<BR>")
    Response.Write("Reason: " + style.parseError.reason + "<BR>")
    Response.Write("Error Source: " + style.parseError.srcText + "<BR>")
    Response.Write("File URL: " + style.parseError.url)
}
else
{
    docOut.transformNodeToObject(style, Response);
}
```

The bulk of the lines here are the XSL itself, and the error-handling block that is almost identical to the one you saw earlier in this chapter to handle errors in the input XML. What's interesting here are the three lines in the middle that create another parser instance and load the XSL into it, and the line at the end that transforms the docOut XML according to the XSLT in style, then writes it to the Response. All in one line.

Figure 18.5 shows the output of this modified ASP page. The source is shown in the small Notepad window. The browser sees only the HTML that resulted from the transformation. There's no indication that any XML or JavaScript were ever involved.

Figure 18.5
When you transform XML into HTML on the server, the browser never sees the original XML.

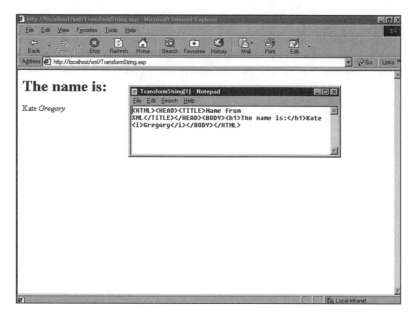

Although the code is really simple, your server is taking on more work than it needs to by doing the transformation in every case. Instead, you could use the browser information in the Request object to detect the browser being used. If it's IE5 or better, send XML with a style sheet tag and let the browser do the work. If not, transform it yourself. You could even use different style sheets for different browsers, so that users viewing your site on a cell phone get readable pages, and so do developers on 21" screens set to 1600 x 1200 resolution.

A COM OBJECT THAT EMITS XML

So far in this chapter you have seen two ASP pages. This combined business logic, such as looking up names in a database or the simplified hard-coded XML in the samples, with presentation details, such as the layout of the input form or the way the XML was transformed into HTML. In general it's not a good idea to mix these two. Ideally an ASP page concentrates on appearance and passes off the calculations, database lookups, and so on to business objects. One example of that is using the MSXML object to parse the input XML, to create the output XML, and to transform the output XML to HTML. Another is to write a COM object of your own and transfer some of the work to that object.

WHY YOU SHOULD USE COM OBJECTS FROM ASP

A good division of the effort involved in this server-side use of XML would be

The ASP page requests XML from the user.

The ASP page passes the XML to another COM object.

The COM object uses the MSXML parser to parse the XML and create output XML (or HTML).

The ASP page gets the output from the COM object and returns it to the browser.

Separating the tasks like this has several important advantages:

The COM object is generally written in a compiled language such as C++ or Visual Basic, which executes far faster than JavaScript.

The COM object can be on another server, or cloned across several servers, reducing the load on the Web server and increasing the scalability of the solution.

The COM object can be written by someone who knows XML and the business problem, and the visual (HTML) aspects of the solution can be written by someone with good user-interface design and HTML skills.

Changes to the visual appearance of the solution usually do not require any changes to the business object. In the same spirit, changes to the operation of the business object do not usually require changes to the HTML and ASP code.

CREATING A COM OBJECT WITH VISUAL BASIC

There are many languages in which you could create a COM object. Visual Basic and Visual C++ are the two most popular. It's a little simpler to work in Visual Basic for the kind of low-key object this chapter demonstrates, but you're welcome to try making a COM object in Visual C++. The concepts are the same as those shown here for Visual Basic.

PART
IV
CH
18

An ActiveX control of the type we've been calling a COM object is, fundamentally, a DLL. The code you've seen that creates instances of the parser object is calling into a DLL called MSXML.DLL. So to build a COM object in VB you start by building a DLL in VB. Here's how:

1. Launch Visual Basic by choosing Start, Programs, Microsoft Visual Studio 6.0, Microsoft Visual Basic 6.0.

2. On the New Project dialog, make sure the New tab is active, then select ActiveX DLL and click Open.

3. Visual Basic creates a new project called Project1. In the Project explorer window at the upper right of your screen, right-click the project name and choose Project1 Properties. The Project Properties dialog box appears. As shown in Figure 18.6, change the name of the project. The name used in the figure is NameXML—the name you use for the project name becomes the filename of your DLL, so choose a name that makes sense in that context.

4. Visual Basic created a class in your project called Class1. In the Project explorer window, select the class by clicking its name. The Properties window just below the explorer shows the properties of the class. Highlight the name and change it to something more appropriate. I called mine ParseString, as shown in Figure 18.7.

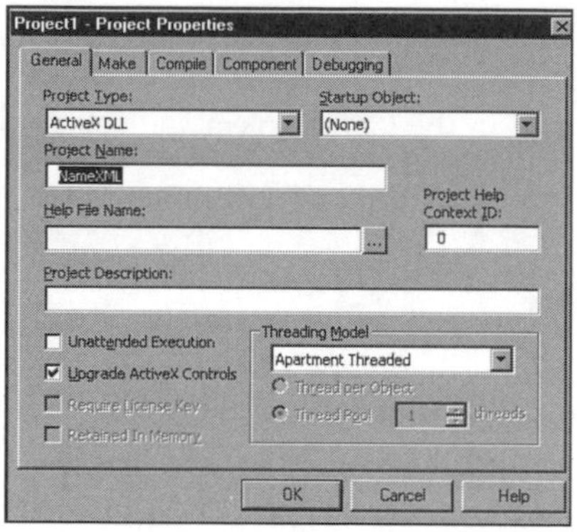

Figure 18.6
Change the name of your Visual Basic project from the default name of Project1.

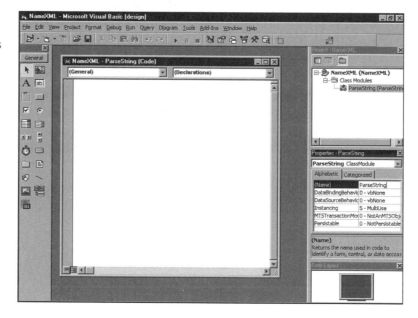

Figure 18.7
Change the name of your Visual Basic class from the default name of Class1 to a more appropriate name, such as ParseString.

At this point, you have an empty shell that can hold the COM object you create. There is no form for you to work with because this ActiveX DLL does not have a visual user interface. Instead, you add code to the class.

An ASP page runs your code by calling a function contained in the DLL. The first thing to do, therefore, is add a public function to the class. In the large code window, enter the code for a suitably-named function. Here's the skeleton of a ProcessName() function for the sample COM object:

```
Public Function ProcessName(xmlin As String) As String

        Dim returnstring As String

        If ((Len(xmlin) > 0) And Not IsNull(xmlin)) Then

        ' process the XML
```

```
        Else
            returnstring = "<error>No Input</error>"
        End If

    ProcessName = returnstring

End Function
```

To process the XML, follow the same basic steps the ASP JavaScript followed:

1. Create a parser object.
2. Load the XML into the parser.
3. If there are no errors, build an output document.
4. If there are errors, write an error string.

The code to create a parser object and load the XML into it is

```
Dim docIn As New MSXML.DOMDocument
docIn.loadXML (xmlin)
```

Notice the name of the DLL, MSXML, is part of the New statement that creates the parser. The second part of this statement, DOMDocument, is the name of the class within the DLL. From here on, the code is very similar to the JavaScript code you saw earlier in this chapter.

The code to check the error condition is

```
If (docIn.parseError.errorCode = 0) Then
```

The code to build an output tree of XML is

```
Dim docOut As New MSXML.DOMDocument
Dim nodeList As IXMLDOMNodeList
Dim node As IXMLDOMNode
Dim person
Dim name
Dim first
Dim last

Set nodeList = docIn.getElementsByTagName("name")
If (nodeList.length > 0) Then
    Dim submittedName As String
    Dim lastName As String
    lastName = ""

    submittedName = nodeList.Item(0).Text

    Set person = docOut.createElement("person")
    docOut.appendChild (person)

    Set name = docOut.createElement("name")
    person.appendChild (name)

    Set first = docOut.createElement("first")
    name.appendChild (first)
    Dim sName
```

```
    Set sName = docOut.createTextNode(submittedName)
    first.appendChild (sName)

    Set last = docOut.createElement("last")
    name.appendChild (last)

    If (submittedName = "Kate") Then
        lastName = "Gregory"
    End If

    Dim lName
    Set lName = docOut.createTextNode(lastName)
    last.appendChild (lName)

    returnstring = docOut.xml
End If
```

The variable types in this code that start with I are COM interface types. This is how the MSXML parser is used from Visual Basic. The Dim statements without types just alert VB that a variable name is beng used—the type is determined at runtime. Because the same object is treated as both a node and an element, it's simpler not to commit to a type.

Other than the types (and the semicolons), this code is just like the JavaScript code used in the ASP page.

The error message, just as in the ASP page, uses the parseError property of the input document:

```
returnstring = "<strong>XML Parsing Error</strong><BR>"
returnstring = returnstring + "File Position: " & docIn.parseError.filepos &
"<BR>"
returnstring = returnstring + "Line Number: " & docIn.parseError.Line & "<BR>"
returnstring = returnstring + "Column Position: " & docIn.parseError.linepos &
"<BR>"
returnstring = returnstring + "Reason: " & docIn.parseError.reason & "<BR>"
returnstring = returnstring + "Error Source: " & docIn.parseError.srcText & "<BR>"
returnstring = returnstring + "File URL: " & docIn.parseError.url
```

After entering your Visual Basic Code, save the project. Then choose Project, References to bring up the References dialog box shown in Figure 18.8. Select the Microsoft XML component from the list—it's in alphabetical order, so scroll to the end of all the Microsoft components. This component was added to your system when you installed IE 5.

Tip from

LeeAnne.com
Words to weave by

If you bring the Project References dialog box up again later, to confirm you added MSXML perhaps, it is at the top of the list—all the references you are using are shown first. It's possible the version number is different from the version you thought you added. In some builds of IE 5 the two strings that identify this DLL to the operating system are different. As long as you are using the "Microsoft XML" component, don't worry about version numbers.

Figure 18.8
Add the XML parser to
the project references.

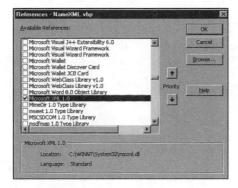

Finally, create the DLL file by choosing File, Make NameXML.dll. You can save the DLL
in your project folder if you want. If the computer on which you're working is also the Web
server on which you test the DLL, you're all set. If not, copy the DLL to the folder of your
choice on the Web server, then register it with the system by opening a command prompt
in that folder and typing regsvr32 NameXML.dll (or whatever you named the DLL). This
registers the DLL on that computer. (VB automatically registers the DLL when you
make it.)

Tip from

LeeAnne.com
Words to weave by

Don't try to use the DLL over a network on a shared drive, for example on a central file
server. VB is happy to save it there, but the Web server won't use it from there. Save a
local copy on the Web server or follow the instructions above for copying the DLL to the
Web server's hard drive.

PART
IV

CH

18

USING A COM OBJECT FROM AN ASP PAGE

The COM object you created in Visual Basic has taken the business logic from the inside of
your ASP page. All that's left is the code to display the form and the code to create and use
the COM object. Here's how it looks:

```
<%@ Language=jscript%>
<%
Response.ContentType ="text/html";

if(Request("submit").Item == "Process Request")
{
    var xml = Request("xmlIn").Item;
    if((xml.length > 0) && (xml != null))
    {
        var parseObj = Server.CreateObject("NameXML.ParseString");
        Response.ContentType ="text/xml";
        Response.Write(parseObj.ProcessName(xml));
    }
    else
    {
        Response.Write("<error>No input</error>");
    }
```

```
}
else
{%>
    <HTML><HEAD><TITLE>Using XML</TITLE></HEAD>
    <BODY><H1>XML from a form</H1>

    Enter some XML in the form &lt;name&gt;Your Name&lt;/name&gt;:<BR>
    <FORM action=ParseStringWithCOM.asp method=post id=form1 name=form1>
    <input name=xmlIn> <BR>
    <input type=submit name=submit value="Process Request">
    </FORM>
    </BODY>
    </HTML>

<%}%>
```

There are three lines here that are worth mentioning:

```
var parseObj = Server.CreateObject("NameXML.ParseString");
Response.ContentType ="text/xml";
Response.Write(parseObj.ProcessName(xml));
```

To create the COM object, use the name of the project, in this case NameXML, followed by a period, followed by the name of the class within the project, in this case ParseString. The CreateObject() method is provided by the Server class for ASP pages and is the same method used to create XML parser objects earlier.

The content type should be set to text/xml because it's XML this page emits, not HTML.

The last line of code uses the name of the method in the ParseString class, ProcessName(). It passes in the string of XML and writes the output straight to the Response object.

At this point if you wanted, you could transform the XML into HTML using an XSLT style sheet, as you saw earlier in this chapter. You should not make that transformation in the COM object, which is concerned only with your business logic. If you transform to HTML, be sure to change the content type.

TROUBLESHOOTING ACTIVEX AND XML

TESTING ACTIVE SERVER PAGES

ASP pages must be served by the server with an http: request. Many developers are in the habit of dragging HTML files onto the browser—this does not work with ASP pages. You must enter a URL to the page, one that starts with http:. Use localhost to refer to your own computer.

DEBUGGING VISUAL BASIC CODE

If something goes wrong in your VB code, the ASP page you'll write shortly just displays a VB error message. To debug your VB code, follow these steps:

1. Stop and restart the Web server. You can use restartwebserver.bat for this, or choose Start, Settings, Control Panel and bring up the Services application. You must stop and restart the Web server so that it "lets go" of the DLL you made.

2. Delete the DLL from the folder you saved it to.

3. In VB, choose Run, Start. Not much appears to happen, but the COM object is now running in the background. Set a breakpoint if you want.

4. Switch to your Web browser and load the ASP page. You can click Refresh if you have the page already loaded.

5. When execution reaches your breakpoint, focus should switch to VB and you can debug your application in the usual way.

6. When your VB application is working perfectly, just make the DLL as before. You should not need to restart the Web server, but it won't hurt if you choose to do so.

CHAPTER 19

USING COMMON OBJECT BROKERS

In this chapter

UNDERSTANDING OBJECT BROKERS

Object brokers, often called *Object Request Brokers* (ORBs), are simply one way to handle complexity on the Internet. By treating everything as an object—users, databases, interfaces, and applications alike—and defining standard ways to send messages back and forth between them, the complexity of distributed applications can be reduced to a manageable level. The object broker helps objects find each other no matter where they are, talk to each other, and (optionally) translate requests for service from one object broker protocol to another.

From the developer's view, easy integration of objects from multiple vendors encourages building applications from best-of-breed components manufactured and made available especially for a given purpose. This makes possible rapid application-development techniques that shorten time to market and enable robust applications to be created from proven technologies without extended integration, testing, and rework.

For example, almost every word processor includes a spelling checker. Most are built from scratch. A developer can make efficient use of that resource by packaging it as an object and reusing it in presentation software, spreadsheets, and other applications. It would also be advantageous if spelling checkers from multiple vendors could be used because that would make it possible to offer the same applications (more or less) to persons writing different languages without making a spelling checker for each one on your own.

No company, however large, is likely to possess in-house linguistic expertise in as many languages as they would like to sell word processors in (that is, *all* languages if they're at all ambitious). By using an object interface, any existing spelling checker can be wrapped in code so that it behaves like an object, even if it wasn't designed to behave that way to begin with.

This chapter examines how this is done, and the how objects distributed across the World Wide Web can coordinate their activities with each other and cooperate to perform complex, even ad hoc, tasks without building expensive custom code for every application. In fact, you'll see how to incorporate small bits of functionality into complete applications without writing anything that might be called traditional programming code. Just as a contractor can build a house without knowing how to pound a nail or install a fuse box by hiring the right people, an object-oriented developer can build an application to an overall design without knowing how to do any of the individual tasks required for the job.

In this chapter, we'll examine object brokers, ubiquitous providers of services on the Web, and show how XML-based applications can interface to objects on the Web. Since object brokers depend on communication and since XML is an excellent communications medium, combining the two is a logical progression in the evolution of the major object broker standards toward XML, the preferred messaging standard on today's Web.

DEFINING OBJECT-ORIENTED INTERFACES

The foundation of the object broker's services depends on a low-level *Interface Definition Language* (IDL) that creates the object-oriented interface that an object presents to the world. An interface describes the entire set of operations that can be performed on an object and the messages that can be passed to it or be expected in response. In object terms, these operations and messages are called *methods*.

Methods prevent any other interaction with the object, so operations not defined by the IDL are not possible. In object-speak, an object is *encapsulated* by its methods, so it really doesn't matter whether the object itself is object-oriented by design. This means that you can easily take legacy programs and databases and turn them into objects by defining a set of methods for them. Since the only way to access the originally non-object-oriented application or database treats it as if it were object-oriented in fact, you can't tell the difference from the outside.

Legacy applications, which aren't object-oriented in and of themselves, are coerced into presenting an object-oriented face to the world by the IDL, which allows only object-oriented methods to be defined. An object broker can then allow those methods to be used by other objects and hide all details of the actual application from the outside. Multiple interfaces can be defined for the same application as well, which allows useful subsets of the total functionality available from the application to be packaged for easy reuse.

Figure 19.1 shows a typical architecture for a distributed component application. The object broker is the glue that ties all the pieces together.

Figure 19.1
The basic distributed object services model is shown here.

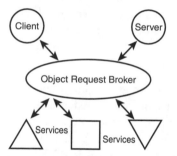

In Figure 19.1, you don't see the IDL layer because it's assumed to be wrapped around the service icon, completely hiding whatever internal processing and representation is used to perform the service and presenting a uniform visage to the world. Of course, the client and server objects can also be defined with the IDL, so the broker can treat these objects transparently as well.

The object broker cloud, which is invisible to the user, is also obscured in the figure. This conceptual single object request broker (ORB) may, in fact, be several brokers located on different machines. They communicate with each other using special protocols that enable the remote ORB to pass requests for services that aren't available on the local machine to another machine where they are.

PART
III

CH
19

Tip from

LeeAnne.com
Words to weave by

One of the advantages of any object-oriented system is the ability to view objects at several levels of abstraction, so your view of the application and its data can vary depending on your need.

Imagine what this generic diagram might represent in the real world. Assume the client object is a graphical user interface (GUI) of some sort and the server object is a legacy database with an object-oriented wrapper around it. You decide to create a simple application that will enable you to query, add new records to, and delete old records from the database. Because those capabilities are available from the object wrapper around the database, you have to find (or code) three modules to

- Read a record from the database.
- Add a new record to the database.
- Delete a record from the database.

The first method will be available to everyone, and the last two will be available only to systems administrators. You don't have to know exactly what the data looks like on the legacy database or even where it is to perform these functions, as long as you have a reliable means of communicating with a service that knows or can find out.

The application then requires only the glue between these component parts. You need some sort of message between your GUI and the object broker requesting a particular service in conjunction with a particular database, and a corresponding message from the object broker returning whatever is to be displayed as a result of the operation. Exactly how the operations are performed is not your concern, and the broker doesn't tell you. Those operations may exist in the code associated with the database itself or may be found at widely separated locations and applied to the database from outside.

Exactly how the database is structured is also not germane to the business at hand. It might be a flat file, fully relational, object-oriented, binary, hashed, sparse array, or any of many other alternatives. The storage medium might be spinning disk, magnetic tape, optical cube, punched cards, or stone tablets. The broker doesn't care because all it wants is the capability to perform a few operations by methods that are uniform across all those database types.

As a general rule, an interface should perform only one task, or a small handful of related tasks. So, if a particular database is ultimately accessed by a native interface that allows hundreds of operations to be performed, the object-oriented interfaces associated with it should abstract small subsets of the total functionality. Trying to pack too much functionality into an object limits its applicability to general problems, so the object is unlikely to be reused. By separating the functions, objects can be more readily used in the future and can be easily debugged by testing their individual functionality. Although the subject of object-oriented systems analysis is beyond the scope of this book, just think of dividing a large problem into small logical tasks that you might assign to an individual without much spare time on her hands and you won't be far wrong.

Good references to this very complex subject include the following:

- *Application (Re)Engineering: Building Web-Based Applications and Dealing With Legacies and Object-Oriented Client/Server Internet Environments* by Amjad Umar
- *Building Application Frameworks: Object-Oriented Foundations of Framework Design* by Mohamed Fayad and Douglas C. Schmidt

- *Design Patterns: Elements of Reusable Object-Oriented Software* by Erich Gamma, Richard Helm, Ralph Johnson, John Vlissides, and Grady Booch
- *COM and CORBA Side by Side: Architectures, Strategies, and Implementations* by Jason Pritchard

REQUESTING BROKER SERVICES

Clients initiate requests for services from an object broker by packaging the request in some manner and sending it to the broker. Two of the most common broker technologies, COM and CORBA, are binary in nature, so their requests are neither transparent nor understandable without extensive knowledge of the interfaces. Debugging a broken interface may require the purchase or development of specialized tools. Also, COM and CORBA cross-platform support runs into translation difficulties. There are internal numeric representation problems, methodological incompatibilities, and other obstacles that prevent rapid deployment, testing, and rework. These two technologies, CORBA and COM, are discussed in the "Understanding CORBA" and "Understanding COM" sections later in this chapter.

XML Transfer Protocol (XMLTP), a new broker standard emerging from the XML world, adds the virtues of full transparency and adherence to an XML DTD so the syntax of the requests can be verified before attempting to execute them. In addition, XMLTP uses an HTTP transport mechanism to get past firewalls and other barriers to network communication. The ready availability of standard XML schema and transformation tools to enable cross-technology support also helps the developer. Although XMLTP is still in a preliminary stage, this new technology may help bridge the XML and object-oriented worlds along with UML and other rapid application development tools. This standard is examined in the "Understanding XMLTP" section later in this chapter, along with a few similar standards suites, SOAP, WIDL plus XML, and XIOP.

And finally, the Java object broker technology, RMI, also a binary standard but very lightweight because it assumes a Java environment on both ends, is discussed in the "Understanding Java RMI" section.

PART
III

CH
19

COMMUNICATING BETWEEN OBJECT BROKERS

A problem with object broker technology is that disparate brokers don't communicate with each other very well, if at all. This has opened the door for vendors of software designed to translate between one object broker format and another, but especially CORBA and COM, because they are the most common broker environments.

IONA, Visual Edge, and Noblenet have all released implementations of COM/CORBA communications packages that enable developers to support mixed environments. Using mixed environments seems to be the most reasonable solution to the dilemma facing developers and large corporations, that is, which standard to choose. The best choice may be both. In fact, SOAP, XMLTP, and other message-transport standards also address the issue of communication between brokers.

Since both COM and CORBA use binary communications protocols, direct conversion between the two object broker message types is difficult, and debugging the conversions requires considerable care. Translating messages to an intermediate format, especially an XML-based standard which is transparent to inspection, makes it more likely that a successful conversion can take place.

Considering the ubiquity of COM on the desktop and in many enterprise servers, coupled with the excellent development tools available for COM, it seems unlikely that COM will ever lose market share completely to CORBA.

At the same time, CORBA is so much more mature as a product and is available on so many platforms that eventual dominance of COM seems equally unlikely. Microsoft has never shown much interest in supporting competing platforms and, although COM does support the Java Virtual Machine (JVM) as an alternative to ActiveX, the Microsoft version of JVM (Microsoft VM) is somewhat Microsoft-specific.

Using proprietary "extensions" in a Java applet or Bean naturally poisons the object when used on the Internet. Extreme care has to be taken to offer alternative non-extended mechanisms. To offer these alternative mechanisms requires testing the environment in which the applet or Bean runs and altering the behavior of the module to suit. This is contrary to the whole idea of a universal virtual machine because it creates multiple versions of the environment. If you have to write to a different virtual machine for each physical or logical platform, what's the point?

On the other hand, if you develop for a Microsoft-only network, Microsoft Java is no more proprietary than ActiveX, so you might justifiably use it when warranted by the situation. Servers handling general Internet traffic are used to the idea of sniffing the browser environment they will run in, so handling one more incompatibility is just more of the same rather than a new problem.

MAKING SENSE OF BROKER CHAOS

Someone once said that the nice thing about standards is that there are so many of them. This is surely true for object brokers. Although we look at only a handful here, many others exist. JavaBeans is an object broker model especially designed for the Java environment, for example, and really subsumes yet another model, Enterprise JavaBeans, which is not quite the same as ordinary Beans. Microsoft's ActiveX is another standard, although closely related to COM, and in turn relates to Universal Plug and Play (UPnP), which adds an XML messaging backbone to the mix. Java Remote Method Invocation (RMI) is yet a third. So the question is, why so many?

The answer is simple: Any object broker introduces a layer of indirection between the multiple objects that may be used in a particular application. The most general brokers, such as CORBA, are also the most inefficient because they handle many types of objects. But if you're working in an exclusively Java environment, for example, you don't need all that complexity because all your objects use the same mechanisms. So the Java RMI interface cuts overhead and makes your Beans cooperate more efficiently. In a world designed from the ground up to use any particular standard, using the native object interface or an object interface designed for that environment can save time and trouble in both coding and debugging, as well as making your overall application smaller.

Unfortunately, most of us don't have the luxury of working in a completely controlled environment. You may come into a situation in which the interface to a small customer database was designed for COM, the main accounting system uses CORBA, a parts inventory system uses a proprietary object interface supplied by the original vendor, and a number of Web applications use JavaBeans. In the real world almost everything costs money, time, or both, and you don't have the luxury of rewriting the entire operating environment at once to try a new programming language.

In fact, by using components from different models, you may simplify your life considerably, because you may discover precoded objects lying around that can be glued together to make an application. So, you might use ActiveX controls and Visual Basic widgets to handle your Windows screen display, and JavaBeans for the Web portion of an application.

UNDERSTANDING CORBA—COMMON OBJECT REQUEST BROKER ARCHITECTURE

CORBA is perhaps the most generic of the object brokers. It fully supports more platforms than any other, including older Windows platforms on which COM and other Microsoft object methods are not available. Perhaps surprisingly, for those familiar with the Microsoft platform only, CORBA is not monolithic, but is made up of many Object Request Brokers (ORBs) from many different vendors such as Inprise (VisiBroker) and IONA (Orbix 2000), to name only two. CORBA provides an interoperability standard, the Internet Inter-ORB Protocol (IIOP) allowing an ORB from one vendor to interact with that from another over TCP/IP with no loss of functionality. IIOP is a particular instantiation of the General Inter-ORB Protocol (GIOP), which isn't mapped to any particular transport medium.

CORBA is under the control of a large consortium of developers and stakeholders in object technology and the architecture supports true object-oriented methods. Unlike COM, described later in this chapter, CORBA was designed from the start to be usable across multiple platforms and languages. CORBA is based on an object technology that encapsulates individual applications or objects comprising a larger application within an interface defined by a common language: the Interface Definition Language (IDL). IDL provides many ways to invoke the basic broker services, depending on the needs of the application as a whole.

The primary means a client uses to call on broker services is an IDL *stub* hard-coded for each client/server object pair. Alternatively the client can construct a similar call through dynamic invocation, although the CORBA Dynamic Invocation Interface (DII) can be very slow. The object is accessed either through a hard-coded *skeleton* or by dynamically creating a similar skeleton. In both cases, neither the client nor the server object can tell the difference between either option from their end of the communication. If the programming language used by the client is object-oriented, a hard-coded stub may not be necessary. Similarly, if the object server is inherently object-oriented, a hard-coded skeleton may not be necessary either, because the programming languages used can dynamically invoke the same interface functionality.

Some basic services may also be offered by an ORB interface directly accessible to clients and by object adaptors containing basic information about server objects. This information might be used, for example, to help the ORB construct dynamic skeletons encapsulating more functionality.

Because all ORBs present the same face to the world and offer the same services, a vendor can distinguish its offerings from those of other vendors by the efficiency of the vendor's implementations or methods of closely integrating its product into an overall programming environment. Closely tracking the latest revisions of the CORBA standard may also confer bragging rights, at least until the rest of the CORBA world catches up.

USING CORBA

The CORBA IDL looks a lot like C++, which may explain why many ORB providers also sell compilers. IDL also makes CORBA relatively inaccessible to nonprogrammers. The following code represents the IDL interface to a simple "hello, world" program so beloved of programmers.

```
module helloWorld {
  interface simpleHelloWorld {
    string sayHello();
    };
  };
```

As you can see, it looks like programming code and, like programming code, it generates a binary interface. Any code that generates the same binary interface is equivalent in the OMG IDL world, so many front-ends have been developed for CORBA to allow easy access from multiple language and operating system platforms. Although this binary focus is traditional in the programming world, it runs contrary to the XML philosophy, which is open, plain-language interfaces that are readily accessible to inspection by anyone. Debugging a traditional CORBA implementation requires special tools or great patience, because the binary code has to be deciphered for each interface.

Nonetheless, CORBA is readily available almost everywhere, and is the lingua franca of distributed development in multi-operating system and multilanguage environments. Because CORBA is also designed to provide encapsulation of legacy code, CORBA offers a clean way to incorporate older technology that still works into reengineered systems.

For further reading on CORBA and related subjects, you might be interested in the following:

- by Dan Harkey (Editor *Client/Server Programming with Java and CORBA, Second Edition*) and Robert Orfali
- *Java Programming with Corba* by Andreas Vogel and Keith Duddy
- *COM and CORBA Side by Side: Architectures, Strategies, and Implementations* by Jason Pritchard
- *Enterprise CORBA* by Dirk Slama, Jason Garbis, and Perry Russell

UNDERSTANDING COM—COMPONENT OBJECT MODEL

COM (Component Object Model) is Microsoft's object broker, providing object communication through a series of predefined binary interfaces. DEC (Digital Equipment Corporation) calls the same technology COM, which in DEC's case always means Common Object Model and probably accounts for the dual terminology, although you see DEC's expansion of the COM acronym in Microsoft literature from time to time. They are the same thing, despite the differing names.

> **Note**
>
> Some controversy exists over whether COM can truly be described as object-oriented because the technology doesn't support inheritance, a basic property of object-orientedness, and the technology builds applications by aggregating smaller COM objects. More than that, COM isn't device- and language-independent, using a fragile and hard-to-understand conglomeration of ad hoc solutions to particular problems. In this view, COM is merely a client-server mechanism and is scorned by object purists.

COM is the basis of Microsoft distributed applications but is combined with several other technologies to make complete systems. Because Microsoft machines are not alone on the Internet, Distributed COM (DCOM) provides COM services on UNIX, IBM MVS, and other mainframe and minicomputer operating systems, as well as a few non-Microsoft microcomputer operating systems. When combined with Microsoft Transaction Server (MTS), Microsoft Internet Information Server (IIS), Active Server Pages (ASP), and Microsoft Message Queue (MSMQ), complex applications spanning multiple platforms can be constructed out of individually simple parts, provided that the center of the application is located on Microsoft machines. Trying to use COM in a non-Microsoft environment is difficult, because most of the COM infrastructure and support is available only on Microsoft platforms.

A huge advantage of COM is that it fully supports the most widely used and available user platform in the world. Although Windows NT servers are not as common, Windows client desktops are almost ubiquitous. But this instant access to most of the desktops in the world comes at a price. COM doesn't interface comfortably with programming languages that don't support pointer arithmetic and, as mentioned before, COM doesn't fit well into non-Windows environments due to lack of support from other vendors and lukewarm support from Microsoft of other architectures. Solaris is about the only competing architecture to which Microsoft has ported COM.

Microsoft has extended COM with Distributed COM, but the distribution is sparse. Software AG produces a product implementing DCOM on UNIX called EntireX, probably a play on the ActiveX underpinnings of DCOM. Several other vendors have DCOM implementations, but they are aftermarket add-ons for the most part, and the primary target machines for DCOM are Windows NT servers at one end and Windows clients at the other.

A few years ago, Microsoft enhanced COM with new features and renamed it COM+, including channels (a publish and subscribe service), better integration of MTS, dynamic load balancing, and COM component queuing.

PART

III

CH

19

Recently, all these Microsoft standards plus BizTalk (Microsoft's XML-based business-to-business communications architecture) and other Microsoft products have been incorporated under the overall term, Windows DNA. Unfortunately, Windows DNA isn't quite done yet and is more of a marketing concept to aim at than a real product.

> **Note**
>
> DNA supposedly stands for *D*istributed *InterNet* Applications *A*rchitecture. As a mnemonic, this seems rather a stretch because half the initial letters are missing and the central "N" is snatched from the middle of the second word. It seems a bit ambitious as well, because presumably Microsoft means to imply that Windows DNA is the genetic material from which Internet applications will be built. Lately, explanation of the mnemonic has quietly vanished from their literature and it's more of an umbrella marketing term than a real product, because you can't actually go out and buy a copy.

COM by itself doesn't support distributed applications, so Microsoft extended the standard with a mechanism called Object Remote Procedure Call (ORPC). ORPC is based on the Open Software Foundation Distributed Computing Environment's Remote Procedure Call (DCE/RPC). Information on DCE/RPC can be found at http://www.opengroup.org/tech/dce/. ORPC is customized for the Microsoft environment but otherwise is an implementation of the cross-platform open standard. DCOM objects can have multiple interfaces, and DCOM clients access the methods exposed by the interface by means of a pointer into the compiled code to the location of the interface itself. This dependency on pointers means that making changes to DCOM clients or objects generally requires recompiling everything.

Most wouldn't call that sort of behavior object-oriented, but it works in the target environments for most DCOM applications, which are homogenous Microsoft platforms with only a few well-defined interfaces to the Internet as a whole. Outside network connections are often passed through interfaces that prevent (or reduce) any possibility of two-way interaction for security reasons in any case, so losing COM/DCOM along the way is often no great loss.

USING COM

COM and DCOM are integrated into the Windows Registry, so it requires the use of Registry UUIDs, which are, quite frankly, ugly. One gets used to them in the Windows world but they're not, to put it mildly, particularly mnemonic.

The following code snippet might implement the DCOM interface to a simple "hello, world" distributed application. You define the interface as dual in line 3 so that the Microsoft IDL compiler will generate both the stub and skeleton (entered into the system Registry by UUID) as well as a dynamic interface library entry:

```
  [
  uuid(2E3BCD48-13AF-D423-167B-437BE6C131DA),
  dual
  ]
library World {
  interface helloWorld : IDispatch {
    HRESULT getHello ([in] BSTR* instr, [out, retval] BSTR* outstr);
    }
```

```
[
  uuid(2E3BCD49-13AF-D423-167B-437BE6C131DA)
  ]
coclass Hello {
  interface helloWorld;
  };
}
```

Because you defined both a library and a class in the preceding snippet, you have a way of finding the class in the library associated with this application. If you don't want to use the dynamic interface, you don't need to access the library and can rely on the stub and skeleton you entered into the Registry. So, COM handily supports both object-oriented languages and procedural languages that don't support object orientation.

Figure 19.2 shows a typical COM architecture with COM as the base layer, MTS and an MTS application as one half of an application, and OLE and/or ActiveX controls accessing the terminal or a database as the other.

Figure 19.2
This is a typical COM-based, transaction-based application architecture.

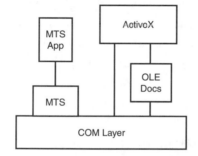

Because COM/DCOM by itself doesn't compensate or attempt to recover from network errors, latency, or other problems that can adversely affect real-world applications, some form of error recovery is needed. A complete process may require a series of tasks to be performed in exact order and, if errors occur, the entire series up to the point of failure must be backed out. Recovery from this sort of failure requires records of each step to be kept so that the reverse steps necessary to restore the initial state can be performed. This is called *transaction processing*.

TRANSACTION PROCESSING

Transaction processing is fairly simple to understand when you consider your own experience with banking. If you walk up to an ATM and draw a hundred dollars out of your checking account, two tasks need to occur in order. One task is that of debiting your account and the other is that of dispensing the money. At any given moment, a failure can occur in either task. If you get the money and your account isn't debited, the bank will be unhappy. If your account is debited and you don't get the money, you'll be unhappy.

By wrapping these two tasks in a transaction wrapper, a failure at any point ensures that neither action is performed. Typically, a transaction processing system maintains a log of every action. First the ATM invokes a trial debit on your account. If that succeeds, the ATM checks to make sure there's money enough in the machine to fulfill the request, often counting it out into an intermediate station with a failsafe dispensing mechanism. If everything seems okay, the trial debit is committed. Finally, your account is a hundred dollars smaller and the ATM receives a signal to release the money.

If not, the transaction is backed out, the money deposited in the intermediate dispensing station is recaptured, and the ATM itself shuts down while awaiting repair. If communication fails before the signal to release the money is received but after it is prepared for dispensing, the ATM should assume that everything went well, because it knows that the bank is aware of the transaction and can reconstruct the transaction if necessary. At state that point the ATM shuts itself down, because it can't communicate with the bank and can't safely dispense any more money.

That's transaction processing in a nutshell, a method of accounting for serialization errors, recovering from them if possible, and minimizing damage if not. COM/DCOM is paired with Microsoft Transaction Server (MTS) to make reliable transaction processing possible in the Microsoft environment.

For further reading on COM you might be interested in the following texts:

- *COM and CORBA Side by Side: Architectures, Strategies, and Implementations* by Jason Pritchard
- *COM Beyond Microsoft : Designing and Implementing Com Servers on Compaq Platforms* by Gene Cronin and Terence P. Sherlock
- *Web Programming with ASP and COM* by Matt J. Crouch
- *Distributed COM Application Development Using Visual Basic 6.0 and MTS* by Jim Maloney
- *COM/DCOM Unleashed* by Randy Abernethy, Jesus Chahin, and Randy Charles Morin

UNDERSTANDING XMLTP—XML TRANSFER PROTOCOL

Interestingly enough, XML has the potential to act as an object broker on its own. Because objects have predefined interfaces that enable you to access them, any interface at all can be defined as long as all the objects are in agreement about what the interface looks like. Although there may seem to be a distinction between interprocess messages and XML documents, the UNIX experience in which everything can be viewed as a file shows that this isn't true.

In fact, XML has significant advantages as an interprocess communications medium because XML (ideally) references a DTD and can be evolved without breaking previous versions. Additional functionality can be incorporated into the document by adding new elements to the DTD or by incorporating other XML documents with their own DTDs into the existing document.

Because every XML document is parsed, it doesn't matter how much information is added to it if the information the target object is looking for remains available. This is a sharp contrast to typical binary communications protocols, because the meaning and size of each field is typically contained in the object itself rather than being inherent in the message. So, whenever an application adds functionality, the application and all objects used by the application will probably have to be recompiled and replaced. In an asynchronous distributed environment such as the Internet, the chance of updating everything at once are slim, and such errors can be almost impossible to track down. Figure 19.3 shows the contrast between the messages passed between closely coupled object mechanisms such as COM and the loosely coupled mechanisms made possible by XML-based protocols such as XMLTP.

Figure 19.3
XMLTP promises inter-process communications that will be easy to understand and debug in the event of failure.

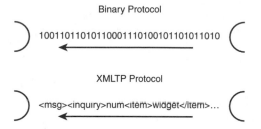

Binary Protocol

10011011010110001110100101101011010

XMLTP Protocol

<msg><inquiry>num<item>widget</item>...

As you can see, a human-readable interface is much easier for programmers (or even ordinary mortals) to understand when creating inter-object methods. Because XMLTP is XML-based, any XML validating parser can be used to ensure that messages conform to the DTD. Initial debugging can be simplified as well, lessening the number of special-purpose tools that have to be created to test the application as a whole.

As you saw in our discussion of COM and CORBA, transaction processing is important in most real-world applications because a number of related activities may have to succeed before an update can be considered complete. Transactions in XML can be represented by simple nesting optionally combined with external document sources, and the XML standard itself prevents documents from being read until the document itself, that is, the message, is complete. So, asynchronous updates can be enforced and automatically rolled back by XML.

The XMLTP home page is located at http://www.xmltp.org/ and future evolution of this standard will be posted there or at the companion development site located on SourceForge at http://sourceforge.net/project/?group_id=1893. SourceForge offers free archival, hosting, and other services to the opensource community.

Many portions of the specification are still undefined, but because it faces the same problems addressed by SOAP as described in the "Understanding SOAP—Simple Object Access Protocol" section later in this chapter, it seems likely that XMLTP will also be carried on top of HTTP to allow the protocol to get past firewall protections.

Firewalls were explained in Chapter 16, "Security and Privacy," but for a quick review, firewalls work (in part) by monitoring the port a request comes in on and preventing all accesses to unauthorized ports. System administrators particularly dislike allowing dynamic port assignments, so many dynamic protocols inevitably fail when they encounter firewalls because security-conscious administrators won't let them past.

→ **See** "Erecting Security Firewalls," **p. 374**.

XMLTP is only one of many efforts underway to integrate XML over HTTP and object broker functionality. For another example, see Anders Tell's XIOP site at `http://xiop.sourceforge.net/`, which is a CORBA-compliant GIOP over HTTP messaging service which is still under development but is open source and extremely interesting.

USING XMLTP

The XMLTP standard is still in a preliminary stage, so it doesn't make a great deal of sense to spend much time on constructing an imaginary example. Please see the example shown in the "Using SOAP" section later in this chapter because the syntax will be similar.

UNDERSTANDING JAVA RMI—REMOTE METHOD INVOCATION

Remote Method Invocation (RMI) is a Sun Microsystems invention and works only in a Java environment. Although the Java Virtual Machine (JVM), Sun's name for the Java runtime environment, is designed to be available and uniform across all platforms, there are notable problems with the Sun strategy. Microsoft, for example, "extended" the Java concept to include hooks to Microsoft-specific features available only on Windows/Intel platforms, so what purported to be Java code written using Microsoft tools wasn't guaranteed to run on other platforms.

> **Note**
>
> RMI is basically an object-oriented remote procedure call mechanism. Although it incorporates much of the functionality of an ORB because it's based on a language that is inherently object-oriented, the only platform independence available is due to the fact that Java is available on most platforms.

Unlike other object broker technologies, RMI is built into the JVM itself. The protocol is lightweight because it doesn't have to take into account different runtime environments. RMI is an object-oriented remote procedure call mechanism and not a full, object-oriented, transaction-processing environment. In any distributed application, you have to take into account the possibility of network failure, latency, concurrency, and other problems associated with an uncertain network environment. In the absence of any transaction wrapper or built-in ways to handle these possibilities, using RMI means taking into account possible error scenarios as well as anticipated success.

RMI forms the basis for Jini, Enterprise JavaBeans(EJB), and JavaSpaces, which each attempt to extend Java into a full distributed transaction-processing system. A complete discussion of the many tools available in the Sun Java universe is not possible in the space allotted to this chapter, but you'll see a short example of RMI in use. Refer to the Sun Java site for further information: `http://java.sun.com/`.

USING RMI

For this example, assume you want to have a server say hello using the facilities of RMI. You need to define RMI interface classes for the client and the server objects and then write the client and server themselves.

Your first Java file creates an instance of the RMI interface class, Remote, which every RMI application must do to use RMI facilities:

```
/* First, get the RMI base class */
import java.rmi.*;
/* Now, declare the interface and the helloRemote method */
public interface helloIF extends Remote {
  String helloRemote(String client)
        throws RemoteException;
  }
```

Your next Java program is the client itself. It has to use the remote interface you declared in the previous code sample:

```
/* First, get the base classes for RMI and RMI servers */
import java.rmi.*;
import java.rmi.server.*;
/* Second, declare the client class */
public class helloClient {
  /* Third, declare the arguments */
  public static void main(String[] arguments) {
    /* Fourth, invoke the RMI security manager */
    System.setSecurityManager(new RMISecurityManager());
    /* Fifth, call the remote server */
    try {
      helloIF x =
        (helloIF)Naming.lookup("//" + getCodeBase().getHost() +
                              "/helloServer");
      System.out.println(x.helloRemote("world."));
      }
    catch(Exception errcode) {
      System.out.println("Error: " + errcode);
      }
    System.exit(0);
    }
  }
```

On the server side, you need a server that uses the same interface as the client:

```
/* First, get the base classes for RMI and RMI servers */
import java.rmi.*;
import java.rmi.server.*;
/* Second, get the base classes for applets and the RMI Registry */
import sun.applet.*;
import java.rmi.registry.LocateRegistry;
/* Third, declare the server class */
public class helloServer {
  public static void main(String args[]){
    if (System.getSecurityManager() == null) {
      System.setSecurityManager(new RMISecurityManager());
      }
```

PART

III

CH

19

```
    try {
      helloObject remoteObject = new helloObject();
      Naming.rebind("helloObject", remoteObject);
      }
    catch(Exception errcode) {
      System.out.println("Error: " + errcode);
      }
    }
  }
```

And on both sides, an you need an object that the client and server can call. Unlike a regular Java file, this file isn't compiled with javac. Instead, we'll use a special RMI compiler, rmic, which generates two files, one suffixed with _stub and one suffixed with _skel. The stub program sits on the client side, and the client program actually calls it. The stub then finds the server using RMI services and passes the client request to it. The server executes the skeleton object, which sits on the server, and passes the result back to the stub on the client side, which passes the returned value to the client. Here's the object code:

```
/* First, get the base classes for RMI and RMI servers */
import java.rmi.*;
import java.rmi.server.*;
/* Second, declare the object class */
public class helloObject
  extends UnicastRemoteObject
  implements helloIF {
    public helloObject() throws RemoteException {
      super();
      }
/* Now do the work */
public String helloRemote(String client)
    throws RemoteException {
      return "Hello, " + client;
      }
    }
```

Before you can register your distributed application, you have to start the RMI Registry on the server. On Windows systems, you open a DOS window and type in

```
start rmiregistry
```

On UNIX systems, type in

```
rimregistry &
```

For those not familiar with UNIX, the ampersand tells the shell to display a system prompt immediately instead of waiting for the rmiregistry program to finish.

Finally, when you run the programs, you have to point at the security files for the client as well as the server. The security files should look like this:

```
grant codeBase
"file:/someURL/" {
  permission java.net.SocketPermission
    "127.0.0.1", "accept, connect, listen, resolve";
  };
```

UNDERSTANDING SOAP–SIMPLE OBJECT ACCESS PROTOCOL

The *Simple Object Access Protocol* (SOAP) is Microsoft's version of an XML interprocess communications and remote procedure call (RPC) mechanism. SOAP is particularly effective at passing through firewalls. Firewalls prevent many RPC and interprocess communications protocols from reaching their destinations because it's piggybacked on top of HTTP, which is available through almost all firewalls. SOAP slips transparently through any firewall that allows Web browser access.

SOAP is an integral part of another Microsoft XML object broker initiative, Universal Plug and Play (UPnP). A consortium of Microsoft partners sponsors UPnP but comparatively little has been heard from UPnP since it was announced in January of 1999, although demonstration products have been presented by consortium vendors. Unlike CORBA and COM/DCOM, UPnP seems primarily designed for the home network or small business LAN rather than as a general Internet-capable product. Network devices make themselves known by broadcasting to a known IP address and port, where a control process registers them as available and collects information about the services they provide. In UPnP terms, this process is known as advertising and discovery.

> **Note**
>
> The UPnP Consortium has a home page at `http://www.upnp.org/` although there's a dearth of information currently available to the general public on the site. This seems reasonable because the users of the product would be hardware vendors primarily, who would presumably join and have access to more information.

UPnP seems to be aimed toward the niche coveted by Jini, home and small office networks. UPnP seems clearly designed to compete with the Sun technology by building on Microsoft's existing relationships with vendors and hardware providers to extend the marketing concept of Plug and Play (PnP) peripherals to networked devices and services. Like Jini, UPnP seems unlikely to scale upward to the Internet as a whole without problems.

The advertising and discovery mechanism, whereby one or more control processes collect and retain information about all devices available on the network based on a series of messages multicast to the network as a whole by each device, seems unwieldy when elaborated to the entire Internet. There seems to be no current mechanism for hierarchical distribution of device information, and little chance that anyone would allow an outsider to use their physical devices anyway. But on a private network, these problems go away or are minimized. The number of devices available on a home or small office network is minimal, and the control process itself can restrict access to devices so programmers, for example, can't use the human resources department printer to run off listings.

A related standard from HP is Appliance Plug and Play (APnP), which integrates UPnP with HP's Chai Java appliance technology, Sun's JVM or Jini, and any other network appliance language that comes along in the future. Although Jini seems fairly well established in certain markets, the vendor base supporting Chai APnP is still unclear but seems likely to be members of the UPnP consortium who want to hedge their bets.

PART

III

CH

19

USING SOAP

Assume a simple order entry program places an order for this book using the title, author name, and ISBN number as well as an arbitrary customer number that can be used by the application to index into a customer database to find the shipping address and billing information. Of course, far more complex messages are possible but not necessary to show for this small example:

```
POST /LeeAnne HTTP/1.1
Host: www.leeanne.com
Content-Type: text/xml
Content-Length: whatever
SOAPMethodName: http://www.leeanne.com/usingxml/OrderEntry
<SOAP:Envelope xmlns:SOAP="urn:SOAP:schemas-soap-org:soap.v1">
  <SOAP:Body>
    <oem:OrderEntry
        xmlns:oem="http://www.leeanne.com/usingxml/OrderEntry">
      <Title>Using XML 1.0</Title>
      <Author>Lee Anne Phillips</Author>
      <ISBN>0-7897-1996-7</ISBN>
    </oem:OrderEntry>
  </SOAP:Body>
</SOAP:Envelope>
```

When the order completes, the same general message can be returned with the addition of a confirmation number and a shipping date or an out-of-stock entry if the title isn't available right now.

```
HTTP/1.1 200 OK
connection: close
Content-Type: text/xml
Content-Length: whatever
SOAPMethodName: http://www.leeanne.com/usingxml/OrderConfirm
<SOAP:Envelope xmlns:SOAP="urn:SOAP:schemas-soap-org:soap.v1">
  <SOAP:Body>
    <oem:OrderConfirm
        xmlns:oem="http://www.leeanne.com/usingxml/OrderConfirm">
      <Title>Using XML 1.0</Title>
      <Author>Lee Anne Phillips</Author>
      <ISBN>0-7897-1996-7</ISBN>
      <Confirm>12345678</Confirm>
      <ShipDate>20000711T163000-8</ShipDate>
    </oem:OrderConfirm>
  </SOAP:Body>
</SOAP:Envelope>
```

The shipping date is in a format supported by XML Schema, so it can be validated easily using standard XML Schema tools. The title, author, and ISBN number are returned so that the order and corresponding confirmation can be manually verified if necessary. Figure 19.4 shows the SOAP transaction as viewed in a browser. In actuality, the transaction would probably be sent directly to another process.

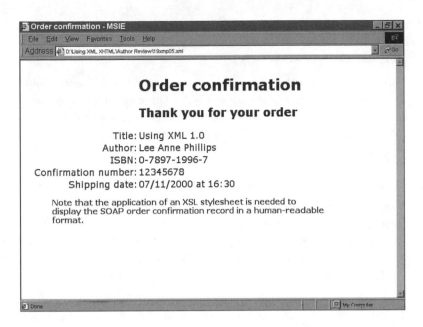

Figure 19.4
This SOAP transaction is being viewed in Microsoft Internet Explorer.

SOAP is currently the only real contender for an XML-based object request broker system; however, there are a pack of alternatives waiting in the wings getting ready to make their entrance. XMLTP, as described briefly in the "Understanding XMLTP—XML Transfer Protocol" section earlier in this chapter, is one example, and XIOP, referenced in the same section, is another.

The combination of XML-based object brokers and XML-based data repositories will eventually make possible the seamless integration of legacy applications and databases with modern object-oriented tools in ways we can hardly imagine today. In particular, SOAP and similar XML-based communications protocols promise a method of leveling the playing field between COM/DCOM and CORBA. At their heart, the two protocols are somewhat similar and implement roughly the same protocol stack although they differ greatly in detail. So it's possible to translate between them.

In the last part of this chapter, you'll look at the ways in which XML data archival systems are changing the way enterprises manage their corporate data assets.

INTEGRATING XML DATA REPOSITORIES— DISTRIBUTED OBJECTS

You have seen many ways to create object-oriented distributed applications in this chapter. However, applications operate on data for the most part, so the remainder of this chapter will focus on object-oriented (or somewhat so) database technologies that allow complete object-oriented applications to include object-oriented database access as well.

Using object wrappers around legacy databases adds a layer of indirection that slows down data access and can preclude their use in real applications. Although this can be valuable as an interim measure to allow rapid development of a reengineered testbed, eventually it may be necessary to convert the database to a more efficient representation that allows the application to access it directly.

The last part of this chapter examines some of the most innovative approaches to XML data access and management currently available. There are many more approaches in development, many under wraps until initial public offerings or a sufficient lead can be developed to give a nascent firm a chance to get a marketing or development plan well underway before everyone in the world knows what it's doing.

PREPARING FOR DATA DISASTER

A significant portion of the assets of modern corporations and even governments are in data form, yet our ability to access and make use of that data is often primitive at best. However, the possibility of losing that data, even with the limited tools we now possess to make use of it, is daunting to the most daring of corporate data specialists. But there are many threats to corporate data, from accidental loss to deliberate sabotage.

With many backup technologies, it's impossible to determine by casual inspection whether the data is valid. It's fairly common for a single failure in a configuration file to invalidate an entire series of backup tapes without anyone knowing. Data audits are an important part of the overall plan, but the most reliable check is the oversight of a human being. Using XML as a backup language enables anyone to glance at the archive and see whether the archived data seems reasonable.

In the event of utter catastrophe, having the data available in XML, a form that allows the data to be recreated no matter what happens, even if the computers and software required to process it have been destroyed, makes it possible to guarantee that recovery is possible. This is not a terribly unlikely scenario. Many applications are running today on legacy computers that aren't made anymore. The source code for the applications that run on them may have been lost or may not run on any other machine. In contrast, XML runs anywhere, and tools to manipulate it can be quickly constructed using available component parts and standards such as XSLT and XML Schema.

PLANNING FOR FAIL-SAFE STORAGE

XML offers a way to store data for generations with every expectation that the data can be used in perpetuity and that data loss is highly unlikely. This contrasts with many previous technologies that have all but disappeared. Even with a simple audio recording, most of us would be hard pressed to decipher an Edison cylinder, much less some of the rarer recording media. Eight-inch floppy disks, common only a few decades ago, are not usually found outside the city dump any more. So, if you find a buried treasure trove of giant floppies containing the entire early documentation of the McDonalds corporation, all of which are labeled to show that they were created on a Wang dedicated word processing machine, you have a problem.

Even if you use a supposedly universal output format such as Rich Text Format (RTF), you're not protected from obsolescence, because data the RTF implementations of many vendors don't work with each other and some won't even work with their own previous incarnations. The format isn't particularly transparent and, because RTF tags aren't explicitly closed, minor data losses can occur without being noticed. Not only that, as you can see in the following snippet, which starts this very paragraph in RTF format, the tagging syntax is obscure to say the least:

```
\par }\pard\plain \s19\ql\li0\ri0\sa240\sl240\slmult0
\widctlpar\tx7920\nooverflow\faroman\rin0\lin0\itap0
\f6\fs24\lang1033\langfe1033\cgrid\langnp1033\langfenp1033 {
Even if you use supposedly universal output formats like …
\par
```

However, modern data asset management tools and XML-based archival media make an ideal combination for maximizing control over your data and making it accessible to the entire enterprise or agency.

MANAGING DATA ASSETS

Asset management tools allow the enterprise to exert effective control over data empires of enormous extent. Even individual users may have trouble keeping track of the amount of data that modern hard disks encourage users to accumulate. When you add up the number of spindles on desktops with the very large disk arrays common on corporate data servers, even moderately sized firms may have many terabits of data scattered across hundreds of locations.

Keeping track of which data is available is difficult in the best of situations, but when you have many employees who may need to update that data, coordinating their efforts can be a daunting task without help. So, data can not only be lost or misplaced, but two people might accidentally decide to update the same file. Whoever finishes first loses, because the last to finish will inadvertently overwrite the work of the first when saving the new work to the changed file.

To avoid this problem, version control systems prevent more than one individual from editing a file at the same time, but that's far too restrictive in many situations. The following section, "Understanding Poet," discusses one solution to the problem of flexible management of complex document systems.

UNDERSTANDING POET

Traditional asset management systems, such as Poet, are aimed primarily at controlling the actions of individuals within a large organization. By keeping track of which documents are in a stable state and which have been checked out by someone, potential chaos is averted. Uncontrolled updates are extremely difficult to control without some sort of formal system that prevents two or more people from editing the document at the same time.

Poet is an asset management system based on XML/SGML documents that enables both SGML/XML documents and binary entities to be managed and versioned, although Poet knows nothing about the internals of non-SGML/non-XML files. Poet manages documents at the entity level but enables the developer to abstract documents into a collection of logical entities if this makes sense for an individual application.

For most purposes, the logical entities defined in a content manager like Poet shouldn't represent elements within a document smaller than what might be edited as a unit. Low-level elements smaller than a section are unlikely to form an editable or reusable unit. So, it might be perfectly logical to define a chapter as a logical entity in a book document but it wouldn't make sense to define an italicized word as an entity because it seems unlikely that a single word, or even a phrase, could profitably be checked out for update. In addition, the more granularity is supported in a document, the longer it will take to process it. However, allowing documents to be sliced and diced like this reaps rewards when it comes time to update it because now component parts of a single document can be edited by teams, with the total document being safely spread among many updaters.

In addition to the version control functions incorporated in the content manager, Poet has some traditional database functions as well. You can construct database queries that enable a selection of documents to be made based on criteria defined by the user. This allows certain documents to be selected for processing using all the power of a modern database inquiry.

Figure 19.5 shows the Poet content management system in the process of checking out a document for update. You can enter a comment detailing the reasons for the update and who did it, although it's also possible to set up the application so that users login and their identities are captured automatically.

Figure 19.5
The Poet content manager shows an XML document checkout in progress.

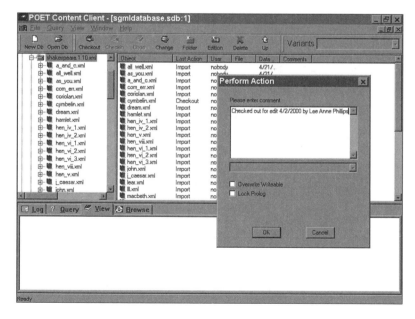

Poet is more than just a version control system in many ways, including its capability to share components among many documents. This capability enables a limited sort of inheritance among the documents in the database, because single components can be used as a base on which to build other documents. If the component is updated, all documents that contain it are automatically updated as well the next time they're used.

This sort of inheritance also allows what document specialists call "boilerplate" to be centrally controlled and used as the basis of other documents by selecting bits of boiler plate to use in a given document and writing glue bits to tie the pieces together. In many situations, this enables a firm to respond quickly to requests for information, because a customized document can be created out of preexisting modular parts.

Looking at dbXML

dbXML is an attempt to redefine the way databases are integrated with XML by making the database fit the XML language rather than wrapping legacy databases in a vaguely XML-related shroud. XML is inherently tree-structured, although most current databases purporting to support XML data repositories are either a collection of flat files or standard indexed tables with or without relational characteristics. This makes data access inefficient, because abstracting a tree structure from a table or flat file requires manipulation of the underlying data before it can be presented at the interface.

In view of this, the dbXML organization aims to create a tree-structured file organization that mirrors the structure of an actual XML file. A typical existing tree-structured file structure is binary in nature, but XML documents are not binary. They can have any number of child branches under each node, so a tree-based file structure has to reflect the multiple branching nature of XML.

The dbXML Web site at http://www.dbxml.org/ eventually will be a good source of the latest information on dbXML and should be checked for ongoing developments. The site is under wraps for a bit while they regroup and decide how much to make public, although dbXML is intended to be open source and available to all. In the reality of the marketplace, however, making too much information available too soon could work against the intentions of the author. A better-funded effort by a commercial firm could quickly overtake a nonfunded or poorly funded development project. The ideas incorporated in the open source code might wind up being hedged about with intellectual property restrictions and patents to the point that no one could use the original concept legally.

Part

III

Ch

19

Understanding Texcel

Texcel Systems of Norway has developed a technology for content management incorporating the idea of object-oriented, DTD-aware objects abstracting an internal document structure independent of the actual document. This is a very object-oriented way to think and has much promise, although the difficulty of understanding documents well enough to be able to encapsulate them in a useful way shouldn't be underestimated.

Very good information on the Texcel Information Manager and other of their data-management products can be found on their Web site at http://www.texcel.no/.

To use a simple example, suppose you want to construct an author database from a large collection of documents in HL7, TEI, and DocBook.

HL7 shows authors like this:

```
<PATIENTINFO>
  <NAME.GRP>
    <FIRSTNAME>Joe</FIRSTNAME>
    <LASTNAME>Blow</LASTNAME>
  </NAME.GRP>
</PATIENTINFO>
```

There may be many authors because HL7 is designed to allow doctors to enter notations on patient records, and any number of doctors can be associated with a patient.

TEI also allows multiple authors, because a document may have several authors, but they look like this

```
<titlePage>
  <byLine>by <docAuthor>Joe Blow</docAuthor></byline>
</titlePage>
```

or like this:

```
<titleStmt>
      <author>Blow, Joe</author>
</titleStmt>
```

DocBook has a slightly different syntax that looks like this:

```
<AUTHORGROUP>
  <AUTHOR>
    <HONORIFIC>Dr.</HONORIFIC>
    <FIRSTNAME>Joe</FIRSTNAME>
    <OTHERNAME>&ldquo;The Jock&rdquo;</OTHERNAME>
    <SURNAME>Blow</SURNAME>
    <LINEAGE>Junior</LINEAGE>
  </AUTHOR>
</AUTHORGROUP>
```

Although you can look at these records and figure out who's who and what's what, an application needs help to do this. The Texcel information management software allows you to define a standard, object-oriented interface that hides all the details of the internal structure of the document and presents methods you can use to extract data transparently as long as the document DTD has been previously decoded and the information retained.

```
interface authorInterface {
  public String Author();
}
```

In use, you could define a document object, Doc, with an access method, getAuthor, which returns the name of an author, no matter which of the three DTDs you've looked at describes the document. Repeated invocations of the method could return secondary authors until an invocation of the method returns a null value. At that point you've extracted all the authors.

```
public class documentInterface implements
  authorInterface {
    public String Author() {
      return Doc.getAuthor();
      }
    }
```

With more work, the same approach can be used for an arbitrary number of document types and extrapolated to any data of interest across a range of documents. This allows documents in a repository to describe themselves, a great improvement over the typical repository descriptive scheme that requires people to insert descriptive data manually. Or the repository might depend on the filename itself to describe the data in sufficient detail to be useful, which is highly unlikely in legacy data from MS-DOS 8.3 file systems. If you wanted to build a bibliography, you could define a series of methods accessing a Doc object that looks something like this:

```
Doc.getTitle();
Doc.getAuthor();
Doc.getPublisher();
Doc.getDate();
Doc.getISBN();
Doc.getLOC();
```

The fact that these methods act exactly the same across multiple document types makes it simple to treat them alike no matter what they look like, just as a library doesn't care what size a book is before it inserts it in the card file.

The same object-oriented techniques can be used to hide the fact that the information a firm needs is scattered across multiple documents, for example, a corpus of text and scholarly annotations of that text with multiple layers of exposition and even multimedia content. Standard XML doesn't allow linking into multimedia documents, but by hiding the actual document behind an object interface, the Texcel repository application can offer a much broader range of services than standard XML can provide:

```
Doc.getTitle();
Doc.getAuthor();
Doc.getPublisher();
Doc.getDate();
Doc.getISBN();
Doc.getLOC();
Doc.getCommentary();
Doc.getCriticism();
Doc.getAudio();
Doc.getVideo();
```

The fact that the conceptual document may include a wide variety of actual source documents is invisible in use because the virtual document can be accessed seamlessly, as if it were an indivisible whole.

PART

III

CH

19

GETTING DOWN TO CASES

Although the wrangling between COM and CORBA partisans is endless, the fact is that each has a proper place. In a primarily Microsoft environment, with Microsoft NT servers in central positions, COM, with the assistance of DCOM, is clearly well worth consideration given the ready availability of specialized development tools and facilities to simplify application design and testing. In a generic Linux or other server environment, especially one in which disparate platforms and operating systems are present, CORBA is equally compelling. There are even situations in which it makes sense to use both, translating between the two standards as needed.

SOAP and other XML-based messaging systems can easily communicate between COM/DCOM applications—for which it supplies many built-in facilities—and those based on CORBA. Since SOAP is XML-based and uses HTTP as a transport mechanism, it can easily pass through most firewalls and onto any platform in the world. SOAP can also use FTP or SMTP as a transport medium, almost guaranteeing that the request-response (Remote Procedure Call) mechanism that SOAP makes available can find some way into any system. SOAP can also be used for initiating requests that require no response, using a fire-and-forget protocol.

In fact, the only thing preventing instant adoption of SOAP is the fact that it was initially developed by Microsoft, DevelopMentor, and UserLand Software. Since the original release, IBM and Lotus have joined in as developers but the deep suspicion that much of the user community holds toward any proposal floated by Microsoft, even with distinguished partners, makes it likely that there will be opposition to SOAP on many levels. Microsoft builds on SOAP for their BizTalk framework, so it's quite clear that adoption of SOAP across the industry would give Microsoft a distinct leg up on its competitors.

Other similar protocols are being proposed without the Microsoft home-court advantage, so it seems likely that some compromise between SOAP and XMLTP—or other competing standard—will be worked out by W3C before the dust settles.

CHAPTER **20**

ENTERPRISE RESOURCE PLANNING AND XML

In this chapter

PART

III

CH

20

UNDERSTANDING HOW XML CAN WORK WITH ERP

Enterprise Resource Planning (ERP) is the current wave of the future in organizations throughout the world. Traditionally, ERP has been associated with application suites that help a firm manage the core components of its business in an integrated manner, whether developed inhouse or purchased as a package. Under this definition, ERP is limited only by what a business thinks of as core components.

Order entry and inventory, as well as manufacturing, purchasing, shipping, customer service, supplier-relationships, and planning are commonly included, but many companies add the human resources and accounting departments to the mix, making a political statement about the importance of the financials and the firm's employees. Because the reach of traditional ERP has been extended to include almost every function the firm could conceivably automate, everything becomes fair game for inclusion and the term ERP becomes somewhat vague.

The glue that binds ERP applications together is often a shared system of relational databases and a communications mechanism that lets the various parts of the system, usually encompassing multiple departments, work as a whole. Because XML is fast becoming a de facto standard for both communications backbones and logical views of database structure, XML is a natural tool to help bind the ERP systems offered by various vendors together as well.

Just as existing ERP systems are becoming more and more Web-enabled, future ERP releases will include XML data transfer facilities as a matter of course. As businesses become more dependent on business-to-business communications and less dependent on traditional brick and mortar facilities, the ability to quickly respond to changing conditions and business relationships becomes critical to the success of the enterprise.

Tip from

Words to weave by

Enterprise Resource Planning is a "hot" term that means pretty much whatever a vendor wants it to mean when trying to sell you a given suite of products that may or may not fit your business. Many systems require the firm to retool and retrain every process and department,   which can take a firm in an undesirable direction. Research many vendors and ask pointed questions before deciding on one supplier. Consider multiple suppliers as well.

Viewing the business process as continuous—fully integrated across departments and even separately owned and managed business partners—creates new opportunities and new challenges for the traditional enterprise. Amalgamating all parts of the enterprise into a seamless continuum is difficult, because the task may include

- Strategic planning
- Staffing and compensation processes
- Accounting and finance
- Sales and marketing
- Order creation and fulfillment
- Manufacturing and delivery

- Design and engineering
- Subcontractor relationships
- Inventory control
- Just-in-time vendor relationships
- Customer satisfaction, service, and support

Heretofore, these activities have been compartmentalized in most firms, with different departments having only partial views of the whole process. If there were links between functions, either human or electronic, they were limited and customized to a particular relationship. The only overall comprehension of the business, if any such understanding exists, is locked away in the heads of an upper management team or even one individual. In some very large enterprises, no one person could be said to understand the whole process.

But current trends toward flattening the management structure, outsourcing many functions entirely, and relying on flexible and constantly-changing relationships with a network of vendors, contractors, distributed sales and marketing organizations, transportation alternatives, and the like has made traditional paper and even EDI communications schemes hopelessly outpaced in the race to succeed in the marketplace.

What ERP needs is a way for applications to exchange information in a structured manner—and XML is just the ticket.

INTEGRATING XML INTO ERP

A new paradigm of interprocess communication is needed so that both ad hoc and permanent links between processes and entities can be facilitated. XML and XML-related standards are the mechanism whereby lengthy time-to-market and communications bottlenecks can be eliminated or streamlined. Building on the Materials Resource Planning and inventory control systems of the '60s, ERP has grown to include a multitude of functions.

Even now, ERP vendors are creating systems which treat the whole enterprise as an integrated unit, together with its suppliers, employees, and customers. Communications between proprietary "chunks" of the entire system take place using XML because the translation and transformation facilities built into XML make it the ideal interface and backbone between the API's and reporting modules of disparate systems. Typically, ERP systems include an integrated relational or other advanced database system to store data, but it's not absolutely necessary if the system provides interfaces to existing database systems.

Oracle, for example, although widely known for its relational database systems, is also an ERP vendor. Buying into the Oracle vision of ERP may require converting to an Oracle database, which may break other parts of existing systems, requiring the firm to incorporate the entire ERP system at once instead of moving incrementally toward a gradual incorporation of legacy systems under an encompassing roof. And vendors and contractors may be unable to change their processes to fit those of the new system, requiring time-consuming design and implementation of custom interfaces between many parts of the whole system.

SAP AG is a major vendor of SAP R/3 ERP systems and is widely regarded as requiring complete re-engineering of existing business processes as part of its installation path, a frightening prospect for many small businesses that deters purchase, even though it may make sense in the long run.

By offering XML data-transfer mechanisms, vendors can make integrating legacy or newly-engineered modules from other vendors easier to incorporate into the complete system. This may make it possible both to more fully accommodate the real needs of the enterprise (as opposed to what the ERP vendor has to offer) and to migrate in a measured manner toward full integration.

MOVING TOWARD THE DREAM OF A COMMON LANGUAGE

In an ideal world, one might suppose that everyone would all speak one language, have one data-sharing mechanism, one government, one set of rules, and one organization for each function. But our own diverse and evolving reality of competing ideas, languages, cultures, and business needs is far more interesting and robust. You can't have evolution without change and you can't have change without difference.

Different business cultures aren't going to go away any more than English speakers are all going to decide to learn Chinese, or vice versa. Part of what makes our world culture strong, what makes our world economy strong, is the enormous diversity of viewpoints and abilities, which are encompassed in a loosely coupled global system.

Translators are the foundation of world commerce as well as world culture. Faced with RosettaNet, cXML, eCo, Biztalk, and countless other "standards," the power of XML to transform one lexicon into another can best be appreciated. With few exceptions, integrating systems from different vendors always entails transforming one internal format into another. If both systems have an XML interface, the basis of an easy transformation is already present. Instead of a lengthy custom coding process to translate one binary data format into another, the combination of XSL and XSLT can resolve differences in nomenclature without ever working with general-purpose programming languages or touching a compiler.

The default method of interfacing two systems is to construct a special program that translates the data stream from one system into the native format of the other. While this is adequate for two or three systems, or even a small handful, when the numbers become large, the number of translation programs increase without limit. Figure 20.1 shows the effect of multiple translation paths. As the number of connections increases, the number of required translation programs increases geometrically. The translation programs are shown as black dots. When there are two applications, one interface is required. When there are three applications, three interfaces are required. With four applications, there are six interfaces; with five, ten; and so on.

Even if only two or three systems need to talk to one another at a particular point in time, as the business grows, that number may increase. Soon the number becomes unmanageable. In most cases, it would be viewed as professional malpractice to recommend or design systems requiring individual interfaces between multiple systems. Likewise, any system that requires such individual interfaces, as opposed to allowing them as a performance option, is badly designed in modern terms. This is one of many reasons every major application manufacturer is building systems that allow interface to a common backbone standard.

Figure 20.1
Five applications require ten interface programs.

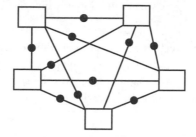

But when all systems can translate to a common format, such as XML, the problem is greatly simplified. Instead of one interface program per application, only one is required to translate to the common backbone. If the manufacturer supplies such an interface natively, the problem is almost trivial. Figure 20.2 shows the architecture of a backbone system. Note that some of the applications translate to the backbone natively (shown by a thin horizontal line within the boundary of the application) and some translate using a custom interface program (shown by a black dot).

Figure 20.2
Because several of the programs translate to and from a backbone format natively, only two custom interfaces (shown as black dots) are required.

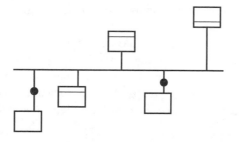

Because XML is designed for the Web and XSL/XSLT is a built-in translation tool meant to interface between different XML dialects, XML or XML-based languages furnish an ideal backbone for Web-enabled applications. In the diagram previously shown in Figure 20.2, XML-enabled applications are represented by the application rectangles with a native interface, so the only systems requiring custom interfaces (black dots) are those without an XML interface.

COMMUNICATION BETWEEN ENTERPRISE SYSTEMS

Because most organizations grow their systems incrementally, different departments within the enterprise have often purchased—and grown to depend on—customized applications systems which don't natively communicate with the rest of the company. Any interface between the customized departmental systems has been accomplished with custom programming. So Purchasing may have one system, Human Resources another, Shipping and Receiving yet another, and so on. Each departmental system that needed to exchange data with another has had a custom interface written especially for that purpose. Although this may have been adequate at the time, imagine what will happen when one department decides to upgrade to a new system.

Every department which had a custom interface now has to coordinate with the one department that has a changed system to rewrite every data exchange program, spreading the pain around and turning a tiny little upgrade into a major project. It's the sort of thing that wakes up Chief Information Officers in the middle of the night with the cold sweats and contributes to the inertia that characterizes many firms.

The following sections show what a well-managed upgrade project might look like.

THE UPGRADE ENVIRONMENT

Imagine a manufacturing organization of some sort. The organization's initial application was CA-Manman Classic (although it wasn't called that then) from Computer Associates. The application was originally written in Fortran but was customized to accommodate real or perceived differences between the organization's operation and the operation of other manufacturing businesses.

At some point, the decision makers in the organization decided to develop an inventory control system on a departmental level, and they chose the COBOL language as a development language. When they integrated manufacturing with the inventory control system, they wrote a custom interface in assembly language for the IBM AS/400 because that's what the inventory control system ran on, and the systems programmer in charge of the machine at that time was an assembly language fanatic who insisted that they needed a low-level language for performance reasons. He's since left the company and nobody understands how it works anymore, although the uncommented source code has been meticulously archived.

In the meantime, members of the sales and marketing department put up a sales support system written in C and running on an HP-3000 mainframe. When they decided to add a link to the inventory control system so the sales staff could check on availability, they wrote the interface in a language that ran on the HP. No one remembers what the language was, and the source code has been lost for some reason. But it works just fine so no one has bothered to do anything about it.

When the members of the accounting department wanted to input accounts receivable data and send out invoices, they just re-keyed the information from sales and marketing because it was too difficult to interface to the marketing system. Their own accounting applications all ran on an Amdahl 5990 running an MVS-compatible operating system and were written in COBOL/CICS/VSAM.

Note

> This example may seem like an exaggeration, but it's actually a fairly typical scenario for any organization that's been around awhile. Past decisions that are almost incomprehensible now are still around to trouble you, even though the decision makers have long since moved on to other companies.

In all, 32 primary applications are running on seven different platforms. Some interface directly to the CA-Manman application and some don't, although they depend indirectly on data obtained from that system. This dependency may be either through manual input or by links to programs that have their own links, which may also be indirect, to the manufacturing system.

Other small applications probably are running on the various platforms, but they're hard to identify because they run only periodically, such as special year-end processing for inventory or accounting purposes. The departments involved may not actually know exactly where the processing takes place.

In this environment, the vice-president of manufacturing decides to migrate his branch of the organization toward a fault-tolerant distributed architecture from Compaq, running on NonStop Integrity systems with a Tru64 UNIX operating system. He believes that CA-Manman/MK, the successor to CA-Manman Classic, can be made to run in that environment, so the problem of actually making a drastic change in environments can be minimized.

THE MIGRATION STRATEGY

Being fair-minded and far-sighted, manufacturing realizes that this will impact many departments, so with the agreement of the chief executive and financial officers, as well as the approval of the board of directors, every department is given the opportunity to buy in or opt out of the proposed migration. The carrot in this plan is that the organization as a whole will partially subsidize the migration for individual departments. The stick is the understanding that if a department opts out, it will be responsible for taking over the costs associated with maintaining the platforms that are being replaced.

Although there are a few holdouts, the majority of the enterprise agrees to the migration in principle, with acceptance accelerating as projected departmental costs of maintaining a platform with fewer and fewer participating co-owner departments start to escalate. This is exactly what manufacturing had foreseen when drafting the plan.

Working with the Compaq eBusiness team and Baan, manufacturing decides to use a mix of Dec Alpha 64-bit and Intel Xeon 32-bit platforms to take advantage of pre-existing business ERP solutions from Baan. They plan to use the Microsoft XML-based BizTalk framework to provide a large portion of the glue to bind the various parts of the system together that are not already able to talk to each other natively. Because Baan provides plug-in turnkey components with its ERP products, the major costs associated with migration for many departments are the purchase and maintenance costs of the system itself, and the conversion costs of existing databases.

PART
III
CH
20

Although final market penetration of BizTalk is still up in the air, the organization hopes that major vendors and subcontractors will adopt the same XML language, although the organization believes that any similar XML language can be substituted at minimal cost if their initially positive assessment of the market proves incorrect. Contingency plans are made to modularize the XML conversion interfaces as much as possible to reduce the impact of any changes.

INITIAL MIGRATION RESULTS

The Baan portions of the system running on Intel Xeon processors drop in almost without a hitch because they're well-tested. Some problems arise in retraining the various departments, because they're being asked to reconceptualize their approach to their respective business processes in many cases, and in some cases requiring reorganization of responsibilities and workflow. Major portions of the documentation supporting these now irrevocably changed business processes were overlooked, so some catch-up work was required to keep the project on schedule.

XML is still in development, so contingency plans have been made to provide interim glue if the proposed solutions don't work out. And the final migration of the manufacturing application that started it all has been delayed, with systems running in parallel in the meantime, because there have been unforeseen problems with the migration from CA-Manman Classic to CA-Manman/MK due to schedule slippages on CA release dates. Nobody's perfect and no major project ever goes entirely according to plan.

CURRENT ERP SYSTEMS

The following sections look in some detail at several vendors but here is a short list of current vendors with ERP or MRP product lines. Some, but not all, of these vendors are discussed in their own sections following this list:

> **Note**
> MRP *(Manufacturing Resource Planning)*, an acronym somewhat out of favor lately, is the ancestor of ERP, which has extended the reach of the methodology into non-manufacturing environments.

- **SAP**—The SAP R/3 product line is perhaps the most famous in the world today. Their Web site is located at http://www.sap-ag.de/.
- **BAAN**—BAAN provides a suite of products for ERP which it claims goes beyond traditional ERP and offers more functionality. Their Web site is found at http://www.baan.com/. Some browsers designed for persons with vision disabilities cannot access the BAAN Web site. BAAN makes heavy use of Adobe PDF files, which have their own horrendous accessibility problems. The layout of the PDF files I've seen seems designed for 21-inch monitors, because the text is too tiny to read on smaller monitors when viewed in the tiny window provided on their Web site.

- **PivotPoint**—PivotPoint is now a part of Mapics, an MRP vendor mentioned in the next bulleted item. Access the PivotPoint Web site at `http://www.pivotpoint.com/`. Some browsers designed for persons with vision disabilities cannot access the PivotPoint Web site.

- **Mapics**—Mapics is a vendor of traditional MRP systems with extensions and application suites that go somewhat beyond traditional MRP. With the acquisition of PivotPoint, they extend their line to include full ERP. Access the Mapics Web site at `http://www.mapics.com/`. Although the Mapics site is accessible in itself, you are sent through an irritating series of screens to make you look at their annoying Macromedia Flash entry screen, a stunning waste of time.

- **Oracle**—Although Oracle is most famous for its relational database technology, they also have a complete suite of ERP products available. Visit the Oracle Web site at `http://www.oracle.com/`. Some browsers designed for persons with vision disabilities cannot access the Oracle Web site. Oracle does provide an accessible, but taunting, message telling the user to upgrade her browser, always an inappropriate suggestion in any context.

- **Manex Systems**—Manex Systems provides an ERP system specifically geared toward electronics manufacturers. Access the Manex Systems Web site at `http://www.manex.com/`.

- **ERP Hub**—This site is a vendor-neutral resource for firms seeking ERP solutions and a good source of more-or-less unbiased opinions. Access the ERP Hub Web site at `http://www.erphub.com/`.

Most of these companies *really* want you to purchase a one-stop solution and scrap every existing tool bearing on their line of expertise, which may require more business process analysis, work procedures analysis, and employee retraining than your firm is willing to undertake at a single sitting. But a key element of the better systems is that they can work with your existing systems and the systems of your suppliers and customers to achieve incremental ERP goals without requiring you to throw out the babies with the bathwater before seeing any return on your investment.

SAP R/3, for example, offers an extensive library of tools designed to enable legacy applications to communicate with SAP R/3 and vice versa. Some vendors specialize in interfacing to SAP R/3 as well, such as HAHT Software, which provides a Web interface to SAP R/3 applications and databases. Visit the HAHT Software site at `http://www.haht.com/`.

Many of these vendors are also able to supply facilities and personnel for outsourcing your ERP requirements. This is a good way to manage the risk of what for many industries and firms is an unproven technology. Some past implementations have been disasters that had to be abandoned; having the vendor on monthly payments gives you quite a bit more power if things go wrong and much less exposure if the project fails.

On the other hand, outsourcing a key component of the strategic planning function of the enterprise might be viewed as an abdication of responsibility. The outsourced capabilities might wither from lack of exercise within the organization itself, permanently damaging the skill sets and knowledgebase of the firm. Also, be sure that the outsourcing project doesn't tie you into a solution that looks like the state of the art today but resembles a less-than-optimal pathetic kludge a few years down the line. It's early days still for ERP, and both outsourcing (with a long term contract) and purchase have the disadvantage of locking in a solution you may be sorry for later.

Be sure also that any choice you make has a clear upgrade path as the technology evolves. You don't want to be stuck with Slowpoke version 1.1 when the rest of the world is using Lightning 2000 because the vendor phased out an old system in favor of a new one.

SAP R3

One of the most famous enterprise systems for designers and integrators is SAP AG, whose R/3 product is widely used in major corporations to create modular application suites using the extensive toolbox of modular R/3 components. SAP is familiar with integrating various components into a complete system. In fact, R/3 is designed as a series of modular plug-in units to furnish discrete portions of the total business logic. These plug-in units are combined into "suites" encompassing all the activities of the enterprise.

By offering a pizza menu approach to ERP, SAP AG promises to minimize disruption and expensive custom integration, because all components are designed to work with each other from the start. They also interface fairly well with legacy applications, so you don't have to do everything at once in many cases, although some custom coding may be required. A company can select from extensive lists of prewritten applications to implement its requirements, with the primary concern being how much it costs rather than how long will it take to develop and whether the project will succeed at all. Elimination of these risks comes at some cost, however, because SAP R/3's way of doing things may not perfectly correspond to your own.

Areas in which SAP will be employing XML include data containers for invoking the R/3 Business API (BAPI) and other programming interfaces. SAP also plans to support XML as content format for electronic forms, such as purchase orders delivered over the Internet in conjunction with online catalogs and XML as a data container for business documents, workflow information, and reports.

SAP plans to enable all its major interfaces with XML, establish XML as a widely used format within its entire product line, and deliver numerous products, including the SAP Business-to-Business Procurement application, which exploits XML as a transfer mechanism. A glance at any major metropolitan newspaper will tell you that SAP R/3 programmers are in considerable demand, and combining XML—another hot item in resumès—with SAP R/3 is probably one of the better career moves.

PEOPLESOFT

PeopleSoft is using what it calls the Open Integration Framework (OIF) to interface both to the Internet and to XML as a transfer medium. Although a programmer still needs to create much of the interface logic, the stability of the XML transfer mechanism means that after the initial interface logic is done, further evolution can take place in the form of XSL transformations of the existing interface. It's far easier to take one XML stream and transform it into another than it is to decipher a binary data stream, which may be compressed and abbreviated in idiosyncratic ways, and transmogrify it into another just as obscure.

BAAN

BAAN provides several levels of business solutions, from customer relations to ERP to supply chain management. Although more or less traditional API's are used for tight integration and to support past integration efforts, XML is also part of BAAN's overall strategy, aimed at what BAAN terms the Business Process Level and the Business Community Level.

The current full ERP solution is called BaanERP. BAAN also offers a product called Baan-on-Board, which packages both software and hardware into a turnkey environment that takes ERP simplification to a new level. Of course, there are still training costs to bring existing employees up to speed in the new environment, and it may be wise to hire people skilled in the new environment to incorporate in-house support capabilities.

SYSTEM CONVERSIONS

In the "Communication Between Enterprise Systems" section earlier in this chapter, you saw the problem of updating an existing system with interfaces to disparate systems within the enterprise or with existing suppliers and customers. But the same problem exists when migrating to a new system. In every migration, at some point there will be a period of parallel operation to ensure that the new system actually does the same work with the same accuracy as the old. In the old days, this often meant hiring duplicate teams to input the same data into each system, because it was a given that no two systems actually talked to each other. But if both systems speak XML, or can be made to speak it, the same data stream could serve both systems, eliminating some possibilities for error and saving at least some staffing costs.

ADDING ERP TO THE ENTERPRISE: HOW XML CAN HELP

To illustrate the issues faced by an enterprise that is adding ERP to its operations, consider the case of Catamount Widget Assembly Group. They have a problem: uncontrolled inventory fluctuations keep happening, because suppliers can't forecast how many widget parts they'll need to supply until the order comes in from Catamount. There is a long lead-time on widget parts and Catamount waits until they have enough coming in to fill a box car to save on shipping costs. This means the suppliers may go weeks without an order and then suddenly have to supply ten thousand widget parts. Often, they can't do it. They have their own inventory problems and can't afford to keep a cushion of ten thousand widget parts around just in case Catamount wants a carload. Inventory is performed manually once per week.

Solution: Let the suppliers see the current state of the widget parts inventory on a daily basis. By looking at the rate at which stock is being drawn down, they can form a good guess about when the next order will come in. In fact, they can just ship a carload at an appropriate inventory point based on the current trend if contractual arrangements can be made. Catamount needs to automate its inventory system because weekly reports don't have sufficient granularity to see trends early enough, but by instituting a ticket control system with barcode readers at the warehouse exit point, every widget that goes out the door of the warehouse is automatically logged.

Because Catamount uses an antique inventory system but one which does the job just fine, it was thought that writing a module to convert inventory reports to an XML-based inventory language made the most sense. These reports can be transmitted to suppliers periodically, and suppliers can also initiate a request more frequently if conditions warrant. As a side effect, it was discovered that the same data feed could be used to inform accounting of the current state of the warehouse stock, which meant that accounting could keep closer track of the cost of sales and capital tied up in inventory at any given time.

Catamount decided on a draft standard from the Electronic Business XML Initiative at http://www.ebxml.org/, which is working to converge the multiplicity of existing XML-based e-business standards into an international standard designed to create a seamless world marketplace. The project is underway.

A real-world example of a similar problem can be found at MRO.com (http://www.mro.com/), which provides XML-based software to simplify the task of communication between trading partners.MRO.com products are used by firms such as Grainger, whose catalog collects information from over 2,000 vendors.

Other suppliers offering or planning similar software include Ariba Technologies, Clarus Corporation, Commerce One, Intelisys, and TRADEX Technologies.

TROUBLESHOOTING ERP SYSTEMS

ERP EITHER WORKS OR IT DOESN'T

ERP is conceptually simple; you exchange data streams and both parties understand them. The chances of failure are small given the verbose nature of XML. You can actually see the data go in and out in real time, so debugging the process that initiates and maintains that data-stream amounts merely to looking at it and verifying that what you deliver isn't garbage and what you receive is error free. Because XML is text-based and transparent by design, the possibilities for error are minimal.

Examine the problem. Here's a step-by-step approach to solving it:

1. Inspect the outgoing data stream. Does it conform to specifications?
2. If yes, proceed to step 4.
3. Notify the programmer to come in and fix the problem. Go back to step 1.
4. Is there any incoming traffic? If yes, proceed to step 6.
5. Is the line dead? If no, proceed to step 7.
6. Notify the network engineer to solve the problem. Go back to step 1.

7. Is the incoming data stream correct?

8. If not, notify the supplier's programmer. Go back to step 1.

9. Go back to sleep.

That's the process in a nutshell and it's very simple. A large part of that simplicity is provided by the transparent XML transfer mechanism, because you don't need complex tables and special display software to inspect the fields in the data-stream.

PART IV

OTHER APPLICATIONS OF XML

CHAPTER 21

RDF—THE RESOURCE DESCRIPTION FRAMEWORK

In this chapter

UNDERSTANDING METADATA

Metadata refers to data *about* data and takes many forms on the Web. In one sense, HTML itself is metadata because it describes the text and other data contained on the page. However, the term usually refers to data one step removed from the HTML or XML code itself. *PICS*, the *Dublin Core*, and *RDF* are all metadata languages or vocabularies, depending on your point of view, that allow Web documents and the elements that make them up to be described in other terms.

Anyone who's had experience with search engines can testify to the enormous amount of data on the Web. Hit counts for many searches mount up into the millions, more references than anyone would want to verify at one sitting. Even ignoring the pernicious effect of deliberate Web spamming—a practice whereby unscrupulous Web hucksters lard their pages with unrelated words in a scheme to bring up their page in response to any search at all— the problem is severe.

Some think XML will solve all the problems by magically ensuring that you can look for information in context, so `<firm>Baker, Inc</firm>` can easily be distinguished from `<individual>Baker, Tom</individual>` and in turn from `<job-title>Baker, First Class</job-title>`. Many people never think beyond that simple observation.

However, XML was deliberately designed to encourage the development of vocabularies appropriate to many disciplines in any number of national languages. DTDs can be created in any language in the world, so `<firm>Baker Corp</firm>` might be easy to find for an English speaker, but `<gesellschaft>Baker GmbH</gesellschaft>` might not.

In a world in which machine translation makes it easier and easier to cross language barriers, does the fact that a company is located in Germany or Japan make them unfit to do business with? Almost everyone would agree that this is clearly not the case.

However, a universal vocabulary is needed that enables certain parts of a page to be labeled unambiguously, no matter what language you speak or what tags you designed in your DTDs. For quite a while that vocabulary has been the library-oriented Dublin Core or something close. In recent years, the basic Dublin Core mechanism has been supplemented with PICS, a standard originally intended to serve the simple purpose of labeling sites as safe for children. However, both use methods that don't fit well into the XML scheme of things, although we'll look at them later in the chapter for hints about what vocabularies might be useful.

→ For more information about the Dublin Core vocabulary, **see** "Understanding the Dublin Core," **p. 495**.

→ For information more about the PICS standard, **see** "Understanding PICS," **p. 500**.

This chapter has few illustrations other than code because the subject is metadata, which by definition is a sort of metaphysical intangible that has few, if any, visible effects. Trying to visualize metadata is like trying to photograph a giant squid at the bottom of the sea. You know that they exist, swimming stealthily somewhere in the dark depths of the ocean, but catching one on film is quite another kettle of fish.

THE RESOURCE DESCRIPTION FRAMEWORK IN CONTEXT

The Resource Description Framework (RDF) is an attempt to fit the plethora of descriptive metadata languages into an XML-based framework (hence the name) that allows describing almost any tagging scheme in terms of triples in a directed graph. The RDF inherits all the XML concepts that allow you to specify element properties. Its schema language duplicates many of the facilities of XML Schema, so encodings are easier to handle as well. RDF is object-oriented, although in a way that's a little hard to grasp, so the benefits of the object-oriented approach may be another advantage.

> **Note**
>
> Every resource can be thought of as an object in an object-oriented sense. An RDF resource represents an instance of an RDF Schema class. RDF property/value pairs act on those resources without affecting whatever properties they inherit from their base class.

Because RDF is based in XML, any XML-aware browser should handle it with ease, requiring no special processing, camouflaging comments, or CDATA elements to hide it from view. RDF has many ways to facilitate automated processing of Web resources, just as search engines of all sorts do. RDF can also be used in a variety of other ways.

For example, the specificity enabled by specific metadata vocabularies can make for better searches in your favorite engine. In the library field, being able to translate or include multiple cataloging schemes provides better access to materials stored in different libraries around the world, a boon to scholarship and science. By enabling intelligent software agents to span the globe looking for resources that fit certain criteria, RDF may facilitate research of all sorts.

For parents and others looking for or trying to avoid sites with or without particular kinds of content, RDF plus PICS may ease their burdened minds and prevent unfortunate incidents. By allowing simple assertion of copyright over an entire site, RDF may simplify the task of the Web designer. And when used with P3P to express the privacy preferences of a user combined with the privacy policies of a Web site, individuals will be better protected from invasive marketing or snooping techniques. Finally, RDF with digital signatures may prove to be the key to building a "Web of Trust" that encourages electronic commerce and other security-sensitive applications.

APPRECIATING THE NEED FOR A SEPARATE DESCRIPTION LANGUAGE

XML is designed to allow everyone to do pretty much as they please with element names. DTD designers can create tags that are meaningful and easy to use in their native language or line of work because different things might be seen in entirely different ways by different industries. A single individual might be `<patient>Sarah Jones</patient>` to her doctor, `<student>Sarah Jones</student>` to the school she attends, `<goruchwyliwr>Sarah Jones</goruchwyliwr>` at her supervisorial job in Wales, and `<taxpayer>Sarah Jones</taxpayer>` to the IRS. No single name can fit all these uses, nor should it. But when data is presented on the Web, it can be used for any number of purposes. The original creator of the data might want to retain their element names for their own purposes, although someone else might want to use other tags for the same data. RDF allows this type of translation.

RDF is not a general-purpose schema translation scheme. The syntax, although fairly succinct considering what it tries to do, is far too verbose to be used around every tag, even with the best of intentions. A page with alternative RDF information surrounding every tag would be ridiculously bloated. Unless the page were automatically generated, maintenance would be a nightmare as well.

What RDF does well is provide a limited tool that allows a limited amount of metadata to be associated with a page in a way that is transparent to the user.

SEEING HOW RDF PINPOINTS DATA MEANING

Searching for any specific thing on the Web can be a frustrating and time-consuming experience. If you know enough about what you want to build, a search string that finds the one treasure in the pile of rubble called the Web, you may not need the information in the first place. It's commonplace to spend a lot of time, sometimes hours, trying to track down a particular piece of information. By providing context, RDF enables you to look for meaningful information as opposed to random bits of fluff.

For example, the XHTML snippet <h1>Ford</h1> is fairly obscure. You don't know whether it refers to automobiles, the Betty Ford Center, a river crossing, or anything else. But when you address an actual resource on the Web with an RDF resource description, it becomes far clearer and potentially offers background information for anyone wanting to explore the subject further:

```
<rdf:Description
  about="http://www.whitehouse.gov/WH/glimpse/presidents/html/gf38.html">
  <h1>Ford</h1>
</rdf:Description>
```

Ford evidently refers to Gerald Ford, the former U.S. President, and the Web reference refers to an actual location where you can find out more about him. You'll find out more about RDF syntax as we continue in this chapter.

COPING WITH CONTEXT-FREE LOOKUP

Until RDF becomes widely available on the Web, most searches have to be narrowed down with the sorts of keywords that may eventually become RDF keywords. So knowing how to search using existing tools will stand you in good stead when RDF descriptions are commonplace.

Tip from

 LeeAnne.com
Words to weave by

While you wait for universal RDF descriptions, learn to use the advanced features of the search engine you use without the help of RDF. Although by no means perfect, cleverly worded queries can hint at some of the context that XML RDF is designed to make clear.

Most of the searching you do is context-free. You can try to supply some sort of context by creating complicated search instructions that attempt to narrow millions of hits into a manageable handful. For example, suppose you want to find out what sort of music system to buy, so you try searching for +"Stereo System" in AltaVista. You'll get a little more than 4,000 hits. It would take a lot of time to search through them all. You notice that many of the sites seem to be on Geocities, which seems an unlikely place to find good advice so you eliminate those entries like this: +"Stereo System" -geocities. The search results only drop out about 200 sites. Your search is still not specific enough.

You ponder for a while. What you want is advice for consumers, right? So, you add a little to your search string: +"Stereo Systems" -geocities +consumer. The hit count drops under a hundred and you have some hope of finding the right stereo before the turn of the next millennium. All this fiddling was made necessary by the fact that the search is context-free. You can't identify any data on the site by any associated metadata scheme.

But what if your search agent knew about some (currently imaginary) metadata standard that tagged consumer advice pages with tags specifically designed to address consumer issues, cost, repair history, sound quality, overall ratings, and so on. Right now, if you type "What's the best stereo system to buy?" you get about 44 million hits. But if the agent were a tiny bit smarter and could figure out that you're looking for advice on stereos, it could initiate a search based on context and turn up your short list in a flash.

That's what XML is for, RDF in particular. By defining special descriptive vocabularies, data can be classified by what it means rather that what it says. So the search we refined at length above might be simply stated in a now imaginary syntax: +"Stereo Systems +RDF:consumerInformation with some hope of achieving an even smaller number of hits. Note that this example assumes that someone, possibly an industry association or consumer awareness organization, has defined an RDF vocabulary that includes consumerInformation and that the search engine being used knows that RDF descriptions have a special meaning. This is not unlikely since most search engines now allow restrictive searches on certain HTML tags.

DEFINING UNIVERSAL RDF VOCABULARIES

In some ways, universal metadata is an impossible dream. For every descriptive scheme you can imagine, there's someone else with a different idea of what a given resource signifies. From the logger who looks at a tree and sees board feet to the conservationist who looks at the same tree and sees a habitat for spotted owls, different communities may imbue the same resources with completely different ideas of what they mean. Metadata works best within clearly defined groups whose members regularly communicate with each other and can agree on a common vocabulary and universe of discourse. Metadata doesn't work nearly as well across boundaries of any kind, so it's never going to be the entire answer. RDF will not enable Star Trek sorts of queries in which you ask for the name of Gilgamesh's mother and the computer goes out and translates never-before-seen material directly from the ancient Sumerian clay tablets to find the answer. It isn't that kind of tool.

Tip from

Words to weave by

If you need a specific search subject, it can be worth your time to look for an organization interested in the same subject. That organization may have solved your search problem on its own by creating metadata descriptions that might aid you in your research.

However, if you're a librarian trying to track down *Genfremstilling af det gamble babyloniske Gilgamesh-epos om venneparret Gilgamesh og Engidu*; København, Nyt nordisk forlag, 1940, in a library halfway across the world, possibly Denmark or Norway but who knows, the Dublin Core was designed to help you do just that.

→ **See** "Understanding the Dublin Core" **p. 495** for an explanation of exactly how the Dublin Core works and how it can be simply redefined as an RDF vocabulary.

The Dublin Core is a librarian's invention that uses an English vocabulary to describe data commonly found in a library card catalog. For scholars and researchers, a Dublin Core entry can be an invaluable tool for identifying particular documents. And in fact, many search engines pay particular attention to indexing data found in Dublin Core fields within existing HTML documents.

Many search engines, however, don't use these fields because of the demonstrated potential for fraud on the part of unscrupulous individuals who deliberately lie about the content of a page in order to lure you to their unrelated sites. So looking for the phrase "corn silage research" will lead you not only to legitimate articles on animal husbandry which might interest farmers but also to a pornography site which uses client-side redirection to instantly transport you to a page of questionable taste. Since the index entry that leads you to this page is a patent lie, it's unclear how anyone of normal intelligence could be other than offended and angry by this sort of venal misdirection. But this problem is precisely why many people distrust search engines and refuse to use them, preferring to navigate from trusted portals which make most of the Web invisible but offer no unpleasant surprises.

And most people don't care about indexing in the first place. Not many people catalog their book collections and place the records on the Web, other than librarians. There might be a thousand copies of a particular book piled in the building next door and you'll never know it. Most people aren't going to do *anything* with *any* of the metadata initiatives unless they are forced to do it or paid to do it. For example, a retail store might want to tag its merchandise like this: `<BeanieBaby>Blackie the Bear</BeanieBaby>` so avid toy collectors can find it and bid up the price, but your average Joe at the corner drugstore couldn't care less. And the potential for abuse means that the most trusted RDF tagging schemes will have to be performed or supervised by third parties with strict controls on their use by individuals.

So for the foreseeable future, RDF and other forms of metadata are going to be the province of specialists, professionals who are, by definition, paid to associate metadata with their work, and a few individuals who just want to use RDF for the heck of it.

UNDERSTANDING THE DUBLIN CORE

Dublin Core is the culmination of years of effort by a group of librarians, computer scientists, and other stakeholders in the publishing world. It describes an ideal bibliographic record suitable for multiple uses, including Union Library Catalogs, search engines, data mining, and other uses. Because it began in the HTML 2.0 days, it originally used only a single mechanism supported by primitive HTML user agents, a standard vocabulary intended for use in meta tags.

> **Note**
>
> Extensive discussion and references to the history of the Dublin Core can be found on the Web site of the Online Computer Library Center, `http://www.oclc.org/` because OCLC has been heavily involved in the planning and development of the standard from the earliest days. OCLC hosts the Dublin Core organization at `http://purl.org/DC/` as well as the Persistent Uniform Resource Locator (PURL) at `http://purl.org/`.

If you are unfamiliar with a meta tag, it's an empty element with three attributes of interest to the purpose here: name, content, and scheme. By filling in the name and content fields, you can instantiate any vocabulary in a machine-readable manner while the `scheme` attribute allows you to identify the vocabulary used. So

```
<meta name="Subject" content="18th century literature">
```

would identify something whose subject was 18th century literature although this isn't the full Dublin Core syntax.

Even in Dublin Core, differences have arisen. The syntax for using Dublin Core, as specified in RFC 2413, Dublin Core Metadata for Resource Discovery, is slightly altered by the AltaVista search engine. The Core element, "Subject," is changed to "Keywords." But there's more—the syntax is slightly different as well. Dublin Core in HTML uses an early version of what became XML namespaces, in which the namespace is identified by a `link` element and then every term belonging to that namespace is identified with a prefix:

```
<link rel="schema.DC"
      href="http://purl.org/DC/elements/1.0/">
<meta name="DC.Subject" content="18th century literature">
```

The equivalent of this syntax rendered in XHTML is

```
<html DC:xmlns="http://purl.org/DC/elements/1.0/">
<DC:meta name="Subject" content="18th century literature" />
```

In RDF it would be

```
<RDF DC:xmlns="http://purl.org/DC/elements/1.0/">
<DC:Subject>18th century literature</DC:Subject>
```

PART

IV

CH

21

In practice, and strongly enforced by the fact that Altavista and other search engines ignore this form, the namespace identifier is dropped or duplicated with a version in which the namespace is omitted. And the standard itself has been revised although the RFC has not. The current version of the standard is 1.1, which adds a few fields here and there and lives at `http://purl.org/DC/`.

Add to this the widespread use of the tags in other countries using native languages and you have a huge mess when it comes to readability. In Denmark, for example, you would have to use the following table of equivalencies to label your pages:

```
Danish Concept            Dublin Core Element Name
  Titel:                    dc.Title
  Udgave:                   dc.Title.Release
  Forfatter eller ophav:    dc.Creator
  Emne og nøgleord:         dc.Subject
  Beskrivelse:              dc.Description
  Udgiver:                  dc.Publisher
  Anden bidragsyder:        dc.Contributor
  Dato :                    dc.Date
  Ressourcetype:            dc.Type
  Format:                   dc.Format
  Identifikator:            dc.Identifier
  Kilde (originalt værk):   dc.Source
  Sprog:                    dc.Language
  Parallel trykt udgave:    dc.Relation.IsVersionOf
  Filiste:                  dc.Relation.HasPart
  Forudsatte programmer:    dc.Relation.Requires
  Dækning:                  dc.Coverage
  Rettigheder:              dc.Rights
```

Note that the Danes extend Dublin Core with some values of their own. This illustrates the pervasive tension between language and labels and between internationalization efforts and practicality. Everyone wants labels to mean something in his native language. If it doesn't mean anything, hardly anyone can use it without help. Although a Dane easily recognizes *sprog* as the concept of *language*, how does he instantly recognize, much less spell, the term on a Web page without a mental shift of gears? The MARC system, used by many national library systems, including the Library of Congress and the Canadian National Library, finesses the issue by labeling every field with an arbitrary number. Therefore, *everyone* is completely at a loss for the meaning of the field without special training, a sort of labeling equalizer.

Given the relative ubiquity of English as opposed to Danish, superficially it makes slightly more sense for the Danes to learn a bit of English rather than for English speakers to learn a bit of Danish, but English is very hard to come by in many areas of the world. Figure 21.1, for example, shows the Dublin Core made slightly more accessible for speakers of Arabic. It uses the English identifiers but tells what they do in Arabic.

Figure 21.1
The Dublin Core is shown here described in Arabic.

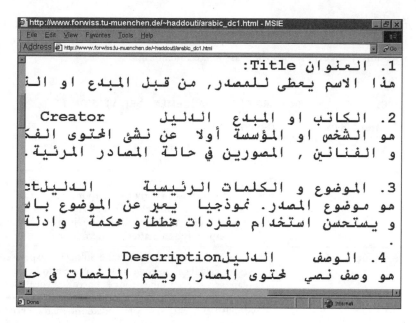

RDF makes handling different languages easy, because you can use the `xml:lang` attribute to identify different versions of the tag names to be rendered in different authoring environments:

```
<rdf:Description about="http://purl.org/dc#Subject">
  <rdfs:label xml:lang="en">Subject</rdfs:label>
  <rdfs:Comment xml:lang="en">The subject of the resource.</rdfs:Comment>
  <rdfs:label xml:lang="dk">Emne</rdfs:label>
  <rdfs:Comment xml:lang="dk">Ressourcens emne.</rdfs:Comment>
  <rdfs:label xml:lang="fr">Suject</rdfs:label>
  <rdfs:Comment xml:lang="fr">Le sujet de la ressource.</rdfs:Comment>
</rdf:Description>
```

So for a Danish audience, a Danish author could use

```
<rdf …
    DC:xmlns="http://purl.org/DC/elements/1.0/">
  <DC:Emne>Bogføringskreds</DC:Emne>
</rdf>
```

instead of

```
<rdf …
    DC:xmlns="http://purl.org/DC/elements/1.0/">
  <DC:Subject>Bogføringskreds</DC:Subject>
</rdf>
```

using the same multilingual Dublin Core namespace by design. Using XSLT, translations between the multiple versions of the Dublin Core in the various supported languages can be handled automatically. In fact, with an appropriate choice of authoring environments, no translation need be made at all because a tag name appropriate to the preferred language of the author can be displayed automatically, although the actual edits are saved in the unqualified (English) Dublin Core syntax. Table 21.1 shows the values of the basic Dublin Core vocabulary together with their associated meanings.

TABLE 21.1   DUBLIN CORE METADATA ELEMENT SET, VERSION 1.1

Element Name	Description
Title	The ordinary name given to the resource, such as the title of a book or the name of a Web site or page.
Creator	The person or entity primarily responsible for the intellectual content of the resource, such as an author or corporate owner of a work made for hire. Be aware that world practice may *require* identifying the human creator of certain objects of art and that the human creator may retain some rights in perpetuity as a matter of international law.
Subject	The topic of the resource. Often the Subject is expressed as keywords, key phrases, or classification codes that describe a topic of the resource. The best plan is to select a value from a controlled vocabulary or formal classification scheme. On the Web, this field should be duplicated with a "Keywords" element, to accommodate the many services that depend on or expect it.
Description	An account of the content of the resource. A description may include, but isn't limited to, an abstract, a table of contents, a reference to a graphical representation of the content, or a free-form text account of the content.
Publisher	The entity responsible for making the resource available, such as the publisher of a book or the entity responsible for a Web site.
Contributor	A person or entity responsible for making contributions to the content of the resource. Examples of a Contributor include a person, such as an illustrator or an editor, an organization, or a service.
Date	A date associated with an event in the life cycle of the resource. Typically, Date is associated with the creation of, or first availability of, the resource. Date encoding should be in ISO 8601 format, if possible, and follow the YYYY-MM-DD format.
Type	The nature or genre of the content of the resource. Type includes terms describing general categories, functions, genres, or aggregation levels for content. Type should be selected from a controlled vocabulary, such as the standard list of Dublin Core Types: collection, dataset, event, image, interactive resource, model, party, physical object, place, service, software, sound, and text. To describe the physical or digital manifestation of the resource, use the Format element.
Format	The physical or digital manifestation of the resource in the real world. Format may include the media-type or dimensions of the resource. Format may be used to determine the software, hardware, or other equipment needed to display or operate the resource (e.g. a microfilm reader). Examples of dimensions include size—important for finding a book in an actual library, since oversized books are often shelved separately—and duration. Format values should be selected from a controlled vocabulary if possible, such as the list of Internet Media (MIME) Types defining computer media formats.

Element Name	Description
Identifier	An unambiguous reference to the resource within a given context. If a string or number identifying the resource and conforming to a formal identification system exists, such as a catalog number, use that. Formal identification systems include the Uniform Resource Identifier (URI), which includes the Uniform Resource Locator (URL); the Digital Object Identifier (DOI); and the International Standard Book Number (ISBN)—the last two are all Uniform Resource Names or URNs.
Source	A reference to a resource from which the present resource is derived. The present resource may be derived from the Source resource in whole or in part. If a string or number identifying the source resource and conforming to a formal identification system exists, use that.
Language	A language of the intellectual content of the resource. You should code values for the Language element as defined by RFC 1766, which includes a two-letter Language Code taken from the ISO 639 standard, followed optionally by a two-letter Country Code taken from the ISO 3166 standard. For example, en for English, fr for French, or en-UK for English as used in the United Kingdom. In the case of a dual language book, two Language elements would be used and so on.
Relation	A reference to a related resource. If a string or number identifying the related resource and conforming to a formal identification system exists, use that.
Coverage	The extent or scope of the content of the resource. Coverage typically includes spatial location (a place name), temporal period (a period label, date, or date range) or jurisdiction (such as a named administrative entity). You should select a value from a controlled vocabulary if possible (for example, the Thesaurus of Geographic Names) and, where appropriate, named places or time periods should be used in preference to numeric identifiers. For Internet content, this value is often "global", but for a city directory, it might be the name of the city and for an internal corporate network, it might be "Company Confidential".
Rights	Information about rights held in and over the resource. The Rights element may contain a rights management statement for the resource or reference a location or service providing this information, such as ASCAP, BMI, or SESAC for musical recordings. Rights information often encompasses copyright and various other intellectual or miscellaneous property rights. If the Rights element is absent, no assumptions can be made about the status of these and other rights with respect to the resource.

To demonstrate how the Dublin Core might be used in an XHTML document, here's an example Dublin Core declaration set from the splash page of my site:

```
<link rel="schema.dc" href="http://purl.org/DC/elements/1.0/">
    <meta name="DC.Title" lang="en" content="White Rose - LeeAnne.com" />
    <meta name="DC.Creator" content="Lee Anne Phillips" />
    <meta name="DC.Type" content="text" />
    <meta name="DC.Language" content="en" />
    <meta name="DC.Coverage" content="global" />
    <meta name="DC.Rights" content="Copyright (c) 1996 Lee Anne Phillips - All
```

PART

IV

CH

21

```
Rights Reserved Worldwide" />
    <meta name="DC.Subject" lang="en" content="Lee Anne Phillips; consultant;
author; networking; telephony; project manager" />
    <meta name="DC.Description" lang="en" content="The Web site of White Rose and
LeeAnne.com Lee Anne Phillips Lee Ann Phillips" />
    <meta name="DC.Date" scheme="WTN8601" content="1999-07-15" />
    <meta name="DC.Source" content="D:\LeeAnne\index.html" />
    <meta name="DC.Format" content="text/html" />
    <meta name="DC.Identifier" content="http://www.leeanne.com/index.html" />
```

Note that the namespace prefixes are consistent with the Warwick Framework, which pre-ceded the current W3C namespace effort by some years.

UNDERSTANDING PICS

PICS, the Platform for Internet Content Selection, arose in response to parental concern about the suitability of many Web sites for children. Many site-rating organizations either solicit voluntary self-ratings or sample actual site content and provide subscribers with "safe lists" of sites considered suitable for children. Several of these sites are mentioned in the following sections.

Tip from  LeeAnne.com Words to weave by	Be aware that many browsers pay absolutely no attention to PICS labels of any sort. If your child is clever, substituting a browser that allows any content to pass its threshold is the work of a moment.

Both these systems are obviously ripe for abuse, although from different perspectives. If an "adult" site catering to persons wanting to view nude pictures of strangers rated their site as having no sexual content, it would pass certain filters although many parents would object to their children having access to the site.

On the other hand, the most restrictive sampling services routinely eliminate any site con-taining any words related to females, such as "breast" or "menstrual." So young girls may be prevented from accessing informational sites expressly designed for them and addressing their natural concerns about puberty with age-appropriate content provided by health professionals.

Others have freedom of expression and speech concerns. It would be easily possible for a ratings service to eliminate sites whose politics it disagreed with, in spite of innocuous content. So PICS, being self-initiated, may be the best compromise for most of us. And the flexibility of the PICS system means that it can be used for almost any selection criteria you can think of, provided that the list of criteria is fairly small.

RSACi: IMPLEMENTING A PICS VOCABULARY

Several organizations provide predefined PICS vocabulary lists, one of the most prominent being RSACi, at http://www.rsac.org/.

In use, the RSACi system is simple; sign on to the Web site, answer a few questions about nudity, sex, violence, and language, and you are given a rating string you can insert on the splash page for your site in the <head> section.

Here's the rating tag for my Web site:

```
<meta http-equiv="PICS-Label"
content='(PICS-1.1 "http://www.rsac.org/ratingsv01.html" l gen true
comment "RSACi North America Server" for "http://www.leeanne.com"
on "1999.11.03T14:41-0800" r (n 0 s 0 v 0 l 0))'>
```

A rating tag like this one should take only a few minutes to generate. Notice that the content is enclosed in one single-quoted string with double-quoted substrings within the main string. This allows the label to contain fairly arbitrary content and still fit the `<meta>` tag archetype. Because XHTML uses the same syntax, there's no reason to suppose that an XHTML page will need any other mechanism, although there are proposals to use RDF as a substitute.

ALTERNATIVE PICS RATING SITES

RSACi is not the only source of PICS vocabularies. Alternative rating sites include the Vancouver Webpages Rating Service at `http://vancouver-webpages.com/VWP1.0/` whose Canadian-aware categories reveal the intellectual and moral poverty of most other PICS vocabulary providers, who focus on vices to the exclusion of virtues. They have separate selection criteria for Multiculturalism, Educational Content, Environmental Awareness, Tolerance, Violence, Sex, Profanity, Safety, Canadian Content, Commercial Content, and Gambling. As a parent, I would much prefer having control over all these things, since it's quite possible for a site advocating the most vicious prejudice and intolerance to do so using the very nicest language and pass the limited concerns of RSACi. Here's the VWP rating for my site:

```
<META http-equiv="PICS-Label"
content='(PICS-1.1 "http://vancouver-webpages.com/VWP1.0/" l gen true
comment "VWP1.0" by "leeanne@leeane.com" on "1999.11.03T12:05-0800" for
"http://www.leeanne.com/"
 r (MC -2 Gam -1 Com 0 SF -1 Edu -1 S 0 Can -1 V 0 Env -1 P 0 Tol -2 ))'>
```

There are, of course, others: Adequate.com focuses on violence at `http://www.adequate.com/ratings/`, but its site doesn't seem well-designed at the present moment. Its splash page, for example, is completely inaccessible to blind users and confusing to everyone else. You might want to take note of it for one reason or another.

Tip from  LeeAnne.com Words to weave by	Never pass up a chance to see what someone else has done wrong. As homework, take a look at `http://www.adequate.com/` and see whether it makes any sense to you or seems easy to use. Hopefully, the company will take a hard look at their design sometime soon and rethink it. There's no excuse for inaccessible design.

SAFE FOR KIDS

The Safe for Kids site at `http://www.weburbia.com/safe/ratings.htm` has only three levels of one category—Safe for Kids, Parental Guidance, and Adults Only—which has the advantage of simplicity if it fails to account for differences of opinion about what those categories might mean.

SAFE SURF

Safe Surf at `http://www.safesurf.com/` has categories that include Age Range, Profanity, Heterosexual Themes, Homosexual Themes, Nudity, Violence, Sex, Violence and Profanity, Intolerance, Glorifying Drug Use, Other Adult Themes, and Gambling. Again, the user's interpretation of what some of these things mean is poorly defined. Does "drug use" include tobacco products? Alcohol? Caffeine? Insulin? What might seem innocuous to some might be distasteful or even immoral to others, depending on personal or religious beliefs. Please note that all the preceding "drugs" are counter to the tenets of one religion or another, and there are many parents in the world who might be upset by a site "glorifying" the use of Pepsi-Cola or iced tea.

EXPLORING RDF SYNTAX

RDF looks pretty much like every other XML application. The trick in RDF is that you typically use multiple namespaces to allow RDF itself, the framework, to coexist with the actual resource description. In many or even most cases, the only RDF syntax you need to know is this:

```
<rdf:Description about="URI">
    stuff pulled in from other XML namespaces
</rdf:Description>.
```

This syntax uses the `about` attribute to point to a URI describing the resource and then lets you put in whatever you want to make the resource easy to use or describe.

Other sites will convert Dublin Core metadata directly into RDF and other metadata formats, such as the U.K. Office for Library and Information Networking at `http://www.ukoln.ac.uk/metadata/dcdot/`.

THE RDF EQUIVALENT OF DUBLIN CORE VALUES

The following is the RDF equivalent of my Dublin Core values as generated automatically by this site:

```
<rdf:RDF
  xmlns:rdf="http://www.w3.org/1999/02/22-rdf-syntax-ns#"
  xmlns:dc="http://purl.org/dc/elements/1.0/">
  <rdf:Description about="http://www.leeanne.com/index.html">
    <dc:title>White Rose - LeeAnne.com</dc:title>
    <dc:creator>Lee Anne Phillips</dc:creator>
    <dc:subject>
      Lee Anne Phillips; consultant; author; telephony; networking; project manager
    </dc:subject>
    <dc:description>
      Home page of Lee Anne Phillips, LeeAnne.com, and White Rose
    </dc:description>
    <dc:publisher>White Rose</dc:publisher>
    <dc:date>26 Oct 1999</dc:date>
    <dc:type>Text.Homepage.Organizational</dc:type>
    <dc:format>text/html</dc:format>
```

```
    <dc:format>6000 bytes</dc:format>
    <dc:language>en-US</dc:language>
    <dc:coverage>global</dc:coverage>
    <dc:rights>Copyright (c) 1999 Lee Anne Phillips</dc:rights>
  </rdf:Description>
</rdf:RDF>
```

Notice that's it basically the same package of information, but the `<meta>` tag elements have been converted into XML elements and both the RDF and Dublin Core namespaces are referenced so that the one RDF tag of real importance, `Description`, can be referenced without confusion. The RDF version is only slightly more verbose than the native HTML version, which is a blessing, but it's still more.

RDF is a little more complicated than that, of course. And it has a schema language as well as a little more syntax that allows you to describe how objects from other namespaces are related to one another. Whether you want to use this facility is up to you. It's simply not necessary for most purposes.

ABBREVIATED RDF SYNTAX

Handiest for HTML documents, however, is an abbreviated syntax that allows you to hide the foreign elements from the HTML parser. You simply treat the elements as if they were attributes and stuff them all into the `Description` tag like this:

```
<rdf:RDF
  xmlns:rdf="http://www.w3.org/1999/02/22-rdf-syntax-ns#"
  xmlns:dc="http://purl.org/dc/elements/1.0/">
  <rdf:Description about="http://www.leeanne.com/index.html"
    dc:title="White Rose - LeeAnne.com"
    dc:creator="Lee Anne Phillips"
    dc:subject="Lee Anne Phillips; author; consultant; telephony;networking;
                ➥project manager"
    dc:description="Home page of Lee Anne Phillips, LeeAnne.com, and White Rose"
    dc:publisher="White Rose"
    dc:date="26 Oct 1999"
    dc:type="Text.Homepage.Organizational"
    dc:format="text/html"
    dc:format="6000 bytes"
    dc:language="en-US"
    dc:coverage="global"
    dc:rights="Copyright (c) 1999 Lee Anne Phillips" />
</rdf:RDF>
```

Tip from	RDF abbreviations are tremendous time savers and solve many problems with interaction between XML/RDF and older browsers.
 LeeAnne.com Words to weave by	

This version is a little more abbreviated and has the huge advantage that the text won't show up in a standard HTML browser because it should ignore the tags it doesn't understand. At best, the browser will see only a few extra spaces that it should ignore per the HTML specification.

MIXING DIFFERENT METADATA SCHEMAS

You can also mix different metadata schemas together in the record, so you're not confined to one or another. In the next example, some information is added for the Global Information Locator Service (GILS). The syntax is exactly the same, except another namespace must be added:

```
<rdf:RDF
  xmlns:rdf="http://www.w3.org/1999/02/22-rdf-syntax-ns#"
  xmlns:gils="http://www.gils.net/"
  xmlns:dc="http://purl.org/dc/elements/1.0/">
  <rdf:Description about="http://www.leeanne.com/index.html"
    gils:Originator="Lee Anne Phillips"
    gils:Abstract="Home page of Lee Anne Phillips, LeeAnne.com, and White Rose"
    dc:title="White Rose - LeeAnne.com"
    dc:creator="Lee Anne Phillips"
    dc:subject="Lee Anne Phillips; author; consultant; telephony; networking;
              ➥project manager"
    dc:description="Home page of Lee Anne Phillips, LeeAnne.com, and White Rose"
    dc:publisher="White Rose"
    dc:date="26 Oct 1999"
    dc:type="Text.Homepage.Organizational"
    dc:format="text/html"
    dc:format="6000 bytes"
    dc:language="en-US"
    dc:coverage="global"
    dc:rights="Copyright (c) 1999 Lee Anne Phillips" />
</rdf:RDF>
```

You could go on adding namespaces and resource descriptions like this for as long as necessary.

USING RDF RESOURCES

RDF can describe any discrete object with a URI, although the object may not necessarily be Web-accessible nor even have a current physical reality. A book, for example, has a unique ISBN identifier, which can function both as an identifier and as a namespace, but that number is assigned long before the book itself comes into existence. Similarly, you can assign a unique identifier to the Pillars of Hercules or the Hanging Gardens of Babylon, both of which ceased to exist millennia ago. So they're resources even though you can't visit them or do anything other than imagine them. In general, anything that you can point at or could conceivably point at, even in metaphor, is a resource. Predicates (that is, properties) are not resources, just as you can't point at "running" in the absence of someone doing it.

Note

> Resources that are not described by a URI are Uniform Resource Names (URN) by default.
> Ideally, a URN should be assigned by a recognized authority to guarantee uniqueness.
> A URN is prefixed by a URN prefix, for example URN:*anyNameAuthority*:
> *anyAssignedName*.

At the present time, few discrete objects on the Web have any metadata associated with them at all. The authors of the RDF specifications hope this situation will gradually change as more stakeholders in various user communities become convinced of the utility of such schemes and as the tools for merging various schemata improve over time.

RDF resources are conceived as objects in the Object-Oriented sense. The description language is designed to support inheritance, even multiple inheritance, opening the possibility of a smart browser being able to trace inheritance family trees to figure out how to process a schema it's never seen before.

USING RDF PROPERTIES

You've seen briefly how you can use the about attribute to point to the resource described by a property/value pair, making the third term of the triple needed for an RDF statement. The resource, in grammatical terms, is the object of the RDF sentence. The property is the predicate, and the literal string in all cases is the subject. The subject might also be a resource, in which case some other property/value pair would be associated with it in yet another sentence with the former subject as an object. You'll see these terms used interchangeably in XML books and documentation, so you should become familiar with them.

In the following example, the members of the RDF triple are defined by descriptive names

```
<rdf:Description about="resourceURI">
    <property>literal</property>
</rdf:Description>.
```

which could be recast as an English sentence: resourceURI has a property whose value is literal.

However, the simple object, predicate, subject triple isn't enough for the real world. Sometimes multiple objects have the same relation to one subject. Must every sentence be duplicated to keep the triples self-contained? RDF allows a shorthand notation to describe these sorts of multiple relationships. So if you wanted to say Lee Anne created all the pages of this book, you could use the following syntax to describe that one-to-many relationship:

```
<lap:Book rdf:about="URN:ISBN-0789719967">
  <rdf:Seq ID="pages">
    <rdf:li resource="page1.doc" />
    <rdf:li resource="page2.doc" />
    <rdf:li resource="page3.doc" />
    <rdf:li resource="and so on …" />
  </rdf:Seq>
  <rdf:Description aboutEach="#pages">
    <DC:Creator>Lee Anne</DC:Creator>
  </rdf:Description>
</lap:Book>
```

The RDF term aboutEach distributes the given description over the RDF sequence container.

If you had used about instead of aboutEach, the statement would only have said that Lee Anne created the sequence itself. That would be true, but wouldn't say enough. Also notice that the URI doesn't have to point to any particular place on the Web. In this instance you're pointing to an object in the real world, even though it doesn't exist yet (at the time of this writing at least) and has a metaphorical referent instead of a path and location. The aboutEach referent is distributive across all the elements of a container, but *only* the elements of a container. You can't use it in any other way.

One more distributive referent can be used to associate a property/value pair with multiple objects. To associate a copyright notice, for example, with every page on a single Web site or directory, use this:

```
<lap:Sites>
  <rdf:Seq ID="pages">
    <rdf:li resource="http://www.leeanne.org/page1.html" />
    <rdf:li resource="http://www.leeanne.com/page1.html" />
    <rdf:li resource="http://www.leeanne.com/page2.html" />
    <rdf:li resource="http://www.leeanne.com/page3.html" />
    <rdf:li resource="and so on …" />
  </rdf:Seq>
  <rdf:Description aboutEachPrefix="http://www.leeanne.com/">
    <DC:Rights>Copyright © 1999 Lee Anne Phillips</DC:Rights>
  </rdf:Description>
</lap:Sites>
```

The first Web location doesn't begin with the same prefix as the rest, so it won't take that property. This is okay because it doesn't exist yet. All the rest are associated with the copyright statement, which is exactly what was intended.

Using RDF Values

There are two special value cases in RDF which might be handy. In the first, you declare that the content is to be treated as an RDF/XML literal, so the RDF processor ignores any enclosed markup. This could be used to hide XHTML code from the RDF processor, for example:

```
<lap:AddressLabel rdf:parseType="Literal">
  <xhtml:ul>
    <xhtml:li>Bill Clinton</xhtml:li>
    <xhtml:li>The White House</xhtml:li>
    <xhtml:li>Washington, DC</xhtml:li>
  </xhtml:ul>
</lap:AddressLabel>
```

In the other case, you might want to refer to an entity defined elsewhere. For example, the following describes the Moon as being made up of so many GigaTonnes of styrofoam, in which the GigaTonne value is defined by the National Institute of Standards and Technology:

```
<RDF
  xmlns:rdf="http://www.w3.org/1999/02/22-rdf-syntax-ns#"
  xmlns:nist="http://www.nist.gov/units/">
    <rdf:Description about="URN:Moon">
      <nist:weight rdf:parseType="Resource">
        <rdf:material>styrofoam</rdf:material>
        <rdf:value>14522204300</rdf:value>
        <nist:units rdf:resource="http://www.nist.gov/units/GigaTonnes"/>
      </nist:weight>
    </rdf:Description>
</RDF>
```

The reference, values, and namespace are almost entirely imaginary, so please don't expect to find them anywhere on the actual National Institute of Standards and Technology site.

RDF COLLECTIONS

RDF has three container models—bag, sequence, and alternative—which correspond roughly to XML content *any*, *sequence*, and *choice*. Note that a bag is not a set, because duplicates are explicitly allowed, but describes an unordered collection of resources.

Using a bag lets you define a triumvirate without specifying any sort of order or ranking. For example, suppose you've defined an ancient history namespace that uses the AH prefix and want to refer to the Triumvirate in ancient Rome without implying that any of the co-rulers had more power or prestige than the others. You could do it like this:

```
<AH:Triumvirate>
  <rdf:Bag>
    <rdf:li>Crassus</rdf:li>
    <rdf:li>Pompeius</rdf:li>
    <rdf:li>Caesar</rdf:li>
  </rdf:Bag>
</AH:Triumvirate>
```

If you wanted to say that there *was* an order, you would use a sequence:

```
<AH:Triumvirate>
  <rdf:Seq>
    <rdf:li>Caesar</rdf:li>
    <rdf:li>Crassus</rdf:li>
    <rdf:li>Pompeius</rdf:li>
  </rdf:Seq>
</AH:Triumvirate>
```

And, if you wanted to show an exclusive choice among alternatives, which in this example it eventually became, you would use a selection:

```
<AH:Triumvirate>
  <rdf:Alt>
    <rdf:li>Caesar</rdf:li>
    <rdf:li>Crassus</rdf:li>
    <rdf:li>Pompeius</rdf:li>
  </rdf:Alt>
</AH:Triumvirate>
```

And finally, if you didn't want the contents of any of your collections exposed to other engines, you could use the abbreviated syntax you saw previously like this, with a special ordinal property also defined in the Recommendation. You have to do it this way because XML doesn't let you have two attributes with the same values in one tag.

```
<AH:Triumvirate>
  <rdf:Alt
    rdf:_1="Caesar"
    rdf:_2="Crassus"
    rdf:_3="Pompeius" />
</AH:Triumvirate>
```

These relationships can be combined in many ways, which would definitely use up more space than it would be worth. The Recommendation is surprisingly readable at http://www.w3.org/TR/REC-rdf-syntax/, and the Schema Proposed Recommendation, which should be a Recommendation by the time you read this, is available on the W3C site as well.

KNOWING WHEN TO SUPPLEMENT XML WITH RDF

One of the uses envisioned for RDF is to supplement XML element names with more universal ones. This theoretical use is still controversial. Although it has benefits for search engines, in that a Danish user, for example, might have an English-based RDF description wrapped around her Danish element names, it seems somewhat doubtful in practice.

Suppose you defined a tiny record in Danish as follows:

```
<Titel>White Rose</Titel>
<Forfatter>Lee Anne Phillips</Forfatter>
```

Is it really worth supplementing this information with

```
<rdf:RDF
  xmlns:rdf="http://www.w3.org/1999/02/22-rdf-syntax-ns#"
  xmlns:dc="http://purl.org/dc/elements/1.0/">
    <rdf:Description about="http://www.leeanne.com/">
      <dc:Title>White Rose</dc:Title>
      <dc:Creator>Lee Anne Phillips</dc:Creator>
    </rdf:Description>
</rdf:RDF>
```

or *any* uniform vocabulary? Why not use the uniform vocabulary to begin with? Although it might irk a Danish speaker to have to use English tags, most Danes know English anyway, as well as German and maybe French. So it's not that big a deal, right? Wrong! Because these things can be defined as XSLT templates and automatically generated after the fact, you don't have to ever see the standard vocabulary your tags will be transformed into. So it's just as easy to code in your native language and leave machines to do the hard part.

On the other hand, it would be just as easy to translate the tags into that standard vocabulary, so why bother with RDF? One reason might be so that naïve users who happen to speak Danish can easily qualify their own searches with a tag that makes sense in context. Of course, that ignores the fact that a Dane might just as easily think *Autor* as *Forfatter*. But at least it narrows it down a bit and you can always look twice. Similar synonyms exist in many languages.

Tip from

LeeAnne.com
Words to weave by

Although you can wait for more tools to become available, the tools won't appear before there's a certain critical mass of marked-up data out there. Start thinking about adding metadata to all your pages and speed the creation of tools at the same time.

It seems likely that eventually browsers will have some form of technology embedded in them that performs these magic translations automatically. So the hypothetical Dane can ask for a *Forfatter* named Lee Anne Phillips and her word will be seamlessly identified as belonging to the class of things called *Creator* in the Dublin Core universe and searched for under that name and several others to boot.

Although we've only scratched the surface in this chapter, you now know how to do 99% of tasks you'll really want to do, as opposed to some books which tell you everything but leave you floundering for something, anything, concrete.

In the next chapter, we'll examine XHTML in some detail, because that's the XML-based language most people will be seeing in the near future.

TROUBLESHOOTING RDF

IS MY RDF WORKING?

You've created your Web resource, rated it with RSACi, described it with Dublin Core metadata, flirted with the special AltaVista metadata forms, and now you're wondering if anything is really happening.

Metadata by nature is slippery stuff. When it's running right, there is no visible effect. Unless you have access to your own search engine or other means of discovering whether the RDF code is actually doing what you meant it to do, you're pretty much stuck. You can open the page in a validating browser/editor and scroll around and see whether it validates, which is a useful exercise for any XML page, but the ultimate test is to try it out. If you're using Internet Explorer, you can put an Adults Only rating on a test Web page and see whether your Content Advisor settings make any difference at all in whether you can see the page. For the rest, it's difficult to say.

Unless you have an existing application that uses metadata, nothing happens when you run into it. It's extraordinarily hard to troubleshoot. Troubleshooting is a matter of running it through your application, whatever that might be, and seeing whether the results are as expected.

CHAPTER **22**

XHTML IN DETAIL

In this chapter

USING XHTML IN AN HTML WORLD

In short, XHTML is a reformulation of HTML as an XML application. However, that simple statement ignores the reality of HTML as it is presently interpreted by most commercial browsers, which ignore many egregious coding errors in favor of trying to display something reasonable in spite of bad syntax. The simple statement also ignores the fact that HTML is basically an application of SGML and, as we've discussed previously, XML is *not* SGML.

Among the things discarded when going from SGML to XML is the capability to exclude elements in the definition of other elements. SGML's capability to abbreviate constructs when the parser can determine that there are missing bits of code while reading the input data stream also was eliminated. That's why you can ignore closing tags on paragraph <P> elements (and many others) in HTML but not in XHTML.

DEMONSTRATING HTML MINIMIZATION

The following code snippet is a complete HTML document and legal in HTML, although I don't recommend doing it this way because it is far too dependent on SGML-style minimization. Although this is legal in XML, it's not terribly clear and is prone to inadvertent error:

```
<TITLE>HTML Example</TITLE>
<H1>HTML Example</H1>
<P>Paragraph One
<P>Paragraph Two
<BR>
<Table>
  <CAPTION>HTML Table</CAPTION>
  <TR>
    <TD>Element A1
    <TD>Element A2
    <TD>Element A3
  <TR>
    <TD>Element B1
    <TD>Element B2
    <TD>Element B3
</TABLE>
```

Notice that there is no <HTML> tag. The HEAD and BODY elements are missing because a true HTML processor will infer their existence from the TITLE and H1 elements and insert virtual equivalents. In fact, the initial <P> tag is actually unnecessary, because it would have been implied by the presence of text in the code. Also, the ending tags on the table elements are missing because they can be easily inferred from the grammar of HTML. In fact, in normal HTML, coding ending tags for table elements are easier to leave out because they muddy the source code with unnecessary tags and make it harder to see the document structure. As a last point, note the mixed case <Table> tag that doesn't match the case of its own closing tag, which is perfectly all right in HTML, but which XML and XHTML would see as an error.

Translating this small example into XHTML using Dave Raggett's Tidy program yields the following well-formed XHTML example:

Tip from

Words to weave by

The Tidy program is available in command-line form from W3C at `http://www.w3.org/People/Raggett/tidy/`; however, for Windows users, an excellent GUI wrapper has been provided by the good folks at Chami, `http://www.chami.com/`, and is combined with a very good HTML/XHTML editor, all provided gratis! Many other ports have been made to many operating systems, and the complete list is maintained on Dave Raggett's W3C site.

```
<?xml version="1.0"?>
<!DOCTYPE html PUBLIC "-//W3C//DTD XHTML 1.0 Strict//EN"
    "http://www.w3.org/TR/xhtml1/DTD/strict.dtd">
<html xmlns="http://www.w3.org/1999/xhtml">
  <head>
    <title>XHTML Example</title>
  </head>
  <body>
    <h1>XHTML Example</h1>
    <p>
      Paragraph One
    </p>
    <p>
      Paragraph Two
    </p>
    <br />
    <table>
      <caption>XHTML Table</caption>
      <tr>
        <td>Element A1</td>
          <td>Element A2</td>
            <td>Element A3</td>
      </tr>
      <tr>
        <td>Element B1</td>
          <td>Element B2</td>
            <td>Element B3</td>
      </tr>
    </table>
  </body>
</html>
```

Note that the Tidy output has been modified slightly to save space and conform to a coding style that makes complex tables easy to comprehend. Table data elements that line up vertically when rendered are indented by hand to line up in the code. Although this is overkill for this tiny sample table, complex tables often become so unwieldy that modifying the table later is irritating and error-prone.

Tip from

Words to weave by

In the case of pages that are generated automatically, you won't have to worry about these table formatting niceties, but a surprising number of pages are partially modified or even entirely written by hand, even on large sites. The addition of formatting hints to the code makes it easier to figure out what's what when you look at the page six months from now.

Tidy also breaks header <h1> elements and puts the contents on a new line, which behaves slightly differently in many browsers than an <h1> element with the content and closing tag all on the same line. This behavior is an annoying bug in the browsers that display the file rather than in the Tidy interpretation of the HTML code. Fortunately, Tidy does allow you to optionally eliminate content indents entirely if this behavior is unwanted. But eliminating content indents has its own problems; so rather than discard indent formatting entirely, I chose here to "tidy" the Tidy output by hand.

Tidy is not the only beautifier program available for the purpose of merely checking HTML code for correctness and reformatting the source into a more structured form. Media++, a German firm (http://mpp.at/pretty/), offers Pretty HTML, which is a beautifier program without the tie-in to XML. Pretty HTML has more features to handle ASP tags and other common additions to standard HTML, so if your target is HTML or Microsoft XML platforms, you might prefer it.

We've also replaced every "HTML" display content with "XHTML" to distinguish one bit of code from another.

Tidy made a lot of changes that you can't fool with. In the first place, the XHTML identifier and doctype elements have been added and the XHTML namespace identified, as required in the XHTML specification. Secondly, every tag is now in lowercase, also a requirement of the XHTML specification. Third, every tag has a corresponding closing tag because XHTML requires XML to be well-formed. The enclosing <html>, <head>, and <body> elements, which can be legally omitted in HTML, are not optional in XHTML. They have to be included in a valid XHTML document, so they were added in their correct locations by Tidy.

The paragraph <p> elements are closed with </p>, <tr> and <td> elements are closed with </tr> and </td>, and the empty break <br> tag is closed with a special format used for empty elements, <br />. Although XHTML actually allows you to close the <br> tag with a closing </br> tag, most existing browsers can't understand this syntax and may do unexpected things. The closing slash at the end of the empty break tag closes the tag as far as XML and XHTML are concerned, although almost all present-day HTML browsers ignore it because they "know" that break tags are empty and close them by default.

CORRECTING HTML IDIOSYNCRASIES

The following HTML idiosyncrasies must be corrected before an HTML file can be considered valid XHTML:

- **Attribute values**—Although SGML (and therefore HTML) requires all text values to be enclosed in single or double quotes in most cases, a few exceptions were made for certain unambiguous strings. So although a string with an enclosed space, such as `"red rubber"`, always had to be enclosed in quotes, the quotes around an unambiguous string, such as `"ball"` were optional. HTML allows `<div align=center>` but not `<p style= font-size: 12pt; >`, because it has no way of knowing where this string is supposed to close. An SGML (or HTML) parser has the ability to do *lookahead*, essentially the power to foretell what comes next in the input stream, and can treat the single-word string as if it were enclosed by quotes even if they are omitted; however, lookahead can't solve every ambiguity. XML (and XHTML) requires all attribute values to be quoted.

- **Minimized attributes**—SGML (and therefore HTML) allows certain attributes to be minimized, so an attribute that takes a single value if present can be indicated by the name alone. The ismap attribute in an `<img>` tag: for example, `<img src="URI" ismap="ismap">` could be indicated by simply writing `<img src="URI" ismap>`; it's actually defined that way in the HTML DTD. This usage is an error in XHTML, which doesn't allow minimalization, so the full value must be spelled out: `<img src="URI" ismap="ismap">`.

- **Closing tags**—All elements must be closed in XHTML, either with an ordinary closing tag, or with a special syntax for empty tags that puts the closing at the end of the empty tag in an XML shorthand like this: `<hr />`. Although XML theoretically allows empty tags to be closed in exactly the same way as a tag with content, using a closing tag on an empty element often breaks HTML browsers. So `<hr></hr>`, though perfectly legal, is highly inadvisable.

- **Case sensitivity**—HTML isn't sensitive to case but XHTML is. Both XHTML element and attribute names must be in lowercase. An exception exists in the XML `<!DOCTYPE…>` element because of the way that particular declaration is defined. XHTML chose not to include uppercase equivalents to the lowercase tags for simplicity, in spite of the huge installed base of uppercase HTML documents.

- **Scripts and style sheets**—Because scripts and style sheets use a different syntax than does HTML, browsers had to know how to process them. Some browsers didn't, and this led to the widespread practice of enclosing the script or style content in SGML comment tags. XHTML may not pass information inside comment tags to the browser at all, so it's better to place both scripts and style sheets in external files if possible. A possible alternative is to place the style sheet or script data inside a CDATA section, much as HTML users can place the same content inside a comment element. However, support for CDATA sections is spotty and unpredictable in HTML browsers, so the content might not be interpreted if passed to the browser in that way. A solution to this problem is discussed in the "Creating an XHTML Web Page" section later in this chapter. The following code shows the CDATA approach but is not recommended:

```
<style>
  <![CDATA[
    Style sheet stuff…
  ]]>
</style>
```

- **Optional tags**—HTML allows a surprising number of tags to be implied by context. In particular, the `<html>` tag itself, the `<head>` tag, and the `<body>` tag are all optional, as shown by the example in the "Demonstrating HTML Minimization" section above. None of these tags are optional in XHTML.

- **Language support**—HTML uses the `lang` attribute to indicate the language used in a document or element; XHTML uses the `xml:lang` attribute to indicate the same thing. Because support for XML is spotty and will likely remain so, use both forms in most situations.

- **Character set support**—HTML expects to see an indication of the character set used in a document in a meta tag in the document head; XHTML expects the same information in the XML declaration. Because support for XML is spotty and will likely remain so, use both forms in most situations. `<meta http-equiv='Content-type' content='text/html; charset="EUC-JP"' />` in the document head should be combined with `<?xml version="1.0" encoding="EUC-JP" ?>`.

- **Special attributes**—For historical reasons, HTML defined the `name` and `id` attributes as meaning more or less the same thing in different elements, allowing a URL fragment to address a particular spot within a document. The confusion is simplified somewhat in XHTML in that the `id` attribute is required in all situations, although the `name` attribute is still allowed on the `<a>` anchor element. Unfortunately, this means that older browsers can no longer reference document fragments correctly if only the `id` attribute is used. So both the `name` and `id` attributes should be used with the same values in every anchor element used as a target like this: `<a name="myid" id="myid"></a>`. Also, because older browsers don't support targets other than anchor elements, you should restrict targets to anchor elements.

- **Element exclusions**—Although HTML contains many SGML-style exclusions governing which elements can be contained within other elements, XHTML has only a few, weakly enforced exclusion rules. Although these rules may save the careless author from a few trivial errors, they don't absolutely prevent them. The exclusion rules have to be applied manually by the author, and a list of excluded elements should be a part of every author's handbook:
  - The `<a>` element cannot contain other `<a>` elements.
  - The `<form>` element cannot contain other `<form>` elements.
  - The `<label>` element cannot contain other `<label>` elements.
  - The `<pre>` element cannot contain `<big>`, `<small>`, `<sub>`, `<sup>`, `<img>`, or `<object>` elements.
  - The `<button>` element cannot contain `<button>`, `<fieldset>`, `<form>`, `<iframe>`, `<input>`, `<label>`, `<select>`, `<isindex>`, or `<textarea>` elements.

HTML RECOVERY MECHANISMS

Another issue is the many HTML recovery mechanisms built into the major browsers, none of which will work with an XHTML parser, because the necessary recoveries result from various common violations of the HTML DTD. Examples are

- **Improperly nested elements**—Although both HTML and XHTML require tags to be closed in reverse of the order in which they were opened, most browsers allow you to close many of them in any order. In particular, the inline elements affecting the appearance of text, such as `<em>`, `<font>`, and so on, are displayed even if closed at random. So the malformed `<b><i>text</b><i>` is incorrectly treated as if it were the correct: `<b><i>text</i><b>`. Only the second, well-formed sequence is legal in XHTML.

- **Whitespace**—Many browsers handle line feeds and extra whitespace within attributes incorrectly. You should avoid line feeds and extra whitespace within attribute values, even though both the HTML and XHTML specifications require extra whitespace and line feeds to be collapsed into a single space.

- **Processing instructions**—Although the XML declaration and processing instructions ought to be ignored by all browsers, because the enclosing < and > should look like an unknown tag, in actuality many browsers become confused by the `<?...?>` syntax and treat the tag as content to be displayed. Avoid processing instructions if possible, although you will need an XML declaration if you want to use anything other than the default character sets.

UNDERSTANDING XHTML EXTENSIBILITY

You learned about extensibility in Chapter 4, "Extending a Document Type Definition with Local Modifications," and saw an exhaustive example of adding a single element, so there's no need to duplicate that effort here. However, you should note that there are many ways to extend an XHTML document. Because XHTML has its own namespace, we can incorporate XML code from other namespaces using the namespace syntax we discussed in Chapter 6, "XML Namespaces." We can also transclude external documents using the XML linking facilities.

XHTML NESTING PROBLEMS

You learned about nesting problems in our discussion of XHTML earlier, but because nesting problems place an onerous burden on the author, it's worth reiterating here:

- The `<a>` element cannot contain other `<a>` elements.
- The `<form>` element cannot contain other `<form>` elements.
- The `<label>` element cannot contain other `<label>` elements.

- The `<pre>` element cannot contain `<big>`, `<small>`, `<sub>`, `<sup>`, `<img>`, or `<object>` elements.
- The `<button>` element cannot contain `<button>`, `<fieldset>`, `<form>`, `<iframe>`, `<input>`, `<label>`, `<select>`, `<isindex>`, or `<textarea>` elements.

The XHTML DTD addresses these limitations directly in the definitions of these elements, but doesn't actually extend the primary level of prohibition to child elements. So the `<a>` element can contain an `<em>` element, according to the DTD, which in turn may contain an `<a>` element, also according to the DTD, in spite of the fact that the `<a>` element is not "allowed" to contain an enclosed `<a>` element by a textual appendix to the Recommendation. Which means that the author is required to keep track of the nesting level of elements as she writes, because a validating parser won't catch such errors, or the XHTML parser must maintain secret knowledge about XHTML files not contained in the DTD, which violates the basic principles of XML.

So the following XHTML code snippet is illegal:

```
<a href="URI-1"><em>Sample <a href="URI-2">nested</a> element</em></a>
```

But the same code is "valid" according to the XHTML DTD. It's forbidden only in the text of an appendix to the recommendation, not the DTD itself. This snippet is also illegal:

```
<a href="URI-1">Sample <a href="URI-2">nested</a> element</a>
```

Because it's not nested, the mistake would be caught by any validating parser and cause a fatal error. Although both examples are errors, only the latter is caught by a simple validating parser.

CUSTOM PREPROCESSING OF XHTML

The only obvious answer to the problem is custom preprocessing when creating large numbers of XHTML files. This is an intentional flaw in the XML design, although it *can* be worked around. Exclusions require look-ahead processing, which increases the complexity of the parser required to handle this feature enormously. Because enormous complexity violates one of the design principles of XML, the tradeoff was thought reasonable. With practice, it's possible to keep the handful of rules in mind. Writing a preprocessor with look-ahead really isn't *all* that hard because the problem is well understood. So the complexity required can be pushed into a tool used rarely at document creation and left out of the parser used to validate against a DTD. On the other hand, the behavior of a browser if such an error gets through is undefined.

Tip from

LeeAnne.com
Words to weave by

Assuming that catching errors is a good thing, implementing a language such as XHTML, that allows undetectable errors, introduces a serious weakness. However, detecting these particular errors is not permitted in XML without restrictions. So the drafters did the best they could with an explicit exclusion in the content model of certain elements; however, that exclusion doesn't go beyond the immediate context of the tag.

The moral of which is don't let such errors happen. One approach to preventing errors is to use one or more HTML or XHTML validators to check the code. The sample code from the initial example makes a good test, with one nested anchor element added to give the validators something bad to find:

```
<?xml version="1.0"?>
<!DOCTYPE html PUBLIC "-//W3C//DTD XHTML 1.0 Strict//EN"
    "http://www.w3.org/TR/xhtml1/DTD/strict.dtd">
<html xmlns="http://www.w3.org/1999/xhtml">
  <head>
    <title>XHTML Example</title>
  </head>
  <body>
    <h1>XHTML Example</h1>
    <p>
      Paragraph One
    </p>
    <p>
      Paragraph Two
    </p>
    <a name="myid" id="myid"><em>Outer Anchor
    <a name="idtwo" id="istwo">Inner Anchor</a></em></a>
    <br />
    <table>
      <caption>XHTML Table</caption>
      <tr>
        <td>Element A1</td>
          <td>Element A2</td>
            <td>Element A3</td>
      </tr>
      <tr>
        <td>Element B1</td>
          <td>Element B2</td>
            <td>Element B3</td>
      </tr>
    </table>
  </body>
</html>
```

Figure 22.1 shows the result of checking the modified XHTML code with the W3C online WebLint validation suite at http://validator.w3.org/. Although several errors are shown, most of them don't seem to be serious because they relate to the XML-specific code rather than to the HTML syntax. One error, however, is revealed just as expected. The added anchor element is described as being improperly nested, which is exactly right.

The W3C SGML validator also shows the nesting error and knows about XHTML, so it doesn't show any other errors. Note that special knowledge not contained in the DTD, as we've mentioned several times earlier, is contained in both validators. This file opens properly in the validating parsers I've tried it on, which makes perfect sense if you actually look at the DTD.

Figure 22.1
The results of validating XHTML code with an HTML validator.

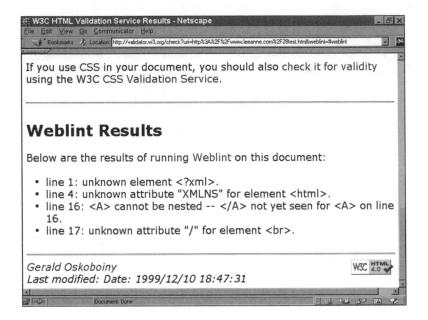

> If you use CSS in your document, you should also check it for validity using the W3C CSS Validation Service.
>
> ## Weblint Results
>
> Below are the results of running Weblint on this document:
>
> - line 1: unknown element <?xml>.
> - line 4: unknown attribute "XMLNS" for element <html>.
> - line 16: <A> cannot be nested -- </A> not yet seen for <A> on line 16.
> - line 17: unknown attribute "/" for element <br>.
>
> *Gerald Oskoboiny*
> *Last modified: Date: 1999/12/10 18:47:31*

CONVERTING HTML TO XHTML

Converting from HTML to XHTML is designed to be easy. In fact, to avoid some of the validation problems of XHTML, it may be best to first create a valid HTML page using any of the excellent validating editors available, most of which are low cost or even free. After the page is tested for appearance in many browsers, just as you would for an ordinary HTML page, you can convert the code to XHTML. Converting to XHTML ensures that many XHTML nesting and other problems are caught early on. Your XHTML pages will also be HTML valid.

Then use a conversion tool such as HTML-Kit from Chami to perform the actual conversion, because almost any automated tool is far more efficient and less error-prone than even the best manual attempts. HTML-Kit uses Tidy, so the Tidy idiosyncrasies must be taken into account and corrected before your code is complete, but it's a simple task to automate even this clean-up step in any decent programmer's editor. I use Visual SlickEdit (http://www.slickedit.com/), which has powerful macro capabilities as well as a complete programming language available that enables tasks of arbitrary complexity to be installed into the editor as if they were natively present.

The Tidy program is even available in source code form, so you could use it as the basis for your own customized version and define your own *pretty-printing* routines if you like.

PART
IV

CH
22

Tip from
LeeAnne.com
Words to weave by

Pretty printing, sometimes called *beautifying,* is a term from software development that refers to automatically formatting a code document according to certain indentation and line break standards to enhance readability and highlight nesting language constructs.

Working backward is also possible, using an HTML validation tool to validate your XHTML pages. This is almost guaranteed to throw a few exception reports, maybe a lot of them, but you should be able to pick out which error messages are valid and which are artifacts of reading bits of XHTML code as incorrect HTML. In the previous example, reading the XHTML file into an HTML validator should generate an error message about the xmlns attribute but nothing else.

CUSTOMIZING XHTML

Although we discussed a simple customization in Chapter 4, eventually there's going to be a lot more to it than that, although exactly what remains to be seen. The XHTML specification is being broken into modules with handy subsets of the complete XHTML functionality in each packet. This is supposed to allow for subsetting the complete language for use in cell phones and other devices, which presumably don't need the full functionality of XHTML, or to encompass the needs of specialized communities. Although subsetting makes considerable sense, it's unclear how any supposed supersetting capability amounts to much more in principle than can already be accomplished with namespaces.

Likewise, the modularization mechanism is unclear. The method whereby the DTD is broken into modular subsets is not defined, and it seems to add considerable complexity to a validating parser to be able to handle conditional processing of the DTD. The same pizza-menu approach used in SGML might serve for XHTML, but the overall complexity of SGML argues against this being a simple task.

UNDERSTANDING THE XML DOCUMENT PROFILE

The XHTML recommendation suggests that something called a document profile will specify the facilities used to process documents of that type. The facilities might include which image formats can be used, levels of scripting support, style sheet support, XHTML modular subsets, extended facilities for other user communities, and so on. The document profile would theoretically allow an XML processor to dynamically create custom DTDs or other document schemas out of many component parts. This may well prove difficult using current DTDs. Again, it's unclear exactly how this supposed facility will improve on namespaces, because presumably the problems that namespaces address will have to be solved in some other way.

Also unclear is what real advantage this approach has over the combination of well-designed specialized DTDs, such as SMIL and MathML when ,used in combination with either CSS or XSL, which already duplicate much of the display formatting functionality of XHTML.

In any case, the problem of supporting older browsers will probably never go away. There are still people on the Web using the original Mosaic browser, and expecting every user to upgrade to a new browser seems optimistic in the extreme. It doesn't seem likely to happen except within particular communities.

CREATING AN XHTML WEB PAGE

In this example, a simple page is converted from HTML into XHTML using HTML-Kit, while maintaining compatibility with existing browsers to the greatest extent possible. Although the exact HTML-Kit settings required to perform these functions are beyond the scope of this chapter, they're easily maintained using the Edit Preferences menu subitem. Here's the source HTML code:

```
<HTML>
  <HEAD>
    <TITLE>Hypatia: A Notable Woman of Science</TITLE>
  <BODY>
    <DIV align="center"><IMG src="Hypatia-text-lc.gif"
        width="300" height="75" border="0"
        hspace="10" alt="[Hypatia's Name]" align="center"></DIV>
    <H1 align="center">Hypatia: A Notable Woman of Science</H1>
    <P>
    <DIV align="center"><IMG src="hypatia6.gif" width="280"
        height="340" border="0" hspace="10"
        alt="[Portrait of Hypatia]" align="center"></DIV>
    <P>
    <DIV align="center"><IMG src="Hypatia-text-uc.gif" width="300"
        height="75" border="0" hspace="10" alt="[Hypatia's Name]"
        align="center"></DIV>
    <A name=hercity></A>
    <P>Hypatia lived in the Egyptian city of Alexandria at the turn
    of the fourth century of the common era. Her father was the last
    director of the great Library of Alexandria and she had been able
    to study mathematics, astronomy, and philosophy to the extent
    that she was renowned as one of the greatest minds of her day,
    surpassing even the scholarship and reputation of her father.
    <A name=herdeath></A>
    <P>She herself was murdered in 415 C.E. at about 45 years of age
    and her work, which included scrolls on Diophantus's
    "Arithmetica," Apollonius's "Conics" and Ptolemy's astronomical
    theories, were systematically destroyed. Her legacy was passed
    down through her students and helped to form the basis of modern
    mathematics.
    <A name=herinventions></A>
    <P>She also invented early astronomical and mechanical devices
    such as the planar astrolabe and the hydroscope.
  </BODY>
</HTML>
```

To "check" the code using Tidy, the file is opened in HTML-Kit under Windows. We're not actually checking the code, because we already know (from prior knowledge—trust me on this) that the original code is valid HTML (with the exception of the align=center attribute on the image tags, which has to be included for compatibility with older versions of many browsers). Instead, Tidy is used to transform the code into XHTML, add style sheet support, and pretty print it.

After the conversion is complete, you select the formatted code in the window to the right, copy it on top of the original code in the window on the left, and then save. You may also want to edit the code slightly at this point. HTML-Kit is a decent HTML/XHTML editor in its own right, and makes this step easy. Figure 22.2 shows the HTML-Kit program at work.

Figure 22.2
HTML-Kit is shown here after converting and pretty printing the Hypatia HTML file.

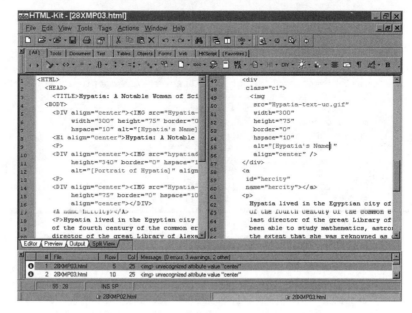

The following code is a slightly edited but syntactically exact rendition of the converted code:

```
<?xml version="1.0"?>
<!DOCTYPE html PUBLIC "-//W3C//DTD XHTML 1.0 Strict//EN"
    "http://www.w3.org/TR/xhtml1/DTD/strict.dtd">
<html xmlns="http://www.w3.org/1999/xhtml">
  <head>
    <title>Hypatia: A Notable Woman of Science</title>
<style type="text/css">
 h1.c2 {text-align: center}
 div.c1 {text-align: center}
</style>
  </head>
  <body>
    <div class="c1">
      <img src="Hypatia-text-lc.gif" width="300" height="75"
      border="0" hspace="10" alt="[Hypatia's Name in Greek]"
      align="center" />
    </div>
    <h1 class="c2">Hypatia: A Notable Woman of Science</h1>
    <p>
    </p>
    <div class="c1">
      <img src="hypatia6.gif" width="280" height="340" border="0"
      hspace="10" alt="[Portrait of Hypatia]" align="center" />
```

```
  </div>
  <p>
  </p>
  <div class="c1">
    <img src="Hypatia-text-uc.gif" width="300" height="75"
     border="0" hspace="10" alt="[Hypatia's Name in Greek]"
     align="center" />
  </div>
  <a id="hercity" name="hercity"></a>
  <p>
    Hypatia lived in the Egyptian city of Alexandria at the turn
    of the fourth century of the common era. Her father was the
    last director of the great Library of Alexandria and she had
    been able to study mathematics, astronomy, and philosophy to
    the extent that she was renowned as one of the greatest
    minds of her day, surpassing even the scholarship and
    reputation of her father.
  <a id="herdeath" name="herdeath"></a>
  </p>
  <p>
    She herself was murdered in 415 C.E. at about 45 years of age
    and her work, which included scrolls on Diophantus's
    "Arithmetica," Apollonius's "Conics" and Ptolemy's
    astronomical theories, were systematically destroyed. Her
    legacy was passed down through her students and helped to
    form the basis of modern mathematics.
  <a id="herinventions" name="herinventions"></a>
  </p>
  <p>
    She also invented early astronomical and mechanical devices
    such as the planar astrolabe and the hydroscope.
  </p>
  </body>
</html>
```

HTML-Kit and Tidy did a good job of converting from HTML to XHTML. Note that the XML declaration and doctype have been added, the anchor target names have been automatically duplicated, all element names and attributes are now in lowercase, attribute values are now quoted, and missing closing tags have been added everywhere.

You can still do a few things, however,and the previous code has been edited slightly to take up less room on the page. But some suggestions from our list of author suggestions have not been followed, and a few things should be explained. First, although the deprecated `align=center` attributes have been replaced with style sheet commands in the `div` elements, they are untouched in the enclosed `img` elements. This makes practical sense because many older browser don't recognize `div` elements but do recognize the `align="center"` syntax, so that should be left alone.

On the other hand, the style sheet is placed in raw form in the document, which will display as text in many browsers. Ideally, you should enclose the style commands in a CDATA section, like this:

```
<style type="text/css">
  <![CDATA[
    h1.c2 {text-align: center}
    div.c1 {text-align: center}
```

```
  ]]>
</style>
```

However, that won't be interpreted by many browsers and may be displayed as data as well, depending on what assumptions the browser makes about what was meant by the construct. An alternative is to place the style information inside comments, as is usually done in HTML, to prevent older browsers from interpreting the code as text content to be displayed.

```
<style type="text/css">
  <!--
    h1.c2 {text-align: center}
    div.c1 {text-align: center}
  // -->
</style>
```

But this method has its own problems. According to the XML Recommendation, XML parsers don't have to pass information inside comments to the application, which means that the style information may disappear before the browser ever sees it, and the style sheet will be empty when the browser tries to apply it to the document.

So, the naive solution might be to place the style sheet in an external file, like this:

```
<style type="text/css" src="hypatia.css"></style>
```

Unfortunately, many browsers don't recognize external style sheets. So the only option left, which seems likely to make the style sheet usable in the greatest number of browsers, is to place the same information in the external style sheet and in the inline code enclosed in comments:

```
<style type="text/css" src="hypatia.css">
  <!--
    h1.c2 {text-align: center}
    div.c1 {text-align: center}
  // -->
</style>
```

Older browsers that don't recognize external style sheets will use the inline information. Still older browsers, such as Mosaic or Netscape 2.0, that don't recognize style sheets at all, will ignore the tags and data completely. Because the external file is supposed to take precedence in any case, if the inline data disappears because the XML parser didn't pass it on to the application, there's no harm done. The style sheet will be applied to the document by every browser likely to be able to interpret it. Here's the final code:

```
<?xml version="1.0"?>
<!DOCTYPE html PUBLIC "-//W3C//DTD XHTML 1.0 Strict//EN"
    "http://www.w3.org/TR/xhtml1/DTD/strict.dtd">
<html xmlns="http://www.w3.org/1999/xhtml">
  <head>
    <title>Hypatia: A Notable Woman of Science</title>
<style type="text/css" src="hypatia.css">
  <!--
    h1.c2 {text-align: center}
    div.c1 {text-align: center}
  // -->
</style>
```

```
    </head>
    <body>
      <div class="c1">
        <img src="Hypatia-text-lc.gif" width="300" height="75"
          border="0" hspace="10" alt="[Hypatia's Name in Greek]"
          align="center" />
      </div>
      <h1 class="c2">Hypatia: A Notable Woman of Science</h1>
      <p>
      </p>
      <div class="c1">
        <img src="hypatia6.gif" width="280" height="340" border="0"
          hspace="10" alt="[Portrait of Hypatia]" align="center" />
      </div>
      <p>
      </p>
      <div class="c1">
        <img src="Hypatia-text-uc.gif" width="300" height="75"
          border="0" hspace="10" alt="[Hypatia's Name in Greek]"
          align="center" />
      </div>
      <a id="hercity" name="hercity"></a>
      <p>
        Hypatia lived in the Egyptian city of Alexandria at the turn
        of the fourth century of the common era. Her father was the
        last director of the great Library of Alexandria and she had
        been able to study mathematics, astronomy, and philosophy to
        the extent that she was renowned as one of the greatest
        minds of her day, surpassing even the scholarship and
        reputation of her father.
      <a id="herdeath" name="herdeath"></a>
      </p>
      <p>
        She herself was murdered in 415 C.E. at about 45 years of age
        and her work, which included scrolls on Diophantus's
        "Arithmetica," Apollonius's "Conics" and Ptolemy's
        astronomical theories, were systematically destroyed. Her
        legacy was passed down through her students and helped to
        form the basis of modern mathematics.
      <a id="herinventions" name="herinventions"></a>
      </p>
      <p>
        She also invented early astronomical and mechanical devices
        such as the planar astrolabe and the hydroscope.
      </p>
    </body>
  </html>
```

This seems to represent the best overall compromise between wide accessibility and confor-
mance to the XML Recommendation. Although there are still a few deprecated attributes,
the code is clean otherwise. Figure 22.3 shows the resulting page in part, using Microsoft
Internet Explorer 5.0.

Figure 22.3
Microsoft Internet Explorer 5.0 shows the completed Hypatia page.

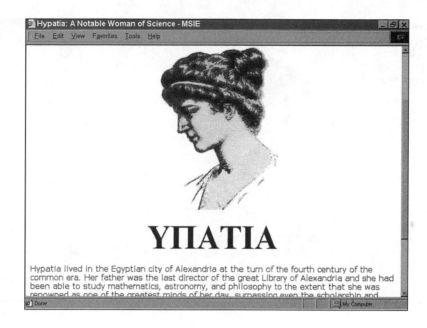

The work isn't finished yet, however; now we have to troubleshoot the result in other browsers.

In one sense, the availability of so many automated tools to convert HTML, which has many available validation tools in itself, to XHTML ought to mean that troubleshooting XHTML should be trivial. However, from the previous example it's obvious that there are still decisions to be made about the code, even though an automated tool produced it. And the sad fact is that browsers are slippery beasts and not to be trusted.

TROUBLESHOOTING XHTML

BROWSER INCOMPATIBILITIES ARE MAKING HASH OF YOUR PAGES

After all that work, when the converted file is opened in Netscape Navigator 4.7, the center alignment doesn't work for some reason. Figure 22.4 shows the anomalous result.

Hmmm. How can this be? Neither version of the style sheet seems to affect the page, at least visibly. Carefully check the code, the name of the CSS file on disk, and everything else you can think of. Now, look at the original code, which worked properly in all browsers (trust me again—it does). The only pertinent difference seems to be the align attribute that was moved out of the code and into a style sheet to begin with. So try it. It works! Those rascally Netscape programmers have used a CSS engine that doesn't recognize and apply text-align properly to the document, so you have to put it back where it was.

Figure 22.4
Netscape Navigator getting lost while trying to display a "standard" page.

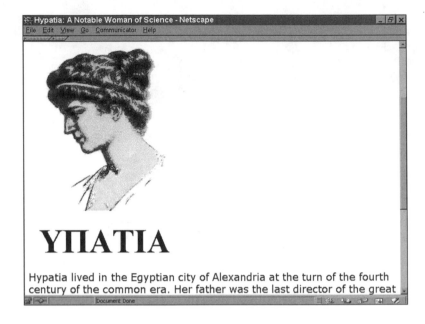

Here's the resulting code:

```
<?xml version="1.0"?>
<!DOCTYPE html PUBLIC "-//W3C//DTD XHTML 1.0 Strict//EN"
    "http://www.w3.org/TR/xhtml1/DTD/strict.dtd">
<html xmlns="http://www.w3.org/1999/xhtml">
  <head>
    <title>Hypatia: A Notable Woman of Science</title>
<style type="text/css" src="hypatia.css">
  <!--
    h1.c2 {text-align: center}
    div.c1 {text-align: center}
 // -->
</style>
  </head>
  <body>
    <div class="c1" align="center">
      <img src="Hypatia-text-lc.gif" width="300" height="75"
      border="0" hspace="10" alt="[Hypatia's Name in Greek]"
      align="center" />
    </div>
    <h1 class="c2" align="center">Hypatia: A Notable Woman of Science</h1>
    <p>
    </p>
    <div class="c1" align="center">
      <img src="hypatia6.gif" width="280" height="340" border="0"
      hspace="10" alt="[Portrait of Hypatia]" align="center" />
    </div>
    <p>
    </p>
    <div class="c1" align="center">
      <img src="Hypatia-text-uc.gif" width="300" height="75"
      border="0" hspace="10" alt="[Hypatia's Name in Greek]"
      align="center" />
```

```
    </div>
    <a id="hercity" name="hercity"></a>
    <p>
       Hypatia lived in the Egyptian city of Alexandria at the turn
       of the fourth century of the common era. Her father was the
       last director of the great Library of Alexandria and she had
       been able to study mathematics, astronomy, and philosophy to
       the extent that she was renowned as one of the greatest
       minds of her day, surpassing even the scholarship and
       reputation of her father.
  <a id="herdeath" name="herdeath"></a>
   </p>
   <p>
       She herself was murdered in 415 C.E. at about 45 years of age
       and her work, which included scrolls on Diophantus's
       "Arithmetica," Apollonius's "Conics" and Ptolemy's
       astronomical theories, were systematically destroyed. Her
       legacy was passed down through her students and helped to
       form the basis of modern mathematics.
  <a id="herinventions" name="herinventions"></a>
   </p>
   <p>
       She also invented early astronomical and mechanical devices
       such as the planar astrolabe and the hydroscope.
   </p>
  </body>
</html>
```

BACK TO PRESENTATION BASICS FOR FULL COMPATIBILITY

Although the only change was to add back the align="center" attributes to the two images and the single header level 1, the page now displays properly. In real life, there might be scores of similar problems and the troubleshooting phase might last quite a bit longer. Figure 22.5 shows the debugged page in Netscape Navigator 4.7.

Figure 22.5
Netscape Navigator is now rendering the page correctly.

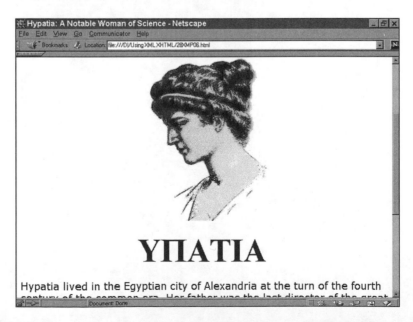

Although specifications are wonderful things, the real world of code development sometimes requires compromises between the way things ought to be done and the way life is. You have the choice of doing things the "right" way or doing them the Microsoft way in many cases, and for a few basic things you might want to compromise somewhat. Because both Netscape and Microsoft are aware of their own history, the `align="center"` value on the `<img>` tag causes no problem in existing browsers from either firm.

You've followed the development of an actual XHTML document from its HTML roots in this section, including a necessary compromise between the standards and browser reality, a common occurrence in document creation on the Web. It's possible to add the `<img align="center" …>` attribute value in the internal DTD if it seems necessary, but it causes more trouble than it's worth at the present time, because including an internal DTD subset breaks many HTML browsers.

CHAPTER **23**

USING SMIL—THE SYNCHRONIZED MULTIMEDIA MARKUP LANGUAGE

In this chapter

UNDERSTANDING SMIL—HYTIME'S DISTANT COUSIN

SMIL, the *Synchronized Multimedia Markup Language* is essentially a list of edits and links to external files that contain the meat of a presentation. SMIL is like a choreographer's dance notes or a theater director's blocking instructions that let the performers make their entrances and exits on cue without actually doing the performance itself. All the metadata and control information is contained in the SMIL document and none of the actual media content, which makes life very easy when it comes time to edit the file.

Most of the functionality of SMIL is contained in only two elements: the par (parallel) element, which describes things that must be done more or less at the same time, and the seq (sequential) element, which describes things that must be done one after the other. The things to be done are referenced with the ubiquitous URI, W3C's successor to the URL. The rest of SMIL is framework and details: defining the playback window, how much of the external file to play, whether there should be any delay in starting playback, and whether playback should wait for a cue from some other event.

In this chapter, you'll learn about the actual SMIL elements, create several working SMIL documents as you go along, and see how the SMIL elements are used to create a show.

Believe it or not, synchronized multimedia isn't a new invention on the Web. The HyTime crowd has been doing it for years. In fact, *HyTime* is short for *Hypermedia Time-based Structuring Language* and is an architecture designed to facilitate the interaction of a wide variety of multimedia documents and tools. The SMIL working group built upon the experience of HyTime, simplifying and rethinking it until SMIL is really quite easy to use and does most of what you want a multimedia director to do.

UNDERSTANDING SYNCHRONIZATION

Synchronizing disparate elements precisely requires some sort of time standard, which can be either externally supplied or maintained in the system executing the synchronized presentation. The most accurate sources of time are external, tied somehow back to a standard time maintained by national standards bodies such as the National Bureau of Standards and many others around the world.

In the United States, the official timekeeper is the U.S. Naval Observatory in Washington, D.C.; however, there are numerous secondary sources. Many universities and private organizations maintain their own clocks, synchronizing them with the USNO clock periodically, so one is rarely at a loss for a time standard somewhere nearby. Within a few hundred miles of most coastal regions throughout the world and around the Great Lakes and other major navigable inland waters, for example, the Loran C navigational system broadcasts a time signal based on the USNO master clock.

GPS (Global Positioning System) satellites broadcast time signals that can be detected by any GPS receiver that can see the sky, anywhere on earth. The accuracy of GPS signals is maintained within 200 nanoseconds for government users, and a random jitter algorithm degrades the signal to within 340 nanoseconds to most civilian users. Because the jitter is random, averaging techniques can be used in combination with a local clock to synchronize very closely to the USNO master clock.

There are also high frequency radio stations around the world that transmit time signals, so there are few places on earth—outside the bottom of mine shafts—that cannot receive radio time signals from somewhere.

Simple and relatively inexpensive radio receivers allow even persons and organizations of modest means to access time only a few steps removed from the USNO Master Clock or similar clocks maintained by many nations around the world. These time sources are highly accurate and can be used from almost anywhere on earth. Users without the need for highly accurate time can use telephone or Internet links to terrestrial sources. The most accurate sources are GPS and Loran C, but not every site needs that amount of accuracy.

PART
IV
CH
23

The radio receivers often use an output port to transmit an ordinary computer data stream, such as 7-bit ASCII over an RS-232c link, to a serial port on your computer. As mentioned previously, it's also possible to receive time signals over the Internet using free or low-cost software such as Cyberkit, Tardis 2000, or YATS. Network latency usually limits accuracy to about 300 milliseconds, which is plenty accurate for many applications, although averaging techniques can shave some of the error to approach (but not equal) the accuracy of the GPS satellite receivers.

Tip from  LeeAnne.com Words to weave by	Online sources, such as TUCOWS (`http://www.tucows.com/`), are good sources for Internet time synchronization software, and there are many excellent candidates, but some software includes time synchronization as a small part of a larger system. A good example is Cyberkit, which is postcardware (the author requests an interesting postcard in payment for using the software) that does NSLookup, keep-alive, ping, network time synchronization, and other network functions. You can search for this name directly on TUCOWS and find it easily.

Networks depend on accurate time synchronization, so anyone on a high-speed network probably has access to an accurate clock if he knows how to extract the data. That's one part of the equation. The other part is maintaining accurate timing records of the media files themselves. The least accurate is obtained by measuring the file directly, called NPT (Normal Play Time) in SMIL. The most accurate is SMPTE (Society of Motion Picture and Television Engineers), which actually timestamps the source so that you can access the file down to individual frames and subframes. A frame is approximately one 30th of a second, and a subframe is measured in one hundredths of a frame, so you can specify begin and end points of a file very accurately indeed. SMPTE-encoded files are not common on the Web, so whereas NPT is most often used with random content, SMPTE requires special equipment to encode an accurate clock signal within the multimedia content itself.

As with many things in life, often the best way to start thinking about a complex multimedia production is with paper and pencil. The professional usually starts with a storyboard, on which she lays out the scenes and transitions in a rough manner together with notes on what audio effects are needed. By doing this on paper—sometimes sheets of graph paper for precise timings but initially on large file cards which can be moved around conveniently—the creative process is facilitated without investing too much time in computer manipulation. Too much detailed effort early on tends to freeze our thinking processes and solidifies ideas before they have time to gestate.

After you have a storyboard you or your customers can live with, it's time to start filling in details. Graph paper is excellent for visualizing tight timings, and it costs nothing to scratch out and modify an entrance or exit. There are a *lot* of books with titles like *Jump Start Your Brain* by Doug Hall, *Orbiting the Giant Hair Ball* by Gordon MacKenzie, *A Whack on the Side of the Head* by Roger von Oech, *Lateral Thinking* by Edward de Bono, and *AHA!* by Jordan Ayan to get you started on becoming more creative, or at least taking a more creative approach to creativity if you need a bit of help, but randomness and fluidity are key concepts. You can't be terribly random nor awfully fluid when using someone else's idea of how to work and organize your thoughts.

USING MULTIMEDIA TOOLS TO CREATE SMIL DOCUMENTS

That said, let's assume you've done all the creative stuff and have a firm idea of what you want to do. Using an automated tool makes more sense, then, because now you're trying to bend someone else's ideas and implementations to fit your own desires. It's a matter of mastery.

There are quite a few multimedia tools out there in the world already, although most are highly proprietary. Macromedia, for example, has several kits available but they all require Macromedia plugins to allow users to view them. An open-source standard such as SMIL means that you're not locked into a few platforms with ports of the rendering engine ready to go, but can pretty much do as you please, confident that almost every platform will be able to use your presentation without hassles.

Microsoft has their own proprietary NetShow, which has a few nice features, but when you use it you're locked into what a single company and a single source thinks is worth doing. So I wouldn't count on a port from NetShow or even PowerPoint to Linux, BeOS, or the Amiga anytime soon. Even Mac OS releases lag Windows production schedules by many months or years.

SMIL—THE SYNCHRONIZED MULTIMEDIA INTERFACE LANGUAGE

SMIL can be implemented in Java, or other open source languages, and run anywhere. W3C periodically updates their own Amaya browser with the latest tidbits from their coffers, and the source is freely available, so ports to any system with a compiler or runtime engine are quite doable, even by individuals.

RealNetworks' RealSlideshow uses SMIL as a non-proprietary scheme, improving its chances of working with future media players and media editing and creation engines. The existing product generates SMIL files and uses RealPlayer as a rendering engine. You can look at the RealNetworks offerings at `http://www.real.com/`. Although they bury proprietary RealNetworks features in external files in shows created using RealSlideshow, they play ordinary SMIL 1.0 files quite nicely but with some limitations. Figure 23.1 shows a slideshow created by hand and played in the RealPlayer 7 basic rendering engine.

Tip from	
LeeAnne.com Words to weave by	If you think of proprietary multimedia technologies such as Flash, Netshow, and Director as the multimedia equivalent of Microsoft Word or WordPerfect, which use what are essentially binary formats to encode and store data, SMIL is like an ASCII plain text editor, which produces files that don't need conversion. In most cases, conversion programs for proprietary multimedia formats don't even exist.

The slideshow handles the images just fine but doesn't deal very well with the `audio` or `textstream` elements. MIDI file types aren't thoroughly supported, so it was necessary to use a WAV file instead. And textstream files aren't supported at all so that statement was commented out in the example. With a little more effort, these files could have been imported into native RealPlayer media types but that would rather beg the question. Complete support is obviously better than no support, but few companies are willing to give up their proprietary advantages and let anyone write files for their rendering engines with no penalty in features or performance.

Figure 23.1
RealPlayer shows a hand-created SMIL slideshow on top of the SMIL code.

The basic code is exactly the same as that used in the sample file used in the "Document Body" section later in this chapter. The only real difference is that the sample filenames have been replaced with real ones.

Apple Quicktime 4.1 is another existing product using SMIL. Apple products can be found at `http://www.apple.com/`.

EXPLORING SMIL SYNTAX

The following sections provide a quick overview of the SMIL elements, so you can see what you're going to be working with. There really aren't all that many tags, and a relative handful are all you need to start doing useful work.

THE smil ELEMENT

The smil element is the root of a SMIL document and can take one attribute, a unique id="value". It may contain two child elements, a head and a body. The document head is mostly meta-information about the display environment, whereas the body does the actual work of the presentation. First, look at the document head in detail.

THE DOCUMENT HEAD

The document head contains information about the exact physical layout of the medium in which the SMIL content is to be rendered and certain metadata about the document, such as who wrote it, when it was written, and so on. It doesn't contain any time-synchronized information whatsoever.

THE head ELEMENT   The head element can take an id attribute, can contain any number of meta children, and can have either a single layout child or a switch child, which can contain an exclusive list of layout children.

THE layout ELEMENT   The layout element can take an id attribute and a type attribute, which defines the layout language used. Although SMIL is one language, SMIL is not limited to itself but can call on the facilities of any other language it understands or has a helper application for. If the type is text/smil-basic-layout, the layout element can contain region and root-layout elements. If not, the layout element can contain any arbitrary text.

For example, instead of using the SMIL layout facilities, you could use CSS2 in addition to SMIL itself, to allow the user agent to choose which mechanism to use for rendering the content, like this:

```
<head>
  <switch title="[Set the banner display window position]">
    <layout type="text/css">
      [region="banner"] { top: 10px; left: 10px }
    </layout>
    <layout>
      <region id="banner" title="[Banner]" top="10" left="10" />
    </layout>
  </switch>
</head>
```

Note that SMIL duplicates many of the layout facilities of CSS using a similar basic syntax. For simplicity, the entirety of the layout elements you might want to specify aren't shown, just the bare essentials, letting the size of the images themselves define the size of the window on the screen. This may or may not be the way you would want an actual show to take place. You'll learn more about the ways you can control the exact placement and size of regions on the screen in the following "SMIL Basic Layout Language" section.

SMIL Basic Layout Language

The SMIL basic layout language is pretty much a duplication of the most commonly used properties of CSS2. The main addition is the `fit` attribute, which has to be simulated in CSS2 but is much handier as a simple attribute. The language consists of attributes associated with the two SMIL layout elements in the `head`, `region`, and `root-layout`. Where `root-layout` elements define the overall rendering window for the presentation, `region` elements optionally subdivide that viewport into whatever smaller segments are required. The whole window can also be used if desired.

If you think of a SMIL document as a series of events similar to what you would experience in a theater, the `root-layout` and `region` elements set up the proscenium and stage and define particular places on it, so you can place actors (the media elements themselves) in their proper positions on the stage. Romeo can be in the garden while Juliet is in the balcony above, and you can coordinate their activities with each other just as a director can block out the actions and sounds an actor makes. Note that the regions defined for the actions may be either visible regions on the screen or aural regions defined by acoustic placement with stereo or surround-sound technology.

The region Element

The region element has no content but controls the position, size, and scaling of media object elements. It takes a required `id` attribute, which allows you to select the region media object elements that should be displayed with a corresponding `region` attribute. Media object elements only appear in the SMIL document body and are `ref`, `animation`, `audio`, `img`, `video`, `text`, and `textstream`.

→ To learn more about the information contained in the document body element, **see** "The Document Body," **p. 538**.

The `region` element can also take the following attributes:

- **background-color**—Very similar to CSS `background-color` except that named colors may or may not be supported.
- **fit**—Describes how the media content fits into the area defined by a region. Possible values are `fill`, which sizes content to fit regardless of aspect ratio; `meet`, which sizes content to fit but retains the original aspect ratio so there may be empty space either to the right or below; `scroll`, which invokes some sort of scrolling mechanism if the media content is larger than the region display window; `slice`, which doesn't; and `hidden`, which displays the media content much as does `slice`, but fills any empty space with the background color. The default value is `hidden`.
- **height**—Identical to the corresponding CSS property.
- **left**—Identical to the corresponding CSS property.

- **skip-content**—This Boolean attribute allows SMIL 1.0 processors to ignore the content of the region element if a later specification changes it from an empty element to one with content.
- **title**—A human-readable description of the region. Although it isn't mandatory, it's strongly advised.
- **top**—Identical to the corresponding CSS property.
- **width**—Identical to the corresponding CSS property.
- **z-index**—Identical to the corresponding CSS property.

THE root-layout ELEMENT

This element has no content but controls the size of the root element, which defines the viewport in which the documents referenced by SMIL are presented. It takes id and title attributes as described previously, as well as height, width, top, and left attributes, which suffice to define a rectangular window. The skip-content Boolean attribute allows SMIL 1.0 processors to ignore the content of the root-layout element if a later specification changes it from an empty element to one with content.

THE meta ELEMENT

The meta element has no content but describes an open-ended list of properties that apply to the document as a whole. It takes mandatory name and content attributes, which describe the property name and value respectively. It also takes optional id and skip-content attributes, as described previously.

Predefined property names include base, the base URI for relative URIs; title, the presentation title; and pics-label (or PICS-Label), which refers to the PICS standard described in Chapter 27, "Summing Up—The Future of the Web."

THE DOCUMENT BODY

The document body contains all time-dependent and linking information associated with the document. The head element sets the stage, as it were, providing the basic frame in which the multimedia show will be performed. But the entrances and exits of every player appearing on that stage are controlled by the body element. Just as a play has a director, a SMIL show has a body element that tells each external multimedia actor in the show when and where to appear, how long to go on, and what role they should play.

For example, the following SMIL fragment would initiate a simple slideshow with unsynchronized captions and background music:

```
<smil>
  <head>
    <layout>
      <root-layout id="Slideshow" title="[Slideshow Window]"
                   width="400" height="400" />
      <region id="slides" title="[Slideshow]" top="10" left="10" />
```

```
          <region id="sound" title="[Audio Track]" />
      </layout>
  </head>
  <body>
    <par>
      <audio src="musicfile" region="sound" />
      <textstream src="captionfile" />
      <seq>
        <img src="slide1file" region="slides" dur="10s" />
        <img src="slide2file" region="slides" dur="10s" />
        <img src="slide3file" region="slides" dur="10s" />
        <img src="slide4file" region="slides" dur="10s" />
        <img src="slide5file" region="slides" dur="10s" />
      </seq>
    </par>
  </body>
</smil>
```

You can replace the generic filenames in this skeleton with any files you have lying about and it should work quite nicely. To be safe in the widest variety of rendering engines, WAV files are pretty generic, although MIDI files are more commonly used on Web pages. The size of the window defined in the root-layout element, and the placement of the actual slides defined in the region element can be tweaked to suit your actual files. You'll learn more about the elements used to coordinate the slideshow in the next section. The show itself was shown in Figure 23.1.

THE body ELEMENT

The body element takes one id attribute and may contain the following optional children:

- **a**—An anchor element equivalent to an HTML `<a src="…" …>linktext</a>` element.

- **animation**—Identifies the referenced file as an animation file.

- **audio**—Identifies the referenced file as an audio file. Note that an audio rendering surface cannot be defined by SMIL basic layout, because CSS2 or above is required to define aural surfaces.

- **img**—Identifies the referenced file as an image file.

- **par**—Tells the SMIL engine to render enclosed children in parallel, that is, simultaneously.

- **ref**—Tells the SMIL engine that the referenced file is a generic media object. This element is used when other media types don't seem appropriate for any reason.

- **seq**—Tells the SMIL engine to render enclosed children sequentially, that is, one after another.

- **switch**—Tells the SMIL engine that the enclosed content should be examined

- **text**—Identifies the referenced file as a text file, that is, a text file that can be displayed in a single window.

- **textstream**—Identifies the referenced file as a textstream file, that is, a text file which should be scrolled through a window.

- **video**—Identifies the referenced file as a video file.

SYNCHRONIZATION ELEMENTS

Simply put, the synchronization elements are the two basic synchronization elements, `par` and `seq`, plus the media object elements, which include `ref`, `animation`, `audio`, `img`, `video`, `text`, and `textstream` elements.

THE `par` ELEMENT

The children of a `par` element form a loosely knit group of media events that can overlap or proceed simultaneously. Exact manipulation of the start and duration or end times can vary the exact effects generated with only your imagination as a limiting factor.

The `par` element can take the following attributes:

- **abstract**—A brief description of the content contained in the element.
- **author**—The name of the author of the content contained in the element.
- **begin**—This attribute specifies the begin time for an element.
- **event-value**—The element begins when a certain event occurs.
- **copyright**—The copyright notice of the content contained in the element.
- **dur**—This attribute specifies the explicit duration of an element.
- **end**—This attribute specifies the explicit end of an element.
- **endsync**—This attribute can have the following values: `first`, `id-ref`, `last`. It lets you synchronize the end of a media play time with another event.
- **id**—This attribute identifies an element with a unique identifier and nothing more.
- **region**—This attribute specifies an abstract rendering surface.
- **repeat**—The attribute value can be an integer, or the string `"indefinite"`. The default value is `1`.
- **system-bitrate**—Evaluate the stated bit rate of the user agent against the bit rate claimed in a given element. This allows you to load beefier files when you have a high-speed connection and skinnier ones on low-speed dialup lines.
- **system-captions**—Based on settings of `on` or `off`, choose to display captions on elements at user option. Because there are two attributes touching on captions, these can be used in combinations to perform fairly sophisticated logic.
- **system-language**—Based on a list of languages set in the user agent, choose the most appropriate language to display or render.
- **system-overdub-or-caption**—Based on settings of `overdub` or `caption`, choose to render overdub audio or display captions on elements at user option. Because there are two attributes touching on captions, these can be used in combinations to perform fairly sophisticated logic.
- **system-required**—Specifies the name of an extension to basic SMIL functionality. If the user agent supports the extension, choose the element that calls upon the facility. This may eventually become an XML namespace.

- **system-screen-size**—Based on the reported screen size of the user agent, choose an appropriate region size and media file.
- **system-screen-depth**—Based on the reported screen depth (color space) of the user agent, choose the most appropriate files to display.
- **title**—A title for the element, which may or may not be rendered, depending on the user agent and the particular needs of the user.

The par element can contain the following children, already defined:

- a
- animation
- audio
- img
- par
- ref
- seq
- switch
- text
- textstream
- video

THE seq ELEMENT

The children of a seq element form a temporal sequence in which one event follows another in strict order. Because events transmitted over a network may arrive out of order, depending completely on start and end times can cause unfortunate overlaps. When elements of the presentation should never overlap, using a seq element to control them lets SMIL itself guarantee that they don't overlap, even if one element is delayed in transmission.

The seq element can take the following attributes:

- **abstract**—A brief description of the content contained in the element.
- **author**—The name of the author of the content contained in the element.
- **begin**—This attribute specifies the begin time for an element.
- **copyright**—The copyright notice of the content contained in the element.
- **dur**—This attribute specifies the explicit duration of an element.
- **end**—This attribute specifies the explicit end of an element.
- **id**—This attribute identifies an element with a unique identifier.
- **region**—This attribute specifies an abstract rendering surface.
- **repeat**—The attribute value can be an integer or the string "indefinite". The default value is 1.

- **system-bitrate**—Evaluate the stated bit rate of the user agent against the bit rate claimed in a given element. This allows you to load beefier files when you have a high-speed connection and skinnier ones on low-speed dialup lines.

- **system-captions**—Based on settings of on or off, choose to display captions on elements at user option. Because there are two attributes touching on captions, these can be used in combinations to perform fairly sophisticated logic.

- **system-language**—Based on a list of languages set in the user agent, choose the most appropriate language to display or render.

- **system-overdub-or-caption**—Based on settings of overdub or caption, choose to render overdub audio or display captions on elements at user option. Because there are two attributes touching on captions, these can be used in combinations to perform fairly sophisticated logic.

- **system-required**—Specifies the name of an extension to basic SMIL functionality. If the user agent supports the extension, choose the element that calls upon the facility. This may eventually become an XML namespace.

- **system-screen-size**—Based on the reported screen size of the user agent, choose an appropriate region size and media file.

- **system-screen-depth**—Based on the reported screen depth (color space) of the user agent, choose the most appropriate files to display.

- **title**—A title for the element which may be rendered or not, depending on the user agent and the particular needs of the user.

The seq element can contain the following children, already defined:

- a
- animation
- audio
- img
- par
- ref
- seq
- switch
- text
- textstream
- video

Media Object Elements

The Media Object elements, which include the `ref`, `animation`, `audio`, `img`, `video`, `text`, and `textstream` elements, allow the inclusion of `media` objects into a SMIL presentation by reference and take the following attributes:

- **`abstract`**—A brief description of the content contained in the element.
- **`alt`**—An alternate description for agents which cannot render the media content or as an aid to persons who cannot use them in a particular situation.
- **`author`**—The name of the author of the content contained in the element.
- **`begin`**—This attribute specifies the begin time for an element.
- **`event-value`**—This element begins when a certain event occurs.
- **`clip-begin`**—Specify a starting offset from the beginning of a media file using SMPTE or NPT.
- **`clip-end`**—Specify an ending offset from the beginning of a media file using SMPTE or NPT.
- **`copyright`**—The copyright notice of the content contained in the element.
- **`dur`**—This attribute specifies the explicit duration of an element.
- **`end`**—This attribute specifies the explicit end of an element.
- **`fill`**—Either `remove` or `freeze`. This attribute controls the behavior of a `par` or terminal `seq` element that ends before an enclosing element does or a non-terminal `seq` element that ends before a following element begins. The value `remove` tells the processor to close the file and the value `freeze` tells the processor to freeze the frame until the enclosing element ends or the following element starts.
- **`longdesc`**—A URI pointing to a long description supplementing the alternate description in the `alt` attribute.
- **`id`**—This attribute identifies an element with a unique identifier.
- **`region`**—This attribute specifies an abstract rendering surface.
- **`src`**—The URI defining the source of the media file.
- **`system-bitrate`**—Evaluate the stated bit rate of the user agent against the bit rate claimed in a given element. This allows you to load beefier files when you have a high-speed connection and skinnier ones on low-speed dialup lines.
- **`system-captions`**—Based on settings of `on` or `off`, choose to display captions on elements at user option. Because there are two attributes touching on captions, these can be used in combinations to perform fairly sophisticated logic.
- **`system-language`**—Based on a list of languages set in the user agent, choose the most appropriate language to display or render.
- **`system-overdub-or-caption`**—Based on settings of `overdub` or `caption`, choose to render overdub audio or display captions on elements at user option. Because there are two attributes touching on captions, these can be used in combinations to perform fairly sophisticated logic.

- **system-required**—Specifies the name of an extension to basic SMIL functionality. If the user agent supports the extension, choose the element that calls upon the facility. This may eventually become an XML namespace.

- **system-screen-size**—Based on the reported screen size of the user agent, choose an appropriate region size and media file.

- **system-screen-depth**—Based on the reported screen depth (color space) of the user agent, choose the most appropriate files to display.

- **title**—A title for the element, which may or may not be rendered, depending on the user agent and the particular needs of the user.

- **type**—The MIME type of the media object referenced in the src attribute.

All Media Objects can contain an anchor child element so that you can construct hyperlinks with them using the anchor, or <a> tag.

SMIL TIME MODEL

When you consider all the things that can go wrong with media transmissions over the Internet, you'll realize that time is a slippery thing. The possibilities for delay are endless, as everyone who's ever tried to access the Web with a dialup modem can tell you, so what happens when things slow to a crawl? The short answer is, "It depends." Timing issues like this can be enormously complex and can vary depending on exactly how the timing was specified. The SMIL 1.0 Recommendation devotes several somewhat unclear pages to examining all the possibilities and coming to essentially the same conclusion. The fact is that sometimes things *do* go wrong and there's very little you can do besides buy a faster Internet connection.

Which, by the way, I highly recommend. In most parts it just isn't all that expensive to get DSL or cable modem service when you consider all the time you save. Anyone buying this book probably does enough work on the Web to justify the expense many times over. Although your line at work may be a T1 or T3, the vagaries of the computing life mean that you'll be spending time solving little emergencies in the middle of the night from time to time. How much nicer not to have to get dressed and drag yourself into work to solve a problem you can fix in ten or twenty minutes online.

TIME MODEL VALUES

There are two types of time values used in SMIL. The NPT, or Normal Playing Time, enables you to measure the playing time from the beginning of the clip and note the exact time you want the subclip to start and end. SMPTE was invented by television and motion picture engineers, and is slightly more confusing than NPT but very accurate. Professional video editing workstations typically measure in SMPTE terms, because the exact *time* is less important than the exact frame of a movie or video clip.

NPT follows this format in your code

`HH:MM:SS.hh`

where HH is any number of hours, MM is 0 to 59 minutes, SS is 0 to 59 seconds, and hh is hundredths of a second. If higher values are `0`, they can be omitted. If the unit of measurement is specified, a numeric range can be as large as necessary to express the length of the interval. `ntp=128.23s` is equivalent to `ntp=02:08.23`.

SMPTE is slightly more complex. In the first place, there are three different kinds of SMPTE to accommodate the needs of various users. `smpte` uses 30 frames per second whereas `smpte-30-drop` uses 23.97 frames per second through a complex "leap" frame arrangement whereby frames are skipped every few minutes. `smpte-25` uses 25 frames per second. They all look the same but vary in how many frames can fit into the frames field.

Tip from

LeeAnne.com
Words to weave by

SMPTE, the Society of Motion Picture and Television Engineers, actually publishes standards by the score relating to every phase of television and motion picture production. They can be found at `http://www.smpte.org/`.

SMPTE looks like this in your code

`HH:MM:SS:ff.hh`

where HH is any number of hours, MM is 0-59 minutes, SS is 0-59 seconds, ff is 0-number of frames in a particular format, and hh is hundredths of a frame.

Each of these standards has a particular use in going to and from various motion picture and television formats. In fact, they missed `smpte-24`, which uses 24 frames per second. The problem is that there are several television systems in use today, and a few motion picture systems as well, which makes it handy to have conversion formats that are related to the source in a more or less integral fashion.

DETERMINING TIMING VALUES OF SMIL 1.0 ELEMENTS

Because everything is so dependent on timing in SMIL, there are quite a few rules telling you exactly which timing values are implicit in every situation in which the actual start and end times may be in doubt. If you specify exact clock times on every element, of course, there's no problem with implied times, but that may not be convenient or practical in a large presentation. Sometimes you want transitions to be under the control of the user, for example, a lecturer might not want to go to the next slide or video until he reaches a particular point in a verbal presentation. Sometimes a user might want to slow down the presentation so it can be more easily understood. And sometimes network latency may delay the start or playing time of a particular element to an unknown extent.

In all these situations, you need a set of rules to flexibly determine what plays at any particular point in the presentation, what follows what, and by how much. The sections immediately following list those rules and give a few examples to clarify the issues.

DETERMINING THE IMPLICIT BEGINNING OF AN ELEMENT

If you don't explicitly set the time at which an element starts, it starts at a time implied by other events according to the following rules:

- The implicit beginning of the first child of the body element is when the document starts playing, which means that elements start playing immediately and on demand unless you alter that behavior explicitly.

- The implicit beginning of any child of a par element is the same as the effective beginning of the par element. In other words, elements within a par section all start at the same time, at least theoretically, which is exactly what you might expect.

- The implicit beginning of the first child of a seq element is the same as the effective beginning of the seq element, which is a fancy way of saying that the first element within a sequence starts playing immediately unless you say something different.

- The implicit beginning of any other child of a seq element is the same as the desired end time of the previous child of the seq element. In other words, they follow one another in strict sequence with no overlap.

So in the following code, the implicit beginning of both elements is the same by rule 2, because they're inside a par element:

```
<par>
  <audio src="audiofile1" />
  <audio src="audiofile2" />
</par>
```

Whereas in the second, the implicit beginning of the second file is immediately after the end of the first file by rule 3, whatever its duration might be, because it's inside a seq element:

```
<seq>
  <audio src="audiofile1" />
  <audio src="audiofile2" />
</seq>
```

If the behavior of the first audio element in the sequence is altered by an explicit end attribute, the implicit beginning of the second audio element is now immediately after the explicit end of the first element by rule 3:

```
<seq>
  <audio src="audiofile1" end="12s" />
  <audio src="audiofile2" />
</seq>
```

This really isn't rocket science. The behavior of elements is quite intuitive when you understand how the media files interact with the volitional behavior of browser users and the vagaries of the network.

DETERMINING THE IMPLICIT END OF AN ELEMENT

If you don't specify an end for an element, it has an implicit end that depends on the interaction of several relationships between the attributes describing the behavior of the element itself and the files the element refers to.

The first description that matches the element in the following list is the one that applies. You can't pick any determinant at random but must proceed through the list step by step:

1. An element with a `repeat` attribute with a value of `indefinite` has an implied end immediately after its beginning. In other words, indefinite means just that. The element can end at any time, depending on some external event, but won't stop by itself.

2. An element with a `repeat` attribute with any value other than `indefinite` has an implied end equal to the implied end of a `seq` element with the same number of copies of the element as children. So repeating an element is the same as inserting a sequence with the same number of duplicate elements as you have repeats.

3. A media element that refers to a continuous object such as an audio or video file has an implied end equal to the sum of the beginning of the element and the duration of the file. So sampling a source with intrinsic duration, such as a .wav file, lasts to the end of the source itself.

4. A media element referring to a file without intrinsic duration, such as a text file or an image, has an implicit end immediately after its effective beginning. Text and image elements display instantly, or at least that's how they are conceptualized.

5. A `seq` element has an implied end equal to the desired end of its last child. So if you set an explicit end time on the last child element, that's when the sequence ends whether any single file has finished playing or not.

6. A `par` element has an implied end that depends on the value of an included `endsync` attribute. If the value of the `endsync` attribute is `last`, the default value that applies if the attribute is missing entirely, the implicit duration of the `par` element is the maximum of the desired durations of its children, so the element will continue playing until the last of its children finishes. But if the value of the `endsync` attribute is `first`, the implicit duration of the `par` element is the minimum of the desired durations of its children, so the element will continue playing until the first of its children finishes. And if the value of the `endsync` attribute is an `id-ref`, the implicit duration of the `par` element is the desired duration of the child referenced by the `id-ref` so you can stop playing when any particular child element finishes.

So in the following example, the duration of the entire `par` element is the same as the duration of the audio file referenced by the ID `fileid` by rule 6. Even if the intrinsic duration of the video file is greater than the audio file, both the audio and video files stop playing at the same time because the enclosing `par` element ends. If the duration of the video file is less than the audio file, then the `par` element continues playing to the end of the audio file even though the video file has finished.

```
<par endsync="id(fileid)">
  <audio id="fileid" src="audiofile" />
  <video src="videofile" />
</par>
```

DETERMINING THE DESIRED END OF AN ELEMENT

If you set either an explicit duration or an explicit end, you define the behavior of the element so that you have a desired end instead of an implicit end. The first situation that applies in the following list must be taken, as in the previous section; you cannot select from the list at random.

1. If a media element has *both* an explicit duration and an explicit end, the desired end is *either* the minimum of the sum of the desired beginning plus the explicit duration *or* the explicit end. If one or the other value is longer, the shorter value rules. In other words, the user agent will determine what you *really* wanted to do whether you like it or not, so add up those values carefully.

2. If the element *has* an explicit duration but *no* explicit end, the desired end is the sum of the desired beginning and the explicit duration, which makes perfect sense when you think about it. If you ask it to play for a certain period of time, it will.

3. If the element *has* an explicit end but *no* explicit duration, the desired end is precisely the explicit end. In other words, unless you say otherwise, a media display stops when you say it does.

4. Otherwise, the desired end is equal to the implicit end, which means that the rendering agent assumes that you know what you're doing and actually want the default behavior to control the timing.

DETERMINING THE DESIRED BEGINNING OF AN ELEMENT

Assuming that you want to control the beginning of a media event in your presentation, you have to insert a timing attribute of some sort. Otherwise the user agent will behave according to default rules. The desired beginning of an element is equal to the explicit beginning if one is given; otherwise the desired beginning is equal to the implied beginning, which again assumes that you know what you're doing and are willing to accept the default behaviors. Specifying an explicit beginning earlier than the implied beginning of an element is an error, so keep careful track of timing.

DETERMINING THE EFFECTIVE BEGINNING OF AN ELEMENT

The effective beginning of an element is equal to the desired beginning of the element, unless the effective end of the parent element is earlier than the beginning of the child, in which case the element is not shown at all. So the video element in the following SMIL fragment won't ever display, because the enclosing par element ends before the video segment starts:

```
<par endsync="id(fileid)">
  <audio id="fileid" end="10s" src="audiofile" />
  <video begin="15s" src="videofile" />
</par>
```

This is perfectly logical but probably a mistake made in creating the SMIL document in this instance. A more sensible scenario would be something like this:

```
<par dur="indefinite">
  <audio src="audiofile" />
  <video begin="15s" src="videofile" />
</par>
```

In this case, the execution of the par element may be interrupted by an external event, say user intervention, in which case the both the audio and the video files will stop playing if they've started, but otherwise the audio file will play for a while and then the video will start playing.

DETERMINING THE EFFECTIVE END OF AN ELEMENT

The effective end of an element is the result of a lot of things beyond your control for the most part. Network delays or errors may alter buffering times for starting play, the speed of either the end user's network connection or the network file server's capability to timely serve the requested files may affect the display, and the user agent itself may introduce delays. Many user agents incorporate pause features, for example, or may automatically slow playing times to accommodate special needs. The method by which elements are synchronized, if they are synchronized at all, is dependent on the user agent itself. You can't count on exact results in an imperfect world.

The following rules all relate to how the final moments of elements appear on the screen when other elements are delayed for any reason. Essentially, the choice is between freeze frame until the effective end or unobtrusively going away.

- The effective end of the last child of the body element is user agent-dependent. The effective end of the last child, and thus of the presentation itself, is at least as late as the desired end, but whether it's any later than that is implementation-dependent. In other words, you can't count on the end occurring at any given moment unless you know how a particular user agent behaves.

- If any child of a par element has a fill attribute with the value freeze, the effective end of the child element is equal to the effective end of the parent, even if the intrinsic duration of the element is less than that of the parent, and the last state of that element is retained on the screen until the effective end of the element. This may or may not be how you want the display to behave but follows from the rule. It would be a reasonable choice if, say, an audio track talks about a video track, and it would be more convenient to have a still image on the screen than for the audio track to blather on about what you're supposed to be looking at when in fact you're looking at a blank screen.

- If any par child element has a fill attribute with the value remove, the effective end of the child element is the lesser of either the effective end of the parent or the desired end of the child element. In other words, if the end of the parent is delayed for any reason the child element will behave nicely and go away anyway.

- If any `par` child element has no `fill` attribute, the effective end of the child depends on whether the child has an explicit duration or end according to the following rules:
  - If any `par` child element has an explicit duration or an explicit end, the effective end of that element is determined as if the element had a `fill` attribute with the value `remove`.
  - If any `par` child element has neither an explicit duration nor an explicit end, the effective end is determined as if the element had a `fill` attribute with the value `freeze`.
  - The effective end of the last child of a `seq` element is derived in the same way as the effective end of any child of a `par` element.
  - The effective end of any non-terminal child of a `seq` element can be derived thusly: If the child has a `fill` attribute with the value `freeze`, the effective end of that child element is equal to the effective beginning of the next element. In other words, the last state of that element will be retained on the display until the next element starts if either the implicit or explicit duration of that element is less than the difference between its start time and the start time of the next element.
  - If any non-terminal `seq` child element has a `fill` attribute with the value `remove`, the effective end of the child element is the minimum of the effective beginning of the next element and the desired end of the next child element.
  - If any non-terminal `seq` child element has no `fill` attribute, the effective end of the child depends on whether or not the child has an explicit duration or end.
  - If any non-terminal `seq` child element has an explicit duration or end, the effective end is determined as if the element had a `fill` attribute with the value `remove`.
  - If any non-terminal `seq` child element has neither an explicit duration nor an explicit end, the effective end of that element is determined as if the element had a `fill` attribute with the value `freeze`.

All of which is a roundabout way of saying that a `fill` attribute with a value of either `remove` or `freeze` *will* be imputed to an element with a parent whether you like it or not, so you should think about it in advance. The rules are quite complex, so it might be wise to define the behavior of each element explicitly rather than to rely on default behavior unless you're very sure what the default behavior is in a given instance.

THE `switch` ELEMENT

A `switch` element allows the designer to select from among multiple media object alternatives depending on tests that can be performed on system variables set by the user or user agent capabilities. In all cases, the first test satisfied is the one whose elements will govern user agent behavior. If no test is satisfied, then nothing will be done. A test is implied by the presence of any system variable, and in fact a one-element switch is implied if any system variable is present. In that case, the `switch` element parent is optional.

The `switch` element can take `id` and `title` attributes and can contain the following child elements, which in turn can take one or more of the system variable attributes that imply a test:

- a
- animation
- audio
- img
- par
- ref
- seq
- switch
- text
- textstream
- video

The following system variable attribute tests are available in SMIL 1.0:

- **system-bitrate**—Tests the speed of the network connection.
- **system-captions**—Tests whether the user wants closed captions displayed.
- **system-language**—Tests the language(s) set by the user.
- **system-overdub-or-caption**—Tests whether an audio or visual alternative content should be displayed.
- **system-required**—Tests the presence of a flag set by the user.
- **system-screen-size**—Tests the screen size of the user agent.
- **system-screen-depth**—Tests the color depth of the screen used by the user agent.

These tests can be combined arbitrarily, so the following switch code would select from among five alternatives: low resolution audio in either French or German; high resolution audio in either French or German; with a default file available if the four test combinations fail for any reason.

```
<switch>
  <audio src="audiofile1" system-language="fr" system-bitrate="2400" />
  <audio src="audiofile2" system-language="de" system-bitrate="2400" />
  <audio src="audiofile3" system-language="fr" system-bitrate="4800" />
  <audio src="audiofile4" system-language="de" system-bitrate="4800" />
  <audio src="audiofile5" />
</switch>
```

But if you want to have a single element executed based on the setting of system variables, you can just put the statement inline:

```
<par>
  <video src="videofile" />
  <audio src="audiofile" />
```

```
        <!-- Content for persons with visual disabilities -->
        <audio src="descriptiveaudiofile"
                system-captions="on"
                system-overdub-or-caption="overdub" />
        <!-- Content for persons with hearing disabilities -->
        <textstream src="closedcaptionfile"
                system-captions="on"
                system-overdub-or-caption="caption" />
</par>
```

This plays a video with an accompanying audio file regardless of user settings. If a user wanted either descriptive audio or closed captioning in addition to the basic program, she would set the `system-captions` variable to `"on"`. Setting the `system-overdub-or-caption` variable would then select whether closed captions or descriptive audio would be rendered.

TEST ATTRIBUTES

The system test attributes seem to make a prima facie statement about what's going to happen in a given case. The two attributes controlling captions and overdub seem to complement each other, for example, with `system-overdub-or-caption` having some logical relation to `system-captions`, but in fact they have no more relationship to each other than any two random semaphores. As you saw in the example in the previous section, they can be used to implement such features, but they could also be used for any other feature if closed captioning or descriptive audio are not required for that particular application.

Some of the attributes invoke Boolean comparisons between mutually exclusive options, and others do comparisons or even select from a list of choices to perform more sophisticated substring comparison.

The following list details the behavior of each of the system variables:

- **system-bitrate**—Evaluate the stated bit rate of the user agent against the bit rate claimed in a given element. This allows you to load beefier files when you have a high-speed connection and skinnier ones on low-speed dialup lines.

- **system-captions**—Based on user or system settings of on or off, choose to display captions on elements at user option. Because there are two attributes touching on captions, these can be used in combinations to perform fairly sophisticated logic.

- **system-language**—Based on a list of languages set in the user agent, choose the most appropriate language file to display or render.

- **system-overdub-or-caption**—Based on settings of overdub or caption, choose to render overdub audio or display captions on elements at user option. Because there are two attributes touching on captions, these can be used in combinations to perform fairly sophisticated logic.

- **system-required**—Specifies the name of an extension to basic SMIL functionality. If the user agent supports the extension, choose the element that calls upon the facility. This may eventually become an XML namespace.

- **system-screen-size**—Based on the reported screen size of the user agent, choose an appropriate region size and media file.
- **system-screen-depth**—Based on the reported screen depth (color space) of the user agent, choose the most appropriate files to display.

HYPERLINKING ELEMENTS

SMIL cries out for excellent linking facilities because it would then be possible to gather media content from all over the Web and integrate it in a seamless multimedia production. But all that's available so far is one a element and an anchor element that behaves like a client-side map with only rectangular areas allowed. SMIL Boston, the planned next generation successor to SMIL 1.0, doesn't seem to be doing much better, although hopefully the XLink people will have finally finished and XLink will be incorporated into SMIL right away.

THE a ELEMENT

This element behaves much like the familiar link element in HTML, except that SMIL adds a show attribute that controls the behavior of the document when a link is followed. The show attribute can take the following values: replace (the default), which pauses the current presentation and replaces it with the destination resource; new, which creates a new presentation context and lets the old presentation continue along in parallel; and pause, which behaves like new except that the original presentation is paused.

Other than that, the a element takes the following attributes: id, href, and title.

The a element can contain the following element children:

- animation
- audio
- img
- par
- ref
- seq
- switch
- text
- textstream
- video

The a element works almost exactly like the a element does in HTML, and can contain any media content other than another a or anchor element:

```
<a href="URI"><video src="videofile" /></a>
```

This is not difficult.

THE anchor ELEMENT

The anchor element is somewhat similar to a client-side image map in that it allows an object to be logically separated into parts. Because this is SMIL, which is time-based, you can not only chop up an object in space, but also in time. This element is always empty and should be contained within a media element to take effect.

The anchor element can take the following attributes:

- **begin**—This attribute specifies the begin time for an element. In combination with the end attribute, this allows the clip to be snipped like a piece of string.

- **coords**—Define a rectangular section of an image using a comma-delimited list of four values. The first two values specify the upper-left corner of the area and the last two specify the lower-right corner. All coordinates are relative to the upper-left corner of the object and can be expressed either in pixels—the default—or as a percentage.

- **end**—This attribute specifies the end time for an element. In combination with the begin attribute, this allows the clip to be snipped like a piece of string.

- **id**—A unique ID.

- **show**—The show attribute can take the following values: replace (the default), which pauses the current presentation and replaces it with the destination resource; new, which creates a new presentation context and lets the old presentation continue along in parallel, just like a new browser window popup doesn't affect the underlying window at all; and pause, which behaves like new except that the original presentation is paused.

- **skip-content**—This Boolean attribute allows SMIL 1.0 processors to ignore the content of the anchor element if a later specification changes it from an empty element to one with content.

- **title**—A title for the element, which may be rendered or not depending on the user agent and the particular needs of the user.

SLIDESHOWS

A slideshow is about the simplest thing you can do with SMIL. A simple seq sequence element is used to control the sequencing of the slides with a five-second duration for each slide.

First, define a viewing area for the slideshow using the layout element and two child elements, root-layout and region, in the SMIL head. Then define the slide sequence in the SMIL body, pointing with a region attribute on each media element to the id of our single defined region, and it's done:

```
<?xml version="1.0" encoding="ISO-8859-1"?>
<!DOCTYPE smil PUBLIC "-//W3C//DTD SMIL 1.0//EN"
        "http://www.w3.org/TR/REC-smil/SMIL10.dtd">
  <smil>
    <head>
      <layout>
        <root-layout id="Slideshow" title="ALS Slideshow Window"
            width="400" height="400" />
```

```
            <region id="slides" title="ALS Slide"
              width="400" height="300" fit="meet" />
          </layout>
        </head>
        <body>
          <seq dur="indefinite" repeat="indefinite">
            <img region="slides" src="29-1.gif" dur="5s" />
            <img region="slides" src="29-2.gif" dur="5s" />
            <img region="slides" src="29-3.gif" dur="5s" />
            <img region="slides" src="29-4.gif" dur="5s" />
            <img region="slides" src="29-5.gif" dur="5s" />
            <img region="slides" src="29-6.gif" dur="5s" />
            <img region="slides" src="29-7.gif" dur="5s" />
          </seq>
        </body>
      </smil>
```

This little SMIL document renders a simple slideshow that repeats indefinitely. You might start it up showing pictures of your collection of distant relatives when you have boring guests that you want to get rid of humanely. But this is where you can start building up a presentation as well. You'll see how to do that in the following section. In this particular document, the xml declaration and DTD reference are optional, although it's a good idea to get into the habit of declaring both items in every XML document, whether they are intended to be used in a validating browser or not.

MULTIMEDIA PRESENTATIONS

Of course, if all you could do with SMIL was make simple slideshows, there wouldn't be much point. The true power of the language comes when you synchronize audio and other multimedia sources to a slideshow, or add slides to a music and video show, or fade in one track of music while fading out another. You add music or narration to the example slideshow like this:

First, enclose each img in an outer par parallel element to make sure they're synchronized with whatever content you want to be rendered simultaneously. Then add the necessary elements to include the added media in the mix. For now, just add an audio tidbit for each slide:

```
<?xml version="1.0" encoding="ISO-8859-1"?>
<!DOCTYPE smil PUBLIC "-//W3C//DTD SMIL 1.0//EN"
          "http://www.w3.org/TR/REC-smil/SMIL10.dtd">
  <smil>
    <head>
      <layout>
        <root-layout id="Slideshow" title="ALS Slideshow Window"
            width="400" height="400" />
        <region id="slides" title="ALS Slide"
          width="400" height="300" fit="meet" />
        <region id="audio" />
      </layout>
    </head>
    <body>
      <seq dur="indefinite" repeat="indefinite">
        <par>
          <img src="29-1.gif" dur="5s" />
          <audio src="29-1.wav" />
```

```
    </par>
    <par>
      <img src="29-2.gif" dur="5s" />
      <audio src="29-2.wav" />
    </par>
    <par>
      <img src="29-3.gif" dur="5s" />
      <audio src="29-3.wav" />
    </par>
    <par>
      <img src="29-4.gif" dur="5s" />
      <audio src="29-4.wav" />
    </par>
    <par>
      <img src="29-5.gif" dur="5s" />
      <audio src="29-5.wav" />
    </par>
    <par>
      <img src="29-6.gif" dur="5s" />
      <audio src="29-6.wav" />
    </par>
    <par>
      <img src="29-7.gif" dur="5s" />
      <audio src="29-7.wav" />
    </par>
  </seq>
 </body>
</smil>
```

Note   Audio files could be RealSystem G2 files or any other audio format supported by your SMIL player.

If this sccms simple from inspecting the code, it is. Almost every multimedia presentation is a combination of things that happen in sequence and things that happen in parallel (more or less). The seq and par elements control this level of temporality.

Figure 23.1 above shows a similar slideshow created by hand and played in the RealPlayer 7 basic rendering engine.

After you get started, you might want to think about using a specialized editor to control what goes where and how everything gets put together. Figure 23.2 shows the GRiNS editor from Oratrix at http://www.oratrix.com/ in action editing the file shown previously, although it has a few problems, as do most editors.

Notice that the actual SMIL code is completely hidden. You can create links and vary timings, even change id names and any other attributes, all by clicking around with a GUI interface. When you're done editing, you can save the finished file and have your SMIL ready to go. Like many proprietary vendors, however, they point to a proprietary DTD, not the standard DTD located at W3C, and use several attributes that don't appear in the standard. So, your spanking new SMIL code may have to be slightly edited by hand to remove idiosyncrasies before it's truly valuable.

Figure 23.2
The GRiNS editor editing a simple SMIL file.

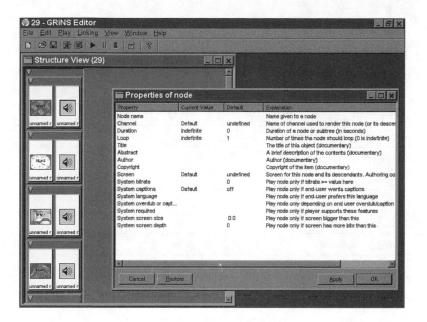

MEDIA TYPES

SMIL uses the standard Internet media types, as a general rule, wherever a type is called for. *MIME*, or *Multipurpose Internet Mail Extensions*, also known as *Internet Media Types* (*IMTs*), is defined in RFC 1521. The seven basic categories are text, multipart, message, image, audio, video, and application, which covers most proprietary media formats. The datatype for SMIL itself is text/smil-basic-layout.

Table 23.1 shows a short list of media types commonly used in presentations together with common suffixes used to describe the file in a DOS legacy environment.

TABLE 23.1   COMMON MEDIA TYPES

Media Type	Common File Suffix
application/octet-stream	bin
application/oda	oda
application/pdf	pdf
application/postscript	ai, eps, ps
audio/32kadpcm audio/basic	au, snd
audio/x-aiff	aif, aiff, aifc
audio/x-wav	wav
image/cgm	cgm
image/gif	gif

TABLE 23.1   CONTINUED

Media Type	Common File Suffix
image/jpeg	jpeg, jpg, jpe
image/naplps	naplps
image/tiff	tiff, tif
image/x-portable-bitmap	pbm
image/x-portable-graymap	pgm
image/x-portable-pixmap	ppm
image/x-rgb	rgb
image/x-xbitmap	xbm
image/x-xpixmap	xpm
text/html	html, htm
text/plain	txt
text/richtext	rtx
video/mpeg	mpeg, mpg, mpe
video/quicktime	qt, mov
video/x-sgi-movie	movie

AUDIO

Audio is important to most of us, which is why few would want to buy a car without a radio. So a big part of the "multi" in multimedia is the addition of sound. Decent graphics have been around on computers for a long time, but quality audio on computers has become available only recently. The technology used to consist of the speaker being rapidly turned on and off in a primitive way that would cause square wave tones to be produced, the sound of which was frankly pathetic.

Today's machines come with sound cards capable of feats only audiophile sound systems could accomplish a few years ago. Audio cards have gone from being an expensive toy to becoming a necessity in today's business environment. The availability of that sound card means that, together with a tiny microphone, you can call home over the Internet. I know a woman who gave her parents a fairly nice machine and paid for it in the space of a year on the savings in telephone charges alone.

And with the addition of a good speaker system—such as the five-box surround sound system I have hooked up to mine, with a single subwoofer that can rattle the windows—and a video card, you're looking at the small-scale equivalent of speaker support systems costing tens of thousands of dollars only a decade ago. With a big screen, or by hooking the box up to a rented projection monitor, you can stage your own professional-level productions, including music and all the trimmings, on a machine costing around a thousand bucks. Of course, the more memory and speed you have the better on systems used for graphic and video development, so you can easily spend more.

But in 1988 I specified and procured a speaker-support system for a major corporation that included a $10,000 video card, a video editing system costing around $60,000, and ancillary systems that brought the price tag well into the low six figures. It was state of the art at the time, but you can do far more, far more quickly with a Windows NT-based Video Toaster nowadays costing less than $15,000 but with a gigabyte of memory, a 600MHz Pentium III processor, and more goodies than you can shake two sticks at. A glance at any modern movie with special effects will tell you what cheap (relatively speaking) processing power has done for the video industry.

And that means that SMIL couldn't have come along at a better time. Just when cheap hardware is making it possible for gifted amateurs to produce movies and multimedia that rival the stuff put out by big studios, an open-source multimedia standard becomes the *lingua franca* of the presentation Web.

The following sections glance at some of the other XML multimedia languages available for presenting audio.

VoxML   There are other markup languages with very specialized target populations, such as VoxML which is designed to render text-to-speech and prerecorded voice in an interactive voice-response system. Although it shares the common XML heritage, the element vocabulary is designed specifically for the voice-response environment. Here's a sample bit of code, just to give you some of the flavor:

```
<?xml version="1.0"?>
  <DIALOG>
    <STEP NAME="initialize">
      <PROMPT>Hello. This is a voice response system.</PROMPT>
    </STEP>
  </DIALOG>
```

This technology can't be covered thoroughly in the space of this short section, but Motorola's VoxML site at http://www.voxml.com/ has a developer's kit available for download if you're interested in exploring further.

VoiceXML   IBM, Lucent Technologies, Motorola, and AT&T have a competing technology, VoiceXML (http://www.voicexml.org/), which optimistically uses a very similar example to the following to illustrate how handy this technology is:

```
<?xml version="1.0"?>
  <vxml>
    <form>
      <field name="drinkrequest">
        <prompt>Would you like coffee, tea, or milk?</prompt>
        <grammar src="drinkrequest.gram"/>
      </field>
      <block>
```

```
        <goto next="http://www.drink.example/drink2.asp"
          submit="drinkrequest" method="get"/>
      </block>
    </form>
  </vxml>
```

In VoiceXML, a field is an input field. The user must provide a "legitimate" value for the field by speaking "correctly" one of a handful of words that the computer "understands" before proceeding to the next element in the form. The processor supplies all the looping logic internally. Although everything may go according to plan if users do not deviate from an "ideal" complaisant user, an accent or other speech peculiarity will prevent understanding completely, and trying to step outside the rigid boundaries defined by the programmer is impossible. A realistic sample interaction with both computer and human speaking aloud, not typing, might be

```
Computer: Would you like coffee, tea, or milk?
Human (in thick Scottish accent): Orange juice.
Computer: I did not understand what you said.
Computer: Would you like coffee, tea, or milk?
Human: Chai with nutmeg.
Computer: I did not understand what you said.
Computer: Would you like coffee, tea, or milk?
Human: I give up! Tea!
Computer: I did not understand what you said.
Computer: Would you like coffee, tea, or milk?
Human: Tea!
Computer: I did not understand what you said.
Computer: Would you like coffee, tea, or milk?
Human: Coffee!
Computer: Thank you.
```

Voice-response systems have significant limitations at the present time, despite all the urgings of their enthusiasts that they're ready for prime time. I personally don't think I've ever had a satisfactory conversation with one. Given the present state of the art, unless the universe of discourse can be severely limited and the users know what to expect and can restrain themselves to thinking like machines, they tend to disappoint and even alienate people.

The technology is a long way from Star Trek, or even HAL right now. But as computer speeds approach 1000 MHz and beyond and main memory storage goes into the terabytes, we can expect to see systems which start to approach the same capability to converse as a reasonably intelligent chimpanzee within the next decade.

Going out on a limb, I would guess that HAL, and perhaps Star Trek, will be possible well before the middle of the next century. But not yet.

When you design an interactive voice response system, always be sure to take into account the fact that some people can't make themselves understood by machines, no matter how hard they try. They may not have TouchTone phones either. Every IVR system needs a few operators standing by to handle people who might fall through the cracks otherwise and a clear way to contact them without rigmarole. I suggest the "Operator" key by default and falling through to an operator after a short time of silence or "odd" noise. It may, after all, be someone trying to communicate with a TDD.

Merely hanging up, as so many IVR systems do, is inexcusably rude and a potential violation of the Americans with Disabilities Act or local equivalent, not to mention being in contemptible bad taste.

VIDEO

There are several video formats on the Web, with RealSystem G2 and QuickTime arguably the most popular in actual use. Both of these systems are currently more or less SMIL compatible. Existing facilities of SMIL allow video clips to be precisely selected from larger files down to the hundredth of a frame level providing SMPTE information is encoded in the file. Failing that, NPT information can provide less-precise positioning information.

TEXT

Text has no intrinsic time associated with it, so there isn't much that can be done with it other than to render it and stop when you are tired of looking at the display. Typically, text is used in titles and descriptive closed captioning, but there's no reason you couldn't use text to make a presentation by itself if you had a mind to.

COORDINATING WITH EXISTING MULTIMEDIA TOOLS (SHOCKWAVE)

Dreamweaver from Macromedia at `http://www.macromedia.com/` is an authoring environment compatible with the RealPlayer 7 player from Real Networks at `http://www.real.com/`. RealSlideshow Basic is available at no cost from their Website and is a simple multimedia editor that allows you to develop SMIL documents easily, as well as use the RealPlayer 7 native language, allowing tight control over video presentations. You can create HTML-based multimedia using RealPlayer 7media types, including RealAudio, RealVideo, RealFlash, RealPix, and RealText. But you will need the RealPlayer 7 player or possibly the Microsoft equivalent as a plug-in, or you won't be able to render these media formats.

Interestingly, RealPlayer 7 also supports SMIL, so the same plug-in can be used for multiple formats, including those that are fully open.

NARRATION AND CLOSED CAPTIONING

Accessibility is a key feature of SMIL, although the author will have to do some work to achieve this for as wide an audience as possible. There are two primary alternative formats available for persons with perceptual disabilities: descriptive narration and captioning.

The narration can possibly be woven into the audio channel so everyone hears the same thing, but for best results it's usually better to provide a second audio track specifically for the narration. Some people have trouble distinguishing words if there is any sound in the background, so having separate channels allows people to choose which tracks will be played. Of course this type of second channel is also an excellent way to provide a second language capability as well.

Captioning allows persons with hearing disabilities to read a description of the audio information being rendered in the SMIL document. Captions can also be used as input to an aural screen reader, so it's another way of providing content to persons with vision disabilities as well. So continuing with the slideshow example, you should add both titles and closed captions to the slideshow.

While you're at it, define and reference specific regions you want the individual pieces to wind up in. Up until now, the chips have been left to fall where they may because the images would all wind up in the same spot anyway. So this file will be a bit bigger and you can start seeing why a dedicated editor might be a good idea at some point.

Notice that in this version the id, title, and alt tags have been added to many of the elements. The current specification encourages the use of title and alt tags, especially on all elements that can carry them. There's only one element in the switch because the closed captions shouldn't display unless someone requests them. However, you could use the switch to select from a number of choices if you wanted to. You could have Spanish and English versions of the caption text, for example:

```
<?xml version="1.0" encoding="ISO-8859-1"?>
<!DOCTYPE smil PUBLIC "-//W3C//DTD SMIL 1.0//EN"
        "http://www.w3.org/TR/REC-smil/SMIL10.dtd">
<smil>
  <head>
    <meta name="title" content="Slideshow"/>
    <layout>
      <root-layout id="Slideshow" width="400" height="450" />
      <region id="slides" title="Slides" width="400" height="300" top="50" />
      <region id="audio" title="Audio" />
      <region id="titles" title="Titles" width="400" height="50" />
      <region id="captions" title="Closed Captions" width="400" height="50"
top="350" />
    </layout>
  </head>
  <body>
    <seq id="Slideshow" dur="indefinite" repeat="indefinite">
      <par id="Slide-1" title="One">
        <img region="slides" src="29-1.gif" dur="5s" alt="Slide 1" />
        <audio region="audio" src="29-1.wav" alt="Slide 1 Audio" />
        <text region="titles" src="29-1.txt" type="text/plain" />
        <switch title="Switch 1">
          <text region="captions" src="29-1cc.txt" type="text/plain"
            system-captions="on" />
        </switch>
      </par>
      <par id="Slide-2" title="Two">
        <img region="slides" src="29-2.gif" dur="5s" alt="Slide 2" />
        <audio region="audio" src="29-2.wav" alt="Slide 2 Audio" />
        <text region="titles" src="29-2.txt" type="text/plain" />
        <switch title="Switch 2">
          <text region="captions" src="29-2cc.txt" type="text/plain"
            system-captions="on" />
        </switch>
      </par>
```

```
      <par id="Slide-3" title="Three">
        <img region="slides" src="29-3.gif" dur="5s" alt="Slide 3" />
        <audio region="audio" src="29-3.wav" alt="Slide 3 Audio" />
        <text region="titles" src="29-3.txt" type="text/plain" />
        <switch title="Switch 3">
          <text region="captions" src="29-3cc.txt" type="text/plain"
          system-captions="on" />
        </switch>
      </par>
      <par id="Slide-4" title="Four">
        <img region="slides" src="29-4.gif" dur="5s" alt="Slide 4" />
        <audio region="audio" src="29-4.wav" alt="Slide 4 Audio" />
        <text region="titles" src="29-4.txt" type="text/plain" />
        <switch title="Switch 4">
          <text region="captions" src="29-4cc.txt" type="text/plain"
          system-captions="on" />
          <text region="titles" src="29-1.txt" type="text/plain" />
        </switch>
      </par>
      <par id="Slide-5" title="Five">
        <img region="slides" src="29-5.gif" dur="5s" alt="Slide 5" />
        <audio region="audio" src="29-5.wav" alt="Slide 5 Audio" />
        <text region="titles" src="29-5.txt" type="text/plain" />
        <switch title="Switch 5">
          <text region="captions" src="29-5cc.txt" type="text/plain"
          system-captions="on" />
        </switch>
      </par>
      <par id="Slide-6" title="Six">
        <img region="slides" src="29-6.gif" dur="5s" alt="Slide 6" />
        <audio region="audio" src="29-6.wav" alt="Slide 6 Audio" />
        <text region="titles" src="29-6.txt" type="text/plain" />
        <switch title="Switch 6">
          <text region="captions" src="29-6cc.txt" type="text/plain"
          system-captions="on" />
        </switch>
      </par>
      <par id="Slide-7" title="Seven">
        <img region="slides" src="29-7.gif" dur="5s" alt="Slide 7" />
        <audio region="audio" src="29-7.wav" alt="Slide 7 Audio" />
        <text region="titles" src="29-7.txt" type="text/plain"/>
        <switch title="Switch 7">
          <text region="captions" src="29-7cc.txt" type="text/plain"
            system-captions="on" />
        </switch>
      </par>
    </seq>
  </body>
</smil>
```

PART

IV

CH

23

Figure 23.3 shows the GRiNS editor from Oratrix at http://www.oratrix.com/ playing this slideshow.

Figure 23.3
The GRiNS editor/player is rendering the completed slideshow with closed captioning.

DESCRIPTIVE AUDIO

Descriptive audio is usually a second track that describes what's going on visually while the primary track carries the default audio portion of the presentation. There are several options to consider when adding descriptive audio: Do you want the descriptive audio interspersed with dialog—as it often is in television production—or done as a voice over the background sound, or should you wait for the end of the default audio and then do your narration? In this case, it makes more sense to wait until the end of the default audio and then add a description.

To add descriptive audio to your multimedia presentation, you need another switch to control the new behavior, of course, and you need to use the `system-overdub-or-caption="overdub"` attribute to selectively play the second audio or not depending on user preference. A new concept will also be introduced—using clips from a single audio source which are assumed to have been encoded with SMPTE (video style) time tics such as might be added by a professional video editing station. The `clip-begin` and `clip-end` attributes take a single value which contains a second equals sign. Pay no attention. These items are all illustrated in the following code sample:

Tip from

Words to weave by

Strictly speaking, you don't need to put a switch around a single element that will either be conditionally rendered or not. But leaving out the switch makes the logic very hard to see so it seems well worth the trouble to highlight the fact that a conditional decision point has been reached.

```
<?xml version="1.0" encoding="ISO-8859-1"?>
<!DOCTYPE smil PUBLIC "-//W3C//DTD SMIL 1.0//EN"
          "http://www.w3.org/TR/REC-smil/SMIL10.dtd">
<smil>
  <head>
    <meta name="title" content="SlideShow"/>
```

```
        <layout>
          <root-layout id="SlideShow" width="400" height="450" />
          <region id="slides" title="Slides" width="400" height="300" top="50" />
          <region id="audio" title="Audio" />
          <region id="audio2" title="Descriptive Audio" />
          <region id="titles" title="Titles" width="400" height="50" />
          <region id="captions" title="Closed Captions" width="400" height="50"
top="350" />
        </layout>
      </head>
      <body>
        <seq id="Slide-Show" dur="indefinite" repeat="indefinite">
          <par id="Slide-1" title="One">
            <img region="slides" src="29-1.gif" dur="5s" alt="Slide 1" />
            <seq id="Slide-1DA" title="One DA">
              <audio region="audio" src="29-1.wav" alt="Slide 1 Audio" />
              <switch title="Switch 1 DA">
                <audio region="audio2" src="29-1-DA.au" alt="Slide 1 Audio DA"
                  clip-begin="smpte=22:11:02.54" clip-end="smpte=22:16:21.33"
                  system-overdub-or-caption="overdub" />
              </switch>
            </seq>
            <text region="titles" src="29-1.txt" type="text/plain" />
            <switch title="Switch 1 CC">
              <text region="captions" src="29-1cc.txt" type="text/plain"
                system-captions="on" />
            </switch>
          </par>
          <par id="Slide-2" title="Two">
            <img region="slides" src="29-2.gif" dur="5s" alt="Slide 2" />
            <seq id="Slide-2DA" title="Two DA">
              <audio region="audio" src="29-2.wav" alt="Slide 2 Audio" />
              <switch title="Switch 2 DA">
                <audio region="audio2" src="29-1-DA.au" alt="Slide 2 Audio DA"
                  clip-begin="smpte=22:34:11.01" clip-end="smpte=22:39:24.57"
                  system-overdub-or-caption="overdub" />
              </switch>
            </seq>
            <text region="titles" src="29-2.txt" type="text/plain" />
            <switch title="Switch 2 CC">
              <text region="captions" src="29-2cc.txt" type="text/plain"
                system-captions="on" />
            </switch>
          </par>
          <par id="Slide-3" title="Three">
            <img region="slides" src="29-3.gif" dur="5s" alt="Slide 3" />
            <seq id="Slide-3DA" title="Three DA">
              <audio region="audio" src="29-3.wav" alt="Slide 3 Audio" />
              <switch title="Switch 3 DA">
                <audio region="audio2" src="29-1-DA.au" alt="Slide 3 Audio DA"
                  clip-begin="smpte=24:21:42.34" clip-end="smpte=24:26:28.11"
                  system-overdub-or-caption="overdub" />
              </switch>
            </seq>
            <text region="titles" src="29-3.txt" type="text/plain" />
```

```
      <switch title="Switch 3 CC">
        <text region="captions" src="29-3cc.txt" type="text/plain"
          system-captions="on" />
      </switch>
    </par>
    <par id="Slide-4" title="Four">
      <img region="slides" src="29-4.gif" dur="5s" alt="Slide 4" />
      <seq id="Slide-4DA" title="Four DA">
        <audio region="audio" src="29-4.wav" alt="Slide 4 Audio" />
        <switch title="Switch 4 DA">
          <audio region="audio2" src="29-1-DA.au" alt="Slide 4 Audio DA"
            clip-begin="smpte=11:31:28.13" clip-end="smpte=11:36:22.21"
            system-overdub-or-caption="overdub" />
        </switch>
      </seq>
      <text region="titles" src="29-4.txt" type="text/plain" />
      <switch title="Switch 4 CC">
        <text region="captions" src="29-4cc.txt" type="text/plain"
          system-captions="on" />
        <text region="titles" src="29-1.txt" type="text/plain" />
      </switch>
    </par>
    <par id="Slide-5" title="Five">
      <img region="slides" src="29-5.gif" dur="5s" alt="Slide 5" />
      <seq id="Slide-5DA" title="Five DA">
        <audio region="audio" src="29-5.wav" alt="Slide 5 Audio" />
        <switch title="Switch 5 DA">
          <audio region="audio2" src="29-1-DA.au" alt="Slide 5 Audio DA"
            clip-begin="smpte=24:21:28.11" clip-end="smpte=24:26:28.11"
            system-overdub-or-caption="overdub" />
        </switch>
      </seq>
      <text region="titles" src="29-5.txt" type="text/plain" />
      <switch title="Switch 5 CC">
        <text region="captions" src="29-5cc.txt" type="text/plain"
          system-captions="on" />
      </switch>
    </par>
    <par id="Slide-6" title="Six">
      <img region="slides" src="29-6.gif" dur="5s" alt="Slide 6" />
      <seq id="Slide-6DA" title="Six DA">
        <audio region="audio" src="29-6.wav" alt="Slide 6 Audio" />
        <switch title="Switch 5 DA">
          <audio region="audio2" src="29-1-DA.au" alt="Slide 6 Audio DA"
            clip-begin="smpte=33:20" clip-end="smpte=39:25"
            system-overdub-or-caption="overdub" />
        </switch>
      </seq>
      <text region="titles" src="29-6.txt" type="text/plain" />
      <switch title="Switch 6 CC">
        <text region="captions" src="29-6cc.txt" type="text/plain"
          clip-begin="smpte=12:33:20" clip-end="smpte=12:33:25"
          system-captions="on" />
      </switch>
    </par>
```

```
        <par id="Slide-7" title="Seven">
          <img region="slides" src="29-7.gif" dur="5s" alt="Slide 7" />
          <seq id="Slide-7DA" title="Seven DA">
            <audio region="audio" src="29-7.wav" alt="Slide 7 Audio" />
            <switch title="Switch 5 DA">
              <audio region="audio2" src="29-1-DA.au" alt="Slide 7 Audio DA"
                clip-begin="smpte=28:21" clip-end="smpte=34:35"
                system-overdub-or-caption="overdub" />
            </switch>
          </seq>
          <text region="titles" src="29-7.txt" type="text/plain"/>
          <switch title="Switch 7 CC">
            <text region="captions" src="29-7cc.txt" type="text/plain"
              system-captions="on" />
          </switch>
        </par>
      </seq>
    </body>
</smil>
```

Notice how this document, which is fairly complex by now, has been built up over a period of time, starting with a very simple slideshow and progressing to more and more features and greater complexity. This is an excellent development method. By getting something up quickly which does a significant amount of the work, you're able to add functionality incrementally without stepping up to the entire megillah at once.

Stepwise development allows you time to sit and think about things and catch mistakes a little at a time instead of all at once and in torrents.

ACCESSIBILITY AND MOBILE COMPUTING ISSUES

The current facilities for accessibility and mobile computing are rather primitive, and the next generation successor to SMIL 1.0—code named "Boston" and still in development—will undoubtedly add many features to support both when the working draft is approved for publication. But there are a number of elements and attributes that address these issues directly. Using the test attributes, you can tailor the display based on user preferences and output device capability:

- **system-bitrate**—Evaluate the stated bit rate of the user agent against the bit rate claimed in a given element. This allows you to load beefier files when you have a high-speed connection and skinnier ones on low-speed dialup lines.

- **system-captions**—Based on settings of on or off, choose to display captions on elements at user option. Because there are two attributes touching on captions, these can be used in combinations to perform fairly sophisticated logic.

- **system-language**—Based on a list of languages set in the user agent, choose the most appropriate language to display or render.

- **system-overdub-or-caption**—Based on settings of overdub or caption, choose to render overdub audio or display captions on elements at user option. Because there are two attributes touching on captions, these can be used in combinations to perform fairly sophisticated logic.

- **system-required**—Specifies the name of an extension to basic SMIL functionality. If the user agent supports the extension, choose the element that calls upon the facility. This may eventually become an XML namespace.

- **system-screen-size**—Based on the reported screen size of the user agent, choose an appropriate region size and media file.

- **system-screen-depth**—Based on the reported screen depth (color space) of the user agent, choose the most appropriate files to display.

Mobile devices are likely to be smaller and have a shallower color depth than your home computer for the foreseeable future. They're also likely to be connected to the Internet using slower connections. This means that the same files are probably not going to be useful in both situations. Figure 23.4 shows an assortment of Web-capable cellular communications devices ranging from an 11-line text only screen on the left to a half-VGA grayscale display at bottom to a full color VGA screen at the right top. These particular devices are available from NeoPoint (the first) and Psion (the others), but similar devices are cropping up all over.

Figure 23.4
Web-capable wireless telecommunications devices from NeoPoint and Psion.

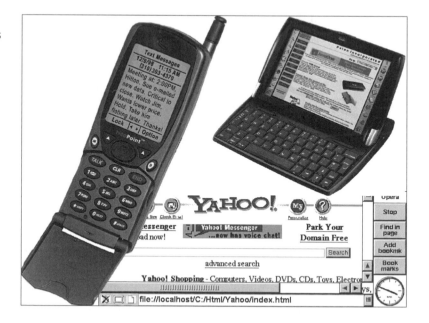

Users with vision disabilities also sometimes use terminals with very small displays, sometimes one line, and the color depth of a Braille terminal is zero. Braille is also a unique language, with spelling and layout rules of its own, so unless an on-the-fly translation can be made, a separate file will have to be supplied.

All this adds up to ever-expanding possibilities for using SMIL to customize multimedia content based on the needs and capabilities of the user and his or her display device.

OUTPUT DEVICE CAPABILITIES

Output devices are proliferating rapidly, from network appliances to mobile phones with integrated display screens and network connections. All these may have different display capabilities.

Several of the system attributes address the capabilities of the output device directly:

- `system-bitrate`—Evaluate the stated bit rate of the user agent against the bit rate claimed in a given element. This allows you to load beefier files when you have a high-speed connection and skinnier ones on low-speed dialup lines.
- `system-required`—Specifies the name of an extension to basic SMIL functionality. If the user agent supports the extension, choose the element that calls upon the facility. This may eventually become an XML namespace.
- `system-screen-size`   Based on the reported screen size of the user agent, choose an appropriate region size and media file.
- `system-screen-depth`—Based on the reported screen depth (color space) of the user agent, choose the most appropriate files to display.

INTO THE UNKNOWN—USER MODIFICATIONS AND FUTURE TECHNOLOGIES

The case of the GRiNS editor is instructive in that even a specification as simple and straightforward as SMIL was tweaked by the designers of the program until many parts of "their" SMIL are clearly not the same as everyone else muddles on with. When you couple that with the planned SMIL Boston changes, you're in for interesting times.

Due to conflicts with DOM, SMIL Boston has defined synonyms for `clip-begin` and `clip-end`. Although the Boston version of SMIL is still very much a work in progress and the details may change, it's clear that some changes can be expected to remain stable through the release. The new attribute names are `clipBegin` and `clipEnd`, which seems minor, but the whole purpose was to get rid of the hyphens. In use, they behave the same. For compatibility, you should always use the new attribute names first followed by the old attribute names. SMIL Boston will see the first instances and, because it knows that it has what it needs already, will ignore the second set of arguments. SMIL 1.0 will ignore the new attributes completely and process the last, because it knows nothing about the new attributes.

Other changes in Boston are quite likely, with changes being made to improve accessibility, animation and multimedia capability, and other improvements to the interface. Among the improvements are modularizing the various components of the specification so that portions can be used in appropriate situations without the overhead of unneeded portions of the specification.

Example applications of the future might include

- Retailers wanting to create sophisticated catalog displays will be able to use a future version of SMIL to create animated displays that adjust to the environment and indicated interests of the user.

- Students could view an interactive presentation and answer questions on the content, with the presentation altering itself based on whether the student had demonstrated understanding of the concepts.

- Users creating presentations will be able to choose exclusive paths through the presentation as questions from the audience dictate the next segment of the presentation.

SMIL is actually one of the easier standards to troubleshoot, because most problems you're likely to run into are due to lack of support rather than incorrect implementation. It remains to be seen how future user agents will support CSS2, because all existing CSS implementations leave so much to be desired, but at least they're starting from relatively clean code to begin with. In Figure 23.1, you saw a simple bug fix for RealPlayer 7 Basic implemented by commenting out a line of code, because the basic player didn't support text streams. You also learned that only a limited number of audio file types were supported, so you had to use a .wav file instead of a MIDI file. In general, that's the sort of problem you'll be finding and fixing, since SMIL itself is fairly straightforward.

TROUBLESHOOTING SMIL

MY PRESENTATION ISN'T WORKING

After coding your presentation, you notice that nothing seems to be happening or what happens is far from what you wanted.

Try these steps to solve the problem:

1. Do you see any errors when you load the code? Try looking there, or in the near vicinity, first. If you're not using a validating authoring tool or parser, try using one. Make sure that the W3C standard DTD hasn't been replaced with a proprietary one, as who knows what bad habits you might fall into given a treacherous guide.

2. If there are no reported errors, consider testing to see whether the tool you're using has errors of its own. Much existing code has bugs, especially for a standard as widely "extended" as SMIL seems to be. W3C is also working on the next version, Boston, and many vendors have started to incorporate bits of Boston into their products before it's even an official Recommendation. This can usually be discerned from the nonstandard DTD used in the DOCTYPE declaration but not always. GRiNS, for example, silently replaces your code with its own idea of what that code should be, including eliminating your DTD statement, even if you don't use it for editing. Figure 23.5 shows the result of allowing GRiNS to edit your code without care. Notice that some of the attributes are completely nonstandard, the xmlns attribute points off into Never Never Land, and the DOCTYPE declaration, which contains the DTD, is out with the trash.

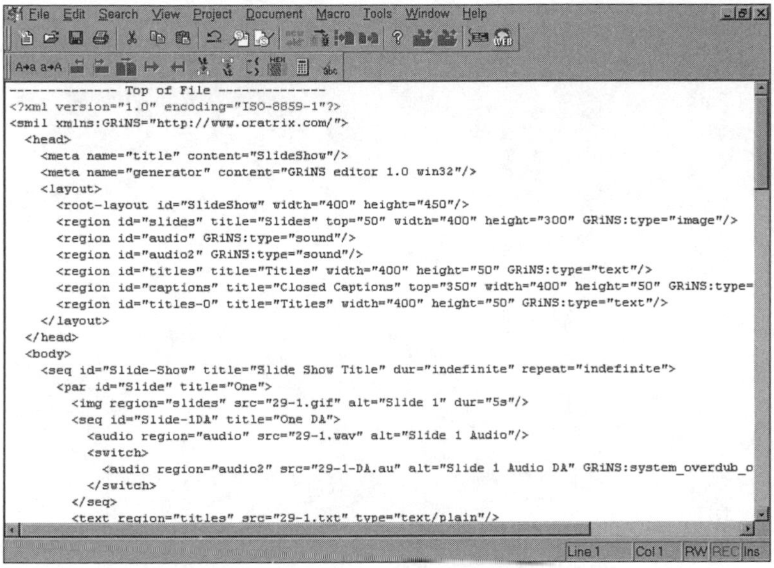

Figure 23.5
The results of letting the GRiNS editor update your code without a backup version to come back to haunt you.

3. Try isolating sections until you find something that either works or doesn't work. Either information can be valuable. If you find a bit that works, you can build on it gradually until you have a complete working program again. If you find a bit that doesn't work, you can try taking it out and see whether the rest is any better.

4. If nothing is appearing, see whether the files are being read by changing a filename to garbage. The parser ought to squawk if you're validating, but you never know. Some authoring tools don't validate the existence of a file until they try reading it.

5. Make sure that your test attributes, if any, are correctly set, both in the SMIL code and in the user agent. The SMIL Recommendation is fairly opaque when describing how these work, and the listed descriptions can be misleading because there is no particular enforcement of the English-language descriptive names possible or contemplated. The user-preference attributes must evaluate to be identical or in a particular relationship with each other if they are tested for, and it doesn't particularly matter what you use them for, at least to SMIL. Although they have a soothingly explicit face value, there's actually nothing in them to ensure that that's the way they're used other than the good intentions of the author. All the logic is created by you. So you (or someone else) can use system-language="fr" to turn on and off the display of graphic images just as easily as it can be used to select the French version of the text.

6. Be sure you're not attempting too much the first time out by creating a vast multimedia edifice with hundreds of files in an intricate choreography of shifting images and sounds right off the bat. The simplest things really are simple, and it's hard to imagine that you couldn't start with a simple presentation and add things to it rather than biting off more than you can chew at one sitting.

CHAPTER 24

USING MATHML—
THE MATH MARKUP LANGUAGE

In this chapter

UNDERSTANDING MATHML

Existing presentation of mathematics using HTML on the Web has been limited to the sorts of things done in grammar school. For anything more serious, you had to create and transmit graphical images. Although many proprietary solutions exist, such as Microsoft's Equation Editor, the interoperability of these tools leaves much to be desired, and the quality of the presentation has also failed to live up to the demands of the mathematical and scientific communities.

MathML, the XML-based Mathematical Markup Language, attempts to meet the needs of a diverse mathematics user community, including teachers of both science and mathematics, working scientists and mathematicians, the math and sciences publishing industry, and vendors of products which allow users to create, manipulate, and display mathematical equations and constructs in various ways. (Not to mention the users for whom all these things are designed, people who want to publish, read, and understand elementary mathematical notations, the most universal of artificial languages and equally as understandable to a Chinese reader as to a German one.)

To meet the needs of these varied groups, it was necessary to create two parallel XML-based markup languages which are subsumed into the specification as a whole, a display language intended primarily to indicate how mathematics should *look* on the page, and a syntax language which indicates what mathematics *mean*. This parallel syntactical language is discussed in the last half of this chapter.

So a user of Mathematica, a professional mathematical editing and problem-solving environment, might want to pass a bit of mathematics to someone who uses MathEQ or MathType, both relatively simple mathematical editors. Using MathML, they should be able to transfer information back and forth in a way that will be useful to both. As mathematics becomes ever more dependent on computer assistance, the possibility of using MathML as a universal interchange format makes possible collaborations that could have been accomplished only with laborious manual transcription before.

The existing standard, although extremely useful, doesn't nearly cover the whole of modern mathematics. However, it can reasonably take users through their first few years of college and allow representation and encoding of most of the mathematics done in daily life outside the theoretical realms of non-Newtonian physics and abstract maths.

In this chapter you look at the current presentation specification, MathML 1.01, in detail, with some comments on the direction the next recommendation, MathML 2.0, will probably take, and examine the tools used to create MathML documents. You also briefly visit a distantly related scientific language, CML, the Chemical Markup Language, which does for chemistry and topological biologists what MathML does for mathematicians. As in all explanations of XML-related standards, the documents and language from W3C are the authoritative reference and should be consulted especially to check any errata that may have been published between the time this book was published—late Summer of the year 2000C.E.—and the time you read this section. Documents relating to MathML can be found at `http://www.w3.org/Math/`.

WHY MathML IS IMPORTANT

Mathematical notations are far more useful and widespread than many people realize. They're used by specialists in almost every field imaginable, from sociology to nuclear physics. None of the modern sciences are accessible without understanding the basic mathematical notations used to describe them; even carpentry has need of the Pythagorean Theorem from time to time. Existing HTML workarounds for these needs have been grossly inadequate and have left persons with vision disabilities at an enormous disadvantage. The ability to communicate between processes and index mathematics for scholarly or scientific research is impaired as well, because in most cases text has to be supplemented with graphical images invisible to both search engines and users without access to visual browsers.

Although MathML may seem verbose in comparison to the terse elegance of mathematical notations, those notations are meant to convey complex ideas in a manner that can be easily grasped by human beings. The shape and orientation of glyphs, the fonts used, and their position in relation to other glyphs all convey information that would be tedious to describe in words.

PART

IV

CH

24

Because MathML is meant in part to be created and used by machines, it makes sense to "unroll" the concepts bundled into terse mathematical notations to some extent, to make it easier for machines to process efficiently. Just as the majority of HTML on the Web today is created with the assistance of graphical editors that both assist in the proper placement of complex tag sequences and hide the messy details of HTML from users who don't care how it works in favor of how it looks, most MathML documents today are created with the assistance of special purpose editors. Hardly anyone expects to actually read the raw MathML code, any more than you ordinarily expect to read HTML and imagine how it should look. Machines can read and render it in various ways depending on whether it's being used as input to a browser or as a transfer mechanism between dedicated mathematics environments or equation editors. But for small things, the expense and steep learning curve of a dedicated mathematical development environment like Mathematica is unwarranted. If you write a Web document on Einstein and want to render his famous $e=mc^2$ formula properly, writing a tiny bit of MathML by hand is fairly simple to do, as the following example shows:

```
<math>
  <mrow>
    <mi>e</mi>
    <mo>=</mo>
    <mrow>
      <mi>m</mi>&it;
      <mrow>
       <apply>
         <power />
         <ci>c</ci>
         <cn>2</cn>
        </apply>
      </mrow>
    </mrow>
  </mrow>
</math>
```

Note that some syntax (content) elements were used to express the exponentiation since these typically render more naturally in an aural browser. In a visual browser, there will be no visible difference between the rendering by presentation elements and the rendering by content (syntax) elements.

Also, in comparison to the widespread practice of using GIF or PNG images to convey mathematics, which are completely obscure for anyone or any processor not capable of visual recognition, total file sizes for MathML pages are considerably smaller than an equivalent graphic image (in spite of the relative verbosity of the source data file). Visually, the rendered file is (or should be) exactly equivalent to a typeset or manually drafted page.

However, the MathML file has considerable advantages for persons with vision disabilities, in that it's completely legible for audio browsers and can be dynamically resized or reformatted to suit users with varying needs.

So a MathML mathematics description meets multiple needs, conforms to a W3C XML standard, supports conversions between many different formats, including proprietary formats if the vendors support it as an interchange medium, and can be conveniently edited, searched, and indexed on the Web. In addition, MathML is suitable for presenting included mathematics fragments in enclosing documents whereas competing technologies are not. As with any embedded XML vocabulary, using the MathML namespace will allow MathML to be included in XHTML or other XML documents without including mathematics capabilities in other XML standards.

Tip from

Words to weave by

The namespace for MathML has been defined as `http://www.w3.org/1998/Math/Math/ MathML`, and this namespace should be used in any XML or HTML document that accesses MathML structures.

The new Working Draft for MathML 2.0 adds a discussion of the W3C Document Object Model and how it may be able to make communication between the document and embedded content possible. This is part of the general problem of how to communicate between browsers and the rendering engines that handle external documents and content.

The next section looks at presentation elements first, because most users will be more concerned with how documents look than what they mean. The syntactical elements are primarily useful with dedicated mathematics environments, which not only allow one to edit and typeset mathematical formulae but actually solve and graph equations.

USING MATHML PRESENTATION ELEMENTS

MathML presentation elements are most similar to Donald E. Knuth's TeX/LaTeX and to ISO 12083 mathematics presentation languages, although they convey far more structure and are more legible to humans. Neither of these languages does a very good job of carrying syntax, however, so MathML represents a quantum leap in capability since it combines both syntactical elements, which allow actual mathematical meaning to be encoded in a document, and presentation elements in one package.

Presentation elements currently have the broadest level of support among vendors of third-party math editors, but development is underway to ensure full coverage of the entire specification for many of the tools you'll use to create mathematics for eventual presentation on the Web.

Tip from
LeeAnne.com
Words to weave by

> Many publishers have a huge investment in proprietary or non-standard mathematical typographical tools for existing documents. Many universities and individual scientists, for example, use TeX and LaTeX, and the publisher of this book, Que, uses Adobe FrameMaker's layout capabilities to typeset mathematics. The MathML standard, and especially most current implementations of it, is probably not mature enough to invest too much in conversion yet. Third-party vendors may soon make tools available that will make conversions far simpler than trying to grow your own.

All the presentation elements begin with the letter "m", perhaps to distinguish them from content elements. In any event, the result is that you can rather easily determine whether a given element is a presentation element because it will have an *extraneous* "m" in front of the name. Presentation elements in MathML are like HTML elements, in that their primary purpose is to define how the resulting rendition looks, rather than what it means mathematically.

The `mfenced` element, for example, algorithmically surrounds an expression with any form of braces, brackets, parentheses, or vertical bars without conveying any information whatsoever about the underlying meaning of the notation or whether, in fact, any such meaning exists. It may be possible to infer a meaning in some cases using common ideas of what notations mean but, because MathML has no knowledge of the universe of mathematical ideas other than those defined using syntax elements, it has no real way of determining what a given notation means for sure without using syntax elements.

Note

> Although the extraneous nature of the initial "m" in the presentation elements may not be obvious until you become slightly more familiar with the MathML elements, the contrast between `mfenced` and the English word "fenced" is quite clear. There's an "m" in front of it. So `mfenced` is a presentation element. Many MathML elements are actual words or trivially obvious concatenations of words in English, so the "m" in `mfenced` is plainly tacked on. The contrast between `mi` and `ci` is less clear, but the fact that `mi` is not a typical English word (other than in musical contexts) offers a clue that it's basically a one-character identifier name, "i," with an "m" tacked on in front. The `ci` it's contrasted with has a "c" tacked on in front to indicate that it's a syntax (or content) element but we haven't gotten to those yet.

Nonetheless, there are habits and conventions of using presentation markup which will help users and processes understand what is meant by a given construct, so even presentation markup can help convey meaning, if appropriately used.

As an example, the `mrow` element can be used to indicate that any number of expressions is to be placed on one line. But this element can also be used to indicate logical groupings, much like invisible parentheses, so that subexpressions, which should be closely tied into a single

PART
IV

CH
24

expression, remain together. For a long line, this capability to nest mrow-delimited expressions means that if the line length of the display is insufficient to render the complete logical line, the break points can be preferentially chosen. Likewise, an aural browser can use mrow delimiters to logically group expressions in a way more meaningful than a simple list.

Tip from
Words to weave by

| The mrow element is so important that many other elements impute an implied mrow container element to an enclosed expression if it doesn't exist. |

Attributes common to all MathML elements are listed in Table 24.1.

TABLE 24.1   COMMON MATHML ATTRIBUTES

Attribute	Possible Value
class	classname
style	stylevalue
id	uniqueid
other	anycontent

The three initial attributes are provided for compatibility with CSS or other style mechanism, although the last, other, is used to pass application-dependent values to other processes without violating the MathML DTD.

Tip from
Words to weave by

| Although the MathML Recommendation allows either double quotes or single quotes to surround attribute values, due to the fact that many rendering engines use Java or any of several scripting languages, double quotes may yield inconsistent results on different platforms. Always use single quotes to enclose attribute values. |

MathML renders mathematics in little nested boxes, of which Figure 24.1 shows a fairly simple example. The mfrac element uses a box that contains two sub-boxes separated by a horizontal line, which is its default behavior. You'll see below how the same mfrac element can be used for other mathematical constructions. The entire mfrac expression is used as the rightmost portion of an equality, which has its own enclosing box and sub-boxes containing the equality operator and the leftmost portion.

The following code generates this expression:

```
<math>
  <mrow>
    <mrow>
      <mi>y</mi>
      <mo>=</mo>
      <mfrac>
        <mrow>
          <mn>1</mn>
        </mrow>
```

```
        <mrow>
            <mi>x</mi>
            <mo>+</mo>
            <mn>1</mn>
        </mrow>
      </mfrac>
    </mrow>
  </mrow>
</math>
```

Figure 24.1
A MathML expression showing the invisible boxes that contain the various subexpressions which comprise the whole.

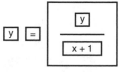

TOKEN ELEMENTS

A token element serves to delineate individual tokens within a MathML text stream. Tokens may represent identifiers (variables or constants), numbers, operators, embedded text, embedded space, and string literals.

Table 24.2 shows the attributes common to token elements.

TABLE 24.2   TOKEN ELEMENT ATTRIBUTES

Attribute	Possible Value	Default Value
fontsize	number v-unit	inherited
fontweight	normal | bold	inherited
fontstyle	normal | italic	normal (except on <mi>)
fontfamily	string | css-fontfamily	inherited
color	#rgb | #rrggbb | html-color-name	inherited

Note

The attributes in Table 24.1 are similar but not exactly equivalent to CSS properties in all cases. The fontstyle attribute, for example, is not inherited in MathML although the CSS property of the same name is. Similarly, many MathML elements change the value of the fontsize attribute automatically, although no such automatic twiddling with properties takes place in CSS.

Token elements are the foundation of presentation, so each token should be carefully identified. The only difference between the sine operation in sin *y* and a multiplication *sin* (*s* times *i* times *n*) is identification of the individual tokens involved in the operation. Although a human being can reason backward from the fact that the latter *sin* is italicized to infer that these letters probably represent one or more variables and puzzle through the exact meaning by the context of surrounding expressions, machines aren't quite that smart. You have to give them more help than that. So, the following list is vital to any presentation that will be rendered in different media:

- **<mi> identifier**—The mi identifier element has two default behaviors. If an enclosed identifier is a single letter, it is rendered in an italic font by default. If the identifier contains more than one letter, it is rendered in an upright font by default. This mirrors the typical rendering in mathematical expressions, in which variables and symbolic constants are single letters and function names are more than a single letter. However, you might also enclose arbitrary text in a mi element, such as an ellipsis indicating omitted terms.

- **<mn> number**—The mn numeric literal element renders content as a numeric literal. There are several situations where an mn element is not appropriate, for example, surrounding a symbolic numeric literal such as *pi* or *e*. Likewise, complex, exponential, imaginary, fractional, or negative numbers require other elements to render the mathematical operations implied in their representations.

- **<mo> operator, fence, or separator**—The mo operator element surrounds mathematical operators, fences, and separators when they should be rendered as operators. Because mathematical operators have complex possible renditions, including no visible rendition at all, the mo element has a large number of attributes in addition to the default attributes listed here. It also makes use of an "operator dictionary" used by the browser or rendering engine. But first, look at the list of attributes shown in Table 24.3. If there is no defined behavior for a particular operator, the default value is used.

TABLE 24.3 ATTRIBUTES FOR <mo> ELEMENTS

Name	Values	Default
form	prefix | infix | postfix	set by position of operator in an <mrow> (rule given following table); used with <mo> content to index operator dictionary
fence	true | false	set by dictionary (false)
separator	true | false	set by dictionary (false)
lspace	number h-unit	set by dictionary (.27777em)
rspace	number h-unit	set by dictionary (.27777em)
stretchy	true | false	set by dictionary (false)
symmetric	true | false	set by dictionary (true)
maxsize	number [v-unit | h-unit] | infinity	set by dictionary (infinity)

Name	Values	Default
minsize	number [v-unit | h-unit]	set by dictionary (1)
largeop	true | false	set by dictionary (false)
movablelimits	true | false	set by dictionary (false)
accent	true | false	set by dictionary (false)

The operator dictionary is implementation dependent, and possibly inaccessible to the user. The rules for operators are so complex that you should refer to the MathML recommendation for a detailed explanation.

For the simple $f(x)$ expression you might pronounce "eff of ex," the corresponding MathML might be <mrow><mi> f </mi><mo> ⁡ </mo><mrow><mo> (</mo><mi> x </mi><mo>) </mo></mrow></mrow>. Note that ⁡ is not rendered visually, although it should be used to ensure proper rendering in an aural browser because the expression could conceivably refer to "'f' times 'x'."

- **<mtext> text**—The mtext element can be used to render enclosed content as text, but there are many situations in which it would not be appropriate to do so. For example, if the following statement were embedded in HTML, "Theorem 1: There exists x such that $f(x) = 0$" it would probably be more reasonable to encode only the first "x" and the expression "$f(x) = 0$" in MathML to ensure that the font size and typeface of the text blended in properly with the rest of the text on the page.

Note

Until a clear mechanism is devised to ensure that HTML and XML documents can communicate this sort of environmental information to included MathML expressions, using the mtext element will probably create islands of odd-looking text in the middle of your document in many browsers. This mechanism is one of the issues being addressed in the next revision of MathML, version 2.0, but full implementation will require full access to the Document Object Model, which is itself in the process of revision. Expect this all to take some considerable time.

Caution

The mtext element can also be used to "tweak" the appearance of the rendered MathML expression using entities such as   or , which is almost always a bad idea because space that renders in a certain way in one browser will probably render differently in another.

- **<mspace /> space**—The mspace element is designed to insert some sort of space into a MathML expression. It takes width, height, and depth attributes to define exactly how big the space should be. Because this is used primarily to "tweak" the appearance of the rendered MathML expression, its use is almost always a bad idea. Space generated in this manner will probably not behave properly if the underlying font size is changed to accommodate user preferences, nor is it guaranteed to be stable across platforms. A better option is to insert spacing with invisible functions using the <mphantom> element.

- `<ms>` **string literal**—The ms element represents a string literal, with the usual XML conventions for escaping special characters and using named entities. Because the content of an ms element is typically rendered with enclosing quote marks, quotes should always be escaped. Because MathML collapses extra whitespace by default, long strings can be broken across lines with no special handling required. The quote marks used can be selected using the rquote and lquote attributes, which override the default values. Although this is possibly handy for languages other than U.S. English, it would be better to choose the value based on the language of a surrounding document, as the <q> tag is *supposed* to do in HTML.

The next section addresses elements that the MathML specification calls "general layout schemata." *Schemata* is merely the plural of schema, and the word is, quite frankly, confusing jargon. It means layout elements.

GENERAL LAYOUT SCHEMATA

These are more complex presentation elements used in MathML to group tokens together in various ways. Before you see what these are, however, you should understand *invisible operators*, which formalize the operations commonly omitted when representing mathematical expressions. MathML supplies these special operators, which usually are not rendered at all in visual browsers, because they might be needed to make sense of a statement when rendered in an aural browser.

An example might be the multiplication implied by the expression $2x$. Although usually spoken as "two ex," the expression really *means* "two times ex." Multiplication is such a common operation that most mathematical notations treat it as a default to save space and make complex expressions easier to grasp.

Another example is the function operator implied in the expression $f(x)$. Using this notation is somewhat ambiguous, because you could conceivably confuse the function f with a variable *f*, without paying rather careful attention to whether the letters are italicized.

And again, sometimes numbers or variables are juxtaposed for the sake of compactness in certain notations even though they're logically disjunct. MathML has special invisible operators that should be used to make the exact relationships between these elements clear, as shown in Table 24.4.

TABLE 24.4 MathML Invisible Operators

Full Name	Short Name	Where to Use Them
&InvisibleTimes;	&it;	$2x$
&ApplyFunction;	&af;	$f(x)$ or $\sin y$
&InvisibleComma;	&ic;	m_{12}

It's a short list, but then there aren't all that many situations in which an operation is understood rather than shown.

- **`<mrow>`**—Horizontally group any number of subexpressions which should be treated as one expression.

  An mrow element is used to group any number of sub-expressions together and, further, to provide browsers and rendering engines clues about the actual structure of the modeled equation. When a long expression needs to be broken across lines or when an aural browser needs to know how to group descriptions, properly nested mrow elements can be crucial. The following example

  ```
  <mrow><mn>2</mn><mo>&it;</mo><mi>x</mi><mrow>
  ```

  displays the expression $2x$. Note the use of an invisible multiplication operator.

- **`<mfrac>`**—Form a fraction from two expressions; numerator and denominator.

  The mfrac element takes a linethickness attribute, which allows the element to be used for fraction-like notations such as binomial expressions (which have a linethickness of zero to eliminate display of the fraction line) or nested fractions (which might use a thicker bar for the outer fraction). This example

  ```
  <mfrac><mn>1</mn><mn>2</mn></mfrac>
  ```

  displays the fraction one-half.

- **`<msqrt>`**—Form a square root from one or more expressions. This example

  ```
  <msqrt><mi>x</mi></msqrt>
  ```

  displays the square root of x.

  If there is more than one expression, an implied mrow element is assumed to contain them.

- **`<mroot>`**—Form a radical from exactly two expressions, base and index.

  It's an error if more or less than two expressions are included. This example

  ```
  <mroot><mn>3</mn><mi>x</mi></mroot>
  ```

  displays the cube root of x.

- **`<mstyle>`**—Style change for any number of subexpressions. This example

  ```
  <mstyle color="blue"><mi>x</mi><mstyle>
  ```

  sets the x variable to display in blue, although this would be invisible in an aural browser or on a monochrome display device and difficult to distinguish from some other colors for persons with color discrimination disabilities.

  The mstyle element can take any attribute accepted by any MathML presentation element. If there is more than one argument, they are treated as if they're enclosed by an implied mrow. In addition to the attributes accepted by every presentation element, mstyle accepts and passes on the following special attributes implicitly inherited by every MathML element as part of its operating environment. These are shown in Table 24.5

TABLE 24.5   mstyle **ATTRIBUTES**

Name	Values	Default
scriptlevel	['+' | '-']	unsigned-integer inherited

TABLE 24.5 CONTINUED

Name	Values	Default
displaystyle	true | false	inherited
scriptsizemultiplier	number	0.71
scriptminsize	number v-unit	8pt
color	#rgb | #rrggbb | html-color-name	inherited
background	#rgb | #rrggbb | transparent | html-color-name	transparent

MathML uses two attributes, displaystyle and scriptlevel, to control certain presentation features. The main effect of the displaystyle attribute is that it determines the effect of other attributes, such as the largeop and movablescripts attributes of <mo>. The main effect of the scriptlevel attribute is to control the font size. Typically, the higher the scriptlevel, the smaller the font size. (Non-visual rendering engines can respond to the font size in an analogous way for their medium.) More sophisticated rendering agents may also choose to use these attributes in other ways, such as rendering expressions with displaystyle='false' in a more vertically compressed manner.

- **<merror>**—Enclose any number of syntax error messages from a preprocessor. These tags presumably would be inserted by the preprocessor itself; it's difficult to imagine why anyone would want to insert them in a document on his own initiative.

  If more than one argument is enclosed, the contents are treated as if surrounded by an implied mrow element.

- **<mpadded>**—Adjust space around any number of content arguments using the attributes shown in Table 24.6. This element, like the mspace element, should be used (if at all) with extreme caution because it's almost guaranteed to give inconsistent results in different browsers, and when using styling mechanisms, to affect the rendering of the expression in any way.

  This has no effect on the rendered size of the enclosed expression but only on the surrounding margins.

  The <mpadded> element accepts any number of arguments; if this number is not 1, the contents are treated as if they were enclosed by an implied mrow.

TABLE 24.6 ATTRIBUTES OF <mpadded>

Name	Values	Default
width	[+ | -] unsigned-number (% [pseudo-unit] | pseudo-unit | h-unit)	same as content

Name	Values	Default
lspace	`[+	-] unsigned-number` `(% [pseudo-unit] |` `pseudo-unit | h-unit)`	0
height	`[+	-] unsigned-number` `(% [pseudo-unit] |` `pseudo-unit | v-unit)`	same as content
depth	`[+	-] unsigned-number` `(% [pseudo-unit] |` `pseudo-unit | v-unit)`	same as content

The `width` and `lspace` attributes are not symmetrical. The `lspace` refers to leading (left margin) space, whereas the `width` attribute refers to the total width of the enclosing box. Likewise, `height` and `depth` are not symmetrical. The `height` is the total height of the enclosing box, whereas `depth` is the amount of vertical space between the bounding box and the baseline.

PART

IV

CH

24

> **Caution**
>
> Like all the elements that insert space, it's unwise to use the `mpadding` element to tweak spacing to improve the look for any particular browser or rendering engine.

- **`<mphantom>`**—Make content invisible but preserve its size.

  This is used to align elements when an element is missing in the actual expression. By creating a phantom element, surrounding elements will space properly without otherwise affecting the rendering of the expression.

- **`<mfenced>`**—Surround content consisting of any number of expressions with a pair of fences. This example

  ```
  <mfenced><mi>x</mi></mfenced>
  ```

  displays (x).

  The `mfenced` element surrounds its argument(s) with some sort of parentheses, braces, curly brackets, vertical bars, or whatever. If there is more than one, arguments are separated by the value of the `separators` attribute, if any. If there is more than one separator, the list is applied sequentially. The last separator is repeated as needed (see Table 24.7).

TABLE 24.7   ATTRIBUTE LIST FOR `mfenced`

Attributes	Values	Default
open	string	(
close	string	)
separators	character *	,

These are most of the ordinary elements used in MathML; however, the following section discusses elements which demand even more complex rendering, scripts and limits, which are usually shown as tiny numbers above and below the baseline of the expression. Again, the jargon word *schemata* makes it somewhat less clear that the things being described are just elements, like any other MathML elements.

SCRIPT AND LIMIT SCHEMATA

- **<msub>**—Attach a subscript to a base; base and subscript. This example

  ```
  <msub><mi>x</mi><mi>y</mi></msub>
  ```

  displays x_y.

  The msub element takes a `subscriptshift` attribute, allowing the exact amount of the shift to be altered from the default, which is automatic and usually about one ex, or x-height value.

- **<msup>**—Attach a superscript to a base; base and superscript. This example

  ```
  <msup><mi>x</mi><mi>y</mi></msup>
  ```

  displays x^y.

  The msub element takes a `superscriptshift` attribute, allowing the exact amount of the shift to be altered from the default, which is automatic and usually about one ex, or x-height value. Because the super- or subscript can apply to an entire expression, it's important to properly structure the code with mrow elements to ensure that it behaves properly in all rendering engines and browsers. So to display $(x+y)^2$, the following code fragment would work:

  ```
  <msup>
    <mrow>
      <mo> ( </mo>
      <mrow>
        <mi> x </mi>
        <mo> + </mo>
        <mi> y </mi>
      </mrow>
      <mo> ) </mo>
    </mrow>
    <mn> 2 </mn>
  </msup>
  ```

- **<msubsup>**—Attach a subscript-superscript pair to a base; base, subscript, and superscript. This example

  ```
  <msubsup><mi>x</mi><mi>y</mi><mi>z</mi></msubsup>
  ```

  displays x with subscript $_y$ and superscript ^{z} properly placed one above the other.

  The msubsup element takes `subscriptshift` and `superscriptshift` attributes, allowing the exact amount of the shift in either direction to be altered from the default, which is automatic and usually about one ex, or x-height value. Although this might seem redundant, the rendering of this element aligns the script elements properly above one another and ensures equal spacing from the enclosed element. Using msup and msub consecutively would offset one from the other improperly.

- **`<munder>`**—Attach an underscript to a base; base and underscript. The under- and over-scripts behave quite similarly to subscripts and superscripts, but are used to show things like limits in summations. To spare my overworked publisher the trouble of typesetting these things, we'll pretend we know what they look like if we actually have need of them.

  Although similar to the `msubscript` element, the underscript is placed directly under the enclosed element. The underscript takes an `accentunder` attribute with values of `true` or `false`, which affect how closely the underscript renders to the base element.

- **`<mover>`**—Attach an overscript to a base; base and overscript.

  `mover` is similar to the `msuperscript` element but the overscript is placed directly over the enclosed element. It takes an `accentover` attribute with values of `true` or `false` which affect how closely the overscript renders to the base element.

- **`<munderover>`**—Attach an underscript-overscript pair to a base; base, underscript, and overscript.

  Although similar to the `msubsup` and `msupscript` elements combined, but the underscript is placed directly under the enclosed element and the overscript is placed directly above. They take the `accentunder` and `accentover` attributes with values of `true` or `false`, which affect how closely the underscript and overscript render to the base element.

- **`<mmultiscripts>`**—Attach one or more prescripts and tensor indices to a base; (base (subscript superscript) * [`<mprescripts />` (presubscript presuperscript) *]).

  This is a complex element that allows an arbitrary number of subscripts and super-scripts, presubscripts, and presuperscripts, to be attached to an argument. The empty `mprescripts` element is the optional marker for prescripts, because they are relatively rare and must be contained within the `mmultiscripts` element. If it isn't present, there are no prescripts. Empty scripts must be identified with the empty element `<none />`. This complex element is used for tensor notation and a few others. If you understand what tensors are, you know how they look.

TABLES AND MATRICES

MathML tables are somewhat more influenced by SGML than XML because they have an assortment of short forms that allow you to omit enclosed rows and data field elements that will be inferred. Allowing elements to be inferred is contrary to general XML practice although quite common in SGML. This makes creation of robust rendering engines for MathML difficult, but mirrors the common conventions of mathematical notations themselves, which often omit important information that a knowledgeable reader can supply from context. A missing `mtr` element, for example, implies a single enclosed row although a missing `mtd` element implies an `mrow` element containing all enclosed elements if there is more than one element.

- **`<mtable>`**—Table or matrix consisting of zero or more rows.

  This element behaves much like an HTML table and takes attributes similar to those found on HTML tables. It's used to render any table-like array or matrix (see Table 24.8).

TABLE 24.8 ATTRIBUTES OF `<mtable>`

Name	Values	Default
align	(top | bottom | center | baseline | axis) [rownumber]	axis
rowalign	(top | bottom | center | baseline | axis) +	baseline
columnalign	(left | center | right) +	center
groupalign	group-alignment-list-list	{left}
alignmentscope	(true | false) +	true
rowspacing	(number v-unit) +	1.0ex
columnspacing	(number h-unit) +	0.8em
rowlines	(none | solid | dashed) +	none
columnlines	(none | solid | dashed) +	none
frame	none | solid | dashed	none
framespacing	number h-unit number v-unit	0.4em 0.5ex
equalrows	true | false	true
equalcolumns	true | false	true
displaystyle	true | false	false

The group-alignment-list-list value contains the list of lists of alignment values that should be applied to all rows and data elements in order.

- **`<mtr>`**—Render a single row in a table or matrix consisting of 0 or more table elements (see Table 24.9).

  This is the rough equivalent of the HTML `<tr>` element. If it's missing, a single row is implied.

TABLE 24.9 ATTRIBUTES OF `<mtr>`

Name	Values	Default
rowalign	top | bottom | center | baseline | axis	inherited
columnalign	(left | center | right) +	inherited
groupalign	group-alignment-list-list	inherited

- **`<mtd>`**—Render one entry in a table or matrix (see Table 24.10).

  This is the rough equivalent of the HTML `<td>` element. If it's missing, a single data entry is implied. If there's more than one expression, an implied mrow element encloses all expressions. The `group-alignment-list-list` value contains the list of lists of alignment values that should be applied to all data elements in order.

TABLE 24.10   ATTRIBUTES OF `<mtd>`

Name	Values	Default
rowspan	number	1
columnspan	number	1
rowalign	top | bottom | center | baseline | axis	inherited
columnalign	left | center | right	inherited
groupalign	group-alignment-list	inherited

- `<maligngroup />`—Specify alignment.

  The `groupalign` attribute of `maligngroup` takes one of four values, `left`, `center`, `right`, or `decimalpoint`. The default value is inherited.

- `<malignmark />`—Specify an alternative alignment marker.

  If `decimalpoint` alignment is specified but the alignment character should be anything other than a decimal point, the `malignmark` element functions as a surrogate for a decimal point. The `edge` attribute can be used to select which character should be aligned. If `edge = 'right'` the alignment takes place on the right edge of the character to the left of the mark. If `edge = 'left'` the alignment takes place on the left edge of the character to the right of the mark.

The `edge` attribute of `malignmark` takes one of two values, `right`, and `left`. The default value is `left`.

ENLIVENING EXPRESSIONS

Perhaps influenced by Dynamic HTML, MathML allows you to explicitly associate actions to a subexpression using a single `maction` element. Of course, more can be done with CSS and XSL, but this guarantees a certain minimal capability in every implementation whether any sort of style sheet is supported or not.

The `<maction>` element binds one or more actions to a subexpression using the `actiontype` attribute.

An example might be to include a balloon help box using an `actiontype='tooltip'` or `actiontype='highlight'` `other='#ff0000'` attribute pair. The `other` attribute is defined for almost every element as a hook for extending the capabilities of MathML. Note that no browser or rendering engine need support any particular action type and can ignore the `other` attribute as well. The value of either attribute is undefined in the MathML specification, and support for any value is entirely dependent on the implementation.

W3C PROPOSED MATHML 2.0 ADDITIONS TO PRESENTATION MARKUP

MathML 2.0 is currently in last call status, although the Recommendation may be released by the time you read this. Any and all of the changes listed here in overview may be dropped, added to, or completely altered before the standard is finalized.

Although the MathML 2.0 specification is in a preliminary state right now, there are surprisingly few proposed changes to the MathML 1.0 specification so far, including the following new elements:

- `<menclose>`—An enclosure element that renders a type of notation surprisingly ignored in the original MathML recommendation. The `longdiv` value is the familiar long division enclosure you learned in grammar school and the `actuarial` enclosure is the mirror image of it used in the insurance industry. The `radical` value renders the equivalent of the `msqrt` element.

  The `menclosure` element takes the `notation` attribute values `longdiv`, `actuarial`, and `radical`. The default value is `longdiv`.

- `<meqno>`—Enter a placeholder for an equation number which can be used to locate and automatically transform the locations into numbers.

  The location can surround an explicit equation number. Because XML allows portions of documents to be transcluded into other documents, it's possible that a correct explicit number may be incorrect as rendered in context. The actual numbering scheme and method is beyond the scope of MathML and must be accomplished by means of XSLT or another transformation language.

  The `meqno` element takes the attribute `eqno` with possible values `string` and `empty`. The default value is `string`.

  The `eqno` attribute allows references to numbered equations to be processed automatically by specifying an arbitrary string to identify the number location. XSLT can be used to transform documents with embedded numbered equations into a series of targets for links, for example, by searching for the string so the enclosed element can be replaced.

- `<mglyph />`—The `mglyph` element allows you to add symbols used in new mathematical notations without relying on the often slow responses of standards bodies such as the Unicode Consortium, which have lengthy comment and distribution periods required before new glyphs can be standardized and used internationally. Although this is adequate for languages, which introduce new characters rarely, mathematics uses new characters all the time as the frontiers of mathematical thinking expand.

  The `mglyph` element takes three required attributes:

  - `alt`, which must contain an alternate representation of the glyph to be used in aural browsers or anywhere the actual glyph is unavailable.
  - `fontfamily`, which is an arbitrary string that may be the name of an actual font or that of a CSS-style font family.

- index, which is a numeric value used to select a single character from the indicated font.

  This example

  ```
  <mglyph alt="[aleph]" fontfamily="HebrewLetters" index="1" />
  ```

  might refer to a Hebrew aleph character.

■ **<mchar />**—The mchar element allows you to refer to non-ASCII characters without using XML named entities, because entities are unreliable when using a non-validating browser. The mchar element takes a single required attribute, name, which must refer to a list of names described in the MathML specification itself. This example

```
<mi><mchar name="aleph" /></mi>
```

displays as the Hebrew aleph character commonly used to represent infinity.

Again, the exact syntax changes slated for MathML 2.0 are still up in the air, but the changes indicated here have been stable for some time and at least indicate the direction the Working Group seems to be moving in. The primary modifications so far have been adding elements and attributes to correct a few oversights and deficiencies in the original specification and accommodating the specification to the difficult reality experienced by implementers of MathML 1.0.

PART

IV

CH

24

DOING MATH WITH MATHML SYNTAX ELEMENTS

In the preceding sections, you looked at MathML presentation elements, which let you publish mathematics in an understandable way. However, mathematics has moved on from the days when most work was done on paper to an era in which machines are regularly used to perform much of the tedious work associated with graphing complex functions, solving difficult mathematical problems, and other vexing tasks that would slow down modern mathematicians to the point of stasis if performed by hand.

Enter Mathematica and other mathematical environments meant to simplify the process of actually *doing* higher math much as electronic calculators have simplified ordinary arithmetic.

In this sort of environment, the presentation elements aren't nearly enough, because they don't really convey meaning other than what a human reader can infer from what they already know about mathematics. So the Greek letter gamma (Γ) means nothing in particular unless you know the context in which it's been used. Machines need far more help than this, because they don't actually understand mathematics at all; they simply apply various rules to exact descriptions they can manipulate according to internal algorithms.

The MathML syntactical, or content, elements make up for this problem by defining a series of mathematical constructs that authors can extend almost at will by defining or redefining custom constructs with external behavioral and semantic descriptions.

USING MATHML CONTENT ELEMENTS

Content (or syntax) elements describe what mathematics means in a way that can be programmatically manipulated and displayed. So as a simple example, not only could you see what an equation looked like, but you could display a graphic representation of the function as it varied. The potentials for education and collaboration are obvious, but even more, the output from such a program could be displayed on alternative tactile output devices for blind users. Such tactile representations now have to be laboriously created by hand and are limited to elementary functions illustrating basic math concepts in textbooks for disabled users.

SYNTACTICAL TOKEN ELEMENTS

The syntactical token elements are similar to their presentation equivalents, with a few differences based on the fact that syntax is different from presentation. So an mn element as described in the previous chapter can be thought of as a string representing a number, whereas a cn element *is* a number.

- **<cn>**—A numerical constant. The following example

  ```
  <cn>42</cn>
  ```

  is the number 42.

  Unlike the mn element, which refers only to content that should be rendered *like* a number, the cn element refers unambiguously to a numerical constant that can be used and manipulated *as* a number.

ATTRIBUTES OF <cn>

- type: real | integer | rational |
  complex-cartesian | complex-polar | constant
- base: number (CDATA for XML DTD) between 2 and 36.
- definitionURL: A URL pointing to an alternative semantic definition.

  By default, a numerical constant is a signed real number in base 10 notation although another base can be chosen with any value between 2 and 36 inclusive. The reasons for this limitation on base values are not immediately obvious. If more parts are needed to create a complex number, the parts should be separated by empty <sep /> elements.

- **<ci>**—A symbolic identifier, for example

  ```
  <ci>x</ci>
  ```

ATTRIBUTES OF <ci>

- type   integer | rational | real |
  float | complex | complex-polar |
  complex-cartesian | constant |
  any container element name (e.g. vector)
  or their type values.
- definitionURL: URL

  The definitionURL attribute allows the default semantics to be overridden with alternative semantics.

BASIC CONTENT ELEMENTS

The basic MathML content elements allow basic functions to be applied to some number of arguments. These elements tend to appear often in MathML documents because they define simple relationships between other elements:

- **`<apply>`**—Apply a mathematical operator to its arguments. Syntax: Operator and zero or more arguments. This example, which represents 2+2, evaluates to 4:

```
<apply> <plus /> <cn>2</cn> <cn>2</cn> </apply>
```

The `apply` semantics enforce a prefixed operator notation which is inherently free of the need for parentheses.

> **Note**
>
> Although there are several algorithms available for evaluating parenthesis-free expressions, in the case of a prefixed notation, the operator and its arguments can be evaluated as they're read from the input stream. Whenever an operator is encountered in the input stream, it marks the leading edge of a complete expression. In the case of a prefixed notation, any previous expression or sub-expression is complete at that point and a new one begins. The ubiquitous Hewlett Packard (HP) scientific and financial calculators use a similarly parenthesis-free postfix notation called Reverse Polish Notation (RPN) which will be familiar to many as stack-based, as opposed to reading the input stream directly, but the general concepts are the same.

- **`<reln>`**—Apply a relation operator to its arguments. Syntax: Operator and arguments. For example, the following represents the Boolean expression 2=2 and would evaluate to `true`:

```
<reln><eq /> <cn>2</ci> <cn>2</cn> </reln>
```

A relation is used in a slightly different way from a function so it has a separate syntax element. This distinction may disappear in MathML 2.0 and `reln` itself may be deprecated. It should be obvious from inspection that the prefix notation used for both `apply` and `reln` is identical, which makes the distinction between them somewhat artificial in practice despite the logical difference; `<apply>` is used for all functions in MathML 2.0.

- **`<fn>`**—Identify a function. For example, the following code describes a simple 2+2 function:

```
<fn><apply> <plus /> <cn>2</cn> <cn>2</cn> </apply></fn>
```

This element takes a `definitionURL` attribute, which allows default semantics to be overridden with alternative semantics if desired but doesn't really do much overall if no overriding semantics are supplied because it's obvious that `<plus />` is being used as a function from context. MathML 2.0 deprecates its use entirely in favor of `csymbol`.

- **`<interval>`**—Defines an interval on the real number line. For example, the following code identifies the interval 5..10:

```
<interval><cn>5</cn> <cn>10</cn></interval>
```

This element takes an attribute, `closure`, which can take any of the following values: `open`, `closed`, `open-closed`, or `closed-open`. The default value is `closed`. This function expects either two child elements which evaluate to real numbers or a single child element which is a condition defining the interval.

- **`<inverse />`**—The generic inverse of a function. This example

  ```
  <apply><inverse /><sin/> <ci>x</ci> </apply>
  ```

  corresponds to $\sin^{-1} x$, the hyperbolic sine of x.

  Not every function has a unique inverse. This element takes a `definitionURL` attribute, which allows the default semantics to be overridden with alternative semantics if necessary.

- **`<sep />`**—Separate the parts of a complex or rational number. For example, the following code identifies the complex number (2,8*i*):

  ```
  <cn type="complex">2<sep />8</cn>
  ```

  The `sep` element is used in a `cn` element to allow tokenizing of the parts so they can be put together by the application.

- **`<condition>`**—Place a condition on a free variable or identifier. This example

  ```
  <condition><apply><in /><ci>x</ci><ci type="set">Y</ci></apply></condition>
  ```

  defines a condition where the variable *x* is restricted to values in the set *Y*.

  The `condition` element is used when you can't conveniently enumerate possible values. It contains either a single `reln` element or an `apply` element used to construct compound conditions. Note that `reln` will probably be deprecated in MathML 2.0.

- **`<declare>`**—Set identifier name and optional attribute values. For example, to declare a set *X*, you'd do this:

  ```
  <declare type="set"> <ci>X</ci> </declare>
  ```

  `declare` has the following attributes:

  - `type` defines the MathML element type of whatever identifier is being declared in this element.
  - `scope` defines the scope of the MathML declaration.
  - `nargs` defines the number of arguments for function declarations in a MathML document or inclusion.
  - `occurrence` defines operator usage as 'prefix', 'infix', or 'function-model'. These indications let a rendering engine decide when to perform the actual operation indicated.
  - `definitionURL` defines a URL pointing to the necessary detailed semantics of the mathematical or logical function being declared.

  The `declare` element has two roles. The first is to change or set the default attribute values for a specific mathematical object. The second is to establish an association between a name and an object using a `ci` element.

- **`<lambda>`**—Construct a user-defined function. This example

  ```
  <lambda><apply><ci>F</ci> <apply><fn><ci>f</ci></fn>
  <ci>x</ci></apply></apply></lambda>
  ```

  defines `[lm](F(f(x))`.

  The `lambda` element is used with an expression and one or more free variables to construct a user-defined function. This is a way of constructing a function you find moderately handy without going to the trouble of creating a new glyph and notation and promulgating the results to the world. Lambda notations are the mathematical equivalent of an ad hoc subroutine or procedure in a programming language.

- **`<compose />`**—Compose a function. This example

  `<apply><compose /><fn><ci>f</ci></fn> <fn><ci>g</ci></fn></apply>`

  defines f _ g.

  The `compose` element is the function composition operator. This element takes a `definitionURL` attribute, which allows the default semantics to be overridden with alternative semantics if desired.

- **`<ident />`**—The identity function. This example

  `<ident />`

  renders as id.

  To override the minimal default semantics for the `<ident/>` element, or to associate a more specific definition, use the `definitionURL` attribute.

Arithmetic, Algebra, and Logic

The following elements are a selection of common functions that behave as you might expect. Each element takes the `definitionURL` attribute, which allows the default semantics to be overridden with alternative semantics. Arithmetic elements default to base ten:

- **`<quotient />`**—The quotient of a division modulo a particular base. This is a binary operator.
- **`<exp />`**—The exponential function. This is a unary operator.
- **`<factorial />`**—The factorial function. This is a unary operator.
- **`<divide />`**—The division operator. This is a binary operator.
- **`<max />`**—The maximum of the enclosed arguments. This is an n-ary operator.
- **`<min />`**—The minimum of the enclosed arguments. This is an n-ary operator.
- **`<minus />`**—The negation or subtraction operator. This is either a unary negation operator or a binary subtraction operator.
- **`<plus />`**—The addition operator. This is an n-ary operator.
- **`<power />`**—The exponentiation operator. This is a binary operator.
- **`<rem />`**—The remainder of a division modulo a particular base. This is a binary operator.
- **`<times />`**—The multiplication operator. This is a binary operator.
- **`<root />`**—Extract the root of the enclosed arguments. The first argument, if present, is a `degree` element with the degree of the root enclosed. If absent, a value of 2 is assumed.
- **`<gcd />`**—The greatest common divisor operator. This is an n-ary operator.
- **`<and />`**—The logical "and" operator. This is an n-ary operator.
- **`<or />`**—The logical "or" operator. This is an n-ary operator.

- `<xor />`—The logical "exclusive or" operator. This is an n-ary operator.
- `<not />`—The logical "not" operator. This is a unary operator.
- `<implies />`—The logical "implies" relational operator. This is a binary operator.
- `<forall />`—The logical "for all" relational operator. The `forall` element represents the universal quantifier of logic. It must be used in conjunction with one or more `bvar` bound variables, an optional `condition` element, and an assertion, which may take the form of either an `apply` or `reln` element although the `reln` element is deprecated in MathML 2.0.
- `<exists />`—The logical "there exists" relational operator. The `exists` element represents the existential quantifier of logic. It must be used in conjunction with one or more `bvar` bound variables, an optional `condition` element, and an assertion, which may take the form of either an `apply` or `reln` element although the `reln` element is deprecated in MathML 2.0.
- `<abs />`—The absolute value operator of a real number or the modulus of a complex quantity. This is a unary operator.
- `<conjugate />`—The complex conjugate of a complex quantity. This is a unary operator.

RELATIONS

These functions define the simple algebraic relationships between values, including equality, inequality, and relative size. They behave as you might expect.

The following elements all take the `definitionURL` attribute, which allows the default semantics to be overridden with alternative semantics:

- `<eq />`—The equality n-ary relation.
- `<neq />`—The negative binary equality relation.
- `<gt />`—The greater than n-ary relation.
- `<lt />`—The less than n-ary relation.
- `<geq />`—The greater than or equal to n-ary relation.
- `<leq />`—The less than or equal to n-ary relation.

Binary relations and operators take two arguments although n-ary operators take any number of arguments including zero.

CALCULUS

These functions are related to calculus in one way or another. The following five functions all take the `definitionURL` attribute, which allows the default semantics to be overridden with alternative semantics. The remainder of this list doesn't take this attribute.

- `<ln />`—The natural logarithm operator. This element takes a single argument.
- `<log />`—The logarithm operator to a given base. If present, the `logbase` element specifies the base. If absent, base 10 is assumed and a single argument is sufficient.

- **`<int />`**—The integral operator. If present, the optional `lowlimit`, `uplimit`, and `bvar` elements enclose the lower limit, the upper limit, and the bound variable respectively. Alternatively, an interval element of a condition element may specify the domain of integration. If a bound variable of integration is intended, it must be specified explicitly.

- **`<diff />`**—The differentiation operator. The `bvar` element defines the bound variable of differentiation whereas an optional `degree` element contained within the `bvar` element specifies the order of the derivative to be taken.

- **`<partialdiff />`**—The partial differentiation operator element for functions of several real variables. The bound variables are given by `bvar` elements, which are children of the containing `apply` element. The `bvar` elements may also contain a `degree` element, which specifies the order of the partial derivative to be taken in that variable.

- **`<lowlimit>`**—A qualifier indicating the lower limit of an element taking qualifiers. This element is a container for the lower limit, if present.

- **`<uplimit>`**—A qualifier indicating the upper limit of an element taking qualifiers. This element is a container for the upper limit, if present.

- **`<bvar>`**—A qualifier indicating the bound variable of an element taking qualifiers. This element is a container for the bound variable, if present.

- **`<degree>`**—A qualifier indicating the degree of an element taking qualifiers. This element is a container for the degree or order of an operation.

ELEMENTS RELATED TO THE THEORY OF SETS

The following elements express set relationships:

- **`<set>`**—Construct a set. The `set` element is a container that constructs a set of elements from its contents. The elements of a set can be defined either by explicitly listing the elements, or by using `bvar` and `condition` elements to define one or more conditions that define values comprising a set.

- **`<list>`**—Construct a list. The `list` element is a container that constructs a list of elements from its contents. The elements of a list can be defined either by explicitly listing the elements, or by using the `bvar` and `condition` elements to define one or more conditions that define values comprising a list.

  Lists differ from sets in that there is an explicit order to the elements. Two orders are supported: `'lexicographic'` and `'numeric'`. You can specify the sort of ordering to be performed by using the `order` attribute.

The following elements all take the `definitionURL` attribute, which allows the default semantics to be overridden with alternative semantics. They behave much as you would expect. Binary relations and operators take two arguments although n-ary operators take any number of arguments:

- **`<union />`**—The union n-ary set operator.

- **`<intersect />`**—The intersection n-ary set operator.

- **`<in />`**—The inclusion binary set relation.
- **`<notin />`**—The exclusion binary set relation.
- **`<subset />`**—The subset n-ary set relation.
- **`<prsubset />`**—The proper subset n-ary set relation.
- **`<notsubset />`**—The "not a subset of" binary set relation.
- **`<notprsubset />`**—The "not a proper subset of" binary set relation.
- **`<setdiff />`**—The difference binary set operator.

Sequences and Series

The following functions are related to sequences and series and all take the `definitionURL` attribute, which allows the default semantics of the element to be overridden with alternative semantics.

- **`<sum />`**—The summation operator. Upper and lower limits for the summation are specified using `uplimit`, `lowlimit`, or a `condition` on bvar elements. The index for the sum is specified by a `bvar` bound variable element.
- **`<product />`**—The product operator. Upper and lower limits for the product are specified using `uplimit`, `lowlimit`, or a `condition` on the bound variables. The index for the product is specified by a `bvar` bound variable element.
- **`<limit />`**—The operation of taking the limit of a sequence. The limit is expressed by specifying a `lowlimit` and a `bvar` bound variable or by specifying a `condition` on one or more bvar bound variable elements.
- **`<tendsto />`**—Stating that a quantity is tending toward a specified quantity. This element takes a `type` attribute with possible values of `above`, `below`, or `two-sided` to indicate the direction from which the limiting value is approached.

Trigonometry

The trigonometric elements are the classic functions almost everyone remembers from high school, sine, cosine, and the rest. Each of the following elements takes the `definitionURL` attribute, which allows the default semantics of the element to be overridden with alternative semantics.

- **`<sin/>`**—Sine
- **`<cos/>`**—Cosine
- **`<tan/>`**—Tangent
- **`<sec />`**—Secant
- **`<csc />`**—Cosecant
- **`<cot />`**—Cotangent
- **`<sinh />`**—Hyperbolic sine
- **`<cosh />`**—Hyperbolic cosine

- **`<tanh />`**—Hyperbolic tangent
- **`<sech />`**—Hyperbolic secant
- **`<csch />`**—Hyperbolic cosecant
- **`<coth />`**—Hyperbolic cotangent
- **`<arcsin />`**—Arcsine
- **`<arcos />`**—Arccosine
- **`<arctan />`**—Arctangent

The preceding elements reference the classic unary trigonometric functions. MathML 2.0 changes the label of these elements from "trigonometric" to "classic" but makes no other changes.

STATISTICS

The statistical elements implement the elementary statistical functions. They each take the `definitionURL` attribute, which allows the default semantics to be overridden with alternative semantics.

- **`<mean />`**—The statistical mean operator. The `mean` element returns the mean of a list of values.
- **`<sdev />`**—The statistical standard deviation operator. The `sdev` element returns the standard deviation of a list of values.
- **`<variance />`**—The statistical variance operator. The `variance` element returns the variance of a list of values.
- **`<median />`**—The statistical median operator. The `median` element returns the median of a list of values.
- **`<mode />`**—The statistical mode operator. The `mode` element returns the mode of a list of values.
- **`<moment />`**—A statistical moment. The `moment` element represents statistical moments. You can use the `degree` element for the n in "nth moment".

The preceding elements reference the classic statistical functions.

LINEAR ALGEBRA

These elements define the classic linear algebraic functions:

- **`<vector>`**—Construct a vector. The `vector` element is the container for a vector. The child elements form the components of the vector.
- **`<matrix>`**—Construct a matrix. The `matrix` element is the container for matrix rows. `matrixrow` elements contain the elements of a matrix.
- **`<matrixrow>`**—Construct a matrix row. The `matrixrow` element is the container for a matrix row.

- **`<determinant>`**—Construct the determinant of a matrix. The `determinant` element is the operator for constructing the determinant of a matrix.

- **`<transpose>`**—Transpose a matrix. The `transpose` element is the operator for constructing the transpose of a matrix.

- **`<selector>`**—Index into a list, vector, array, or matrix.

  This element takes the ID of a list, vector, array, or matrix and the next two identify the column and row. If there is a third argument and a list or vector is identified, the third argument is ignored. If an array or matrix is identified and there are only two arguments, the elements of the array are arranged first by column and then by row as a simple vector and the appropriate element is returned.

SEMANTIC MAPPING ELEMENTS

These elements allow you to alter the semantics of predefined functions:

- **`<annotation>`**—A non-XML-based alternative semantics. The `annotation` element is always contained within a `semantics` element if present. It takes an encoding attribute used to identify the encoding used for a non-XML semantic annotation format. An example might be `<annotation encoding='TeX'> TeX statements </annotation>`. Whether a browser can actually do anything with this information is application dependent.

- **`<semantics>`**—Provide alternative semantics for a MathML expression. The first element is always a content-based MathML construct and is rendered by default. Any number of alternative formats can be included following the first construct using either annotation element for each following format.

  The `semantics` element allows alternative rendering mechanisms to be attached to a content-based MathML expression. For example, you could include a MathML presentation element alternative using an included

  ```
  <annotation-xml encoding='MathML-Presentation'>
     …
  </annotation-xml>
  ```

  This element takes the `definitionURL` attribute, which allows the default semantics to be overridden with alternative semantics.

- **`<annotation-xml>`**—An XML-based alternative semantics. The `annotation-xml` element is always contained within a `semantics` element if present. It takes an encoding attribute used to identify the encoding used for XML-based semantic annotations. An example might be `<annotation-xml encoding='OpenMath'> OpenMath statements </annotation-xml>`. Whether a browser can actually do anything with this information is application dependent.

PROPOSED MATHML 2.0 CHANGES AND ADDITIONS TO CONTENT ELEMENTS

MathML 2.0 is still very much in development, with at least two more Working Drafts due before advancing up the ladder toward full Recommendation status. Any and all of the changes listed here in overview may be dropped, added to, or completely altered before the standard is finalized.

`<reln>` is supported but deprecated in favor of `<apply>`, which now supports relational elements.

The trigonometric functions have been renamed to elementary classical functions.

The following elements are added:

- **`<csymbol>`**—Define a mathematical symbol.

  The `csymbol` element uses the `definitionURL` attribute to point to the mathematical definition of the new symbol. In addition, it uses the encoding element to identify the mathematical application used to define the new symbol.
- **`<arg>`**—New arithmetic, algebraic, or logical element.
- **`<real>`**—New arithmetic, algebraic, or logical element.
- **`<imaginary>`**—New arithmetic, algebraic, or logical element.
- **`<equivalent>`**—New calculus and vector calculus element.
- **`<approx>`**—New relation element.
- **`<divergence>`**—New relation element.
- **`<grad>`**—New calculus and vector calculus element.
- **`<curl>`**—New calculus and vector calculus element.
- **`<laplacian>`**—New calculus and vector calculus element.
- **`<size>`**—New set element.
- **`<vectorproduct>`**—New linear algebra element.
- **`<scalarproduct>`**—New linear algebra element.
- **`<outerproduct>`**—New linear algebra element.

The definitions of the preceding elements haven't been formalized as of this writing.

PART

IV

CH

24

UNDERSTANDING THE MATHML INTERFACE ELEMENT

The top level or interface element for all MathML content is the `math` element. It's the equivalent of any top level XML element and it's an error to include a `math` element within another `math` element. Because MathML is designed to be included within HTML or XML documents, it's also an error to include MathML statements in a document without enclosing `<math>` tags.

In cut and paste operations involving MathML expressions, the enclosing `math` element may not be included, so the user agent should supply these tags if they're missing. Likewise, if a cut and paste operation inserts a complete MathML expression including `math` elements into an existing complete MathML expression, the included `math` elements must be removed.

The attributes of the `math` element are

`class='value'`—Provided for style sheet compatibility.

`id='value'`—Provided for style sheet compatibility.

`style='value'`—Provided for style sheet compatibility.

`macros='URL URL ...'`—The `macros` attribute provides a way of pointing to external macro definition files. Macros are not currently part of the MathML specification, but it's anticipated that in the future, many uses of macros in MathML can be accommodated by XSL transformations (`http://www.w3.org/TR/xslt`). However, the `macros` attribute is provided to make possible future development of more streamlined, MathML-specific macro mechanisms.

`mode='display|inline'`—The `mode` attribute specifies whether the enclosed MathML expression should be rendered in a display style or an inline style. The default is `mode='inline'`. This attribute is deprecated in favor of the standard CSS2 `display` property.

SYNTAX VERSUS PRESENTATION

This chapter has already discussed the two primary sorts of MathML elements: presentation and content. Although ideally, MathML rendering engines should understand content and render it appropriately based on its meaning, the reality of mathematics research and development means that new notations will constantly be invented to meet new needs, and even existing notations can be used in different contexts to express different meanings. So x^2 might indicate "x squared" or the second component of the vector x.

Rendering mathematical meaning is also dependent on context. The notations used by mathematicians to express factorial(x) differ in different situations depending on what they want to do with the information. A rendering engine has no way to know whether it should be $x!$, arguably the most common notation, $\Gamma(x+1)$, the equivalent gamma function, or $(1)_x$, the Pochhammer symbol for the same mathematical concept.

Presentation markup is needed to tell the rendering engine how the MathML `<apply>` `<factorial/><ci>x</ci></apply>` statement should be rendered unless the rendering happens to correspond to the default notation specified in the operator dictionary.

MIXING PRESENTATION AND CONTENT DIRECTLY

There are many reasons you might want to include presentation elements within content elements or vice versa. The first might be to allow special formatting to be applied to a `ci` element like this:

```
<ci><mi fontweight='bold'>x</mi></ci>
```

Because the `ci` element doesn't allow a `fontweight` attribute, this is a simple way to render the variable in boldface.

The reverse might also be true. In a presentation-oriented document, it might be advisable to use content tags to allow people using aural browsers, for example, to easily distinguish a power from a vector using browser settings:

```
<mrow>
  <apply>
    <power/>
    <ci>x</ci><cn>2</cn>
  </apply>
  <mo>+</mo>
  <msup>
    <mi>x</mi><mn>2</mn>
  </msup>
</mrow>
```

Because the default display of a number raised to a power is very likely to be identical to that of a generic superscript, or nearly so, the display will appear normally when viewed in a visual browser. However, using the two different tagging schemes will allow aural browsers to distinguish them by using different tones.

USING PRESENTATION ELEMENTS WITHIN CONTENT MARKUP

To avoid problems decoding meaning when using presentation elements within content markup, using presentation elements is forbidden except

- Within `ci` or `cn` token elements
- Within the `fn` element
- Within the `semantics` element

The `semantics` element in particular is designed to allow arbitrary visualizations or semantic mappings to be attached to content elements.

USING CONTENT ELEMENTS WITHIN PRESENTATION MARKUP

The only content elements allowed in presentation markup are container tags such as `ci`, `cn`, `<apply>`, `<fn>`, `<lambda>`, `<reln>`, `<interval>`, `<list>`, `<matrix>`, `<matrixrow>`, `<set>`, `<vector>`, and `<declare>`.

Other elements depend for part of their meaning on context, so they are forbidden in this context.

PROPOSED MATHML CHANGES AND ADDITIONS TO MIXING PRESENTATION AND CONTENT

The `xref` attribute can be combined with the `id` attribute to allow unambiguous reference between presentation elements and content elements. In use you would simply identify each presentation element with an XML ID and then add an `xref` to the corresponding presentation element in every syntax element.

MIXING MATHS AND TEXT IN MATHML

MathML is designed to be used in math fragments inside larger documents, so the top level math element is a key component of the complete rendering strategy. Because the math element is stable, all a browser has to do is know that everything inside should be rendered specially or ignored, with no middle ground. Unfortunately, it probably won't be working that way any time soon, since legacy browsers often attempt to render everything.

Because MathML fragments (and all XML documents or document fragments) contain text data exposed to many browsers, some means has to be provided to avoid rendering the exposed data inappropriately. There will always be this tension between new facilities and older ones in the HTML world, and the impossibility of supporting (or even properly ignoring) new capabilities in old browsers means that some things just cannot be done. Although every HTML browser should ignore unknown tags, the only way to hide exposed text content is to remove it from the document entirely.

This means that you'll have to create external documents containing the new features and link to them using features that aren't supported in older browsers. The new XLink linking mechanisms are a good example. Presumably, a browser that supports XLink also supports the capability to ignore exposed content when surrounded by unknown tags. The only alternative is to use scripting languages or server facilities to feed dynamic content based on the make and revision level of the browser. Both strategies may be required in particular instances. Figure 24.2 illustrates the problem using the MathML example, which is then shown properly displayed in Figure 24.3 in the next section. The display is, quite frankly, filled with irritating junk. The text that's displayed in Figure 24.2 *should* be invisible because it's part of the code that generates the three dimensional image in Figure 24.3. This is a problem of language design, not the browser manufacturer's error. Ideally, you could work around the problem with nested HTML or XHTML object tags, but many browsers don't support that syntax either.

Figure 24.2
The Opera browser showing exposed MathML text content.

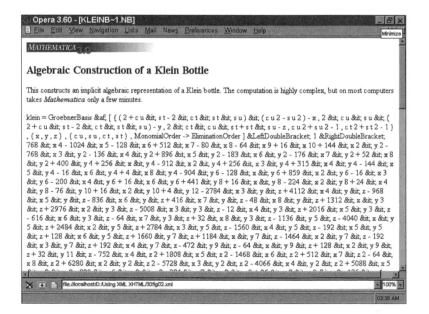

Although the designers of new languages assume that older browsers will be replaced soon, the fact is that most people don't upgrade their browser until they buy a new computer and a new browser is supplied with the machine. Programmers tend to be "early adopters," and assume that other people either are or ought to be the same. This won't happen. As a Web designer, you'll have to deal with that fact forever unless you're on an internal network with strict configuration control and can guarantee the make and revision level of every browser on the network.

The techniques for supporting multiple browsers are beyond the scope of this book but widely available in almost every book on HTML design and coding. In general, client-side code slows down your browser although server-side code slows down your server. It's possible to have a little bit of the best of both worlds by judiciously distributing server-side and client-side programming with basic support for your site's most common browsers built in and rare-browsers supported by server-side creation of custom pages.

This has the disadvantage of defeating most caching schemes, so more hits will go through to the server. But nothing's perfect, eh?

MathML Tools

One of the easiest MathML tools to find is the W3C browser, Amaya. Best of all, it's free. Unfortunately, the range of MathML features Amaya supports is limited. In this it mirrors most display and editing tools. Support for MathML will be available in Mozilla, and in fact the presentation tags are already there in the pre-release milestones.

After you get into the range of professional tools, the possibilities become much more enticing. Figure 24.3 shows a sample drawn from the Mathematica program from Wolfram Research at http://www.wolfram.com/ illustrating the extensive formula graphing capabilities of this package. Mathematica is geared toward both scientific exploration and publication and has an extensive library of prewritten applications for specialized scientific fields.

Listing 24.1 shows the MathML code for the complex formula, exported from the Mathematica software environment. Although this listing may seem intimidating at first because of its size, even a cursory glance will show you that it's contructed of quite ordinary MathML elements such as mrow, mo, and mi for the most part. Rendering the equation by hand might be boring but certainly not impossible for anyone likely to actually use MathML professionally. Using TeX and LaTeX to typeset mathematics is at least as complex and time-consuming and scientists do it every day.

Figure 24.3
A graph of the surface
of the formula dis-
played here using
Mathematica 4.0.

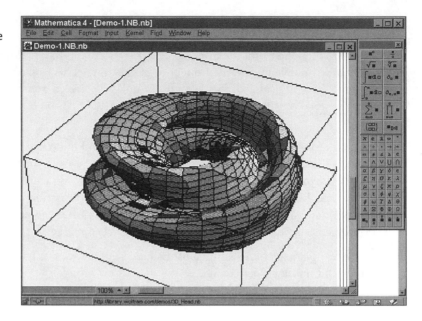

LISTING 24.1   A MathML Formula Exported from Mathematica

```
<math>
  <mrow>
    <mi>klein</mi>
    <mo>=</mo>
    <mrow>
      <mrow>
        <mi>GroebnerBasis</mi>
        <mo>&af;</mo>
        <mrow>
          <mo>[</mo>
          <mrow>
            <mrow>
              <mo>{</mo>
              <mrow>
                <mrow>
                  <mrow>
                    <mrow>
                      <mo>(</mo>
                      <mrow>
                        <mn>2</mn>
                        <mo>+</mo>
                        <mrow>
                          <msub>
                            <mi>c</mi>
                            <mi>u</mi>
                          </msub>
                          <mo>&it;</mo>
                          <msub>
                            <mi>s</mi>
                            <mi>t</mi>
```

```
                    </msub>
                </mrow>
                <mo>-</mo>
                <mrow>
                  <mn>2</mn>
                  <mo>&it;</mo>
                  <msub>
                    <mi>c</mi>
                    <mi>t</mi>
                  </msub>
                  <mo>&it;</mo>
                  <msub>
                    <mi>s</mi>
                    <mi>t</mi>
                  </msub>
                  <mo>&it;</mo>
                  <msub>
                    <mi>s</mi>
                    <mi>u</mi>
                  </msub>
                </mrow>
              </mrow>
              <mo>)</mo>
            </mrow>
            <mo>&it;</mo>
            <mrow>
              <mo>(</mo>
              <mrow>
                <msubsup>
                  <mi>c</mi>
                  <mi>u</mi>
                  <mn>2</mn>
                </msubsup>
                <mo>-</mo>
                <msubsup>
                  <mi>s</mi>
                  <mi>u</mi>
                  <mn>2</mn>
                </msubsup>
              </mrow>
              <mo>)</mo>
            </mrow>
          </mrow>
          <mo>-</mo>
          <mi>x</mi>
        </mrow>
        <mo>,</mo>
        <mrow>
          <mrow>
            <mn>2</mn>
            <mo>&it;</mo>
            <msub>
              <mi>c</mi>
              <mi>u</mi>
            </msub>
            <mo>&it;</mo>
            <msub>
```

```
        <mi>s</mi>
        <mi>u</mi>
      </msub>
      <mo>&it;</mo>
      <mrow>
        <mo>(</mo>
        <mrow>
          <mn>2</mn>
          <mo>+</mo>
          <mrow>
            <msub>
              <mi>c</mi>
              <mi>u</mi>
            </msub>
            <mo>&it;</mo>
            <msub>
              <mi>s</mi>
              <mi>t</mi>
            </msub>
          </mrow>
          <mo>-</mo>
          <mrow>
            <mn>2</mn>
            <mo>&it;</mo>
            <msub>
              <mi>c</mi>
              <mi>t</mi>
            </msub>
            <mo>&it;</mo>
            <msub>
              <mi>s</mi>
              <mi>t</mi>
            </msub>
            <mo>&it;</mo>
            <msub>
              <mi>s</mi>
              <mi>u</mi>
            </msub>
          </mrow>
        </mrow>
        <mo>)</mo>
      </mrow>
    </mrow>
  </mrow>
  <mo>-</mo>
  <mi>y</mi>
</mrow>
<mo>,</mo>
<mrow>
  <mrow>
    <mn>2</mn>
    <mo>&it;</mo>
    <msub>
      <mi>c</mi>
      <mi>t</mi>
    </msub>
    <mo>&it;</mo>
    <msub>
```

```
            <mi>c</mi>
            <mi>u</mi>
          </msub>
        <mo>&it;</mo>
        <msub>
          <mi>s</mi>
          <mi>t</mi>
        </msub>
      </mrow>
      <mo>+</mo>
      <mrow>
        <msub>
          <mi>s</mi>
          <mi>t</mi>
        </msub>
        <mo>&it;</mo>
        <msub>
          <mi>s</mi>
          <mi>u</mi>
        </msub>
      </mrow>
      <mo>-</mo>
      <mi>z</mi>
    </mrow>
    <mo>,</mo>
    <mrow>
      <msubsup>
        <mi>c</mi>
        <mi>u</mi>
        <mn>2</mn>
      </msubsup>
      <mo>+</mo>
      <msubsup>
        <mi>s</mi>
        <mi>u</mi>
        <mn>2</mn>
      </msubsup>
      <mo>-</mo>
      <mn>1</mn>
    </mrow>
    <mo>,</mo>
    <mrow>
      <msubsup>
        <mi>c</mi>
        <mi>t</mi>
        <mn>2</mn>
      </msubsup>
      <mo>+</mo>
      <msubsup>
        <mi>s</mi>
        <mi>t</mi>
        <mn>2</mn>
      </msubsup>
      <mo>-</mo>
      <mn>1</mn>
    </mrow>
  </mrow>
</mrow>
```

```
                    <mo>}</mo>
                  </mrow>
                  <mo>,</mo>
                  <mrow>
                    <mo>{</mo>
                    <mrow>
                      <mi>x</mi>
                      <mo>,</mo>
                      <mi>y</mi>
                      <mo>,</mo>
                      <mi>z</mi>
                    </mrow>
                    <mo>}</mo>
                  </mrow>
                  <mo>,</mo>
                  <mrow>
                    <mo>{</mo>
                    <mrow>
                      <msub>
                        <mi>c</mi>
                        <mi>u</mi>
                      </msub>
                      <mo>,</mo>
                      <msub>
                        <mi>s</mi>
                        <mi>u</mi>
                      </msub>
                      <mo>,</mo>
                      <msub>
                        <mi>c</mi>
                        <mi>t</mi>
                      </msub>
                      <mo>,</mo>
                      <msub>
                        <mi>s</mi>
                        <mi>t</mi>
                      </msub>
                    </mrow>
                    <mo>}</mo>
                  </mrow>
                  <mo>,</mo>
                  <mrow>
                    <mi>MonomialOrder</mi>
                    <mo>-></mo>
                    <mi>EliminationOrder</mi>
                  </mrow>
                </mrow>
                <mo>]</mo>
              </mrow>
            </mrow>
            <mo>&LeftDoubleBracket;</mo>
            <mn>1</mn>
            <mo>&RightDoubleBracket;</mo>
          </mrow>
        </mrow>
      </math>
```

Figure 24.4 shows the same formula imported into the WebEQ equation editor, which is a specialized tool from Geometry Technologies (http://www.webeq.com/) that addresses MathML specifically. This demonstrates that you could easily pass work done on one platform to a colleague using an entirely different tool in the universal transfer medium that MathML represents.

Figure 24.4
The formula created in Mathematica is displayed in WebEQ.

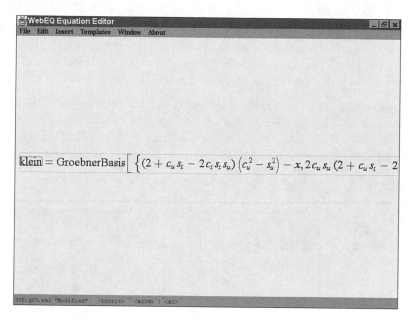

Other tools include Maple, from Waterloo Maple at http://www.maplesoft.com/, MathCAD from http://www.mathcad.com/, Macsyma from Macsyma at http://www.macsyma.com/, and many more. Computer algebra systems are widely available, many free or very low cost, and most of high quality. By no means do all of these currently support MathML, but support should be forthcoming for most algebra systems in the near future.

CML AND OTHER SCIENTIFIC XML APPLICATIONS

The Chemical Markup Language, CML, is another XML-based application designed for working scientists. It allows scientists to define the exact structure of molecules and visualize the results using special purpose editor/browsers. Like MathML, CML is designed to be created with power assistance and to serve as a transfer medium between different chemical editing and display environments.

This section shows a single example of CML to show some of the power of scientific XML applications in general. CML is only standing in for this wide range of applications and not special in itself. In particular, this section won't explain what CML elements mean or how they're put together, because by now you know roughly how XML works and all XML vocabularies obey identical rules.

The CML site at http://www.xml-cml.org/ contains information on existing software, including Jumbo, the CML browser, but is slightly dated. Peter Murray-Rust's site at http://www.ch.ic.ac.uk/omf/cml/ also contains much of interest although it too hasn't been updated in a while. Peter Murray-Rust is planning on updating CML and is working toward improving and extending its reach in the scientific community.

Examples of similar scientific software include MOLMOL, the Molecule Analysis and Molecule Display program from http://www.mol.biol.ethz.ch/wuthrich/software/molmol/ and hundreds more, most of which cannot currently communicate with one another. Another site with links to many software packages for the biological and scientific communities is http://www.infochem.co.uk/software/bio/index.htm.

An example of CML in action is available from Mr. Murray-Rust's site at http://www.ch.ic.ac.uk/omf/cml/doc/examples/csd.html and is here used by permission from Mr. Murray-Rust himself, who has performed yeoman service to the XML community in many capacities, both with his CML language and the inestimable services he's performed for XML-DEV.

Figure 24.5 shows a molecular display generated by a CML document.

Figure 24.5
The Jumbo CML browser displaying the molecule described by the CML code.

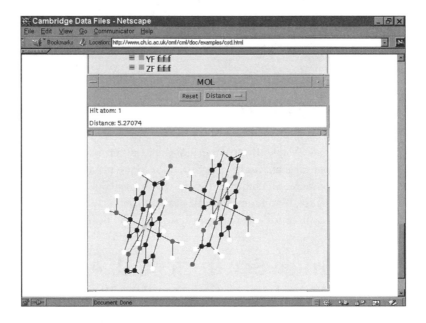

Figure 24.5 was generated by the CML code in Listing 24.2, which demonstrates how nicely specialized browsers can make very complex XML documents accessible for improved understanding and visualization of scientific data, in this case the structure of molecules:

LISTING 24.2   A CML DOCUMENT SUPPLIED BY THE AUTHOR OF THE TOOL

```
<?XML VERSION='1.0'?>
<!DOCTYPE CML PUBLIC '-//CML//DTD CML/EN'>
  <CML>
```

```
<MOL>
  <BIB TITLE='Citation'>
    <PERSON>
      <XVAR BUILTIN='LASTNAME'>
        PROUT
      </XVAR>
      <XVAR BUILTIN='INITIALS'>
        C.K
      </XVAR>
    </PERSON>
    <PERSON>
      <XVAR BUILTIN='LASTNAME'>
        ARMSTRONG
      </XVAR>
      <XVAR BUILTIN='INITIALS'>
        R.A
      </XVAR>
    </PERSON>
    <PERSON>
      <XVAR BUILTIN='LASTNAME'>
        CARRUTHERS
      </XVAR>
      <XVAR BUILTIN='INITIALS'>
        J.R
      </XVAR>
    </PERSON>
    <PERSON>
      <XVAR BUILTIN='LASTNAME'>
        FORREST
      </XVAR>
      <XVAR BUILTIN='INITIALS'>
        J.G
      </XVAR>
    </PERSON>
    <PERSON>
      <XVAR BUILTIN='LASTNAME'>
        MURRAY-RUST
      </XVAR>
      <XVAR BUILTIN='INITIALS'>
        P
      </XVAR>
    </PERSON>
    <PERSON>
      <XVAR BUILTIN='LASTNAME'>
        ROSSOTTI
      </XVAR>
      <XVAR BUILTIN='INITIALS'>
        F.J.C
      </XVAR>
    </PERSON>
    <XVAR BUILTIN='JOUR'>
      J.CHEM.SOC.A
    </XVAR>
  </BIB>
  <FORMULA CONVENTION='CCDC'>
  <XVAR BUILTIN='STOICH'>
    C16 H18 CU1 O8
```

LISTING 24.2   CONTINUED

```
    </XVAR>
    <ARRAY BUILTIN='ELSYM'>
      CU 'O ' 'O ' 'O ' 'O ' 'O ' 'O ' 'C ' 'C ' 'C ' 'C ' 'C ' 'C '
      'C ' 'C ' 'C ' 'C ' 'O ' 'O ' 'C ' 'C ' 'C ' 'C ' 'C ' 'C '
    </ARRAY>
    <ARRAY BUILTIN='NONH'>
      6 3 3 2 2 1 1 3 2 3 2 3 3 2 2 2 2 1 1 2 2 2 2 2 2
    </ARRAY>
    <ARRAY BUILTIN='NUMH'>
      0 0 0 0 0 2 2 0 2 0 2 0 0 1 1 1 1 0 0 1 1 1 1 1 1
    </ARRAY>
    <ARRAY BUILTIN='FORMCHARGE'>
      0 0 0 0 0 0 0 0 0 0 0 0 0 0 0 0 0 0 0 0 0 0 0 0 0
    </ARRAY>
    <ARRAY BUILTIN='ATID1'>
      1 1 1 1 1 1 2 2 3 3 4 5 8 8 9 10 10 11 12 13 14 15 16 17
      20 21 22 23
    </ARRAY>
    <ARRAY BUILTIN='ATID2'>
      2 3 4 5 6 7 8 9 10 11 12 13 14 15 12 16 17 13 18 19 20
      21 22 23 24 24 25 25
    </ARRAY>
    <ARRAY BUILTIN='ORDER'>
      -1 -1 -1 -1 1 1 1 -1 1 -1 -1 -1 -5 -5 -1 -5 -5 -1 2 2
      -5 -5 -5 -5 -5 -5 -5 -5
    </ARRAY>
  </FORMULA>
  <CRYST>
    <XVAR BUILTIN='ACELL' TYPE='FLOAT' UNITS='ANGSTROM'>
      16.26
    </XVAR>
    <XVAR BUILTIN='BCELL' TYPE='FLOAT' UNITS='ANGSTROM'>
      7.28
    </XVAR>
    <XVAR BUILTIN='CCELL' TYPE='FLOAT' UNITS='ANGSTROM'>
      23.99
    </XVAR>
    <XVAR BUILTIN='ALPHA' TYPE='FLOAT' UNITS='DEGREES'>
      90
    </XVAR>
    <XVAR BUILTIN='BETA' TYPE='FLOAT' UNITS='DEGREES'>
      90
    </XVAR>
    <XVAR BUILTIN='GAMMA' TYPE='FLOAT' UNITS='DEGREES'>
      110.4
    </XVAR>
    <XVAR BUILTIN='RFACTOR' TYPE='FLOAT'>
      0.113
    </XVAR>
    <XVAR BUILTIN='COMMENT'>
      Atom H16 removed from ATOM-list, for suspected coordinate error(s)
    </XVAR>
    <XVAR BUILTIN='COMMENT'>
      C15 z -0.1763, not 0.1763 C5 z 0.1742, not 0.1762 C7 z 0.2151,
      not 0.2171 C14 z -0.138, not -0.135 C18 z -0.1739, not -0.1729
```

```
          O13 y -0.1588, not 0.1588. Phenyl ring defined by C23-C28 have been
          interchanged in figure 2, the correct values are C23-C24 1.38,C24-C25
          1.46, C25-C26 1.38, C26-C27 1.35, C27-C28 1.43 and C28-C231.40
        </XVAR>
      </CRYST>
      <SYMMETRY TITLE='Symmetry'>
        <ARRAY BUILTIN='SYMOP' ROWS='4' COLUMNS='3' TYPE='FLOAT'
STRUCT='RECTANGULAR'>
          1 0 0 0 0 1 0 0 0 0 1 0
        </ARRAY>
        <ARRAY BUILTIN='SYMOP' ROWS='4' COLUMNS='3' TYPE='FLOAT'
STRUCT='RECTANGULAR'>
          -1 0 0 0.5 0 -1 0 0.5 0 0 1 0.5
        </ARRAY>
      </SYMMETRY>
      <ATOMS>
        <ARRAY BUILTIN='ELSYM'>
          CU CU C C C C C C C C C C C C C C C C C C C C C C C C C H H H
          H H H H H H H H H H H H H H H H H H H H H H H O O O O O O O O
          O O O O O O O C C C H H O H H C C C H C H C H H
        </ARRAY>
        <ARRAY BUILTIN='ATID'>
          CU1 CU2 C1 C11 C12 C13 C14 C15 C16 C17 C18 C2 C21 C22 C23 C24
          C25 C26 C27 C28 C3 C4 C5 C6 C7 C8 H1 H11 H12 H13 H14 H15 H17
          H18 H19 H2 H21 H22 H23 H24 H25 H26 H27 H28 H29 H3 H4 H5 H6 H7
          H8 H9 O1 O11 O12 O13 O14 O2 O21 O22 O23 O24 O3 O4 O1B O3B O4B
          C1B C2B C3B H3B H9B O2B H1B H2B C4B C8B C5B H4B C7B H8B C6B H5B
          H7B H6B
        </ARRAY>
        <ARRAY BUILTIN='XF' TYPE='FLOAT'>
          0 0.3292 -0.053 0.3892 0.324 0.237 0.2049 0.1403 0.1165 0.1507
          0.2112 0.0131 0.2774 0.3414 0.4266 0.4544 0.5173 0.5431 0.5154
          0.4556 0.0961 0.1246 0.1858 0.211 0.182 0.1237 0.0691 0.3569
          0.2702 0.2334 0.2277 0.1126 0.1303 0.2363 0.1759 -0.0163 0.3955
          0.3087 0.4271 0.43 0.5429 0.5469 0.5401 0.4333 0.4776 -0.0954
          0.1008 0.2114 0.2553 0.2038 0.1013 -0.152 -0.0681 0.4004 0.4312
          0.2922 0.2316 -0.0929 0.2626 0.2369 0.3725 0.4251 0.0414 -0.0968
          0.0681 -0.0414 0.0968 0.053 -0.0131 -0.0961 0.0954 0.152 0.0929
          -0.0691 0.0163 -0.1246 -0.1237 -0.1858 -0.1008 -0.182 -0.1013
          -0.211 -0.2114 -0.2038 -0.2553
        </ARRAY>
        <ARRAY BUILTIN='YF' TYPE='FLOAT'>
          0 0.0344 0.3147 -0.2747 -0.3182 -0.1653 -0.0155 -0.0114 -0.1569
          -0.307 -0.315 0.344 0.3453 0.3634 0.192 0.0341 0.015 0.151 0.306
          0.331 0.1754 0.0196 0.0056 0.1478 0.304 0.3214 0.4738 -0.3337 -0.45
          -0.3034 0.1028 0.1031 -0.4211 -0.4338 -0.2175 0.3622 0.497 0.3636
          0.3765 -0.0762 -0.1041 0.1341 0.414 0.4542 0.2929 -0.3382 -0.0962
          -0.1127 0.1365 0.4148 0.4448 -0.2505 0.1738 -0.133 -0.387 -0.1588
          -0.1673 0.4345 0.2098 0.4648 0.2034 0.2392 0.1788 -0.2018 -0.1738
          -0.1788 0.2018 -0.3147 -0.344 -0.1754 0.3382 0.2505 -0.4345 -0.4738
          -0.3622 -0.0196 -0.3214 -0.0056 0.0962 -0.304 -0.4448 -0.1478 0.1127
          -0.4148 -0.1365
        </ARRAY>
        <ARRAY BUILTIN='ZF' TYPE='FLOAT'>
          0 0.0004 0.0397 -0.0325 -0.0817 -0.1327 -0.138 -0.1763 -0.2162
          -0.2146 -0.1739 0.0867 0.0426 0.0897 0.132 0.1302 0.1709 0.2134
          0.2149 0.1744 0.1344 0.135 0.1742 0.2175 0.2151 0.1757 0.0782 -0.1192
```

LISTING 24.2   CONTINUED

```
        -0.0735 0.0397 -0.1048 -0.1755 -0.2461 -0.1726 0.0169 0.1252 0.085
         0.1285 -0.0349 0.0981 0.1678 0.2459 0.2477 0.1769 -0.0149 0.0376
         0.1037 0.1752 0.2504 0.2493 0.1757 0.0159 0.0051 0.0005 -0.0272
        -0.0889 0.0389 0.0363 0.0055 0.0415 0.089 -0.0393 0.0904 0.0384
        -0.0051 -0.0904 -0.0384 -0.0397 -0.0867 -0.1344 -0.0376 -0.0159
        -0.0363 -0.0782 -0.1252 -0.135 -0.1757 -0.1742 -0.1037 -0.2151
        -0.1757 -0.2175 -0.1752 -0.2493 -0.2504
      </ARRAY>
    </ATOMS>
  </MOL>
</CML>
```

The full details of CML are far too complex to go into here and I recommend following up by individual research if you're interested in this solution domain. Likewise, JUMBO and CML are not the be-all and end-all of molecular science. Many proprietary applications exist which facilitate specialized activities such as "docking"—discovering how molecules "fit" together in simulation—to determine possible activities of the molecule without laborious laboratory synthesis and testing, and others.

Similar scientific packages are or will be available for many other problem domains as XML gains acceptance in the scientific community. Already under development are AML, the Astronomical Markup Language, AIML, the Astronomical Instrument Markup Language, IML, the Instrument Markup Language, and many others.

GETTING DOWN TO CASES

MathML and CML have a lot of similarities, despite their different appearance, in that the fields they address are highly specialized, the studies of science professionals rather than being part of the general information that almost anyone would expect to know. If you need these facilities, you need them badly since communication between scientists is one of the cornerstones of modern research.

What these languages have in common is the ability to communicate and transfer information seamlessly over the Web using an XML-based application language. As a transfer medium, or even as a storage format, XML-based documents have the advantage of human legibility and extreme robustness. In an environment in which a single software update can break binary data formats, MathML and other XML-based languages retain the ability to decode the data easily without knowing the format in advance. In the case of MathML, a mathematician looking at the code in Listing 24.1 could easily deduce the meaning of the tags since they obey the ordinary rules of mathematical notation and are English-based for the most part, a language widely known and used in scientific circles. Even in some distant time when English is a forgotten relic of ancient history, the regularity of the tags and the universality of mathematics would ensure that the entire structure of XML, and MathML in particular, could be inferred from a few simple examples like this one.

CHAPTER 25

ACCESSIBILITY

In this chapter

WEB ACCESSIBILITY OVERVIEW

In the brave new XML world, accessibility as defined in the W3C Web Accessibility Initiative (WAI) should be universal. The whole point of XML is to make documents available in a platform-independent form that is "evolution proof," based on text and descriptive tags so that anyone can look at the file and figure out what the document is and what the pieces are. The WAI is designed to extend that transparency to everyone, so that browsers, authoring tools, and the entire Web experience is equally enjoyable or useful for persons with visual, motor, or cognitive disabilities. But that doesn't mean your troubles are over. It's unlikely that the world will have universal access to XML-capable browsers anytime soon. So part of your job is going to be thinking of ways to make your XML content visible to the large numbers of persons without direct XML support.

Tip from	One of the banes of software development is dealing with incompatible binary file formats. Oftentimes, the format has evolved to the point that it's currently unrecognizable and, because it's binary, nearly impossible to figure out without exhaustive analysis of many record types. XML is designed to solve this problem by explicitly labeling every field, so that even an archeologist five thousand years from now could decipher your XML data structures from scratch without access to the DTD.

 LeeAnne.com
Words to weave by

In a modern context, this means that you'll have to take into account display devices with many levels of display capability. Devices may include

- Text-only or aural displays with a simple keyboard.
- Web-TVs with only a pointing device.
- High-resolution graphics terminals with keyboard plus a graphics tablet plus whatever.
- Internet appliances, devices intended to address a few specialized needs.
- Text-only includes both terminals, such as those used by persons with vision disabilities, and PDAs or even cell phones.

This wide range of potential output devices means that either you'll have to supply documents dynamically, based on sniffing browser capability, or provide lowest-common-denominator documents using interim technologies. Those technologies will include XHTML along with the capability to embed (or transclude) XML or other content along with XSL style information to allow dynamic modification of the incoming data stream by XML-aware devices. Like scripts today, browsers not capable of supporting advanced capabilities will ignore them.

With similar techniques, users could use the Net as easily with low vision or no vision as others can with 20/20 eyesight. If you can't distinguish blue from green, why shouldn't your computer know this and compensate in appropriate ways? With CSS or XSL style sheets, the compensation is trivial as long as the underlying meaning of every data item is encoded in the page.

Tip from

Words to weave by

Accessibility makes sense for everyone. Just as people with baby strollers benefit from so-called "wheelchair ramps," providing accessible content can make your site more usable in ways you might not be able to imagine.

All these things are possible. The technology exists today. The means includes universal use of XML in Web pages. For example, it's quite common now for Web document authors to use visual clues, like color, font, or point size, to highlight meaning in particular data fields. Since HTML doesn't allow you to easily identify meaningful distinctions between types of data, the highlighting mechanisms tend to be coded directly into the page. Just as calendars are customarily printed with weekend and holiday dates in red, which is meaningless unless you already know the red-letter-day convention, HTML authors tried to duplicate the conventions of their national languages by brute force rather than letting meaning flow from the tags themselves as is possible in XML.

So an HTML author might naively encode information too specifically and too uninformatively like this·

```
<p>Click on the red text to select a link an explanation <a href="URL"><font
color-"red">here</font></a>.</p>
```

An XML author, on the other hand, should be aware that not everyone will have a mouse so "click" is a poor description of selecting a link, and using the word "here" to describe a link doesn't give much of a clue to whatís on the other end when presented as an isolated list of links, as some aural browsers do automatically. So in XML you might want to do something more like this:

```
<paragraph>Select the following link to see a <a href="URL">further explanation of
</link> of this subject.</paragraph>
```

Note that this XML version doesnít assume anything about how links are highlighted or displayed and offers the phrase "further explanation" to describe what one finds on the other end of the link. In a longer example, you might want the link descriptions to be even more formal, since they may be presented separately as an outline as mentioned above.

THE HUMAN CASE FOR ACCESSIBILITY

XML-enabled browsers will enable you to define XSL style sheets that take into account your own abilities, those of your current interface device, the speed of the connection, and a host of other variables to format every page based on what's right for you.

There are a host of excellent reasons to make pages accessible widely. For one thing, the world is full of people with different capabilities. Even language is becoming more easily compensated for, with automatic translation making it possible to surf through sites in French or Russian as easily as you read this book. A French speaker might use your English page in the same way, with the intervening Web interface functioning as a sort of universal Babel Fish to take input data and transform it into a format you can use.

HANDLING LANGUAGE DIFFERENCES IN XML

Have you ever considered publishing an XHTML document in a language other than English? If you have a large customer base in Germany, for example, it would probably be in your best interest to have a version of your site, or at least part of it, translated into the German language.

As you may be aware, the German alphabet—although mostly similar to the English alphabet—has a few additional letter characters, as well as the accent, umlaut, and other features that distinguish it from English.

A common workaround when writing German is to substitute two-character digraphs for certain distinctive German characters. Ess tzet, sometimes called scharfes ess (β) is usually represented as "ss". O umlaut (ö) is usually printed as "oe." And so on. This kind of workaround is suitable for a page that has world-wide distribution, because the special characters needed for German may not be available on any particular browser, especially browsers used by persons with vision impairments. On the other hand, XML provides facilities to print any character in almost any human language using Unicode encodings, and the encodings themselves are often accessed by means of mnemonic character entities rather than directly as numeric values. This means that the value of any particular mnemonic entity can be overridden in the internal subset of the DTD, so the appropriate characters for any browser can be supplied by means of overriding the default values in the internal subset of the DTD, which every XML parser is required to recognize, like this:

```
Default value:     <!ENTITY szlig  CDATA "&#223;" -- latin small letter
                                   ➥sharp s = ess-zed, U+00DF ISOlat1-->
Override value:    <!ENTITY szlig  CDATA "sz" -- latin small letter--
                                   ➥sharp s transliteration in ASCII  -->
```

Of course, many companies offer translation software as well. Although the resulting translation may not be as idiomatic and correct as a human translator is capable of, it's usually understandable at least. If image is vital, consider hiring a translator to go over the results and fix up the rough spots.

You can get more information on using different languages either by searching Help in Internet Explorer or Netscape Navigator, or from their Web sites. The Opera Browser site has an extensive list of European language versions at http://www.opera.com/. Alis Technologies also offers multilingual capabilities in their Tango browser including Arabic and Chinese: http://www.alis.com/. The W3C http://www.w3c.org/WAI is working on language and accessibility standards for the Internet. If this is an important part of your overall Web site, you will benefit from checking their information and resources at http://www.w3.org/WAI/ and http://www.w3.org/International/.

To handle a German quote within an XML document, for example, the following fragment would give the user agent clues about how to handle a mixed-language document gracefully:

```
<paragraph xml:lang="en" lang="en">Goethe once said in
<citation>Rechenschaft</citation>, <quote xml:lang="de" lang="de">Nur die Lumpen
sind bescheiden,/ Brave freuen sich der Tat.</quote></paragraph>
```

Although this would probably have no visible effect, the above `lang` attributes tells an aural browser that the quoted text obeys different pronunciation rules than the English rules that govern the enclosing paragraph and tells all browsers that there is an enclosed quote.

A style sheet associated with an XML document might take into account the fact that different languages use different quoting rules and characters, so to account for four major European styles you could do this:

```
:lang(en) > quote {quotes: '&lsquo;' '&rsquo;' '&ldquo;' '&rdquo;'}
:lang(en-US) > quote {quotes: '&ldquo;' '&rdquo;' '&lsquo;' '&rsquo;'}
:lang(fr) > quote { quotes: '&laquo; ' ' &raquo' }
:lang(de) > quote { quotes: '&raquo;' '&laquo;' '&rsaquo;' '&lsaquo;' }
```

The above CSS code snippet succinctly says that quotes in running English text use single quotes to begin a quote and double quotes for enclosed quotes whereas English as written in the United States does the opposite. If the running text is French, quotes use angled quotes (guillemets) pointing outward with an enclosed space at either end, whereas quotes in German text use two levels of angled quotes pointing inward without an enclosed space. Because the language encoded in the running text of the fragment was not specified as American English, the default English single quote marks are used like this:

```
Goethe once said in Rechenschaft, 'Nur die Lumpen sind bescheiden,/ Brave freuen
sich der Tat.'
```

THE BUSINESS CASE FOR ACCESSIBILITY

PART
IV
CH
25

As the ways in which people use the Internet evolve, you can't assume anything about the environment your pages will run in anymore. A user might "read" your page cruising down the road in his car with an aural browser, from a PDA on a street corner, from a cell phone, from a smart refrigerator or cooking range, or from a wheelchair in Braille. Figure 25.1 shows a Neopoint cellular phone accessing email; the same phone can browse simple Web pages. It will take special care on your part to ensure that your page will survive being displayed on a tiny 11-line screen.

According to statistics published by the U.S. Bureau of the Census, `http://www.census.gov/`, about a fifth of the U.S. population is currently disabled in some way and the proportion is expected to rise to one quarter of the total or more as the population ages. In fact, when you take into account the normal aging process, most people will have some sort of physical or mental impairment eventually since more than half of all persons over 65 have some level of disability and fully a third are severely disabled. Similar ratios affect most of the countries in the world, with many developing nations having far higher rates of disability.

Tip from

LeeAnne.com
Words to weave by

As people age, they often have more free time on their hands to learn and use the Internet. The availability of online services and information makes it possible for persons with limited mobility to independently access a much wider community than in previous times. So the proportion of older individuals using the Internet is rising at a faster rate than their actual numbers are.

Figure 25.1
This shows a Neopoint cellular phone accessing the Internet to read e-mail.

That doesn't mean people stop spending money. Far from it. As people age, they become *more* dependent on services, including online services, not less, as their capabilities change. Where they might once have mowed their own lawn, now they engage yard services. Where they might once have battled traffic to shop, they now order in. This is a market waiting to be tapped in many ways. Current targeted marketing is crude compared with what will be possible in the future.

Companies will have to think fast to keep up with the new ways they can serve a changing customer base and make money while they're doing it. As real information becomes easier to access, brand loyalty may take a drubbing. When you or your intelligent agent can easily compare price, service history, and customer satisfaction over the Web, why buy from the people you bought from last time? It's far more likely that people will develop loyalties to reliable sources of information, to responsible data clearing houses that offer the straight skinny about the best sources for a small fee.

Business strategies that address these issues might first include making sure that your information is available and accessible in every possible media type, to ensure the broadest possible coverage. For example, you can provide linked price comparisons and service histories for every item you offer, including competitor's data; and strive to provide a service on your Web site that people will come back to. You can't depend on Burma Shave style billboards touting your product anymore. You have to back up your claims with facts and figures, just as you would in responding to a request for a quote from a major corporation.

THE LEGAL CASE FOR ACCESSIBILITY

In the United States, the Americans with Disabilities Act places requirements on businesses, governmental agencies, and educational institutions to offer equivalent access to disabled persons whenever that access is readily achievable. If a technology exists that would make equivalent access achievable and you don't use it, even if you don't know about it, but use another technology instead, you may be required to make access available even if your spanking new technology makes providing that equivalent access expensive and difficult. As a Web designer, it's your business to know the tools of your trade, and it could be considered professional malpractice to recommend or use inappropriate technologies.

In spite of the fact that the Americans with Disabilities Act (ADA) has been around for years, many sites that ought to know better persist in creating page content that is completely inaccessible to persons with disabilities. It's *easy* to design accessibility into a site from the outset, and you automatically gain ease-of-use and speed for everyone. It's another story to go back and try to figure out what to do when an ADA lawsuit is filed against your organization for failure to provide "reasonable accommodations" for persons with disabilities.

PART
IV
CH
25

When that happens, you're faced with hard choices. Do you immediately pay to rethink and rework every page or do you pay professional malpractice or ADA lawyers to explain why you think you shouldn't have to and *then* possibly pay to rework every page anyway? You should *definitely* consult a lawyer experienced in disabilities law before betting your job and livelihood on whether you can get away with *not* doing the right thing.

Tip from

LeeAnne.com
Words to weave by

Here is the URL of an excellent discussion of some of the legal issues involved in providing accessibility by Cynthia D. Waddell, JD, an attorney and ADA Coordinator for the City of San Jose, California: `http://www.consumerlawpage.com/article/ada.shtml`.

You might be surprised at how little effort is required to make a site fully accessible if you approach the issue with good will and an appreciation of the issues involved. And with the burgeoning variety of browsing devices available, considering accessibility at the start gives you a leg up on developing pages that will work just as well with portable and handheld devices.

LOW-VISION DISPLAY TECHNIQUES

There is a small repertoire of techniques you can use to ensure good usability for low-vision and blind users. Many of the same techniques will make life considerably safer for sighted people driving down the road in a car who can't spare their attention to thoughtfully peruse a visually complex Web page to determine how to proceed while simultaneously trying to avoid crashing into the cars around them.

Tip from

LeeAnne.com
Words to weave by

For easier handling of accessibility problems, validate your HTML and XHTML pages with CAST's Bobby validator at `http://www.cast.org/bobby/` and follow the suggestions it makes to ensure wide accessibility. Another simple validation tool is Dave Raggett's (W3C) Tidy program which not only checks your code for accessibility errors but fixes common mistakes. You can find Tidy at `http://www.w3.org/People/Raggett/tidy/` and it is also incorporated in Chami's HTML-Kit, a free XHTML editor at `http://www.chami.com/html-kit/` to add "optional" closing tags and eliminate many common coding errors. It will also "prettyprint" your code into a stylized format that is easier to read. Such a deal!

HANDLING BACKGROUNDS AND TEXT FOR LOW-VISION USERS

XML tries to separate content from rendering and display as much as possible, but CSS and XSL are part of the complete XML-related standards and have to be addressed by someone eventually, even though an individual XML author may have no presentation choices to make. However, the document presentation designer responsible for creating XML style sheets should consider the following issues:

- Think about using a white or very light off-white background. If you must use a colored background, choose a single, solid color, rather than textured or patterned.

- Although light background colors work best, it's possible to use dark colors if you increase the size of the text to compensate for the eye's poor ability to distinguish light text on a dark background. Make sure that there is good contrast between the background and the text.

- Avoid italic text. This text treatment is difficult for some low-vision people to read and flummoxes many automatic screen readers as well.

- Don't make the default text too large or too small and don't set it in absolute measures. Standard (medium) size text is preferable, so visitors to your page can adjust the text size to suit their needs by altering their browser settings.

- Underlining of text should be avoided. Underlined text is difficult to read for many people and confusing to those who associate underlines with hypertext links. There's a reason most people who know how to do so have underlining turned off for links.

- Capitalizing whole sentences looks like shouting to people schooled in "netiquette." And it's hard to read in any case. All caps headlines have to be much larger to ensure legibility so be frugal in their use. Look at your newspaper or magazine. They have the benefit of hundreds of years experience balancing the need for legibility with the desire to squeeze as much onto the page as possible.

The same techniques that make pages more accessible for low-vision users make the page more usable for those with monochrome or low-resolution display devices, such as hand-held digital assistants or cell phones. In general, incorporating accessibility into your design at the beginning yields many unforeseen benefits for everyone as technology evolves and application designers take advantage of "accessibility" features to implement new ways of doing things.

USING IMAGES AND OTHER NOTATIONS

Other than in XHTML, XML doesn't have dedicated notations associated with graphics. But for most documents, graphic images are integral, or at least ancillary, to the information content of the page. But some user agents don't support graphics, and some users can't see them; every XML document should provide alternative means of conveying the information provided in graphic images.

HTML and XHTML provide a built-in mechanism for conveying this information, in a handful of attributes that provide different information about the non-text portions of a document. The primary HTML mechanisms are the `alt` and `longdesc` attributes, but the `title` attribute can also be used. In generalized XML documents, these mechanisms don't exist by default but can be easily provided in the DTD.

Tip from

Words to weave by

Because there's already a widely recognized convention in the HTML and XHTML worlds, it makes sense in terms of readability and ease of use to replicate the HTML attributes in XML instantiations of notations unless there are overriding considerations.

Notations used as imagemaps should always be accompanied by a text only navigation alternative.

All notations should contain succinct alternative text (`alt="text"`) attributes. In XML, there are no predefined attributes to rely on, so an `alt` attribute should be declared explicitly on every notation instantiation. Use a short description of the image itself. It's often a good idea to use a standard format for these descriptions, to distinguish them from running text. A common syntax is to surround the text with brackets, like

```
<img alt="[image description]" ...>
```

or to add a tag at the beginning to make it even clearer:

```
<img alt="[IMAGE: image description]" ...>
```

The capitalized letters will be spoken at a different pitch than running text in many aural browsers, which will give a good indication that the text is special in some way.

A fuller description of the image may be provided by a `longdesc="url"` attribute or a dedicated "description link." Because XML doesn't provide a `longdesc` attribute on notations, you should declare an explicit `longdesc` attribute on every notation instantiation so this information can be provided to the user if needed. As a workaround for `longdesc`, you can use a link. Place a 'D' adjacent to the image, and link the 'D' to a separate page containing a detailed description of the image. No current mainstream browser supports the longdesc attribute, but that is its intended use. In XHTML, you'd provide the image and associated "D" like this:

```
<img src="imageURI" alt="[IMAGE: image description]" /><a
href="textDescriptionURI">D</a>
```

This will provide both an alternative label, which may be useful in text mode browsers, and a fuller description which might be as simple as a paragraph describing a photograph or as complex as an alternative format for a graphical table.

USING LINKS ACCESSIBLY

Links, whether implemented with the XML linking mechanisms or an XHTML hyperlink anchor element, should contain enough text to make it clear where the link will take the user. "Click here" is singularly uninformative when abstracted from surrounding context, which many aural user agents do to provide a quick navigation map of the page. In JAWS, for example, the entire list of links is presented when the page is first accessed, before the actual text of the page is read. This speeds navigation when you're trying to get from one page to another. If graphical links are used, these should be accompanied or supplemented by text links for those who cannot interpret graphics.

Another consideration is making your links large enough that users can easily maneuver a pointing device to select them. Users with motor or vision disabilities sometimes find it difficult to see or select tiny targets. Providing keyboard access for link elements is also thoughtful, although not all browsers implement keyboard shortcuts using an accesskey attribute. Browsers that depend on Dynamic HTML to handle keyboard access simultaneously disallow it for users with browsers that don't support DHTML, which seems to miss the point.

USING FRAMES ACCESSIBLY

Many people have difficulty with frames, either because the frames themselves are confusing or because the software they're using doesn't do frames. When using frames in XHTML, always offer a NOFRAMES alternative. Use NOFRAMES properly—smug little "upgrade your browser" messages are of no help at all. NOFRAMES should either contain the entry page content itself or should contain links to frames-free versions of your pages.

USING FRAMES RESPONSIBLY

Frames have no independent existence in XML, but can be easily implemented if desired. XHTML provides a frames DTD and SMIL uses a near equivalent. However, frames are difficult to use in many situations. Some older browsers don't support them, aural browsers can't render frames, and miniaturized displays don't have enough room to make them meaningful even if they could. It's up to the page designer to accommodate all users when designing a framed site. The following guidelines offer suggestions and are described in terms of XHTML frames but can as easily be applied to SMIL layout regions:

■ Provide alternative access. De-frame the site for browsers that don't support frames. Copy all the pertinent information from each of the frames and add it to the <NOFRAMES> section of an appropriate page. The <FRAME> and <FRAMESET> tags are completely ignored when the site is being viewed from a browser that does not support frames, so these elements will disappear. But when viewed with a frames-capable browser, the <NOFRAMES> tag tells the HTML interpreter to ignore everything within its scope while displaying the FRAMESET and FRAME locations. That's why you must remember to use the <FRAMESET> and <FRAME> tags first, and then the <NOFRAMES> alternative HTML can follow. When you're done, you'll have a page with all the navigation elements and information on one page.

■ Save the new document. After the information from the various framed pages of the site is added into the main pages in their logical order, you will save the file as the new default page.

■ Upload the new file. Having made and saved the new version of the framed page incorporating a no-frames option, you need to make it available or replace any old version— if this is a fix-it job—already available on the Net.

■ If the site is well designed, you may only need to change one or two pages to make the entire site work well in both frames and non-frames browsers. Remember to isolate frame information as much as possible to ensure this.

Frames and SMIL share common characteristics in that they imbed layout information in the document itself, although SMIL reuses a large part of the CSS2 layout mechanism. In both cases, it's not terribly easy for users to alter the imposed view of the designer to suit their own needs. So it's up to the designer to allow for alternative views explicitly, rather than demanding that users alter themselves or their environment to suit the page.

USING JAVASCRIPT AS A RENDERING ENGINE

JavaScript is often used to modify or create a document display and often presents a problem, because most of the software low-vision and blind Net users use cannot understand or execute JavaScript. Wherever JavaScript is offered, ensure that script-free pages are available or that the document is not altered by whatever it is you do with it. So a JavaScript decorative element can be ignored, whereas a JavaScript navigation mechanism needs a text-only alternative.

The same caveats apply to Java, Perl, VBScript, Python, Tcl, and other scripting languages. If they constitute a part of the total client-side rendering environment, provide alternatives. If they're used on the server side, be sure their actions take all users into account, either by browser sniffing or programming to a lowest common denominator.

AVOIDING PORTABLE DOCUMENT FORMAT (PDF) FILES

In general, avoid using or linking to PDF files like the plague. They're almost always troublesome for blind and low-vision users, requiring time-consuming fiddling before anything is readable because the text can't be read by screen-reader software without conversion. The author can and quite often does set a flag (provided by Adobe) in the file that prevents any form of accessible rendering of the document. It ought to be labeled "Place a Stumbling Block Before the Blind" but isn't. In fact, Adobe encourages its use to prevent users from easily copying portions of the text, which simultaneously disallows decoding to accessible format.

So a very few PDF documents are readable by Net users using access technology with the help of Access Adobe. Access Adobe translates PDF into ASCII or HTML, making it readable if you are unable to access PDF in the usual way. If you do offer PDF files on your site, ensure that a link to http://access.adobe.com/ is available and that the flags are properly set to allow users to extract the text. However, the vast majority of Adobe PDF files available on the Web were deliberately intended to be opaque to this utility, so it's next to worthless in real life.

When you add to this the fact that most users, not only visually disabled users, find PDF files irritating and slow to download, it's really difficult to understand why anyone would expose their site to so much justifiable criticism in return for such dubious value.

AVOIDING MULTIMEDIA PLUG-IN CONTENT

Shockwave, Flash, Java applets, Dynamic HTML, and other multimedia plug-ins are mostly worthless in terms of accessibility. Either provide alternative content or, better, rethink their necessity. They tend to be slow to load and often don't contribute all that much to the information content of the page.

There's no simple way to provide accessible content using most of these technologies. The only safe way to provide multimedia content is through SMIL and even then only if alternative formats are incorporated at document creation time. Few sites seem to take the trouble, so encouraging their use is irresponsible.

In addition, although this doesn't directly impact accessibility, the use of Java, JavaScript, and other technologies in header files and many Dynamic HTML techniques destroys the usefulness of Internet search engines, because they don't typically know what to do with the error messages or content of such files when accessed by a spider. Although you may have lovely content, if the description of your page entry in a search result says `Error: JavaScript incompatibility Please enable JavaScript in your Browser preferences, or download the latest version of Netscape or Internet Explorer...` instead of a clear description of content, you've lost a good portion of the value of your listing in the search engine.

Using Dynamic HTML to implement jumping text boxes, window shade effects, scrolling displays, or automatically refreshing text at short intervals is hard to deal with if you have low vision. Aural browsers lose their place as well. Avoid doing it if you possibly can.

TABLES

Use tables in XML documents with extreme caution. Some software providing computer and Web access for users with visual disabilities cannot read tables reliably, and may turn your nifty table into a jumbled mess. If tables are used to format running text on your site, consider providing alternative content for people using screen-reading software. In XHTML and HTML, tables have been provided with attributes to make navigation and comprehension easier for persons using aural or other browsers that don't render the document graphically:

- The summary attribute of the table element allows the author to provide a short description of the purpose of the table and what it shows.

- The title attribute of almost every element allows the table to be titled and every cell to be identified unambiguously.

- The accesskey and tabindex attributes allow tables to be navigated without the use of a mouse or other pointing device.

- The abbr attribute provides an abbreviated reference that can be substituted for the contents of a header cell, to simplify and shorten aural rendering.

- The axis attribute allows data cells to be identified in secondary ways, in addition to the basic header structure of the table, and allows a category annotation describing the exact function of the cell in the containing table.

- The headers and id attributes allow individual data cells to be associated with any number of header information cells identified by id attributes.

- The scope attribute allows a header cell to define which data cell span it refers to, either col, row, colgroup, or rowgroup.

If using tables in generalized XML documents, attributes equivalent to the XHTML attributes listed above should be provided in the DTD, probably with the same names for the sake of clarity and standardization, and used throughout the table. Listing 25.1 shows how these attributes might be used in practice.

LISTING 25.1 AN XHTML TABLE SHOWING ACCESSIBLE ATTRIBUTE USE

```
<table summary="Table of rare books showing title, author,
 publication date, accession date, and location">
<caption>Rare Books in our Collections</caption>
<thead>
 <tr>
  <th id="title">Title</th>
   <th id=author">Author</th>
    <th id="PubDate">Publication Date</th>
     <th id="AccDate">Accession Date</th>
      <th id="CatNum">Catalog Number</th>
       <th id="Location">Location</th></tr>
</thead>
<tbody>
 <tr>
  <td id="Rerum" headers="Title">De rerum naturis</td>
   <td headers="Rerum Author">Rabanus Maurus</td>
    <td headers="Rerum PubDate">c. 1466 C.E.</td>
     <td headers="Rerum AccDate">1947 C.E.</td>
      <td headers="Rerum CatNum">RB1078</td>
```

LISTING 25.1 CONTINUED

```
      <td headers="Rerum Location">Locked Cabinet</td></tr>
 <tr>
  <td id="EtymOrig" headers="Title">Etymologiarum siue Originum</td>
   <td headers="EtymOrig Author">Isidorus Hispalensis</td>
    <td headers="EtymOrig PubDate">1186 C.E.</td>
     <td headers="EtymOrig AccDate">1967 C.E.</td>
      <td headers="EtymOrig CatNum">RB6721</td>
       <td headers="EtymOrig Location">Rare Book Room</td></tr>
 <tr>
  <td id="PropRerum" headers="Title">Liber de proprietatibus rerum</td>
   <td headers="PropRerum Author">Bartholomaeus Anglicus</td>
    <td headers="PropRerum PubDate">1372 C.E.</td>
     <td headers="PropRerum AccDate">1887 C.E.</td>
      <td headers="PropRerum CatNum">RB008</td>
       <td headers="PropRerum Location">Rare Book Room</td></tr>
</tbody>
</table>
```

Although this is only one level of categorization, an aural agent could identify each cell by its complete location in the table matrix to prevent confusion. So an aural browser asked to list the fourth cell for the first book might say, "De rerum naturis, Accession Date, 1947 C.E." For a larger table, it might also be advisable to provide abbreviations for the header information to shorten the aural rendering time. The following fragment shows the sort of information you can add to do this using an abbr attribute:

```
<thead>
 <tr>
  <th id="title">Title</th>
   <th id=author>Author</th>
    <th id="PubDate" abbr="Publish">Publication Date</th>
     <th id="AccDate" abbr="Accession">Accession Date</th>
      <th id="CatNum" abbr="Catalog">Catalog Number</th>
       <th id="Location">Location</th></tr>
</thead>
<tbody>
 <tr>
  <td id="Rerum" headers="Title" abbr="Rerum">De rerum naturis</td>
   <td headers="Rerum Author">Rabanus Maurus</td>
    <td headers="Rerum PubDate">c. 1466 C.E.</td>
     <td headers="Rerum AccDate">1947 C.E.</td>
      <td headers="Rerum CatNum">RB1078</td>
       <td headers="Rerum Location">Locked Cabinet</td></tr>
```

In this case, an aural agent could identify the same location as "Rerum, Accession, 1947 C.E." Other slices of the data could be identified with an axis attribute.

COPING WITH BRAILLE

As screen readers and other technical solutions for the blind have gotten better, fewer people are willing to devote the committed hours of practice necessary for Braille fluency. This is a pity, because without the ability to read and write without computerized help, more and more blind and low-vision people are functionally illiterate. However, Braille is the universal and quickest system to read after you become good at it. It's far faster than screen readers even when the speech rate is speeded to the point of gibberish. And it's far easier and quicker to scan a page looking for a particular piece of information using Braille than it is to hunt and peck about with a screen reader. Perhaps the availability of inexpensive Braille terminals may help reverse this trend toward essential illiteracy among the blind.

XML and its related standards have built-in support for Braille output devices, although implementation of the drivers for these devices is dependent on user agents. CSS2 and XSL have particular style mechanisms for creating or supporting Braille output devices. In CSS2, the media types braille and embossed, as well as the media group tactile, refer to Braille displays. braille refers to continuous displays, mostly single line Braille output devices, whereas embossed refers to hardcopy embossed Braille output on Braille paper. Although the XSL draft is still under development, the primary XSL accessibility mechanism at present seems to be the source-document property, which points back to the XML source documents that were used as input. Presumably, this would allow a Braille-aware user agent to undertake its own style modifications and transformation of the original document(s), possibly including translation to Grade 2 Braille and above with a separate process.

Braille is not a monolithic system although work is in progress to help unify the many Braille codes presently in use. Despite sharing a common name, there are in fact different Braille systems for different languages and purposes. Even within languages, there are six-dot character-for-character systems, a sort of basic level called grade one, and grade two systems and above using extensive contractions, abbreviations, and idioms that mark the difference between primer-level schoolbook language and adult literacy.

When you add the Nemeth computer and scientific code, grade three Braille, special eight-dot systems which extend the basic characters with non-alphabetic or formatting symbols, rules for indenting, shift in and out symbols, and more, you're talking about enormous complexity. There are even special Braille systems for music, computer codes, and mathematics, that make translating a page to well-formed literary or technical Braille about as difficult as translating into any foreign language. You can't usually do it with a style sheet, although there's widespread belief that this is so. In most cases, you have to escape to a program because lookahead and backtracking are necessary for implementation of many rules.

Nevertheless, with the introduction of MathML, ChemML, and other specialized XML-based markup languages, the possibilities for machine translation of technical texts are very exciting. Although far more tedious to read, character-by-character systems can make technical publications accessible to blind and visually impaired users who would have needed the assistance of a human reader.

It's beyond the scope of this book to discuss the rules and conventions of Braille printing. See the many publications of the American Printing House for the Blind for further discussion if you want to find out how to do Braille grade two or technical transcribing for a particular purpose on your site.

USING AURAL STYLE SHEETS AND AUDIO BROWSERS

Appendix E, "CSS1, CSS2 Reference," lists the style sheet properties used for aural style sheets; they're duplicated on the enclosed CD-ROM so you can easily search for properties with the [aural] tag. You'll notice that there are properties that control how the rendered voice sounds, its position in space, and how loud the voice is.

You can use these properties to make document elements more plain to persons viewing it without the aid of vision. So headings might be louder than normal text whereas fine print might have less volume. A note could be positioned in space way off to the right and below the listener. The columns of a table, which are difficult to understand without some sort of aid, can be located in space as if they were spread out before you, with the first column off to the left and proceeding across the aural field to the right. The characters in a play could have their own voices, rate and style of speaking, intonation pattern, and so on while their positions on the virtual stage could be followed stereophonically.

So a fragmentary XML style sheet for Hamlet, Prince of Denmark, might read:

```
dialog[speaker~="hamlet"] {pitch: 120Hz; pitch-range: 45; }
dialog[speaker~="polonius"] {pitch: 100Hz; pitch-range: 35; }
dialog[speaker~="gertrude"] {pitch: 200Hz; pitch-range: 60; }
dialog[speaker~="ophelia"] {pitch: 220Hz; pitch-range: 70; }
dialog[speaker~="ghost"] {pitch: 80Hz; pitch-range: 20; }
```

So Hamlet would have a normal male voice, Polonius would sound deeper and more ponderous, and the ghost would be a *basso profundo* with a monotonous pitch range. Gertrude and Ophelia could be distinguished by the fact that Gertrude's voice was more womanly and Ophelia's held a hint of girlishness. The play could actually be blocked aurally, placing the characters in three-dimensional space as they moved about on the imaginary stage.

```
<dialog speaker="hamlet" style="azumith: left; ">To be or not to be,</dialog>
<dialog speaker="hamlet" style="azumith: center; ">that is the question.</dialog>
<dialog speaker="hamlet" style="azumith: right; ">Whether tis nobler …</dialog>
```

For simplicity and clarity, the style elements that move Hamlet's soliloquy in space are placed inline on portions of the dialog, although they would be far better placed in an associated style sheet. Unfortunately, that would mean glancing back and forth from the style sheet to the document.

This discussion only touches the surface of what's possible. Most aural rendering engines have named voice patterns, say Karen, George, and Frank, which can be modified in complex ways. Unfortunately, the named voices aren't consistent across engines, no more than alphabetic fonts are, so eventually some sort of generic labeling system must be created to identify a typical ingenue, a clown, a doctor, and the other stereotypes of the *commedia del-l'arte*. This would provide a dependable pallet of voices to work with. Until then voices must be synthesized based on the cruder characteristics allowed by the CSS2 property list.

Listing 25.2 shows a more extended example using Hamlet again, using the XML markup of the play kindly placed in the public domain by Jon Bosak, with more aural properties added to make the experience richer and using the fragmentary style sheet from the first example.

The speeches have also been rendered into lines, so the rendering software can properly enunciate the meter of the Shakespearean blank verse. Using deprecated inline styles in this way is, again, only for the sake of showing what's going on, to avoid looking back and forth from a style sheet to the document.

LISTING 25.2   THE GHOST SCENE FROM HAMLET RENDERED IN XML

```
<dialog speaker="hamlet" style="azumith: left; ">
<line>Where wilt thou lead me? speak; I'll go no further.</line>
</dialog>
<dialog speaker="ghost" style="azumith: center; elevation: -45deg ">
<line>Mark me.</line>
</dialog>
<dialog speaker="hamlet">
<line>I will.</line>
</dialog>
<dialog speaker="ghost">
<line>My hour is almost come,</line>
<line>When I to sulphurous and tormenting flames</line>
<line>Must render up myself.</line>
</dialog>
<dialog speaker="hamlet">
<line>Alas, poor ghost!</line>
</dialog>
<dialog speaker="ghost">
<line>Pity me not, but lend thy serious hearing</line>
<line>To what I shall unfold.</line>
</dialog>
<dialog speaker="hamlet">
<line>Speak; I am bound to hear.</line>
</dialog>
<dialog speaker="ghost">
<line>So art thou to revenge, when thou shalt hear.</line>
</dialog>
<dialog speaker="hamlet">
<line>What?</line>
</dialog>
<dialog speaker="ghost">
<line>I am thy father's spirit,</line>
<line>Doom'd for a certain term to walk the night,</line>
<line>And for the day confined to fast in fires,</line>
<line>Till the foul crimes done in my days of nature</line>
<line>Are burnt and purged away. But that I am forbid</line>
<line>To tell the secrets of my prison-house,</line>
<line>I could a tale unfold whose lightest word</line>
<line>Would harrow up thy soul, freeze thy young blood,</line>
<line>Make thy two eyes, like stars, start from their spheres,</line>
<line>Thy knotted and combined locks to part</line>
<line>And each particular hair to stand on end,</line>
<line>Like quills upon the fretful porpentine:</line>
<line>But this eternal blazon must not be</line>
<line>To ears of flesh and blood. List, list, O, list!</line>
<line>If thou didst ever thy dear father love--</line>
</dialog>
<dialog speaker="hamlet" style="volume: loud; ">
```

LISTING 25.2   CONTINUED

```
<line>O God!</line>
</dialog>
<dialog speaker="ghost">
<line>Revenge his foul and most unnatural murder.</line>
</dialog>
<dialog speaker="hamlet" style="azumith: center; volume:x-loud; ">
<line>Murder!</line>
</dialog>
<dialog speaker="ghost" style="azumith: right; ">
<line>Murder most foul, as in the best it is;</line>
<line>But this most foul, strange and unnatural.</line>
</dialog>
<dialog speaker="hamlet" style="azumith: far-right; volume: medium; ">
<line>Haste me to know't, that I, with wings as swift</line>
<line>As meditation or the thoughts of love,</line>
<line>May sweep to my revenge.</line>
</dialog>
```

In this snippet of dialog, the voice of the ghost is placed in its traditional location below the level of the stage and they move about individually, Hamlet pacing from one side of the stage to the other while the ghost moves away, again traditional blocking. Hamlet also raises his voice when he gets excited.

Existing software for voice synthesis includes JAWS from Henter-Joyce at `http://www.hj.com/`, recently upgraded to provide better Web accessibility, as well as pwWebSpeak from Productivity Works at `http://www.prodworks.com/`.

Tip from

LeeAnne.com
Words to weave by

pwWebSpeak has received very good reviews in the low vision/blind community. Productivity Works also has *existing* products for non-traditional Web browsing, including pwTelephoneSpeak, a browser designed for use over the telephone. See `http://www.prodworks.com` for more information.

VOICE EDITING FOR AURAL RENDERING

Fine tuning of XML style sheets can be done by varying the allowable parameters within CSS2 and XSL themselves, or by building on a base voice already present within the aural package, if you know that voice will be available. So you could select Shelly, a *JAWS* character, with a default female value if Shelly weren't present in the aural engine. Because Shelly's voice might not be perfect for Ophelia, you can set her normal speaking pitch to slightly higher than average and her animation level to very high, so the range of pitches she uses is fairly large:

```
dialog[speaker="ophelia"] { voice-family: shelly, female; pitch: 230hz; pitch-range: 80; }
```

Almost every voice synthesis package allows you to vary voice parameters. *JAWS*, for example, comes with a small selection of characters, Reed, Shelly, Rocko, Bobby, Glen, Sandy, Grandma, and Grandpa. You can set rate and pitch, although no other parameters are available other than a generic pitch level change for capitalized letters, those typed with Shift or Caps Lock on. Shelly, Sandy, and Grandma are female voices and the rest are male, a typical weighting by gender. You can also set the pronunciation rules used, so if you're reading Spanish, the pronunciation will sound closer to what a native speaker would use. You even have a choice of American or British English.

From the keyboard, you can set *JAWS* to handle different events with different voices, so system messages, for example, sound different from the global setting used to read text. In use, the product is easy to use and intuitive for the most part. To read a line, move your cursor to any point on the line using up- or down-arrow keys. To spell out words, move your cursor with the left- or right-arrow keys.

HANDLING MULTIPLE TARGET MEDIA

At the present time, there are few reliable mechanisms for providing variable style sheets for different media. Until XML browsers that support media types become available, you'll have to depend on hard-coded media, such as the aural style sheet examples discussed previously, on user style sheets, and on the ingenuity of users to handle multiple media.

In the next section, you'll learn the steps involved in actually creating an accessible document.

MAKING AN XML DOCUMENT ACCESSIBLE

For this case study, you'll design a page that will be accessible using multiple browsers, provide good navigation clues for everyone, including persons with vision disabilities, and provide alternative content and navigation even for persons with text-only browsers, such as Lynx, which don't support frames. You'll use plain XHTML for widest compatibility with existing browsers, although the document could be created on-the-fly from an XML template using XSLT. To verify that your site is accessible, you'll use the Bobby validation suite, a widely available tool designed to identify potential problems that low-vision and blind users might face in using a site.

The following Web site is available at `http://www.igc.apc.org/women/bookstores/` `feminist-frames.html` and is used as the content for the all-browser XHTML document.

A WOMAN'S BOOKSTORE IN AFRICA

Listing 25.3 represents a real XHTML page designed to be accessible to multiple browsers although it uses frames, ordinarily difficult for many aural browsers to handle. It achieves this by using the `noframes` tag to identify content to be rendered by non-frames-capable browsers.

LISTING 25.3   THE BOOKSTORE INDEX TEXT

```
Feminist Bookstores Index
    SUB-SAHARAN AFRICA
    (Including Madagascar)
    Countries Indexed:
        Kenya
    Kenya
    Country Telephone Code 254
    Nairobi, Nairobi Province, Kenya
        Binti Legacy
        (Feminist Bookstore)
        Loita House
        Loita Street
        Nairobi
        Kenya
        +254.2.33.0854 FAX
        +254.2.33.0854
    Contact for Binti Legacy in the USA:
        Dan Hoffman
        597 San Luis Road
        Berkeley, CA  94707
        USA
        +1.510.527.7651 FAX
        +1.510.528.9900
    African Feminist Publishers
        (None Known)
```

This little tidbit is taken from a real example on the Web that includes many more bookstores; I used this one because it's the shortest list. When I created the list, I used an aggressively Lynx-compatible format, which isn't as pretty as it could be because it was completely graphics and formatting free. At the same time, I didn't want to add too many bells and whistles because the purpose of the page is purely informational. So I compromised. But this is a new age of Web development and I thought the site needed a little more "pizzazz" so I wanted to modernize.

To update the format, I used frames, which aren't really that difficult to handle correctly, and to spice up the presentation a little I used JavaScript to create a navigation bar that highlighted whatever the mouse was pointing to. This seemed cool enough for a simple page but it immediately raised several issues that couldn't easily be avoided. The first was what to do about browsers that didn't support frames.

HANDLING FRAMES IN NON-FRAMES BROWSERS

That one was easy. When Netscape created the frame tags, they designed them so they would be backward-compatible with other browsers. Because the `<frame>` and `<frameset>` tags include no inline content, they are ignored by browsers that don't understand them. And, browsers that do support frames ignore any inline content surrounded by a `<noframes>` tag pair. So all you have to do is include the non-framed version of the page in a `<noframes>` container.

The other issue was what to do with Microsoft Internet Explorer. For a variety of reasons, Microsoft didn't track the development of JavaScript very well and didn't handle the more advanced features of JavaScript in early versions of their browser. I could introduce complex scripts to handle everything in one document but that quickly becomes a maintenance nightmare. Any time you put in code to handle bugs, you have the problem of whether to track bugs as they develop, a logistic hassle because your development cycle is now being driven by the whims of another company, or to fix one bug and ignore any future bugs, another less than satisfactory solution.

What I chose to do, because Microsoft was the browser with the problem, was to split off the Microsoft bug handling and put it into navigation pages designed just for Microsoft. That way, if I felt like it, I could track their bugs or ignore them safely.

So all I need is a tiny little piece of JavaScript to switch Microsoft browsers into their version of the framed navigation system and, for completeness, to switch every other browser out of the Microsoft versions if they happen to stumble in for any reason. Here's the fragment to detect Microsoft browsers. It works by scanning the name of the browser for the word "Microsoft" and, if it finds it, switching to the Microsoft version:

```
<?xml version="1.0"?>
<!DOCTYPE html PUBLIC "-//W3C//DTD XHTML 1.0 Transitional//EN"
    "http://www.w3.org/TR/xhtml1/DTD/transitional.dtd">
<html
 xmlns="http://www.w3.org/TR/xhtml1">
  <head>
    <script language="JavaScript">
      <!--
        var browser = navigator.appName;
        if (browser.indexOf ("Microsoft") != -1)
          location = "feminist-frames-msie.html";
      // -->
    </script>
```

...

The corresponding fragment to switch to the standard version also looks for the word "Microsoft" but switches only if the word is not found. This sounds complex but it works for most browsers. Those browsers that don't support JavaScript will ignore the switch, but these browsers won't see any difference between the two versions anyway, because the only variations are in how the JavaScript works:

```
<?xml version="1.0"?>
<!DOCTYPE html PUBLIC "-//W3C//DTD XHTML 1.0 Transitional//EN"
    "http://www.w3.org/TR/xhtml1/DTD/transitional.dtd">
<html
 xmlns="http://www.w3.org/TR/xhtml1">
  <head>
    <script language="JavaScript">
      <!--
        var browser = navigator.appName;
        if (browser.indexOf ("Microsoft") == -1)
          location = "feminist-frames-msie.html";
      // -->
    </script>
```

PART
IV
CH
25

DEFINING HOW THE PAGE WILL LOOK

Now we're ready to start the real work, defining how the page will look. First, I coded the basic Africa page. I always start with the simplest things first so I know they work and then start adding tags and functionality. I kept the Bobby guidelines (`http://www.cast.org/`) in mind while I was coding and validated it several times while I was working just to make sure I didn't forget anything.

Because many visually impaired users will see the information page by itself, using my alternative navigation system, I wanted to be particularly sure that it was accessible. When I was finished and had passed the Bobby tests I inserted the code fragment they make available to signal compliance with their guidelines and patted myself on the back. The first task was done!

Note

> It wouldn't hurt to remind yourself of what good accessible design practices are. There is a list at `http://www.w3.org/WAI/` that has a capsule summary as well as a lot of other information. The basics are really obvious when you think about them but some things are more subtle. As a start, you should use no more than one link per line, descriptive `alt` attributes on all images or an explicit null description, good contrast between text and background, no patterned or textured backgrounds, and alternative means of accessing visual navigation elements.
>
> There's a lot more useful information on the site, so do visit before you spend a lot of time on design. Many favorite tricks of some designers are either forbidden or not recommended so it pays to study the issue before plowing ahead with a big project. On the other hand, sometimes you must use features that cause problems. In that case you need to provide alternative pages.

After the information page was in the bag, I started on the surrounding frames, working from the base page to the navigation pages, so the whole process was sort of inside out and then outside in.

I decided to make the navigation bar run down the left hand margin, a popular choice, and then put in a little secondary navigation bar along the bottom of the page for the heck of it. Both navigation bars live in their own little frames and the rest of the browser screen is devoted to the information.

Frames and JavaScript have already been covered, so I'll just show fragments here. The entire site is visible on the Web at `http://www.igc.apc.org/women/bookstores/feminist-frames.html` if you want to explore the code further. Parts of the graphics files and code for this book are also available on my Web site: `http://www.leeanne.com/practical/`.

Listing 25.4 shows the first portion of the main entry to the framed site at

LISTING 23.4   THE BOOKSTORE INDEX XHTML ENTRY PAGE

```
<?xml version="1.0"?>
<!DOCTYPE html PUBLIC "-//W3C//DTD XHTML 1.0 Transitional//EN"
    "http://www.w3.org/TR/xhtml1/DTD/transitional.dtd">
```

```
<html
 xmlns="http://www.w3.org/1999/xhtml">

<frameset
    cols="100,*"
    frameborder="0"
    framespacing="0"
    border="0">
  <frame
   src="bookmenu.html"
   marginheight="0"
   marginwidth="0"
   noresize="noresize"
   name="MenuBar"
   noresize="noresize"
   scrolling="no" />
  <frameset
   rows="*,20"
   frameborder="0"
   framespacing="0"
   border="0">
   <frame
    src="bookmain.html"
    marginheight="0"
    marginwidth="0"
    noresize="noresize"
    name="MainWindow"
    noresize="noresize" />
   <frameset
    frameborder="0"
    framespacing="0"
    border="0">
    <frame
     src="booknavigate.html"
     marginheight="0"
     marginwidth="0"
     noresize="noresize"
     name="Navbar2"
     scrolling="no" />
   </frameset>
  </frameset>
  <noframes>
    <body
     bgcolor="FFFFFF">
     <!--Begin Index-->

     <p>
       <br />
     </p>
     <blockquote>
       <a href="#Index"><img src="fembooks.gif" height="124"
        width="354" align="left"
        alt="Feminist Bookstore Index Menu" border="0" /></a>
     </blockquote>
     <h1 align="center">Feminist Bookstores Index</h1>
     <p>
       <br clear="clear" />
```

LISTING 23.4   CONTINUED

```
        </p>
        <p align="right">
          <a href="widehtml.html" target="_top"><img src="textonly.gif"
          height="25" width="80" align="right" border="0" hspace="10"
          vspace="0" alt="Text Only Version" /></a><a
          href="feminist-text.html" target="_top">Text Only Version</a>
        </p>
        <p align="right">
          <a href="feminist-frames.html" target="_top"><img
          src="frames.gif" height="25" width="80" align="right"
          border="0" hspace="10" vspace="0"
          alt="Frames Version" /></a><a href="feminist-noframes.html"
          target="_top">Frames Version</a>
        <a name="Top"></a>
        </p>
        <blockquote>
          <h2>Welcome! </h2>
        </blockquote>
        <blockquote>
          <p>
            You've reached this page from a browser without frames
            support. That's fine with me. All the information on
            this site is accessible to all browsers that I'm aware
            of, including text browsers like Lynx and as accessible
            for the vision-impaired as possible.
          </p>
```

   ...

The code can stop here, although the page itself continues at some length, because there's little more to be learned by the data actually contained on the page.

The navigation pages for browsers that either properly support JavaScript (or properly ignore it) look like Listing 25.5.

LISTING 25.5   THE NAVIGATION PAGE FOR THE BOOKSTORE SITE

```
<?xml version="1.0"?>
<!DOCTYPE html PUBLIC "-//W3C//DTD XHTML 1.0 Transitional//EN"
    "http://www.w3.org/TR/xhtml1/DTD/transitional.dtd">
<html
 xmlns="http://www.w3.org/1999/xhtml">
  <head>
<script
 language="JavaScript"
 type="text/javascript">
<!--
var browser = navigator.appName;
if (browser.indexOf ("Microsoft") != -1)
        location = "feminist-frames-msie.html";
// -->
</script>
<script
 language="JavaScript"
 type="text/javascript">
```

```
<!--
var image1 = new Image(88,86);
var image2 = new Image(88,30);
var image3 = new Image(88,30);
var image4 = new Image(88,30);
var image5 = new Image(88,30);
var image6 = new Image(88,30);
var image7 = new Image(88,30);
var image8 = new Image(88,30);
var image9 = new Image(88,30);
var image10 = new Image(88,30);
function init() {
   image1.src = "menu-logohigh.gif";
   image2.src = "menu-africahigh.gif";
   image3.src = "menu-asiahigh.gif";
   image4.src = "menu-austrnzhigh.gif";
   image5.src = "menu-canadahigh.gif";
   image6.src = "menu-europehigh.gif";
   image7.src = "menu-mideasthigh.gif";
   image8.src = "menu-samericahigh.gif";
   image9.src = "menu-usahigh.gif";
   image10.src = "menu-linkshigh.gif";
   }
init();
function highlight(image) {
   document[image].src = image + "high.gif";
   }
function unhighlight(image) {
   document[image].src = image + "low.gif";
   }
// -->
</script>
    <title></title>
  </head>
  <body bgcolor="#00ffff">
    <a href="bookmain.html" target="MainWindow"
       onmouseover="highlight('menu-logo'); self.status='Feminist \
       Bookstores Index Worldwide Home'; return true;"
       onmouseout="unhighlight('menu-logo'); self.status=''; return
       true;"><img name="menu-logo" src="menu-logolow.gif" hspace="0"
       vspace="0" width="88" height="86" border="0"
       alt="Feminist Bookstores Index Worldwide Home" /></a><a
       href="africa.html" target="MainWindow"
       onmouseover="highlight('menu-africa');
       self.status='Sub-Saharan Africa - Feminist Bookstores';
       return true;"
       onmouseout="unhighlight('menu-africa'); self.status='';
       return true;"><img name="menu-africa" src="menu-africalow.gif"
       hspace="0" vspace="0" width="88" height="30" border="0"
       alt="Africa - Feminist Bookstores" /></a><a
       ...
```

PART

IV

CH

25

I won't show the whole navigation bar, and the second bar at the bottom of the screen is pretty much the same, so if you're curious, you can look at the site on the Web to see the whole megillah in action.

At every step, I tested each page using the Bobby validation tool. The entire site has to pass the tests to display the logo so it's important to test each page, not just the main pages.

The end result is shown in Figure 25.2

Figure 25.2
The Framed Women's
Bookstore Site shows
the Africa page.

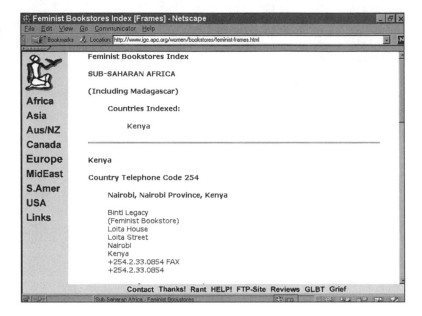

On the entry page, the visitor has the option of going to a non-framed or text-only version of the site. Figure 25.3 shows the framed version of the site with links to non-framed and text-only versions. For the most part, all these versions use the same files or are created by automatically modifying a base file. There are only a few files which handle the various versions and these files rarely change.

Figure 25.3
The Framed Women's
Bookstore Site.

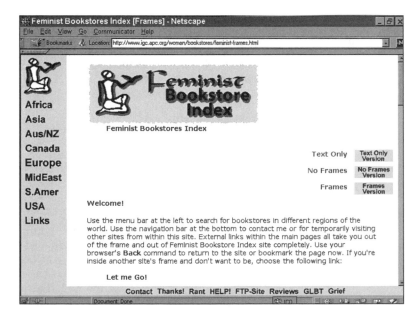

Finally, I'm going to show you a screen shot of the Bobby logo in Figure 25.4 so you can see what you'll receive as the reward for all your hard work, besides the satisfaction of doing the right thing.

Figure 25.4
The Bobby logo on the Women's Bookstore Site.

That's it! Accessibility in a nutshell. Although the example shown is in XHTML, since the available tools for automatically testing accessibility are all HTML/XHTML-based, the same techniques can be used to implement accessible pages in any XML vocabulary.

Accessibility is both easy and difficult to handle. There are resources on the Web, such as the Bobby site mentioned in the Women's Bookstore site example, to automate the process for HTML and XHTML pages. XML is more problematic, but the totality or a representative sample of the site can be converted to HTML using XSLT and that in turn can be validated using Bobby or other tools listed on the W3C Web Accessibility Initiative Web site at `http://www.w3.org/WAI/`.

Many authoring tools encourage accessibility, and some are quite insistent. If you follow the hints and suggestions provided by such tools you can hardly go wrong. Among HTML tools, HoTMetaL is perhaps most notable for its devotion both to ensuring accessibility and in making the authoring tool itself accessible. The co-founder of SoftQuad Inc., Yuri Rubinsky, whose Yuri Rubinsky Insight Foundation at `http://128.100.250.10/yuri/` is active in disability issues to this day, was devoted to ensuring that the products produced by his company were accessible to all.

PART
IV
CH
25

TROUBLESHOOTING ACCESSIBILITY PROBLEMS

HANDLING COMPLAINTS BY DISABLED USERS

Unless you're very careful in your testing, your site may attract a complaint from a disabled user who feels, quite justly, aggrieved and doesn't hesitate to let you know it.

Pay close attention. If there is anything you don't understand, reply with a polite question showing willingness to learn. Disabled individuals have a lot more experience dealing with their disability than you have. Quite often, they are rich sources of information on how to easily and inexpensively deal with the issue they raise. Also consider that they've done you a tremendous favor. Many of your potential customers, perhaps hundreds, may have clicked on through rather than take the time to pen a note. Or perhaps they couldn't find anyone to send the note to. Make sure you have clearly labeled contact information on your splash page.

Note

> A splash page is the home page of a site, the first page someone sees that establishes the identity and overall look of a site. Of course, you know by now that using a vestibule page with redirection to display a glitzy entry page, or worse a series of such entry pages, is a stunning waste of time and resources.

Although all sites should maintain a webmaster@{sitename} email identity to simplify life for persons with visual disabilities who may need assistance, it's surprising how many sites make it difficult to contact a human being. Some use forms located on a page which may itself be inaccessible, which is, quite frankly, unconscionable.

HANDLING CUSTOMER DEMANDS FOR INACCESSIBLE CONTENT

Your customer decides that she wants every page to have all-singing, all-dancing Shockwave navigation elements, a black background with dark grey text, because it looks "arty," and other features you know will cause trouble for disabled users.

First, try reasoning with the customer. Point out some of the potential problems with the proposed feature set and the cost of maintaining alternative navigation for every page. If that doesn't work, consider having her sign a release from liability on your behalf and leaving your name as designer off the page in favor of blessed anonymity. These things get around and when the customer is sued, you don't want to be around to take the blame.

→ For more information about displaying content for low-vision users, **see** "Low Vision Display Techniques," **p. 624**.

CHAPTER 26

INDUSTRY COOPERATION AND RESOURCES

In this chapter

MOVING TOWARD XML IN COMMERCIAL APPLICATIONS

The prospects for widespread acceptance of XML DTDs and Schemas as a common language of exchange are both very good and very bad, depending on who you are as a potential user of the new XML standards. The most successful DTDs have been related to vendor/purchaser channels in which the XML schema is enforced by the party with the most economic power. In the case of the U.S. Government, it had no trouble getting CALS accepted whatsoever; the government simply told vendors that if they didn't submit bids using this standard they wouldn't be considered. Likewise, almost any major purchaser can impose data interchange formats on its suppliers. And the suppliers are fairly happy to accept these formats because there's a pile of money to be made on the other end when serving very large customers who place very large orders.

The opposite situation exists when large suppliers sell to many small customers. There, the economic power is weighted on the side of the vendor, so every buyer has to learn the unique cataloging, ordering, and billing procedures of each supplier the buyer uses. The customer has all the burden of complying with vendor requirements but little power to enforce change. The vendor has little or no desire to align its procedures with other vendors because it would make it easier for a customer to change suppliers. So, a bookstore which orders from a major book wholesaler such as Ingram is perforce required to use Ingram's ordering system. And if you want to order a pair of trousers from Land's End, you'll have little luck unless you use their system.

But on the other hand, where industry trade groups exist, a group of otherwise small companies can band together and create a schema designed to facilitate commerce between members of the group as well as vendors. With enough purchasing power to affect even large vendors, a cooperative relationship based on common standards can result.

In many industries, trading information is a requirement of doing business. Healthcare, insurance, banking, credit reporting agencies, auto wreckers, financial markets, and even the IRS have built-in incentives to facilitate communication, so it comes as no surprise that there are already XML standards or study groups in most of these fields. In fact, the greatest barrier to the new XML technology in some of these industries is that the communications problems they face were solved once already using old non-XML technology; everyone bought into the solution, and now no one wants to rock the boat to move to a better alternative. If it ain't broke, don't fix it is a guiding principle for many corporate and institutional executives, and unless they can see clear benefits from moving to a new format, they're unwilling to spend the money and effort required to move forward from the status quo.

However, at the retail level, in which physical store front owners vie for every customer nickel, there's no such incentive. In fact there's a positive disincentive. Even on the Web, where prices have to be available if a company expects to sell anything, posting prices in a manner which invites comparison by an automated search agent rather than by a consumer already on the advertising page and ready to buy might give the hardiest retailer pause. Although universal deep discounts may be used to draw people to a site initially, the discount angle has quietly faded away from many sites, which now stress convenience and lack of sales tax rather than low price.

Asking a company to post prices in an easily accessible format on the Web invites robotic comparison shopping, which most bricks and mortar companies prefer their customers to never, ever do. The only company that can possibly benefit from price comparisons is the one with the lowest price. Everyone else must meet that price or try to persuade customers that the premium is worth it. That sort of thing quickly sets off a downward spiral which companies fight hard to prevent with advertising that stresses the value of intangibles—convenience, reliability—or extraneous reasons that justify spending $50,000 on an automobile when a $500 bicycle might do.

Note

The only way to see the price on most retail sites is to read the ads since they're not identified with XML tags. At least one major online retailer started off guaranteeing lowest prices but quietly backed off this claim for large numbers of their non-best-seller titles, leaving the distinct but false impression that one is getting the best price on their site. In fact, they quite often have the highest prices on the Web and now stress how convenient everything is and the advantages of a huge inventory rather than how inexpensive things are. Making this information easily accessible to robots might well kill them, since everyone with a suitable robot would buy only the loss leaders and ignore the non-bargains.

So, don't hold your breath waiting for every company to start posting prices. The early adopters may be discount firms who honestly try to deliver the best price and make up for slim profit margins by high volume. However, there will always be those companies whose panache depends on saying to the customer, figuratively at least, "If you need to know how much it costs, you can't afford it."

A common model for Web sites is to first present a selling page, which gives you many reasons to buy the product, whatever it is, and then presents a link to an order page, on which you finally learn the price.

PART
IV
CH
26

Looking at Successful DTDs

The following section describes one of the first successful DTDs, which provided a huge impetus for SGML development and thus ultimately set the stage for XML. The sections immediately after describe other approaches to the same problem space, cooperatively authoring and publishing large and complex documents which look very much like books.

The CALS DTD

One of the first DTDs was a series of SGML standards promulgated by the U.S. Department of Defense and named with typical military efficiency, CALS, the Continuous Acquisition and Life-cycle Support system, Military Standard (MIL-STD) 196 et al. CALS is designed to inter-operate with other DOD standards, including FLIS, the Federal Logistics Information System containing type designation data for over a million items of military hardware and spare parts for both the U.S. Armed Forces and many NATO members, and National Stock Numbers (NSN), which is a sort of Uniform Product Code for military parts and supplies.

There are a host of other military SGML standards, which the Pentagon is able to demand that its suppliers comply with, that govern the procurement of everything from canned soup to battleships.

> **Note**
>
> As an example of the complexity of these systems, FLIS alone contains the National Stock Number (NSN), standard item name, approved manufacturers, manufacturers' part numbers, interchangeable and substitutable items, freight and shipping data, hazardous materiel indicators, ecological and environmental characteristics, energy efficiency, material characteristics codes, management data, and physical and performance characteristics.

CALS was initiated in 1984 and designed to help the military cope with the enormous piles of paperwork demanded by mission-critical and life-critical systems, which in the military tend to be one and the same. Since then it's grown to include many related standards, including the Joint Computer-aided Acquisition and Logistics Support (JCALS) system as the information infrastructure, work flow manager, and global data manager. JCALS is integrated with the Joint Engineering Data Management Information and Control System (JEDMICS) to store digital data and several government owned applications, such as the Configuration Management Information System (CMIS) and Multi-user Engineering Change Proposal Automated Review System (MEARS). The glue that binds all these processes together is a set of SGML DTDs that enable seamless data transfer between systems.

Because the military has purchasing and support requirements that cover decades rather than years, a key element in the success of CALS has been the robust tool set provided by SGML and the CALS DTDs. Because the DTD is intended to cover all the purchasing and supply requirements of the entire Department of Defense, the CALS-related DTDs are huge and numerous. They help maintain our military procurement systems today and are likely to continue in this role for many years. At least some CALS-related DTDs are being converted to XML, to enable the military to take advantage of the new standards and tools becoming available thereby lowering their costs of procurement. A Navy site which has a lot of information, including Navy CALS DTDs, is located at `http://navycals.dt.navy.mil/cals.html`.

Figure 26.1 shows a Navy CALS DTD being used to edit an operating manual for the Beatles' Yellow Submarine in XMetaL 1.0, surely an appropriate use for ths DTD. The text of course, is Top Secret and is grayed out.

You'll notice a great deal of similarity between this DTD, which is designed for naval manuals, ISO-12083, Doc-Book, and other book-like document DTDs. This makes sense because the SGML community has had a great deal of influence on XML; similar problem spaces often yield similar schemas.

Figure 26.1
XMetaL 1.0 editing an operating manual for the Yellow Submarine.

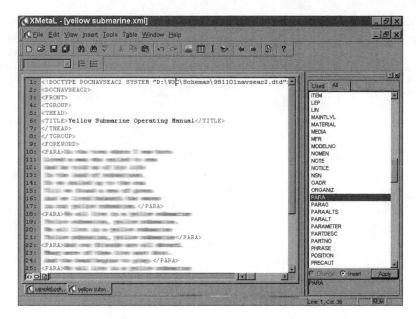

ISO-12083—A PRIVATE PUBLIC DTD

This standard illustrates one of the problems with private, or even semi-public, development of DTDs. Although widely supported in the publishing industry, this DTD describing books and periodicals is not available without paying ISO for the privilege of reading it. This limits free debate and makes evaluations more difficult, because the only people qualified to talk about it are the people who have access to the standard. If you don't work for a company with an existing interest in ISO-12083, it can be difficult to persuade the powers that be to part with the cash required just to look it over.

Some draft versions of XML recreations of the ISO-12083 standards are publicly available at http://www.xmlxperts.com/12083xml.htm, but the full existing SGML spec is available only from the International Standards Organization (ISO) at http://www.iso.ch/.

Figure 26.2 shows a small part of the payload of the ISO-12083 Book DTD translated into XML as a working draft. Because the same basic elements are needed as were needed in the Navy manual DTD, the same general sorts of data structures apply: author, title, chapters, paragraphs, and so on. You can see the XML draft of all three ISO-12083 standards at the XMLXperts site, http://www.xmlxperts.com/12083xml.htm.

PART
IV

CH
26

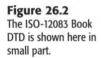

Figure 26.2
The ISO-12083 Book DTD is shown here in small part.

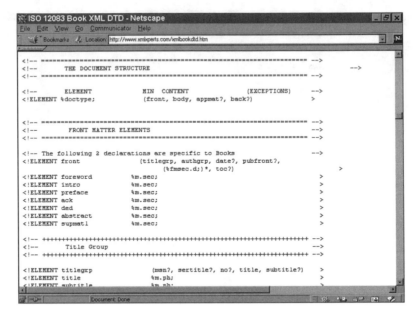

TEI—TEXT ENCODING INITIATIVE FOR SCHOLARS

Another approach was taken by the people in charge of the Text Encoding Initiative. TEI developed out of the desire to have basic texts available in a form useful to scholarly research without having to reinvent the wheel every time some new area of inquiry was opened. In 1987, the Association for Computers and the Humanities convened the Poughkeepsie Planning Conference to explore the possibility of creating a universal encoding scheme for marking up electronic texts to provide free interchange and use in the educational and research environments. TEI is now under the control of a consortium of scholarly organizations and has a home at Oxford University.

The Text Encoding Initiative home page is at `http://www.hcu.ox.ac.uk/TEI/` and I won't bore you with details. If you need to see the DTDs, you should look to the source, which provides guidance in using TEI in both its SGML and XML forms, as well as shows you how to construct a "pizza" of modular DTD portions to construct a custom DTD.

DOCBOOK—DOCUMENTATION MADE PORTABLE

DocBook is another variation on the book DTD theme lately maintained by OASIS at `http://www.oasis-open.org/docbook/` but originally created in 1991 by HaL Computer Systems and O'Reilly & Associates. DocBook has fairly wide support among authors and publishers and is directly supported by some SGML authoring environments. Of course, this may have something to do with its being available, because so many DTDs are locked away behind copyrights and standards bodies who fund their activities by selling the results of their labor. Because I too, make my living at writing, I sympathize with this desire. But in the case of standards bodies it sometimes means that people are tempted to reinvent wheels just to avoid dependence on them. Updating a manual set can be a significant expense for a small company, and in the case of a large company with many users—all of whom want their own manuals—it can be significant even to a large company.

> **Note**
>
> OASIS, the Organization for the Advancement of Structured Information Standards, has emerged as a major repository of XML standards, and promotes XML and other industry standards through programs of education and cooperation. OASIS also hosts `XML.org`.

MARC 21—MACHINE READABLE CATALOGING

The Library of Congress delivers catalog and name authority content to thousands of local libraries, so they have a data transfer standard, MARC 21, which they cosponsor along with the British Library, the National Library of Canada, the International Federation of Library Associations (IFLA), and others. Although MARC is neither XML nor SGML, the tagging mechanism used in MARC is easily transmutable to both SGML and XML so it should be mentioned here at least as a prominent EDI format related to publishing and books. A simple XML conversion already exists, MARCXML, from Logos Research Systems at `http://www.logos.com/marc/`.

This concludes the in-depth look at XML-related publishing standards. In the next section, you look at other industry consortiums in brief, explaining generally what sort of communication is facilitated by the standards disseminated by each organization.

OTHER XML-RELATED INDUSTRY GROUPS

The above sections don't exhaust the industries similarly cooperating toward improving communication between diverse environments and operating systems. The following list briefly describes many more:

PART
IV
CH
26

- **Acord** at `http://www.acord.org/`—An insurance industry group promoting common XML interchange formats between insurers. Insurers talk to each other a lot because that's one of the ways they control fraud. It wouldn't do if you could insure your car with a dozen companies and then collect from all of them when it's mysteriously smashed flat by a steam roller.

- **Astronomical Markup Language (AML)** at `http://pioneer.gsfc.nasa.gov/public/xml/` and `http://monet.astro.uiuc.edu/~dguillau/these/`—A markup language that encourages sharing of astronomical data between observatories worldwide. Because any given observatory can only see part of the sky, observatories and research astronomers have to cooperate to ensure a complete picture of the universe.

- **Astronomical Instrument Markup Language (AIML)** at `http://pioneer.gsfc.nasa.gov/public/aiml/` and `http://monet.astro.uiuc.edu/~dguillau/these/`—An astronomical instrument markup language.

- **The Australia New Zealand Land Information Council (ANZLIC) Metadataat** `http://www.erin.gov.au/database/metadata/anzmeta/`—A Mapping/GIS (Geographic Information System) metadata language from down under.

- **Bank Internet Payment System (BIPS) at** `http://www.fstc.org/projects/bips/`— Yet another e-payment and funds transfer system aimed at the banking market.

- **Bioinformatic Sequence Markup Language (BSML) at http://www.visualgenomics. com/**—A "bioinformatics" proprietary markup language. Bioinformatics refers to data collected and disseminated for the purpose of genome research and reporting. It allows easy markup of DNA sequencing information, among other things.

- **Bio.Perl at** `http://bio.perl.org/Projects/XML/`—A site developing tools to translate biological markup languages, such as BSML and BIOML, from one form to another.

- **The BIOpolymer Markup Language (BIOML)at** `http://www.proteometrics. com/BIOML/`—Yet another markup language for the life sciences.

- **Centre de recherche en droit public (CRDP)at** `http://www.droit.umontreal.ca/ crdp/en/equipes/technologie/index.html`—A Canadian legal database in SGML.

- **Chemical Markup Language (CML) at** `http://www.xml-cml.org/`—Home page for CML.

- **Coins: Tightly Coupled JavaBeans and XML Elements at** `http://www.jxml.com/ coins/index.html`—A JavaXML vendor's site.

- **Cold Fusion Modeling Language (CFML) at** `http://www.allaire.com/developer/ index.cfm`—Cold Fusion markup language. See the link.

- **CommerceNet Home Page at** `http://www.commerce.net/`—Industry e-commerce standards consortium.

- **Component Information Dictionary Specification (CIDS) at** `http://www.si2.org/ ecix/cids/index.html`—An electronic component standard developed by the Electronic Component Information Exchange (ECIX).

- **The Corpus Legis Project at** `http://www.juridicum.su.se/iri/corpus/`—A Swedish legal database.

- **Customer Support Consortium at** `http://www.customersupport.org/`—An XML standards body for customer support organizations.

- **cXML, Commerce XML at** `http://www.cxml.org/home/`—An E-commerce DTD.

- **Data Documentation Initiative at** `http://www.icpsr.umich.edu/DDI/`—An XML DTD for data documentation.

- **DDML/XSchema at** `http://simonstl.com/xschema`—An XML Schema alternative or evolutionary step claiming to be far better than XML Schema.

- **Digital Receipt Infrastructure Initiative at** `http://www.receipt.org/`—Home page for the Digital Receipt Consortium, an e-commerce standards organization made up of vendors and financial institutions.

- **DISA, Data Interchange Standards Association at** `http://www.disa.org/`— An e-commerce standards site.

- **DMTF Common Information Model (CIM)** at `http://www.dmtf.org/spec/index.html`—The Distributed Management Task Force standards page describes CIM, WBEM, DMI, and customer support XML standards.

- **DTMF Desktop Management Interface (DMI)** at `http://www.dmtf.org/spec/index.html`—The Distributed Management Task Force standards page describes CIM, WBEM, DMI, and customer support XML standards.

- **DMTF Web-Based Enterprise Management (WBEM)** at `http://www.dmtf.org/spec/index.html`—The Distributed Management Task Force standards page describes CIM, WBEM, DMI, and customer support XML standards.

- **ECIX—Electronic Component Information Exchange** at `http://www.si2.org/ecix/`—Home page of the QuickData (QuickData Protocol and Quick Evaluation Data Specifications), PCIS, CIDS, and TDML specifications.

- **Educom Instructional Management Systems Project (IMS) Metadata Specification** at `http://www.imsproject.org/metadata/index.html`—XML educational metadata language.

- **EEMA EDI/EC Work Group: UN-XML** at `http://www.edi-tie.nl/edifact/xml-edi.htm`—European XML Repository proposal to be organized under the auspices of the United Nations.

- **Encoded Archival Description (EAD) Home Page** at `http://www.loc.gov/ead/ead.html`—Home page for a Library of Congress SGML standard related to MARC.

- **EUROMATH Project** at `http://stork.ukc.ac.uk/computer_science/EMT/`— European mathematics editor.

- **European XML/EDI Pilot Project** at `http://www.cenorm.be/isss/workshop/ec/xmledi/isss-xml.html`—Electronic Data Interchange from a European perspective.

- **Exchange Table Model** at `http://www.oasis-open.org/html/publtext.htm`—A subset of the CALS table model for interchange between vendors.

- **Frontier 5 and XML** at `http://frontier.userland.com/stories/storyReader$1124`— Describes the XML tools a publisher is using to manage content creation and storage.

- **GCA, Graphic Communications Association** at `http://www.gca.org/`—Publishers association with a strong interest in standards relating to the printing trade. It is the source of several standards of little interest to anyone except printers and paper manufacturers.

- **GCA, Graphic Communications Association Paper DTD** at `http://www.mulberrytech.com/MT99/mtxmldtd.html`—A GCA DTD for submitted papers.

- **GedML: [GEDCOM] Genealogical Data in XML** at `http://home.iclweb.com/icl2/mhkay/gedml.html`—Genealogical XML DTD.

- **Georgia State University Electronic Court Filing Project** at `http://gsulaw.gsu.edu/gsuecp/`—Court document system from Georgia.

- **Health Level Seven** at `http://www.hl7.org/`—A health services industry group standardizing the transfer of health records between health-services providers.

- **HR-XML Consortium** at `http://www.hr-xml.org/`—XML standards for Human Resources Departments.

- **HTTP Distribution and Replication Protocol (DRP)** at `http://www.w3.org/TR/NOTE-drp`—An HTTP standard under development.

- **IEEESTD V3.0 DTD** at `http://standards.ieee.org/resources/spasystem/dtd/index.html`—The IEEE standard for standards.

- **Information & Content Exchange (ICE)** at `http://www.w3.org/TR/NOTE-ice`—A proposal to W3C for a content syndication protocol. The complete ICE DTD is a part of the submission.

- **Interactive Financial Exchange (IFX)** at `http://www.IFXForum.org/`—XML financial data and processing information standard. Subsumes the older Open Financial Exchange (OFX/OFE) standard.

- **JSML, Java Speech Markup Language** at `http://java.sun.com/products/java-media/speech/`—Although Sun still promotes JSML, the Sable language is supposed to replace it.

- **Meta Content Framework (MCF)** at `http://www.textuality.com/mcf/NOTE-MCF-XML.html`—Netscape's version of RDF.

- **Newspaper Association of America (NAA) - Standard for Classified Advertising Data** at `http://www.naa.org/`—Home page for NAA. See also: `http://www.naa.org/technology/index.html`.

- **Ontology Markup Language** at `http://wave.eecs.wsu.edu/CKRMI/OML.html`—Ontological site with DTDs.

- **Open Content Syndication (OCS)** at `http://alchemy.openjava.org/ocs/`—A Netcenter Channel format.

- **OpenMLS, Real Estate DTD Design** at `http://www.openmls.com/`—Multiple Listing Service markup language for the real estate industry.

- **Open Software Description Format (OSD)** at `http://www.marimba.com/products/whitepapers/osd-wp.html`—Marimba/Microsoft proposal to W3C for describing software.

- **Open Trading Protocol (OTP)** at `http://www.otp.org/`—Home page for the OTP Consortium, a group of vendors and financial institutions trying to standardize methods of trading and electronic payment.

- **OpenTag** at `http://www.opentag.org/`—A common mark-up format to encode text extracted from documents of varying formats.

- **Platform for Internet Content Selection (PICS)** at `http://www.w3.org/PICS/`—A metadata standard created to enable parents to control which sites are available over the Internet to their children.

- **Process Interchange Format XML (PIF-XML)** at `http://www.xmls.com/dtd/pif.html`—An XML translation of a Lisp-based standard.

- **Rich Site Summary (RSS)** at `http://my.netscape.com/publish/help/quickstart.html`—Netscape's syndication package.

- **RosettaNet at `http://www.rosettanet.org/`**—E-commerce standards consortium.

- **Sable, Speech Synthesis Markup Language at `http://www.cstr.ed.ac.uk/projects/ssml.html`**—Sable is a speech synthesis markup language and the successor to SSML, JSML, and STML.

- **SAE J2008, Automotive Industry Standard at `http://www.xmlxperts.com/sae.htm`**—An XML standard for the automotive industry. California will require SAE J2008 service records for all new cars sold in the state starting in 2002.

- **Schema.net, The XML Schema Site at `http://www.schema.net/`**—A repository of XML Schemas.

- **SIM SGML Database Technology, Royal Melbourne Institute of Technology (RMIT) at `http://www.mds.rmit.edu.au/sim_2.1/welcome.html`**—Structured Information Manager from Australia.

- **SmartX at `http://www.smartxml.com/`**—Smart card markup language.

- **SSML, Speech Synthesis Markup Language: Sable at `http://www.cstr.ed.ac.uk/projects/ssml.html`**—Sable is a speech synthesis markup language and the successor to SSML, JSML, and STML.

- **TalkML at `http://www.w3.org/Voice/TalkML/`**—An experimental XML language for voice browsers using voice recognition.

- **Telecommunications Interchange Markup (TCIF/IPI) at `http://www.atis.org/atis/tcif/index.htm`**—A telecommunications standards consortium. Look under committees for TCIF activities which include e-commerce.

- **Theological Markup Language (ThML) at `http://www.ccel.org/`**—A theological markup language with special tags for scripture references, Strong's Exhaustive Concordance numbers, and so on.

- **Translation Memory eXchange at `http://www.lisa.org/tmx/index.html`**—A DTD for the exchange of translation memory data between translation tools or vendors with little or no loss of data.

- **UML eXchange Format (UXF) at `http://www.yy.cs.keio.ac.jp/~suzuki/project/uxf/`**—XML exchange format for Unified Modeling Language models.

- **UIML, User Interface Markup Language at `http://uiml.org/`**—A markup language for user interfaces.

- **Virtual Hyperglossary (VHG) at `http://www.vhg.org.uk/`**—A glossary of terms used on the Web from the UK.

- **VoiceXML at `http://www.alphaworks.ibm.com/tech/voicexml`**—Voice recognition language from IBM.

- **Weather Observation Markup Format(OMF) at `http://zowie.metnet.navy.mil/~spawar/JMV-TNG/`**—Home page for meteorological markup language.

- **Web Standards Project (WSP) at `http://www.webstandards.org/`**—User group trying to standardize browsers. They're focused on CSS right now, a noble, if bravely futile, battle in my opinion.

PART

IV

CH

26

- **Web-based Distributed Authoring and Versioning (WEBDAV) at `http://www.ics.uci.edu/pub/ietf/webdav/`**—A DTD designed for collaborative documents which lets authors keep track of who did what and when.

- **Wireless Markup Language (WML) at `http://www.wapforum.org/`**—Markup language for cell phones, PDAs, and pagers.

- **XFDL, Extensible Forms Description language at `http://www.uwi.com/xfdl/`**—A forms description language which enables the signing of the form among other things.

- **XLF (Extensible Log Format) Initiative at `http://www.docuverse.com/xlf/`**—Log format for XML-based servers.

- **XML Court Interface (XCI) at `http://www.nmcourt.fed.us/xci/xcihome.htm`**—XML Court document system from New Mexico.

- **XML/EDI Group at `http://www.geocities.com/WallStreet/Floor/5815/`**—A Geocities page (need we say more?) describing an electronic data interchange standard. The list of endorsers is surprisingly long.

- **XML/EDI Repository at `http://www.xmledi.com/repository/`**—A more believable site from the Geocities XML/EDI Group listed previously. The intent is to foster the development of public domain DTDs and make them freely available on the Web.

- **XMLNews at `http://www.xmlnews.org/`**—XML News DTDs.

- **XML NITF at `http://www.iptc.org/iptc/` and `http://www.nitf.org/`**—The News Industry Text Format DTD.

- **XML-RPC Home Page at `http://www.xmlrpc.com/`**—Remote procedure calls mediated through XML!

- **Simple Object Access Protocol (SOAP) at `http://www.ietf.org/internet-drafts/draft-box-http-soap-01.txt`**—Another Remote Procedure Call language from Dave Winer.

DTD ARCHIVES AND STANDARDS BODIES

The following references represent standards or proposed standards from W3C and a few other standards bodies. By far the greatest number are from W3C since that body is responsible for a large part of the total XML effort, but the International Standards Organization (ISO) and other organizations are also represented.

Note

Although the descriptions listed here are accurate at the time of this writing, Proposed Recommendations and a few of the Working Drafts as well in the following list are very likely to be Recommendations by the time you read this. If this is so, their Web locations will have changed. Please refer to the main W3C site at `http://www.w3.org/` for updated information.

- **Annotated XML Specification** at `http://www.xml.com/axml/axml.html`—The very slick XML 1.0 Recommendation annotated by Tim Bray.

- **APPEL** at `http://www.w3.org/TR/WD-P3P-preferences`—A W3C Working Draft describing one approach to P3P.

- **Associating Style Sheets with XML documents Version 1.0** at `http://www.w3.org/TR/xml-stylesheet`—A W3C Recommendation describing a standard way to associate a style sheet with a document.

- **CSS1, Cascading Style Sheets level 1** at `http://www.w3.org/TR/REC-CSS1`—The revised CSS1 Recommendation from W3C.

- **CSS2, Cascading Style Sheets level 2** at `http://www.w3.org/TR/REC-CSS2`—The CSS2 Recommendation from W3C.

- **Canonical XML** at `http://www.w3.org/TR/xml-c14n`—A W3C Working Draft describing a canonical XML form used to compare XML documents for differences or equivalencies.

- **Common Markup for micropayment per-fee-links** at `http://www.w3.org/TR/WD-Micropayment-Markup/`—A W3C Working Draft.

- **DOM Level 1** at `http://www.w3.org/TR/REC-DOM-Level-1/`—The W3C DOM level 1 Recommendation.

- **DOM Level 2** at `http://www.w3.org/TR/WD-DOM-Level-2/`—The W3C DOM level 2 Working Draft.

- **Extensible Stylesheet Language (XSL) Specification** at `http://www.w3.org/TR/WD-xsl`—The W3C XSL Working Draft.

- **HTML 4.0** at `http://www.w3.org/TR/REC-html40/`—The W3C HTML 4.0 Recommendation.

- **HTML 4.01** at `http://www.w3.org/tr/html40`—The W3C HTML 4.01 Proposed Recommendation, which adds more multimedia options, scripting languages, style sheets, better printing facilities, better accessibility for users with disabilities, and internationalization enhancements.

- **ISO/IEC FCD 13250:1999 - Topic Maps** at `http://www.ornl.gov/sgml/sc34/document/0058.htm/`—An ISO proposed standard describing a method of mapping resources used to define topics.

- **International Layout in CSS** at `http://www.w3.org/TR/WD-i18n-format/`—A W3C Working Draft describing additional internationalization (i18n) requirements for printing some East Asian (Korean, Japanese, Chinese) and bi-directional languages.

- **MathML (Mathematical Markup Language)** at `http://www.w3.org/TR/REC-MathML/`—The W3C Recommendation describing MathML.

- **Namespaces in XML** at `http://www.w3.org/TR/REC-xml-names/`—The W3C Namespaces Recommendation.

- **P3P, Platform for Privacy Preferences** at `http://www.w3.org/tr/wd-p3p`—The W3C Working Draft for P3P.

PART

IV

CH

26

- **PICS Signed Labels at** `http://www.w3.org/TR/REC-DSig-label/`—The Platform for Internet Content Selection Singed Labels Recommendation.

- **Paged Media Properties for CSS3 at** `http://www.w3.org/TR/css3-page`—The W3C Working Draft describing proposed extensions to the CSS standards.

- **RDF Model and Syntax at** `http://www.w3.org/TR/1999/REC-rdf-syntax-19990222/`— The W3C Recommendation for RDF.

- **RDF Schema at** `http://www.w3.org/TR/PR-rdf-schema/`—The W3C Proposed Recommendation for RDF Schmea.

- **RFC-2112, MIME Multipart/Related at** `http://www.faqs.org/rfcs/rfc2112.html`— Internet RFC replacing the older RFC-1872 Multipart MIME document.

- **Ruby at** `http://www.w3.org/TR/WD-ruby/`—The W3C Working Draft describing "ruby" text support as needed in Chinese and other East Asian languages. The term "ruby" actually refers to 5.5 point type and, by extension, any tiny type face. Ruby text is used to indicate pronunciation or other annotations to a base word or phrase, the usage being understood in context.

- **SMIL, Synchronized Multimedia Integration Language at** `http://www.w3.org/TR/REC-smil/`—The W3C SMIL Recommendation.

- **SMIL Boston at** `http://www.w3.org/TR/SMIL-Boston`—The W3C Working Draft describing the next level of SMIL.

- **SVG, Scalable Vector Graphics at** `http://www.w3.org/TR/SVG/`—The W3C SVG Working Draft.

- **SVG Requirements at** `http://www.w3.org/TR/WD-SVGReq`—The W3C SVG Requirements Working Draft.

- **String Identity/Matching at** `http://www.w3.org/TR/WD-charreq`—The W3C Working Draft describing requirements for indexing and comparing strings.

- **Unicode in XML and other Markup Languages at** `http://www.w3.org/TR/unicode-xml`—The W3C Working Draft for using Unicode in XML.

- **User Interface for CSS3 at** `http://www.w3.org/TR/css3-userint`—W3C Working Draft describing the CSS3 user interface.

- **VoiceXML at** `http://www.voicexml.org/`—Yet another speech synthesis markup language.

- **WAI, Web Accessibility Initiative at** `http://www.w3.org/WAI/`—Home page for the WAI at W3C.

- **WAI Authoring Tools Guidelines at** `http://www.w3.org/TR/WAI-AUTOOLS/`—W3C Proposed Recommendation describing authoring tools guidelines for WAI.

- **Web Content Accessibility Guidelines 1.0 at** `http://www.w3.org/TR/WAI-WEBCONTENT/`—The W3C WAI Content Guidelines Recommendation.

- **User Agent Accessibility Guidelines 1.0 at** `http://www.w3.org/TR/WAI-USERAGENT/`— The W3C WAI User Agent Guidelines Working Draft.

- **Web Characterization at** `http://www.w3.org/TR/NOTE-WCA/`—The W3C Activity working on ways to collect statistical data about Web use in HTTP-NG.

- **WebCGM Profile** at `http://www.w3.org/TR/REC-WebCGM`—The W3C Recommendation for WebCGM, Computer Graphics Metafile.

- **XHTML 1.0** at `http://www.w3.org/TR/xhtml1/`—W3C Proposed Recommendation for XHTML 1.0.

- **XML 1.0** at `http://www.w3.org/TR/REC-xml`—The W3C XML 1.0 Recommendation.

- **XML Canonicalization Requirements** at `http://www.w3.org/TR/NOTE-xml-canonical-req`—The W3C Note describing the requirements for XML canonicalization.

- **XML Fragment Interchange** at `http://www.w3.org/TR/WD-xml-fragment`—The W3C XML Working Draft for XML fragment interchange.

- **XML Information Set** at `http://www.w3.org/TR/xml-infoset`—W3C Working Draft describing the information available in an XML document.

- **XML Path Language (XPath) Version 1**.0 at `http://www.w3.org/TR/xpath`—The W3C Proposed Recommendation for XPath.

- **XML Pointer Language (XPointer)** at `http://www.w3.org/TR/WD-xptr`—The W3C XPointer Working Draft.

- **XML Schema Part 1: Structures** at `http://www.w3.org/TR/xmlschema-1/`—The XML Schema structures Working Draft.

- **XML Schema Part 2: Datatypes** at `http://www.w3.org/TR/xmlschema-2`—The XML Schema datatypes Working Draft.

- **XML Signature** at `http://www.w3.org/Signature/`—The W3C XML Signature home page.

- **XLink** at `http://www.w3.org/TR/WD-xlink`—The W3C XLink Working Draft.

- **XML.org** at `http://www.xml.org/`—An industry portal which primarily offers a list of standards bodies actually creating XML standards.

- **XSL, Extensible Stylesheet Language Specification** at]`http://www.w3.org/TR/WD-xsl/`—The W3C XSL Working Draft.

- **XSLT, XSL Transformations Version 1.0** at `http://www.w3.org/TR/xslt`—The W3C XSLT Recommendation.

XML-RELATED SOFTWARE

The following sites offer important resources for XML developers and Web designers. Everything from XML tools to test suites and tutorials is represented and almost all offer unexpected riches to the diligent explorer.

- **Academia Sinica Computing Centre** at `http://www.ascc.net/`—The Academia Sinica Computing Centre Home page. Host to Chinese XML Now!

- **Chinese XML Now! Site** at `http://www.ascc.net/xml/`—The definitive resource for programmers wanting to test or develop Chinese applications in XML. Figure 26.3 shows one of their XML-encoded test files in Microsoft Internet Explorer. There is an excellent step-by-step testing suite here as well that will be useful for any XML developer.

Figure 26.3
This is one of the many excellent test files on the Chinese XML Now! Web site hosted by Academia Sinica Computing Centre.

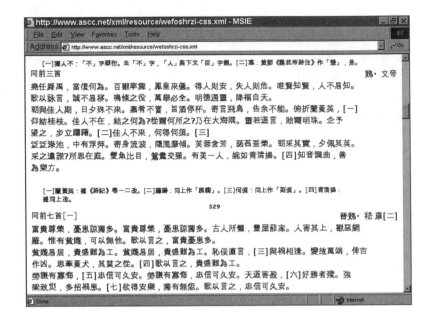

- **developerWORKS, IBM at `http://www.ibm.com/developer/xml/`**—IBM's XML programmer's resource site.

- **GNOME, Gnu Network Object Model Environment at `http://www.gnome.org/`**— The Gnu source for much free XML software including dia, a diagramming tool; go, an editor; gXaio, an XML image album organizer; tim, a Web browser that supports selected XML languages; and more.

- **Free XML software at `http://www.garshol.priv.no/download/xmltools/`**—A collection of XML software by Lars Marius Garshol from Norway.

- **Microsoft Internet Explorer at `http://msdn.microsoft.com/xml/`**—Microsoft's general XML site.

- **Mozilla at `http://www.mozilla.org/rdf/doc/`**—Mozilla.org's plans for RDF and XML.

- **Python at `http://www.python.org/`**—Parsers and more in Python.

- **XMLephant at `http://xmlephant.com/`**—A programmer's resource site. Bills itself as the BIG XML Resource.

- **XMLSOFTWARE at `http://xmlsoftware.com/`**—A programmer's resource site.

- **XML Toolkit at `http://csmctmto.interpoint.net/didx/xml.html`**—A Python tool set for XML development.

- **Café Con Leche: XML News and Resources at `http://metalab.unc.edu/xml/`**— An XML-related news and resource site.

- **XML Hack: Developer news from the XML Community at `http://www.xmlhack.com/`**—A news site for the XML developer community.

- **DTD.com: XML-based Language Standards Center at `http:www.dtd.com/`**—An XML-based language standards center with an extensive archive of XML DTDs.
- **Perl XML: XML news for Perl developers at `http://www.perlxml.com`**—The home of the Perlmonth E-zine.
- **The Apache XML Project at `http://xml.apache.org/`**—The homepage of Cocoon, an XML-based Web publisher; Xalan, an XSLT style sheet processor; Xerces, XML parsers; and FOP, an XSL formatting objects parser.

GETTING DOWN TO CASES

From the wealth of references and links provided in this chapter, it's easy to see that there's been quite a lot of activity going on in the past few years since the release of the XML 1.0 Recommendation by W3C. In fact, there's so much out there it can be hard to decide what's relevant and what's not for a given purpose. As a rule of thumb, links provided by the W3C home page related to a particular XML-related subject are current and being actively worked on, but there are also many independent authors and groups developing XML vocabularies in many fields.

You'll have to use your best judgment to decide which leads or industry standards to follow, if any, or whether to develop your own standard precisely suited to your purpose. In that case, looking at related work done by others may inspire your own creativity or possibly avoid mistakes or oversights present in existing standards or tools.

XML encourages both experimentation and evolution, with the transparency and ease-of-use of XML vocabularies removing many barriers to development, while the simple methods by which existing vocabularies can be extended or modified makes it easy to use prior work as a springboard to new development.

→ For an in-depth look at how to extend existing DTDs, **see** "Extending a DTD," **p. 94**.

But with so much development going on in so many areas, it's quite likely that there is existing work available in almost any field. Conducting a Web search in your field of endeavor may well yield surprising results. A search on the combination of XML and a random word which sprang to mind, "etymology," brought forth 72 results in the Altavista search engine. At least some of them suggested that DTDs for dictionary and encyclopedia makers already exist, or are under development, which contain etymological elements. It would be foolish not to pursue this further if your project involved etymological information, which of course is unlikely. But a similar search on important keywords in your field combined with the word "XML" or "SGML" might well produce valuable references.

CHAPTER 27

SUMMING UP—
THE FUTURE OF THE WEB

In this chapter

XML CHOREOGRAPHY

To some extent, you know what's *planned* for XML, because W3C has published position papers describing the direction *they* see the Web taking in the future. That direction, of course, features XML in a starring role. Because XML is meant to be accessible anytime and anywhere on any Web-capable device, Web designers will have to incorporate a few changes into their thought patterns before *you're* as ready for the future as is XML.

Among the skills required is the ability to act as an information choreographer, staging a complete presentation that can interactively adapt our pages to the flux of the ever-changing Web environment. But XML is still evolving, and if the evolution of HTML is any guide, no one knows exactly what's coming on down the road.

The current state of XML and its related standards is reminiscent of the early days of "talking" pictures. Many people guessed that the new technology would change things, but none could have foreseen the latest high- tech special effects version of *Godzilla* after seeing the first talking pictures. Similarly, it *is* clear that XML "data islands"—as used by Microsoft to embed snippets of XML in HTML documents—aren't going to cut it in the long run. Any interim solution that involves hiding the underlying XML document or breaking it up into bite size chunks is mere hubris on the author's part. Hiding the XML document by transforming it into some sort of HTML implies that the author of the transformation already knows what every user wants to do with the information contained in the native XML and can offer a canned HTML solution that fits all needs, in which case XML is redundant to begin with, but we know better than that by now.

No individual or group can possibly foresee what another might want to do with information or how that other might use published information to make new discoveries or inventions. Progress in science comes about because of the free flow of ideas. Progress on the Web will be made in spite of data filters and transformations, not because of them.

Converting an underlying XML document to HTML for rendering on the Web caters to the lowest common denominator, the legacy HTML browser. Unfortunately, it also throws away many of the advantages of XML at the same time. Although making information available to the widest number of users might require the HTML equivalent of a child's primer for those who aren't quite ready for anything more, no one bothers to pretend that a primer is a good substitute for the real thing. Although much of the current rhetoric about the future of XML focuses on placing control in the hands of authors, there comes a time when even the most clever author has to give up control. Letting users do what they want with the information an author has supplied, or even organized, is the real wave of the future, not schemes to let the dead hand of an author dictate how information is served in perpetuity.

PLACING POWER IN THE HANDS OF THE USER

One of the real advances of XML is that it places power in the hands of the user, or an intelligent user agent, and frees the user to define what kind of publication she needs rather than scan the shelves looking for a prepackaged glop of information that *might* come close. So the users of the future will include *information engineers* as well as *information consumers*, and the dichotomy between them will be as clear as that between people who *play* football and people who *watch* the game. An information engineer will design and coordinate the construction of Web documents as an architect designs and coordinates the construction of a building, bringing disparate materials and technologies into a coherent and eloquent whole.

An information consumer may be anyone, from a research scientist performing an exhaustive literature search to a teenager looking for the latest hot tracks and videos for pure entertainment.

Not everyone will want to learn how to generate interactive XML publications, and it's clear that current tools don't even allow it, being mostly frozen into a lockstep from the unimaginative demands of large corporations, which ignore the dreams of artists and inventors. But creativity will eventually allow the creation of real versions of devices that are only science fiction now.

Star Trek-like voice-activated inquires to "computer" are only the beginning of what's possible. A random instruction such as "Calculate the statistical relationship between blood type and dominant hand and create a graph showing how that relationship varies based on distance and great circle direction from Denali," might lead to another question that leads to a cure for the common cold or a working warp drive for starships. Who knows?

But we do know that information in HTML files is a nearly worthless homogenous mass, and information in proprietary databases is nearly inaccessible from the outside. Without XML or something so similar that it's indistinguishable, you can't ask these potentially breakthrough questions without extensive and expensive data collection and preparation work in advance. Whether you will ever be able to walk up to a computer, talk to it, and reasonably expect it to answer a natural-language question isn't clear, but already users are beginning to ask those questions on a keyboard.

PART

IV

CH

27

Note

Natural language voice recognition is waiting primarily on a few orders of magnitude improvement in memory and processing speed to approximate the capacities of the human brain. Many now believe that processing speeds of 1000MHz and 1GB or so of memory would allow at least a primitive level of trainable voice recognition, with full speaker-independent recognition still out of reach for the next few years at least. But a decade from now, keyboards may be a quaint as buggy whips and wooden pitchforks. You may see them hanging on walls in trendy restaurants.

What's certain is that no one will have created the answer to that question, or countless others, in advance; the answer will be found by searching raw data, pulling together information from thousands of different sources, synthesizing order out of chaos, and expanding knowledge out of relative ignorance.

XML is the glue that holds all these data sources together. XML-based languages describe and identify data, whereas style sheets describe rendering options available for different devices and users.

MULTIPLE LANGUAGES

One thing that may change in the near future is the dependence on one language per site, one language per browser, and one language per user. Internationalization (I18N) is already part of the XML philosophy, with substantial improvements already made over older I18N schemes, which demanded a localized operating system before foreign language support was possible. Mozilla—the open source incarnation of Netscape Navigator and primarily funded by Netscape but with significant input from other parts of the user community as well—is taking it very seriously, and Microsoft Internet Explorer already has a large number of language support modules available. The difficulty so far is that older operating systems, such as Windows versions before Windows 2000 and Windows NT, don't natively support the ISO/Unicode character sets. Windows 95 and later allow applications to handle Unicode support on their own, but memory limitations on most older Windows machines make this solution problematic. Although it's fairly easy to enable the user to see a site using a given character set, enabling interactivity (such as filling out a form) in that language is another kettle of fish unless the application has been specially written with Unicode support in mind.

LOCALIZATION

Localization (L10N) is the capability to alter the user interface to suit the native (or most comfortable) language of a given user. Microsoft has excellent coverage of the "big" languages, but Mozilla is interesting in their planned coverage of "little" languages as well. It's a measure of the commitment of their user community that people have signed up to produce user interface instances for so many languages spoken by relatively small populations. The Opera browser from Opera Software in Norway has good coverage of European languages but relatively little support of languages outside the European community. If language is an important consideration for you, you might want to glance at current support before committing to a purchase.

Figure 27.1 shows the Egyptian *El Shaab* newspaper in Arabic. Because browser support is so poor for the Arabic alphabet, the entire site is made up of graphic images. So the only way for a user to cut and paste a quote is to find a pen and paper!

Figure 27.1
Arabic speakers
deserve browsers
that understand how
to present Arabic
natively and databases
which can be
queried in their
own languages.

LANGUAGE SUPPORT IN THREE BROWSERS

The internationalization of the Web is sure to continue with or without the help of the W3C, but their I18N initiative is providing the impetus behind many efforts, not the least of which is strongly encouraging I18N support from the browser makers. Previous to the W3C standards effort, language support required a confusing mix of proprietary fonts, each with its own encoding standards. Although special purpose browsers existed for many languages, such as Sakhr's Sindbad browser for Arabic at http://www.sakhr.com/ each had its own limitations and idiosyncrasies. No single solution existed.

Among mainstream browsers, no single browser supports all languages. Only languages with enough potential users to justify the effort from the viewpoint of the makers of browser software are supported.

MOZILLA (NETSCAPE) LANGUAGES

Mozilla surely leads the pack in support for languages no one else would even think of supporting because the economic base simply doesn't exist to justify the expense of development. But one of the great strengths of the open software philosophy is that almost anything can and will be supported if someone wants to do it.

The other side of the open source equation is that a language won't be supported unless someone steps up to the plate and actually does it, so Mozilla's initial support of languages is apt to be somewhat spotty at first. But Mozilla differs from many open source projects in that it has a major corporate sponsor, so whatever language support is economically justified will surely be supplied eventually.

Netscape will undoubtedly provide support for their existing language base, which includes Brazilian Portuguese, Czech, Danish, Dutch, English (UK), English (US), French non-SMIME, French, Finnish, German, Greek, Hungarian, Italian, Japanese, Korean, Norwegian, Polish, Russian, Simplified Chinese, Slovenian, Spanish, Swedish, Traditional Chinese, and Turkish. Conspicuous by their absence in the existing browser are Arabic and Hebrew, which represent major concentrations of political and/or economic power. Also missing is coverage of the Indian subcontinent, another major linguistic and cultural grouping of many languages that is sure to be extremely important in the future.

Mozilla is the development name for the next generation Netscape browser, open source in concept and supported with help from the user community. Mozilla has been a Netscape name from the very beginning, and is being reused here for both historic and cultural reasons.

Languages you should expect to see supported in Mozilla include

- Bosnian
- Brazilian Portuguese
- Bulgarian
- Catalan
- Chinese Simplified
- Chinese Traditional
- Czech
- Danish
- Dutch
- English
- French
- Georgian
- German
- Greek
- Hawaiian
- Hebrew
- Hungarian
- Indonesian
- Italian
- Norwegian (Nynorsk and Bokma°)
- Japanese
- Malay
- Polish
- Romanian

- Russian
- Swedish
- Thai
- Turkish
- Ukranian
- Welsh

MICROSOFT INTERNET EXPLORER LANGUAGES

Microsoft Internet Explorer covers, by population and economic power, most of the major markets in the world. For sheer breadth, they surely take the prize, because every "major" language group is well represented. However, if your native tongue doesn't fit into the major category, it's unlikely to be added to the list any time soon. The supported languages are

- Arabic
- Chinese (Simplified)
- Chinese (Traditional)
- English
- German
- Hebrew
- Korean
- Japanese
- Thai
- Vietnamese
- Chinese, Korean, and Japanese require special entry methods for forms because their character sets are too large for entry by any practical keyboard without multiple keystrokes.

OPERA LANGUAGES

The Opera browser has excellent support for European languages as well as Afrikaans, which is somewhat similar to Dutch, but doesn't extend much beyond the borders of continental Europe otherwise. The only exception, of course, is the extension of support into those lands touched by European colonialism, which has left English and a handful of other European languages spoken throughout the world as either second or first languages.

Opera's list of supported languages is

- Afrikaans
- English
- French

- German
- Italian
- Norwegian (Bokma°)
- Norwegian (Nynorsk)
- Portuguese
- Romanian
- Spanish (European)
- Spanish (Latin American)
- Swedish Opera

MULTIPLE ALPHABETS AND OTHER SCRIPTS

Cascading Opera Style Sheets Level 3 promises to enable full support of multiple text encodings, print directions, and character transformation algorithms. Just as in English we have a handful of common ligatures, which represent two characters combined as a single glyph, such as the fi ligature we sometimes see in fine typography, many languages have extremely complex combining forms that have to be presented properly for legibility. In English these combinations are a nicety we've learned to do without, because few computers know how to do them, but not every language is quite that rough and ready.

In the larger sense, XML itself will support Chinese, Burmese, Devangari scripts, Arabic, Coptic, and all the rest. HTML supported only Western European languages and could be said to *really* be English, because USASCII was at its heart and every tag made sense in English, at least as an abbreviation, and was an arbitrary code in any other.

XML supplies the data while CSS3 and beyond supplies the formatting. XSL and XSLT are destined to remain specialized tools, probably sitting on the server or invoked after other processes have decided how to render information based on ready-made CSS "thumbnail sketches" of existing data. With XSL, too much has to be designed rather than guessed at as you can with CSS. By coordinating the style sheet edits with periodic reloading of the document in a browser, or even using a style sheet editor with a built-in display, you can modify a style sheet while you sit and look at the results in real time.

MULTIPLE MEDIA

The Web is becoming Opera more and more diverse as devices capable of accessing it become smaller and more ubiquitous. Already, cell phones are reading email and Personal Digital Assistants are surfing the Web. Cell phone browsers and even wristwatch browsers are starting to appear. Several developments make that possible: the development of tiny XML-based browser languages especially designed for particular applications and devices, CSS2 and CSS3 support for multiple media types, and XSL/XSLT transformations to convert XML information into palatable forms for each of these devices.

INTERACTIVE MEDIA

The next generations Opera of CSS will eliminate the bonds that tie the display to a static rendition of a single subject. Style sheet awareness of user actions will enable designers to free users to wander off down any path they want, simplifying the production of training media, interactive educational displays, repair manuals, and other learning and research tools that work best when you can turn the page to another view.

Coupled with voice response, we'll even be able to control a heads-up display with floating schematics and parts lists by talking to it. "No, not that one. The next. That's it! Order it." With a wireless network and a display built into your contact lenses, you could easily wipe out the competition on *Jeopardy*.

Imagine too, an article without old-fashioned hypermedia links, which would let you branch out from a concept dynamically by simply pointing at a word or phrase and asking for more information with a gesture. Circling the letters "IBM" might link you to their home page, and underlining the letters could fetch the current stock price and breaking news. Truly interactive media will take care of its own links and decide what sorts of information you want based on long experience.

But in the meantime, the major manufacturers, Netscape and Microsoft, are trying to bring us closer to that future with interim solutions that are, unfortunately, still proprietary.

NETSCAPE CASCADING ACTION SYSTEM

Scripts have become annoying on many pages, with lengthy load times required before anything happens. Netscape created a system called Cascading Action Systems that promises to unload some of the load time from the client and place the behaviors into reusable bundles that could be cached on the client or even the server. Of course, they're playing this game with themselves, because Microsoft has a similar scheme it calls Scriptlets and behaviors that package HTML and XML in reusable ways.

MICROSOFT DHTML BEHAVIORS

Remember Dynamic HTML? This so-called standard caused the war between Netscape and Microsoft and nearly destroyed and slowed the pace of innovation while driving up development costs for years. Now it's back as an extension of CSS that lets you build custom tags that use scripts to define page actions or events. A behavior could set an element's position on a screen, for example, so it swings from side to side as the user moves a mouse under it. The object could be a mouse that followed the cursor around. The behavior tags could serve as reusable components that encapsulate functionality or behavior on a Web page. As an extension of CSS, DHTML behaviors combine action attributes and style attributes in the same code. This means that Microsoft style sheets are that much further away from obeying any sort of standard except that of licentious excess.

The next section looks at how to do some of the same things in a controlled and standardized way that is consistent with the goals of XML.

VRXML—VIRTUAL REALITY MODELING AND XML

VRML, the Virtual Reality Modeling Language, is an ISO standard allowing three-dimensional surfaces to be modeled and manipulated using a standard interface. The combination of the XML-based Chemical Markup Language, CML, and VRML enables scientists to automatically generate VRML representations of CML objects in a way well-suited to understanding the three-dimensional structure of the compounds and molecules in the CML database. With that done, an intelligent agent could "mine" the existing knowledgebase looking for interesting new ways that molecules might fit together.

Which means, in turn, that a doctor looking for a cure for cancer could describe significant bits of protein from the cancer and start an agent to look for potential interactions with other molecules. Likewise, after candidates were found, similar 3D animations would enable the researcher to manipulate both molecules looking for potential bond sites.

Although we don't *know* everything yet, we're quickly approaching the point at which all the data is in and all we have to do is think about it in many fields. The complete human genome (the DNA that makes up the basis of our genetic selves) is being mapped. What we're able to do with that universe of information depends largely on the tools we can bring to bear on it. Metaphysics aside, understanding the approximately three billion bases of the genome will tax present capabilities. We'll need better integration and interoperability of databases for a start, something XML may well be able to provide, and communication among researchers and medical practitioners, which XML/CML is already facilitating.

At the present time, we suspect that many more diseases have a genetic basis than we can actually prove. Rapidly using VRML techniques to scan through the genome looking for specific structures may vastly improve our ability to both predict and cure disease. With certain knowledge of the susceptible gene, gene therapies could be designed to fix that tiny bit and eliminate the root cause of the disease before an individual actually became ill.

MICROSOFT CHROME

Chrome is Microsoft's next take on exposing their proprietary technologies, ActiveX, DNA, ASP, Exchange, OLE DB, and IE4 DHTML, to the Web. Chrome lets HTML and XML authors access DirectX from HTML, allowing them to directly integrate multimedia content, high-fidelity graphics, media streaming, and hardware acceleration into their Web pages for a new level of pizzazz on the desktop. Current system requirements include 350MHz or higher Pentium II processors, a 100MHz bus, 4MB of video memory, 64MB of RAM, and DVD capability that, if past history is any indication, means you'll probably need about twice as much of everything to have a real system. Luckily, this is going to be cheap.

On the other hand, using Chrome is going over to the dark side of the Web. Fancy 3D effects tied to a single operating system and primarily designed to entertain a passive audience doesn't do much for people with work to do. Although Chrome could theoretically be used to do useful work, it seems primarily intended to increase the attractiveness and flash of advertising, the excitement of games, and the interactivity of DVD and other multimedia content.

XML itself is moving in the direction of combining multiple technologies and data streams into documents designed in part by the combination of user and device requirements. The next section describes how multiple data streams, which currently require multiple application programs to render them for your display, could be merged into single XML documents and displayed in a single window.

MULTIPLE DATA STREAMS

We can already have a news feed from our stock broker run continuously in a window while we casually keep track of a televised sports spectacular in another little window on our screen while sending email with one hand and updating our sales figures with the other. Unfortunately, all these things currently take place in multiple windows. It would be even better to incorporate everything into one window. There's no particular reason that every application requires a separate window other than the habits of the designers of monolithic applications who see no particular reason to devote any screen real estate to the needs of other applications.

XML documents, which can be almost anything we want them to be by design—from the Dialogs of Plato to the Final Inning of the Big Giants Game—can be easily merged into single documents. These documents can pretty much look like anything we want. So we could theoretically set up one document that would accept our input into the sales figures and, by switching focus slightly, handle our email at the same time without ever losing track of the score. And all this can take place on the same page.

The ability to merge and handle multiple data streams goes beyond that trivial example, of course, because a similar ambidexterity can let the same screen serve as an order entry screen, an inventory control display, and an interactive video deck. This ability strikes terror into the hearts of operating systems designers, since an XML browser designed to run on any hardware platform can create a uniform look and feel and consistent user interface that hides system services from the user or bypasses them altogether.

What's bad for operating systems vendors will be very good for applications designers, since they could write to a uniform XML browser interface and run on any platform in the world without recoding or doing extra development work.

In current practice, one could do this by defining notations for each input feed and then placing the document portion on the page with either CSS or XSL. In future, you may be able to do the same thing with a more generic mechanism, pointing to the type of input you want and letting the server decide through interaction with your browser which data stream would best suit you.

SERVING MULTIPLE KINDS OF USERS

The Web of the future will have a broad cross-section of every kind of person in the world, speaking different languages, with different abilities and understanding of what they want the Internet to do for them.

PART

IV

CH

27

Appliances will be hooked up to the Web, with a disembodied diagnostician able to monitor the temperature of a refrigerator over time to notify the owner that the door seal is faulty and needs replacement. Just in time, inventory control systems already are in place in large industry. A similar system could scan what goes into and out of our kitchen and access a customized database so that orders for staples could be made automatically. Special dishes could be ordered by name, and the "food processor" (an old term with a new referent) could generate an ingredients list and notify the market of what is needed for a meal and when it should arrive.

Although grocery shopping can be a great way to meet people, most people have other things they want to spend their time on. For many, the time is worth more than the groceries. A market with no physical customers inside the store could go the "big box" warehouses one better. They could eliminate most aisle space, all the checkout counters, and a potent source of food spoilage and waste: shoppers with no regard for the ultimate recipient of the avocado they just put their thumb through.

LOOKING AT THE FUTURE OF HTML

Even in the long run, HTML is unlikely to disappear. It's too handy and addresses too large an audience. Just as television didn't wipe out radio, XML is not going to wipe out HTML. What *will* happen, however, is that HTML will become more of a niche product, not the end-all and be-all we've tried to make of it today. The number of display languages will increase as specialized devices proliferate, and the tools for dealing with multiple markup languages will become ubiquitous.

So we're all going to have different experiences with the same basic data. If you're plugged into your virtual reality console, you'll have a vastly different experience than I will accessing the same site on my cell phone. But our roles and viewpoints may switch from day to day. Your console is left behind when you're in your car, and you're now experiencing the Web and its databases in a similar fashion to the low-vision person next door, and when you get to the office with a gigabit network connection, things change again.

What will change for sure is the present assault on our time by designers who make a site really hum when it's sitting on their desktop and then stick it onto an antiquated server off in a closet somewhere connected to the Net through a straw. I can't imagine going back to a dial-up modem now that I've experienced DSL, and we won't be able to imagine going back to the way things are right this minute when we've really seen what XML can do.

TROUBLESHOOTING THE FUTURE

THINGS HAVEN'T TURNED OUT THE WAY WE PLANNED

After careful planning, the preparation of several White Papers, a Business Plan, a Prospectus, a stock offering, or a marriage proposal, things didn't turn out quite like we expected.

The freeway is agood metaphor for the planning process. Based on a known roadmap, you can plan a route well in advance, like your coming vacation to the Grand Canyon. Based on daily highway information from the highway patrol or state trooper's office you can make medium-term changes in those plans before you start the day's journey. Radio reports may help you update your plans en route. But the most current information is what you see before your eyes, and that information may require either swerving or slamming on the brakes.

Some unexpected events require only a leisurely reverie or focus group from time to time, no hurry, if they don't affect current plans. But other surprises demand an instant response. A good planner, like a good driver, doesn't ever lose sight of the ultimate goal but is quick to respond safely to changing conditions.

With XML, as with any human endeavor, the rewards will be reaped by the ones who are quickest, luckiest, and smartest, in that order. You'll note that quick beats smart in this list, as does lucky. If you can manage to be all three at once, you'll be sitting in the catbird seat.

Right now, XML is limited by the notation mechanism to multimedia mechanisms that can be imagined today. If technology advances, as it always seems to, taking advantage of that new technology requires making a new document. But this may change. Where we now face the pain of updating entire sites to allow change to take place, it may be soon be possible to make the future plug-compatible with the present to some extent.

It may soon be possible to seamlessly replace GIF images with PNGs and those in turn with holographic three dimensional images or even virtual windows onto actual objects in real time. We already see the primitive beginnings of this sort of technology in Web cams and 3-D gaming. All we're waiting for is new inventions of the human imagination and new products engineered from bits and pieces of the old inventions leavened with a healthy admixture of the newest ideas.

It's interesting when thinking about XML to compare visions of the future.

On one hand, we have futuristic worlds like that of *Star Trek* and its descendents, where technology is highly visible. *Star Trek*, even in its earliest days, had talking computers, electronic books, and highly complex machines whose functionality and science is known even to children and at the service of all living beings. This world is characterized by a clear distinction between machines and humans, for the most part, and a humane and hopeful outlook. Even intelligent machines in this worldview aspire, like Pinocchio, to be human. XML seems to fit well into this world since it basically is aimed at directly serving human needs. XML seems appropriate to implement a talking computer, or an electronic book, and XML communication channels may make it possible to control complex machines appropriately in language even children can understand.

On the other hand, we have more inhumane worlds, those of *Bladerunner*, cyberpunk visionaries, perhaps even *Dune* and *Star Wars*. In these technology is mysterious, almost muted, invisible or anthropomorphized to the point that even machines walk around and talk like people with no attempt to transcend that status, or people have internalized machines so that the line between machine and human is blurred. In this worldview, the most successful people aspire to be machines, or secretly are, and humanity is doomed. Since XML is just technology and neutral in that sense, either scenario seems possible depending on whether your outlook is optimistic, but XML seems democratic in a deep sense, and possibly more appropriate for the first alternative than the second. But one never knows.

Right now we can see only the beginnings of possibilities. What really happens is up to you.

EVERYTHING HAPPENED JUST AS WE PREDICTED!

When you bought the lottery ticket on the advice of a wandering Gypsy witch and promptly won the jackpot, you thought things just couldn't get any better. And now this!

Okay, so now you're wealthy beyond the feeble dreams of avarice. This is a dangerous time. More people have been ruined in the throes of triumph than you might imagine. Keep thinking about what's coming down the road. It might be a truck.

Although the success of XML as a whole seems assured, there are many issues that have more than technical importance. Legislation may affect e-commerce in general through potential taxes on revenues or sales levied by various jurisdictions worldwide. Privacy concerns make take center stage as well, with entire segments of the industry forced to restructure their revenue streams if the USA and the European Union, in particular, can't hammer out a compromise between US inaction on privacy and European concern. We may move toward the US model or wind up moving toward a European privacy model worldwide. Which model prevails will make all the difference.

At the present time, powerful forces in every country are intent on maintaining the status quo. They may succeed in the short run. But in a global marketplace, in which the USA is not as prominent as in former days but still a force to be reckoned with, even great powers may move toward compromise rather than hegemony. Eventually, we will probably move toward a worldwide marketplace in which everyone plays by the same rules, more or less. But whose rules prevail is still very much up in the air.

Domestic politics may intervene as well, if our own electorate decides to take legislative notice of the Internet and impose restrictions from without. A large portion of the Web is funded by advertising revenue whose total value is based on how much identifying information can be delivered with each interaction a user makes with a server. If restrictive legislation lowers the value of that particular clickstream, it may be your company either left holding the bag or poised to take advantage of new opportunities for revenue and marketing. Exactly what those opportunities might be is known by none but those with the most active imaginations and vigorous curiosity. Creativity can never sleep.

APPENDIX

XML/XHTML REFERENCE

In this appendix

XML TECHNICAL REFERENCE

XML 1.0 is more or less described in the W3C XML 1.0 Recommendation by its 89 Extended Backus-Naur Form productions, with a few caveats called validity constraints and well-formedness constraints and a built-in attribute or two thrown in for good measure. But Backus-Naur form is not terribly transparent to those unaccustomed to extracting usable information from an obscure shorthand description. In fact, many of the tools out there, written by real programmers, fail to completely execute the specification correctly, either from marketing pressures to hurry a product to early release or flaws in design. To fully understand the Recommendation, one must understand a syntax about as complex as XML 1.0 itself and twice as obscure, which only begs the question. And finally, W3C threw quite a lot of specification into the words that accompany the EBNF so beloved of programmers. The document has really to be read in its entirety, with the care one might well use in holy orders, before its real profundities emerge from terse obscurity.

This appendix shows the Backus-Naur rules and explains them simply, then gives some examples to give you a good idea of what it all means. It should be used as a short reference to supplement the longer treatments of DTDs in other chapters of this book. In all cases, you are advised to study the specification itself and not depend on any explanation other than as a crib sheet to illustrate or expand on the words therein. The entire official specification can be found at `http://www.w3.org/TR/REC-x`.

Surprisingly, or maybe not when you consider that design simplicity was a major goal of the developers, XML can be defined by only 89 Extended Backus-Naur productions plus very careful reading of the text of the recommendation. The productions describe the decomposition of each variable. When you reach productions with quote marks around them, you've found one of the terminal nodes and quite possibly a key word or constant.

Listing A.1 shows each of the EBNF productions described in the XML 1.0 Recommendation. The notation used in Productions [13] (`[-'()+,./:=?;!*#@$_%]`) and [26] (`[a-zA-Z0-9_.:]`) is not specifically described, although it is, in fact, the same as that used in Unix-style Regular Expressions, an enumerated list compromising a set of characters surrounded by square brackets. The hyphenated notation in Production 26 is a shorthand way of enumerating a range precisely equivalent to "abcdefghijklmnopqrstuvwxyz" and "ABCDEFGHIJKLMNOPQRSTUVWXYZ" and "0123456789" respectively, although the alphabetic ordering and range conventions assumed don't translate well to the IBM EBCDIC world. Note, too, that the first hyphen in Production 13 is not ambiguous because it's the first character in the list.

In the listing, validity and well-formedness constraints are identified within square brackets in a concise mnemonic form. For a full explanation, see the explanation in Chapters 2 and 3 or the XML 1.0 Recommendation itself.

→ **See** "Understanding the Well-Formedness Constraints," **p. 39**.
→ **See** "Understanding the Well-Formed and Valid XML" **p. 84**.

In Listing A.1, the validity and well-formedness constraints are shown in this form:

```
[VC: Validity Constraint]
[WFC: Well-Formedness Constraint]
```

VC stands for Validity Constraint and is followed by the terse description of the constraint. WFC stands for Well-Formedness Constraint and is similarly followed by the terse description of the constraint. These are meant as mnemonic reminders of the actual constraint only. One has to read the text describing the constraint and sometimes the accompanying text before jumping to conclusions.

LISTING A.1   XML GRAMMAR IN EXTENDED BACKUS-NAUR FORM

```
[1]    document          ::= prolog element Misc*
[2]    Char              ::= #x9 | #xA | #xD | [#x20-#xD7FF] | [#xE000-#xFFFD]
                             | [#x10000-#x10FFFF]
      /* any Unicode character, excluding the surrogate blocks, FFFE, and FFFF. */
[3]    S                 ::= (#x20 | #x9 | #xD | #xA)+
                             /* Whitespace is space, tab, cr, lf */
[4]    NameChar          ::= Letter | Digit | '.' | '-' | '_' | ':'
                             | CombiningChar | Extender
[5]    Name              ::= (Letter | '_' | ':') (NameChar)*
[6]    Names             ::= Name (#x20 Name)*
[7]    Nmtoken           ::= (NameChar)+
[8]    Nmtokens          ::= Nmtoken (#x20 Nmtoken)*
[9]    EntityValue       ::= '"' ([^%&"] | PEReference | Reference)* '"'
                             | "'" ([^%&'] | PEReference | Reference)* "'"
[10]   AttValue          ::= '"' ([^<&"] | Reference)* '"' |  "'" ([^<&']
                             | Reference)* "'"
[11]   SystemLiteral     ::= ('"' [^"]* '"') | ("'" [^']* "'")
[12]   PubidLiteral      ::= '"' PubidChar* '"' | "'" (PubidChar - "'")* "'"
[13]   PubidChar         ::= #x20 | #xD | #xA | [a-zA-Z0-9]
                             | [-'()+,./:=?;!*#@$_%]
[14]   CharData          ::= [^<&]* - ([^<&]* ']]>' [^<&]*)
[15]   Comment           ::= '<!--' ((Char - '-') | ('-' (Char - '-')))* '-->'
[16]   PI                ::= '<?' PITarget (S (Char* - (Char* '?>' Char*)))? '?>'
[17]   PITarget          ::= Name - (('X' | 'x') ('M' | 'm') ('L' | 'l'))
[18]   CDSect            ::= CDStart CData CDEnd
[19]   CDStart           ::= '<![CDATA['
[20]   CData             ::= (Char* - (Char* ']]>' Char*))
[21]   CDEnd             ::= ']]>'
[22]   prolog            ::= XMLDecl? Misc* (doctypedecl Misc*)?
[23]   XMLDecl           ::= '<?xml' VersionInfo EncodingDecl? SDDecl? S? '?>'
[24]   VersionInfo       ::= S 'version' Eq ("'" VersionNum "'" | '"' VersionNum '"')
[25]   Eq                ::= S? '=' S?
[26]   VersionNum        ::= ([a-zA-Z0-9_.:] | '-')+
[27]   Misc              ::= Comment | PI | S
[28]   doctypedecl       ::= '<!DOCTYPE' S Name (S ExternalID)?
                             S? ('[' (markupdecl | PEReference | S)* ']' S?)? '>'
                                    [ VC: Root Element Type ]
[29]   markupdecl        ::= elementdecl | AttlistDecl | EntityDecl
                             | NotationDecl | PI | Comment
                                    [ VC: Proper Declaration/PE Nesting ]
                                    [ WFC: PEs in Internal Subset ]
```

```
[30] extSubset         ::= TextDecl? extSubsetDecl
[31] extSubsetDecl     ::= ( markupdecl | conditionalSect | PEReference | S )*
[32] SDDecl            ::= S 'standalone' Eq (("'" ('yes' | 'no') "'")
                            | ('"' ('yes' | 'no') '"'))
                                           [ VC: Standalone Document Declaration ]
[33] LanguageID        ::= Langcode ('-' Subcode)*
[34] Langcode          ::= ISO639Code | IanaCode | UserCode
[35] ISO639Code        ::= ([a-z] | [A-Z]) ([a-z] | [A-Z])
[36] IanaCode          ::= ('i' | 'I') '-' ([a-z] | [A-Z])+
[37] UserCode          ::= ('x' | 'X') '-' ([a-z] | [A-Z])+
[38] Subcode           ::= ([a-z] | [A-Z])+
[39] element           ::= EmptyElemTag | STag content ETag
                                           [ WFC: Element Type Match ]
                                           [ VC: Element Valid ]
[40] STag              ::= '<' Name (S Attribute)* S? '>'
                                           [ WFC: Unique Att Spec ]
[41] Attribute         ::= Name Eq AttValue
                                           [ VC: Attribute Value Type ]
                                           [ VC: Valid xml:lang ]
                                           [ WFC: No External Entity References ]
                                           [ WFC: No < in Attribute Values ]
[42] ETag              ::= '</' Name S? '>'
[43] content           ::= (element | CharData | Reference | CDSect
                            | PI | Comment)*
[44] EmptyElemTag      ::= '<' Name (S Attribute)* S? '/>'
                                           [ WFC: Unique Att Spec ]
[45] elementdecl       ::= '<!ELEMENT' S Name S contentspec S? '>'
                                           [ VC: Unique Element Type Declaration ]
[46] contentspec       ::= 'EMPTY' | 'ANY' | Mixed | children
[47] children          ::= (choice | seq) ('?' | '*' | '+')?
[48] cp                ::= (Name | choice | seq) ('?' | '*' | '+')?
[49] choice            ::= '(' S? cp ( S? '|' S? cp )+ S? ')'
                                           [ VC: Proper Group/PE Nesting ]
[50] seq               ::= '(' S? cp ( S? ',' S? cp )* S? ')'
                                           [ VC: Proper Group/PE Nesting ]
[51] Mixed             ::= '(' S? '#PCDATA' (S? '|' S? Name)* S? ')*'
                            | '(' S? '#PCDATA' S? ')'
                                           [ VC: Proper Group/PE Nesting ]
                                           [ VC: No Duplicate Types ]
[52] AttlistDecl       ::= '<!ATTLIST' S Name AttDef* S? '>'
[53] AttDef            ::= S Name S AttType S DefaultDecl
[54] AttType           ::= StringType | TokenizedType
                            | EnumeratedType
[55] StringType        ::= 'CDATA'
[56] TokenizedType     ::= 'ID'
                                           [ VC: ID ]
                                           [ VC: One ID per Element Type ]
                                           [ VC: ID Attribute Default ]
                            | 'IDREF'
                                           [ VC: IDREF ]
                            | 'IDREFS'
                                           [ VC: IDREF ]
                            | 'ENTITY'
                                           [ VC: Entity Name ]
                            | 'ENTITIES'
```

```
                                      [ VC: Entity Name ]
                          | 'NMTOKEN'
                                      [ VC: Name Token ]
                          | 'NMTOKENS'
                                      [ VC: Name Token ]
[57] EnumeratedType       ::= NotationType | Enumeration
[58] NotationType         ::= 'NOTATION' S '(' S? Name (S? '|' S? Name)* S? ')'
                                      [ VC: Notation Attributes ]
                                      [ VC: One Notation per Element Type ]
[59] Enumeration          ::= '(' S? Nmtoken (S? '|' S? Nmtoken)* S? ')'
                                      [ VC: Enumeration ]
[60] DefaultDecl          ::= '#REQUIRED' | '#IMPLIED' | (('#FIXED' S)? AttValue)
                                      [ VC: Required Attribute ]
                                      [ VC: Attribute Default Legal ]
                                      [ WFC: No < in Attribute Values ]
                                      [ VC: Fixed Attribute Default ]
[61] conditionalSect      ::= includeSect | ignoreSect
[62] includeSect          ::= '<![' S? 'INCLUDE' S? '[' extSubsetDecl ']]>'
[63] ignoreSect           ::= '<![' S? 'IGNORE' S? '[' ignoreSectContents* ']]>'
[64] ignoreSectContents   ::= Ignore ('<![' ignoreSectContents ']]>' Ignore)*
[65] Ignore               ::= Char* - (Char* ('<![' | ']]>') Char*)
[66] CharRef              ::= '&#' [0-9]+ ';' | '&#x' [0-9a-fA-F]+ ';'
                                      [ WFC: Legal Character ]
[67] Reference            ::= EntityRef | CharRef
[68] EntityRef            ::= '&' Name ';'
                                      [ WFC: Entity Declared ]
                                      [ VC: Entity Declared ]
                                      [ WFC: Parsed Entity ]
                                      [ WFC: No Recursion ]
[69] PEReference          ::= '%' Name ';'
                                      [ VC: Entity Declared ]
                                      [ WFC: No Recursion ]
                                      [ WFC: In DTD ]
[70] EntityDecl           ::= GEDecl | PEDecl
[71] GEDecl               ::= '<!ENTITY' S Name S EntityDef S? '>'
[72] PEDecl               ::= '<!ENTITY' S '%' S Name S PEDef S? '>'
[73] EntityDef            ::= EntityValue | (ExternalID NDataDecl?)
[74] PEDef                ::= EntityValue | ExternalID
[75] ExternalID           ::= 'SYSTEM' S SystemLiteral
                            | 'PUBLIC' S PubidLiteral S SystemLiteral
[76] NDataDecl            ::= S 'NDATA' S Name [ VC: Notation Declared ]
[77] TextDecl             ::= '<?xml' VersionInfo? EncodingDecl S? '?>'
[78] extParsedEnt         ::= TextDecl? content
[79] extPE                ::= TextDecl? extSubsetDecl
[80] EncodingDecl         ::= S 'encoding' Eq ('"' EncName '"'
                            | "'" EncName "'" )
[81] EncName              ::= [A-Za-z] ([A-Za-z0-9._] | '-')*
                            /* Encoding name contains only Latin characters */
[82] NotationDecl         ::= '<!NOTATION' S Name S (ExternalID
                            | PublicID) S? '>'
[83] PublicID             ::= 'PUBLIC' S PubidLiteral
[84] Letter               ::= BaseChar | Ideographic
[85] BaseChar             ::= [#x0041-#x005A] | [#x0061-#x007A] | [#x00C0-#x00D6]
                            | [#x00D8-#x00F6]
                            | [#x00F8-#x00FF] | [#x0100-#x0131] | [#x0134-#x013E]
                            | [#x0141-#x0148] | [#x014A-#x017E] | [#x0180-#x01C3]
                            | [#x01CD-#x01F0] | [#x01F4-#x01F5] | [#x01FA-#x0217]
```

LISTING A.1 CONTINUED

```
| [#x0250-#x02A8] | [#x02BB-#x02C1] | #x0386
| [#x0388-#x038A]
| #x038C | [#x038E-#x03A1] | [#x03A3-#x03CE]
| [#x03D0-#x03D6]
| #x03DA | #x03DC | #x03DE | #x03E0 | [#x03E2-#x03F3]
| [#x0401-#x040C] | [#x040E-#x044F] | [#x0451-#x045C]
| [#x045E-#x0481] | [#x0490-#x04C4] | [#x04C7-#x04C8]
| [#x04CB-#x04CC] | [#x04D0-#x04EB] | [#x04EE-#x04F5]
| [#x04F8-#x04F9] | [#x0531-#x0556] | #x0559
| [#x0561-#x0586]
| [#x05D0-#x05EA] | [#x05F0-#x05F2] | [#x0621-#x063A]
| [#x0641-#x064A] | [#x0671-#x06B7] | [#x06BA-#x06BE]
| [#x06C0-#x06CE] | [#x06D0-#x06D3] | #x06D5
| [#x06E5-#x06E6]
| [#x0905-#x0939] | #x093D | [#x0958-#x0961]
| [#x0985-#x098C]
| [#x098F-#x0990] | [#x0993-#x09A8] | [#x09AA-#x09B0]
| #x09B2
| [#x09B6-#x09B9] | [#x09DC-#x09DD] | [#x09DF-#x09E1]
| [#x09F0-#x09F1] | [#x0A05-#x0A0A] | [#x0A0F-#x0A10]
| [#x0A13-#x0A28] | [#x0A2A-#x0A30] | [#x0A32-#x0A33]
| [#x0A35-#x0A36] | [#x0A38-#x0A39] | [#x0A59-#x0A5C]
| #x0A5E
| [#x0A72-#x0A74] | [#x0A85-#x0A8B] | #x0A8D
| [#x0A8F-#x0A91]
| [#x0A93-#x0AA8] | [#x0AAA-#x0AB0] | [#x0AB2-#x0AB3]
| [#x0AB5-#x0AB9] | #x0ABD | #x0AE0 | [#x0B05-#x0B0C]
| [#x0B0F-#x0B10] | [#x0B13-#x0B28] | [#x0B2A-#x0B30]
| [#x0B32-#x0B33] | [#x0B36-#x0B39] | #x0B3D
| [#x0B5C-#x0B5D]
| [#x0B5F-#x0B61] | [#x0B85-#x0B8A] | [#x0B8E-#x0B90]
| [#x0B92-#x0B95] | [#x0B99-#x0B9A] | #x0B9C
| [#x0B9E-#x0B9F]
| [#x0BA3-#x0BA4] | [#x0BA8-#x0BAA] | [#x0BAE-#x0BB5]
| [#x0BB7-#x0BB9] | [#x0C05-#x0C0C] | [#x0C0E-#x0C10]
| [#x0C12-#x0C28] | [#x0C2A-#x0C33] | [#x0C35-#x0C39]
| [#x0C60-#x0C61] | [#x0C85-#x0C8C] | [#x0C8E-#x0C90]
| [#x0C92-#x0CA8] | [#x0CAA-#x0CB3] | [#x0CB5-#x0CB9]
| #x0CDE
| [#x0CE0-#x0CE1] | [#x0D05-#x0D0C] | [#x0D0E-#x0D10]
| [#x0D12-#x0D28] | [#x0D2A-#x0D39] | [#x0D60-#x0D61]
| [#x0E01-#x0E2E] | #x0E30 | [#x0E32-#x0E33]
| [#x0E40-#x0E45]
| [#x0E81-#x0E82] | #x0E84 | [#x0E87-#x0E88]
| #x0E8A | #x0E8D
| [#x0E94-#x0E97] | [#x0E99-#x0E9F] | [#x0EA1-#x0EA3]
| #x0EA5
| #x0EA7 | [#x0EAA-#x0EAB] | [#x0EAD-#x0EAE] | #x0EB0
| [#x0EB2-#x0EB3] | #x0EBD | [#x0EC0-#x0EC4]
| [#x0F40-#x0F47]
| [#x0F49-#x0F69] | [#x10A0-#x10C5] | [#x10D0-#x10F6]
| #x1100
| [#x1102-#x1103] | [#x1105-#x1107] | #x1109
| [#x110B-#x110C]
| [#x110E-#x1112] | #x113C | #x113E | #x1140 | #x114C
```

```
                              |  #x114E
                              |  #x1150 | [#x1154-#x1155] | #x1159 | [#x115F-#x1161]
                              |  #x1163
                              |  #x1165 | #x1167 | #x1169 | [#x116D-#x116E]
                              |  [#x1172-#x1173]
                              |  #x1175 | #x119E | #x11A8 | #x11AB | [#x11AE-#x11AF]
                              |  [#x11B7-#x11B8] | #x11BA | [#x11BC-#x11C2] | #x11EB
                              |  #x11F0
                              |  #x11F9 | [#x1E00-#x1E9B] | [#x1EA0-#x1EF9]
                              |  [#x1F00-#x1F15]
                              |  [#x1F18-#x1F1D] | [#x1F20-#x1F45] | [#x1F48-#x1F4D]
                              |  [#x1F50-#x1F57] | #x1F59 | #x1F5B | #x1F5D
                              |  [#x1F5F-#x1F7D]
                              |  [#x1F80-#x1FB4] | [#x1FB6-#x1FBC] | #x1FBE
                              |  [#x1FC2-#x1FC4]
                              |  [#x1FC6-#x1FCC] | [#x1FD0-#x1FD3] | [#x1FD6-#x1FDB]
                              |  [#x1FE0-#x1FEC] | [#x1FF2-#x1FF4] | [#x1FF6-#x1FFC]
                              |  #x2126
                              |  [#x212A-#x212B] | #x212E | [#x2180-#x2182]
                              |  [#x3041-#x3094]
                              |  [#x30A1-#x30FA] | [#x3105-#x312C] | [#xAC00-#xD7A3]
[86] Ideographic    ::= [#x4E00-#x9FA5] | #x3007 | [#x3021-#x3029]
[87] CombiningChar  ::= [#x0300-#x0345] | [#x0360-#x0361] | [#x0483-#x0486]
                              |  [#x0591-#x05A1]
                              |  [#x05A3-#x05B9] | [#x05BB-#x05BD] | #x05BF
                              |  [#x05C1-#x05C2]
                              |  #x05C4 | [#x064B-#x0652] | #x0670 | [#x06D6-#x06DC]
                              |  [#x06DD-#x06DF] | [#x06E0-#x06E4] | [#x06E7-#x06E8]
                              |  [#x06EA-#x06ED] | [#x0901-#x0903] | #x093C
                              |  [#x093E-#x094C]
                              |  #x094D | [#x0951-#x0954] | [#x0962-#x0963]
                              |  [#x0981-#x0983]
                              |  #x09BC | #x09BE | #x09BF | [#x09C0-#x09C4]
                              |  [#x09C7-#x09C8]
                              |  [#x09CB-#x09CD] | #x09D7 | [#x09E2-#x09E3] | #x0A02
                              |  #x0A3C
                              |  #x0A3E | #x0A3F | [#x0A40-#x0A42] | [#x0A47-#x0A48]
                              |  [#x0A4B-#x0A4D] | [#x0A70-#x0A71] | [#x0A81-#x0A83]
                              |  #x0ABC
                              |  [#x0ABE-#x0AC5] | [#x0AC7-#x0AC9] | [#x0ACB-#x0ACD]
                              |  [#x0B01-#x0B03] | #x0B3C | [#x0B3E-#x0B43]
                              |  [#x0B47-#x0B48]
                              |  [#x0B4B-#x0B4D] | [#x0B56-#x0B57] | [#x0B82-#x0B83]
                              |  [#x0BBE-#x0BC2] | [#x0BC6-#x0BC8] | [#x0BCA-#x0BCD]
                              |  #x0BD7
                              |  [#x0C01-#x0C03] | [#x0C3E-#x0C44] | [#x0C46-#x0C48]
                              |  [#x0C4A-#x0C4D] | [#x0C55-#x0C56] | [#x0C82-#x0C83]
                              |  [#x0CBE-#x0CC4] | [#x0CC6-#x0CC8] | [#x0CCA-#x0CCD]
                              |  [#x0CD5-#x0CD6] | [#x0D02-#x0D03] | [#x0D3E-#x0D43]
                              |  [#x0D46-#x0D48] | [#x0D4A-#x0D4D] | #x0D57 | #x0E31
                              |  [#x0E34-#x0E3A] | [#x0E47-#x0E4E] | #x0EB1
                              |  [#x0EB4-#x0EB9]
                              |  [#x0EBB-#x0EBC] | [#x0EC8-#x0ECD] | [#x0F18-#x0F19]
                              |  #x0F35
                              |  #x0F37 | #x0F39 | #x0F3E | #x0F3F | [#x0F71-#x0F84]
                              |  [#x0F86-#x0F8B] | [#x0F90-#x0F95] | #x0F97
                              |  [#x0F99-#x0FAD]
```

| LISTING A.1 | CONTINUED |

```
                        | [#x0FB1-#x0FB7]  | #x0FB9  | [#x20D0-#x20DC]  | #x20E1
                        | [#x302A-#x302F]  | #x3099  | #x309A
[88] Digit     ::= [#x0030-#x0039]  | [#x0660-#x0669]  | [#x06F0-#x06F9]
                        | [#x0966-#x096F]
                        | [#x09E6-#x09EF]  | [#x0A66-#x0A6F]  | [#x0AE6-#x0AEF]
                        | [#x0B66-#x0B6F]  | [#x0BE7-#x0BEF]  | [#x0C66-#x0C6F]
                        | [#x0CE6-#x0CEF]  | [#x0D66-#x0D6F]  | [#x0E50-#x0E59]
                        | [#x0ED0-#x0ED9]  | [#x0F20-#x0F29]
[89] Extender  ::= #x00B7  | #x02D0  | #x02D1  | #x0387  | #x0640  | #x0E46
                        | #x0EC6  | #x3005
                        | [#x3031-#x3035]  | [#x309D-#x309E]  | [#x30FC-#x30FE]
```

XML CRIB NOTES

When trying to understand EBNF productions, it helps to have a printed copy and many colored pens so you can trace the exact sequence of replacement steps for a given production as you go along. You wind your way through the maze of production rules until you come to a final leaf, which has no names and only quoted text or text rules of some sort.

The characters *, +, and ? have special meaning in an EBNF production when they appear after an element or group of elements enclosed in parentheses. An asterisk (*) means there can be zero or more instances of this element. A plus (+) means that there can be one or more instance of this element. And a question mark (?) means that there can be zero or one instance of this element. No suffix means that a single element is mandatory and cannot be repeated at that level. These are the same conventions used in regular expressions, a Unix concept slowly making its way into the hearts and minds of the general public, and used in XML DTD documents as well.

XML markup is constrained by a requirement that, whatever entity substitutions and parsing might do to a particular markup entity, the result has to be complete in itself. So if any markup includes the leftmost < character of any markup, it must also include the rightmost > character which closes the markup. All XML keywords, such as ENTITY, NOTATION, ELEMENT, and so on must be in uppercase. This also includes datatypes and tokenized types such as #PCDATA, IDREF, and so on.

THE XML DECLARATION

If you combine productions 1, 22, 23, and 28, you see that every XML DTD begins with a prolog that might or might not have any meaningful content. The prolog might contain a formal processing command statement that declares it to be XML and has three useful attributes:

```
<?xml version="1.0" encoding="ISO-8859-1"? standalone="no">
```

XML files might omit this declaration at their discretion although there is not a good reason to and W3C says you should include it anyway. It was made optional only because they found that there were quite a few HTML and SGML files that were perfectly good XML as well. They saw no sense in breaking all those pages out of pique.

If you want to specify your encoding, which you should, you need to have a DTD anyway. Both the encoding and standalone attributes are optional, however. Processors that see `standalone="yes"` might ignore external references when validating the document, which might be vaguely useful for something or another. But their behavior is hard to depend on as they're not actually required to do much of anything at all with this information.

The version number is mandatory if you use the declaration at all and identifies the version of XML your code conforms to. Processors that see a version they don't support should stop and tell you so. Currently, there's only one version, 1.0, but it should always be specified anyway.

The encoding is optional but allows you to specify which of several character encoding standards the document uses. Typical are the values "UTF-8", "UTF-16", "ISO-10646-UCS-2", and "ISO-10646-UCS-4", which are used for parts of Unicode / ISO/IEC 10646. "ISO-8859-1", "ISO-8859-2", and so on through "ISO-8859-9" are used for ISO 8859 character spaces. And "ISO-2022-JP", "Shift_JIS", and "EUC-JP" can be used for the Japanese JIS X-0208-1997 character space. The full list of options can be found in the XML 1.0 Recommendation at W3C, `http://www.w3.org/XMl/`. Appendix D, Character Entities, lists the entity values of the ISO-8859-1 characters most commonly used in Western European languages.

Standalone allows you to declare whether your document uses external markup or not. This is mainly useful for allowing a processor to decide whether or not to convert the document into a standalone document if it's going to be sent somewhere else before use. This statement has a validity constraint. The value must be "no" if any of the following statements is true:

- External markup contains attributes with default values if your document uses the elements those attributes apply to without setting those values explicitly in the internal DTD subset.

- You reference character entities other than amp, lt, gt, apos, and quot in your document, which aren't defined or included by reference in the internal subset of the DTD.

- Your external markup contains any attributes that must be *normalized*, that is, parsed to resolve entity and character references and to substitute a space for whitespace characters.

- Element types exist in the external document containing whitespace. This means any opening element that immediately follows another opening element with a carriage return or a space in between them.

THE XML DOCTYPE STATEMENT

The prolog might also contain a DOCTYPE statement. Every complete XML DTD has a single DOCTYPE statement that names the root of the XML document description tree (the DTD being defined) and encloses the DTD itself as internal and external subsets, either of which is optional:

```
<!DOCTYPE docname SYSTEM "mydocname.dtd" [
<!ELEMENT docname {next level(s) of tree} >
… etc.
]>
```

DTD fragments, those meant to be included in other DTDs, must omit this declaration as there can be only one DOCTYPE per XML DTD. In this case the DOCTYPE might be declared in another file that references the external DTD fragments:

```
<!DOCTYPE docname SYSTEM "mydocname.dtd" [
<!ENTITY % subdtd1 SYSTEM "mysubdtd1.dtd">
%subdtd1;
<!ENTITY % subdtd2 SYSTEN "mysubdtd2.dtd">
%subdtd2;
]>
```

Note that the square brackets enclosing inline XML code delimit the internal subset of the complete XML document that can be used to override the default attribute lists and entity declarations in the external DTD subset. This is a primary mechanism for changing or customizing external DTDs although you can also do it from another DTD.

Note that the root of the document description tree (DTD) must have exactly the same name as the DOCTYPE.

THE XML ENTITY

You can think of an XML ENTITY as you might a macro facility in a programming language, although it is subject to a complex set of rules that govern when and how the macro is executed or interpreted. Table A.1 shows a quick reference list of entities as shown in the W3C XML 1.0 Recommendation.

TABLE A.1 ENTITY QUICK REFERENCE

Entity Type	Parameter	Internal General	External Parsed General	Character Unparsed
Reference in Content	Not recognized	Included	Included if validating	Forbidden
Reference in Attribute Value	Not recognized	Included in literal	Forbidden	Forbidden
Occurs as Attribute Value	Not recognized	Forbidden	Forbidden	Notify
Reference in EntityValue	Included in literal	Bypassed	Bypassed	Forbidden
Reference in DTD	Included as PE	Forbidden	Forbidden	Forbidden

ENTITY declarations are required to be there when they are used, so the order in which cascading entities are declared is critical. Their exact placement in the DTD is also critical because entities are severely restricted in the internal subset.

In a nutshell, the internal subset was simplified so that non-validating parsers, which don't do much with the DTD anyway, don't have to be very smart. To accomplish this laudable goal, they allow character entities quite freely, and prevent use of parameter entities except at the topmost level, where you can use markup.

THE XML NOTATION

Notations identify the format of unparsed entities, elements that carry a NOTATION attribute, and the helper applications to which a processing instruction is directed. Typical uses are to tell an application how to handle binary files, such as a JPEG graphic, or what to do with chunks of other data, such as TeX or Postscript files.

Notations must be declared before use, which in practice means that it's a good idea to include them toward the start of your file. It makes life a little easier if all the notations are located in one place, but this is not a requirement. I like to put all the ENTITY declarations first, then NOTATION and ELEMENT declarations in that order. I prefer keeping the ATTLISTs with their ELEMENTs. It makes sense to me that way, because I can instantly see what attributes an element carries and I know exactly where to look for the attributes when considering an element, but whatever logical grouping makes sense to you is okay too.

There are two types of NOTATION declarations. The first allows you to identify how particular kinds of objects are to be handled by an application that resides on your system:

```
<!NOTATION notation-name SYSTEM "data-handler.exe ">
```

This might be used to declare, for example, that an application should use Adobe Photoshop to view GIF files:

```
<!NOTATION gif SYSTEM "ps.exe ">
```

You can assume that the PhotoShop directory is in your path, but you could as easily have used a full path name. Of course this assumes that the helper application you use will never change and that everyone else who might use your DTD will have access to the same helper application. This sort of assumption is not terribly safe but might be justified in a particular situation.

A variation of this method works in Microsoft Windows and might work in some other systems but is not guaranteed:

```
<!NOTATION gif SYSTEM "GIF">
```

This lets Windows look in its Registry for an application that can handle files of type "GIF" and pass the information along to it.

A second strategy might be to refer to a public standard and let the application figure out how to use this information to handle the file. So in our GIF example, you would use two NOTATION declarations to handle the two types of GIF files:

```
<!NOTATION gif87a PUBLIC "-//CompuServe//NOTATION Graphics Interchange Format
87a//EN">
<!NOTATION gif89a PUBLIC "-//CompuServe//NOTATION Graphics Interchange Format
89a//EN">
```

This approach has problems of its own. Although almost all GIF handlers automatically recognize the two types of GIFs and behave properly when they find either version, you now have to know what kind of GIF files you're talking about before referencing them unless our application handles both. Bummer. Also, you're depending on the good offices of the SGML directory, which strictly speaking doesn't exist for XML other than by default, to locate applications from public identifiers. XML really requires you to follow the public identifier with the URI identifying an application that can handle this type of file. So the syntax looks like this:

```
<!NOTATION gif87a PUBLIC "-//CompuServe//NOTATION Graphics Interchange Format
87a//EN" "ps.exe ">
<!NOTATION gif89a PUBLIC "-//CompuServe//NOTATION Graphics Interchange Format
89a//EN" "ps.exe ">
```

After you've declared a notation, you can use it in an attribute with an enumerated list like this:

```
<!ELEMENT img EMPTY>
<!ATTLIST img
        src  %URL  #REQUIRED
        alt  CDATA #REQUIRED
        type NOTATION (gif89a | gif87a) "gif89a">
```

You could also use it like this as a default datatype:

```
<!ELEMENT img EMPTY>
<!ATTLIST img
        src  %URL  #REQUIRED
        alt  CDATA #REQUIRED
        type NDATA gif89a>
```

Every notation name must be declared before use.

THE XML ELEMENT

ELEMENTs are often parsed and arranged in an internal tree structure, a lookup table essentially, as they are read. This means that the order they arrive in within the data stream is not terribly important as long as there are no duplicates, which is a fatal error.

Every complete document description tree (DTD) must have a single root element. The ELEMENT name must be the same as the name of the DOCTYPE used to identify the DTD.

Note that this doesn't prevent a DTD fragment from being used as a leaf in an enclosing tree, either as an external subset or as a parameter entity.

An ELEMENT with content looks like

```
<!ELEMENT elementname (content)>
```

where content can be any number of data types and or other elements given in a syntax that allows you to declare a content model specifying what elements can occur in what order and how many times they can be repeated.

An ELEMENT without content looks like this:

```
<!ELEMENT elementname EMPTY>
```

An empty element behaves much like an empty element in HTML; that is it uses a single tag with optional attributes to do all the work. Unlike HTML, however, XML expects and demands that empty tags be closed, either like

```
<emptyelement />
```

or like

```
<emptyelement></emptyelement>
```

The second form can be a little confusing, because you might think that the element might possibly contain content just looking at it. I recommend the single tag with integral closing slash.

The opposite of an empty element is an unrestricted element that can take any content at all without restriction. The syntax is simple:

```
<!ELEMENT elementname ANY>
```

As you might expect, this doesn't allow much in the way of validity checking.

XML PROCESSING INSTRUCTIONS

The XML processing command allows you to embed information specific to a particular application inside your XML document. Any content within the instruction is ignored by XML and by any processor unable to interpret the command. So you could, for example, insert a Perl script into your document like this:

```
… <?perl  use Date::DateCalc; if (Date::DateCalc::Version() eq "3.2") {print
"OK\n";} else {print "Fail\n";} … ?> …
```

If you're not sure what processors might be available on a given target system, you can provide several choices, although what happens if several are present is a bit up in the air. There is no syntax (so far) that tells an XML processor to ignore alternatives when one processing instruction is successfully interpreted.

XML COMMENTS

The XML comment is the familiar HTML or SGML comment but narrowed somewhat to exclude the possibility of including multiple comments within one set of comment delimiters. So the following is a legal comment:

```
<!-- Comment text -->
```

And these are not

```
<!-- Comment text --    -- Second comment -- -->
<!-- Comment text --
  -- Second comment -->
```

although they are legal in both SGML and HTML 4.0

XML processors are not required to pass comments along to any external application, so inserting script or style commands inside comments is not recommended although it's standard practice in HTML. For the purpose of hiding information from the XML processor, use a CDATA section or a processing instruction instead of a comment.

XML CDATA SECTIONS

When you want to hide text from the XML processor, the CDATA section is pretty much ideal. Whatever sits inside the CDATA section is completely ignored. No entity resolutions are made, no markup is recognized, and nothing gets done besides transferring the text as-is to the application:

```
<[CDATA[Anything at all can sit in here … ]]>
```

CDATA sections are useful when you want to pass along data that might be mistaken for XML, such as an HTML tag for instance, or use text containing reserved characters, such as the ampersand (&) or angle bracket (<) signs and don't want to escape them for any reason. The sequence]]> must not occur within the included text or the CDATA section will be prematurely terminated.

THE XML CATALOG FILE

Although one should officially use the XML quoted system identifier syntax when using PUBLIC identifiers, there is an SGML legacy file called the catalog file located in the same directory as the XML document or another location that is application dependent. If your XML processor supports this file, it will be filled with lists of PUBLIC identifiers and unnamed SYSTEM identifiers that your processor can use to resolve PUBLIC identifier references. This is a better way to support external references because, if an external file moves or changes, you can update all references to it in one fell swoop instead of tediously searching through hundreds or thousands of documents looking for possible references and changing every location found. In an environment that enforces change control, that "simple" change might result in weeks of work checking everything back in.

The catalog file looks something like this:

```
-- catalog -
-- comments --
PUBLIC "-//CompuServe//NOTATION Graphics Interchange Format 87a//EN" "ps.exe "
PUBLIC "-//CompuServe//NOTATION Graphics Interchange Format 89a//EN" "ps.exe "
PUBLIC "-//W3C//DTD XHTML Transitional//EN"
       "http://www.w3.org/TR/xhtml1/DTD/transitional.dtd"
PUBLIC "-//W3C//DTD XHTML 1.0 Transitional//EN"
       "http://www.w3.org/TR/xhtml1/DTD/transitional.dtd"
…
```

where each PUBLIC identifier is paired with a URI that defines an application or other external reference that corresponds. It's the same sort of data you use in a DOCTYPE declaration or, for that matter, the same XML quoted system identifier syntax mentioned above. The advantage of the catalog is that it saves quite a bit of typing and removes at least one opportunity for errors:

```
PUBLIC "-//W3C//DTD XHTML 1.0 Transitional//EN"
       http://www.w3.org/TR/xhtml1/DTD/transitional.dtd
```

The whole issue of how to find XML external documents is still a bit up in the air, although work is being done on trying to maintain stable locations on the Web (see the article on Cool URIs at http://www.w3.org/Provider/Style/URI), the problem of naming and locating documents is very difficult. It requires the cooperation of millions of sites, most of which are in a constant state of chaos and turmoil as new administrators (or old administrators with new ideas) change file locations at the drop of a hat.

Using link checkers periodically is a good idea, but that doesn't usually help find the new location. In fact, many sites never post a change notice at the old location. In a stunning display of hubris and ego-centricity, they assume that everyone in the world is motivated to use internal search engines to find where the old page went. So benevolent cooperation seems a bit much to hope for.

Like the rest of the Web community, XML is going to have to muddle along with imperfect methods of linking to documents until some theoretical breakthrough takes place.

In the meantime, let's look at an XHTML DTD.

XHTML TECHNICAL REFERENCE

Only the Transitional DTD will be included in the book for reasons of length. The full DTD set is available as a link from http://www.w3.org/TR/xhtml1/ and is contained on the CD-ROM accompanying this book, but the actual DTDs might change slightly as the standard evolves.

XHTML VERSION 1 TRANSITIONAL DTD

The XHTML Transitional DTD shown in Listing A.2 is the one most likely to be appropriate for random HTML documents. Although it doesn't support frames, they seem to be relatively rare on the Web and are strongly discouraged, both by user preference and by the proper consideration of the difficulties they place before persons with visual and motor disabilities.

LISTING A.2 THE XHTML 1.01 TRANSITIONAL DTD

```
<!--
   Extensible HTML version 1.0 Transitional DTD
   This is the same as HTML 4.0 Transitional except for
   changes due to the differences between XML and SGML.
   Namespace = http://www.w3.org/1999/xhtml
```

APP
A

LISTING A.2   CONTINUED

```
    For further information, see: http://www.w3.org/TR/xhtml1
    Copyright (c) 1998-2000 W3C (MIT, INRIA, Keio),
    All Rights Reserved.
    This DTD module is identified by the PUBLIC and SYSTEM identifiers:
    PUBLIC "-//W3C//DTD XHTML 1.0 Transitional//EN"
    SYSTEM "http://www.w3.org/TR/xhtml1/DTD/xhtml1-transitional.dtd"
    $Revision: 1.1 $
    $Date: 2000/01/26 14:08:56 $

-->

<!--======= Character mnemonic entities =============-->

<!ENTITY % HTMLlat1 PUBLIC
    "-//W3C//ENTITIES Latin 1 for XHTML//EN"
    "xhtml-lat1.ent">
%HTMLlat1;

<!ENTITY % HTMLsymbol PUBLIC
    "-//W3C//ENTITIES Symbols for XHTML//EN"
    "xhtml-symbol.ent">
%HTMLsymbol;

<!ENTITY % HTMLspecial PUBLIC
    "-//W3C//ENTITIES Special for XHTML//EN"
    "xhtml-special.ent">
%HTMLspecial;

<!--========== Imported Names ====================-->

<!ENTITY % ContentType "CDATA">
    <!-- media type, as per [RFC2045] -->

<!ENTITY % ContentTypes "CDATA">
    <!-- comma-separated list of media types, as per [RFC2045] -->

<!ENTITY % Charset "CDATA">
    <!-- a character encoding, as per [RFC2045] -->

<!ENTITY % Charsets "CDATA">
    <!-- a space separated list of character encodings, as per [RFC2045] -->

<!ENTITY % LanguageCode "NMTOKEN">
    <!-- a language code, as per [RFC1766] -->

<!ENTITY % Character "CDATA">
    <!-- a single character from [ISO10646] -->

<!ENTITY % Number "CDATA">
    <!-- one or more digits -->

<!ENTITY % LinkTypes "CDATA">
    <!-- space-separated list of link types -->
```

```
<!ENTITY % MediaDesc "CDATA">
    <!-- single or comma-separated list of media descriptors -->

<!ENTITY % URI "CDATA">
    <!-- a Uniform Resource Identifier, see [RFC2396] -->

<!ENTITY % UriList "CDATA">
    <!-- a space separated list of Uniform Resource Identifiers -->

<!ENTITY % Datetime "CDATA">
    <!-- date and time information. ISO date format -->

<!ENTITY % Script "CDATA">
    <!-- script expression -->

<!ENTITY % StyleSheet "CDATA">
    <!-- style sheet data -->

<!ENTITY % Text "CDATA">
    <!-- used for titles etc. -->

<!ENTITY % FrameTarget "NMTOKEN">
    <!-- render in this frame -->

<!ENTITY % Length "CDATA">
    <!-- nn for pixels or nn% for percentage length -->

<!ENTITY % MultiLength "CDATA">
    <!-- pixel, percentage, or relative -->

<!ENTITY % MultiLengths "CDATA">
    <!-- comma-separated list of MultiLength -->

<!ENTITY % Pixels "CDATA">
    <!-- integer representing length in pixels -->

<!-- these are used for image maps -->

<!ENTITY % Shape "(rect|circle|poly|default)">

<!ENTITY % Coords "CDATA">
    <!-- comma separated list of lengths -->

<!-- used for object, applet, img, input and iframe -->
<!ENTITY % ImgAlign "(top|middle|bottom|left|right)">

<!-- a color using sRGB: #RRGGBB as Hex values -->
<!ENTITY % Color "CDATA">

<!-- There are also 16 widely known color names with their sRGB values:

        Black  = #000000    Green  = #008000
        Silver = #C0C0C0    Lime   = #00FF00
        Gray   = #808080    Olive  = #808000
        White  = #FFFFFF    Yellow = #FFFF00
        Maroon = #800000    Navy   = #000080
        Red    = #FF0000    Blue   = #0000FF
```

```
    Purple = #800080    Teal  = #008080
    Fuchsia= #FF00FF    Aqua  = #00FFFF
-->

<!--=========== Generic Attributes ===============-->

<!-- core attributes common to most elements
  id        document-wide unique id
  class     space separated list of classes
  style     associated style info
  title     advisory title/amplification
-->
<!ENTITY % coreattrs
 "id         ID            #IMPLIED
  class      CDATA         #IMPLIED
  style      %StyleSheet;  #IMPLIED
  title      %Text;        #IMPLIED"
  >


<!-- internationalization attributes
  lang          language code (backwards compatible)
  xml:lang      language code (as per XML 1.0 spec)
  dir           direction for weak/neutral text
-->
<!ENTITY % i18n
 "lang         %LanguageCode; #IMPLIED
  xml:lang     %LanguageCode; #IMPLIED
  dir          (ltr|rtl)      #IMPLIED"
  >


<!-- attributes for common UI events
  onclick     a pointer button was clicked
  ondblclick  a pointer button was double clicked
  onmousedown a pointer button was pressed down
  onmouseup   a pointer button was released
  onmousemove a pointer was moved onto the element
  onmouseout  a pointer was moved away from the element
  onkeypress  a key was pressed and released
  onkeydown   a key was pressed down
  onkeyup     a key was released
-->
<!ENTITY % events
 "onclick     %Script;      #IMPLIED
  ondblclick  %Script;      #IMPLIED
  onmousedown %Script;      #IMPLIED
  onmouseup   %Script;      #IMPLIED
  onmouseover %Script;      #IMPLIED
  onmousemove %Script;      #IMPLIED
  onmouseout  %Script;      #IMPLIED
  onkeypress  %Script;      #IMPLIED
  onkeydown   %Script;      #IMPLIED
  onkeyup     %Script;      #IMPLIED"
  >
```

```
<!-- attributes for elements that can get the focus
  accesskey    accessibility key character
  tabindex     position in tabbing order
  onfocus      the element got the focus
  onblur       the element lost the focus
-->
<!ENTITY % focus
 "accesskey    %Character;    #IMPLIED
  tabindex     %Number;       #IMPLIED
  onfocus      %Script;       #IMPLIED
  onblur       %Script;       #IMPLIED"
  >

<!ENTITY % attrs "%coreattrs; %i18n; %events;">

<!-- text alignment for p, div, h1-h6. The default is
     align="left" for ltr headings, "right" for rtl -->

<!ENTITY % TextAlign "align (left|center|right) #IMPLIED">

<!--=========== Text Elements ============-->

<!ENTITY % special
    "br | span | bdo | object | applet | img | map | iframe">

<!ENTITY % fontstyle "tt | i | b | big | small | u
                       | s | strike |font | basefont">

<!ENTITY % phrase "em | strong | dfn | code | q | sub | sup |
                    samp | kbd | var | cite | abbr | acronym">

<!ENTITY % inline.forms "input | select | textarea | label | button">

<!-- these can occur at block or inline level -->
<!ENTITY % misc "ins | del | script | noscript">

<!ENTITY % inline "a | %special; | %fontstyle; | %phrase; | %inline.forms;">

<!-- %Inline; covers inline or "text-level" elements -->
<!ENTITY % Inline "(#PCDATA | %inline; | %misc;)*">

<!--========== Block level elements ===============-->

<!ENTITY % heading "h1|h2|h3|h4|h5|h6">
<!ENTITY % lists "ul | ol | dl | menu | dir">
<!ENTITY % blocktext "pre | hr | blockquote | address | center | noframes">

<!ENTITY % block
    "p | %heading; | div | %lists; | %blocktext; | isindex |fieldset | table">

<!ENTITY % Block "(%block; | form | %misc;)*">

<!-- %Flow; mixes Block and Inline and is used for list items etc. -->
<!ENTITY % Flow "(#PCDATA | %block; | form | %inline; | %misc;)*">

<!--========== Content models for exclusions ==============-->
```

APP

A

LISTING A.2 CONTINUED

```
<!-- a elements use %Inline; excluding a -->

<!ENTITY % a.content
    "(#PCDATA | %special; | %fontstyle; | %phrase; | %inline.forms; | %misc;)*">

<!-- pre uses %Inline excluding img, object, applet, big, small,
     sub, sup, font, or basefont -->

<!ENTITY % pre.content
    "(#PCDATA | a | br | span | bdo | map | tt | i | b | u | s |
      %phrase; | %inline.forms;)*">

<!-- form uses %Flow; excluding form -->

<!ENTITY % form.content "(#PCDATA | %block; | %inline; | %misc;)*">

<!-- button uses %Flow; but excludes a, form, form controls, iframe -->

<!ENTITY % button.content
    "(#PCDATA | p | %heading; | div | %lists; | %blocktext; |
      table | br | span | bdo | object | applet | img | map |
      %fontstyle; | %phrase; | %misc;)*">

<!--======== Document Structure ===================-->

<!-- the namespace URI designates the document profile -->

<!ELEMENT html (head, body)>
<!ATTLIST html
  %i18n;
  xmlns        %URI;          #FIXED 'http://www.w3.org/1999/xhtml'
  >

<!--======== Document Head =======================-->

<!ENTITY % head.misc "(script|style|meta|link|object|isindex)*">

<!-- content model is %head.misc; combined with a single
     title and an optional base element in any order -->

<!ELEMENT head (%head.misc;,
    ((title, %head.misc;, (base, %head.misc;)?) |
     (base, %head.misc;, (title, %head.misc;))))>

<!ATTLIST head
  %i18n;
  profile      %URI;          #IMPLIED
  >

<!-- The title element is not considered part of the flow of text.
     It should be displayed, for example as the page header or
     window title. Exactly one title is required per document.
   -->
<!ELEMENT title (#PCDATA)>
```

```
<!ATTLIST title %i18n;>

<!-- document base URI -->

<!ELEMENT base EMPTY>
<!ATTLIST base
  href          %URI;         #IMPLIED
  target        %FrameTarget; #IMPLIED
  >

<!-- generic metainformation -->
<!ELEMENT meta EMPTY>
<!ATTLIST meta
  %i18n;
  http-equiv    CDATA         #IMPLIED
  name          CDATA         #IMPLIED
  content       CDATA         #REQUIRED
  scheme        CDATA         #IMPLIED
  >

<!--
  Relationship values can be used in principle:

    a) for document specific toolbars/menus when used
       with the link element in document head e.g.
         start, contents, previous, next, index, end, help
    b) to link to a separate style sheet (rel="stylesheet")
    c) to make a link to a script (rel="script")
    d) by stylesheets to control how collections of
       html nodes are rendered into printed documents
    e) to make a link to a printable version of this document
       e.g. a PostScript or PDF version (rel="alternate" media="print")
-->

<!ELEMENT link EMPTY>
<!ATTLIST link
  %attrs;
  charset       %Charset;       #IMPLIED
  href          %URI;           #IMPLIED
  hreflang      %LanguageCode;  #IMPLIED
  type          %ContentType;   #IMPLIED
  rel           %LinkTypes;     #IMPLIED
  rev           %LinkTypes;     #IMPLIED
  media         %MediaDesc;     #IMPLIED
  target        %FrameTarget;   #IMPLIED
  >

<!-- style info, which may include CDATA sections -->
<!ELEMENT style (#PCDATA)>
<!ATTLIST style
  %i18n;
  type          %ContentType;   #REQUIRED
  media         %MediaDesc;     #IMPLIED
  title         %Text;          #IMPLIED
  xml:space     (preserve)      #FIXED 'preserve'
  >
```

Listing A.2   Continued

```
<!-- script statements, which may include CDATA sections -->
<!ELEMENT script (#PCDATA)>
<!ATTLIST script
  charset     %Charset;       #IMPLIED
  type        %ContentType;   #REQUIRED
  language    CDATA           #IMPLIED
  src         %URI;           #IMPLIED
  defer       (defer)         #IMPLIED
  xml:space   (preserve)      #FIXED 'preserve'
  >

<!-- alternate content container for non script-based rendering -->

<!ELEMENT noscript %Flow;>
<!ATTLIST noscript
  %attrs;
  >

<!--=============== Frames ========================-->

<!-- inline subwindow -->

<!ELEMENT iframe %Flow;>
<!ATTLIST iframe
  %coreattrs;
  longdesc     %URI;          #IMPLIED
  name         NMTOKEN        #IMPLIED
  src          %URI;          #IMPLIED
  frameborder  (1|0)          "1"
  marginwidth  %Pixels;       #IMPLIED
  marginheight %Pixels;       #IMPLIED
  scrolling    (yes|no|auto)  "auto"
  align        %ImgAlign;     #IMPLIED
  height       %Length;       #IMPLIED
  width        %Length;       #IMPLIED
  >

<!-- alternate content container for non frame-based rendering -->

<!ELEMENT noframes %Flow;>
<!ATTLIST noframes
  %attrs;
  >

<!--=========== Document Body ====================-->

<!ELEMENT body %Flow;>
<!ATTLIST body
  %attrs;
  onload       %Script;       #IMPLIED
  onunload     %Script;       #IMPLIED
  background   %URI;          #IMPLIED
  bgcolor      %Color;        #IMPLIED
  text         %Color;        #IMPLIED
```

```
   link        %Color;        #IMPLIED
   vlink       %Color;        #IMPLIED
   alink       %Color;        #IMPLIED
   >

<!ELEMENT div %Flow;>   <!-- generic language/style container -->
<!ATTLIST div
   %attrs;
   %TextAlign;
   >


<!--=========== Paragraphs ========================-->

<!ELEMENT p %Inline;>
<!ATTLIST p
   %attrs;
   %TextAlign;
   >


<!--=========== Headings ==========================-->

<!--
   There are six levels of headings from h1 (the most important)
   to h6 (the least important).
   >

<!ELEMENT h1  %Inline;>
<!ATTLIST h1
   %attrs;
   %TextAlign;
   >

<!ELEMENT h2 %Inline;>
<!ATTLIST h2
   %attrs;
   %TextAlign;
   >

<!ELEMENT h3 %Inline;>
<!ATTLIST h3
   %attrs;
   %TextAlign;
   >

<!ELEMENT h4 %Inline;>
<!ATTLIST h4
   %attrs;
   %TextAlign;
   >

<!ELEMENT h5 %Inline;>
<!ATTLIST h5
   %attrs;
   %TextAlign;
   >
```

Listing A.2   Continued

```
<!ELEMENT h6 %Inline;>
<!ATTLIST h6
  %attrs;
  %TextAlign;
  >

<!--=========== Lists ===============================-->

<!-- Unordered list bullet styles -->

<!ENTITY % ULStyle "(disc|square|circle)">

<!-- Unordered list -->

<!ELEMENT ul (li)+>
<!ATTLIST ul
  %attrs;
  type         %ULStyle;       #IMPLIED
  compact      (compact)       #IMPLIED
  >

<!-- Ordered list numbering style

    1    arabic numbers      1, 2, 3, ...
    a    lower alpha         a, b, c, ...
    A    upper alpha         A, B, C, ...
    i    lower roman         i, ii, iii, ...
    I    upper roman         I, II, III, ...

    The style is applied to the sequence number which by default
    is reset to 1 for the first list item in an ordered list.
-->
<!ENTITY % OLStyle "CDATA">

<!-- Ordered (numbered) list -->

<!ELEMENT ol (li)+>
<!ATTLIST ol
  %attrs;
  type         %OLStyle;       #IMPLIED
  compact      (compact)       #IMPLIED
  start        %Number;        #IMPLIED
  >

<!-- single column list (DEPRECATED) -->
<!ELEMENT menu (li)+>
<!ATTLIST menu
  %attrs;
  compact      (compact)       #IMPLIED
  >

<!-- multiple column list (DEPRECATED) -->
<!ELEMENT dir (li)+>
<!ATTLIST dir
```

```
  %attrs;
  compact       (compact)      #IMPLIED
  >


<!-- LIStyle is constrained to: "(%ULStyle;|%OLStyle;)" -->
<!ENTITY % LIStyle "CDATA">


<!-- list item -->

<!ELEMENT li %Flow;>
<!ATTLIST li
  %attrs;
  type          %LIStyle;      #IMPLIED
  value         %Number;       #IMPLIED
  >


<!-- definition lists - dt for term, dd for its definition -->

<!ELEMENT dl (dt|dd)+>
<!ATTLIST dl
  %attrs;
  compact       (compact)      #IMPLIED
  >


<!ELEMENT dt %Inline;>
<!ATTLIST dt
  %attrs;
  >


<!ELEMENT dd %Flow;>
<!ATTLIST dd
  %attrs;
  >


<!--=========== Address ===========================-->

<!-- information on author -->

<!ELEMENT address %Inline;>
<!ATTLIST address
  %attrs;
  >


<!--=========== Horizontal Rule ====================-->

<!ELEMENT hr EMPTY>
<!ATTLIST hr
  %attrs;
  align         (left|center|right) #IMPLIED
  noshade       (noshade)      #IMPLIED
  size          %Pixels;       #IMPLIED
  width         %Length;       #IMPLIED
  >


<!--=========== Preformatted Text ==================-->

<!-- content is %Inline; excluding
```

LISTING A.2 CONTINUED

```
            "img|object|applet|big|small|sub|sup|font|basefont" -->

<!ELEMENT pre %pre.content;>
<!ATTLIST pre
  %attrs;
  width        %Number;        #IMPLIED
  xml:space    (preserve)      #FIXED 'preserve'
  >


<!--=========== Block-like Quotes ==================-->

<!ELEMENT blockquote %Flow;>
<!ATTLIST blockquote
  %attrs;
  cite         %URI;           #IMPLIED
  >


<!--=========== Text alignment ====================-->

<!-- center content -->
<!ELEMENT center %Flow;>
<!ATTLIST center
  %attrs;
  >


<!--=========== Inserted/Deleted Text =============-->

<!--
  ins/del are allowed in block and inline content, but its
  inappropriate to include block content within an ins element
  occurring in inline content.
-->
<!ELEMENT ins %Flow;>
<!ATTLIST ins
  %attrs;
  cite         %URI;           #IMPLIED
  datetime     %Datetime;      #IMPLIED
  >


<!ELEMENT del %Flow;>
<!ATTLIST del
  %attrs;
  cite         %URI;           #IMPLIED
  datetime     %Datetime;      #IMPLIED
  >


<!--=========== The Anchor Element ==================-->

<!-- content is %Inline; except that anchors shouldn't be nested -->

<!ELEMENT a %a.content;>
<!ATTLIST a
  %attrs;
  charset      %Charset;       #IMPLIED
  type         %ContentType;   #IMPLIED
```

```
    name        NMTOKEN        #IMPLIED
    href        %URI;          #IMPLIED
    hreflang    %LanguageCode; #IMPLIED
    rel         %LinkTypes;    #IMPLIED
    rev         %LinkTypes;    #IMPLIED
    accesskey   %Character;    #IMPLIED
    shape       %Shape;        "rect"
    coords      %Coords;       #IMPLIED
    tabindex    %Number;       #IMPLIED
    onfocus     %Script;       #IMPLIED
    onblur      %Script;       #IMPLIED
    target      %FrameTarget;  #IMPLIED
    >


<!--============== Inline Elements ================-->

<!ELEMENT span %Inline;> <!-- generic language/style container -->
<!ATTLIST span
  %attrs;
  >


<!ELEMENT bdo %Inline;>  <!-- I18N BiDi over-ride -->
<!ATTLIST bdo
  %coreattrs;
  %events;
  lang        %LanguageCode; #IMPLIED
  xml:lang    %LanguageCode; #IMPLIED
  dir         (ltr|rtl)      #REQUIRED
  >


<!ELEMENT br EMPTY>   <!-- forced line break -->
<!ATTLIST br
  %coreattrs;
  clear       (left|all|right|none) "none"
  >


<!ELEMENT em %Inline;>   <!-- emphasis -->
<!ATTLIST em %attrs;>

<!ELEMENT strong %Inline;>   <!-- strong emphasis -->
<!ATTLIST strong %attrs;>

<!ELEMENT dfn %Inline;>   <!-- definitional -->
<!ATTLIST dfn %attrs;>

<!ELEMENT code %Inline;>   <!-- program code -->
<!ATTLIST code %attrs;>

<!ELEMENT samp %Inline;>   <!-- sample -->
<!ATTLIST samp %attrs;>

<!ELEMENT kbd %Inline;>  <!-- something user would type -->
<!ATTLIST kbd %attrs;>

<!ELEMENT var %Inline;>   <!-- variable -->
<!ATTLIST var %attrs;>
```

APP

A

LISTING A.2   CONTINUED

```
<!ELEMENT cite %Inline;>   <!-- citation -->
<!ATTLIST cite %attrs;>

<!ELEMENT abbr %Inline;>   <!-- abbreviation -->
<!ATTLIST abbr %attrs;>

<!ELEMENT acronym %Inline;>   <!-- acronym -->
<!ATTLIST acronym %attrs;>

<!ELEMENT q %Inline;>   <!-- inlined quote -->
<!ATTLIST q
  %attrs;
  cite        %URI;           #IMPLIED
  >

<!ELEMENT sub %Inline;> <!-- subscript -->
<!ATTLIST sub %attrs;>

<!ELEMENT sup %Inline;> <!-- superscript -->
<!ATTLIST sup %attrs;>

<!ELEMENT tt %Inline;>   <!-- fixed pitch font -->
<!ATTLIST tt %attrs;>

<!ELEMENT i %Inline;>   <!-- italic font -->
<!ATTLIST i %attrs;>

<!ELEMENT b %Inline;>   <!-- bold font -->
<!ATTLIST b %attrs;>

<!ELEMENT big %Inline;>   <!-- bigger font -->
<!ATTLIST big %attrs;>

<!ELEMENT small %Inline;>   <!-- smaller font -->
<!ATTLIST small %attrs;>

<!ELEMENT u %Inline;>   <!-- underline -->
<!ATTLIST u %attrs;>

<!ELEMENT s %Inline;>   <!-- strike-through -->
<!ATTLIST s %attrs;>

<!ELEMENT strike %Inline;>   <!-- strike-through -->
<!ATTLIST strike %attrs;>

<!ELEMENT basefont EMPTY> <!-- base font size -->
<!ATTLIST basefont
  id          ID            #IMPLIED
  size        CDATA         #REQUIRED
  color       %Color;       #IMPLIED
  face        CDATA         #IMPLIED
  >

<!ELEMENT font %Inline;> <!-- local change to font -->
<!ATTLIST font
```

```
    %coreattrs;
    %i18n;
    size        CDATA           #IMPLIED
    color       %Color;         #IMPLIED
    face        CDATA           #IMPLIED
    >


<!--=========== Object =======================-->
<!--
  object is used to embed objects as part of HTML pages.
  param elements should precede other content. Parameters
  can also be expressed as attribute/value pairs on the
  object element itself when brevity is desired.
-->

<!ELEMENT object (#PCDATA | param | %block; | form | %inline; | %misc;)*>
<!ATTLIST object
    %attrs;
    declare     (declare)       #IMPLIED
    classid     %URI;           #IMPLIED
    codebase    %URI;           #IMPLIED
    data        %URI;           #IMPLIED
    type        %ContentType;   #IMPLIED
    codetype    %ContentType;   #IMPLIED
    archive     %UriList;       #IMPLIED
    standby     %Text;          #IMPLIED
    height      %Length;        #IMPLIED
    width       %Length;        #IMPLIED
    usemap      %URI;           #IMPLIED
    name        NMTOKEN         #IMPLIED
    tabindex    %Number;        #IMPLIED
    align       %ImgAlign;      #IMPLIED
    border      %Pixels;        #IMPLIED
    hspace      %Pixels;        #IMPLIED
    vspace      %Pixels;        #IMPLIED
    >


<!--
  param is used to supply a named property value.
  In XML it would seem natural to follow RDF and support an
  abbreviated syntax where the param elements are replaced
  by attribute value pairs on the object start tag.
-->
<!ELEMENT param EMPTY>
<!ATTLIST param
    id          ID              #IMPLIED
    name        CDATA           #REQUIRED
    value       CDATA           #IMPLIED
    valuetype   (data|ref|object) "data"
    type        %ContentType;   #IMPLIED
    >


<!--=========== Java applet ===================-->
<!--
  One of code or object attributes must be present.
  Place param elements before other content.
-->
```

LISTING A.2   CONTINUED

```
<!ELEMENT applet (#PCDATA | param | %block; | form | %inline; | %misc;)*>
<!ATTLIST applet
  %coreattrs;
  codebase      %URI;           #IMPLIED
  archive       CDATA           #IMPLIED
  code          CDATA           #IMPLIED
  object        CDATA           #IMPLIED
  alt           %Text;          #IMPLIED
  name          NMTOKEN         #IMPLIED
  width         %Length;        #REQUIRED
  height        %Length;        #REQUIRED
  align         %ImgAlign;      #IMPLIED
  hspace        %Pixels;        #IMPLIED
  vspace        %Pixels;        #IMPLIED
  >

<!--=========== Images ============================-->

<!--
    To avoid accessibility problems for people who aren't
    able to see the image, you should provide a text
    description using the alt and longdesc attributes.
    In addition, avoid the use of server-side image maps.
-->

<!ELEMENT img EMPTY>
<!ATTLIST img
  %attrs;
  src           %URI;           #REQUIRED
  alt           %Text;          #REQUIRED
  name          NMTOKEN         #IMPLIED
  longdesc      %URI;           #IMPLIED
  height        %Length;        #IMPLIED
  width         %Length;        #IMPLIED
  usemap        %URI;           #IMPLIED
  ismap         (ismap)         #IMPLIED
  align         %ImgAlign;      #IMPLIED
  border        %Length;        #IMPLIED
  hspace        %Pixels;        #IMPLIED
  vspace        %Pixels;        #IMPLIED
  >

<!-- usemap points to a map element which may be in this document
    or an external document, although the latter is not widely supported -->

<!--=========== Client-side image maps =============-->

<!-- These can be placed in the same document or grouped in a
        separate document although this isn't yet widely supported -->

<!ELEMENT map ((%block; | form | %misc;)+ | area+)>
<!ATTLIST map
  %i18n;
  %events;
  id            ID              #REQUIRED
```

```
    class         CDATA           #IMPLIED
    style         %StyleSheet;    #IMPLIED
    title         %Text;          #IMPLIED
    name          CDATA           #IMPLIED
    >

<!ELEMENT area EMPTY>
<!ATTLIST area
    %attrs;
    shape         %Shape;         "rect"
    coords        %Coords;        #IMPLIED
    href          %URI;           #IMPLIED
    nohref        (nohref)        #IMPLIED
    alt           %Text;          #REQUIRED
    tabindex      %Number;        #IMPLIED
    accesskey     %Character;     #IMPLIED
    onfocus       %Script;        #IMPLIED
    onblur        %Script;        #IMPLIED
    target        %FrameTarget;   #IMPLIED
    >

<!--======== Forms ================================-->

<!ELEMENT form %form.content;>   <!-- forms shouldn't be nested -->

<!ATTLIST form
    %attrs;
    action        %URI;           #REQUIRED
    method        (get|post)      "get"
    name          NMTOKEN         #IMPLIED
    enctype       %ContentType;   "application/x-www-form-urlencoded"
    onsubmit      %Script;        #IMPLIED
    onreset       %Script;        #IMPLIED
    accept        %ContentTypes;  #IMPLIED
    accept-charset %Charsets;     #IMPLIED
    target        %FrameTarget;   #IMPLIED
    >

<!--
    Each label must not contain more than ONE field
    Label elements shouldn't be nested.
-->
<!ELEMENT label %Inline;>
<!ATTLIST label
    %attrs;
    for           IDREF           #IMPLIED
    accesskey     %Character;     #IMPLIED
    onfocus       %Script;        #IMPLIED
    onblur        %Script;        #IMPLIED
    >

<!ENTITY % InputType
    "(text | password | checkbox |
      radio | submit | reset |
      file | hidden | image | button)"
    >
```

```
<!-- the name attribute is required for all but submit & reset -->

<!ELEMENT input EMPTY>       <!-- form control -->
<!ATTLIST input
  %attrs;
  type         %InputType;    "text"
  name         CDATA          #IMPLIED
  value        CDATA          #IMPLIED
  checked      (checked)      #IMPLIED
  disabled     (disabled)     #IMPLIED
  readonly     (readonly)     #IMPLIED
  size         CDATA          #IMPLIED
  maxlength    %Number;       #IMPLIED
  src          %URI;          #IMPLIED
  alt          CDATA          #IMPLIED
  usemap       %URI;          #IMPLIED
  tabindex     %Number;       #IMPLIED
  accesskey    %Character;    #IMPLIED
  onfocus      %Script;       #IMPLIED
  onblur       %Script;       #IMPLIED
  onselect     %Script;       #IMPLIED
  onchange     %Script;       #IMPLIED
  accept       %ContentTypes; #IMPLIED
  align        %ImgAlign;     #IMPLIED
  >

<!ELEMENT select (optgroup|option)+> <!-- option selector -->
<!ATTLIST select
  %attrs;
  name         CDATA          #IMPLIED
  size         %Number;       #IMPLIED
  multiple     (multiple)     #IMPLIED
  disabled     (disabled)     #IMPLIED
  tabindex     %Number;       #IMPLIED
  onfocus      %Script;       #IMPLIED
  onblur       %Script;       #IMPLIED
  onchange     %Script;       #IMPLIED
  >

<!ELEMENT optgroup (option)+>   <!-- option group -->
<!ATTLIST optgroup
  %attrs;
  disabled     (disabled)     #IMPLIED
  label        %Text;         #REQUIRED
  >

<!ELEMENT option (#PCDATA)>      <!-- selectable choice -->
<!ATTLIST option
  %attrs;
  selected     (selected)     #IMPLIED
  disabled     (disabled)     #IMPLIED
  label        %Text;         #IMPLIED
  value        CDATA          #IMPLIED
  >
```

```
<!ELEMENT textarea (#PCDATA)>      <!-- multi-line text field -->
<!ATTLIST textarea
  %attrs;
  name        CDATA           #IMPLIED
  rows        %Number;        #REQUIRED
  cols        %Number;        #REQUIRED
  disabled    (disabled)      #IMPLIED
  readonly    (readonly)      #IMPLIED
  tabindex    %Number;        #IMPLIED
  accesskey   %Character;     #IMPLIED
  onfocus     %Script;        #IMPLIED
  onblur      %Script;        #IMPLIED
  onselect    %Script;        #IMPLIED
  onchange    %Script;        #IMPLIED
  >


<!--
  The fieldset element is used to group form fields.
  Only one legend element should occur in the content
  and if present should only be preceded by whitespace.
-->
<!ELEMENT fieldset (#PCDATA | legend | %block; | form | %inline; | %misc;)*>
<!ATTLIST fieldset
  %attrs;
  >


<!ENTITY % LAlign "(top|bottom|left|right)">


<!ELEMENT legend %Inline;>      <!-- fieldset label -->
<!ATTLIST legend
  %attrs;
  accesskey   %Character;     #IMPLIED
  align       %LAlign;        #IMPLIED
  >


<!--
 Content is %Flow; excluding a, form, form controls, iframe
-->
<!ELEMENT button %button.content;>  <!-- push button -->
<!ATTLIST button
  %attrs;
  name        CDATA           #IMPLIED
  value       CDATA           #IMPLIED
  type        (button|submit|reset) "submit"
  disabled    (disabled)      #IMPLIED
  tabindex    %Number;        #IMPLIED
  accesskey   %Character;     #IMPLIED
  onfocus     %Script;        #IMPLIED
  onblur      %Script;        #IMPLIED
  >


<!-- single-line text input control (DEPRECATED) -->
<!ELEMENT isindex EMPTY>
<!ATTLIST isindex
  %coreattrs;
  %i18n;
  prompt      %Text;          #IMPLIED
  >
```

```
<!--=============== Tables ========================-->

<!-- Derived from IETF HTML table standard, see [RFC1942] -->

<!--
 The border attribute sets the thickness of the frame around the
 table. The default units are screen pixels.

 The frame attribute specifies which parts of the frame around
 the table should be rendered. The values are not the same as
 CALS to avoid a name clash with the valign attribute.
-->
<!ENTITY % TFrame "(void|above|below|hsides|lhs|rhs|vsides|box|border)">

<!--
 The rules attribute defines which rules to draw between cells:

 If rules is absent then assume:
     "none" if border is absent or border="0" otherwise "all"
-->

<!ENTITY % TRules "(none | groups | rows | cols | all)">

<!-- horizontal placement of table relative to document -->
<!ENTITY % TAlign "(left|center|right)">

<!-- horizontal alignment attributes for cell contents

  char        alignment char, e.g. char=':'
  charoff     offset for alignment char
-->
<!ENTITY % cellhalign
  "align        (left|center|right|justify|char) #IMPLIED
   char         %Character;    #IMPLIED
   charoff      %Length;       #IMPLIED"
  >

<!-- vertical alignment attributes for cell contents -->
<!ENTITY % cellvalign
  "valign       (top|middle|bottom|baseline) #IMPLIED"
  >

<!ELEMENT table
     (caption?, (col*|colgroup*), thead?, tfoot?, (tbody+|tr+))>
<!ELEMENT caption  %Inline;>
<!ELEMENT thead    (tr)+>
<!ELEMENT tfoot    (tr)+>
<!ELEMENT tbody    (tr)+>
<!ELEMENT colgroup (col)*>
<!ELEMENT col      EMPTY>
<!ELEMENT tr       (th|td)+>
<!ELEMENT th       %Flow;>
<!ELEMENT td       %Flow;>
```

```
<!ATTLIST table
  %attrs;
  summary     %Text;          #IMPLIED
  width       %Length;        #IMPLIED
  border      %Pixels;        #IMPLIED
  frame       %TFrame;        #IMPLIED
  rules       %TRules;        #IMPLIED
  cellspacing %Length;        #IMPLIED
  cellpadding %Length;        #IMPLIED
  align       %TAlign;        #IMPLIED
  bgcolor     %Color;         #IMPLIED
  >

<!ENTITY % CAlign "(top|bottom|left|right)">

<!ATTLIST caption
  %attrs;
  align       %CAlign;        #IMPLIED
  >

<!--
colgroup groups a set of col elements. It allows you to group
several semantically related columns together.
-->
<!ATTLIST colgroup
  %attrs;
  span        %Number;        "1"
  width       %MultiLength;   #IMPLIED
  %cellhalign;
  %cellvalign;
  >

<!--
 col elements define the alignment properties for cells in
 one or more columns.

 The width attribute specifies the width of the columns, e.g.

    width=64        width in screen pixels
    width=0.5*      relative width of 0.5

 The span attribute causes the attributes of one
 col element to apply to more than one column.
-->
<!ATTLIST col
  %attrs;
  span        %Number;        "1"
  width       %MultiLength;   #IMPLIED
  %cellhalign;
  %cellvalign;
  >

<!--
    Use thead to duplicate headers when breaking table
    across page boundaries, or for static headers when
    tbody sections are rendered in scrolling panel.
```

LISTING A.2   CONTINUED

```
      Use tfoot to duplicate footers when breaking table
      across page boundaries, or for static footers when
      tbody sections are rendered in scrolling panel.

      Use multiple tbody sections when rules are needed
      between groups of table rows.
-->
<!ATTLIST thead
  %attrs;
  %cellhalign;
  %cellvalign;
  >

<!ATTLIST tfoot
  %attrs;
  %cellhalign;
  %cellvalign;
  >

<!ATTLIST tbody
  %attrs;
  %cellhalign;
  %cellvalign;
  >

<!ATTLIST tr
  %attrs;
  %cellhalign;
  %cellvalign;
  bgcolor       %Color;           #IMPLIED
  >

<!-- Scope is simpler than headers attribute for common tables -->
<!ENTITY % Scope "(row|col|rowgroup|colgroup)">

<!-- th is for headers, td for data and for cells acting as both -->

<!ATTLIST th
  %attrs;
  abbr          %Text;            #IMPLIED
  axis          CDATA             #IMPLIED
  headers       IDREFS            #IMPLIED
  scope         %Scope;           #IMPLIED
  rowspan       %Number;          "1"
  colspan       %Number;          "1"
  %cellhalign;
  %cellvalign;
  nowrap        (nowrap)          #IMPLIED
  bgcolor       %Color;           #IMPLIED
  width         %Pixels;          #IMPLIED
  height        %Pixels;          #IMPLIED
  >
```

```
<!ATTLIST td
  %attrs;
  abbr        %Text;       #IMPLIED
  axis        CDATA        #IMPLIED
  headers     IDREFS       #IMPLIED
  scope       %Scope;      #IMPLIED
  rowspan     %Number;     "1"
  colspan     %Number;     "1"
  %cellhalign;
  %cellvalign;
  nowrap      (nowrap)     #IMPLIED
  bgcolor     %Color;      #IMPLIED
  width       %Pixels;     #IMPLIED
  height      %Pixels;     #IMPLIED
  >
```

XHTML Crib Notes

XHTML 1.0 has been designed to look and function very much like HTML 4.0. Because HTML is an application of SGML, however, while XHTML is an application of XML, some things which were allowed in HTML 4.0 are not permitted in XHTML 1.0. Oddly, the opposite is true as well.

SGML allows one to enforce what SGML calls *exclusions*, which allow you to simply declare that certain elements are not allowed within other elements. XML doesn't allow this level of simplicity as it turns out to be very complex to actually do. An anchor tag (<A …> … </A>), for example, is not allowed to nest within another anchor in HTML 4.0. XHTML 1.0 relies on the good will and fond intentions of the XHTML designer not to do it in XHTML 1.0. This is somewhat less than satisfactory but will have to do for a while. One can always enforce these unguarded error points with external XHTML syntax checkers.

A big change from HTML is that XHTML, like XML itself, is case sensitive. The XHTML DTDs use lowercase tag and attribute names throughout and will not accept uppercase tags or attributes.

All attribute values must be enclosed in quotes and are treated as characters. Any processing of the values is an application responsibility.

Every tag must be properly closed, even empty tags. For compatibility, the suggested syntax for empty tags is to add a space and a slash (/) to the end of the empty tag. So the proper XHTML equivalent for HTML <br> is <br /> and so on. Paragraph tags must be closed, which hardly any of us do, and all the rest. I recommend using a good XML syntax checker such as HTML-Kit / Tidy to automatically insert the proper end tags as it can be quite tedious to insert them by hand. Tidy will also convert all your tags and attributes to lower-case, eliminating a huge chore for those of us with a lot of code out in the world.

Tip from

 LeeAnne.com
Words to weave by

Dave Raggett's Tidy is a command-line program that validates and optionally converts HTML legacy code into the XHTML equivalent. It can be found at http://www.w3.org/People/Raggett/tidy/ as well as incorporated in the HTML-Kit graphical (Windows) interface and editor found at http://www.chami.com/.

NAMING THE XHTML NAMESPACE

Among the very first ELEMENT declarations you see in the XHTML DTD above is definition of the `<html>` tag set which should enclose every html or xhtml document. Notice that the xmlns namespace attribute is pre-declared as FIXED. This means that you cannot override this value, even if you try to supply a different namespace value. It's roughly the same effect as entering it manually like this:

```
<html xmlns="http://www.w3.org/1999/xhtml">
```

The xmlns attribute should always be added to the root tag. In fact it's required, and this version of the XHTML DTD takes care of it for you. With other DTDs you might have to enter it, and with any DTD that's located in several locations, you won't have the luxury of making a FIXED declaration.

With the xmlns attribute you identify the namespace of the document. In the future, when multiple namespaces are supported in each document and the namespace will help applications access the object model of the page, the presence of a valid namespace will facilitate that access and other processing.

RECURSION

If you start taking apart the XHTML DTD, you'll notice some ENTITY declarations that set up what they call content models for exclusions. Remember I said that the anchor tag was one of the troublesome ones? Well there is an ENTITY called `%a.content` that sets up a list of possible elements for inclusion in an anchor tag. It looks like `<a>` is not among them, having been excluded quite properly by the special content list. But wait! Let's look at the tags that do appear on the list. We'll pick one at random, say `<i>`. If we look at that tag's permitted content, `%Inline`, we see that you can include an anchor tag inside it. Most of the potential anchor enclosures are the same way. So the incorrect construction below is obviously illegal and will be caught by the parser:

```
… <a href=" … "><a href=" … "></a></a> …
```

This snippet will be caught when the document is validated but the close cousin, which is equally illegal, probably won't:

```
… <a href=" … "><i><a href=" … "></a><i></a> …
```

It seems to be fine as far as the XHTML DTD is concerned.

This is a general problem with XML, and one I think will have to be addressed someday, but it's been thrashed about for quite some time already and the decision was made to do it that way, so we're stuck with it for a while.

EXTENSIBILITY

This DTD is a model of what you need to do to enable your own DTDs to be easily extended, either by others or by yourself, when you want to experiment with a feature without touching the actual code.

Every major structure is described in an ENTITY before it's declared so it can be overridden by another DTD, either in the internal subset or another DTD entirely that brings in the XHTML DTD after making its own declarations.

It's well-structured, with all the ENTITY declarations at the top of the file, well-commented, and the ELEMENT declarations grouped by function with their associated ATTLIST directly beneath.

APP

A

Tools for XML/XHTML Editing and Conversion

In this appendix

This appendix lists a number of tools you might find useful when working with XML and XML-related standards. They range from simple command-line programs donated to the XML developer community by public-spirited—and usually very talented—XML developers to elaborate graphical document or DTD editing environments created by major corporations. In many cases, each tool description is accompanied by an example of the program in use or a short description of how it works.

This appendix is divided into sections which categorize the general nature of the tools included in that section, although the categories sometimes overlap. When this is so, a utility will be listed in both sections.

XML VALIDATORS

An XML validator checks a well-formed XML document against the DTD that defines it to determine whether it obeys all the rules. If it doesn't, it returns a fatal error. In some cases, the validation behavior can be turned off to make it easier to initially check a new document. The following are several good validators:

- **TclXML**—A validating parser written in the Tcl programming language.
  `http://www.zveno.com/zm.cgi/in-tclxml/`

- **Xerces-J**—Xerces-J is the Apache Project's Java open source XML parser.
  `http://xml.apache.org/xerces-j/`

- **fxp**—The Functional XML Parser from The University of Trier in Germany. An XML parser written in Standard ML. It supports XML Catalog and a document tree visualization module.
  `http://www.informatik.uni-trier.de/~neumann/Fxp/`

- **Ælfred**—A simple Java-based validating XML parser and free for non-commercial use.
  `http://www.opentext.com/services/content_management_services/`
  `xml_sgml_solutions.html#aelfred_and_sax`

XML EDITORS

XML editors allow you to create XML content in a user-friendly environment. Although it's possible to create XML using any text editor, the added support offered by a good authoring environment makes it much harder to make mistakes. The following list is not exhaustive but only a selection of the many fine XML editors available:

- **XMLwriter**—This is one of the best validating XML editors available as shareware at `http://xmlwriter.net/`. XMLWriter allows the author to edit and validate an XML document against a DTD or an XML Schema. The author can also convert an XML document into HTML using an XSL style sheet. CSS is also supported, permitting either XSL or CSS to be used to format documents. XMLWriter can also be used from the command line to validate and translate XML documents.

- **XML Spy**—Another very good validating XML editor available as shareware at `http://www.xmlspy.com/`. XML Spy is an XML, XHTML, XSL, and 3DML editor using a grid layout view of the document. Although it allows the user to edit a version of the source file as well, the actual source file is regenerated every time the views are changed, so formatting is lost every time.

- **Amaya**—Amaya (`http://www.w3.org/Amaya/`) is the W3C HTML/XML editor and Web browser with partial MathML editing support and display capabilities. Amaya is free and among the few HTML/XML editors that edit and display MathML, the mathematics modeling language. In use, you can easily and seamlessly switch between editing and browsing, as well displaying editable source, structure, link, and other views of the document, so checking your work is easy and you can work at whatever level seems appropriate for the task at hand. Amaya is available for many common platforms.

- **Microsoft XMLNotePad**—This is Microsoft's simple XML editor. XML Notepad is well-integrated into the Microsoft version of XML.

- **Emacs**—Emacs is probably the most versatile and widely available programmer's editor in the world, with ports to all the major Unix boxes, Windows in various flavors, Mac OS, and many more. Emacs is a general-purpose engine that supports modes—add-in modules that handle specific languages and tasks. Modes available for XML are psgml, tdtd, and as many more as programmers have a mind to make.

XML-ENABLED BROWSERS

- **InDelv XML Client**—XML Client is an XML/XSL-enabled browser that also supports CSS for XML. Although it's currently in beta, it looks like a tremendous product. There'll be a new version available for download by the time you read this. Visit InDelv at `http://www.indelv.com/`.

- **Microsoft Internet Explorer release 5**—MSIE supports a partially non-standard version of XML. The browser is widely available and will not be included here, but is well worth exploring because by far the greatest number of browsers active on the Web are from Microsoft. Unfortunately, a large percentage of them are older versions and don't support XML at all.

- **Mozilla**—The Mozilla (Netscape) open source development project constitutes a radical rethinking of the Netscape position. Long committed to innovation and proprietary extensions as a source of product differentiation, Netscape has become a late convert to the standards process, and when Mozilla is turned into Netscape version 5—the next generation browser—it promises to be the most full-featured, standards-compliant browser around. Instead of bells and whistles in the code, one of their areas of innovation and differentiation will be to allow the user to define and replace his own chrome, the decorative frame and interface in which the browser window is placed. Full support for XML, CSS1 and XML, MathML, and other XML technologies is promised.

- **Panorama SGML Viewer**—Panorama is an SGML and XML-enabled browser with a long history in the SGML community. It's currently available as a plugin which supports both Netscape and Microsoft browsers from Interleaf at `http://www.interleaf.com/products/sgml.htm` along with a suite of related SGML authoring and publishing products.

- **Plume**—This experimental Web browser written in the Tcl programming language allows you to view XML documents in tree form. The product is available from `http://tcltk.anu.edu.au/` but the site is often unavailable. The author, Steve Ball, now works at Zveno: `http://www.zveno.com/`.

- **Amaya**—Amaya is the experimental W3C HTML/XML editor and Web browser with partial MathML editing support and display capabilities (`http://www.w3.org/Amaya/`). A more complete description is listed under the previous "XML Editors" section.

- **JUMBO**—JUMBO is the first XML browser from Peter Murray-Rust and is still one of the very few that lets one view CML (Chemical Markup Language) files. Peter Murray-Rust is planning to develop and promote the use of the Chemical Markup Language as a universal means of transferring and rendering chemical information on the Web. Get more information on this at `http://www.nottingham.ac.uk/~pazpmr/`.

XML DEVELOPMENT TOOLS

Here is a collection of tools incorporating multiple functions in an interactive development environment of some sort. Many support the development of DTDs, XSL style sheets for display, and other parts of a complete XML document. The following are some good development tools:

- **Near & Far Designer**—Microstar's (Recently acquired by `OpenText Corporation`) DTD development tool is available in a bundle with Vervet Logic's XML <PRO> XML editor to form a complete DTD and XML authoring environment. See it at `http://www.opentext.com/near_and_far/`.

- **XML <PRO>**—Vervet Logic's XML editor is available in a bundle with Microstar's Near & Far Designer. Check out Vervet at `http://www.vervet.com/`.

- **XMLwriter**—This is one of the best validating XML editors, available as shareware at `http://xmlwriter.net/`.

- **XMetaL 1.2**—This is a commercial authoring product rather than a DTD development tool as such, although it can be used to develop new DTDs. Find out more at `http://www.xmetal.com/`.

- **Visual XML**—A Java-based tool for creating and editing XML documents and DTDs. Visual XML offers support for Java Document handlers as well as pure XML applications and is available from from Bluestone Software at `http://www.bluestone.com/Xml/Visual-XML/`.

- **Python and XML Processing**—This site contains links to Python tools for XML, including PyPointers, LT PyXML, tmproc, and XML Toolkit. See them at `http://www.python.org/topics/xml/`.

- **XML Spy**—Another very good validating XML editor available as shareware at `http://www.xmlspy.com/`.

- **XML Testbed**—Steve Withall's XML Testbed is a general development and testing environment including an XML parser, a grove, an editor, and a tree viewer. See it at `http://www.w3.org/XML/1998/08withall/`.

- **MultiDoc Pro Publisher**—An XML/SGML Browser and editor from Citec Information. Citec also makes Doczilla and the The SGML Offshore Toolbox. See it at `http://www.citec.fi/company/products/`.

- **Cocoon**—The Apache Project's XML publishing framework. Cocoon includes support for Extensible Server Pages (XSP), Xerces-J, Xalan, XT, FOP (XSL FO to PDF generation), and more. Find more information at `http://www.apache.org/`.

XML PARSING ENGINES

A parsing engine is simply a tool for generating an XML document tree from an XML document and optional DTD. Many parsers also validate but it's not required. The examples shown range from simple but effective command-line tools to elaborate graphical display environments with integrated debugging and editing facilities. Many are also usable as parts of larger tool sets, enabling the developer to avoid using a home-grown parser and concentrate on exactly what he wants to do with the parsed data. The following are several XML parsing engines:

- **XP**—A non-validating parser from James Clark. See it at `http://www.jclark.com/xml/`.

- **SAX**—The Simple API for XML. Sax is not exactly a parser in the ordinary sense but an event-based engine for traversing the XML tree and outputting modifications of the input. It can be used to perform conversions from XML to HTML and tons of other useful things. SAX is written in Java but has a Python implementation as well. See it at `http://www.megginson.com/SAX/`.

- **Lark**—Lark and Larval are Tim Bray's nonvalidating and validating parsers respectively. See them at `http://www.textuality.com/Lark/`.

- **TclXML**—A validating parser written in tcl. See it at `http://www.zveno.com/zm.cgi/in-tclxml/`.

XML/SGML CONVERSION TOOLS

Conversion tools allow existing documents in various formats to be converted to XML although there are several listed under the next section, "Miscellaneous XML Tools," that convert from XML to other formats such as PDF or HTML. These are three good conversion tools:

- **David Raggett's HTML Tidy**—An excellent command-line tool for checking your HTML or XHTML code for many common errors. Tidy will also attempt to fix many of these errors, saving the designer enormous amounts of time. Find Tidy in many forms at `http://www.w3.org/people/Raggett/tidy/` and, if you find it useful, please send David an interesting souvenir postcard at 73b Ground Corner, Holt, Wiltshire, BA14 6RT, United Kingdom. Remember to affix proper postage if mailing from outside the UK.

- **HTML-Kit from Chami.com**—HTML-Kit is a free Windows HTML/XHTML graphical editor and wrapper for Tidy, David Raggett's error checker and pretty printer. The latest version (they update often) can be found at `http://www.chami.com/html-kit/`.

- **Microstar FastTAG**—A batch and interactive conversion program suitable for automatically turning almost any structured file into an XML or other structured file type using a proprietary rule file. Rules can be set up to convert certain parts of the file automatically and break out to an interactive editing session for difficult conversions. Microstar was recently acquired by OpenText Corporation, so the product should now be available from them at: `http://www.opentext.com/`.

MISCELLANEOUS XML TOOLS

The following tools are directed toward various XML-related standards, Cascading Style Sheets, XSL/XSLT, RDF, Content Management, and other tools. Included in this section is the entire suite of IBM XML tools. Although parts of the suite address tasks that belong in other categories, such as editing, XML validation against a DTD, DTD editing, and so on, there are so many tools in the set that the entire set fits better here:

- **XT**—James Clark's XSLT processor using the XP XML parser. See it at `http://www.jclark.com/xml/`.

- **Style One**—Style One is a CSS1/CSS2 style sheet editor for Win98/NT. See it at `http://www.3-t.com/3-T/products/styleone/Homepage.html`.

- **4DOM**—The FourThought LLC. Python library for manipulating XML documents using the W3C Document object. Model. See it at `http://fourthought.com/4Suite/4DOM/`.

- **4XPath**—The FourThought LLC. Python library for processing the XPath language. See it at `http://fourthought.com/4Suite/4XPath/`.

- **4XSLT**—The FourThought LLC. Python transformation processor for a useful subset of W3C XSLT. See it at `http://fourthought.com/4Suite/4XSLT/`.

- **Xalan**—The Apache Project's XSLT style sheet processors in Java and C++. See it at `http://www.apache.org/`.

- **FOP**—Turn XSL Formatting Objects into PDF files. See it at `http://www.apache.org/`.

- **Extensibility XML Authority**—Build and translate DTDs into SOX and BizTalk. XML authority is slated to support other XML Schema dialects. See it at `http://www.extensibility.com/`.

- **Poet Content Management Suite**—A professional level database system which allows a large business to keep track of their information assets. See it at `http://www.poet.com`.

- **BladeRunner**—An XML-based content management suite available from Interleaf at `http:www.interleaf.com/products/`. The suite includes X-WAP, Interleaf's XML Wireless Application Product, which uses the XML Wireless Application Protocol (WAP) standard and XSL to publish XML documents to the Web-enabled cellphone and pocket organizer market.

- **IBM alphaWorks Tool Suite**—An extensive library of tools from the IBM research labs around the world. See it at `http://www.alphaworks.ibm.com/`. The current toolkit includes

  - **IBM alphaWorks BML**—Bean Markup Language is an XML-based scripting language to use Java Beans to implement an application.
  - **IBM alphaWorks DDbE**—Data Descriptors by Example takes a well-formed XML document and constructs a DTD.
  - **IBM alphaWorks DataCraft**—DataCraft provides an XML database view and enables the designer to publish XML forms to the Web.
  - **IBM alphaWorks DXMLJ**—Dynamic XML for Java allows the designer to add dynamic behavior to XML pages using namespace annotations.
  - **IBM alphaWorks LotusXSL**—An implementation of a subset of the W3C XSL specification in Java.
  - **IBM alphaWorks P3P parser**—An implementation of the P3P (Platform for Privacy Preferences) protocol in 100% pure Java.
  - **IBM alphaWorks PatML**—A rule-based pattern matching and replacement processor for XML in embeddable Java Beans.
  - **IBM alphaWorks SVGView**—A prototype viewer for Scalable Vector Graphics (SVG) files in Java.
  - **IBM alphaWorks TaskGuide Viewer**—An XML-based tool for creating and viewing wizards, knowledge-based help guides that explain complex tasks in simple, easy-to-follow steps.
  - **IBM alphaWorks TeXML**—This XSLT/Java tool publishes XML documents in TeX—Donald Knuth's formatting and typesetting language—in a two part process. Before the conversion can occur, you must first write an XSLT transformation style sheet to convert the XML to a TeXML document type. Then an included Java tool, TeXMLatte, performs the initial parsing to a TeXML DOM. A second Java tool, TeXML, takes a TeXML DOM and outputs TeX.
  - **IBM alphaWorks TSpaces**—An e-commerce and data exchange toolkit supporting XML and other protocols. The toolkit handles buffering and other communications needs automatically, setting up anonymous, asynchronous communications between clients and servers with no requirements for handling semaphores or other artifacts of pseudo-simultaneity.

- **IBM alphaWorks Visual XML Tools**—A prototype XML toolkit for the Application Framework for e-Business. Packages include Visual XML Query, which helps you construct an XML query expression allowing you to open an XML document, construct an XPath expression for an XML document, execute the XPath expression using the Lotus XSLT-based XML Query engine, and save the XPath expression to a file. The second package is Visual XML Creation, which enables you to connect to a DB2 database and retrieve a list of tables, execute an SQL query statement, generate an XML document and DTD, and generate an XSL style sheet for the XML document. The third package is Visual DTD, a tool for creating and editing DTDs. The fourth is Visual XML Transformation, which enables you to create a new XML document from existing XML documents using XSLT.

- **IBM alphaWorks VoiceXML**—A Java-based XML interactive voice response platform being widely adopted in the voice industry. VoiceXML can be used as the basis for voice and DTMF (TouchTone) interaction with Web documents and data.

- **IBM alphaWorks X-IT**—A batch processing application for XML files which allows you to process them in interactive or non-interactive mode.

- **IBM alphaWorks Xeena**—A visual XML editor.

- **IBM alphaWorks XMI Toolkit**—Share Java objects using XML, generate DTDs, and convert code between Java, UML, and Rational Rose.

- **IBM alphaWorks XML BeanMaker**—Generate a Java Bean from a DTD.

- **IBM alphaWorks XML Diff and Merge Tool**—Compares two XML documents, generates a list of changes, and interactively accepts or rejects them.

- **IBM alphaWorks XML EditorMaker**—Automatically generate a custom visual editor from an XML DTD.

- **IBM alphaWorks XML XLE**—XML Lightweight Extractor allows the user to mark up a DTD with proprietary annotations and extract data from an underlying database without processing specific database queries.

- **IBM alphaWorks XML XMas**—XML Master generates custom Java Beans for a particular XML document. XMas also comes with a selection of useful Java beans.

- **IBM alphaWorks XML Enabler**—A Java servlet implementing LotusXSL style sheets on the server side. This allows users with any browser to view an XSL formatted XML document based on the type of browser being used. Separate style sheets must be defined for each type of browser conversion performed.

- **IBM alphaWorks XML for C++**—Two C++ libraries for parsing, validating, and manipulating XML documents.

- **IBM alphaWorks XML Generator**—Generate "random" XML documents from a DTD for the purpose of testing.

- **IBM alphaWorks XML Parser for Java**—A validating XML parser for Java.

- **IBM alphaWorks XML Productivity Kit for Java**—A companion set of Java Beans for the validating XML parser for Java listed previously. Using the productivity kit, the designer can quickly craft simple but effective e-commerce, order entry, shopping basket, and other XML applications.

- **IBM alphaWorks XML Security Suite**—A Java implementation of various security features such as digital signatures, data encryption, and access control.

- **IBM alphaWorks XML Translator Generator**—This application development utility generates special-purpose translators for translating XML documents based on DTD to XML documents based on another DTD. Although the same thing could be done with XSLT, these might be handier in actual use.

- **IBM alphaWorks XML TreeDiff**—This package of Java Beans provides a way to compare and update DOM trees.

- **IBM alphaWorks XML Viewer**—This Java display tool lets you view XML data from the source of the XML, the DTD, or the hierarchical structure of the document.

- **IBM alphaWorks Xplorer**—A companion to XML Viewer that lets you search for XML files meeting specified criteria, validate them, and then view them using XML Viewer.

XML-Enabled Applications

An XML-enabled application is primarily designed to perform some other application, such as typesetting and editing mathematical text, but uses XML as an output or transfer mechanism either by default or as an option.

- **MathType**—A mathematical equation editor for XML at `http://www.mathtype.com/`.

- **WebEQ**—A mathematical equation editor from Geometry Technologies for XML available at `http://www.webeq.com/`.

- **Mathematica**—Mathematica is a fantastic product if you're a mathematician, scientist, or student who uses mathematics extensively. Far from being a simple equation editor, it's a complete mathematical programming environment that let's you enter, evaluate, and graph functions of almost any size and complexity. It also generates MathML code so you can share files with scientists using other engines, or use it for other purposes. See it at `http://www.wolfram.com/`.

- **Amaya**—The experimental W3C HTML/XML editor and Web browser with partial MathML editing support and display capabilities. See it at `http://www.w3.org/Amaya/`.

- **Breeze Commerce Studio**—Breeze Commerce Studio generates Java code to integrate XML and XML-related files such as DTDs, XML Schemas, and more with ODBC/JDBC database sources into complete e-commerce solutions. See it at `http://www.vsi.com/breeze/`.

CONTENTS OF THE CD

In this appendix

The CD accompanying this book contains many useful files and programs arranged in several directories for your convenience with regard to understanding what you're looking at and how you can use it.

USEFUL FILES

Useful files include the whole information content of Appendix A, "XML/XHTML Reference," Appendix D, "Character Entities," and Appendix E, "CSS1, CSS2 Reference." In addition, the CD contains the full HTML text of all W3C XML and XML-related Recommendations, a convenience if your connection to the Internet is not a high-speed one. Although we've tried in this book to cover everything you'll really need, sometimes looking at the source is the only way to handle a tricky question. As always, even Recommendations may be revised so you'll want to keep abreast of the W3C site at `http://www.w3.org/` from time to time. The year 2000 and beyond promises to see a great many XML-related Recommendations issued and you'll want to keep current:

- **Associating Style Sheets with XML documents (29 June 1999)**—This describes the official way to link to an external style sheet from an XML document.

- **Cascading Style Sheets (CSS1) Level 1 Specification (17 December 1996)**—This is the original specification for CSS. It should be noted that it has not been fully, or even reliably, implemented by any major manufacturer in more than three years.

- **Cascading Style Sheets, Level 2 (CSS2) Specification (12 May 1998)**—This specifies the facilities of an extension to basic CSS, allowing more rendering options for more output media to be utilized by the layout designer or typographer. Among the notable new media types supported are aural browsers, as might be used in a cell phone, automobile, or by a user with vision disabilities; hardcopy printers; handheld devices; and others.

- **Document Object Model (DOM) Level 1 (October 1998)**—This is the first level of the Document Object Model, a method of describing the parts of an HTML document in an object-oriented way. DOM Level 1 is not fully capable of describing an XML document, which will require DOM Level 2 and above, but parts of the specification are applicable to XML documents as well as HTML documents.

- **Extensible Markup Language (XML) 1.0 Specification (10 February 1998)**—This is the description of XML itself. AS in all W3C documents, there is an errata document linked to the main document, which contains mistakes and reinterpretations found after the specification was published. The list for XML is particularly extensive and it's not possible to fully understand the document without also reading the errata.

- **Mathematical Markup Language (MathML") 1.01 Specification (7 April 1998, revised 7 July 1999)**—This is an XML application allowing mathematicians, scientists, and others who work with non-trivial mathematical statements to format and edit equations and formulae using tags instead of graphic images. Among other benefits, this allows a mathematical expression to be indexed and searched, a well as referenced by individual part.

- **Namespaces in XML (14 January 1999)**—This specification addresses how parts of a composite XML document using portions using different DTDs can be safely and unambiguously referenced. Namespaces are used by a great number of XML-related specifications and in a wide variety of ways.

- **Resource Description Framework (RDF) Model and Syntax Specification (22 February 1999)**—This is a metalanguage allowing resources to be described using any of a number of standard vocabularies.

- **Synchronized Multimedia Integration Language (SMIL) 1.0 Specification (15 June 1998)**—This specification addresses the need to coordinate and synchronize the timing of many output media types in a single presentation as well as to allow multiple optional parts of a presentation. It is a distantly-related successor to HyTime, the very complex SGML tool capable of similar effects in the SGML world.

- **Web Content Accessibility Guidelines 1.0 (5 May 1999)**—This Recommendation offers guidelines for ensuring that your documents are usable by users with a wide variety of output media types. Although it specifically addresses the needs of persons with disabilities, the guidelines are applicable to every user not using a "standard" interface to the Web with a high-resolution graphic display, a pointing device, and a full keyboard. As the number of alternative output devices continue to multiply, these guidelines will become more and more important to Web designers.

- **XML Path Language (XPath) Version 1.0 (16 November 1999)**—This is a method of describing the location of individual elements and attributes of an XML document in terms of their relationship to the root, each other, or values.

- **XSL Transformations (XSLT) Version 1.0 (16 November 1999)**—This is the document describing the transformation portion of the XSL style sheet specification.

- **HTML 4.01 Specification (24 December 1999)**—This is the revised specification for HTML itself, still used by XML as a target translation medium.

- **XHTML 1.0: The Extensible HyperText Markup Language—A Reformulation of HTML 4 in XML 1.0. (26 January 2000)**—This specification redefines the HTML markup language as a vocabulary of XML. This allows existing HTML documents to be easily reformulated as XML documents with all the accompanying benefits in extensibility and robust error checking available with a DTD.

- **Authoring Tool Accessibility Guidelines 1.0 (3 February 2000)**—Although the Web Content Accessibility guidelines specify methods of ensuring that all users can access the information content of Web pages, there are few content creation tools similarly accessible. This recommendation gives guidelines which should be followed to ensure that all designers can access content-creation tools.

We won't include Working Drafts or other XML-related standards still in development on the CD-ROM. Because these documents are still subject to drastic revision, the best place to view them is on the W3C site itself. You can look at specific areas of interest on the W3C main page at http://www.w3.org/, or look for publications only at http://www.w3.org/TR/.

APP
C

PROPOSED RECOMMENDATION

A Proposed Recommendation has passed several levels of review and comment and is well on its way to becoming a Recommendation. Although substantial changes are much less likely at this point, the reason for this stage is to solicit final comments before publication. It's not unheard of for Proposed Recommendations to be sent back to the Working Group for further study and modification, or even withdrawn and redrafted. The only current proposed recommendations is User Agent Accessibility Guidelines 1.0. These are a set of guidelines to help programmers make sure that user agents (browsers) are more easily accessible to persons with vision and motor disabilities.

CANDIDATE RECOMMENDATIONS

A Candidate Recommendation is a step away from Proposed status. At this point, it's expected that implementations of the Candidate will be developed so that informed comment based on real experience can be collected and understood by the community as a whole. In practice, such implementations have already been partially developed, but advancing to Candidate status implies that the specification is in a state that warrants more complete investigation.

- **Document Object Model (DOM) Level 2 Specification Version 1.0**—The Level 2 DOM extends DOM Level 1 to include specific support for XML and modularizes the specification to make it possible for smaller subsets to be implemented for specific uses.
- **Resource Description Framework (RDF) Schemas**—This describes a method of declaring RDF properties and the relationships between RDF data sets.

WORKING DRAFTS

A Working Draft is a standard, or portion of a standard, still in development. By publishing the Working Draft, the W3C working group responsible for the specification exposes their thinking to the user community for comments, suggestions, and criticisms. At this point, the specification is quite often revised extensively, based on the scrutiny and comments of other interested parties. Parts may even be scrapped and reworked, or the entire draft may be incorporated in another document, although the drafts are usually somewhat stable in overall architecture. Details are never at all dependable, however. This is the W3C scrap book and scratch pad. The following are the Working Drafts:

- **XHTML 1.1 (Module-based XHTML)**—This is part of a larger modularization effort within W3C. Because it's expected that smaller devices may not use the entire HTML specification, identifying modular parts may help make it easier to identify and use appropriate parts of HTML without taking on the whole recommendation.
- **Modularization of XHTML**—Another part of the previously mentioned effort.
- **Building XHTML Modules**—Yet another part of the previously mentioned effort.
- **XML-Signature Core Syntax and Processing**—A portion of XML Signature, under development as a way to irrefutably identify the author of an XML document and ensure that it hasn't been modified.

- **Model Architecture for Voice Browser Systems**—Self-explanatory overall architecture for voice browsers.

- **Speech Synthesis Markup Requirements for Voice Markup Languages**—A requirements document for incorporating speech synthesis into voice browsers.

- **Natural Language Processing Requirements for Voice Markup Languages**—An attempt to identify the current state of the art in machine understanding of natural speech and define what will be required by any language processor.

- **Grammar Representation Requirements for Voice Markup Languages**—Still more parts of the total voice markup language universe.

- **Dialog Requirements for Voice Markup Languages**—And more…

- **Voice Browsers, Introduction**—And more…

- **Mathematical Markup Language (MathML) Version 2.0**—An extension of MathML to handle more mathematical constructs and glyphs. This is waiting for, among other things, some resolution of the request for a larger mathematical character space in the Unicode specification.

- **XHTML Basic**—An initial module of modular XHTML.

- **XHTML Events Module**—Another initial module of modular XHTML.

- **XML Information Set**—An abstract model of the information available in an XML document.

- **XML Base (XBase)**—A method of including the capabilities of HTML Base in XML documents.

- **XML Linking Language (XLink)**—Allows elements to be inserted into XML documents that describe various sorts of links between documents.

- **XML Schema Part 1: Structures**—The structural part of the XML Schema specification. XML Schema is a method of specifying the data content of XML elements and attributes.

- **XML Schema Part 2: Datatypes**—The datatype portion of the XML Schema specification. XML Schema is a method of specifying the data content of XML elements and attributes.

- **Ruby Annotation**—Describes a method of annotating documents with (usually) smaller marginal descriptions or explanations. Usually, this form of notation is used in Chinese, Japanese, and other Eastern scripts.

- **Canonical XML Version 1.0**—Canonical XML is an attempt to define a least common denominator to which "identical" XML documents should resolve. The work is important for digital signatures and other applications of XML.

- **Synchronized Multimedia Integration Language (SMIL) Boston Specification**—The next generation of SMIL. Among other things, Boston attempts to allow portions of SMIL to be embedded in other XML document languages.

- **Synchronized Multimedia Integration Language Document Object Model**—An extension of the DOM to handle SMIL documents.

- **XML Pointer Language (XPointer)**—The language used as an XML document fragment identifier in URIs.

- **User Agent Accessibility Guidelines 1.0**—A definition of requirements for making user agents (loosely, browsers) accessible to all users.

- **Techniques for User Agent Accessibility Guidelines 1.0**—Methods of implementing accessibility in user agents (loosely, browsers).

- **SMIL Animation**—A method of including animations in SMIL documents.

- **Techniques for Authoring Tool Accessibility**—Methods of implementing accessibility in authoring tools.

- **XML-Signature Requirements**—A requirements definition for XML-Signature, a way of irrefutably identifying the authorship and integrity of an XML document.

- **Paged Media Properties for CSS3**—A portion of the CSS3 specification. Current CSS levels offer little support for paged media, which can include hardcopy and other formats with limited and non-scrollable display options. Paper bound in books or magazines is inherently non-scrollable, in contrast to the original scrolling mechanism, the paper or papyrus scroll.

- **Unicode in XML and other Markup Languages**—Accessing Unicode glyphs from XML and other languages.

- **User Interface for CSS3**—A portion of the CSS3 next generation Cascading Style Sheets.

- **International Layout**—A description of international layout requirements, including top to bottom layout as used in Chinese and other text layout conventions.

- **XHTML Document Profile Requirements**—A modular part of XHTML describing document profile requirements in an XHTML document.

- **XHTML Extended Forms Requirements**—A modular part of XHTML describing forms in an XHTML document.

- **Behavioral Extensions to CSS**—Describes standalone behaviors that can be attached to XML documents without modifying the DTD. The XML integrated equivalent of scripts or Dynamic HTML.

- **CSS3 module: W3C selectors**—Describes the new and extended selectors required for CSS3 and XML.

- **XML Fragment Interchange**—Defines a standard method of exchanging XML document fragments, small portions of documents that can be included in other documents.

- **CSS Namespace Enhancements (Proposal)**—A proposal to extend CSS to make it namespace-aware.

- **Color Profiles for CSS3**—A method of defining display characteristics of output media, so that corrected color can be approximated to the extent possible for a particular device.

- **Multi-column layout in CSS**—An extension of CSS to allow true column layout with text flow from one column to the next and embedded pull quotes and the like for documents.

- **Web Characterization Terminology & Definitions Sheet**—A prolegomena to the study of Web Characterization.

- **Extensible Stylesheet Language (XSL)**—The actual formatting objects specification for XSL, which has been eagerly awaited.

- **A P3P Preference Exchange Language (APPEL)**—A language for sharing P3P rule sets between agents, proxies, and other devices that require knowledge of a user's privacy preferences.

- **Requirements for String Identity Matching and String Indexing**—A requirements document for sophisticated pattern matching, especially using character sets with multiple representations possible for the "same" string.

- **XSL Requirements Summary**—An overall architecture document describing what XSL may eventually look like.

CODE SAMPLES

This directory contains the code samples from the book that have the form CCxmpNN.SSS, where CC is the chapter number, xmp is a literal string, NN is the example number in the text, and SSS is a descriptive suffix which depends on the type of file. So x.css would be a Cascading Style Sheets file, x.xml would be an XML file, x.html would be an HTML or XHTML file, x.xsl would be an Extensible Style Language file, and so on. The second XML code example from Chapter 12 would be 12xmp02.xml, and so on.

All files associated with a particular example use the same name format, so it's easy to see which files belong with which others and what they are. If there are several files of a particular type associated with a particular example, succeeding files will be suffixed with -X, where X is a lowercase alphabetic character assigned in ascending order from a to z. So the first HTML file from the first example in Chapter 7 would be 07xmp01.html, the second would be 07xmp01-a.html, the third 07xmp01-b.html, and so on.

If the same file is used several times in different examples, it will be duplicated so you never have to guess about the numbering scheme or which files are needed for a particular example.

FREEWARE

This directory contains software that is really, truly free. It doesn't expire and there are no limitations on its use. In most cases freeware is a labor of love on the part of its maker. It may also be a way to demonstrate programming skills, or represent a commitment to the idea of free software as a way of exchanging ideas and paying back the software development community for the free software an author has benefited from in the past.

Certainly, if you've used free software over the years and it's been of use to you, perhaps made money for you, there may well be a moral obligation of some sort to pass on the favor in some way. If one has no particular programming skills, perhaps a donation to a charity would help balance the karmic books, and a short note of thanks is almost always appreciated.

Freeware ranges from tiny little utilities to entire operating systems and suites of ancillary products. There are several variations on copyright schemes used to protect freeware, many of them demanding that, if the freeware is incorporated into a commercial product, the descendent product inherits the copyright conditions of the original source.

The following sites contain a wide range of software in addition to those related to XML, from compilers to operating systems and more. They really can't be categorized but are available for exploration.

- **GNU**—The GNU's Not Unix (GNU) site with the complete substance of the GNU Project open source software. From Linux to compilers, editors, and everything else one could think of, it's all here and it's all free. Although the GNU distributions are not here, if you find that you need something in order to make any of the other tools work, it may well be found here at `http://www.gnu.org/`.

- **Apache**—The Apache Software Foundation specializes in free server systems software. Their distributions will be found here and at many mirror sites around the world. If you're setting up your own server, the combination of GNU and Apache pretty much covers everything you need. Check it out at `http://www.apache.org`.

The following two sites primarily offer a single tool but are worth mentioning because they're so useful for XHTML development.

- **David Raggett's HTML Tidy**—An excellent tool for checking your HTML or XHTML code for many common errors. Tidy will also attempt to fix many of these errors, saving the designer enormous amounts of time. Find Tidy in many forms at `http://www.w3.org/people/Raggett/tidy/` and, if you find it useful, please send David an interesting souvenir postcard at: 73b Ground Corner, Holt, Wiltshire, BA14 6RT, United Kingdom. Remember to affix proper postage if mailing from outside the UK.

- **HTML-Kit from Chami.com**—HTML-Kit is a free Windows HTML/XHTML editor and wrapper for Tidy, David Raggett's error checker and pretty printer. The latest version (they update often) can be found at `http://www.chami.com/html-kit/`.

The following sites offer a single product which facilitates some phase of XML development. In some cases the site also offers a version with more features that must be purchased.

- **TopStyle Lite**—A style sheet editor and validation tool. The full version, TopStyle, is mentioned with approval in this text and is an excellent choice for editing style sheets and checking for known (many not obvious to inspection) problems. Bradsoft's TopStyle Lite is a scaled-down, free version of the full TopStyle program. For information about the full version of TopStyle, please stop by at `http://www.bradsoft.com/`.

- **Amaya**—The experimental W3C HTML/XML editor and Web browser with partial MathML editing support and display capabilities. See it at `http://www.w3.org/Amaya/`.

- **TclXML**—A validating parser written in tcl. See it at `http://www.zveno.com/zm.cgi/in-tclxml/`.

- **FOP**—Turn XSL Formatting Objects into PDF files. See it at `http://xml.apache.org/fop/`.

- **XT**—James Clark's XSLT processor. See it at `http://www.jclark.com/xml/`.

- **XP**—A non-validating parser from James Clark. See it at `http://www.jclark.com/xml/`.

- **Emacs**—Emacs is probably the most versatile and widely available programmer's editor in the world with ports to all the major Unix boxes, Windows in various flavors, Mac OS and many more. Emacs is a general-purpose engine that supports what are called "modes," add-in modules that handle specific languages and tasks. Modes available for XML are `psgml`, `tdtd`, and as many more as programmers have a mind to make. See it at `http://www.gnu.org/software/emacs/emacs.html` and `http://www.cs.indiana.edu/elisp/w3/docs.html`.

- **Plume**—An experimental Web browser written in tcl which allows you to view XML documents in tree form. See it at `http://plume.browser.org/` or `http://tcltk.anu.edu.au/`.

- **JUMBO**—The first XML browser from Peter Murray-Rust and still one of the very few which let's one view CML (Chemical Markup Language) files. See it at `http://www.nottingham.ac.uk/~pazpmr/`.

- **SAX**—The Simple API for XML. Sax is not exactly a parser in the ordinary sense but an event-based engine for traversing the XML tree and outputting modifications of the input. It can be used to perform conversions from XML to HTML and tons of other useful things. SAX is written in Java but has a Python implementation as well. See it at `http://www.megginson.com/SAX/`.

- **Lark**—Lark and Larval are Tim Bray's non-validating and validating parsers. See it at `http://www.textuality.com/Lark/`.

- **TclXML**—A validating parser written in tcl. See it at `http://www.zveno.com/zm.cgi/in-tclxml/`.

- **IBM alphaWorks Tool Suite**—An extensive library of tools from the IBM research labs around the world. See it at `http://www.alphaworks.ibm.com/`. The current toolkit includes
  - **IBM alphaWorks Bean Markup Language**
  - **IBM alphaWorks Data Descriptors by Example**
  - **IBM alphaWorks DataCraft**
  - **IBM alphaWorks Dynamic XML for Java**
  - **IBM alphaWorks LotusXSL**
  - **IBM alphaWorks P3P parser**

- **IBM alphaWorks PatML**
- **IBM alphaWorks RDF for XML**
- **IBM alphaWorks Speech Markup Language**
- **IBM alphaWorks SVGView**
- **IBM alphaWorks TaskGuide Viewer**
- **IBM alphaWorks TeXML**
- **IBM alphaWorks TSpaces**
- **IBM alphaWorks Visual XML Tools**
- **IBM alphaWorks VoiceXML**
- **IBM alphaWorks X-IT**
- **IBM alphaWorks Xeena**
- **IBM alphaWorks XMI Toolkit**
- **IBM alphaWorks XML BeanMaker**
- **IBM alphaWorks XML Diff and Merge Tool**
- **IBM alphaWorks XML EditorMaker**
- **IBM alphaWorks XML Enabler**
- **IBM alphaWorks XML for C++**
- **IBM alphaWorks XML Generator**
- **IBM alphaWorks XML Parser for Java**
- **IBM alphaWorks XML Productivity Kit for Java**
- **IBM alphaWorks XML Security Suite**
- **IBM alphaWorks XML Translator Generator**
- **IBM alphaWorks XML TreeDiff**
- **IBM alphaWorks XML Viewer**
- **IBM alphaWorks Xplorer**

SHAREWARE

This directory contains software that can be used for an unlimited time but asks you to pay the author if you find the product useful. Sometimes the software nags you about payment periodically, and sometimes it just exhibits a reproachful "Evaluation Version" on the menu bar somewhere.

Shareware authors depend on the honesty of their customers, sort of like the fresh produce and fruit stands by the side of the road you see in some farming communities. There's a shoebox full of money to make change from and baskets of fruit or vegetables but no sales clerk. It's enough to restore your faith in the essential goodness of humanity if you've been made hard and cynical by too close confinement in the urban environment.

Please help these authors continue their efforts, and their optimistic view of human nature, by paying the usually trivial price they ask for their software. Often, they ask no more than what it would cost to take a date to the movies and if more, about the cost of a meal afterward.

The sole inhabitant of this directory is XML Spy, which is an excellent validating XML editor available as true shareware at `http://www.xmlspy.com/`.

DEMOWARE

Demoware either shuts itself down after a predetermined number of uses or after a predetermined time has passed and demands payment or even re-downloading before the program will work again. Sometimes the program is limited in functionality instead.

Although not as nice to have as free or shareware, demoware is an excellent "try before you buy" strategy for experimenting with software that interests you before plunking down your cash for it. Demoware is also a sign of pride and confidence on the part of the vendor, as their income depends on people who pay after they decide whether they're satisfied.

The sole inhabitant of this directory is XMLwriter, which is one of the best validating XML editors available as demoware at `http://xmlwriter.net/`.

MISCELLANY

We would be remiss if we failed to point out that there are many excellent online resources that may help you with particular problems. Included on the CD-ROM are self-explanatory XHTML files with pointers to mailing lists and other resources addressing particular aspects of XML development. The following resources are part of those lists:

- **XML-List**—The most general list for XML and XML-related standards. XML-List will generate quite a lot of mail but most of it will be extremely useful. You can ask questions, offer opinions, and generally participate in the life of the XML development community on this list. I highly recommend it. To subscribe to or unsubscribe from the list, send the message "subscribe" or "unsubscribe" without quotes to `xsl-list-request@mulberrytech.com`.

- **XSL-List**—A list devoted to XSL style sheets. Far more specialized than XML-List, this is the place to go for questions related to XSL or XSLT. To subscribe, `mailto:majordomo@ic.ac.uk` the following message; subscribe xml-dev. To unsubscribe, `mailto:majordomo@ic.ac.uk` the following message; "unsubscribe xml-dev".

- **www-mobile@w3.org**—This is an archived public mailing list for technical discussion about mobile access. To subscribe, send email to `www-mobile-request@w3.org` with the subject "subscribe", or leave the subject line blank and put in the body of the email subscribe `yourname@yourhost`. DO NOT send subscribe/unsubscribe request to `www-mobile@w3.org` itself! See the W3C Mailing List Administrativia for more detail.

APP

C

CHARACTER ENTITIES

In this appendix

XML AND XHTML CHARACTER SETS

Unlike HTML, which is firmly grounded in standard Western European alphabetic conventions, XML and XHTML are international in scope and design. This means that, unlike HTML, there are no default extended character sets that can be assumed by the developer aside from the basic ASCII/ISO-IEC 646 character set used to describe the language itself. Any special character entities you need have to be declared. So a Russian designer calls for Cyrillic entity sets, a Chinese designer chooses from several Chinese character set variations, and speakers of Western European languages such as English have to identify a particular extended character set just like everyone else in the world.

Of course, if your application doesn't need any characters beyond ASCII, you don't need to do anything. And you can explicitly name almost any character in any character space numerically as long as it is a tab (09), a carriage return (0D), a line feed (0A), or in the ranges 0020-D7FF or 010000-10FFFF, the legal characters of Unicode and ISO 10646. Your operating system and that of your viewers might not be able to support and use these characters, or you might have to find and use some sort of support for extended character sets, but the capability is there in the language. Literally a billion or two characters are at your beck and call.

REFERENCING CHARACTER SETS

Referencing and using character sets by mnemonic name as opposed to numerically is quite simple, following the entity declaration format used for substitutions in XML. Here's how to call up the ISO Latin-1 and a few other standard character sets, assuming you have them stashed somewhere on your system or have some way of pointing to them otherwise:

```
<!ENTITY % ISOnum PUBLIC "ISO 8879:1986//ENTITIES Numeric and  Special
         Graphic//EN" "ISOnum.ent">
%ISOnum;
<!ENTITY % ISOpub PUBLIC "ISO 8879:1986//ENTITIES Publishing//EN"
         "ISOpub.ent>
%ISOpub;
<!ENTITY % ISOtech PUBLIC "ISO 8879:1986//ENTITIES General Technical//EN"
         "ISOtech.ent">
%ISOtech;
<!ENTITY % ISOdia PUBLIC "ISO 8879:1986//ENTITIES Diacritical Marks//EN"
         "ISOdia.ent">
%ISOdia;
<!ENTITY % ISOlat1 PUBLIC "ISO 8879:1986//ENTITIES Added Latin 1//EN"
         "ISOlat1.ent">
%ISOlat1;
<!ENTITY % ISOlat2 PUBLIC "ISO 8879:1986//ENTITIES Added Latin 2//EN"
         "ISOlat2.ent">
%ISOlat2;
<!ENTITY % ISOamso PUBLIC "ISO 8879:1986//ENTITIES Added Math Symbols:
         Ordinary//EN" "ISOamso.ent">
%ISOamso;
<!ENTITY % ISOgrk1 PUBLIC "ISO 8879:1986//ENTITIES Greek Letters//EN"
         "ISOgrk1.ent">
%ISOgrk1;
```

```
<!ENTITY % ISOgrk3 PUBLIC "ISO 8879:1986//ENTITIES Greek Symbols//EN"
         "ISOgrk3.ent">
%ISOgrk3;
```

Or here's how to point to a version of ISO Latin-1 on the W3C site remotely:

```
<!ENTITY % ISOlat1 PUBLIC "-//W3C//ENTITIES Latin1 for XHTML//EN"
       "http://www.w3.org/TR/xhtml1/DTD/xhtml-lat1.ent">
%ISOlat1;
```

Both entries are needed for each character set declaration. The first tells the system where to find the character set whereas the second actually inserts the characters into the document so they can be used.

I've included several of these entity sets on the accompanying CD-ROM as they can be difficult to find when you need them. I've also listed them in the "Standard XHTML Character Sets" section immediately following.

STANDARD XHTML CHARACTER SETS

Although XML enables many character sets to be used in a document, the XHTML redefinition includes the three standard HTML extended character entity sets by default so that XHTML behaves a bit more like HTML.

ISO LATIN-1 ENTITIES

ISO Copyright Notice

Portions (C) International Organization for Standardization 1986

Permission to copy in any form is granted for use with conforming SGML systems and applications as defined in ISO 8879, provided this notice is included in all copies.

Standard ASCII doesn't contain enough characters to allow Web page designers to render most European languages with appropriate accents and special characters. The Latin 1 character set extends ASCII with accents, special characters, and a few common typographical symbols that make it possible to display and print French, German, Danish, Spanish and many other languages. Although extensive, this extended character set doesn't address the full range of languages found in the world:

```
<!-- Latin-1 characters for XHTML -->

<!-- Character entity set. Typical invocation:
    <!ENTITY % HTMLlat1 PUBLIC
       "-//W3C//ENTITIES Latin1 for XHTML//EN"
       "http://www.w3.org/TR/xhtml1/DTD/xhtml-lat1.ent">
    %HTMLlat1;
-->

<!ENTITY nbsp   " "> <!-- no-break space = non-breaking space, U+00A0
ISOnum -->
<!ENTITY iexcl  "&#161;"> <!-- inverted exclamation mark, U+00A1 ISOnum -->
<!ENTITY cent   "&#162;"> <!-- cent sign, U+00A2 ISOnum -->
```

APP

D

```
<!ENTITY pound  "&#163;"> <!-- pound sign, U+00A3 ISOnum -->
<!ENTITY curren "&#164;"> <!-- currency sign, U+00A4 ISOnum -->
<!ENTITY yen    "&#165;"> <!-- yen sign = yuan sign, U+00A5 ISOnum -->
<!ENTITY brvbar "&#166;"> <!-- broken bar = broken vertical bar, U+00A6
➥ISOnum -->
<!ENTITY sect   "&#167;"> <!-- section sign, U+00A7 ISOnum -->
<!ENTITY uml    "&#168;"> <!-- diaeresis = spacing diaeresis, U+00A8 ISOdia -->
<!ENTITY copy   "&#169;"> <!-- copyright sign, U+00A9 ISOnum -->
<!ENTITY ordf   "&#170;"> <!-- feminine ordinal indicator, U+00AA ISOnum -->
<!ENTITY laquo  "&#171;"> <!-- left-pointing double angle quotation mark = left
➥pointing guillemet, U+00AB ISOnum -->
<!ENTITY not    "&#172;"> <!-- not sign = discretionary hyphen, U+00AC
➥ISOnum -->
<!ENTITY shy    "&#173;"> <!-- soft hyphen = discretionary hyphen, U+00AD
➥ISOnum -->
<!ENTITY reg    "&#174;"> <!-- registered sign = registered trade mark sign,
➥U+00AE ISOnum -->
<!ENTITY macr   "&#175;"> <!-- macron = spacing macron = overline = APL
➥overbar, U+00AF ISOdia -->
<!ENTITY deg    "&#176;"> <!-- degree sign, U+00B0 ISOnum -->
<!ENTITY plusmn "&#177;"> <!-- plus-minus sign = plus-or-minus sign, U+00B1
➥ISOnum -->
<!ENTITY sup2   "&#178;"> <!-- superscript two = superscript digit two = v
squared, U+00B2 ISOnum -->
<!ENTITY sup3   "&#179;"> <!-- superscript three = superscript digit three =
➥cubed, U+00B3 ISOnum -->
<!ENTITY acute  "&#180;"> <!-- acute accent = spacing acute, U+00B4 ISOdia -->
<!ENTITY micro  "&#181;"> <!-- micro sign, U+00B5 ISOnum -->
<!ENTITY para   "&#182;"> <!-- pilcrow sign = paragraph sign, U+00B6
➥ISOnum -->
<!ENTITY middot "&#183;"> <!-- middle dot = Georgian comma = Greek middle dot,
➥U+00B7 ISOnum -->
<!ENTITY cedil  "&#184;"> <!-- cedilla = spacing cedilla, U+00B8 ISOdia -->
<!ENTITY sup1   "&#185;"> <!-- superscript one = superscript digit one,
➥U+00B9 ISOnum -->
<!ENTITY ordm   "&#186;"> <!-- masculine ordinal indicator, U+00BA ISOnum -->
<!ENTITY raquo  "&#187;"> <!-- right-pointing double angle quotation mark =
➥right pointing guillemet, U+00BB ISOnum -->
<!ENTITY frac14 "&#188;"> <!-- vulgar fraction one quarter = fraction one
➥quarter, U+00BC ISOnum -->
<!ENTITY frac12 "&#189;"> <!-- vulgar fraction one half = fraction one half,
➥U+00BD ISOnum -->
<!ENTITY frac34 "&#190;"> <!-- vulgar fraction three quarters = fraction three
➥quarters, U+00BE ISOnum -->
<!ENTITY iquest "&#191;"> <!-- inverted question mark = turned question mark,
➥U+00BF ISOnum -->
<!ENTITY Agrave "&#192;"> <!-- latin capital letter A with grave = latin
➥capital
➥letter A grave, U+00C0 ISOlat1 -->
<!ENTITY Aacute "&#193;"> <!-- latin capital letter A with acute, U+00C1
➥ISOlat1 -->
<!ENTITY Acirc  "&#194;"> <!-- latin capital letter A with circumflex, U+00C2
➥ISOlat1 -->
➥<!ENTITY Atilde "&#195;"> <!-- latin capital letter A with tilde, U+00C3
➥ISOlat1 -->
<!ENTITY Auml   "&#196;"> <!-- latin capital letter A with diaeresis,
➥U+00C4 ISOlat1 -->
```

```
<!ENTITY Aring  "&#197;"> <!-- latin capital letter A with ring above = latin
➥capital letter A ring, U+00C5 ISOlat1 -->
<!ENTITY AElig  "&#198;"> <!-- latin capital letter AE = latin capital
➥ligature AE, U+00C6 ISOlat1 -->
<!ENTITY Ccedil "&#199;"> <!-- latin capital letter C with cedilla,
➥U+00C7 ISOlat1 -->
<!ENTITY Egrave "&#200;"> <!-- latin capital letter E with grave, U+00C8
➥ISOlat1 -->
<!ENTITY Eacute "&#201;"> <!-- latin capital letter E with acute, U+00C9
➥ISOlat1 -->
<!ENTITY Ecirc  "&#202;"> <!-- latin capital letter E with circumflex,
➥U+00CA ISOlat1 -->
<!ENTITY Euml   "&#203;"> <!-- latin capital letter E with diaeresis, U+00CB
➥ISOlat1 -->
<!ENTITY Igrave "&#204;"> <!-- latin capital letter I with grave, U+00CC
➥ISOlat1 -->
<!ENTITY Iacute "&#205;"> <!-- latin capital letter I with acute, U+00CD
➥ISOlat1 -->
<!ENTITY Icirc  "&#206;"> <!-- latin capital letter I with circumflex,
➥U+00CE ISOlat1 -->
<!ENTITY Iuml   "&#207;"> <!-- latin capital letter I with diaeresis, U+00CF
➥ISOlat1 -->
<!ENTITY ETH    "&#208;"> <!-- latin capital letter ETH, U+00D0 ISOlat1 -->
<!ENTITY Ntilde "&#209;"> <!-- latin capital letter N with tilde, U+00D1
➥ISOlat1 -->
<!ENTITY Ograve "&#210;"> <!-- latin capital letter O with grave, U+00D2
➥ISOlat1 -->
<!ENTITY Oacute "&#211;"> <!-- latin capital letter O with acute, U+00D3
➥ISOlat1 -->
<!ENTITY Ocirc  "&#212;"> <!-- latin capital letter O with circumflex, U+00D4
➥ISOlat1 -->
<!ENTITY Otilde "&#213;"> <!-- latin capital letter O with tilde, U+00D5
➥ISOlat1 -->
<!ENTITY Ouml   "&#214;"> <!-- latin capital letter O with diaeresis, U+00D6
➥ISOlat1 -->
<!ENTITY times  "&#215;"> <!-- multiplication sign, U+00D7 ISOnum -->
<!ENTITY Oslash "&#216;"> <!-- latin capital letter O with stroke = latin
➥capital letter O slash, U+00D8 ISOlat1 -->
<!ENTITY Ugrave "&#217;"> <!-- latin capital letter U with grave, U+00D9
➥ISOlat1 -->
<!ENTITY Uacute "&#218;"> <!-- latin capital letter U with acute, U+00DA
➥ISOlat1 -->
<!ENTITY Ucirc  "&#219;"> <!-- latin capital letter U with circumflex, U+00DB
➥ISOlat1 -->
<!ENTITY Uuml   "&#220;"> <!-- latin capital letter U with diaeresis, U+00DC
➥ISOlat1 -->
<!ENTITY Yacute "&#221;"> <!-- latin capital letter Y with acute, U+00DD
➥ISOlat1 -->
<!ENTITY THORN  "&#222;"> <!-- latin capital letter THORN, U+00DE ISOlat1 -->
<!ENTITY szlig  "&#223;"> <!-- latin small letter sharp s = ess-zed, U+00DF
➥ISOlat1 -->
<!ENTITY agrave "&#224;"> <!-- latin small letter a with grave = latin small
➥letter a grave, U+00E0 ISOlat1 -->
<!ENTITY aacute "&#225;"> <!-- latin small letter a with acute, U+00E1
➥ISOlat1 -->
<!ENTITY acirc  "&#226;"> <!-- latin small letter a with circumflex, U+00E2
➥ISOlat1 -->
```

```
<!ENTITY atilde "&#227;"> <!-- latin small letter a with tilde, U+00E3
➥ISOlat1 -->
<!ENTITY auml   "&#228;"> <!-- latin small letter a with diaeresis, U+00E4
➥ISOlat1 -->
<!ENTITY aring  "&#229;"> <!-- latin small letter a with ring above = latin
➥small letter a ring, U+00E5 ISOlat1 -->
<!ENTITY aelig  "&#230;"> <!-- latin small letter ae = latin small ligature
➥ae, U+00E6 ISOlat1 -->
<!ENTITY ccedil "&#231;"> <!-- latin small letter c with cedilla, U+00E7
➥ISOlat1 -->
<!ENTITY egrave "&#232;"> <!-- latin small letter e with grave, U+00E8
➥ISOlat1 -->
<!ENTITY eacute "&#233;"> <!-- latin small letter e with acute, U+00E9
➥ISOlat1 -->
<!ENTITY ecirc  "&#234;"> <!-- latin small letter e with circumflex, U+00EA
➥ISOlat1 -->
<!ENTITY euml   "&#235;"> <!-- latin small letter e with diaeresis, U+00EB
➥ISOlat1 -->
<!ENTITY igrave "&#236;"> <!-- latin small letter i with grave, U+00EC
➥ISOlat1 -->
<!ENTITY iacute "&#237;"> <!-- latin small letter i with acute, U+00ED
➥ISOlat1 -->
<!ENTITY icirc  "&#238;"> <!-- latin small letter i with circumflex, U+00EE
➥ISOlat1 -->
<!ENTITY iuml   "&#239;"> <!-- latin small letter i with diaeresis, U+00EF
➥ISOlat1 -->
<!ENTITY eth    "&#240;"> <!-- latin small letter eth, U+00F0 ISOlat1 -->
<!ENTITY ntilde "&#241;"> <!-- latin small letter n with tilde, U+00F1
➥ISOlat1 -->
<!ENTITY ograve "&#242;"> <!-- latin small letter o with grave, U+00F2
➥ISOlat1 -->
<!ENTITY oacute "&#243;"> <!-- latin small letter o with acute, U+00F3
➥ISOlat1 -->
<!ENTITY ocirc  "&#244;"> <!-- latin small letter o with circumflex, U+00F4
➥ISOlat1 -->
<!ENTITY otilde "&#245;"> <!-- latin small letter o with tilde, U+00F5
➥ISOlat1 -->
<!ENTITY ouml   "&#246;"> <!-- latin small letter o with diaeresis, U+00F6
➥ISOlat1 -->
<!ENTITY divide "&#247;"> <!-- division sign, U+00F7 ISOnum -->
<!ENTITY oslash "&#248;"> <!-- latin small letter o with stroke, = latin
➥small letter o slash, U+00F8 ISOlat1 -->
<!ENTITY ugrave "&#249;"> <!-- latin small letter u with grave, U+00F9
➥ISOlat1 -->
<!ENTITY uacute "&#250;"> <!-- latin small letter u with acute, U+00FA
➥ISOlat1 -->
<!ENTITY ucirc  "&#251;"> <!-- latin small letter u with circumflex, U+00FB
➥ISOlat1 -->
<!ENTITY uuml   "&#252;"> <!-- latin small letter u with diaeresis, U+00FC
➥ISOlat1 -->
<!ENTITY yacute "&#253;"> <!-- latin small letter y with acute, U+00FD
➥ISOlat1 -->
<!ENTITY thorn  "&#254;"> <!-- latin small letter thorn with, U+00FE
➥ISOlat1 -->
<!ENTITY yuml   "&#255;"> <!-- latin small letter y with diaeresis, U+00FF
➥ISOlat1 -->
```

ISO SPECIAL CHARACTER ENTITIES

ISO Copyright Notice

Portions (C) International Organization for Standardization 1986

Permission to copy in any form is granted for use with conforming SGML systems and applications as defined in ISO 8879, provided this notice is included in all copies.

This small character set extends ASCII to include special characters used in XML and it's related standards, including XHTML, as well as a handful of rarely used characters used in some European languages and fairly extensive typographical elements used in formatting and marking text:

```
<!-- Special characters for XHTML -->

<!-- Character entity set. Typical invocation:
     <!ENTITY % HTMLspecial PUBLIC
        "-//W3C//ENTITIES Special//EN//HTML"
        "http://www.w3.org/TR/xhtml1/DTD/xhtml-special.ent">
     %HTMLspecial;
-->

<!-- Relevant ISO entity set is given unless names are newly introduced.
     New names (i.e., not in ISO 8879 list) do not clash with any
     existing ISO 8879 entity names. ISO 10646 character numbers
     are given for each character, in hex. values are decimal
     conversions of the ISO 10646 values and refer to the document
     character set. Names are Unicode names.
-->

<!-- C0 Controls and Basic Latin -->
<!ENTITY quot    "&#34;"> <!--  quotation mark = APL quote, U+0022 ISOnum -->
<!ENTITY amp     "&#38;"> <!--  ampersand, U+0026 ISOnum -->
<!ENTITY lt      "&#60;"> <!--  less-than sign, U+003C ISOnum -->
<!ENTITY gt      "&#62;"> <!--  greater-than sign, U+003E ISOnum -->
<!ENTITY apos    "&#39;"> <!--  apostrophe mark, U+0027 ISOnum -->

<!-- Latin Extended-A -->
<!ENTITY OElig   "&#338;"> <!--  latin capital ligature OE, U+0152 ISOlat2 -->
<!ENTITY oelig   "&#339;"> <!--  latin small ligature oe, U+0153 ISOlat2 -->
<!-- ligature is a misnomer, this is a separate character in some languages -->
<!ENTITY Scaron  "&#352;"> <!--  latin capital letter S with caron, U+0160
➥ISOlat2 -->
<!ENTITY scaron  "&#353;"> <!--  latin small letter s with caron, U+0161
➥ISOlat2 -->
<!ENTITY Yuml    "&#376;"> <!--  latin capital letter Y with diaeresis, U+0178
➥ISOlat2 -->

<!-- Spacing Modifier Letters -->
<!ENTITY circ    "&#710;"> <!--  modifier letter circumflex accent, U+02C6
➥ISOpub -->
<!ENTITY tilde   "&#732;"> <!--  small tilde, U+02DC ISOdia -->

<!-- General Punctuation -->
<!ENTITY ensp    " "> <!--  en space, U+2002 ISOpub -->
```

```
<!ENTITY emsp    " "> <!-- em space, U+2003 ISOpub -->
<!ENTITY thinsp  " "> <!-- thin space, U+2009 ISOpub -->
<!ENTITY zwnj    "&#8204;"> <!-- zero width non-joiner, U+200C NEW RFC 2070 -->
<!ENTITY zwj     "&#8205;"> <!-- zero width joiner, U+200D NEW RFC 2070 -->
<!ENTITY lrm     "&#8206;"> <!-- left-to-right mark, U+200E NEW RFC 2070 -->
<!ENTITY rlm     "&#8207;"> <!-- right-to-left mark, U+200F NEW RFC 2070 -->
<!ENTITY ndash   "&#8211;"> <!-- en dash, U+2013 ISOpub -->
<!ENTITY mdash   "&#8212;"> <!-- em dash, U+2014 ISOpub -->
<!ENTITY lsquo   "&#8216;"> <!-- left single quotation mark, U+2018 ISOnum -->
<!ENTITY rsquo   "&#8217;"> <!-- right single quotation mark, U+2019 ISOnum -->
<!ENTITY sbquo   "&#8218;"> <!-- single low-9 quotation mark, U+201A NEW -->
<!ENTITY ldquo   "&#8220;"> <!-- left double quotation mark, U+201C ISOnum -->
<!ENTITY rdquo   "&#8221;"> <!-- right double quotation mark, U+201D ISOnum -->
<!ENTITY bdquo   "&#8222;"> <!-- double low-9 quotation mark, U+201E NEW -->
<!ENTITY dagger  "&#8224;"> <!-- dagger, U+2020 ISOpub -->
<!ENTITY Dagger  "&#8225;"> <!-- double dagger, U+2021 ISOpub -->
<!ENTITY permil  "&#8240;"> <!-- per mille sign, U+2030 ISOtech -->
<!ENTITY lsaquo  "&#8249;"> <!-- single left-pointing angle quotation mark,
➥U+2039 ISO proposed -->
<!-- lsaquo is proposed but not yet ISO standardized -->
<!ENTITY rsaquo  "&#8250;"> <!-- single right-pointing angle quotation mark,
➥U+203A ISO proposed -->
<!-- rsaquo is proposed but not yet ISO standardized -->
<!ENTITY euro    "&#8364;"> <!--  euro sign, U+20AC NEW -->
```

ISO MATHEMATICAL, GREEK, AND SYMBOLIC CHARACTER ENTITIES

The third major lack in the ASCII character set, at least as far as Western Europeans are concerned, is lack of support for mathematics and scientific typography. So this set of characters defines the unaccented Greek alphabet, mathematical, and certain scientific characters:

Note

Of course these are not enough for serious mathematics; mathematicians invent new symbols as fast as they discover new ways of looking at things, but it does allow the basics. Neither are the Greek characters suitable for printing modern Greek.

ISO Copyright Notice

Portions (C) International Organization for Standardization 1986

Permission to copy in any form is granted for use with conforming SGML systems and applications as defined in ISO 8879, provided this notice is included in all copies.

```
<!-- Mathematical, Greek and Symbolic characters for XHTML -->

<!-- Character entity set. Typical invocation:
     <!ENTITY % HTMLsymbol PUBLIC
       "-//W3C//ENTITIES Symbols for XHTML//EN"
       "http://www.w3.org/TR/xhtml1/DTD/xhtml-symbol.ent">
     %HTMLsymbol;
-->

<!-- Relevant ISO entity set is given unless names are newly introduced.
     New names (i.e., not in ISO 8879 list) do not clash with any
```

```
        existing ISO 8879 entity names. ISO 10646 character numbers
        are given for each character, in hex. values are decimal
        conversions of the ISO 10646 values and refer to the document
        character set. Names are Unicode names.
-->


<!-- Latin Extended-B -->
<!ENTITY fnof       "&#402;"> <!-- latin small f with hook = function
                                    = florin, U+0192 ISOtech -->


<!-- Greek -->
<!ENTITY Alpha      "&#913;"> <!-- greek capital letter alpha, U+0391 -->
<!ENTITY Beta       "&#914;"> <!-- greek capital letter beta, U+0392 -->
<!ENTITY Gamma      "&#915;"> <!-- greek capital letter gamma, U+0393 ISOgrk3 -->
<!ENTITY Delta      "&#916;"> <!-- greek capital letter delta, U+0394 ISOgrk3 -->
<!ENTITY Epsilon    "&#917;"> <!-- greek capital letter epsilon, U+0395 -->
<!ENTITY Zeta       "&#918;"> <!-- greek capital letter zeta, U+0396 -->
<!ENTITY Eta        "&#919;"> <!-- greek capital letter eta, U+0397 -->
<!ENTITY Theta      "&#920;"> <!-- greek capital letter theta, U+0398 ISOgrk3 -->
<!ENTITY Iota       "&#921;"> <!-- greek capital letter iota, U+0399 -->
<!ENTITY Kappa      "&#922;"> <!-- greek capital letter kappa, U+039A -->
<!ENTITY Lambda     "&#923;"> <!-- greek capital letter lambda, U+039B
➥ISOgrk3 -->
<!ENTITY Mu         "&#924;"> <!-- greek capital letter mu, U+039C -->
<!ENTITY Nu         "&#925;"> <!-- greek capital letter nu, U+039D -->
<!ENTITY Xi         "&#926;"> <!-- greek capital letter xi, U+039E ISOgrk3 -->
<!ENTITY Omicron    "&#927;"> <!-- greek capital letter omicron, U+039F -->
<!ENTITY Pi         "&#928;"> <!-- greek capital letter pi, U+03A0 ISOgrk3 -->
<!ENTITY Rho        "&#929;"> <!-- greek capital letter rho, U+03A1 -->
<!-- there is no Sigmaf, and no U+03A2 character either -->
<!ENTITY Sigma      "&#931;"> <!-- greek capital letter sigma, U+03A3 ISOgrk3 -->
<!ENTITY Tau        "&#932;"> <!-- greek capital letter tau, U+03A4 -->
<!ENTITY Upsilon    "&#933;"> <!-- greek capital letter upsilon, U+03A5
➥ISOgrk3 -->
<!ENTITY Phi        "&#934;"> <!-- greek capital letter phi, U+03A6 ISOgrk3 -->
<!ENTITY Chi        "&#935;"> <!-- greek capital letter chi, U+03A7 -->
<!ENTITY Psi        "&#936;"> <!-- greek capital letter psi, U+03A8 ISOgrk3 -->
<!ENTITY Omega      "&#937;"> <!-- greek capital letter omega, U+03A9 ISOgrk3 -->


<!ENTITY alpha      "&#945;"> <!-- greek small letter alpha, U+03B1 ISOgrk3 -->
<!ENTITY beta       "&#946;"> <!-- greek small letter beta, U+03B2 ISOgrk3 -->
<!ENTITY gamma      "&#947;"> <!-- greek small letter gamma, U+03B3 ISOgrk3 -->
<!ENTITY delta      "&#948;"> <!-- greek small letter delta, U+03B4 ISOgrk3 -->
<!ENTITY epsilon    "&#949;"> <!-- greek small letter epsilon, U+03B5 ISOgrk3 -->
<!ENTITY zeta       "&#950;"> <!-- greek small letter zeta, U+03B6 ISOgrk3 -->
<!ENTITY eta        "&#951;"> <!-- greek small letter eta, U+03B7 ISOgrk3 -->
<!ENTITY theta      "&#952;"> <!-- greek small letter theta, U+03B8 ISOgrk3 -->
<!ENTITY iota       "&#953;"> <!-- greek small letter iota, U+03B9 ISOgrk3 -->
<!ENTITY kappa      "&#954;"> <!-- greek small letter kappa, U+03BA ISOgrk3 -->
<!ENTITY lambda     "&#955;"> <!-- greek small letter lambda, U+03BB ISOgrk3 -->
<!ENTITY mu         "&#956;"> <!-- greek small letter mu, U+03BC ISOgrk3 -->
<!ENTITY nu         "&#957;"> <!-- greek small letter nu, U+03BD ISOgrk3 -->
<!ENTITY xi         "&#958;"> <!-- greek small letter xi, U+03BE ISOgrk3 -->
<!ENTITY omicron    "&#959;"> <!-- greek small letter omicron, U+03BF NEW -->
<!ENTITY pi         "&#960;"> <!-- greek small letter pi, U+03C0 ISOgrk3 -->
<!ENTITY rho        "&#961;"> <!-- greek small letter rho, U+03C1 ISOgrk3 -->
<!ENTITY sigmaf     "&#962;"> <!-- greek small letter final sigma, U+03C2
➥ISOgrk3 -->
```

```
<!ENTITY sigma    "&#963;"> <!-- greek small letter sigma, U+03C3 ISOgrk3 -->
<!ENTITY tau      "&#964;"> <!-- greek small letter tau, U+03C4 ISOgrk3 -->
<!ENTITY upsilon  "&#965;"> <!-- greek small letter upsilon, U+03C5 ISOgrk3 -->
<!ENTITY phi      "&#966;"> <!-- greek small letter phi, U+03C6 ISOgrk3 -->
<!ENTITY chi      "&#967;"> <!-- greek small letter chi, U+03C7 ISOgrk3 -->
<!ENTITY psi      "&#968;"> <!-- greek small letter psi, U+03C8 ISOgrk3 -->
<!ENTITY omega    "&#969;"> <!-- greek small letter omega, U+03C9 ISOgrk3 -->
<!ENTITY thetasym "&#977;"> <!-- greek small letter theta symbol,
➥U+03D1 NEW -->
<!ENTITY upsih    "&#978;"> <!-- greek upsilon with hook symbol, U+03D2 NEW -->
<!ENTITY piv      "&#982;"> <!-- greek pi symbol, U+03D6 ISOgrk3 -->

<!-- General Punctuation -->
<!ENTITY bull     "&#8226;"> <!-- bullet = black small circle, U+2022
➥ISOpub  -->
<!-- bullet is NOT the same as bullet operator, U+2219 -->
<!ENTITY hellip   "&#8230;"> <!-- horizontal ellipsis = three dot leader,
➥U+2026 ISOpub  -->
<!ENTITY prime    "&#8242;"> <!-- prime = minutes = feet, U+2032 ISOtech -->
<!ENTITY Prime    "&#8243;"> <!-- double prime = seconds = inches, U+2033
➥ISOtech -->
<!ENTITY oline    "&#8254;"> <!-- overline = spacing overscore, U+203E NEW -->
<!ENTITY frasl    "&#8260;"> <!-- fraction slash, U+2044 NEW -->

<!-- Letterlike Symbols -->
<!ENTITY weierp   "&#8472;"> <!-- script capital P = power set = Weierstrass p,
➥U+2118 ISOamso -->
<!ENTITY image    "&#8465;"> <!-- blackletter capital I = imaginary part,
➥U+2111 ISOamso -->
<!ENTITY real     "&#8476;"> <!-- blackletter capital R = real part symbol,
➥U+211C ISOamso -->
<!ENTITY trade    "&#8482;"> <!-- trade mark sign, U+2122 ISOnum -->
<!ENTITY alefsym  "&#8501;"> <!-- alef symbol = first transfinite cardinal,
➥U+2135 NEW -->
<!-- alef symbol is NOT the same as hebrew letter alef, U+05D0 although the
➥same glyph could be used to depict both characters -->

<!-- Arrows -->
<!ENTITY larr     "&#8592;"> <!-- leftwards arrow, U+2190 ISOnum -->
<!ENTITY uarr     "&#8593;"> <!-- upwards arrow, U+2191 ISOnum-->
<!ENTITY rarr     "&#8594;"> <!-- rightwards arrow, U+2192 ISOnum -->
<!ENTITY darr     "&#8595;"> <!-- downwards arrow, U+2193 ISOnum -->
<!ENTITY harr     "&#8596;"> <!-- left right arrow, U+2194 ISOamsa -->
<!ENTITY crarr    "&#8629;"> <!-- downwards arrow with corner leftwards =
➥carriage return, U+21B5 NEW -->
<!ENTITY lArr     "&#8656;"> <!-- leftwards double arrow, U+21D0 ISOtech -->
<!-- Unicode does not say that lArr is the same as the 'is implied by' arrow
➥but also does not have any other character for that function. So ? lArr can be
➥used for 'is implied by' as ISOtech suggests -->
<!ENTITY uArr     "&#8657;"> <!-- upwards double arrow, U+21D1 ISOamsa -->
<!ENTITY rArr     "&#8658;"> <!-- rightwards double arrow, U+21D2 ISOtech -->
<!-- Unicode does not say this is the 'implies' character but does not have
➥another character with this function so ? rArr can be used for 'implies' as
➥ISOtech suggests -->
<!ENTITY dArr     "&#8659;"> <!-- downwards double arrow, U+21D3 ISOamsa -->
<!ENTITY hArr     "&#8660;"> <!-- left right double arrow, U+21D4 ISOamsa -->
```

```
<!-- Mathematical Operators -->
<!ENTITY forall    "&#8704;"> <!-- for all, U+2200 ISOtech -->
<!ENTITY part      "&#8706;"> <!-- partial differential, U+2202 ISOtech   -->
<!ENTITY exist     "&#8707;"> <!-- there exists, U+2203 ISOtech -->
<!ENTITY empty     "&#8709;"> <!-- empty set = null set = diameter, U+2205
➥ISOamso -->
<!ENTITY nabla     "&#8711;"> <!-- nabla = backward difference, U+2207
➥ISOtech -->
<!ENTITY isin      "&#8712;"> <!-- element of, U+2208 ISOtech -->
<!ENTITY notin     "&#8713;"> <!-- not an element of, U+2209 ISOtech -->
<!ENTITY ni        "&#8715;"> <!-- contains as member, U+220B ISOtech -->
<!-- should there be a more memorable name than 'ni'? -->
<!ENTITY prod      "&#8719;"> <!-- n-ary product = product sign, U+220F
➥ISOamsb -->
<!-- prod is NOT the same character as U+03A0 'greek capital letter pi' though
➥the same glyph might be used for both -->
<!ENTITY sum       "&#8721;"> <!-- n-ary sumation, U+2211 ISOamsb -->
<!-- sum is NOT the same character as U+03A3 'greek capital letter sigma'
➥though the same glyph might be used for both -->
<!ENTITY minus     "&#8722;"> <!-- minus sign, U+2212 ISOtech -->
<!ENTITY lowast    "&#8727;"> <!-- asterisk operator, U+2217 ISOtech -->
<!ENTITY radic     "&#8730;"> <!-- square root = radical sign, U+221A
➥ISOtech -->
<!ENTITY prop      "&#8733;"> <!-- proportional to, U+221D ISOtech -->
<!ENTITY infin     "&#8734;"> <!-- infinity, U+221E ISOtech -->
<!ENTITY ang       "&#8736;"> <!-- angle, U+2220 ISOamso -->
<!ENTITY and       "&#8743;"> <!-- logical and = wedge, U+2227 ISOtech -->
<!ENTITY or        "&#8744;"> <!-- logical or = vee, U+2228 ISOtech -->
<!ENTITY cap       "&#8745;"> <!-- intersection = cap, U+2229 ISOtech -->
<!ENTITY cup       "&#8746;"> <!-- union = cup, U+222A ISOtech -->
<!ENTITY int       "&#8747;"> <!-- integral, U+222B ISOtech -->
<!ENTITY there4    "&#8756;"> <!-- therefore, U+2234 ISOtech -->
<!ENTITY sim       "&#8764;"> <!-- tilde operator = varies with = similar
➥to, U+223C ISOtech -->
<!-- tilde operator is NOT the same character as the tilde, U+007E, although
➥the same glyph might be used to represent both   -->
<!ENTITY cong      "&#8773;"> <!-- approximately equal to, U+2245 ISOtech -->
<!ENTITY asymp     "&#8776;"> <!-- almost equal to = asymptotic to, U+2248
➥ISOamsr -->
<!ENTITY ne        "&#8800;"> <!-- not equal to, U+2260 ISOtech -->
<!ENTITY equiv     "&#8801;"> <!-- identical to, U+2261 ISOtech -->
<!ENTITY le        "&#8804;"> <!-- less-than or equal to, U+2264 ISOtech -->
<!ENTITY ge        "&#8805;"> <!-- greater-than or equal to, U+2265 ISOtech -->
<!ENTITY sub       "&#8834;"> <!-- subset of, U+2282 ISOtech -->
<!ENTITY sup       "&#8835;"> <!-- superset of, U+2283 ISOtech -->
<!-- note that nsup, 'not a superset of, U+2283' is not covered by the Symbol
➥font encoding and is not included. Should it be, for symmetry? It is in
➥ISOamsn   -->
<!ENTITY nsub      "&#8836;"> <!-- not a subset of, U+2284 ISOamsn -->
<!ENTITY sube      "&#8838;"> <!-- subset of or equal to, U+2286 ISOtech -->
<!ENTITY supe      "&#8839;"> <!-- superset of or equal to, U+2287 ISOtech -->
<!ENTITY oplus     "&#8853;"> <!-- circled plus = direct sum, U+2295 ISOamsb -->
<!ENTITY otimes    "&#8855;"> <!-- circled times = vector product, U+2297
➥ISOamsb -->
<!ENTITY perp      "&#8869;"> <!-- up tack = orthogonal to = perpendicular,
➥U+22A5 ISOtech -->
<!ENTITY sdot      "&#8901;"> <!-- dot operator, U+22C5 ISOamsb -->
<!-- dot operator is NOT the same character as U+00B7 middle dot -->
```

```
<!-- Miscellaneous Technical -->
<!ENTITY lceil    "&#8968;"> <!-- left ceiling = apl upstile, U+2308
➥ISOamsc  -->
<!ENTITY rceil    "&#8969;"> <!-- right ceiling, U+2309 ISOamsc  -->
<!ENTITY lfloor   "&#8970;"> <!-- left floor = apl downstile, U+230A
➥ISOamsc  -->
<!ENTITY rfloor   "&#8971;"> <!-- right floor, U+230B ISOamsc  -->
<!ENTITY lang     "&#9001;"> <!-- left-pointing angle bracket = bra, U+2329
➥ISOtech -->
<!-- lang is NOT the same character as U+003C 'less than' or U+2039 'single
➥left-pointing angle quotation mark' -->
<!ENTITY rang     "&#9002;"> <!-- right-pointing angle bracket = ket, U+232A
➥ISOtech -->
<!-- rang is NOT the same character as U+003E 'greater than' or U+203A 'single
➥right-pointing angle quotation mark' -->

<!-- Geometric Shapes -->
<!ENTITY loz      "&#9674;"> <!-- lozenge, U+25CA ISOpub -->

<!-- Miscellaneous Symbols -->
<!ENTITY spades   "&#9824;"> <!-- black spade suit, U+2660 ISOpub -->
<!-- black here seems to mean filled as opposed to hollow -->
<!ENTITY clubs    "&#9827;"> <!-- black club suit = shamrock, U+2663 ISOpub -->
<!ENTITY hearts   "&#9829;"> <!-- black heart suit = valentine, U+2665
➥ISOpub -->
<!ENTITY diams    "&#9830;"> <!-- black diamond suit, U+2666 ISOpub -->
```

XHTML ENTITIES SORTED ALPHABETICALLY

Because it can be hard to find or quickly understand a mnemonic character reference, I've included a list of all three of the standard XHTML entity sets sorted alphabetically so you can look them up easily:

```
Symbols

[LS] = Latin 1 Characters
[SS] = Special Characters
[XS] = Symbols

Alphabetic sort of combined XHTML symbol sets
Note that lower case letters sort after all uppercase letters

AElig    &#198;   latin capital letter AE = latin capital ligature AE,
➥U+00C6 ISOlat1 [LS]
Aacute   &#193;   latin capital letter A with acute, U+00C1 ISOlat1 [LS]
Acirc    &#194;   latin capital letter A with circumflex, U+00C2 ISOlat1 [LS]
Agrave   &#192;   latin capital letter A with grave = latin capital letter A
➥grave, U+00C0 ISOlat1 [LS]
Alpha    &#913;   greek capital letter alpha, U+0391 [XS]
Aring    &#197;   latin capital letter A with ring above = latin capital
➥letter A ring, U+00C5 ISOlat1 [LS]
Atilde   &#195;   latin capital letter A with tilde, U+00C3 ISOlat1 [LS]
Auml     &#196;   latin capital letter A with diaeresis, U+00C4 ISOlat1 [LS]
Beta     &#914;   greek capital letter beta, U+0392 [XS]
Ccedil   &#199;   latin capital letter C with cedilla, U+00C7 ISOlat1 [LS]
Chi      &#935;   greek capital letter chi, U+03A7 [XS]
```

```
Dagger    &#8225;  double dagger, U+2021 ISOpub [SS]
Delta     &#916;   greek capital letter delta, U+0394 ISOgrk3 [XS]
ETH       &#208;   latin capital letter ETH, U+00D0 ISOlat1 [LS]
Eacute    &#201;   latin capital letter E with acute, U+00C9 ISOlat1 [LS]
Ecirc     &#202;   latin capital letter E with circumflex, U+00CA ISOlat1 [LS]
Egrave    &#200;   latin capital letter E with grave, U+00C8 ISOlat1 [LS]
Epsilon   &#917;   greek capital letter epsilon, U+0395 [XS]
Eta       &#919;   greek capital letter eta, U+0397 [XS]
Euml      &#203;   latin capital letter E with diaeresis, U+00CB ISOlat1 [LS]
Gamma     &#915;   greek capital letter gamma, U+0393 ISOgrk3 [XS]
Iacute    &#205;   latin capital letter I with acute, U+00CD ISOlat1 [LS]
Icirc     &#206;   latin capital letter I with circumflex, U+00CE ISOlat1 [LS]
Igrave    &#204;   latin capital letter I with grave, U+00CC ISOlat1 [LS]
Iota      &#921;   greek capital letter iota, U+0399 [XS]
Iuml      &#207;   latin capital letter I with diaeresis, U+00CF ISOlat1 [LS]
Kappa     &#922;   greek capital letter kappa, U+039A [XS]
Lambda    &#923;   greek capital letter lambda, U+039B ISOgrk3 [XS]
Mu        &#924;   greek capital letter mu, U+039C [XS]
Ntilde    &#209;   latin capital letter N with tilde, U+00D1 ISOlat1 [LS]
Nu        &#925;   greek capital letter nu, U+039D [XS]
OElig     &#338;   latin capital ligature OE, U+0152 ISOlat2 [SS]
Oacute    &#211;   latin capital letter O with acute, U+00D3 ISOlat1 [LS]
Ocirc     &#212;   latin capital letter O with circumflex, U+00D4 ISOlat1 [LS]
Ograve    &#210;   latin capital letter O with grave, U+00D2 ISOlat1 [LS]
Omega     &#937;   greek capital letter omega, U+03A9 ISOgrk3 [XS]
Omicron   &#927;   greek capital letter omicron, U+039F [XS]
Oslash    &#216;   latin capital letter O with stroke = latin capital letter
➥O slash, U+00D8 ISOlat1 [LS]
Otilde    &#213;   latin capital letter O with tilde, U+00D5 ISOlat1 [LS]
Ouml      &#214;   latin capital letter O with diaeresis, U+00D6 ISOlat1 [LS]
Phi       &#934;   greek capital letter phi, U+03A6 ISOgrk3 [XS]
Pi        &#928;   greek capital letter pi, U+03A0 ISOgrk3 [XS]
Prime     &#8243;  double prime = seconds = inches, U+2033 ISOtech [XS]
Psi       &#936;   greek capital letter psi, U+03A8 ISOgrk3 [XS]
Rho       &#929;   greek capital letter rho, U+03A1 [XS]
Scaron    &#352;   latin capital letter S with caron, U+0160 ISOlat2 [SS]
Sigma     &#931;   greek capital letter sigma, U+03A3 ISOgrk3 [XS]
THORN     &#222;   latin capital letter THORN, U+00DE ISOlat1 [LS]
Tau       &#932;   greek capital letter tau, U+03A4 [XS]
Theta     &#920;   greek capital letter theta, U+0398 ISOgrk3 [XS]
Uacute    &#218;   latin capital letter U with acute, U+00DA ISOlat1 [LS]
Ucirc     &#219;   latin capital letter U with circumflex, U+00DB ISOlat1 [LS]
Ugrave    &#217;   latin capital letter U with grave, U+00D9 ISOlat1 [LS]
Upsilon   &#933;   greek capital letter upsilon, U+03A5 ISOgrk3 [XS]
Uuml      &#220;   latin capital letter U with diaeresis, U+00DC ISOlat1 [LS]
Xi        &#926;   greek capital letter xi, U+039E ISOgrk3 [XS]
Yacute    &#221;   latin capital letter Y with acute, U+00DD ISOlat1 [LS]
Yuml      &#376;   latin capital letter Y with diaeresis, U+0178 ISOlat2 [SS]
Zeta      &#918;   greek capital letter zeta, U+0396 [XS]
aacute    &#225;   latin small letter a with acute, U+00E1 ISOlat1 [LS]
acirc     &#226;   latin small letter a with circumflex, U+00E2 ISOlat1 [LS]
acute     &#180;   acute accent = spacing acute, U+00B4 ISOdia [LS]
aelig     &#230;   latin small letter ae = latin small ligature ae, U+00E6
➥ISOlat1 [LS]
agrave    &#224;   latin small letter a with grave = latin small letter a
➥grave, U+00E0 ISOlat1 [LS]
alefsym   &#8501;  alef symbol = first transfinite cardinal, U+2135 NEW [XS]
```

```
alpha      &#945;    greek small letter alpha, U+03B1 ISOgrk3 [XS]
amp        &#38;     ampersand, U+0026 ISOnum [SS]
and        &#8743;   logical and = wedge, U+2227 ISOtech [XS]
ang        &#8736;   angle, U+2220 ISOamso [XS]
apos       &#39;     apostrophe mark, U+0027 ISOnum [SS]
aring      &#229;    latin small letter a with ring above = latin small letter
➥a ring, U+00E5 ISOlat1 [LS]
asymp      &#8776;   almost equal to = asymptotic to, U+2248 ISOamsr [XS]
atilde     &#227;    latin small letter a with tilde, U+00E3 ISOlat1 [LS]
auml       &#228;    latin small letter a with diaeresis, U+00E4 ISOlat1 [LS]
bdquo      &#8222;   double low-9 quotation mark, U+201E NEW [SS]
beta       &#946;    greek small letter beta, U+03B2 ISOgrk3 [XS]
brvbar     &#166;    broken bar = broken vertical bar, U+00A6 ISOnum [LS]
bull       &#8226;   bullet = black small circle, U+2022 ISOpub [XS]
cap        &#8745;   intersection = cap, U+2229 ISOtech [XS]
ccedil     &#231;    latin small letter c with cedilla, U+00E7 ISOlat1 [LS]
cedil      &#184;    cedilla = spacing cedilla, U+00B8 ISOdia [LS]
cent       &#162;    cent sign, U+00A2 ISOnum [LS]
chi        &#967;    greek small letter chi, U+03C7 ISOgrk3 [XS]
circ       &#710;    modifier letter circumflex accent, U+02C6 ISOpub [SS]
clubs      &#9827;   black club suit = shamrock, U+2663 ISOpub [XS]
cong       &#8773;   approximately equal to, U+2245 ISOtech [XS]
copy       &#169;    copyright sign, U+00A9 ISOnum [LS]
crarr      &#8629;   downwards arrow with corner leftwards = carriage return,
➥U+21B5 NEW [XS]
cup        &#8746;   union = cup, U+222A ISOtech [XS]
curren     &#164;    currency sign, U+00A4 ISOnum [LS]
dArr       &#8659;   downwards double arrow, U+21D3 ISOamsa [XS]
dagger     &#8224;   dagger, U+2020 ISOpub [SS]
darr       &#8595;   downwards arrow, U+2193 ISOnum [XS]
deg        &#176;    degree sign, U+00B0 ISOnum [LS]
delta      &#948;    greek small letter delta, U+03B4 ISOgrk3 [XS]
diams      &#9830;   black diamond suit, U+2666 ISOpub [XS]
divide     &#247;    division sign, U+00F7 ISOnum [LS]
eacute     &#233;    latin small letter e with acute, U+00E9 ISOlat1 [LS]
ecirc      &#234;    latin small letter e with circumflex, U+00EA ISOlat1 [LS]
egrave     &#232;    latin small letter e with grave, U+00E8 ISOlat1 [LS]
empty      &#8709;   empty set = null set = diameter, U+2205 ISOamso [XS]
emsp           em space, U+2003 ISOpub [SS]
ensp           en space, U+2002 ISOpub [SS]
epsilon    &#949;    greek small letter epsilon, U+03B5 ISOgrk3 [XS]
equiv      &#8801;   identical to, U+2261 ISOtech [XS]
eta        &#951;    greek small letter eta, U+03B7 ISOgrk3 [XS]
eth        &#240;    latin small letter eth, U+00F0 ISOlat1 [LS]
euml       &#235;    latin small letter e with diaeresis, U+00EB ISOlat1 [LS]
euro       &#8364;   euro sign, U+20AC NEW [SS]
exist      &#8707;   there exists, U+2203 ISOtech [XS]
fnof       &#402;    latin small f with hook = function = florin, U+0192
➥ISOtech [XS]
forall     &#8704;   for all, U+2200 ISOtech [XS]
frac12     &#189;    vulgar fraction one half = fraction one half, U+00BD
➥ISOnum [LS]
frac14     &#188;    vulgar fraction one quarter = fraction one quarter, U+00BC
➥ISOnum [LS]
frac34     &#190;    vulgar fraction three quarters = fraction three quarters,
➥U+00BE ISOnum [LS]
frasl      &#8260;   fraction slash, U+2044 NEW [XS]
```

```
gamma      &#947;   greek small letter gamma, U+03B3 ISOgrk3 [XS]
ge         &#8805;  greater-than or equal to, U+2265 ISOtech [XS]
gt         &#62;    greater-than sign, U+003E ISOnum [SS]
hArr       &#8660;  left right double arrow, U+21D4 ISOamsa [XS]
harr       &#8596;  left right arrow, U+2194 ISOamsa [XS]
hearts     &#9829;  black heart suit = valentine, U+2665 ISOpub [XS]
hellip     &#8230;  horizontal ellipsis = three dot leader, U+2026 ISOpub [XS]
iacute     &#237;   latin small letter i with acute, U+00ED ISOlat1 [LS]
icirc      &#238;   latin small letter i with circumflex, U+00EE ISOlat1 [LS]
iexcl      &#161;   inverted exclamation mark, U+00A1 ISOnum [LS]
igrave     &#236;   latin small letter i with grave, U+00EC ISOlat1 [LS]
image      &#8465;  blackletter capital I = imaginary part, U+2111 ISOamso [XS]
infin      &#8734;  infinity, U+221E ISOtech [XS]
int        &#8747;  integral, U+222B ISOtech [XS]
iota       &#953;   greek small letter iota, U+03B9 ISOgrk3 [XS]
iquest     &#191;   inverted question mark = turned question mark, U+00BF
➥ISOnum [LS]
isin       &#8712;  element of, U+2208 ISOtech [XS]
iuml       &#239;   latin small letter i with diaeresis, U+00EF ISOlat1 [LS]
kappa      &#954;   greek small letter kappa, U+03BA ISOgrk3 [XS]
lArr       &#8656;  leftwards double arrow, U+21D0 ISOtech [XS]
lambda     &#955;   greek small letter lambda, U+03BB ISOgrk3 [XS]
lang       &#0001;  left-pointing angle bracket = bra, U+2329 ISOtech [XS]
laquo      &#171;   left-pointing double angle quotation mark = left pointing
➥guillemet, U+00AB ISOnum [LS]
larr       &#8592;  leftwards arrow, U+2190 ISOnum [XS]
lceil      &#8968;  left ceiling = apl upstile, U+2308 ISOamsc [XS]
ldquo      &#8220;  left double quotation mark, U+201C ISOnum [SS]
le         &#8804;  less-than or equal to, U+2264 ISOtech [XS]
lfloor     &#8970;  left floor = apl downstile, U+230A ISOamsc [XS]
lowast     &#8727;  asterisk operator, U+2217 ISOtech [XS]
loz        &#9674;  lozenge, U+25CA ISOpub [XS]
lrm        &#8206;  left-to-right mark, U+200E NEW RFC 2070 [SS]
lsaquo     &#8249;  single left-pointing angle quotation mark, U+2039 ISO
➥proposed [SS]
lsquo      &#8216;  left single quotation mark, U+2018 ISOnum [SS]
lt         &#60;    less-than sign, U+003C ISOnum [SS]
macr       &#175;   macron = spacing macron = overline = APL overbar,
➥U+00AF ISOdia [LS]
mdash      &#8212;  em dash, U+2014 ISOpub [SS]
micro      &#181;   micro sign, U+00B5 ISOnum [LS]
middot     &#183;   middle dot = Georgian comma = Greek middle dot, U+00B7
➥ISOnum [LS]
minus      &#8722;  minus sign, U+2212 ISOtech [XS]
mu         &#956;   greek small letter mu, U+03BC ISOgrk3 [XS]
nabla      &#8711;  nabla = backward difference, U+2207 ISOtech [XS]
nbsp           no-break space = non-breaking space, U+00A0 ISOnum [LS]
ndash      &#8211;  en dash, U+2013 ISOpub [SS]
ne         &#8800;  not equal to, U+2260 ISOtech [XS]
ni         &#8715;  contains as member, U+220B ISOtech [XS]
not        &#172;   not sign = discretionary hyphen, U+00AC ISOnum [LS]
notin      &#8713;  not an element of, U+2209 ISOtech [XS]
nsub       &#8836;  not a subset of, U+2284 ISOamsn [XS]
ntilde     &#241;   latin small letter n with tilde, U+00F1 ISOlat1 [LS]
nu         &#957;   greek small letter nu, U+03BD ISOgrk3 [XS]
oacute     &#243;   latin small letter o with acute, U+00F3 ISOlat1 [LS]
ocirc      &#244;   latin small letter o with circumflex, U+00F4 ISOlat1 [LS]
```

```
oelig     &#339;    latin small ligature oe, U+0153 ISOlat2 [SS]
ograve    &#242;    latin small letter o with grave, U+00F2 ISOlat1 [LS]
oline     &#8254;   overline = spacing overscore, U+203E NEW [XS]
omega     &#969;    greek small letter omega, U+03C9 ISOgrk3 [XS]
omicron   &#959;    greek small letter omicron, U+03BF NEW [XS]
oplus     &#8853;   circled plus = direct sum, U+2295 ISOamsb [XS]
or        &#8744;   logical or = vee, U+2228 ISOtech [XS]
ordf      &#170;    feminine ordinal indicator, U+00AA ISOnum [LS]
ordm      &#186;    masculine ordinal indicator, U+00BA ISOnum [LS]
oslash    &#248;    latin small letter o with stroke, = latin small letter
➥o slash, U+00F8 ISOlat1 [LS]
otilde    &#245;    latin small letter o with tilde, U+00F5 ISOlat1 [LS]
otimes    &#8855;   circled times = vector product, U+2297 ISOamsb [XS]
ouml      &#246;    latin small letter o with diaeresis, U+00F6 ISOlat1 [LS]
para      &#182;    pilcrow sign = paragraph sign, U+00B6 ISOnum [LS]
part      &#8706;   partial differential, U+2202 ISOtech [XS]
permil    &#8240;   per mille sign, U+2030 ISOtech [SS]
perp      &#8869;   up tack = orthogonal to = perpendicular, U+22A5
➥ISOtech [XS]
phi       &#966;    greek small letter phi, U+03C6 ISOgrk3 [XS]
pi        &#960;    greek small letter pi, U+03C0 ISOgrk3 [XS]
piv       &#982;    greek pi symbol, U+03D6 ISOgrk3 [XS]
plusmn    &#177;    plus-minus sign = plus-or-minus sign, U+00B1 ISOnum [LS]
pound     &#163;    pound sign, U+00A3 ISOnum [LS]
prime     &#8242;   prime = minutes = feet, U+2032 ISOtech [XS]
prod      &#8719;   n-ary product = product sign, U+220F ISOamsb [XS]
prop      &#8733;   proportional to, U+221D ISOtech [XS]
psi       &#968;    greek small letter psi, U+03C8 ISOgrk3 [XS]
quot      &#34;     quotation mark = APL quote, U+0022 ISOnum [SS]
rArr      &#8658;   rightwards double arrow, U+21D2 ISOtech [XS]
radic     &#8730;   square root = radical sign, U+221A ISOtech [XS]
rang      &#9002;   right-pointing angle bracket = ket, U+232A ISOtech [XS]
raquo     &#187;    right-pointing double angle quotation mark = right
➥pointing guillemet, U+00BB ISOnum [LS]
rarr      &#8594;   rightwards arrow, U+2192 ISOnum [XS]
rceil     &#8969;   right ceiling, U+2309 ISOamsc [XS]
rdquo     &#8221;   right double quotation mark, U+201D ISOnum [SS]
real      &#8476;   blackletter capital R = real part symbol, U+211C
➥ISOamso [XS]
reg       &#174;    registered sign = registered trade mark sign, U+00AE
➥ISOnum [LS]
rfloor    &#8971;   right floor, U+230B ISOamsc [XS]
rho       &#961;    greek small letter rho, U+03C1 ISOgrk3 [XS]
rlm       &#8207;   right-to-left mark, U+200F NEW RFC 2070 [SS]
rsaquo    &#8250;   single right-pointing angle quotation mark, U+203A
➥ISO proposed [SS]
rsquo     &#8217;   right single quotation mark, U+2019 ISOnum [SS]
sbquo     &#8218;   single low-9 quotation mark, U+201A NEW [SS]
scaron    &#353;    latin small letter s with caron, U+0161 ISOlat2 [SS]
sdot      &#8901;   dot operator, U+22C5 ISOamsb [XS]
sect      &#167;    section sign, U+00A7 ISOnum [LS]
shy       &#173;    soft hyphen = discretionary hyphen, U+00AD ISOnum [LS]
sigma     &#963;    greek small letter sigma, U+03C3 ISOgrk3 [XS]
sigmaf    &#962;    greek small letter final sigma, U+03C2 ISOgrk3 [XS]
sim       &#8764;   tilde operator = varies with = similar to, U+223C
➥ISOtech [XS]
spades    &#9824;   black spade suit, U+2660 ISOpub [XS]
```

```
sub        &#8834;    subset of, U+2282 ISOtech [XS]
sube       &#8838;    subset of or equal to, U+2286 ISOtech [XS]
sum        &#8721;    n-ary sumation, U+2211 ISOamsb [XS]
sup        &#8835;    superset of, U+2283 ISOtech [XS]
sup1       &#185;     superscript one = superscript digit one, U+00B9 ISOnum [LS]
sup2       &#178;     superscript two = superscript digit two = squared, U+00B2
➧ISOnum [LS]
sup3       &#179;     superscript three = superscript digit three = cubed,
➧U+00B3 ISOnum [LS]
supe       &#8839;    superset of or equal to, U+2287 ISOtech [XS]
szlig      &#223;     latin small letter sharp s = ess-zed, U+00DF ISOlat1 [LS]
tau        &#964;     greek small letter tau, U+03C4 ISOgrk3 [XS]
there4     &#8756;    therefore, U+2234 ISOtech [XS]
theta      &#952;     greek small letter theta, U+03B8 ISOgrk3 [XS]
thetasym   &#977;     greek small letter theta symbol, U+03D1 NEW [XS]
thinsp          thin space, U+2009 ISOpub [SS]
thorn      &#254;     latin small letter thorn with, U+00FE ISOlat1 [LS]
tilde      &#732;     small tilde, U+02DC ISOdia [SS]
times      &#215;     multiplication sign, U+00D7 ISOnum [LS]
trade      &#8482;    trade mark sign, U+2122 ISOnum [XS]
uArr       &#8657;    upwards double arrow, U+21D1 ISOamsa [XS]
uacute     &#250;     latin small letter u with acute, U+00FA ISOlat1 [LS]
uarr       &#8593;    upwards arrow, U+2191 ISOnum [XS]
ucirc      &#251;     latin small letter u with circumflex, U+00FB ISOlat1 [LS]
ugrave     &#249;     latin small letter u with grave, U+00F9 ISOlat1 [LS]
uml        &#168;     diaeresis = spacing diaeresis, U+00A8 ISOdia [LS]
upsih      &#978;     greek upsilon with hook symbol, U+03D2 NEW [XS]
upsilon    &#965;     greek small letter upsilon, U+03C5 ISOgrk3 [XS]
uuml       &#252;     latin small letter u with diaeresis, U+00FC ISOlat1 [LS]
weierp     &#8472;    script capital P = power set = Weierstrass p, U+2118
➧ISOamso [XS]
xi         &#958;     greek small letter xi, U+03BE ISOgrk3 [XS]
yacute     &#253;     latin small letter y with acute, U+00FD ISOlat1 [LS]
yen        &#165;     yen sign = yuan sign, U+00A5 ISOnum [LS]
yuml       &#255;     latin small letter y with diaeresis, U+00FF ISOlat1 [LS]
zeta       &#950;     greek small letter zeta, U+03B6 ISOgrk3 [XS]
zwj        &#8205;    zero width joiner, U+200D NEW RFC 2070 [SS]
zwnj       &#8204;    zero width non-joiner, U+200C NEW RFC 2070 [SS]
```

XHTML ENTITIES SORTED NUMERICALLY

Because it can be hard to convert a numeric character reference made inline, I've included a list of all three of the standard XHTML entity sets sorted numerically together so you can look them up easily:

```
Symbols

[LS] = Latin 1 Characters
[SS] = Special Characters
[XS] = Symbols

Numeric sort of combined XHTML symbol sets

quot       &#34;      quotation mark = APL quote, U+0022 ISOnum [SS]
amp        &#38;      ampersand, U+0026 ISOnum [SS]
apos       &#39;      apostropher mark, U+0027 ISOnum [SS]
lt         &#60;      less-than sign, U+003C ISOnum [SS]
```

```
gt          &#62;    greater-than sign, U+003E ISOnum [SS]
nbsp            no-break space = non-breaking space, U+00A0 ISOnum [LS]
iexcl       &#161;   inverted exclamation mark, U+00A1 ISOnum [LS]
cent        &#162;   cent sign, U+00A2 ISOnum [LS]
pound       &#163;   pound sign, U+00A3 ISOnum [LS]
curren      &#164;   currency sign, U+00A4 ISOnum [LS]
yen         &#165;   yen sign = yuan sign, U+00A5 ISOnum [LS]
brvbar      &#166;   broken bar = broken vertical bar, U+00A6 ISOnum [LS]
sect        &#167;   section sign, U+00A7 ISOnum [LS]
uml         &#168;   diaeresis = spacing diaeresis, U+00A8 ISOdia [LS]
copy        &#169;   copyright sign, U+00A9 ISOnum [LS]
ordf        &#170;   feminine ordinal indicator, U+00AA ISOnum [LS]
laquo       &#171;   left-pointing double angle quotation mark = left pointing
➥guillemet, U+00AB ISOnum [LS]
not         &#172;   not sign = discretionary hyphen, U+00AC ISOnum [LS]
shy         &#173;   soft hyphen = discretionary hyphen, U+00AD ISOnum [LS]
reg         &#174;   registered sign = registered trade mark sign, U+00AE
➥ISOnum [LS]
macr        &#175;   macron = spacing macron = overline = APL overbar, U+00AF
➥ISOdia [LS]
deg         &#176;   degree sign, U+00B0 ISOnum [LS]
plusmn      &#177;   plus-minus sign = plus-or-minus sign, U+00B1 ISOnum [LS]
sup2        &#178;   superscript two = superscript digit two = squared, U+00B2
➥ISOnum [LS]
sup3        &#179;   superscript three = superscript digit three = cubed,
➥U+00B3 ISOnum [LS]
acute       &#180;   acute accent = spacing acute, U+00B4 ISOdia [LS]
micro       &#181;   micro sign, U+00B5 ISOnum [LS]
para        &#182;   pilcrow sign = paragraph sign, U+00B6 ISOnum [LS]
middot      &#183;   middle dot = Georgian comma = Greek middle dot, U+00B7
➥ISOnum [LS]
cedil       &#184;   cedilla = spacing cedilla, U+00B8 ISOdia [LS]
sup1        &#185;   superscript one = superscript digit one, U+00B9 ISOnum [LS]
ordm        &#186;   masculine ordinal indicator, U+00BA ISOnum [LS]
raquo       &#187;   right-pointing double angle quotation mark = right
➥pointing guillemet, U+00BB ISOnum [LS]
frac14      &#188;   vulgar fraction one quarter = fraction one quarter, U+00BC
➥ISOnum [LS]
frac12      &#189;   vulgar fraction one half = fraction one half, U+00BD
➥ISOnum [LS]
frac34      &#190;   vulgar fraction three quarters = fraction three quarters,
➥U+00BE ISOnum [LS]
iquest      &#191;   inverted question mark = turned question mark, U+00BF
➥ISOnum [LS]
Agrave      &#192;   latin capital letter A with grave = latin capital letter
➥A grave, U+00C0 ISOlat1 [LS]
Aacute      &#193;   latin capital letter A with acute, U+00C1 ISOlat1 [LS]
Acirc       &#194;   latin capital letter A with circumflex, U+00C2 ISOlat1 [LS]
Atilde      &#195;   latin capital letter A with tilde, U+00C3 ISOlat1 [LS]
Auml        &#196;   latin capital letter A with diaeresis, U+00C4 ISOlat1 [LS]
Aring       &#197;   latin capital letter A with ring above = latin capital
➥letter A ring, U+00C5 ISOlat1 [LS]
AElig       &#198;   latin capital letter AE = latin capital ligature AE,
➥U+00C6 ISOlat1 [LS]
Ccedil      &#199;   latin capital letter C with cedilla, U+00C7 ISOlat1 [LS]
Egrave      &#200;   latin capital letter E with grave, U+00C8 ISOlat1 [LS]
Eacute      &#201;   latin capital letter E with acute, U+00C9 ISOlat1 [LS]
```

```
Ecirc      &#202;    latin capital letter E with circumflex, U+00CA ISOlat1 [LS]
Euml       &#203;    latin capital letter E with diaeresis, U+00CB ISOlat1 [LS]
Igrave     &#204;    latin capital letter I with grave, U+00CC ISOlat1 [LS]
Iacute     &#205;    latin capital letter I with acute, U+00CD ISOlat1 [LS]
Icirc      &#206;    latin capital letter I with circumflex, U+00CE ISOlat1 [LS]
Iuml       &#207;    latin capital letter I with diaeresis, U+00CF ISOlat1 [LS]
ETH        &#208;    latin capital letter ETH, U+00D0 ISOlat1 [LS]
Ntilde     &#209;    latin capital letter N with tilde, U+00D1 ISOlat1 [LS]
Ograve     &#210;    latin capital letter O with grave, U+00D2 ISOlat1 [LS]
Oacute     &#211;    latin capital letter O with acute, U+00D3 ISOlat1 [LS]
Ocirc      &#212;    latin capital letter O with circumflex, U+00D4 ISOlat1 [LS]
Otilde     &#213;    latin capital letter O with tilde, U+00D5 ISOlat1 [LS]
Ouml       &#214;    latin capital letter O with diaeresis, U+00D6 ISOlat1 [LS]
times      &#215;    multiplication sign, U+00D7 ISOnum [LS]
Oslash     &#216;    latin capital letter O with stroke = latin capital letter
➥O slash, U+00D8 ISOlat1 [LS]
Ugrave     &#217;    latin capital letter U with grave, U+00D9 ISOlat1 [LS]
Uacute     &#218;    latin capital letter U with acute, U+00DA ISOlat1 [LS]
Ucirc      &#219;    latin capital letter U with circumflex, U+00DB ISOlat1 [LS]
Uuml       &#220;    latin capital letter U with diaeresis, U+00DC ISOlat1 [LS]
Yacute     &#221;    latin capital letter Y with acute, U+00DD ISOlat1 [LS]
THORN      &#222;    latin capital letter THORN, U+00DE ISOlat1 [LS]
szlig      &#223;    latin small letter sharp s = ess-zed, U+00DF ISOlat1 [LS]
agrave     &#224;    latin small letter a with grave = latin small letter a
➥grave, U+00E0 ISOlat1 [LS]
aacute     &#225;    latin small letter a with acute, U+00E1 ISOlat1 [LS]
acirc      &#226;    latin small letter a with circumflex, U+00E2 ISOlat1 [LS]
atilde     &#227;    latin small letter a with tilde, U+00E3 ISOlat1 [LS]
auml       &#228;    latin small letter a with diaeresis, U+00E4 ISOlat1 [LS]
aring      &#229;    latin small letter a with ring above = latin small letter
➥a ring, U+00E5 ISOlat1 [LS]
aelig      &#230;    latin small letter ae = latin small ligature ae, U+00E6
➥ISOlat1 [LS]
ccedil     &#231;    latin small letter c with cedilla, U+00E7 ISOlat1 [LS]
egrave     &#232;    latin small letter e with grave, U+00E8 ISOlat1 [LS]
eacute     &#233;    latin small letter e with acute, U+00E9 ISOlat1 [LS]
ecirc      &#234;    latin small letter e with circumflex, U+00EA ISOlat1 [LS]
euml       &#235;    latin small letter e with diaeresis, U+00EB ISOlat1 [LS]
igrave     &#236;    latin small letter i with grave, U+00EC ISOlat1 [LS]
iacute     &#237;    latin small letter i with acute, U+00ED ISOlat1 [LS]
icirc      &#238;    latin small letter i with circumflex, U+00EE ISOlat1 [LS]
iuml       &#239;    latin small letter i with diaeresis, U+00EF ISOlat1 [LS]
eth        &#240;    latin small letter eth, U+00F0 ISOlat1 [LS]
ntilde     &#241;    latin small letter n with tilde, U+00F1 ISOlat1 [LS]
ograve     &#242;    latin small letter o with grave, U+00F2 ISOlat1 [LS]
oacute     &#243;    latin small letter o with acute, U+00F3 ISOlat1 [LS]
ocirc      &#244;    latin small letter o with circumflex, U+00F4 ISOlat1 [LS]
otilde     &#245;    latin small letter o with tilde, U+00F5 ISOlat1 [LS]
ouml       &#246;    latin small letter o with diaeresis, U+00F6 ISOlat1 [LS]
divide     &#247;    division sign, U+00F7 ISOnum [LS]
oslash     &#248;    latin small letter o with stroke, = latin small letter
➥o slash, U+00F8 ISOlat1 [LS]
ugrave     &#249;    latin small letter u with grave, U+00F9 ISOlat1 [LS]
uacute     &#250;    latin small letter u with acute, U+00FA ISOlat1 [LS]
ucirc      &#251;    latin small letter u with circumflex, U+00FB ISOlat1 [LS]
uuml       &#252;    latin small letter u with diaeresis, U+00FC ISOlat1 [LS]
yacute     &#253;    latin small letter y with acute, U+00FD ISOlat1 [LS]
```

```
thorn      &#254;    latin small letter thorn with, U+00FE ISOlat1 [LS]
yuml       &#255;    latin small letter y with diaeresis, U+00FF ISOlat1 [LS]
OElig      &#338;    latin capital ligature OE, U+0152 ISOlat2 [SS]
oelig      &#339;    latin small ligature oe, U+0153 ISOlat2 [SS]
Scaron     &#352;    latin capital letter S with caron, U+0160 ISOlat2 [SS]
scaron     &#353;    latin small letter s with caron, U+0161 ISOlat2 [SS]
Yuml       &#376;    latin capital letter Y with diaeresis, U+0178 ISOlat2 [SS]
fnof       &#402;    latin small f with hook = function = florin, U+0192
➥ISOtech [XS]
circ       &#710;    modifier letter circumflex accent, U+02C6 ISOpub [SS]
tilde      &#732;    small tilde, U+02DC ISOdia [SS]
Alpha      &#913;    greek capital letter alpha, U+0391 [XS]
Beta       &#914;    greek capital letter beta, U+0392 [XS]
Gamma      &#915;    greek capital letter gamma, U+0393 ISOgrk3 [XS]
Delta      &#916;    greek capital letter delta, U+0394 ISOgrk3 [XS]
Epsilon    &#917;    greek capital letter epsilon, U+0395 [XS]
Zeta       &#918;    greek capital letter zeta, U+0396 [XS]
Eta        &#919;    greek capital letter eta, U+0397 [XS]
Theta      &#920;    greek capital letter theta, U+0398 ISOgrk3 [XS]
Iota       &#921;    greek capital letter iota, U+0399 [XS]
Kappa      &#922;    greek capital letter kappa, U+039A [XS]
Lambda     &#923;    greek capital letter lambda, U+039B ISOgrk3 [XS]
Mu         &#924;    greek capital letter mu, U+039C [XS]
Nu         &#925;    greek capital letter nu, U+039D [XS]
Xi         &#926;    greek capital letter xi, U+039E ISOgrk3 [XS]
Omicron    &#927;    greek capital letter omicron, U+039F [XS]
Pi         &#928;    greek capital letter pi, U+03A0 ISOgrk3 [XS]
Rho        &#929;    greek capital letter rho, U+03A1 [XS]
Sigma      &#931;    greek capital letter sigma, U+03A3 ISOgrk3 [XS]
Tau        &#932;    greek capital letter tau, U+03A4 [XS]
Upsilon    &#933;    greek capital letter upsilon, U+03A5 ISOgrk3 [XS]
Phi        &#934;    greek capital letter phi, U+03A6 ISOgrk3 [XS]
Chi        &#935;    greek capital letter chi, U+03A7 [XS]
Psi        &#936;    greek capital letter psi, U+03A8 ISOgrk3 [XS]
Omega      &#937;    greek capital letter omega, U+03A9 ISOgrk3 [XS]
alpha      &#945;    greek small letter alpha, U+03B1 ISOgrk3 [XS]
beta       &#946;    greek small letter beta, U+03B2 ISOgrk3 [XS]
gamma      &#947;    greek small letter gamma, U+03B3 ISOgrk3 [XS]
delta      &#948;    greek small letter delta, U+03B4 ISOgrk3 [XS]
epsilon    &#949;    greek small letter epsilon, U+03B5 ISOgrk3 [XS]
zeta       &#950;    greek small letter zeta, U+03B6 ISOgrk3 [XS]
eta        &#951;    greek small letter eta, U+03B7 ISOgrk3 [XS]
theta      &#952;    greek small letter theta, U+03B8 ISOgrk3 [XS]
iota       &#953;    greek small letter iota, U+03B9 ISOgrk3 [XS]
kappa      &#954;    greek small letter kappa, U+03BA ISOgrk3 [XS]
lambda     &#955;    greek small letter lambda, U+03BB ISOgrk3 [XS]
mu         &#956;    greek small letter mu, U+03BC ISOgrk3 [XS]
nu         &#957;    greek small letter nu, U+03BD ISOgrk3 [XS]
xi         &#958;    greek small letter xi, U+03BE ISOgrk3 [XS]
omicron    &#959;    greek small letter omicron, U+03BF NEW [XS]
pi         &#960;    greek small letter pi, U+03C0 ISOgrk3 [XS]
rho        &#961;    greek small letter rho, U+03C1 ISOgrk3 [XS]
sigmaf     &#962;    greek small letter final sigma, U+03C2 ISOgrk3 [XS]
sigma      &#963;    greek small letter sigma, U+03C3 ISOgrk3 [XS]
tau        &#964;    greek small letter tau, U+03C4 ISOgrk3 [XS]
upsilon    &#965;    greek small letter upsilon, U+03C5 ISOgrk3 [XS]
phi        &#966;    greek small letter phi, U+03C6 ISOgrk3 [XS]
```

```
chi       &#967;    greek small letter chi, U+03C7 ISOgrk3 [XS]
psi       &#968;    greek small letter psi, U+03C8 ISOgrk3 [XS]
omega     &#969;    greek small letter omega, U+03C9 ISOgrk3 [XS]
thetasym  &#977;    greek small letter theta symbol, U+03D1 NEW [XS]
upsih     &#978;    greek upsilon with hook symbol, U+03D2 NEW [XS]
piv       &#982;    greek pi symbol, U+03D6 ISOgrk3 [XS]
ensp          en space, U+2002 ISOpub [SS]
emsp          em space, U+2003 ISOpub [SS]
thinsp        thin space, U+2009 ISOpub [SS]
zwnj      &#8204;   zero width non-joiner, U+200C NEW RFC 2070 [SS]
zwj       &#8205;   zero width joiner, U+200D NEW RFC 2070 [SS]
lrm       &#8206;   left-to-right mark, U+200E NEW RFC 2070 [SS]
rlm       &#8207;   right-to-left mark, U+200F NEW RFC 2070 [SS]
ndash     &#8211;   en dash, U+2013 ISOpub [SS]
mdash     &#8212;   em dash, U+2014 ISOpub [SS]
lsquo     &#8216;   left single quotation mark, U+2018 ISOnum [SS]
rsquo     &#8217;   right single quotation mark, U+2019 ISOnum [SS]
sbquo     &#8218;   single low-9 quotation mark, U+201A NEW [SS]
ldquo     &#8220;   left double quotation mark, U+201C ISOnum [SS]
rdquo     &#8221;   right double quotation mark, U+201D ISOnum [SS]
bdquo     &#8222;   double low-9 quotation mark, U+201E NEW [SS]
dagger    &#8224;   dagger, U+2020 ISOpub [SS]
Dagger    &#8225;   double dagger, U+2021 ISOpub [SS]
bull      &#8226;   bullet = black small circle, U+2022 ISOpub [XS]
hellip    &#8230;   horizontal ellipsis = three dot leader, U+2026 ISOpub [XS]
permil    &#8240;   per mille sign, U+2030 ISOtech [SS]
prime     &#8242;   prime = minutes = feet, U+2032 ISOtech [XS]
Prime     &#8243;   double prime = seconds = inches, U+2033 ISOtech [XS]
lsaquo    &#8249;   single left-pointing angle quotation mark, U+2039 ISO
➥proposed [SS]
rsaquo    &#8250;   single right-pointing angle quotation mark, U+203A ISO
➥proposed [SS]
oline     &#8254;   overline = spacing overscore, U+203E NEW [XS]
frasl     &#8260;   fraction slash, U+2044 NEW [XS]
euro      &#8364;   euro sign, U+20AC NEW [SS]
image     &#8465;   blackletter capital I = imaginary part, U+2111 ISOamso [XS]
weierp    &#8472;   script capital P = power set = Weierstrass p, U+2118
➥ISOamso [XS]
real      &#8476;   blackletter capital R = real part symbol, U+211C
➥ISOamso [XS]
trade     &#8482;   trade mark sign, U+2122 ISOnum [XS]
alefsym   &#8501;   alef symbol = first transfinite cardinal, U+2135 NEW [XS]
larr      &#8592;   leftwards arrow, U+2190 ISOnum [XS]
uarr      &#8593;   upwards arrow, U+2191 ISOnum [XS]
rarr      &#8594;   rightwards arrow, U+2192 ISOnum [XS]
darr      &#8595;   downwards arrow, U+2193 ISOnum [XS]
harr      &#8596;   left right arrow, U+2194 ISOamsa [XS]
crarr     &#8629;   downwards arrow with corner leftwards = carriage return,
➥U+21B5 NEW [XS]
lArr      &#8656;   leftwards double arrow, U+21D0 ISOtech [XS]
uArr      &#8657;   upwards double arrow, U+21D1 ISOamsa [XS]
rArr      &#8658;   rightwards double arrow, U+21D2 ISOtech [XS]
dArr      &#8659;   downwards double arrow, U+21D3 ISOamsa [XS]
hArr      &#8660;   left right double arrow, U+21D4 ISOamsa [XS]
forall    &#8704;   for all, U+2200 ISOtech [XS]
part      &#8706;   partial differential, U+2202 ISOtech [XS]
exist     &#8707;   there exists, U+2203 ISOtech [XS]
```

```
empty    &#8709;    empty set = null set = diameter, U+2205 ISOamso [XS]
nabla    &#8711;    nabla = backward difference, U+2207 ISOtech [XS]
isin     &#8712;    element of, U+2208 ISOtech [XS]
notin    &#8713;    not an element of, U+2209 ISOtech [XS]
ni       &#8715;    contains as member, U+220B ISOtech [XS]
prod     &#8719;    n-ary product = product sign, U+220F ISOamsb [XS]
sum      &#8721;    n-ary sumation, U+2211 ISOamsb [XS]
minus    &#8722;    minus sign, U+2212 ISOtech [XS]
lowast   &#8727;    asterisk operator, U+2217 ISOtech [XS]
radic    &#8730;    square root = radical sign, U+221A ISOtech [XS]
prop     &#8733;    proportional to, U+221D ISOtech [XS]
infin    &#8734;    infinity, U+221E ISOtech [XS]
ang      &#8736;    angle, U+2220 ISOamso [XS]
and      &#8743;    logical and = wedge, U+2227 ISOtech [XS]
or       &#8744;    logical or = vee, U+2228 ISOtech [XS]
cap      &#8745;    intersection = cap, U+2229 ISOtech [XS]
cup      &#8746;    union = cup, U+222A ISOtech [XS]
int      &#8747;    integral, U+222B ISOtech [XS]
there4   &#8756;    therefore, U+2234 ISOtech [XS]
sim      &#8764;    tilde operator = varies with = similar to, U+223C
➥ISOtech [XS]
cong     &#8773;    approximately equal to, U+2245 ISOtech [XS]
asymp    &#8776;    almost equal to = asymptotic to, U+2248 ISOamsr [XS]
ne       &#8800;    not equal to, U+2260 ISOtech [XS]
equiv    &#8801;    identical to, U+2261 ISOtech [XS]
le       &#8804;    less-than or equal to, U+2264 ISOtech [XS]
ge       &#8805;    greater-than or equal to, U+2265 ISOtech [XS]
sub      &#8834;    subset of, U+2282 ISOtech [XS]
sup      &#8835;    superset of, U+2283 ISOtech [XS]
nsub     &#8836;    not a subset of, U+2284 ISOamsn [XS]
sube     &#8838;    subset of or equal to, U+2286 ISOtech [XS]
supe     &#8839;    superset of or equal to, U+2287 ISOtech [XS]
oplus    &#8853;    circled plus = direct sum, U+2295 ISOamsb [XS]
otimes   &#8855;    circled times = vector product, U+2297 ISOamsb [XS]
perp     &#8869;    up tack = orthogonal to = perpendicular, U+22A5
➥ISOtech [XS]
sdot     &#8901;    dot operator, U+22C5 ISOamsb [XS]
lceil    &#8968;    left ceiling = apl upstile, U+2308 ISOamsc [XS]
rceil    &#8969;    right ceiling, U+2309 ISOamsc [XS]
lfloor   &#8970;    left floor = apl downstile, U+230A ISOamsc [XS]
rfloor   &#8971;    right floor, U+230B ISOamsc [XS]
lang     &#9001;    left-pointing angle bracket = bra, U+2329 ISOtech [XS]
rang     &#9002;    right-pointing angle bracket = ket, U+232A ISOtech [XS]
loz      &#9674;    lozenge, U+25CA ISOpub [XS]
spades   &#9824;    black spade suit, U+2660 ISOpub [XS]
clubs    &#9827;    black club suit = shamrock, U+2663 ISOpub [XS]
hearts   &#9829;    black heart suit = valentine, U+2665 ISOpub [XS]
diams    &#9830;    black diamond suit, U+2666 ISOpub [XS]
```

CSS1, CSS2 Reference

INSPECTING A STYLE SHEET EXAMPLE

CSS2 is backwards compatible with CSS1 with minor or logical exceptions although it adds quite a bit of functionality. All style sheets follow roughly the same pattern, so here's a sample showing how you might set up your own page with an inline style sheet, as well as override some default values with the style attribute on a tag.

```
<html>
  <head>
    <style type="text/css">
      <--
      body { margin-left: 3%; margin-right: 3%; color: black;
             font-family: serif; background-color: #def ;
             background: url(background.jpg) ; }
      a:link { color: blue }
      a:visited { color: purple }
      a:active { color: red }
      div.block { margin-left: 9%; }
      div.block H2, DIV.block H3 { margin-left: -9%; }
      h1 { clear: left; margin-top: 2em; text-align: center; }
      pre { font-family: monospace; }
      img { border: 0; }
      -->
    </style>
  </head>
  <body text="black" bgcolor="#ddeeff" background="background.jpg"
        link="blue" vlink="purple" alink="red">
    <h1 style="color:red background-color:yellow">Main Heading</H1>
```

This style sheet sets up standard margins of 3% of the browser window, sets text color to black, chooses a serif font without specifying a particular one, and sets the background color to #ddeeff using a shorthand three hexadecimal digit notation, #def. Each single hexadecimal digit is doubled to make the final number, #ddeeff. It also loads an image into the background after the color was set to a close match, so the transition from blank page to background is smooth. Multiple property and value pairs are separated by semicolons so the browser can keep them straight in its tiny brain.

Tip from

Words to weave by

The W3C has an excellent CSS2 validation service available at http://jigsaw.w3.org/ css-validator/ and it's always a very good idea to validate a style sheet before use. You might also use their HTML/XHTML validation service at http://validator.w3.org/ before spending too much time scratching your head when things go wrong. It's always irritating when the source of a problem turns out to be a simple coding error, and using validation tools is good design and coding practice.

Note that I've argued pretty much the same effects in the BODY tag. Because the implementation of style sheets is uneven at best, as a general rule you should always argue the old styles as well as the new during the transition between the two different ways of doing things although the older mechanism is now deprecated.

The margin changes might or might not take place, depending on the browser. Right margins are less commonly implemented than left margins, but the page will be readable without margin information so we can let that slide. If they appear, we're happy. If not, we truck on with our lives.

The rest of the style commands are also niceties which we would prefer to see, and some of them can be argued in the body as a fall-back position. You can see what the effect of each should be by looking up the keywords in the reference list below.

CSS QUICK REFERENCE

The numbers found at the end of each CSS property description below refer to the actual section headings in the Cascading Style Sheets, Level 1 (CSS1) and Cascading Style Sheets, Level 2 (CSS2) style sheet recommendations of the World Wide Web Consortium (W3C). Some numbers are skipped because they discuss issues that have no properties. CSS2 section numbers are also presented in italics, either directly above the property or above the group of properties covered in the CSS2 section, although they might skip around to follow the CSS1 order. In all cases the actual CSS1 and CSS2 Recommendations of the W3C are primary. This précis is merely a handy crib sheet for quick reference, not a manual for study.

Each entry consists of a selector, usually an HTML element followed by a property/value pair enclosed in curly braces, followed by an optional example, description, or explanation. The value can be a list of values that the property can take.

I left out examples for almost all the properties after "font-family" as they're all the same and it gets not only boring but fills up space that could be better spent on other things. The initial (and more complex) items all have examples to help you figure out what's going on.

I've shown ellipses (…) after the property and value pairs to show that you could add more properties if you wanted to, always remembering to separate the pairs by a semicolon as shown in the earlier example.

A TECHNICAL EXPLANATION OF CSS1 AND CSS2

The text of the CSS1 and CSS2 recommendations are surprisingly readable, so if you want a more technical explanation, and don't mind reading documents on your computer, you can look it up on the Web on the W3C Web site at http://www.w3.org/Style/css/.

W3C also has online tutorials and background information to make life easier for the budding style sheet *maven*. (That's *guru* to those whose metaphors for expertise are more influenced by the Far East than by Middle Europe.)

The conventions used in this appendix are illustrated in Table E.1.

APP

E

TABLE E.1   TEXT FORMATTING CONVENTIONS USED IN THIS APPENDIX

Text Format Conventions	Meaning
CSS1 x.x	Refers to paragraphs in the W3C CSS1 Style Sheet Recommendation
CSS2 x.x	Refers to paragraphs in the W3C CSS2 Style Sheet Recommendation
Boldface	Style properties and values safe across all browsers
Lightface	Style properties and values not supported across all browsers
Italics	Comments and explanations—also CSS2 section headings
[adv]	Marks advanced features that are not required to claim CSS compliance and are not supported in most browsers
[s2]	Marks features introduced with CSS2
[ns2]	Marks features whose behavior has been modified and whose classification is changed in CSS2
`<element1>`	Refers to HTML elements (tags)
classid	Refers to a value entered in a class attribute in the HTML tag
id	Refers to a value entered in an ID attribute in the HTML tag
angle brackets < >	Surround HTML elements but are also used to surround a property value to indicate that the entire element, including the brackets, should be replaced by a single word
Curly Braces { }	Surround property/value pairs and are mandatory
property	Refers to CSS properties found in front of the colon
value	Refers to CSS values found after the colon

Most entries consist of a selector followed by the property/value pair enclosed in curly braces ({}). The selector defines the scope of the following property/value pair while the property/value pair defines how the browser will render text selected by the selector used. In a few cases the description also shows inline styles.

Note

The numbers in parentheses found at the end of every heading below refer to the actual section headings in the Cascading Style Sheets, Level 1 (CSS1) and Cascading Style Sheets, Level 2 (CSS2) style sheet Recommendations of the World Wide Web Consortium (W3C). Some numbers are skipped because they discuss issues that have no properties.

BASIC CONCEPTS

CONTAINMENT IN HTML (CSS1 1.1)

```
<LINK rel="stylesheet" type="text/css" href="importedstylesheet" ... >
```

External style sheet.

```
@import importedstylesheet
```

External style sheet imported into an inline style element.

```
<STYLE type="text/css" ... ><-- style sheet commands --></STYLE>
```

Inline style sheet with style commands contained within SGML comments.

```
<STYLE><-- commands --></STYLE>
```

```
<XXX style=" ... ">
```

Style commands added directly to an HTML element.

GROUPING (CSS1 1.2, CSS2 5.2.1)

```
element1, element2, element3 { property: value }
```

Save space in style sheets by grouping elements that will be treated in the same fashion together in a comma-separated list.

INHERITANCE (CSS1 1.3)

```
element1 { property: value ... }
```

```
<element1> <element2> (same as outer) </element2> </element1>
```

If an element is not otherwise declared, it takes on the values of an enclosing element.

CLASS AS SELECTOR (CSS1 1.4 CSS2 5.8.3)

```
element1.classid { property: value ... }
```

```
<element1 class="classid">
```

Elements can be grouped and selected according to class attributes on the HTML or XHTML tags themselves. If the element name only is omitted, the selector selects all elements with the same class. This dotted notation is not available in general XML documents.

ID AS SELECTOR (CSS1 1.5, CSS2 5.9)

```
#xxx { property: value ... }
```

```
element1#xxx { property: value ... }
```

```
<element1 id=#xxx>
```

> Elements can be addressed directly by means of a unique ID attribute on the individual HTML tag.

CONTEXTUAL SELECTORS (CSS1 1.6)

```
element1 element2 { property: value ... }
```

```
<element1><element2>this text is affected</element2></element1>
```

```
<element2>this text is not</element2>
```

> Commands can be limited in scope to elements within the scope of a containing tag.

COMMENTS (CSS1 1.7)

```
/* comment */
```

> Comments can be inserted in the style sheet to explain the code.

DESCENDANT SELECTORS (CSS2 5.5)[S2]

> `<element1>` * `<element2>` Matches a grandchild or later.

CHILD SELECTORS (CSS2 5.6)[S2]

> `<element1>` > `<element2>` Matches a child.

ADJACENT SIBLING SELECTORS (CSS2 5.7)[S2]

> `<element1>` + `<element2>` Matches an adjacent sibling.

MATCHING ATTRIBUTES AND ATTRIBUTE VALUES (CSS2 5.8.1)[S2]

> [att]   Match when the element sets the "att" attribute, whatever the value of the attribute.

> [att=value]   Match when the element's "att" attribute value is exactly "val".

> [att~=value]   Match when the element's "att" attribute value is a space-separated list of "words", one of which is exactly "value". If this selector is used, the words in the value must not contain spaces.

> [att|=val]   Match when the element's "att" attribute value is a hyphen-separated list of "words", beginning with "val". The match starts at the beginning of the attribute value.

PSEUDO-CLASSES AND PSEUDO-ELEMENTS (CSS1 2, CSS2 5.10)

FIRST-CHILD PSEUDO-CLASS (CSS2 5.11.1)[S2]

E:first-child { *property*: *value* ... }[s2]

> Matches the first child of any element.

ANCHOR PSEUDO-CLASSES (CSS1 2.1, CSS2 5.11.2)

A:link { *property*: *value* ... }

A:active { *property*: *value* ... }[ns2]

A:visited { *property*: *value* ... }

> Anchors can be styled based on their browser status.

DYNAMIC PSEUDO-CLASSES (CSS2 5.11.2)[S2]

A:hover { *property*: *value* ... }[s2]

A:active { *property*: *value* ... }[s2]

A:focus { *property*: *value* ... }[s2]

> Anchors can be styled based on their dynamic browser status.

THE LANGUAGE PSEUDO-CLASS (CSS2 5.11.4)[S2]

E:lang(xx) { *property*: *value* ... }[s2]

> Elements can be styled based on the language in use.
> ```
> HTML:lang(de) { quotes: '»' '«' '\2039' '\203A' }[s2]
> :lang(de) > Q { quotes: '»' '«' '\2039' '\203A' }[s2]
> ```

TYPOGRAPHICAL PSEUDO-ELEMENTS (CSS1 2.2, CSS2 5.12)

THE :FIRST-LINE PSEUDO-ELEMENT (CSS2 5.12.1)[S2]

FIRST-LINE (CSS1 2.3)[ADV]

E:first-line { *property*: *value* ... }

> The first line of any element can be selected directly.

THE :FIRST-LETTER PSEUDO-ELEMENT (CSS2 5.12.2)[S2]

FIRST-LETTER (CSS1 2.4)[ADV]

E:first-letter { *property*: *value* ... }

> The first letter of any element can be selected directly.

THE :BEFORE AND :AFTER PSEUDO-ELEMENTS (CSS2 5.12.3)[S2]

E:before { content: *value* ... }[s2]

E:after { content: *value* ... }[s2]

> Content can be generated before or after an element.

APP

E

PSEUDO-ELEMENTS IN SELECTORS (CSS1 2.5)

```
element1 element2:pseudo-element { property: value ... }
```

Pseudo-elements must be last in a contextual list of   selectors.

MULTIPLE PSEUDO-ELEMENTS (CSS1 2.6)

```
element1 { property: value ... }

element1:pseudo-element1 { property: value ... }

element1:pseudo-element2 { property: value ... }
```

Several pseudo-elements that have overlapping effects can be defined.

THE @IMPORT RULE (CSS2 6.3)[s2]

@import url("pathname") modifier[s2]

Import an external stylesheet. @import commands must precede any other stylesheet rule. If any media type variations exist in the source, the modifier lets you select them like this:

```
@import url("bigscreen.css") projection, tv;
```

IMPORTANT *(CSS1 3.1, CSS2 6.4.2)*

```
element1 { ! important property: value ... }
```

Add weight to a style command, promoting it over conflicting commands that would otherwise override it. There are very few times that you'd be justified in using this command as it's one method whereby persons with special visual needs can override your style sheet with a high contrast or large print alternative rendering. In moving to CSS2, W3C made an important change in the order in which this modifier is interpreted, thereby correcting a design bug. CSS2 quite properly follows a user's estimation of what's important before the author's opinion. Until CSS2 support is universal, though, using this weighting command is still unwise.

CASCADING ORDER (CSS1 3.2, CSS2 6.4)

Weight sorting

! Important commands are more important than unmarked ones.

Origin sorting

CSS1: Author style sheets are more important than the reader's style sheets, which are more important than the default style sheet for the browser.

CSS2: Author style sheets are more important than the reader's style sheets, which are more important than the default style sheet for the browser. Except that reader's ! important modifiers take precedence over an author's. This allows people with special needs to have more control over the presentation of documents on their browser.

Specificity sorting

Resolve conflicts by means of a complex algorithm that attempts to discover how "specific" a command is.

Order sorting

Resolve remaining conflicts by means of a last-seen algorithm. If two commands are otherwise equal, the last-seen takes precedence.

THE @MEDIA RULE (CSS2 7.2.1)[S2]

@media mediatype { stylesheet ruleset }

Delimit stylesheet rulesets by supported media type. Multiple stylesheets can be included in a single document to support different media.

```
@import url("bigscreen.css") projection, tv;
```

RECOGNIZED MEDIA TYPES (CSS2 7.3)[S2]

Table E.2 describes the media types recognized in CSS2.

TABLE E.2 CSS2 MEDIA TYPES

Media Type	Description
all	Suitable for all devices[s2]
aural	Intended for speech synthesizers[s2]
braille	Intended for Braille tactile feedback devices[s2]
embossed	Intended for paged Braille printers[s2]
handheld	Intended for handheld devices[s2]
print	Intended for paged, opaque material and for documents viewed in print preview mode[s2]
projection	Intended for projected presentations[s2]
screen	Intended primarily for color computer screens[s2]
tty	Intended for media using a fixed-width character display, such as teletypes, some older computer terminals, and portable devices with limited display capabilities. You shouldn't use pixel units with the "tty" media type.[s2]
tv	Intended for television-type devices[s2]

APP

E

MEDIA GROUPS (CSS2 7.3.1)[S2]

TABLE E.3   CSS2 MEDIA GROUPS

Media group	Media types included in group
continuous	aural, braille, handheld, screen, tty, tv[s2]
paged	embossed, handheld, print, projection, tv[s2]
visual	handheld, print, projection, screen, tty, tv[s2]
aural	aural, tv[s2]
tactile	braille, embossed[s2]
grid	braille, embossed, handheld, tty[s2]
bitmap	handheld, print, projection, screen, tv[s2]
interactive	aural, braille, embossed, handheld, screen, tty, tv[s2]
static	aural, braille, embossed, handheld, print, projection, screen, tty, tv[s2]

Used in defining which media types a property applies to.

Font Properties (CSS1 5.2)

PROPERTY: FONT-FAMILY (CSS1 5.2.2, CSS2 15.2.2)[VISUAL]

```
element1 { font-family: value ... }
```

<family-name>

> Specify a font family name like Garamond or Beppo.

```
<generic-family>
```

serif

sans-serif

cursive

fantasy

monospace

```
inherit[s2]
```

> Specify a font family by generic characteristics.

PROPERTY: FONT-STYLE (CSS1 5.2.3, CSS2 15.2.3)[VISUAL]

```
normal
```

```
italic
```

```
oblique
```

```
inherit[s2]
```

> Specify a text treatment. Oblique is similar to italic but only slants the characters. True italics also alter the shape of the characters.

PROPERTY: FONT-VARIANT (CSS1 5.2.4, CSS2 15.2.3)[VISUAL]

```
normal
small-caps
inherit[s2]
```

> Specify a text treatment. Small caps are required in the core functionality but may turn into regular caps in text-based browsers, and browsers may ignore the command in non-Western European alphabets for which capital letters are not defined or whose techniques for emphasizing words are different.

PROPERTY: FONT-WEIGHT (CSS1 5.2.5, CSS2 15.2.3)[VISUAL]

```
normal
bold
bolder
lighter
100-900
inherit[s2]
```

> Specify a text treatment. The language allows for nine weights but, if there are fewer available, they might be mapped onto the missing weights in some logical way.

PROPERTY: FONT-STRETCH[VISUAL][S2]

```
normal[s2]
wider[s2]
narrower[s2]
ultra-condensed[s2]
extra-condensed[s2]
condensed[s2]
semi-condensed[s2]
semi-expanded[s2]
expanded[s2]
extra-expanded[s2]
ultra-expanded[s2]
inherit[s2]
```

> Specify the relative width of a font.

PROPERTY: FONT-SIZE (CSS1 5.2.6)

<absolute-size>

`xx-small`

`x-small`

`small`

`medium`

`large`

`x-large`

`xx-large`

<relative-size>

`larger`

`smaller`

<length>

<percentage>

`inherit[s2]`

> Specify a text treatment. Font size can be specified in absolute terms or relative to the current size, whichever is convenient.

PROPERTY: FONT-SIZE ADJUST[S2]

<number>[s2]

none[s2]

inherit[s2]

> Specify the adjustment target for a font. Number is the ratio of font size to x-height.

PROPERTY: FONT (CSS1 5.2.7)

<font-family>

<font-style>

<font-variant>

<font-weight>

<font-size>

<font-height>

inherit[s2]

> Specify several text treatments. This property is a shorthand notation for `<font-style>`, `<font-variant>`, `<font-weight>`, `<font-size>`, `<line-height>`, and `<font-family>`. The values each can take can be entered after this property without worrying about which goes with which. The browser will figure it out. Added in CSS2 are the keywords, *caption, icon, menu, message-box, small-caption,* and *status-bar* which refer to system font groups.

COLOR AND BACKGROUND PROPERTIES (CSS1 5.3, CSS2 14.1)

PROPERTY: **COLOR** (CSS1 5.3.1)[VISUAL]

<color>

inherit[s2]

Specify a foreground (text) color on an element.

PROPERTY: BACKGROUND-COLOR (CSS1 5.3.2, CSS2 14.2.1)[VISUAL]

<color>

transparent

inherit[s2]

Specify a background color on an element. Unlike traditional HTML, style sheets allow you to add "spot color" behind any visible element. This can be either wonderful or annoying, depending on how well one uses the capability.

PROPERTY: BACKGROUND-IMAGE (CSS1 5.3.3, CSS2 14.2.1)[VISUAL]

<url>

inherit

Specify a background image on an element.

PROPERTY: BACKGROUND-REPEAT (CSS1 5.3.4, CSS2 14.2.1)[VISUAL]

repeat

repeat-x

repeat-y

no-repeat

inherit[s2]

Specify a repeat value and method. repeat tiles the available area both horizontally and vertically. repeat-x tiles horizontally only. repeat-y tiles vertically only.

PROPERTY: BACKGROUND-ATTACHMENT (CSS1 5.3.5, CSS2 14.2.1)[VISUAL]

scroll

fixed [adv]

inherit[s2]

Specify how the background moves while scrolling. The default is to scroll with the text, but you can specify that a logo, for example, remains centered and immovable on the page while the rest of the page scrolls over it.

APP

E

PROPERTY: BACKGROUND-POSITION (CSS1 5.3.6, CSS2 14.2.1)[VISUAL]

```
<percentage>
<length>
top
center
left
bottom
right
inherit[s2]
```

Specify an initial position for a background image. Values can be combined, and if two numeric values are present, the horizontal value is presumed to be first. So background-position: 10pc 40pc ; would set the image 10% in from the left margin and 40% down from the top.

PROPERTY: BACKGROUND (CSS1 5.3.7)[VISUAL]

```
<background-color>
<background-image>
<background-repeat>
<background-attachment>
<background-position>
inherit[s2]
```

Specify several background values at once. This property is a shorthand notation for <background-color>, <background-image>, <background-repeat>, <background-attachment>, and <background-position>. The values each can take can be entered after this property without worrying about which goes with which. The browser will figure it out.

TEXT[S2]

TEXT PROPERTIES (CSS1 5.4, CSS2 16.4)

PROPERTY: WORD-SPACING (CSS1 5.4.1)[VISUAL]

```
normal
<length> [adv]
inherit[s2]
```

Specify the default whitespace between words.

PROPERTY: LETTER-SPACING (CSS1 5.4.2)[VISUAL]

```
normal
<length> [adv]
inherit[s2]
```

> Specify the default whitespace between letters. This is useful in old-style German Fraktur fonts, where emphasis is usually made by spacing out the letters more widely than normal.

PROPERTY: TEXT-DECORATION (CSS1 5.4.3, CSS2 16.3.1)[VISUAL]

```
none
underline
overline
line-through
blink
inherit[s2]
```

> Specify a text treatment. Line-through text is what we would ordinarily call strikeout or strike-through. This is useful for turning off link underlining globally, among other things.

TEXT SHADOWS: THE 'TEXT-SHADOW' PROPERTY (CSS2 16.3.2)[VISUAL][S2]

PROPERTY: TEXT-SHADOW[S2]

```
none[s2]
<color>? <length> <length> <length>?[s2]
inherit[s2]
```

> Specify one or more shadow text treatments. The lengths are horizontal, vertical, and optional blur. Succeeding shadows are separated by commas. It doesn't matter whether the color is before or after the lengths.[s2]

PROPERTY: VERTICAL-ALIGN (CSS1 5.4.4, CSS2 10.8)[VISUAL]

```
baseline
sub
super
top
text-top
middle
bottom
```

APP

E

      `text-bottom`

      `<length>``[s2]`

      `<percentage>`

      `inherit[s2]`

> Specify the vertical alignment of an element in relation to the surrounding text.

PROPERTY: TEXT-TRANSFORM (CSS1 5.4.5, CSS2 16.5)[VISUAL]

      `capitalize`

      `uppercase`

      `lowercase`

      `none`

      `inherit[s2]`

> Specify a text transformation treatment. Transformations are required in the core functionality, since capitalization is a basic text treatment in most Western European languages, but may be ignored by browsers in the case of many non-Western European alphabets, for which capital letters are not defined, or whose techniques for emphasizing words are substantially different.

PROPERTY: TEXT-ALIGN (CSS1 5.4.6, CSS2 16.2)[VISUAL]

      `left`

      `right`

      `center`

      `justify[adv]`

      `string[s2]`

      `inherit[s2]`

> Specify a text treatment. Justification refers to spacing out the text to precisely fit within the left and right margins, which browser makers hate to do because it's complicated and difficult.

PROPERTY: TEXT-INDENT (CSS1 5.4.7, CSS2 16.1)[VISUAL]

      `<length>`

      `<percentage>`

      `inherit[s2]`

> Specify a text treatment that occurs at the beginning of an element. This is useful for indenting (or outdenting) the first line of a paragraph, for one example. Hanging (outdented) paragraphs are quite common in technical materials.

PROPERTY: LINE-HEIGHT (CSS1 5.4.8, CSS2 10.8)[VISUAL]

```
normal

<number>

<length>

<percentage>

inherit[s2]
```

Specify the line height in relation to the font. In typographical terms this is called the body of the text. So you could set a 12-point font on a 14-point body to achieve a set separation between lines. Or you could set the same font on a 12-point body to jam them together rather tightly. Ordinarily the browser will set the text with a reasonably loose fit to allow easy legibility, but you can use this property to gain complete control, as when you want to bring the top of a following line up to meet the bottom of the current one to achieve a special typographic effect in a logo or headline.

BOX PROPERTIES (CSS1 5.5)

All the following properties specify how the "invisible" boxes that surround each element are treated, including being made visible by means of rules or changing the color of the background. Using spot background color to emphasize a headline, for example, looks rather ill-done unless you also expand the "invisible" border box the headline sits in to allow the background to make a nice border around it.

Margins are the outermost piece of the nested puzzle. They affect the whitespace gutter around an element and are always transparent to allow the background to show through. Borders come next. They affect the "elbow room" inside the box and take on the characteristics of the background set for the element itself. The border values affect whether the "invisible" box is made visible by the addition of a visible border. They appear between the margin and the border boxes if present.

PROPERTY: MARGIN-TOP (CSS1 5.5.01, CSS2 8.3)[VISUAL]

```
<length>

<percentage>

auto

inherit[s2]
```

Specify the exterior top margin or gutter of an element.

PROPERTY: MARGIN-RIGHT (CSS1 5.5.02, CSS2 18.3)[VISUAL]

```
<length>

<percentage>
```

APP

E

```
auto

inherit[s2]
```
> Specify the exterior right margin or gutter of an element.

PROPERTY: MARGIN-BOTTOM (CSS1 5.5.03, CSS2 18.3)[VISUAL]

```
<length>

<percentage>

auto

inherit[s2]
```
> Specify the exterior bottom margin or gutter of an element.

PROPERTY: MARGIN-LEFT (CSS1 5.5.04, CSS2 18.3)[VISUAL]

<length>

<percentage>

```
auto

inherit[s2]
```
> Specify left exterior margin or gutter of an element.

PROPERTY: MARGIN (CSS1 5.5.05, CSS2 18.3)[VISUAL]

```
<length>

<percentage>

auto

inherit[s2]
```
> Specify one or more exterior margins or gutters of an element. If four length values are specified, they apply to top, right, bottom, and left respectively. If there is only one value, it applies to all sides; if there are two or three, the missing values are taken from the opposite side.

PROPERTY: PADDING-TOP (CSS1 5.5.06, CSS2 18.4)[VISUAL]

```
<length>

<percentage>

auto

inherit[s2]
```
> Specify the top interior margin or gutter of an element. It sets the amount of space between one "invisible" border of an element and the element itself.

PROPERTY: PADDING-RIGHT (CSS1 5.5.07, CSS2 18.4)[VISUAL]

> *<length>*
>
> *<percentage>*
>
> auto
>
> inherit[s2]
>
>> Specify the right interior margin or gutter of an element. It sets the amount of space between one "invisible" border of an element and the element itself.

PROPERTY: PADDING-BOTTOM (CSS1 5.5.08, CSS2 18.4)[VISUAL]

> *<length>*
>
> *<percentage>*
>
> auto
>
> inherit[s2]
>
>> Specify the bottom interior margin or gutter of an element. It sets the amount of space between one "invisible" border of an element and the element itself.

PROPERTY: PADDING-LEFT (CSS1 5.5.09, CSS2 18.4)[VISUAL]

> *<length>*
>
> *<percentage>*
>
> auto
>
> inherit[s2]
>
>> Specify the left interior margin or gutter of an element. It sets the amount of space between one "invisible" border of an element and the element itself.

PROPERTY: PADDING (CSS1 5.5.10, CSS2 18.4)[VISUAL]

> *<length>*
>
> *<percentage>*
>
> auto
>
> inherit[s2]
>
>> Specify one or more interior margins or gutters of an element. They set the amount of space between the "invisible" borders of an element and the element itself. If four length values are specified, they apply to top, right, bottom and left respectively. If there is only one value, it applies to all sides, and if there are two or three, the missing values are taken from the opposite side.

APP

E

PROPERTY: BORDER-TOP-WIDTH (CSS1 5.5.11, CSS2 8.5.1)[VISUAL]

thin

medium

thick

<length>

inherit[s2]

Specify the thickness (and visibility) of the top border of an element.

PROPERTY: BORDER-RIGHT-WIDTH (CSS1 5.5.12, CSS2 8.5.1)[VISUAL]

thin

medium

thick

<length>

inherit[s2]

Specify the thickness (and visibility) of the right border of an element.

PROPERTY: BORDER-BOTTOM-WIDTH (CSS1 5.5.13, CSS2 8.5.1)[VISUAL]

thin

medium

thick

<length>

inherit[s2]

Specify the thickness (and visibility) of the bottom border of an element.

PROPERTY: BORDER-LEFT-WIDTH (CSS1 5.5.14, CSS2 8.5.1)[VISUAL]

thin

medium

thick

<length>

inherit[s2]

Specify the thickness (and visibility) of the left border of an element.

PROPERTY: BORDER-WIDTH (CSS1 5.5.15, CSS2 8.5.1)[VISUAL]

thin

medium

thick

<length>

inherit[s2]

Specify the thickness (and visibility) of one or more borders of an element. This property is a shorthand property for setting 'border-width-top,' 'border-width right,' 'border-width-bottom,' and 'border-width-left' in one fell swoop. There can be from one to four values, with the following interpretation: one value—all four border widths are set to that value; two values—top and bottom border widths are set to the first value, right and left are set to the second; three values—top is set to the first, right and left are set to the second, bottom is set to the third; four values—top, right, bottom, and left, respectively.

PROPERTY: BORDER-COLOR (CSS1 5.5.16, CSS2 8.5.2)[VISUAL]

`<color>`

`transparent[s2]`

`inherit[s2]`

Specify the color of one or more borders of an element. There can be from one to four values, with the following interpretation: one value—all four border colors are set to that value; two values— top and bottom border colors are set to the first value, right and left are set to the second; three values—top is set to the first, right and left are set to the second, bottom is set to the third; four values—top, right, bottom, and left, respectively. The CSS2 value `transparent` means that the border is transparent (invisible) although it still takes up space on the page. The CSS2 value `inherit` means that whatever value was set by an ancestor is explicitly accepted in this descendent.

PROPERTY: BORDER-STYLE (CSS1 5.5.17, CSS2 8.5.3)[VISUAL]

`none`

`dotted[adv]`

`dashed[adv]`

`solid`

`double[adv]`

`groove[adv]`

`ridge[adv]`

`inset[adv]`

`offset[adv]`

`inherit[s2]`

Specify the rule style of one or more borders of an element. There can be from one to four values, with the following interpretation: one value—all four border rules are set to that value; two values—top and bottom border rules are set to the first value, right and left are set to the second; three values—top is set to the first, right and left are set to the second, bottom is set to the third; four values—top, right, bottom, and left, respectively.

PROPERTY: BORDER-TOP (CSS1 5.5.18, CSS2 8.5.4)[VISUAL]

`<border-top-width>`

`<border-style>`

`<color>`

`inherit[s2]`

Set the width, color, and rule styles of the top border (only) at one time.

PROPERTY: BORDER-RIGHT (CSS1 5.5.19, CSS2 8.5.4)[VISUAL]

`<border-right-width>`

`<border-style>`

`<color>`

`inherit[s2]`

Set the width, color, and rule styles of the right border (only) at one time.

PROPERTY: BORDER-BOTTOM (CSS1 5.5.20, CSS2 8.5.4)[VISUAL]

`<border-bottom-width>`

`<border-style>`

`<color>`

`inherit[s2]`

Set the width, color, and rule styles of the bottom border (only) at one time.

PROPERTY: BORDER-LEFT (CSS1 5.5.21, CSS2 8.5.4)[VISUAL]

`<border-left-width>`

`<border-style>`

`<color>`

`inherit[s2]`

Set the width, color, and rule styles of the left border (only) at one time.

PROPERTY: BORDER (CSS1 5.5.22, CSS2 8.5.4)[VISUAL]

`<border-width>`

`<border-style>`

`<color>`

```
inherit[s2]
```

Set the width, color, and rule styles of all borders at one time and to the same values. You can't use multiple values to set different values for the four sides.

PROPERTY: WIDTH (CSS1 5.5.23, CSS2 10.2)[VISUAL]

```
<length>

<percentage>

auto

inherit[s2]
```

Override the default width of an element.

PROPERTY: MIN-WIDTH (CSS2 10.4)[VISUAL][S2]

```
<length>[s2]

<percentage>[s2]

inherit[s2]
```

Set the minimum width of an element.

PROPERTY: MAX-WIDTH (CSS2 10.4)[VISUAL][S2]

```
<length>[s2]

<percentage>[s2]

none[s2]

inherit[s2]
```

Set the maximum width of an element.

PROPERTY: HEIGHT (CSS1 5.5.24, CSS2 10.5)[VISUAL][S2]

```
<length>

<percentage>[s2]

auto

inherit[s2]
```

Override the default height of an element.

PROPERTY: MIN-HEIGHT (CSS2 10.7)[VISUAL][S2]

```
<length>[s2]

<percentage>[s2]

inherit[s2]
```

Set the minimum height of an element.

PROPERTY: MAX-HEIGHT (CSS2 10.7)[VISUAL][S2]

`<length>`[s2]

`<percentage>`[s2]

`inherit`[s2]

Set the maximum height of an element.

PROPERTY: FLOAT (CSS1 5.5.25, CSS2 9.5.1)[VISUAL]

`left`

`right`

`none`

`inherit`[s2]

Override the default behavior of an element to cause text to flow around it as if it were a bump on the left or right margin. It also overrides the display property and causes the element to behave as a block element regardless of type.

PROPERTY: CLEAR (CSS1 5.5.26, CSS2 9.5.2)[VISUAL]

`left`

`right`

`both`

`none`

`inherit`[s2]

Fix the behavior of an element in relation to floating elements by listing sides on which the element will refuse to float. none says the element will float on either side. both says it will always clear down to the next available free space on both margins. left says it will clear down to the left margin but ignore the right and vice versa for right.

CLASSIFICATION PROPERTIES (CSS1 5.6)

PROPERTY: DISPLAY [ADV] (CSS1 5.6.1, CSS2 5.6)[VISUAL]

`block`

`inline`

`list-item`

`none`

`run-in`[s2]

`compact`[s2]

`marker`[s2]

```
table[s2]

inline-table[s2]

table-row-group[s2]

table-header-group[s2]

table-footer-group[s2]

table-row[s2]

table-column-group[s2]

table-column[s2]

table-cell[s2]

table-caption[s2]

inherit[s2]
```

Override the default behavior of an element to make it behave however one wants. Very cool. Unfortunately only Netscape Navigator for Windows 95 does much about it so far and only the CSS1 stuff. Mozilla may well be better by far.

PROPERTY: WHITE-SPACE [ADV] (CSS1 5.6.2, CSS2 16.6)[VISUAL]

```
normal

pre

nowrap

inherit[s2]
```

Override the default whitespace behavior of an element to make white-space behave however you want. This is very cool because it lets you typeset poetry and other text requiring exact placement of whitespace without fooling around with non-break spaces and breaks while retaining the ability to control the look of the font. Unfortunately, only Netscape Navigator for Windows 95 and Mac does much about it so far.

PROPERTY: LIST-STYLE-TYPE (CSS1 5.6.3, CSS2 12.6.2)[VISUAL]

```
disc

circle

square

decimal

decimal-leading-zero[s2]

lower-roman

upper-roman

lower-alpha
```

```
upper-alpha

lower-greek[s2]

lower-latin[s2]

upper-latin[s2]

hebrew[s2]

armenian[s2]

georgian[s2]

cjk-ideographic[s2]

hiragana[s2]

katakana[s2]

hiragana-iroha[s2]

katakana-iroha[s2]

none

inherit[s2]
```

This sets the default numeration type of a list element, similar to the way the type attribute can be used on a list tag.

PROPERTY: LIST-STYLE-IMAGE (CSS1 5.6.4, CSS2 12.6.2)[VISUAL]

```
<url>

none

inherit[s2]
```

Override the numeration type of a list element by picking up an image to be used as a bullet.

PROPERTY: LIST-STYLE-POSITION (CSS1 5.6.5, CSS2 12.6.2)[VISUAL]

```
inside

outside

inherit[s2]
```

Override the default display of list elements by specifying whether the bullet or number will be displayed as a hanging indent (outdent), as usual, or inline, as if it were part of the text.

PROPERTY: LIST-STYLE (CSS1 5.6.6, CSS2 12.6.2)[VISUAL]

```
<keyword>

<position>

<url>

inherit[s2]
```

A shorthand notation for setting all list style values at once.

GENERATED CONTENT, AUTOMATIC NUMBERING, AND LISTS (CSS2 12)[S2]

THE 'CONTENT' PROPERTY (CSS2 12.2)[ALL][S2]

PROPERTY: CONTENT[S2]

> *<string>*[s2]
>
> *<url>*[s2]
>
> *<counter>*[s2]
>
> attr(X) [s2]
>
> open-quote[s2]
>
> close-quote[s2]
>
> no-open-quote[s2]
>
> no-close-quote[s2]
>
> inherit[s2]
>> Used with the :before and :after pseudo-elements to generate content. attr(X) returns the value of attribute X for the subject of the selector only. Counters may be generated with either the counter() function or the counters() function. Use an @media rule when content is media sensitive.

QUOTATION MARKS (CSS2 12.4)[VISUAL][S2]

PROPERTY: QUOTES[S2]

> *<string>* *<string>* ...[s2]
>
> none[s2]
>
> inherit[s2]
>> Used to set the value or values of beginning and ending quote marks and nested quote marks. These values must be used with a content property which specifies open-quote and close-quote values. There are also two values, no-open-quote and no-close-quote, which affect the nesting level but produce no visible display to handle the elision of quote marks used in certain typographical styles.

APP

E

AUTOMATIC COUNTERS AND NUMBERING (CSS2 12.5)[ALL][S2]

PROPERTY: COUNTER-RESET[S2]

> *<identifier>* *<integer>*? ...[s2]
>
> none[s2]
>
> inherit[s2]
>> Reset the value of one or more counters to zero or to an optional *<integer>* value.

PROPERTY: COUNTER-INCREMENT (CSS2 12.5)[ALL][S2]

      <identifier> <integer>? ...[s2]

      none[s2]

      inherit[s2]

          Set the increment value of one or more counters to one or to an optional *<integer>* value.

PROPERTY: COUNTER(*<IDENTIFIER>* 'LIST-STYLE-TYPE') (CSS2 12.5.2)[ALL][S2]

PROPERTY: COUNTERS(*<IDENTIFIER>* 'LIST-STYLE-TYPE'...) (CSS2 12.5.2)[ALL][S2]

SET THE LIST STYLE TYPE OF ONE OR MORE COUNTERS.

PROPERTY: MARKER-OFFSET (CSS2 12.6.1)[VISUAL][S2]

      length[s2]

      auto[s2]

      inherit[s2]

          Set the marker-offset of a counter whose containing element has the display property set to marker.

PAGED MEDIA (CSS2 13)[S2]

PAGE BOXES: THE @PAGE RULE (CSS2 13.2)[VISUAL][PAGED][S2]

   @page *<identifier>*? { pageproperty: pageattribute ; ... }

          Define a page.

PAGE SIZE: THE 'SIZE' PROPERTY (CSS2 13.2.2)[VISUAL][PAGED][S2]

PROPERTY: SIZE[S2]

      <length><length>?[s2]

      auto[s2]

      portrait[s2]

      landscape[s2]

      inherit[s2]

          Set the page size and orientation.

CROP MARKS: THE 'MARKS' PROPERTY (CSS2 13.2.3)[VISUAL][PAGED][S2]

PROPERTY: MARKS[S2]

      crop[s2]

      cross[s2]

none[s2]

inherit[s2]

> Toggle crop or alignment marks.

LEFT, RIGHT, AND FIRST PAGE PSEUDO-CLASSES (CSS2 13.2.4)[VISUAL][PAGED][S2]

left pseudo-class[s2]

Example: @page <*identifier*>:left { *property*: *value* ... }[s2]

Example: @page :left { *property*: *value* ... }[s2]

> Matches an element on a right-facing page in a page context.

right pseudo-class[s2]

Example: @page :right { *property*: *value* ... }[s2]

> Matches an element on a left-facing page in a page context.

first pseudo-class[s2]

Example: @page :first { *property*: *value* ... }[s2]

> Matches an element on the first page in a page context.

PAGE BREAKS (CSS2 13.3)[VISUAL][PAGED][S2]

> Break before/after elements: 'page-break-before', 'page-break-after', 'page-break-inside' (CSS2 13.3.1)[visual][paged][s2]

PROPERTY: PAGE-BREAK-BEFORE[S2]

auto[s2]

always[s2]

avoid[s2]

left[s2]

right[s2]

inherit[s2]

> Set page-break behavior before an element.

PROPERTY: PAGE-BREAK-AFTER[S2]

auto[s2]

always[s2]

avoid[s2]

left[s2]

right[s2]

inherit[s2]

> Set page-break behavior after an element.

PROPERTY: PAGE-BREAK-INSIDE[S2]

> auto[s2]
>
> avoid[s2]
>
> inherit[s2]
>
>> Set page-break behavior within an element.

USING NAMED PAGES: 'PAGE' (CSS2 13.3.2)[VISUAL][PAGED][S2]

PROPERTY: PAGE

> <identifier>
>
> auto
>
>> Use the named page.

BREAKS INSIDE ELEMENTS: 'ORPHANS', 'WIDOWS' (CSS2 13.3.3)[VISUAL][PAGED][S2]

PROPERTY: ORPHANS[S2]

> *<integer>*[s2]
>
> inherit[s2]
>
>> Set orphan (bottom of page) control.

PROPERTY: WIDOWS[S2]

> *<integer>*[s2]
>
> inherit[s2]
>
>> Set widow (top of page) control.

TABLES (CSS2 17)[S2]

17.2 The CSS table model[s2]

The following CSS2 keyword attributes can be assigned to the display property described in section CSS1 5.6.1 and CSS2 9.2.5. These are designed to let you make any XML element behave as if it's a table for the purposes of display but are only available in CSS2.

> table[s2] (In HTML: TABLE)
>
>> Specifies that an element defines a block-level table: It is a rectangular block that participates in a block formatting context.
>
> inline-table[s2] (In HTML: TABLE)
>
>> Specifies that an element defines an inline-level table: It is a rectangular block that participates in an inline formatting context).

`table-row[s2]` (In HTML: TR)

> Specifies that an element is a row of cells.

`table-row-group[s2]` (In HTML: TBODY)

> Specifies that an element groups one or more rows.

`table-header-group[s2]` (In HTML: THEAD)

> Like 'table-row-group', but for visual formatting, the row group is always displayed before all other rows and rowgroups and after any top captions. Print user agents may repeat footer rows on each page spanned by a table.

`table-footer-group[s2]` (HTML: TFOOT)

> Like 'table-row-group', but for visual formatting, the row group is always displayed after all other rows and rowgroups and before any bottom captions. Print user agents may repeat footer rows on each page spanned by a table.

`table-column[s2]` (HTML: COL)

> Specifies that an element describes a column of cells.

`table-column-group[s2]` (HTML: COLGROUP)

> Specifies that an element groups one or more columns.

`table-cell[s2]` (HTML: TD, TH)

> Specifies that an element represents a table cell.

`table-caption[s2]` (HTML: CAPTION)

> Specifies a caption for the table.

So a default CSS2 style sheet for XHTML would look like this:

```
TABLE     { display: table }
TR        { display: table-row }
THEAD     { display: table-header-group }
TBODY     { display: table-row-group }
TFOOT     { display: table-footer-group }
COL       { display: table-column }
COLGROUP  { display: table-column-group }
TD, TH    { display: table-cell }
CAPTION   { display: table-caption }
```

Anonymous table objects (CSS2 17.2.1)[s2]

Because table display properties do not necessarily follow the CSS2 display model, anonymous table objects will be generated automatically to contain them if there are missing elements.

App

E

COLUMN SELECTORS (CSS2 17.3)[S2]

The following properties may apply to column and column-group elements:

PROPERTY: BORDER[S2]

PROPERTY: BACKGROUND[S2]

PROPERTY: WIDTH[S2]

PROPERTY: VISIBILITY[S2]

Caption position and alignment (CSS2 17.4.1)[visual][s2]

PROPERTY: CAPTION-SIDE[S2]

```
top[s2]
bottom[s2]
left[s2]
right[s2]
inherit[s2]
```
Set the position of the caption.

Table width algorithms: the 'table-layout' property (CSS2 17.5.2)[visual][s2]

PROPERTY: TABLE-LAYOUT[S2]

```
auto[s2]
fixed[s2]
inherit[s2]
```
Set the algorithm used to lay out the table.

Borders (CSS2 17.6)[visual][s2]

PROPERTY: BORDER-COLLAPSE[S2]

```
collapse[s2]
separate[s2]
inherit[s2]
```
Set the model used for borders.

The separated borders model (CSS2 17.6.1)[visual][s2]

PROPERTY: BORDER-SPACING[S2]

```
<length> <length>?[s2]
inherit[s2]
```
Set the distance between cell borders.

PROPERTY: EMPTY-CELLS[S2]

    show[s2]

    hide[s2]

    inherit[s2]

Audio rendering of tables (CSS2 17.7)[aural][s2]

PROPERTY: SPEAK-HEADER[S2]

    once[s2]

    always[s2]

    inherit[s2]

        Set behavior of aural rendering.

18 USER INTERFACE (CSS2 18)[S2]

Cursors: the 'cursor' property (CSS2 18.1)[visual][interactive][s2]

PROPERTY: CURSOR[S2]

    <url>[s2]

    auto[s2]

    crosshair[s2]

    default[s2]

    pointer[s2]

    move[s2]

    e-resize[s2]

    ne-resize[s2]

    nw-resize[s2]

    n-resize[s2]

    se-resize[s2]

    sw-resize[s2]

    s-resize[s2]

    w-resize[s2]

    text[s2]

    wait[s2]

    help[s2]

    inherit[s2]

        Set the type of cursor. URL is image. Keyword is the cursor context.

APP
E

User preferences for colors(CSS2 18.2)[visual][interactive][s2]

Any color property can take the following keyword attributes relating to system colors as a value similar to a named color. This is designed to let you make the user agent display look like the default user interface colors.[s2]

ActiveBorder[s2]

> Active window border.

ActiveCaption[s2]

> Active window caption.

AppWorkspace[s2]

> Background color of multiple document interface.

Background[s2]

> Desktop background.

ButtonFace[s2]

> Face color for three-dimensional display elements.

ButtonHighlight[s2]

> Dark shadow for three-dimensional display elements (for edges facing away from the light source).

ButtonShadow[s2]

> Shadow color for three-dimensional display elements.

ButtonText[s2]

> Text on push buttons.

CaptionText[s2]

> Text in caption, size box, and scrollbar arrow box.

GrayText[s2]

> Grayed (disabled) text. This color is set to #000000 if the current display driver does not support a solid gray color.

Highlight[s2]

> Item(s) selected in a control.

HighlightText[s2]

> Text of item(s) selected in a control.

InactiveBorder[s2]

> Inactive window border.

InactiveCaption[s2]

> Inactive window caption.

InactiveCaptionText[s2]

> Color of text in an inactive caption.

InfoBackground[s2]

Background color for tooltip controls.

InfoText[s2]

Text color for tooltip controls.

Menu[s2]

Menu background.

MenuText[s2]

Text in menus.

Scrollbar[s2]

Scroll bar gray area.

ThreeDDarkShadow[s2]

Dark shadow for three-dimensional display elements.

ThreeDFace[s2]

Face color for three-dimensional display elements.

ThreeDHighlight[s2]

Highlight color for three-dimensional display elements.

ThreeDLightShadow[s2]

Light color for three-dimensional display elements (for edges facing the light source).

ThreeDShadow[s2]

Dark shadow for three-dimensional display elements.

Window[s2]

Window background.

WindowFrame[s2]

Window frame.

WindowText[s2]

Text in windows.

Dynamic outlines: the 'outline' property(CSS2 18.4)[visual][interactive][s2]

PROPERTY: OUTLINE[S2]

<outline-color><outline-style><outline-width>[s2]

inherit[s2]

Shorthand property to set border attributes. Outlines are like borders but take up no space on the page.

PROPERTY: OUTLINE-WIDTH[S2]

> `<border-width>`[s2]
>
> `inherit`[s2]
>
>> Set outline width. See Border properties. Outlines are like borders but take up no space on the page.

PROPERTY: OUTLINE-STYLE[S2]

> `<border-style>`[s2]
>
> `inherit`[s2]
>
>> Set outline style. See Border properties. Outlines are like borders but take up no space on the page.

PROPERTY: OUTLINE-COLOR

> `<color>`[s2]
>
> `invert`[s2]
>
> `inherit`[s2]
>
>> Set outline color. See Border properties. Outlines are like borders but take up no space on the page.

AURAL STYLE SHEETS (CSS2 19)[AURAL][S2]

Volume properties: 'volume' (CSS2 19.2)[aural][s2]

PROPERTY: VOLUME[S2]

> `<number>`[s2]
>
> `<percentage>`[s2]
>
> `silent`[s2]
>
> `x-soft`[s2]
>
> `soft`[s2]
>
> `medium`[s2]
>
> `loud`[s2]
>
> `x-loud`[s2]
>
> `inherit`[s2]
>
>> Set volume.

Speaking properties: 'speak' (CSS2 19.3)[aural][s2]

PROPERTY: SPEAK

> normal[s2]
>
> none[s2]
>
> spell-out[s2]
>
> inherit[s2]
>> Set style of speech.

Pause properties: 'pause-before', 'pause-after', and 'pause' (CSS2 19.4)[aural][s2]

PROPERTY: PAUSE-BEFORE[S2]

> <time>[s2]
>
> <percentage>[s2]
>
> inherit[s2]
>> Set pause before speaking value.

PROPERTY: PAUSE-AFTER[S2]

> <time>[s2]
>
> <percentage>[s2]
>
> inherit[s2]
>> Set pause after speaking value.

PROPERTY: PAUSE[S2]

> <time>[s2]
>
> <percentage>[s2]
>
> inherit[s2]
>> Shorthand property to set pause-before and pause-after.

Cue properties: 'cue-before', 'cue-after', and 'cue' (CSS2 19.5)[aural][s2]

PROPERTY: CUE-BEFORE[S2]

> <url>[s2]
>
> none[s2]
>
> inherit[s2]
>> Set cue before speaking sound.

APP

E

PROPERTY: CUE-AFTER[S2]

    <url>[s2]

    none[s2]

    inherit[s2]

        Set cue after speaking sound.

PROPERTY: CUE[S2]

    <url>[s2]

    none[s2]

    inherit[s2]

        Shorthand property to set cue-before and cue-after sounds.

Mixing properties: 'play-during' (CSS2 19.6)[aural][s2]

PROPERTY: PLAY-DURING[S2]

    <url>[s2]

    mix?[s2]

    repeat?[s2]

    auto[s2]

    none[s2]

    inherit[s2]

        Set volume.

Spatial properties: 'azimuth' and 'elevation' (CSS2 19.7)[aural][s2]

PROPERTY: AZIMUTH[S2]

    <angle>[s2]

    left-side[s2]

    far-left[s2]

    left[s2]

    center-left[s2]

    center[s2]

    center-right[s2]

    right[s2]

    far-right[s2]

    right-side[s2]

    behind[s2]

leftwards[s2]

rightwards[s2]

inherit[s2]

> Set simulated location of sound source or speaker.

PROPERTY: ELEVATION[S2]

<angle>[s2]

below[s2]

level[s2]

above[s2]

higher[s2]

lower[s2]

inherit[s2]

> Set simulated height of sound source or speaker.

Voice characteristic properties: 'speech-rate', 'voice-family', 'pitch', 'pitch-range', 'stress', and 'richness' (CSS2 19.8)[aural][s2]

PROPERTY: SPEECH-RATE[S2]

<number>[s2]

x-slow[s2]

slow[s2]

medium[s2]

fast[s2]

x-fast[s2]

faster[s2]

slower[s2]

inherit[s2]

> Set speech rate. Number is words per minute.

PROPERTY: VOICE-FAMILY[S2]

<specific voice>[s2]

<generic voice>[s2]

inherit[s2]

> Set voice family. Specific voices are dependent on user agent.

PROPERTY: PITCH[S2]

    `<frequency>`[s2]

    `x-low`[s2]

    `low`[s2]

    `medium`[s2]

    `high`[s2]

    `x-high`[s2]

    inherit[s2]

        Set average speech pitch (frequency). Average Male=120Hz, Female=210Hz, Child=300Hz.

PROPERTY: PITCH-RANGE[S2]

    `<number>`[s2]

    inherit[s2]

        Set pitch range. Number is 0–100. 50=average.

PROPERTY: STRESS[S2]

    `<number>`[s2]

    inherit[s2]

        Set intonation pattern. Number is 0–100.

PROPERTY: RICHNESS[S2]

    `<number>`[s2]

    inherit[s2]

        Set overtone pattern. Number is 0–100.

Speech properties: 'speak-punctuation' and 'speak-numeral' (CSS2 19.9)[aural][s2]

PROPERTY: SPEAK-PUNCTUATION[S2]

    `code`[s2]

    `none`[s2]

    inherit[s2]

        Set spoken punctuation or inferred from pause and tone.

PROPERTY: SPEAK-NUMERAL[S2]

    `digits[s2]`

    `continuous[s2]`

    `inherit[s2]`

        Set digit-by-digit (telephone) or natural (money).

UNITS (CSS1 6)

CSS1 and CSS2 units follow the number they modify with no intervening space. So 10px is correct but 10 px is not.

Length Units (CSS1 6.1, CSS2 4.3.2)

em	em-quad, the point size of the current font.
ex	*x*-height, the height of the letter x in the current font.
px	pixels
in	inches
cm	centimeters
mm	millimeters
pc	percent
pt	points, a typographical measure equal to one seventy-second of an inch. In other words, there are 72 points to the inch.

Percentage Units (CSS1 6.2, CSS2 4.3.3)

<percentage>

    Percentage values are not inherited. The result of a percentage calculation is inherited.

Color Units (CSS1 6.3, CSS2 4.3.6)

#000

#000000

`(RRR,GGG,BBB)`

`(R%,G%,B%)`

keyword

    Style sheet colors do not affect images.

URLs and URNs (CSS1 6.4, CSS2 4.3.4)

`url("url")`

    URLs are always enclosed in parentheses and may be surrounded by optional single or double quote marks. Parentheses, commas, whitespace characters, single quotes ('), and double quotes (") appearing in an URL must be escaped with a backslash (\). Partial URLs are interpreted relative to the source of the style sheet, not relative to the document. CSS2 introduces the concept of URIs, Uniform Resource

Identifiers, which consist logically of a URN, Uniform Resource Name plus a URL. They're still accessed by the url("url") syntax, however.

Angles (CSS2 4.3.7)[aural][s2]

deg degrees

grad grads

rad radians

Angles may be negative or, with a "-" or "+" prefix, relative.

Times (CSS2 4.3.8)[aural][s2]

ms milliseconds

s seconds

Times, alas, may not be negative.

Frequencies (CSS2 4.3.9)[aural][s2]

Hz Hertz

kHz kiloHertz

Frequencies may not be negative.

Strings (CSS2 4.3.10)[all][s2]

Strings can either be written with double quotes or with single quotes. Double quotes cannot occur inside double quotes, unless escaped (as '\"' or as '\22'). Single quotes can be escaped likewise with ("\'" or "\27") inside single quotes.

CSS document representation (CSS2 4.4)[all][s2]

@charset "<ISO Identifier>"

Referring to characters not represented in a character encoding (CSS2 4.4.1)[all][s2]

\<hexvalue>

UNDERSTANDING WHY CSS IS IMPORTANT

Cascading style sheets are the wave of the future on the Web although they might soon be supplemented in XML by XSL, the Extensible Stylesheet Language, or other initiatives. Designers are pushing hard for the ability to control all variables on the page, from typeface to line spacing and exact layout and control of whitespace, just as they're used to in print media. They're not quite there yet, but they're getting closer with each new browser release.

- Style sheets are easy to use and accessible to all users, while XSL is somewhat difficult for non-programmers to understand, even though XSL is much more powerful.

- Style sheets have the official backing of W3C, which means really all the W3C member organizations, which include most major software developers in the world, so they will eventually be supported well and everywhere. We fondly hope.

- Style sheets are available to both HTML and XML documents, so they have wider applicability to the millions of pages of legacy data already existing on the Web.

- Style sheet support can easily be modularized, so rendering engines can incorporate whatever parts are appropriate for a particular kind of device, which makes it feasible to use a style sheet even in a hand-held device or cell phone.

All these reasons are compelling, so style sheets seem far more likely to be widely supported than XSL, which is more complex and less modular at the present time.

The theory behind style sheets is simple: You can create a master style sheet for an entire site and then override or extend the style sheet on any particular page while not altering global settings not specifically addressed.

Likewise, a user can create a style sheet that overrides the default style sheet the browser uses to display pages while allowing the page designer to override those settings to format a particular page.

For the designer, this means that you should usually specify sizes in terms of relative size and not force a user to accept your idea of what's "big enough." For the most part you're free to play around with whatever you want, though, and you can really do quite stunning things with fairly simple commands.

STYLE SHEET COMMANDS

The style sheet commands consist of simple text strings with each command consisting of an HTML element, special pseudo-element, or subclass of elements followed by a curly bracketed list of properties and values. If there is more than one property and value pair listed, they should be separated by semicolons. Styles can be further refined by declaring what context they would apply to by listing elements in order or by applying pseudo-elements or attributes to modify the HTML element.

So a style referring to anchor elements might be modified by saying this style applies only to anchor elements which are also links, `A:link { color:blue }`, have been visited, `A:visited { color:red }`, or occur within the scope of a paragraph, `P A { color:green }`.

The commands can be placed in a separate file, which is very convenient for controlling an entire site from one uniform location, in the head section of a file, or inline, attached to an individual tag. In the case of an inline style, there is no need of an element description because the style affects the element to which it is attached. Likewise, you don't bracket the style with curly braces but just list the style commands in a comma-separated list within quote marks.

This section has addressed the bright theory of CSS, but now let's take a somber look at reality as implemented by actual browsers in the field.

BROWSER SUPPORT FOR CSS

Quite frankly, support for CSS1 has thus far been a dismal failure and CSS2 is only a shadow of its possibility. The few things available across multiple platforms are almost not worth doing because of the difficulty of maintaining compatibility across multiple browsers and some property value combinations cause browsers to crash at random intervals. We can only hope the situation will improve over time. There is every reason to hope that it will if the browser makers will only get behind existing standards and concentrate on getting *at least* the defined syntax and commands right before heading off after quirky or non-standard "features" and "extensions" to attain some hoped-for Nirvana of product differentiation.

You'll note that I put the two terms, "features" and "extensions," much bandied-about by both major manufacturers, in wry quotes. It's my considered opinion that you can't make an extension to a standard until you've done it right to begin with, and an extension without a stable and agreed-upon base is merely a fancy and disingenuous name for a bug.

Overall, the best cross-platform support in a main-stream browser is with Netscape Navigator/Communicator 4.0, although the forthcoming release of the Mozilla beta as Netscape 5.0 promises vastly improved support for CSS1 and CSS2. Their coverage of Windows platforms and the Macintosh is even-handed for the most part, and what works in one will pretty much work in the other. They also support UNIX rather well, which accounts for pretty much all the major platforms. Because they still have a substantial market share and people with Macintoshes are known to be easily distressed regarding page design issues and matters of typographical taste, this might be a good platform to concentrate on as the most common denominator, despite the 55% overall market penetration of MSIE, which includes both current and obsolete versions of the Microsoft browser.

On the other hand, if you're only interested in Windows 95, Microsoft's Internet Explorer 4.0 has very good coverage for Windows and Intel PCs. Unfortunately, their implementation of CSS1 on the Macintosh is terrible, and their UNIX support is an afterthought at best and a slight at worst.

If you're willing to go against the main stream, the GNU version of Emacs-W3 (GnuScape Navigator) is probably the most complete and up-to-date implementation of CSS1 available. Although configuring Gnu Emacs-W3 is not for the faint of heart, it being assumed that you have not one, but two shirt pockets with many colored pens and pencils safely ensconced in unmatched pocket protectors, it's easily the most powerful and extensible Web browser around. It has many features built in, including out-of-the-box integration with Emacspeak, a marvelous audio browser package by T.V. Raman entirely suitable for surfing the Web without the assistance of vision.

Since Emacs-W3 is built around an editor, importing information from the Web and incorporating it into documents is a trivial task. Since it's Emacs, you can do sophisticated filtering and rearranging of the data you get off the Web without fighting with what the designers thought you *should* be doing every step of the way.

Gnu Emacs-W3 can be found at `http://www.cs.indiana.edu/elisp/w3/docs.html`.

T.V. Raman's Emacspeak can be found at `http://cs.cornell.edu/home/raman/emacspeak/emacspeak.html`.

On the Web, things sometimes move around, so a quick visit to a search engine can often lead you to a current source when a document "disappears." Most useful pages are quickly reincarnated when they vanish from a former location.

Now that we've seen the problems associated with CSS in the real world, let's think about how to handle the inevitable problems, and even whether we really want to.

HANDLING BUGS GRACEFULLY

I'm of two minds about this. On one hand, it's not right for the designers of Web pages to spend countless hours trying to account for the vagaries and oversights of the manufacturers.

In that frame of mind, I tend to think that we should code for the way it *ought* to work and let people see just how bad most browsers are. Let the chips fall where they may.

On the other hand, people will judge your page based on how well you use the tools at hand, and using features that break some browsers just makes your pages look bad. Few people are sophisticated enough to realize that the terrible-looking page they're trying to read is due to the failure of the maker of the browser they're reading it with and not the errors of the page's creator. Just as people who need new glasses tend to think that print is getting smaller, people who need new browsers tend to think that pages are looking sloppier.

In practice this means that you have to do the best job you can with traditional tags first and then apply a style sheet after the fact. This makes sense because there are still lots of browsers out there for whom your style sheet is so much gobbledygook, and you should probably try to account for them as well.

That can mean arguing typographical elements several times, calling for a background color and image and link colors in the `<BODY>` tag as well as the body selector, and so on.

It can also mean asking for things that don't really affect the look of the page drastically. Calling for a particular font, for example, is a nice touch, but failure to actually *use* the font is unlikely to affect readability unless it's Russian Cyrillic or something like that.

REFERENCE

Although the information in this appendix is current as of this writing, the most up-to-date source for information is the World Wide Web Consortium at `http://www.w3.org/Style/`.

This directory contains both the latest thinking on cascading style sheets and research projects showing where they might be headed.

In addition, browser capabilities change rapidly and both major manufacturers are committed to supporting style sheets. This means we can expect that some of the features marked as questionable for actual use may be less undependable in the future. My own recommendation is to take a yellow highlighter to those elements that you've personally tested and found to be safe or that have been recommended as safe to you by some credible resource. In most cases, failure to honor a style sheet command won't result in any harm other than to mess up your formatting a bit. But in the worst cases, the formatting will be trashed and the document will be rendered unreadable. It's even possible to crash your browser.

Tip from

 **LeeAnne.com**
Words to weave by

Always remember to use the excellent W3C CSS2 validation service available at `http://jigsaw.w3.org/css-validator/` before using (or even testing) a style sheet. You might also use their HTML/XHTML validation service at `http://validator.w3.org/` before spending too much time testing. It's always irritating when the source of a problem turns out to be a simple coding error and using validation tools is good design and coding practice.

In short, style sheets are not quite ready for prime time unless you have lots of spare time on your hands to fiddle and tweak your pages as new and possibly less buggy implementations appear.

NOTES ON CSS2, THE NEXT GENERATION OF STYLE SHEETS

CSS2, the next version of style sheets, takes some of the characteristics of the existing specification and extends them to include many more pseudo-elements to allow even finer control of the document, as well as providing specific properties for affecting the rendering of audio browsers.

These changes track the increasing importance of network information retrieval in daily life. As Web browsers become ubiquitous, appearing everywhere from luxury cars to home theater systems, the possible best renderings for information multiply far beyond the simple tricks we ask of them now.

If you're under the car trying to fix some doohickey according to instructions on the manufacturer's Web site, you probably want the text to be spoken and the pictures to be as large as possible so you can see them with your neck at an awkward angle peering around a wheel.

In the car tooling down the road at high speed, you don't want anything to distract you at all. Perhaps the car itself will apply a style sheet while in motion that restricts output to spoken material, but lets you look at maps and text descriptions while at a full stop.

For a surgeon accessing medical records in the midst of an operation, perhaps a very telegraphic and rapid-fire aural rendering might be needed to keep up with the exigencies of the medical moment.

We can only guess at what the future may look like once we get more than a few years out, but I think it's safe to say that the Web will still be around in some form, and that it will be integrated into our daily lives in ways we can only dimly imagine today.

Terms Used in This Book

How to Use This Glossary

When reading the definitions in the body of the glossary below, you'll encounter words or phrases in **bold face**. These refer to glossary entries that may contain related or additional information. The referenced item may help create a clearer picture of how that definition is related to others in the glossary or expand upon the meaning of the entry by directing you to a more general or specific definition. It may also point to a synonym or antonym.

Glossary

abstract syntax   In **XML Schema**, a formal specification of the information provided for each declaration and definition in the schema language. *See also* **concrete syntax**.

accessible   Capable of being viewed by persons in a wide variety of circumstances. Although the word has a specific legal meaning and requirements in relation to the Americans with Disabilities Act, it actually applies to everyone. Information should be equally accessible to person using Macs, PCs, or Unix systems, for example, or using a grayscale monitor designed for the graphic arts. *See also* **accessible design**.

accessible design   Broadly, egoless design that doesn't assume that the designer is the center of the universe and embodies in the environment the epitome of hardware, software, abilities, and skills that everyone should either possess or aspire to. Narrowly, presentation design that allows persons with motor, vision, or hearing disabilities to use a document without artificial barriers. *See also* **accessible**.

aggregate datatype   In **XML Schema**, a complex datatype made up of other datatypes. *See also* **atomic datatype**.

all content model group   In **XML Schema**, a content model that includes everything. *See also* **any content model group**.

ancestor   In **XPath**, any of the direct sequence of **parent** nodes from which a context node depends. *See also* **self**.

application   The software layer that receives output from an XML processor and does something useful with it.

ANY content   In an XML DTD, an element declaration keyword that indicates that the element can contain all kinds of markup and data in any mixture. `<!ELEMENT elementname ANY>`

any content model   In **XML Schema**, a content model that allows any content to be included. *See also* **seq content model** and **choice content model**.

any content model group   In **XML Schema**, a content model group enabling any content to be included. *See also* **seq content model group** and **choice content model group**.

arc   In **RDF**, the representation of a **predicate** or **property** edge in directed graph form.

archetype   In **XML Schema**, a reusable content description of element types and attributes that can then be instantiated or declared as a particular element.

atomic datatype   In **XML Schema**, a simple datatype which has not been constructed from other datatypes. *See also* **aggregate datatype**.

ATTLIST   In a DTD, markup that defines an **attribute list**. `<!ATTLIST attribute datatype {"default"} >`

attribute   Information contained within a tag as a `name="value"` pair rather than as content between the start and end tags. An **empty element tag** carries no information other than that in its attributes.

attribute group   In **XML Schema**, a group of **attributes** that might be treated as a reusable unit of attribute declarations.

attribute list   A list of attribute names with datatypes and possible default values. *See also* **ATTLIST**.

beautifying   Processing a code file so that it obeys certain formatting conventions that make it easier to understand or edit. *See* **prettyprinting**.

bound variable   In mathematics, a variable whose value depends on those taken by other variables. Roughly, the variable on the lefthand side of an equation. *See* **free variable**.

Cascading Style Sheets (CSS)   A method of separating content from presentation based on tag context or position in the **document tree**. CSS uses a hierarchical model of the document to affect how the browser **renders** page content by means of inheritance.

CDATA section   Information to be passed on to the application without being parsed for markup, a handy shorthand means of escaping an entire block of text without searching for and escaping individual characters that might otherwise be mistaken for markup. `<![CDATA[ anything ]]>`

character   Any Unicode / ISO 8879 / ISO 10646 character excluding single characters from the **surrogate blocks**, #xFFFE, and #xFFFF. Legal characters are #x9 | #xA | #xD | [#x20-#xD7FF] | [#xE000-#xFFFD] | [#x10000-#x10FFFF]. For an excellent and inexpensive guide to the wonderful world of legal characters, I highly recommend purchasing the authoritative Unicode Standard Version 3.0, a lovely coffee table book with enclosed CD-ROM available at http://www.unicode.org/ and sure to delight anyone with an interest in human languages and writing systems. It's also a reference guide to commonly used mathematical and scientific symbols used worldwide.

character data   The text of an XML document considered apart from its markup; whatever would be left over after stripping all tags, processing instructions, and XML declarations from the document. In other words, raw text before being marked up in any way.

character reference   A numeric entity of the form &#DDDD; or &#xHHHH; representing a character in the Unicode / ISO 8879 / ISO 10646 character space. The decimal entities are probably the most familiar from our experience with ASCII. But the hexadecimal equivalents can be used without conversion as an entry into the **Unicode Standard Version 3.0** and vice versa.

child   In **XPath** and **XML** generally, the immediate descendent of a node. *See also* **descendent**.

choice content model   In **XML Schema**, a content model that allows a choice from listed elements but not more than one. *See also* **seq model group** and **any model group**.

choice content model group   In **XML Schema**, a content model group that allows a choice from listed elements but not more than one. *See also* **seq content model group** and **any content model group**.

client   A distributed object that sends requests to a **server** and receives the response.

comment   In a **DTD** or **XML** document, explanatory text not meant to be parsed or acted upon. <!-- comment text -->

composition   In **XML Schema**, the method used to construct a complete schema out of components from any of several namespaces.

concrete syntax   In **XML Schema**, the element and attribute names used in a schema. *See also* **abstract syntax**.

conditional section   In a DTD, a method of using paired parameter entities to switch between variant logical DTD structures. <![INCLUDE[anything]]> <![IGNORE[anything]]>

constraint   In **XML Schema**, the limitations placed on the possible values which can be taken by an element or attribute. In **XML** generally, any of the limitations placed on content including **well-formedness** and **validity**.

content   Either a **datatype** or a **content model**.

content model In a **DTD**, the template describing legal **descendents** of a particular node.

content type Either a **datatype** or a **content model**. *See also* **content**.

context In **CSS** and **XML Schema**, the sequential list of parent elements that locate any particular node in the document tree.

CORBA Common Object Request Broker Architecture. An object-oriented standard allowing distributed applications to communicate with each other.

datatype Any item of content that is not another element. Atomic or terminal data. One of the two varieties of **content type**.

datatype reference In **XML Schema**, a reference to the datatype or datatypes that an **element** contains.

declaration In **XML Schema**, a statement which lets an element or attribute with a specific name and type appear in a document.

default value In **XML**, the default value taken by an **attribute**.

definition In **XML Schema**, a statement which creates a new **archetype** or **datatype**.

dereference To replace a pointer with the value that pointer refers to. In **XML Schema**, to read and process an external schema file. While a legitimate programming term, in the context of the wide audience of the XML standards it seems more like jargon. *See also* **include**.

descendent In **XPath** and generally, any of the direct sequence of **child** nodes branching from a **node**. Alternatively, all the elements contained within a given element.

DOCTYPE In an **XML** document, a statement that declares the name of the document and optionally identifies the DTD that defines its format and contents. `<!DOCTYPE name "public id" "url" [ XML declarations ]>`

document Any discrete entity containing information, of which an **XML document** is one example.

document element *See* **root**.

document fragment Any portion of an **XML** document.

document root *See* **root**.

document tree The abstract model of a hierarchical document that allows individual nodes, elements, and sections to be addressed by processing and style instructions.

Document type declaration *See* **DOCTYPE**.

Document Type Definition *See* **DTD**.

DSSSL Document Style Semantics and Specification Language. A style sheet language of tremendous power and complexity designed originally for **SGML**.

DSSSL-o   A stripped-down version of DSSSL designed to be easier to use online with XML.

DTD   Document Type Definition. The collection of **XML** declarations that defines the format and contents of an **XML** document.

DTD declaration   In **XML** generally, the statement that contains the internal DTD subset and/or points to the external DTD subset.

Dublin Core   A resource description framework developed in Dublin, Ohio. One of many series of defined **triples** that can be used to make a **statement** about **resource** objects in **RDF**. Also used as **metadata** in existing HTML and **XHTML** documents.

ELEMENT   In XML, a tag, or the name of its definition declaration in a DTD.

element content   In a DTD, a content model that allows only other elements inside an element.

element reference   In **XML Schema**, a reference to an **element** as opposed to a **datatype**.

empty content   *See* **empty element**.

empty element   An element with no inline content.

empty element tag   The single tag marking an empty element consisting of a combined **start tag** and **end tag** that adds a space and a final slash to the element name like this: `<elementname />`.

encoding declaration   In a DTD or external entity, an ISO value identifying a character encoding.

end tag   The ending tag of an element containing the name of the element preceded by a slash and surrounded by angle brackets: `</elementname>`. There is a special form of the end tag for **empty elements** that consists of a combined start and end tag that adds a space and a final slash to the element name like this: `<elementname />`. *See also* **empty element tag**.

ENTITY   Any storage unit that makes up any part of an **XML document**.

entity declaration   In a DTD, a name followed either by a replacement string or by a public ID and URL that points to external XML declarations. `<!ENTITY name "pubid" "url">`

entity reference   A reference to a previously-declared **entity** on an **XML document**.

error   A violation of the rules of a specification that might be detected and reported to the application and from which it might be possible to recover and continue processing. *See also* **fatal error**.

export   In **XML Schema**, making a constraint available to an outside process.

export control   In **XML Schema**, any restrictions placed on the making a constraint available to an outside process.

extended link   A link contained outside an **XML document**.

Extensible Stylesheet Language   *See* **XSL**.

external DTD subset   The portion of a DTD that lies outside an XML document. *See also* **internal DTD subset**.

external entity   An entity, whether parsed or unparsed, general or parameter, located outside the **XML document** proper.

facet   In **XML Schema**, a facet is a defining feature of a concept or object.

fatal error   An error that an **XML processor** is obliged to detect and report to the application and from which it is impossible to recover. *See also* **error**.

fixed value   In **XML Schema**, content that doesn't vary in value.

flow object   An **XSL** container into which data can be poured.

flow object tree   The set of **XSL** flow objects that comprise an **XML document**.

forest   *See* **grove**.

fragment   A portion of an XML document. Document fragments are required to be well-formed.

free variable   In mathematics, a variable whose value can vary without regard to others. Roughly, the variables on the righthand side of an equation. *See* **bound variable**.

general entity   An **entity** of the form &name; which can be used within **XML document** content. *See also* **parameter entity**.

generic identifier   The name of an element. The string associated with the tag when used in an XML document. `<!ELEMENT genericid … > <genericid> stuff </genericid>`

GIOP   General Inter-ORB Protocol. In **CORBA**, the media-independent communications protocol used between **ORB**s. *See* **IIOP**.

glyph   The physical representation of a letter, numeral, **ideograph**, non-alphabetic character, or other symbol in any of the **Unicode** character sets.

grove   A canonical view of an information tree or directed graph in which every node is a property of that information set and there is one and only one root node. The concept is much used in **DSSSL**, **SGML**, and **HyTime** and corresponds roughly to the DOM in **XSL** but has no exact equivalent. A grove is essentially a view into an information object that can vary by the type of notation used to describe it and can serve to link different XML DTDs (namespaces) that might describe the same data sets. Also known as a **forest**.

HTML   The Hypertext Markup Language, an application of **SGML** designed to **render** and **hyperlink** documents on the World Wide Web.

hyperlink   The foundation linking mechanism of the World Wide Web. A far memory reference.

HyTime   The HyperMedia Time-based Structuring Language, ISO/IEC 10744, an application or enhancement of SGML that extends SGML capabilities to synchronized multimedia and more eloquent addressing mechanisms.

identical   Exactly the same according to the rules for identity in XML **Namespaces**.

ideograph   A language character that represents meaning instead of pronunciation.

IIOP   General Inter-ORB Protocol. In **CORBA**, the TCP/IP-based communications protocol used between **ORB**s. *See* **GIOP**.

import   In **XML** generally, to include data or entire documents from outside a document into the document itself.

include   In **XML** generally, those things that form the content of an element.

information set   In **XML** generally, a dataset describing the content of an XML document. The format of this dataset is not defined but is left to the discretion of the designer. *See* **Infoset**.

Infoset   The W3C Working Draft describing the **XML** Information Set. *See* **information set**.

inline link   A simple link contained in the document itself as opposed to existing outside the document in an **extended link**.

instance   A particularization of an abstract object.

internal DTD subset   That part of the **DTD** contained in the document itself. Every **XML** processor, whether **validating** or not, is expected to parse and act upon the statements in the internal subset with certain exceptions.

internal entity   An **entity** defined within the **internal DTD subset** or one of those predefined by **XML**.

Internet   The network of interconnected machines on which the **World Wide Web** is based. The Internet hosts many services besides the **Web**, such as email, IRC, WAIS, Gopher, and much more.

ISO 10646   The international standard that defines unique numeric representations for the **glyphs** used in writing most of the commonly-used languages of the world. Roughly equivalent to **Unicode**.

kludge   A hastily designed, awkward, or inelegant means of accomplishing a given task.

literal   In **RDF**, an object, typically a string of characters. The content of a literal is not interpreted by RDF itself and might contain additional XML markup. The RDF model doesn't permit literals to be the subject of a **statement**.

locator   In **XLink**, an object that visibly fixes one end of a link in a document.

lookahead   In a parser, the ability to read ahead and backtrack if it finds an ambiguity which it can heuristically resolve by examining the input stream in a non-sequential manner. XML doesn't do lookahead.

logical structure   The structure defined by the sum total of XML declarations in a document, including both those defined as internal entities and as external entities. The external DTD subset is a special type of external entity.

markup   The tags and processing commands that comprise the structure of an XML document.

metadata   A **statement** about a **resource**. *See also* **RDF**.

Meta-language   Language whose reference is the structure of a document or element rather than its literal meaning.

metaphor   An underlying organizational and operational principle that allows an application to be more easily understood in terms of concepts pre-existing in a user's mind.

mixed content   In a DTD, a content model that allows character data as well as other elements inside an element.

model   The **constraint** place upon element content. *See also* **content type**.

model group   In **XML Schema**, a group of content models that might be treated as a reusable unit.

model group reference   In **XML Schema**, a reference to a model group.

name   In a **DTD**, a string consisting of a letter, an underscore, or a colon followed by letters, digits, underscore, hyphen, period, colon, half colon, triangular colon, middle dot, combining accent, combining diacritic, or non-Latin1 equivalent. Use of a colon is restricted to namespaces and internal **XML** mechanisms. Use of the initial string "xml" in any case combination is prohibited except in predefined attribute names like `xml:lang`. Letters refer to any ISO or Unicode glyph that functions as a letter, syllable, or ideographic unit of meaning in any of the defined languages of the world. Digits arc the glyphs of any numbering system likewise.

name token   In a **DTD**, a string like a **name** except that there is no restriction on the first character.

namespace   An arbitrary identifier used to avoid name collisions between different DTDs or an abbreviated equivalent. In certain XML-related standards, like **XML Schema**, an abbreviation for the root of a tree upon which an applicable document file (such as a schema) might be found. Namespaces are sometimes used as internal switches to indicate to an XML parser or user agent that certain types of processing are to be performed. *See also* **scope**.

NCName   A **name** with no namespace qualification, as defined in **XML Namespaces**. That is, a name without an included colon.

nmtoken, nmtokens   *See* **name token**.

node   In general, a branching point or leaf on a document tree. In **RDF**, a representation of a subject resource or an object **literal** in a directed graph format; specifically, a vertex in a directed labeled graph. *See also* **XPath**, **arc**, and other related entries found at those locations.

notation   In mathematics, a method of rendering mathematical concepts in a concise form suitable for display and publication. Notations often make it possible to communicate extremely complex ideas with a few symbols or special two-dimensional arrangements of pre-existing symbols on the page.

NOTATION   A link to an external unparsed entity.

occurrence   In **XML Schema**, the number of times an element or content model can occur.

ORB   Object Request Broker. In **CORBA**, the infrastructure that enables distributed objects to communicate with each other.

origin   *See* **root**.

out-of-line link   A link that is not contained within a document.

parameter entity   In a **DTD**, an entity of the form %name; used only within the DTD. The term and form are meaningless outside the DTD. *See also* **general entity**.

parent   The immediate ancestor of a **node**.

parser   A program which understands the syntax of a language and can read an input file and output intermediate productions or modified data streams that another program can use. XML parsers may also be able to **validate** the input file based on a defining **schema**.

Persistent Uniform Resource Locator (PURL)   A **URL** intermediated through a resolution server that redirects references to their current locations. This supplies a level of persistence to resources that might otherwise change physical addresses on the Web.

physical structure   The total collection and arrangement of data storage units that forms an XML document.

PICS   The Platform for Internet Content Selection. Originally developed for facilitating parental control of children's access to Web sites, this metadata label syntax also supports Internet privacy and digital signatures.

preamble   The optional introductory portion of an XML Document containing any combination of an XML declaration, a DTD declaration, and processing instructions.

predefined entity   One of a handful of character entities so important to XML processing that their corresponding general entities are predefined. They are "<", ">", "&", "'", and '"'. They can theoretically be used without declaring them like this: &, <, >, ', and &quot. For compatibility with some older processors, they should be declared anyway. Their declarations should look like this: <!ENTITY lt "&#60;">, <!ENTITY gt ">">, <!ENTITY amp "&#38;">, <!ENTITY apos "'">, and <!ENTITY quot """>.

predicate   In logic, a term indicating a property or relationship. Also, whatever is affirmed or denied in a logical proposition. In a sentence, a verb or verb phrase with or without an object. In **RDF**, a specific attribute with defined meaning that might be used to describe an RDF **resource**. *See* **property**.

presence In **XML Schema**, the occurrence in the XML document content of an optional element, attribute, or data.

prettyprinting Processing a code file so that it obeys certain formatting conventions that make it easier to understand or edit. Usually this is performed by placing complete statements on separate lines and indenting each line to reflect the current nesting level. *See* **beautifying**.

processing instruction In a **DTD**, a special instruction of the form `<?proccessor data ?>` that instructs the XML processor to pass the enclosed data directly to an external processor.

prolog In a **DTD**, that part of an XML DTD or document that precedes and includes the DOCTYPE declaration. It consists of the XML declaration, optional comments, and the document type declaration.

property In **RDF**, another name for a **predicate**. A specific attribute with defined meaning that might be used to describe an RDF **resource**. *See also* **arc**, **literal**, and **metadata**.

PURL *See* **Persistent Uniform Resource Locator**.

RDF Resource Description Framework. A W3C method of describing resources in a **meta-language** that doesn't alter the native behavior of the resource. RDF can be used to tag existing documents with supplemental information to allow greater granularity and precision in searches without modifying existing applications. A generalization in XML of such key metadata frameworks as the Dublin Core and other descriptions of data objects.

refinement In **XML Schema**, the process of building on base datatypes to further constrain the values taken by the enclosing element.

render To display or otherwise present a document or part of a document in a manner suitable for a given display device. Aural rendering of documents originally intended for visual display might make them more accessible to persons with vision disabilities, but careful consideration and design is needed to make that feasible and useful.

resource Generally, any addressable unit of information or service located anywhere in the information space of your computer, network, or the World Wide Web. Anything that can be addressed by a **URI**. In RDF, the **node** that represents the subject in an RDF **statement**. *See also* **arc**, **literal**, and **metadata**.

Resource Description Framework *See* **RDF**.

root The base of an XML document tree. Also called **origin**.

RUE A Reference to Undefined Entity information item as defined in **XML-Infoset**.

schema A schema generally defines the structure and content of an XML file. Particular schema languages are **XML Schema**, **RDF**, and the XML **DTD**.

scope In **XML Schema** and elsewhere, the range of validity of an element name. Also, the **XML Namespace** device that allows elements to mix without scope collisions. *See also* **Namespace**.

self   In **XPath**, the **node** that is one's self. The context node from which other nodes are selected.

seq content model   In **XML Schema**, a content model that forces all the members of a list to appear in the content of an element in sequence. *See also* **any content model** and **choice content model**.

seq content model group   In **XML Schema**, a content model group that forces all the members of a list to appear in the content of an element in sequence. *See also* **any content model group** and **choice content model group**.

sequence content model   In XML, a content model that forces all the members of a list to appear in the content of an element in sequence.

server   A distributed object that receives requests from a **client** and responds to them.

SGML   Standard Generalized Markup Language, ISO 8879. A very complex markup definition language used only on very large projects for the most part. **XML** tries to incorporate the most valuable features of SGML in a way that can be easily used and implemented on the Web.

sibling   In **XPath**, a **node** that has the same **parent**.

skeleton   In **CORBA**, the communications module that interfaces between the **ORB** core and the **server** implementation.

standalone declaration   A theoretical notification to an application that there are no external markup declarations that affect the data passed from the XML processor to the application. There is no required action to be taken in either case. `<?xml standalone=` `"no" | "yes"?>`

start tag   The starting tag of an element that optionally contains attribute settings: `<ele-` `mentname {attributes} >` There is a special form of the start tag for **empty elements** that consists of a combined start and end tag that adds a space and a final slash to the element name like this: `<elementname />`. *See also* **empty element tag**.

statement   In RDF, an expression that names a specific **resource** (subject), a specific **property** (predicate or attribute), and gives the value of that property (object or **literal**) for that resource. *See also* **metadata**.

structure   In **XML Schema**, the range of possible content models and datatypes.

stub   In **CORBA**, the communications module that interfaces between the **ORB** core and the **client** implementation.

style sheet   A list of instructions that associate display properties with document elements.

surrogate blocks   Two blocks of 16-bit character sequences set aside for encoding rarely used or obscure characters. They are the ranges [#xD800-#xDBFF] and [#xDC00-#xDFFF] and are always used in pairs, one from each block.

symbol space   In **XML Schema**, the scope of names used in defining objects.

text entity   In **XML**, an entity in the form &name; that can function as a mnemonic replacement for a character or string.

topology   The allowable connectivity between nodes, anchors and links. For example, one to one, or many to one; one directional or bi-directional, and so on.

transaction processing   A data processing technology whereby an entire series of operations must complete as a whole or the steps leading up to the point of failure will be undone, restoring the system to its initial state.

transclude   To process and include the contents of a hyperlink within the body of a document. In HTML, images, objects, and style sheets are commonly transcluded. In XML, other documents, and portions of other documents can be rendered within a document as well.

triple   In **RDF**, the representation of a **statement** consisting of the **property** (predicate), the **resource** identifier (subject), and the property value (object or **literal**) in that order. *See also* **metadata**.

type   The datatype of an element.

type reference   In **XML Schema**, a reference to the datatype of an element.

Unicode   The international standard that defines unique numeric representations for the **glyphs** used in writing most of the commonly-used languages of the world. Roughly equivalent to **ISO 10646**.

Unicode Standard Version 3.0   The latest draft of the Unicode standard as published by Addison-Wesley, ISBN: 0201616335. This is an essential tool for anyone in the XML field who cares about being able to handle worldwide communications. *See* **character**.

unparsed entity   A binary or other entity not understood by an XML processor. Common examples would be graphics files, audio, video, and other multimedia files, programming language files, and executable object files.

URI   Uniform Resource Identifier. A generalization of both URN and URL methods of addressing information or services to include any short string that refers to a resource anywhere in the information space of the Web.

URL   Uniform Resource Locator, RFCs 1738 and 1808. A method of addressing information on the Web by means of a short identifier that gives explicit directions on where the information is on the Web.

URN   Uniform Resource Name, RFC 2141. A mechanism for allowing the owners of a particular namespace, typically a **Web** location but not always, to provide a method of resolving names into locations.

valid   A **well-formed XML** document that also obeys all the rules defined in the associated **DTD**.

validation   The process whereby a well-formed **XML** document is parsed and tested to ensure conformity with the rules of the **DTD** that defines it.

validating   *See* **validation**.

vocabulary   In **XML Schema**, a pre-existing collection of datatypes and constraints that can be reused by other documents.

W3C   The World Wide Web Consortium. A standards body made up of representatives from the vendor and user communities that defines and promulgates standards relating to the **World Wide Web**. http://www.w3.org/

Web   The **World Wide Web**. Loosely, the **Internet**.

well-formed   An **XML document** that nests properly, has a correct tagging structure, and meets other criteria defined in the **W3C XML** 1.0 Recommendation. It is possible to generate a **DTD** based on any well-formed document that would make it a valid document, although not every well-formed document is valid as an instance of a particular DTD. *See also* **valid**.

World Wide Web   The interconnected network of machines and transport mechanisms that constitute the interactive hyperlinked **Internet** environment most familiar today.

XHTML   Extensible HTML 1.0. HTML 4.0 redefined as an application of XML. One of the subjects of this book.

XLink   The **XML** linking language used to define **hyperlinks**.

XML   Extensible Markup Language 1.0. The main subject of this book. XML allows an abstract hierarchical data tree to be described serially.

XML declaration   The optional instruction at the top of an XML file that identifies it as an XML document of a particular version, currently always set to "1.0," and might further identify the character set encoding used and whether the document depends on external files. <?xml version="1.0" … ?>

XML document   A document describing an abstract information tree created according to the rules of the XML Recommendation from W3C. XML documents extend and generalize the familiar concept of tagging, as used in HTML 4.0, to include full context and meaning information. XML documents can be **well-formed**, meaning that they are syntactically correct, or **valid**, meaning that they follow the rules of an existing **DTD**.

XML Namespaces   A mechanism whereby elements from different **DTD**s can share an **XML document** without name collisions.

XML processor   The software layer that reads and interprets XML documents, including any required DTD declarations, checks them for well-formedness, possibly validates them, and makes their parsed contents known to an **application**.

xml:lang   An attribute used to declare the language used within a given element or entity. The declaration follows RFC 1766 for language identification tags, ISO 639 for language name codes, and ISO 3166 for country name codes), name codes, and ISO 3166 for country name codes). `<name xml:lang="xx">`. This attribute is predefined but not declared in any element.

xml:space   An attribute used to declare the intention to preserve white space within elements that might otherwise ignore it. `<!ATTLIST name xml:space (default|preserve) 'preserve'>` This attribute is predefined but not declared in any element.

XPath   A compact language designed to address the parts of an XML or other XML-like document in an unambiguous manner. Part of **XLink**, **XPointer**, **XSL**, **XSLT**, and other W3C Recommendations.

XPointer   The extended locator for a document identified by a **URI** that allows precise identification of a position within a document or a selected portion of that document. *See also* **XPath**.

XSL   Extensible Stylesheet Language. A reformulation and extension of **CSS2** as an **XML document** with significant additions to allow it to refer to a wider range of documents and a more powerful page model. Simply put, CSS2-style properties and values are converted into XML-style attributes and values with significant additions to the **CSS2** functionality.

XSLT   Extensible Stylesheet Language Transformations. An **XSL** adjunct facility that allows the conversion of one **XML** document into another.

INDEX

UPnP, 463
Web site, 656
XML-based data protocols,
465

**Society of Motion Picture
and Television Engineers
(SMPTE), 545**

sockets
SSL (Secure Sockets
Layer), 393-395
XML, 424

software
Academia Sinica
Computing Centre, 659
Apache XML Project, 661
Cafe Con Leche:XML
News and Resources, 660
Chinese XML Now! Web
Site, 659
developersWORKS, IBM,
660
DTD.com, 661
GNOME, 660
Java, 400
JAWS screen reader, 312
Microsoft Internet
Explorer, 660
Mozilla, 660
Perl XML, 661
Psion platform, 317
Python, 660
XML, 660
XML Hack:Developer
News from the XML
Community, 660
XML Toolkit, 660
XMLephant, 660
XMLSoftware, 660

sorting (XSL), 338-339

sound (CSS), 796-801

**source code, testing validity,
101-102**

**SOX (Schema for Object-
Oriented XML), 170**
XML schemas, 170

**special attributes (HTML),
516**

specifying
default data, 77
versions, declarations, 685

speech pitch, 314
**Speech Synthesis Markup
Language (SSML), 655**

spell checkers, 448

spoofing, 372-373

**src attribute (Media Object
elements), 543**

**SSL (Secure Sockets Layer),
393-395**

**SSML (Speech Synthesis
Markup Language), 655**
Web site, 655

stacks, 369

standalone attribute
DTDs, 685
validity constraints, 685

**standalone documents,
43-44**

**Standard Generalized
Markup Language. *See*
SGML**

**standards, open standards
(Microsoft), 429**

start tags, 47-49

start-point() function, 210

**startDocument() method,
262-263**

startElement() method, 263

**startPrefixMapping()
method, 263**

**starts-with() function
(XPath), 183**

**STATEMENT element
(P3P), 357**

statements
Dim statements (COM
objects), 442
DOCTYPE, 685

steganography, 391-392

**Steganography Info and
Archive pages, 392**

**stopping Java Web Server,
426**

storing data, 466
RTFs, 467

strategies (ERP), 479, 483

**strengths, XML schemas,
149**

string functions (XPath)
concat(), 183
contains(), 183
normalize-space(), 184
starts-with(), 183
string(), 183
string-length(), 184
substring(), 184
substring-after(), 183
substring-before(), 183
translate(), 184

**String Identity/Matching
Web site, 658**

**string() function (XPath),
183**

**string-length() function
(XPath), 184**

strings
selecting, 211
W3C XML Schema
Working Group, 162

**strong encryption, restoring,
386-387**

Stronghold, 386

structure (XML), 11-12, 28
exclusion, 11-12
logical structure, 47
physical structure, 47-48

structures, servlets, 414

**style languages. *See* style
sheets**

Style One tools, 722
Web site, 722

**style sheet interfaces
(DOM), 220**

**style sheet references
(XML), 418**

style sheets, 270
aural style sheets, 632-634
browser implementations,
300
browser support, 281-292,
340, 804-805

System Requirements for This Macmillan USA CD-ROM

Processor:	486DX or higher
OS:	Microsoft Windows 95/98/NT
Memory (RAM):	24 MB
Monitor:	VGA, 640×480 or higher with 256 color or higher
Storage Space:	10 MB Minimum (will vary depending on installation)
Other:	Mouse or compatible pointing device

Internet connection and Web browser

If you have "AutoPlay" enabled, your computer will automatically run the CD-ROM Interface. If "AutoPlay" is disabled, please follow these instructions:

1. Insert the CD-ROM in your CD-ROM Drive. (Because you are reading this, it is likely this step is completed.)
2. From the Windows Desktop, double-click the "My Computer" icon.
3. Double-click the icon representing your CD-ROM drive.
4. Double-click the icon titled START or START.EXE to begin.

READ THIS BEFORE OPENING THE SOFTWARE

By opening this package, you are agreeing to be bound by the following agreement:

You may not copy or redistribute the entire CD-ROM as a whole. Copying and redistribution of individual software programs on the CD-ROM is governed by terms set by the licensors or individual copyright holders.

This software is sold as-is, without warranty of any kind, either expressed or implied, including but not limited to the implied warranties of merchantability and fitness for a particular purpose. Neither the publisher nor its dealers or distributors assumes any liability for any alleged or actual damages arising from the use of this program. (Some states do not allow for the exclusion of implied warranties, so the exclusion may not apply to you.)

NOTE: This CD-ROM may use long and mixed-case filenames requiring the use of a protected-mode CD-ROM Driver.

What's on the CD-ROM?

CD-ROM Contents

Browsing the CD-ROM via the CD-ROM Interface

Author Examples

Third-Party Evaluation Software

User Services Information

Browsing the CD-ROM via the CD-ROM Interface

System Requirements for the Macmillan USA CD-ROM	
Processor:	486DX or higher
OS:	Microsoft Windows 95/98/NT
Memory (RAM):	24MB
Monitor:	VGA, 640x480 or higherwith 256 color or higher
Storage Space:	10 MB Minimum (will vary depending on installation)
Other:	Mouse or compatible pointing device
Internet connection and Web browser:	For your convenience, on this disk you will find some Web browsers and ISP software

If you have AutoPlay turned on, your computer will automatically run the CD-ROM Interface. If AutoPlay is off, please follow these instructions:

1. Insert the CD-ROM in your CD-ROM Drive. (Because you are reading this, it is likely this step is completed.)
2. From the Windows Desktop, double-click the My Computer icon.
3. Double-click the icon representing your CD-ROM drive.
4. Double-click the icon titled START or START.EXE to begin.

Author Examples

To install the author's XML examples on this CD, double click `ExamplesCode.EXE`.

THIRD-PARTY EVALUATION SOFTWARE

If you are not using the CD-ROM interface, you can find these products in /3RDPARTY.

Although we have tried our best, it is possible that newer versions have been released between the time this book was finished and the date you purchased it. Please check with each manufacturer to insure that your products are up to date.

Here is a list of the programs you will find on this CD-ROM:

XML PRO V.2 DEMO© BY VERVET LOGIC

XML Pro offers an easy to use, affordable XML editing solution as a standalone application or as a complement to many more expensive XML suites. Features include

- Full integration of the IBM XML 4J Parser
- Drag and Drop support
- Undo
- New advanced Find
- Document Encoding support
- View DTD
- Cutting and pasting of elements
- And a native Java application!

To install or explore, go to 3rdParty\Vervet\xmlpro2.0.1-demo.EXE.

NEAR & FAR DESIGNER DEMO© BY VERVET LOGIC

As the only industrial-strength DTD modeling tool available on the market today, Near & Far Designer is the ideal product for those who are new to structured information, as well as those who are already realizing the benefits of structured corporate content. Using Near & Far Designer, DTDs can be created and modified graphically without prior knowledge of the language syntax.

To install or explore, go to 3rdParty\Vervet\NearandFarDemo\nfddemo.zip.

VISUAL-XML© BY BLUESTONE, INC.

Bluestone Visual-XML is one of the world's first visual toolkits for creating dynamic XML applications for data integration and content management applications. These applications run as pure Java document handlers inside the Bluestone XML-Server and enable developers to tie XML documents to any database or back-end data and business object. Visual-XML is a wizard-based, visual drag-and-drop environment that enables developers to bind XML, DTD, and DOM elements to databases. Visual-XML ships with a complete communications configuration framework as well as database access capabilities for creating and executing SQL and stored procedures.

XMETAL© BY SOFTQUAD

Xmetal is an advanced XML authoring tool that delivers unprecedented ease of use to authors while shielding them from the complexeties of XML.

To install or explore, go to `3rdParty\SoftQuad\sqxm12.EXE`.

XML AUTHORITY© BY EXTENSIBILITY, INC.

XML Authority is the premier solution to the development and deployment of e-business grammars for your company and trading partners. XML Authority provides a comprehensive design environment that accelerates the creation, conversion, and management of XML schemas. XML Authority's intuitive and graphical environment provides users a powerful environment for the creation of e-business infrastructures.

To install or explore, go to `3rdParty\Extensibility\XML Authority\XA_Setup_12Trial.EXE`.

XML INSTANCE© BY EXTENSIBILITY, INC.

XML Instance is a comprehensive solution for the creation, editing, and management of XML business documents, messages, and configuration files. It is the ideal platform for the creation of XML-based documents and messages for use in XML application development. The support of multiple dialects creates flexibility for the implementation of XML initiatives internally and with trading partners.

To install or explore, go to `3rdParty\Extensibility\XMLInstance\XI_Setup_max.EXE`.

XML SPY© BY ICON INFORMATION SYSTEMS GMBH

XML Spy is the first true IDE for XML that includes all major aspects of XML in one powerful, easy to use product.

To install or explore, go to `3rdParty\Icon Information Systems GmbH\xmlspy30c.EXE`.

ACROBAT READER 4.05© BY ADOBE

The free Adobe Acrobat Reader allows you to view, navigate, and print PDF files across all major-computing platforms. Acrobat Reader is the free viewing companion to Adobe Acrobat and to Acrobat Capture software.

For more information, visit the Web site at `http://www.adobe.com`.

To install Acrobat Reader 4.05, go to `3rdParty\Adobe\Acrobat4\rs405eng`.

WINZIP 8.0© BY NICO MAK

WinZip brings the convenience of Windows to the use of Zip files and other archive and compression formats. The optional wizard interface makes unzipping easier than ever. WinZip features built-in support for popular Internet file formats, including TAR, gzip, Unix compress, UUencode, BinHex, and MIME. ARJ, LZH, and ARC files are supported via external programs. WinZip interfaces to most virus scanners.

To order, visit the Web site at http://www.winzip.com.

To install WinZip 8.0, go to 3rdParty\NICOMAK\Winzip8\winzip8.EXE.

WS_FTP PRO6.5© BY IPSWITCH

Quickly and easily upload and manage your Web site, download graphics and games, and transfer files with the world's most popular FTP client for Windows.

To order, visit the Web site at http://www.ipswitch.com.

To install WS_FTP Pro 6.5, go to 3rdParty\IPSwitch\WS_ftppro\f_x86t32.EXE.

XSPLIT SHAREWARE VERSION©PERCUSSION SOFTWARE

XSpLit is leading edge technology that allows you to go backward from HTML to XSL and XML; and to define the content by adding labels to the HTML. XSpLit parses the HTML page, automatically separating the content definition into an XML DTD and formatting it into an XSLT style sheet. Style sheets produce an HTML page when applied to any XML content conforming to the associated DTD. Any content now trapped inside HTML files can be easily split from formatting for use as raw XML.

To install or explore, go to 3rdParty\Percussion\.

RHYTHMYX INTEGRATOR TRIAL©PERCUSSION SOFTWARE

The Rhythmyx Integrator, a native XML Application Server, simplifies building dynamic content management applications for the Web. The Workbench maps data sources to content objects and content objects to formatting style sheets. The Server assembles content from various sources, creates an XML file, and applies an XSL style sheet to format it for any output type.

To install or explore, go to 3rdParty\Percussion\.

USER SERVICES INFORMATION

Sometimes you will need help. We are here for you; however, our help can only assist with information about the book, help with the CD-ROM, things that may be missing, and the like.

We, unfortunately, are not authorized to assist with computer malfunction, system errors, or third-party applications.

If you need help, or are unsure where to go for help, you can contact us through our Web site. You should get a response within 24–48 hours. Go to www.mcp.com/support to submit an email. You will need to provide the following information:

1. Full title of the book (Special Edition Using XML)
2. The ISBN of the book (0789719967)

3. Your name

4. Your email address

5. Your problem or question

6. System information

Sometimes we will have already resolved problems, such as file updates or errata. You can find this information and more at www.mcp.com/info. You will need the ISBN of the book (0789719967) to access that information.